TACKLING INEQUALITY

Tackling Inequality

Richard Layard
Director
Centre for Economic Performance
London School of Economics and Political Science

First published in Great Britain 1999 by
MACMILLAN PRESS LTD
Houndmills, Basingstoke, Hampshire RG21 6XS and London
Companies and representatives throughout the world

A catalogue record for this book is available from the British Library.

ISBN 0–333–72231–0

First published in the United States of America 1999 by
ST. MARTIN'S PRESS, INC.,
Scholarly and Reference Division,
175 Fifth Avenue, New York, N.Y. 10010

ISBN 0–312–21576–2

Library of Congress Cataloging-in-Publication Data
Layard, P. R. G. (P. Richard G.)
Tackling inequality / Richard Layard.
p. cm.
Includes bibliographical references (p.) and index.
ISBN 0–312–21576–2 (cloth)
1. Poor—Employment—Great Britain. 2. Poor-
-Employment—Europe, Eastern. 3. Labor supply—Effect
of education on—Great Britain. 4. Labor supply-
-Effect of education on—Europe, Eastern. 5. Post
-communism—Europe, Eastern. I. Title.
HD5765.A6L378 1998
331.11'423'0941—dc21   98–16544
                                          CIP

This book is printed on paper suitable for recycling and made from fully managed and sustained forest sources.

10   9   8   7   6   5   4   3   2
08   07   06   05   04   03   02   01   00   99

Printed and bound in Great Britain by
Antony Rowe Ltd, Chippenham, Wiltshire

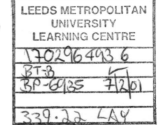

To David Blunkett

Contents

vii

PART II   ECONOMIC TRANSITION

Preface

This is one of two books, *Tackling Unemployment* and *Tackling Inequality*, which reproduce my main articles on these issues. A complete list of publications appears at the end.

I am grateful to Tim Farmiloe of Macmillan for proposing the idea of publication. He also suggested I write a personal credo which appears at the beginning of the volume.

RICHARD LAYARD

Acknowledgements

The author and publishers acknowledge with thanks permission from the following to reproduce copyright material:

Chapter 3: Macmillan for R. Layard, 'On measuring the redistribution of lifetime income', from M.S. Feldman and R.P. Inman (eds), *The Economics of Public Services* (1977).

Chapters 4, 9, 10, 13: *Journal of Political Economy* for R. Layard and A. Zabalza, 'Family income distribution: explanation and policy evaluation' (1979); for R. Layard and G. Pscharopoulos, 'The screening hypothesis and the return to education' (1974); for R. Layard and P. Fallon, 'Capital–skill complementarity, income distribution, and output accounting' (1975); for R. Layard, 'On the use of distributional weights in social cost-benefit analysis' (1980): all © The University of Chicago Press.

Chapter 5: *Journal of Public Economics* for R. Layard, 'Education versus cash redistribution: the lifetime context' (1979).

Chapter 6: *National Westminster Bank Quarterly Review* for R. Layard, D. Piachaud and M. Stewart, 'The causes of poverty' (1979).

Chapter 7: *British Journal of Industrial Relations* for R. Layard, D. Metcalf and S. Nickell, 'The effect of collective bargaining on relative and absolute wages' (1978).

Chapter 8: *Review of Economic Studies* for G. Psacharopoulos and R. Layard, 'Human capital and earnings: British evidence and a critique', (1979).

Chapter 11: *Economica* for R. Layard, M. Barton and A. Zabalza, 'Married women's participation and hours' (1980).

Chapter 12: *Journal of Labour Economics* for H. Joshi, R. Layard and S. Owen, 'Why are more women working in Britain?' (1985).

Chapter 14: *Economic Journal* for R. Layard, 'Human satisfactions and public policy' (1980).

Chapter 16: Longman for R. Layard and R. Jackman, 'University efficiency and university finance', in *Essays in Modern Economics* (1973).

Chapter 17: Elsevier for R. Layard and M. Oatey, 'The cost-effectiveness of the new media in higher education' (1974).

Chapter 18: HMSO for 'The pool of ability', in Committee on Higher Education, Appendix One, Part III, *The Demand for Places in Higher Education* (1963): Crown copyright is reproduced with the permission of the Controller of Her Majesty's Stationery Office.

Chapter 19: *American Economic Review, Papers and Proceedings* for R. Layard and S. Nickell, 'The Thatcher miracle?' (1989).

Chapter 20: Centre for Economic Performance, LSE for R. Layard, P. Robinson and H. Steedman, 'Lifelong learning' (1995).

Chapter 22: University of Kiel for O. Blanchard and R. Layard, 'How to privatise', in H. Siebert (ed.), *The Transformation of the Socialist Economies: Symposium 1991* (1991).

Chapter 23: The World Bank for O. Blanchard and R. Layard, 'Post-stabilisation inflation in Poland', in F. Coricelli and A. Revenga (eds), Wage Policy during the Transition to a Market Economy. Poland 1990–91' (1992), World Bank Discussion Paper No. 158.

Chapter 24: Carfax Publishing Ltd, Abingdon, UK, for R. Layard and A. Richter, 'Who gains and who loses from Russian credit expansion?', in *Communist Economies and Economic Transformation*, Vol. 6, No. 4, pp. 459–472 (1994).

Chapter 25: Kluwer Academic Publishers for R. Layard, 'Can Russia control inflation?', in J.A.H. de Beaufort Wijnholds, S.C.W. Eijffinger and L.A. Hoogduin (eds), *A Framework for Monetary Stability* (1994).

Chapter 26: Oxford University Press for R. Layard and A. Richter, 'How much unemployment is needed for restructuring? The Russian experience' in *Economics of Transition*, Vol. 3 (1), pp. 39–58 (1995).

Chapter 27: The MIT Press for R. Layard, 'Why so much pain? An Overview', in P. Boone, S. Gomulka and R. Layard (eds), *Emerging from Communism: Lessons from Russia, China and Eastern Europe.*

Every effort has been made to contact all the copyright-holders, but if any have been inadvertently omitted the publishers will be pleased to make the necessary arrangement at the earliest opportunity.

I am extremely grateful to Richard Barwell, Marion O'Brien, Sunder Katwala and Keith Povey for help in preparing this volume for publication.

1 Why I am an Economist*

I turned to economics because I wanted a framework for thinking about the problems of society. I was already in my early 30s, so it was quite a decision. But I was not disappointed.

As an undergraduate I had read history and then begun a part-time masters' degree in sociology while teaching in a comprehensive school. I remember well at that stage thinking that I understood how society and the economy worked. In fact I even began to write a sixth-form textbook on the subject.

But then I was asked to become the research officer for the Robbins Committee on Higher Education, which was to launch the great university expansion of the 1960s. In the first few weeks of our work, a memorandum came from the Treasury asking 'Should extra public money be spent on higher education or on renovating the decaying cities of the North?' I realised I had no framework at all for thinking about such a question.

So, when the Committee's work was done, I set about learning economics – not easy at any age and certainly not at 31. I was comforted to be told that James Meade had not understood the subject for the first five years, until he suddenly realised what it was all about. Fortunately I was well motivated and I already had questions I wanted answering.

It was a real culture shock. Though I had always believed in the mixed economy, I had never much liked the profit motive. To be among people who thought it wonderful was at first quite uncomfortable, but I soon took it on board. The majority of the British intelligentsia did not do so until quite recently. What they perceived as a new philosophy of 'market economics' was in fact the stock-in-trade of mainstream economists throughout my working life.

But what I really liked about economics was the breadth of the issues it could handle – from taxation and transport to education, health and crime. Since many people question this universalism of economics, let me try to explain what I think economics can and cannot do. I shall do it in the form of seven propositions, beginning with positive economics and moving on to policy.

---

* Prepared for this volume.

WHAT I BELIEVE

Economics is about rational choice and about systems

Economics is about two things – rational choice and systems. Positive economics begins with rational choice which tells us how individuals and companies will change their behaviour if faced with different alternatives. These responses can be predicted because to a degree individuals and companies are maximising some objective function subject to constraints. When altered circumstances change the constraints, behaviour changes in predictable ways. In common parlance, people compare the benefits and costs of different actions and adjust until there is no scope for increasing the excess of benefit over cost.

From this approach to the different agents in the economy, we then model the working of the system when all the agents interact. When they come together in a 'market', this determines the terms ('prices') which constitute the opportunities for the individual agents. Thus the 'market' determines the prices and also the allocation of resources – of which the most important is the use of human time. There can be no coherent economic analysis of any problem without an equilibrium model of how agents interact to determine a set of prices and quantities.

Too much of empirical economics is conducted without a theory of how the system is working. People run wage equations which show that house prices affect wages without reference to what causes house prices. And so on. There has to be theory, but the theory must be driven by facts.

Positive economics should start from facts

When we set up the Centre for Labour Economics in 1980, we discussed what were the big issues we should investigate. One distinguished theorist said we should investigate 'why unemployment was too high'. But most of us jumped on him, saying we should investigate first why unemployment was what it was. Only if we understood that could we fruitfully discuss whether it was too high.

This means that we must start from facts. Of course some facts are more interesting than others – and generally the things we want to explain will be things which have a big impact on human welfare or on people's ability to make money. But that is a matter of motivation. The research strategy must be driven only by facts – many facts. And the aim of the research is to find an explanation which is as consistent as possible with all of them.

Thus economics which starts with one fact and looks for a theoretical explanation of it is unlikely to be fruitful. I once taught a labour economics course jointly with a distinguished theorist, who claimed to have revolutionised contract theory by insisting that workers must in fact be indifferent to being laid off. I asked him why he believed this. He replied that it must be so, and offered an anecdote about a case where an involuntary separation became voluntary through the offer of increased redundancy pay.

Economics cannot be based on the odd anecdote. It should start from a serious body of facts and try to find a theory which encompasses them. Theory is vital in economics and too few applied economists work on it. But the reverse is equally true. Unfortunately in our profession too little prestige is derived from knowledge of facts. But facts should be as important for theory as they are for empirical work.

The best kind of theory is theory which leads to estimable equations, so that we can find out whether the theory is true. It took me years to learn this, and without the shining example of Stephen Nickell I might never have learned it.

But how scientific can economics ever be?

Positive economics should aspire to be a science

We have to be realistic. At present we have few controlled experiments. So most of our evidence comes from non-experimental data where too many variables are changing across the different observations for us to get very precise estimates of causal effects. In practice we proceed in a Bayesian fashion, basing our views on many pieces of evidence, and modifying them as further evidence accumulates. We rarely base our views on one test or estimation. Thus when we report standard errors on coefficients the reason is not usually to test whether the coefficients are different from zero, but to help us form some estimate of what the effect is – taking into account other estimates we know of and their standard errors.

One of the striking differences between economists and many other social scientists is that they are not usually testing whether a relationship exists but what it is. The aim is to build a coherent explanation. Economists generally focus on the coefficients in their equations (how much y changes as a result of a given change in x), while many other social scientists find it enough to ask whether an association exists. In addition, economists realise that most relationships are multi-variate and get frustrated by the bivariate correlations still produced by so many other social scientists. It is one of the glories of economics that econometrics has set a standard which is now being followed more widely in the social sciences.

Even so the controlled experiment and the natural experiment generally provide clearer evidence than non-experimental data. I greatly admire economists like Orley Ashenfelter and David Card who have tried so hard to find good quasi-experimental evidence and to make sense of it. Unfortunately there is so far only limited evidence of this type. As time passes, we shall get more of it and the information revolution will also yield much larger numbers of observations on non-experimental data. So the future for economics as a science is bright.

But for the moment we are still in the Middle Ages. Economists are better placed than others to make sense of economic reality and, if we do not do it, others even more ignorant will take over. So it is right that economists should go beyond pure science and offer the most coherent explanation they can of what is happening – even when the evidence is contradictory and a judgement has to be made. It is perfectly proper that the judgement should be based not only on systematic research but also on personal experience of life. Certainly this is the spirit in which Stephen Nickell, Richard Jackman and I have approached the explanation of European unemployment.

The key requirement is that the explanation be consistent with the main facts. Not only must it explain the thing of greatest interest (for example, aggregate unemployment or inflation) but it must be consistent with more detailed facts (such as the structure of unemployment or price movements). Many theories fall at this first hurdle. For example, Paul Krugman has hypothesised that 'US inequality and European unemployment are two sides of the same coin'. The idea is that the demand for labour has shifted towards skilled labour. In response to this, relative wages of the unskilled fell in the USA, while in Europe they did not, so that unemployment rose. But the corollary of this mismatch explanation is that for skilled workers in Europe the unemployment rate should have fallen. But in fact it rose by at least the same multiple as did unskilled unemployment. So Krugman's theory of why European unemployment rose falls at the first hurdle. Without checking on the intermediate predictions the theory would have appeared consistent with the facts.

The separation between theory and empirical work in the profession is unfavourable to the spirit of checking against the facts. For a theory article to be published it is often sufficient that it be clever and internally consistent. There is no soupçon of requirement to provide evidence. Even worse, I discover from the chairman of one editorial board that it is generally dangerous to include evidence when submitting a theory article because the evidence might not be of equivalent standard to the theory. If this is true, it cannot be good for the development of economic understanding.

In my opinion there is another criterion for a plausible explanation of events.

A plausible explanation describes the behaviour of people and companies in ways they themselves would recognise

There are two polar styles in economics, with a spectrum in between. At one pole are those who are content with explanations that appeal to economists but not to anyone else. An example is the theory that unemployment fluctuates due to intertemporal substitution in labour supply. This was never remotely plausible to any unemployed person, but wasted the time of millions of economics students. Our profession is so sheltered that it is quite possible for it to play its own games without worrying when there are literally no spectators from outside the profession.

But in the end the theories which prevail are those where the economist has checked his model with practitioners. He has said to an economic actor, 'Here is my model of why you do what you do', and the actor has said, 'Yes, that makes sense'. Surely every economist should perform such checks.

It is nice to be an economist because on the whole it has been the most successful social science – in predictive ability and therefore in public prestige. Yet in many ways this is surprising because the theory of rational choice explains such a small part of human behaviour.

Human wellbeing depends on more than individual opportunities

Economics explains the behaviour of individuals with given tastes as their opportunities change. It does not explain their tastes. Thus economics is much better at explaining *changes* in behaviour than the *levels* of, say, consumption or time use. Culture is a key factor here, though as the world becomes more homogeneous there will be fewer such differences to explain.

A second major weakness of standard economics is that it ignores many key variables that affect utility and therefore affect behaviour. For example, if you get a pay rise and I do not, I become unhappy. This may affect my work effort. The simplest form of efficiency wage theory is one where effort depends on the individual's wage relative to some concept of the fair wage. In that case, work effort will not be correctly predicted by a utility function that ignores these externalities.

This is extremely unfortunate from the point of view of positive economics. It is even more serious from the point of view of normative or 'public' economics. For example, if I work harder and earn more and this hurts other people, then this provides an extra argument in favour of income taxes.

It is most unfortunate that the thousands of economists who think about how to maximise a social welfare function $W(u_1, \ldots, u_n)$ should have devoted so little attention to what actually generates utility. It is one reason why politicians often disregard the advice of economists – because they know better what affects utility than the economists who think that income and prices say it all. Obviously psychologists and social psychologists have to come to the rescue here, but they will not provide the insights that we need unless we work with them. Among the few honourable examples of economists who do this are Richard Thaler and Andrew Oswald. One of Oswald's most important findings is that being unemployed reduces a person's happiness by much more than the cost of the income loss. This means that social welfare depends not only on output but also negatively on unemployment. The usual welfare triangle will give quite the wrong idea, especially if we treat leisure as a normal good.

Thus any sensible policy analysis is bound to use an eclectic approach. Most of the economists I most respect do just this, rather than using one simple model as a guide. They also recognise that any policy choice must allow for issues of fairness as well as efficiency.

Public choices must always involve issues of income distribution

When I took up economics in the 1960s the common view was that 'economic policy' was about how to achieve efficiency – maximising the size of the cake. It was then the task of 'social policy' to decide how the cake should be distributed and used. This distinction between economic and social policy was a disaster, since every policy decision affects both the size of the cake and its distribution. The focus on efficiency had been rationalised by the Kaldor criterion, which said that a change was good if the gainers gained enough to be able (hypothetically) to compensate the losers, by lump-sum transfers. The criterion was philosophically absurd since a change could be morally justified along these lines only if the compensation were actually paid. It is also practically unhelpful since in the practical world lump-sum transfers (with no incentive effects) are impossible to orchestrate and any policy generates losers as well as gainers.

Yet in the early postwar period much of the thinking of economists about the problems of distribution was conducted as if lump-sum transfers were possible. Thus arose the postwar welfare state which considered that poverty was best dealt with through cash redistribution, rather than by enabling people (where possible) to be productive and earn a decent living.

Thinking improved greatly through the work of James Meade, Britain's greatest postwar economist and founder of the subject of 'public economics', and his great successors Jim Mirrlees, Tony Atkinson, Joe Stiglitz and Amartya Sen who was a great influence for good at LSE during the 1970s. They all started from the point that lump-sum transfers were impossible and we are in the world of second-best. It followed that if the objective was to maximise a social welfare function $W(u_1, ..., u_n)$ subject to behavioural constraints, we should always find that the marginal social value of a pound was different in the hands of different people. Normally the value would be higher in the hands of the poor than of the rich. So income distribution must be taken into account in evaluating every policy.

I stressed this in my first textbook, on *Cost-Benefit Analysis* (1972), and I felt it so strongly that, when I later wrote a microeconomics textbook with Alan Walters (1978), we put welfare economics at the front of the book. The result was that Amartya Sen called it the most left-wing micro text available. But a second result was that it never captured the market. However, I still think that no policy remarks should be included in micro textbooks until the issues of welfare economics have been properly discussed.

Thus policy choices depend on a well specified social welfare function involving ethical judgements, and on sound knowledge of behavioural relationships. The policy problem will suggest which behavioural relationships most need understanding. For example, income tax policy obviously requires knowledge of labour supply responses. But the spirit in which the behavioural relationships are studied should be totally detached. And indeed it is a very good thing that many economists have no interest in advocating policies or in making a fortune – they just want to explain what happens.

If the economics I learned in the 1960s was a little confused on issues of income distribution, in most other ways it was remarkably sound. Some people say that economists have totally changed their tune since the 1960s. This is simply untrue.

Little has happened to make economists change their political philosophy

There was in fact little wrong with the mainstream approach of the majority of British economists in the 1960s. They accepted the profit motive and favoured private production of most goods and services (at least three-quarters of GDP). They were unenthusiastic about trade unions and believed that redistribution was a key role for the state. They also believed that, where individuals are ignorant or exposed (as in education and health), state provision is necessary for efficiency and fairness. Most of them thought competition was important in the private economy and were suspicious of 'industrial policy'. Almost all believed in free trade, except for some development economists. As regards macroeconomics, they considered the key instruments of short-run policy were fiscal policy and interest rates.

So what has changed? For most of the economists I respect, only two things of importance. First, in 1970–2 we switched from the Phillips curve to the expectations-augmented Phillips curve – an important change technically, leading to a de-emphasising of demand as opposed to supply-side issues. But it was hardly a change of political philosophy. Second, we became more aware of government failure as well as market failure, and in the 1980s were converted to the privatisation of telecoms and the debureaucratising of many state functions through the establishment of public agencies.

But the idea that the economics profession in Britain has changed its basic tune is quite simply untrue. The profession has surely been at fault in not explaining clearly enough what it believed – leaving this too often to people at either extreme. Hence people have the impression that economists always disagree with each other – an impression largely overstated by the media because anything else makes the analysis too tame.

At least I can honestly say that my own position has changed little except in the ways I have said. As early as 1980 I was writing that the welfare state had taken the wrong tack in its approach to unemployment, and needed instead a Welfare-to-Work approach.

I also have the impression that most of those who hold more right-wing opinions than myself now also held similar positions in the 1960s. The main change has been a reduced number of left-wingers; most have moved to the centre while a few have unhelpfully proclaimed that economics has died, rather than noting that it was always a complicated business.

Compared with people from some other disciplines, most British economists are now polite and helpful to each other. When they disagree with each other, they usually understand why – rather than simply failing to make contact. This comradeliness makes it a pleasant profession to work in, and is perhaps at its best in Britain's leading economics department at the London School of Economics (LSE), where I have had the pleasure to work throughout my professional life.

THE BOOKS

The sequence of my interests has been heavily influenced by problems of concern in the external world, and perhaps I should describe the sequence briefly as an explanation of the papers gathered together in *Tackling Inequality* and *Tackling Unemployment*.

Education and income distribution

I became an economist in the 1960s. This was a time of strong educational expansion caused by the rapidly rising demand for educated people, coming partly from the space race. This raised the stock of educated people, which in time depressed graduate earnings. So in the 1970s educational expansion largely stopped. In consequence, there was eventually a shortage of educated people, and the rewards to educated people again rose. This produced a second great expansion from the late 1980s, and at the time of writing education is the top priority of all three British political parties.

I have always believed that most people can reach a good educational level if the motivation and opportunities are there. The motivation is largely affected by the pay of people with different types of skill, which is in turn determined by the interaction of demand and supply. But it is also affected by the degree of subsidisation provided by the state.

A key issue in educational policy is therefore the degree of subsidisation at different levels. This can be resolved only by taking into account considerations of equity as well as efficiency. In the 1960s the discussion of education and income distribution focused on the impact of education on annual earnings. This was the great contribution of Becker and Mincer. They showed how the variance of education helped to explain the inequality of annual earnings. But the policy implications went largely unanalysed. On the one side more educated people earned more. But on the other side students were poor. What followed?

It was clear that one could think about the distributional issues only by looking at the incomes of different people over their whole lifetimes. Philosophically, the same applied to issues like health, child support and pensions where one function of the state is to redistribute between different points of life, but another is to redistribute between lifetimes. I therefore developed a cost-benefit framework for analysing the efficiency and equity impact of policies, where equity is evaluated in terms of lifetime income.

When Lyndon Johnson launched the War on Poverty, he believed that education was the key to a more equal society. But then Jencks pointed out that education explains only a small fraction of the variance of annual earnings, making it appear a weak tool of equalisation. But if, as I argued, annual earnings was the wrong concept and it was lifetime earnings that mattered, then a key role for education was re-established.

I tried to show this using relevant empirical material – and comparing the effects of different educational policies with cash redistribution. Since people live in families the analysis has to be done using family income per head rather than individual income. It requires also a knowledge of supply responses.

This led me into the study of family labour supply, since the scope for redistribution is limited by the size of the labour supply response. On the other side, however, I was struck by the consideration that, in trying to keep up with the Joneses, people might be induced to work excessively.

I had the good fortune at this time to meet Orley Ashenfelter who played an important role in bringing the rigour of American labour economics to Britain. I was also asked by the Royal Commission on the Distribution of Income and Wealth to write a report on the causes of poverty, which enabled me to set many of these issues in perspective. At the same time I wrote the microeconomics textbook with Alan Walters to make sure I understood the subject.

In the area of education my other interest was in education as an industry and its incentives (or lack of them) to be efficient. The dominant technology in the education industry has changed little since the invention of book and blackboard, while the technology of communication has been totally revolutionised by post, radio, television, cassette player and computer where there are huge economies of scale. I argued that to be cost-effective the industry had to change. But the problem was, and remains, the incentives facing teachers. Now at last there is some sign that things are changing.

By the late 1970s I was thinking of writing a book about economics and human nature – in other words about what makes people happy and what this implies for policy. But, instead, the second oil shock sent unemployment rocketing up and I thought it would be more useful to work on unemployment.

Unemployment

Though I knew little about the subject, in 1980 I signed a contract to write a book called *Unemployment*. The book was published in 1991 with three authors – Richard Jackman, Stephen Nickell and myself. Working with them has been the most satisfying experience of my working life. Throughout the 1980s we were developing our ideas in a series of articles, but I always felt (and continue to feel) that the idea of a book is always the best incentive for getting a real perspective on an issue. Partly for that reason, but also in order to stimulate debate, I wrote a smaller popular book in 1986 called *How to Beat Unemployment*, reflecting where we had got to at that point.

Looking back, I think our main contributions on unemployment were these.

1   We focused attention on the average level of unemployment over the cycle (the NAIRU) and tried to explain this. We insisted that both positive and normative analysis of unemployment should start from a *general equilibrium* framework, in which the artificial distinction between macro and micro had no place. All the various factors at work should fit into a single model, which could handle the reality of individuals flowing through unemployment as well as the other forces at work. The most fruitful model turned out to involve a function for wages (or more strictly labour cost), a price function and a hiring function.

2   We argued that a key clue to higher European unemployment was the outward shift of unemployment at given *vacancies*. This suggested that something was making the unemployed less effective as fillers of vacancies.

3   One possible explanation for this was increased *mismatch* by skill, region or industry. But we rigorously derived an appropriate measure of mismatch, between the pattern of jobs and the characteristics of job seekers – and this suggested that mismatch had not increased.

4   A more plausible explanation was the huge increase in the proportion of the unemployed who were *long-term* unemployed. We were able to show how for a given unemployment level, vacancies and wage pressure were higher the higher was the proportion of long-term unemployed within the total. This has now become the conventional wisdom, and there is growing support for the corollary – that the welfare state should be re-designed to prevent people entering long-term unemployment.

5   The key issue to focus upon was the wage curve – i.e. the level of real wage cost associated with any given level of unemployment. The main factors influencing unemployment could all be analysed through their influence on the wage curve. Important factors included are *wage bargaining*, where we developed a plausible model of decentralised bargaining (perhaps the first) which explained why (despite the turnover of workers) firms tended not to

contract but to adjust their employment in response to the size of the labour force.

6   For all the main *policies* we tried to develop relevant models. For active labour market policy we developed models to analyse the degree of substitution and displacement (much exaggerated in public discussion), and we showed in a plausible way how a tax-based incomes policy would work. George Johnson was a great stimulus to all our policy analysis.

Meantime I was fortunate enough in 1982 to be appointed to the Macroeconomic Policy Group set up by the European Commission, and including Rudi Dornbusch (as its first chairman) and Olivier Blanchard. Both have been wonderful colleagues. They focused my mind on the absolute necessity of a blending of macro and micro. They also forced me to think about problems on a wider international canvas, and in my time in the group we produced four reports urging a more proactive employment strategy in Europe.

Economic reform

In 1989 Dornbusch and I formed a new group including also Olivier Blanchard, Larry Summers, Paul Krugman and Andrei Shleifer. This was the time of economic transition, and our group produced three books on reform, including one on its impact on migration.

In 1991 I was invited to become an economic adviser to the Russian government and spent much of 1992 there. Thereafter my monthly visits became shorter and shorter, but we still had a strong team in Moscow producing *Russian Economic Trends* and contributing to the Russian policy debate within the government and the media. We had a monthly press conference. The work I did on Russia was largely macroeconomic, including writing a macroeconomic textbook about the Russian economy. But I also studied the labour market and analysed the remarkable labour market flexibility there which helped to keep unemployment in check.

Progress in Russia was always going to be difficult, given Russia's unique legacy of 75 years of Communism. Up to the end of 1996 I was fairly optimistic and progress was indeed being made. John Parker and I recorded our views in a co-authored book which we titled *Russia Reborn?* but the publisher insisted on calling it *The Coming Russian Boom*. From December 1996 onwards I became more pessimistic, as reflected in the monthly updates of *Russian Economic Trends*. The problem was not, as is often said, that Russia was having inappropriate market solutions foisted on it, but that local and national governments were intefering in every aspect of the economy and preventing new firms from developing. From autumn 1997 my anxieties increased, as it became obvious that Russia was next in line for a speculative attack after the

Far East. Early and resolute action by the West could have preserved financial order, but it was not taken.

In the meantime the British policy world has become a lot more attractive to someone like myself. The Labour Party has adopted on a large scale the kinds of policy in which I believe – preventing long-term unemployment and ensuring a minimum level of skill for all. We now have a real opportunity to put our ideas to the test.

I cannot end without a tribute to the LSE which has been my working home. It provides a wonderfully stimulating environment, in which there is always someone who knows the answer to your questions and someone who will help. The hand of management is light, so that if you have an idea you can implement it.

I came to LSE in 1964 to set up with Claus Moser the Higher Education Research Unit. In 1974 it became the Centre for Labour Economics and in 1990 the Centre for Economic Performance.[1] Since 1980 it has had a block grant from the ESRC, whose support has been constant and unswerving. And it has attracted the best in-house research group of economists in Europe and two fine deputy directors Charles Bean and David Metcalf. I am deeply grateful for their help. But equally important has been the wonderful administrative support over the years of Pam Mounsey, Bettie Jory, Phyllis Gamble, Joanne Putterford, Philomena McNicholas and, above all, Marion O'Brien and Nigel Rogers. I have been truly lucky.

Note

1.   Strictly, from 1964–7 it was called the Unit for Economic and Statistical Studies on Higher Education, and from 1974–7 it was the Centre for the Economics of Education. But the key break points were 1964, 1974 and 1990.

References

Layard, R. (ed.) (1972) *Cost-Benefit Analysis* (Penguin Modern Economics Readings); Second Edition (edited with S. Glaister) 1994 (Cambridge University Press).
Layard, R. (1986) *How to Beat Unemployment* (Oxford: Oxford University Press).
Layard, R. (from 1992) *Russian Economic Trends*, 4 quarterly issues (London: Whurr).
Layard, R., S. Nickell and R. Jackman (1991) *Unemployment: Macroeconomic Performance and the Labour Market* (Oxford: Oxford University Press).
Layard, R. and J. Parker (1996) *The Coming Russian Boom* (New York: The Free Press).
Layard, R. and A. Walters (1978) *Microeconomic Theory* (New York: McGraw-Hill) reissued as McGraw-Hill International edition, 1987.

Part I
Education and Inequality

2 Introduction

Two key questions for any society are: what determines average income, and what determines its distribution? I devoted most of the 1970s to working on these issues.

LIFETIME INEQUALITY

We begin with four chapters on major strategic issues. Chapter 3 deals with the question of how to measure the effects of the state on social welfare. Since there is continuity of the personality, our idea of fairness cannot treat every person-year as a separate event. The basic units for thinking about inequality are lifetimes. We have to find some way of summarising lifetime income, and this chapter is one of the first which presents such estimates.

We then want to analyse the impact of policy changes upon social welfare in a way that distinguishes between their effects on efficiency and equity. This is easy to do if we use the Atkinson equality index, since social welfare then equals average income *times* equality. Using this approach the chapter evaluates different educational and cash transfer policies.

The approach is extended in Chapter 4 to allow for the fact that people live in families. This means that inequality depends on marriage functions, fertility functions, earnings functions, and of course labour supply functions. All of these are estimated first, followed by policy analyses. These show, for example, that it would be possible to increase both equality and efficiency by shifting public expenditure on education away from higher education towards education that was more universal.

The lifetime framework has a profound impact on the relative impact of educational policy and cash redistribution upon the final distribution of welfare – because so much cash redistribution is between different periods in the same lifetime or is related to temporary fluctuations of income. This is shown clearly in Chapter 5.

So what are the main instruments for the state to reduce poverty? As Chapter 6 brings out, the distribution of income depends not only on education and on cash redistribution, but also on institutions like trade unions, minimum wages and of course the way in which individuals choose their hours of work. These topics are treated in the chapters which follow.

EARNINGS

Chapters 7 and 8 deal with the determinants of individual earnings. Chapter 5 shows the important role of trade unions in raising the earnings of their members relative to average earnings. Whether this leads to more or less equality depends on who belongs to unions.

Chapter 8 focuses on the impact of education, and shows that the measured impact of education is much greater when one focuses on actual educational achievement measured by qualifications obtained (including those through part-time study) rather than on years of full-time schooling. The chapter also punctures some of the more unreasonable claims made by Mincer about the share of earnings variance explained by human capital.

PRODUCTIVITY

If extra education raises an individual's earnings, this does not necessarily imply that it raises his productivity. There might be a pure screening effect, whereby education was used as a signal for pre-existing ability. Chapter 9 tackles this problem. It gives three powerful reasons for questioning the importance of the screening issue. Thus we can fairly safely assume that, when education raises a person's earnings, it is also raising that person's contribution to the national product.

So how far do educational differences explain the differences in productivity between countries? Chapter 10 attempts an answer.[1] It estimates the parameters of a CES production function where output depends on physical capital, human capital and raw labour. This shows that human and physical capital are complementary. As each of them accumulates, it raises the marginal product of the other more (proportionately) than it raises the marginal product of raw labour. Using this production function, the finding is that human capital per head 'explains' an important part of the income differences between countries, but less than physical capital per head explains.

LABOUR SUPPLY

Labour supply responses are crucial when thinking about the efficiency costs of cash redistribution. Chapters 11 and 12 are concerned with female labour supply. Changes in women's work are among the most profound changes in postwar history and it appears that women's labour supply elasticities are higher than men's – adding to the efficiency costs of cash redistribution. Chapter 11 is a cross-sectional study of female participation in Britain. The resulting supply elasticities explain about one-third of the time-series growth of women's work in the 1950s and 1960s, though more since the Equal Pay Act of 1970. Chapter 12 is a time-series study, which implies a rather higher estimate of labour supply elasticities. But its chief focus is on the role of children in explaining the lifecycle of women's work and the historical changes in women's work.

The higher the supply elasticity, the more inefficiency occurs in the process of cash redistribution. As Harberger (1971) once put it, the process of redistribution is like the process of sending ice cream from the rich to the poor on camelback across the desert – how much you will send depends on how much is lost in transit. But how much is in fact lost? Harberger argued that not much was lost. It followed that society must value a dollar almost equally whether it was in the hand of a rich man or a poor one – since otherwise it would transfer still more from rich to poor. The conclusion of all this was that cost-benefit analysis could ignore distributional considerations.

However, Harberger had made a simple error – see Chapter 13. Even if the compensated labour supply elasticity is as low as 0.15, the marginal cost of redistributing one dollar is around 30 cents – once you allow for the efficiency effects on both rich and poor.

Efficiency arguments thus put an important limit on redistribution. But there is another argument going in the opposite direction – the problem of keeping up with the Joneses. If Jones works harder and earns more in order to outshine his neighbours, the neighbours feel worse off. They therefore work harder also. In the end it is possible that none of them feels better off because of their higher income, but all are working harder. So all are worse off. As Chapter 14 argues, this is one reason why economic growth often leads to no increase in self-reported happiness. There is one obvious exception – when people's income exceeds what they expected it to be. This is what happened in the golden age of the 1950s and 1960s.

EDUCATIONAL POLICY AND TEACHING METHODS

The next three chapters deal with the planning and organisation of education. Chapter 15 sets out the basic rate of return approach to education planning, and hints at how this can be used as a guide to policy in a dynamically changing world.

The next two chapters deal with the organisation of education as an industry. Chapter 16 discusses the problem of perverse incentives in universities. This comes from the problems of measuring output, either of teaching or research – leading to the organisation of universities as labour-managed enterprises. The result is a teaching system which no firm or army would consider, where bought-in materials (except books) are grossly underused. The reason for this appears to be that teachers like to spend their teaching time on activities like lectures which they enjoy and which help their own research rather than on organising things in the way in which students will learn at least cost.

The worst reflection on universities is their failure to take advantage of the new media of film, tape and computer-aided learning. The economies of scale here are truly enormous and are examined in some detail in Chapter 17. Without a better use of the new media, there is no way in which we can today provide the wider educational opportunities which are needed.

REALISING OUR EDUCATIONAL POTENTIAL

The last three chapters are of mainly historical interest and reflect my belief in the huge importance of education in the development of people and of nations. Chapter 18 is a section from the Robbins Report on Higher Education. When the Committee began its work, there was a growing literature on the pool of ability, in which people tried to calculate the maximum number of people with the ability to benefit from university. One calculation suggested that it was only 7 per cent of the population! I reviewed this literature and came to the conclusion that there was no meaningful limit to the numbers who could be educated. The Committee accepted this view, and recommended an ambitious plan for expanding the system.

By 1987 it was widely believed that there had been a 'Thatcher revolution', so that Britain's productivity record had been turned around, with Britain moving up towards the North European level. In Chapter 19 Nickell and I questioned whether this improvement would last – owing to the poor quality of education offered to the bottom half of the workforce. Unfortunately we have been proved right. Over the period 1979–96 output per hour in Britain rose no faster than in France and Germany: the gap remained as wide as ever.[2] And British inequality increased.

It became clear that most countries with good productivity growth took good care to ensure an adequate minimum level of skill for all their people. In Chapter 20 Steedman and I set out what is needed in Britain for people aged over 16. In 1996 the Labour Party put forward as Target 2000 a programme for 16–18 year olds, similar to that which we had advocated.

I will end with my conclusions on the pool of ability which I wrote for the Robbins Committee, but which remain true to this day:[3] 'Much untapped ability exists in this country. But little is known about ultimate human capacities. The levels of education already achieved would have surprised those alive even fifty years ago, and it is impossible to circumscribe with a formula the potentialities of the future.'

Notes

1. An earlier attempt by estimating a translog production function appears in Layard, Sargan, Ager and Jones (1971).
2. Layard (1997) Chapter 3.
3. Layard (1963).

References

Harberger, A.C. (1971) 'Three basic postulates for applied welfare economics', *Journal of Economic Literature* (September).

Layard, R. (1963) *Appendix Volumes One – Three of Higher Education. Report of the Robbins Committee* (London: HMSO).

Layard, R. (1997), *What Labour Can Do* (London: Warner Books).

Layard, R., D. Sargan, M. Ager and D. Jones (1971) *Qualified Manpower and Economic Performance: An Inter-Plant Study in the Electrical Engineering Industry* (London: Allen Lane, The Penguin Press).

3 On Measuring the Redistribution of Lifetime Income (1977)*

I INTRODUCTION

How far, if at all, does the State reduce inequality? Or, how far does a particular policy affect it? To answer these questions one has to compare the *actual* distribution of income after taxes and benefits (a vector $\underline{V}^A$) with some *hypothetical* alternative distribution ($\underline{V}^H$).[1] The measure of income normally used in such analyses is current annual income, regardless of the past or future income of those concerned (Nicholson, 1964; Musgrave, 1964). But this is unsatisfactory, partly because a person's current income is a bad measure of his underlying real income, and especially because much government activity redistributes a person's lifetime income over his lifetime more than it alters its total. The 'annual-income approach' thus gives the wrong impression in two ways: first, it exaggerates the basic inequality of incomes and then it exaggerates the amount of redistribution.

It is particularly important to take the lifecycle perspective when considering social service expenditures, since, unlike such programmes as roads and defence, the social services typically involve payments by workers to support non-workers such as children, pensioners, the sick or the unemployed. Since individuals do not remain in these dependent categories throughout their lives, current beneficiaries will, at other times, be supporting people who are similar to themselves but at a different stage of their lifecycle or of their fortunes. One may speculate on why such transfers are actually made or may be desirable. In terms of welfare economics many of them may be defended on grounds of the

* Chapter 4 in M.S. Feldstein and R.P. Inman (eds), *The Economics of Public Services* (London: Macmillan, 1977). This paper arises from work done jointly with Mark Stewart, who did the computing with superb efficiency. The author is also most grateful to M.J. Bowman, P. Dasgupta, A. Flowerdew, R. Jackman, A.R. Prest, G. Psacharopoulos, A.K. Sen, C. von Weizsäcker and B.A. Weisbrod for comments and helpful discussions on various points, and to the Social Science Research Council for financial support.

failure of capital and insurance markets or as merit wants, rather than on grounds of equity, and Arrow (1963) has argued that

> a good part of the preference for redistribution expressed in government taxation and expenditure policies and private charity can be reinterpreted as desire for insurance. It is noteworthy that virtually nowhere is there a system of subsidies that has as its aim simply an equalization of income.

This paper, however, is not concerned with how to explain or justify State action, but with how to measure its effects on the inequality of *ex post* lifetime incomes.

Section II justifies the use of lifetime rather than annual income to measure V^A and considers the problems of measuring it when capital markets are imperfect and some people live longer than others. Section III discusses how to measure V^H using relevant alternative policy assumptions with clearly defined non-steady-state time dimensions; it also considers the distinction between the effects of policy on *ex ante* and *ex post* income. Section IV deals briefly with the parametric representation of redistribution and adopts a framework within which the distributional and efficiency effects of policies can be computed in a commensurable way. It also rehearses some handy rules of thumb for measuring distributional effects, subject to one caution, which is often overlooked. Section V applies these ideas to education. First it contrasts approaches that look at effects on parents with those that look at effects on children, and supports Jencks's argument that education may not be a very suitable means towards income equalisation. It then proceeds to compute the equity and efficiency effects of various possible policies in Britain, using a newly estimated earnings function. It tentatively concludes that new cash subsidies to upper secondary education might be efficient and not too inequitable, but that a reduction in higher education subsidies might be efficient and equitable.

II LIFETIME INCOME AS THE MEASURE OF INDIVIDUAL WELFARE

Why lifetime income?

There are well known objections to using income within a limited time period as an indicator of economic welfare. First, it includes transitory income, which, according to Friedman (1957, p. 189) accounts for between 15 per cent and 30 per cent of the cross-sectional variance in the annual incomes of urban families. Then, there are the earnings variations that reflect differential investments in human capital; if we include in this category the effects of schooling and on-the-job training, these compensating differentials account for at least 30 per cent of the cross-sectional variance of the log of earnings in the work force (Mincer, 1974). However, there is no obvious reason why earnings distribution should exclude those who have zero earnings because they are still at school, and, if all aged over, say, sixteen were included, differential human capital investment would explain an even greater share of earnings inequality. Then there is the problem of retirement, which means that the economic welfare of a man with a given income at 60 is quite different from that of a man with the same income but with 20 more years of work ahead of him. Finally, there is the effect on welfare of the ownership of wealth, as opposed to the receipt of income from it.

However, various ways around these problems have been suggested that focus on annual consumption rather than on income as a measure of welfare. One is to compute for each individual the annuity that he could take out on the strength of his current wealth and expected earnings (Weisbrod and Hansen, 1969).[2] This is the standard of consumption that the person could maintain for the rest of his life if he planned no bequest. An alternative is to take a person's actual current consumption as the measure of his welfare (Kaldor, 1955), though this is less good since it ignores any satisfaction he may be getting from accumulation for purposes of bequest.

These ideas are certainly more consistent with standard theory than is the notion that individual welfare depends on current income. However, in measuring inequalities in welfare one must have some social welfare function in mind, in which both justice and efficiency play a part. The measures of welfare proposed in the last paragraph imply that the justice of the current-period distribution of consumption can be assessed independently of the past consumption of each of those currently consuming.[3] If one accepts the continuity of the personality, this would seem impossible. Additive utilitarians would, of course, argue that the social welfare in one period depends only on the sum of happinesses, regardless of their distribution among persons. If this were so, social welfare over many periods should also be independent of the grouping of sequential states of mind within individuals. But additive utilitarianism is morally unattractive (Sen, 1973a). Thus, if social welfare in one period depends not only on the sum of happiness, but also on its inequality, intertemporal social welfare must take into account the grouping of 'happinesses' in different periods as between individuals. So we may say, fairly generally, that

$$W = W[U_1(C_{11}, \ldots, C_{1T_1}), \ldots, U_n(C_{n1}, \ldots, C_{nT_n})]$$

where C_{ij} is the consumption (including gifts to others) of the ith person in the jth year of his life, T_i is his age when he dies and U_i is a cardinal measure of his lifetime welfare. W measures social welfare and is a symmetric and concave function of the Us. In practice, of course, there is no general way of taking into account the different utility functions of different members of society. So we assume a common utility function for all men. Ignoring, for the moment, the problem of varying lengths of life, we might write this utility function, for an individual living T periods, as

$$U = U[V(C_1, \ldots, C_T)]$$

where V is a linear homogeneous function, and U increases with V but at a declining rate.

The discount-rate problem

The first practical problem, then, would then be to find an index that approximately measures V for each individual. In a perfect capital market we could take the present value of his consumption plus gifts to others, which would necessarily be equal to the present value of his after-tax earnings plus gifts from others.[4] But if capital markets are imperfect, two people with consumption streams having the same present value at some discount rate may differ both in utility and in the present value of their discounted incomes. If we knew the individual consumption streams this would pose no problem: we could simply assume some reasonable functional form for V. But we generally know only people's income streams. If, in addition, we knew their capital-market positions, we should again have no problem: we could either infer their maximal V or compute the consumption annuity that would give the same satisfaction.

But we normally know nothing about people's capital-market positions. Assuming, therefore, that we use a common discount rate, how should it be selected? There is probably greater variation among people in borrowing rates than in lending rates. Suppose, for a moment, two borrowers of equal ability and owning no non-human capital. Would we get better measures of their real income differences by using high or low discount rates? The individual with the lower borrowing rate will invest more in human capital and will, therefore, have a higher ratio of earnings in later life to earnings in earlier life.[5] If we evaluate their incomes using high discount rates we shall overlook this advantage. This is illustrated in Figure 3.1 for the traditional two-period case. Individual I has a lower borrowing rate than has individual II. They have the same original endowment and investment opportunities. I is better off than II. Yet, at a rate of interest equal to II's borrowing rate, II has a higher present value of income than I has, and, at a rate of interest equal to I's borrowing rate, the discounted incomes stand in a ratio that understates V^I/V^{II}.[6]

Only at a rate less than the lower of the two rates, do we get a ratio of present values that correctly measures V^I/V^{II}. This argument suggests that, so long as interest rates and ability are independent, we should use low discount rates for

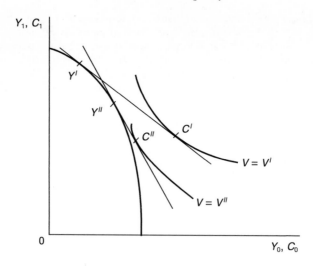

Figure 3.1

borrowers. In fact, of course, people of higher-than-average ability tend to come from relatively well favoured families and therefore will be using lower discount rates. But higher ability, defined as a higher marginal rate of return on a given amount of human capital (Becker, 1967) will, other things being equal, lead a man to choose a higher ratio of later to earlier earnings; this provides a second reason for using low discount rates to make real income comparisons. The rates should perhaps be similar to those used for lenders, who have unearned incomes, so far ignored. In the empirical work in this paper, I concentrate on the estimates using a 5 per cent real rate.[7]

The length-of-life problem

The next inescapable problem is the variation in length of life. Suppose that the length of individual lives was the same under all hypothetical distributions of income. Now, compare two people with the same present value of income, one of whom lives to 80 and the other to 60. Which is better off? All of our normal judgements about inequality imply that the one who lives to be 80 is worse off, as he will have had a lower standard of living for most of his life. The most natural solution might be to measure a person's income by the annuity that, taken over his actual lifespan, has the same present value as his actual income stream, both being evaluated at some uniform rate of discount.[8] This is still not altogether satisfactory, since people have different needs at different ages. If these are known, or can be inferred from the chosen time paths of consumption, we might first deflate consumption at each age by some relevant weight before taking the equivalent annuity.

Some will object to this whole argument and assert that life, as such, is good (Meade, 1956). In this case, those who live long are richer than we have allowed. Likewise, State activity that lengthens life may add to income, even though each person's annual standard of living falls. I do not find this plausible. Those who do so might wish to compute individual welfare as the annuity already described times the length of life.

We now have the elements of our actual income distribution vector V^A. The other practical problem is to measure its level of welfare $[W(V^A)]$ and its inequality. However, we postpone this until we have looked at the problems of constructing the alternative vector V^H, corresponding to some alternative set of policies.

III THE EFFECTS OF GOVERNMENT POLICY

What alternatives are we to hypothesise and how do we compute their effects? The lifetime approach immediately raises problems that are concealed in the cross-section.[9] The chief new problems are, first, to identify a 'policy' and, second, to define the time period and historical context over which we consider substituting one policy for another.

Identifying policies

If we follow the 'annual income' approach, we need only note that in the current year the government is paying out £x per pensioner, educating y students at a subsidy of £z per student, and so on. But if we want to know the future pensions that current policy implies for today's workers, or how much education today's students will have to supply to the next generation, we need to know the underlying principles governing today's policies. This raises questions such as: Do present pensions reflect a decision on the relative incomes of pensioners or on the tax rate out of which pensions are to be paid? The problems of defining a pension policy have been discussed by Asimokopoulos and Weldon (1968), though in fact, in Britain at any rate, government pension policies are spelt out in more explicit time streams than are most other policies (Atkinson, 1970a; Prest, 1970). As regards education, we are rarely given any explicit commitment. For example, ten years ago British students thought their maintenance grants had been fixed relative to the wage level, five years ago they thought they had been fixed relative to the price level, and now they appear to have been fixed relative to the nominal pound.

Education and Inequality

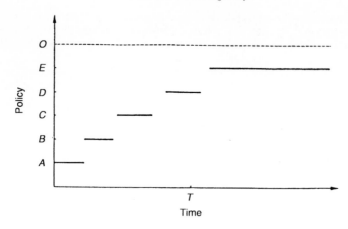

Figure 3.2(a)

This makes it peculiarly difficult to define present educational policies, and to examine their distributional effect, assuming them to be continued. One can, however, attempt to examine the impact of specified changes in policy, as is done in section V.

The time path and context of alternative policies

When alternative policies are being considered, there is also the question of the timing of their substitution. This must depend on the question being asked. For example, economic historians might ask how State activity in education has affected the distribution of lifetime incomes. To answer this, they might attempt to compare the effect of the whole set of policies in force up to now (and those expected from now on) with the effects of zero State activity. This is illustrated in Figure 3.2(a), which indicates that, since State activity began (in year 0) and up to now (year T), varying policies (A to D) have been in force, and now we have policy E. This set of policies is to be compared with no policy (policy 0). For this purpose, the inner rationale of past policies need not be discovered, and we need only ask what happened from year to year.

If, however, we are interested in evaluating policy options, we can be interested only in policies that are real options now or in the future. The most natural way to evaluate an additional expenditure option X would be to imagine introducing it now in addition to the policies E that already appear to be in force. We thus compare $(X + E)$ with E as in Figure 3.2(b), taking into account the whole population that will be affected by the introduction of X. The change will have these main types of effect:

(a) intra-cohort redistribution within each cohort;
(b) inter-cohort redistribution between each pair of future cohorts whose education is not complete; and
(c) inter-cohort redistribution due to the impact effect on current earners (assuming, as I do throughout, that the expenditure is tax-financed).

Effect (c) can be wished away either by pretending that the expenditure is financed by borrowing that is to be repaid by the benefiting cohort, or by pretending to compare policies $(X + E)$ and E as if they were in force for ever (see Figure 3.2c).

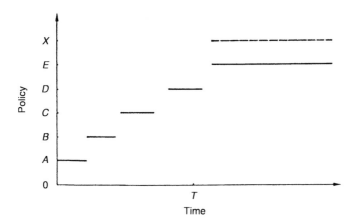

Figure 3.2(b)

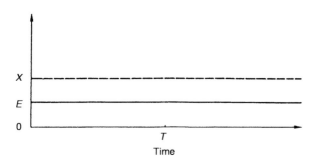

Figure 3.2(c)

Effect (b) can be simplified by further assuming, as the context of the comparison, either steady-state growth or, in the case of pure consumption transfers between generations, exogenously-given constant rates of growth of income and population. In these cases, many policies, constantly maintained, will affect all generations in the same way.[10] However, as regards steady-state growth, the historical record shows that the increase of measured inputs gives a good explanation of growth in output in the United States (Jorgesen and Griliches, 1967). Thus, little is gained by resorting to the steady-state fiction when attempting quantitative measure of redistribution. As regards exogenous growth, it does not seem credible, for example, that a tax-financed increase in pensions would not alter the rate of saving. Moreover, as soon as we return to historical time and introduce policy X at time T, we find that a tax-financed increase in educational outlays is bound to hurt present adults and a decrease in pensions is bound to hurt present pensioners. It is worth noting how many cohorts would actually be subject to these impact effects. A policy involving increased educational expenditure would, perhaps, have a harmful impact effect on 50-year cohorts of existing adults, whose education is finished and who could never gain from educational expansion; the impact would continue, in the case of the youngest cohort, for 50 years.

However, even though a historical context seems preferable for applied work on redistribution, some simplifying assumptions have to be made. In section V, I estimate the effects of various possible educational changes on the lifetime incomes of only one cohort of currently young people. I ignore the one-for-all effect of the additional taxes on existing adults. I also ignore, for lack of data, the impact of the changes on the incomes of the parents of the currently young cohort. Finally, I make a simplifying assumption about the extra taxes that the current cohort will need to pay in order to finance the extra expenditure on succeeding generations. As regards the tax adjustment, there are two problems. First, there is the new problem, introduced by the lifecycle approach, of determining the future numbers who will benefit from the policy, and the size of the tax bases from which these benefits could be financed. Second, there is the old problem of the tax instruments that would actually be chosen to finance the policy. Some, like Hansen and Weisbrod (1970), argue that it is impossible to answer this latter question – which is the same as saying that it is impossible to assess the distributional impact of a policy. Others (Pechman, 1970) have assumed (reasonably, in my view) that, unless there is good ground for assuming otherwise, expenditure changes will be financed by a mix of taxes equal to the average currently prevailing. Since, in Britain, taxation (including National Insurance) on families of a given size is roughly proportional (CSO, 1972), I assume that all tax changes affect the present values of all incomes equiproportionately. Since the inequality measure used is invariant with respect to scalar multiplication of all incomes, it is not necessary to compute the amount of the tax change; and, thus, the first problem (of projecting future expenditures and tax bases) can be avoided.

Ex ante and *ex post* redistribution

Before coming to education, I shall make a brief digression to consider the effects of other social services and, in particular, the issue of *ex ante* versus *ex post* redistribution. Clearly, many social services have an insurance aspect – health care and sickness benefit (against disease), pensions (against longevity), family support (against unwanted children?). Any insurance scheme redistributes *ex post* income, from the lucky to the unlucky. In a cross-section or lifetime analysis that measures actual individual income, it would thus appear as equalising when compared with the absence of insurance.[11] However, if there were no State insurance, there would be private insurance. State insurance can, therefore, be redistributive *ex post*, as compared with no State insurance, for either of two reasons. First, it could simply have a wider coverage than the private scheme it displaces, even though each is equally redistributive *ex ante*. Second, it could be more redistributive *ex ante*. A private insurance company will, of course, redistribute towards people who have defects it does not know about. But it cannot redistribute to people who have defects that are known in advance; otherwise, it will be bankrupted by 'adverse selection'. For example, a scheme that included benefits in excess of premiums to people with multiple sclerosis would soon have no takers other than sufferers from that affliction.

To illustrate the distinction between these two possible effects of State insurance, we may suppose that, at birth, the income that we should predict for the ith individual from our knowledge of his and his family's characteristics (a vector X_i), together with some general knowledge of the world as it will be during his life, is $f^A(X_i)$. Multiplied with this is random term, U_i^A, with mean unity, which we may suppose independent of the person's characteristics.
So

$$Y_i^A = f^A(X_i)U_i^A$$

and the inequality of income, as measured by the variance of log income, is, if $\log X$ and $\log U^A$ are independent,

$$\text{var}\,[\log Y^A] = \text{var}\,[\log f^A(X)] + \text{var}\,[\log(U^A)]$$

The left-hand expression measures inequality *ex post*, and the expression in the middle measures it *ex ante*. If we now construct the hypothetical alternative distribution, we have

$$\text{var}\,[\log Y^H] = \text{var}\,[\log f^H(X)] + \text{var}\,[\log U^H]$$

Ex post inequality reduction consists of *ex ante* redistribution (var $[\log f^A(X)]$ − var $[\log f^H(X)]$) plus the effects of extended insurance (var $[(\log U^A]$ − var $[\log U^H]$).

Should the analysis of redistribution be confined to *ex ante* income? Surely not.[12] The misfortunes of life are in no way either more or less serious than the misfortunes of birth. Arrow (1963) implies that governments tend, in fact, to be more concerned with the former. It would certainly be interesting to partition the effects of government activity into the two components above. But casual inspection suggests that most governments run many programmes that are *ex ante* equalising. Most government health-care and sickness-benefit schemes are not financed in a way related to a person's health risk but, rather, in relation to income, which is inversely related to health risk. Programmes of poor relief are the same. Likewise child-aid programmes such as family allowances, child tax credits, and universal education must equalise *ex ante* income, for they raise the standard of living of children in larger families, where the standard of living is, on average, lower than in smaller families.[13] (They also, of course, raise the standard of living of the parents, but parents who choose larger families cannot necessarily be considered worse off than those parents of the same income who have smaller families.)

IV   THE PARAMETRIC REPRESENTATION OF REDISTRIBUTION

Suppose we have now constructed our two income vectors $\underline{V}^A$ and $\underline{V}^H$. What is an appropriate way to compare them? We could of course compare them for social welfare, using some explicit concave social welfare function. In this case, we prefer $\underline{V}^H$ to $\underline{V}^A$ if $W(\underline{V}^H)$ exceeds $W(\underline{V}^A)$. However, suppose, as is often the case, that we want to look separately at the equity and efficiency aspects of the policy. The efficiency effects can be measured by the ratio of the average present values $\overline{V}^A/\overline{V}^H$. The equity effects could be measured by any of a number of inequality measures (Sen, 1973a). However, it would be desirable if the inequality measure implied some specific trade-off between equality and efficiency so that, if we knew both equality and efficiency effects, we could say whether social welfare had improved. This is the virtue of the Atkinson (1970b) inequality measure, as opposed to, for example, the coefficient of variation of income or the standard deviation of the logs.[14] The trade-off is as follows. Social welfare (W) is a concave function of $\underline{V}$. Equally-distributed equivalent income (V_{EDE}) is defined as that income which, if everybody had it, would produce the same social welfare as the actual income distribution vector $\underline{V}$. So

$$W(V_{EDE}, \ldots, V_{EDE}) = W(V_1, \ldots, V_n)$$

Because the welfare function is concave,

$$V_{EDE} < \overline{V}$$

The Atkinson inequality measure is then

$$I = 1 - \frac{V_{EDE}}{\overline{V}} \qquad 0 \le I \le 1$$

To get the trade-off we note that

$$V_{EDE} = (1 - I)\overline{V}$$

If social welfare increases under the hypothetical alternative policy, then

$$V_{EDE}^H > V_{EDE}^A$$

Therefore, $\qquad \dfrac{1 - I^H}{1 - I^A} > \dfrac{\overline{V}^A}{\overline{V}^H}$

or, for small changes $\qquad \Delta \ell n (1 - I) > - \Delta \ell n \, \overline{V}$

The proportional increase in 'equality' must exceed the proportional fall in total output.

In Section V, I compute measures of both of these for each policy change, using for the inequality measure the Atkinson welfare function

$$W = \frac{1}{\alpha} \sum V_i^\alpha \alpha < 1$$

Taking $\alpha = -1$. The combined effect of any two policies can be roughly inferred by adding their separate effects, provided that the effects of both policies on a given individual are small and additive.

Rules of thumb

However, in speculating about the effects of policy it is also helpful to have some principles that enable one to infer, where possible, without doing detailed calculations, whether a policy is equalising or not. It often happens that policies are of a form that enables one to make such inferences. One such case is when a policy clearly shifts the Lorenz curve either in or out along its whole length, so that inequality rises or falls using any concave W. An example is where a policy confers benefits (B) and imposes costs (C) in a way uniquely related to income (V), so that

$$B(V_{min}) - C(V_{min}) > 0 \tag{3.1}$$

$$-1 < \frac{dB}{dV} - \frac{dC}{dV} < 0 \qquad \text{(all } V) \tag{3.2}$$

$$\Sigma B(V_i) - \Sigma C(V_i) = 0 \tag{3.3}$$

In this case the Lorenz curve after the policy lies wholly along or above the previous Lorenz curve, for the policy can be achieved entirely by transfers from richer to poorer.[15]

For practical purposes it is often easier to analyse redistribution by looking not at the absolute change of B and C per unit change in income, but at the proportional change. Supposing that within the relevant range $B = aV^{\alpha}$ and $C = V^{\beta}$, and that conditions (3.1)–(3.3) hold within that range, then we can say that a policy raises the Lorenz curve throughout if $\alpha < \beta$.[16] This is an extremely useful approach.[17] It says, for example, that, if a programme is financed by a proportional tax, it equalises if benefits rise more slowly than income does.

A proposition about group benefits

However, when we turn to real world policies, there is one caveat. Most policies produce benefits that are not uniquely related to income. Suppose, instead, that a policy confers a given small benefit (α) on all members of a group (group 1) financed by a proportional tax on the whole population (groups 1 and 2). One might suppose that, if the average income of group 1 were above the average income of group 2, the policy would necessarily be disequalising, since group 1 has net gains and group 2 (with lower average income) loses. But this does not follow if the income distributions of the two groups overlap sufficiently. Intuitively, one can see this by supposing initially that the two groups have the same distribution. Then, a given small benefit to either group is definitely equalising (and the tax that finances it leaves inequality unchanged). Now move one rich man from group 2 to group 1. Provided that both groups are large, the policy is still equalising, although group 1 is, on average, richer than group 2. In fact, the policy may be equalising for many more different compositions of the groups. Suppose that there are only two income classes in the population, the poor (with uniform incomes Y_p) and the rich (with uniform incomes Y_R), and the group 1 comprises a proportion p_1 of the poor and a proportion r_1 of the rich ($p_1 < r_1$). The policy is equalising if the proportional increase in the average income of the poor (in groups 1 and 2) exceeds that of the rich (in groups 1 and 2), i.e. if

$$\frac{\alpha p_1}{Y_p} > \frac{\alpha r_1}{Y_R} \quad \text{or} \quad \frac{p_1}{r_1} > \frac{Y_P}{Y_R}$$

The groups must be not too dissimilar (p_1/r_1 too low), but can be more dissimilar the greater the relative poverty of the poor. For, the poorer the poor, the greater the proportional improvement in their income resulting from the gift of α to the few of them in the privileged group 1.

To complete the story, a gift of α to the members of group 2 is necessarily equalising, since

$$\frac{p_2}{r_2} > 1 > \frac{Y_P}{Y_R}$$

Thus, it is perfectly possible that, if the population consists of two (or more) mutually exclusive groups, it is equalising to provide each of them in turn with a given benefit financed by a proportional tax.[18] However, this requires that the groups be not too dissimilar. With the caveat of the preceding paragraph in mind, we can turn to the specific analysis of public support for education.

V EDUCATION AND REDISTRIBUTION

Analysis by parents' income

The traditional approach has been to allocate the estimated benefits of this between individuals according to the income class of their parents. Individual benefits have been estimated as the cost of the subsidy, as would be appropriate if the subsidy had no effect on private choice. Examples of this approach applied to higher education may be found in Glennerster (1972) for Great Britain, and Pechman (1970) for California. The Glennerster analysis showed that, as one goes up the occupational scale and, presumably, the (average) income scale, the probability of having a child at university, and receiving a (uniform) benefit thereby, rises faster than the level of taxes paid per family. If we suppose that this process can be represented by

$$P(B) = aV^{\alpha}; C = bV^{\beta}$$

It is likely to be disequalising, since $\alpha > \beta$.

In the case of California, the position is more complicated, partly because there exist different levels of benefits, but mainly because the probability of receiving a benefit is not a monotonic function of income. This has led to a somewhat confused debate. Hansen and Weisbrod (1969, 1971) grouped the population according to their level of benefits and then showed that those who received higher levels of benefit had higher average incomes and paid, on average, (total) taxes less than the benefits they received. By contrast, Pechman

(1970) grouped the population by income level and showed that the higher education benefits received by the richest income groups were, on average, less than the taxes they paid that could be attributed to higher education.[19] Finally, Hartman (1970) explained how these apparently contradictory findings could be consistent with a given set of data. However, he did not offer a criterion for deciding whether the system was equalising or not and concluded that it was both '(a) regressive and (b) progressive'. This paradox could easily be settled, of course, by the simple device of measuring the inequality of $\underline{V}^A$ and $\underline{V}^H$.

Analysis by child's income

It is, in any case, unsatisfactory to suppose that the incidence of educational expenditures is wholly on parents, so, running to the opposite extreme, Jencks (1972) proceeds on the assumption that the relevant impact is on children. His argument is by now so notorious that, were it not still misunderstood, it could be taken as read. Jencks *et al.* start from the low correlation (0.35) between income and years of schooling for native, white, non-farm males in the United States.[20] According to some economist critics, this is the wrong place to start, the right place being the estimated effect of education on income (the regression coefficient) and not the power of education to explain income. However, for distributional purposes, the correlation coefficient *is* the right place to start. For, whatever education can do to income, a low correlation indicates that many people with low education have high incomes, and vice versa. So, steps to augment the incomes of people with little education will involve many transfers from richer to poorer people. They would, of course, be equalising, but only mildly so.

To clarify the issue, let us review a few possible policies. First, imagine giving each child a better-quality elementary education (of the same value for each child). Suppose that this were financed by a tax rising with income. Then, the net benefit of the policy would fall with income ($dB/dV - dC/dV < 0$) and the policy, if efficient, would be redistributive. But the redistribution comes from the fact that taxes rise with income. Now, imagine a compensatory educational policy where more education was given only to those who had least of it, again financed by a tax rising with income. This might, or might not, be more equalising, depending on how many of the poor had more than the minimum of education. But, since there will certainly be some in this category, such a policy will involve many transfers from poorer to richer, even though these are outweighed by transfers from richer to poorer. Though equalising, the policy will reduce inequality relatively little, compared with the use of the same tax receipts as income transfers. By the same token, expenditure on higher education would involve many transfers from richer to poorer and might not be as disequalising as one might suppose.

There is, however, one point that Jencks overlooks with regard to the incidence of educational expenditure on children. He assumes that social mobility (i.e. the correlation of fathers' and sons' incomes) is not directly relevant to the problem of income distribution. However, this is not the case if we are interested in lifetime income. For a child's standard of living in youth is determined by his father's income and in adulthood by his own. The inequality of lifetime income may thus be substantially reduced by reducing this correlation.[21]

Incidence on parents and children

However, viewed more widely, educational spending must be seen as affecting both parents and children (Stiglitz, 1973). According to Bowles (1972), the correlation between father's income and son's schooling is much higher (0.60) than the correlation between son's income and schooling (0.36).[22] This means that, in so far as educational expenditure affects income distribution, it may do so at least as much through its effects on parents' incomes as on children's. In discussing the incidence of possible policy changes in Great Britain, we shall consider both types of effect. For numerical purposes, however, we unfortunately have to ignore the effects on parents, since no data are available on the income of the parents of children with different completed years of schooling. Since children's schooling, parents' income and children's income are all positively correlated, a policy that has similar effects on a child and on his parents is likely to (dis)equalise through its effects on both sets of incomes. But this is not necessarily the case. For example, a subsidy to the brilliant child of poor parents could disequalise through its effect on the child's income but equalise through its effects on that of the parents. A policy that has opposite effects on a child and his parents (like a reduction in the minimum compulsory school leaving age – see below) could also have this same set of results.

Computing lifetime income in the United Kingdom ($\underline{V}^A$)

The numerical analysis is for the cohort of working males aged 25–29 in 1971 and relies on cross-sectional data from the 1971 General Household Survey.[23] First, we compute their $\underline{V}^A$, and then their $\underline{V}^H$ under different policy assumptions. Getting $\underline{V}^A$ involves two steps. First we run an earnings function for all working males aged 15–65. This (the first earnings function for Britain that includes education)[24] comes out as follows (SEs are shown in brackets; $R^2 = 0.496$, and $SE = 0.344$):

$$\ln Y = 2.777 + 0.948 \ \ln W + 0.092C + 0.110T$$
$$ (0.028) (0.041) (0.024)$$
$$+ \ 0.114F_1 + 0.053F_2 + 0.163F_3 + 0.184F_4 + 0.139F_s$$
$$ (0.044) (0.044) (0.052) (0.046) (0.050)$$
$$+ \ 0.093S_{15} + 0.140S_{16} + 0.214S_{17} + 0.300S_{18} + 0.507S_{19+}$$
$$ (0.024) \phantom{S_{15}} (0.033) \phantom{S_{16}} (0.047) \phantom{S_{17}} (0.052) \phantom{S_{18}} (0.043)$$
$$+ \ 0.030(A - S) - 0.00052(A - S)^2 + e \qquad\qquad (3.4)$$
$$ (0.003) (0.00005)$$

where the variables are

Y after-tax earnings in previous 12 months (using tax rates for married men with no children)
W weeks worked in previous 12 months
C country of birth (1 = British Isles, 0 = other)
T type of secondary school (1 = selective entry, 0 = other)
F father's socio-economic group
  F_1 1 = semi-skilled manual, 0 = other
  F_2 1 = skilled manual and self-employed non-professional, 0 = other
  F_3 1 = intermediate and junior non-manual, 0 = other
  F_4 1 = employers and managers, 0 = other
  F_5 1 = professionals, 0 = other
  (omitted group is unskilled manual)
S age on completing full-time education
  $S_{15}, S_{16}, S_{17}, S_{18}, S_{19+}$ indicate age shown by subscript
  (omitted group is those who completed at 14 and under)
A age last birthday

This function is broadly similar to that used by Mincer (1974), but differs in three important respects. First, the dependent variables is after-tax earnings, which would be quite appropriate in a supply-side model such as Mincer's, and is the concept relevant to distribution. Second, schooling is treated as a dummy variable to avoid imposing equal private rates of return to each level of schooling.[25] Third, we include a dummy variable for type of secondary school (selective or non-selective); this is intended to catch at least some small part of the important effect of ability on income.

Once the earnings function is obtained, we confine ourselves to those members of the sample aged 25–29 in 1971. For each individual we then estimate his income at each age (A) from $(S + 1)$ to 65, using equation (3.4) but replacing $\ln W$ by $\ln 52$, and multiplying the resulting estimate by $(1.02)^{A-27}$, 2 per cent being the assumed rate of growth of real age–education-specific earnings. We thus assume that the individual's error (e) computed from the regression equation stays with him for life, but attempt to eliminate transitory components of annual income in 1971 by replacing ln W by ln 52.[26] The present value of the individual's earnings (V^A) is got by discounting this stream back to age 15 and then adding to it the present value of any maintenance grants paid. (No tuition fees are paid by British students in Britain, except in private schools.) Unfortunately, no data are available on inherited wealth; otherwise, the discounted stream of bequests ought to be added in. The expected value of pensions should also be added in, but would involve many assumptions. If it is proportional to the included items, the exclusion of pensions does not affect the measurement of inequality. In addition, since we know little about how long the different individuals will live, no adjustment is made for length of life. The computed inequality of lifetime income at a 5 per cent discount rate is 0.0707.[27]

The impact of educational policy change (computing $\underline{V}^H$)

We now construct various hypothetical vectors $\underline{V}^H$ by examining various possible educational policy changes.[28] As already explained, in all cases we assume that the additional taxes paid by the cohort to finance the same educational changes for succeeding generations are in the form of taxes proportional to consumption. So these are ignored altogether in obtaining our measures of inequality change $\Delta \ln (1 - I)$ shown in Table 3.1. Adjacent to these measures is shown the fall in total output ($- \Delta \ln \overline{V}$). This needs some explaining. The policy changes experienced by the current cohort also affect the elder generation, who partially pay for them. Though we cannot allocate this burden among people, its total must be taken into account in evaluating the efficiency effects of the project. $\overline{V}^H$ is therefore computed as follows. First, we compute the social present value (S) of the policy per person whose quantity of education was affected by it. The constituent elements in this calculation are shown in Table 3.2. If the project affected the quantity of education of a proportion p of the cohort, we then compute[29]

$$\overline{V}^H = \overline{V}^A + pS$$

Finally, Table 3.1 shows, on the right-hand side, the relative total cost of the policy to public funds. This includes only the outlays by taxpayers and not any additional tax receipts resulting from higher incomes generated by the project. It may not be a very important magnitude but is often looked at closely by governments. We can now examine the policies to be evaluated in this way.

Qualitative improvements in universal education ((a))

These affect children and not parents. We examine the effects of an investment of £20 extra per annum on each child's education throughout his compulsory

Table 3.1 Inequality and efficiency effects of different educational policies

Policy	i = 0			i = 0.02			i = 0.05			Cost to public funds Policy (a) = 1		
	I	$\frac{\Delta \ln (1-I)}{\%}$	$\frac{-\Delta \ln V}{\%}$	I	$\frac{\Delta \ln (1-I)}{\%}$	$\frac{-\Delta \ln V}{\%}$	I	$\frac{\Delta \ln (1-I)}{\%}$	$\frac{-\Delta \ln V}{\%}$	$i = 0$	$i = 0.02$	$i = 0.05$
Present policy (I^A)	0.079101	–	–	0.075676	–	–	0.070574	–	–	–	–	–
(a) Qualitative improvement in universal schooling	0.078760	+0.037	−0.130	0.075282	+0.043	−0.008	0.070068	+0.377	+0.377	1.00	1.00	1.00
(b) Qualitative improvement for early leavers	0.078723	+0.041	−0.083	0.075262	+0.045	−0.005	0.070113	+0.050	+0.242	0.64	0.64	0.64
(c) Raising minimum school leaving age	0.075839	+0.354	−8.152	0.073543	+0.231	−6.195	0.070022	+0.059	−2.010	0.93	0.84	0.71
(d) Maintenance grants in 16th year $\eta = 0$	0.079152	−0.005	0	0.075722	−0.005	0	0.070490	+0.009	0	0.54	0.47	0.39
$\eta = 1$(I)	0.079127	−0.003	−0.175	0.075686	−0.001	−0.116	0.070440	+0.014	+0.015	0.78	0.70	0.59
(II)	0.078637	+0.050	−0.778	0.075303	+0.040	−0.727	0.070266	+0.033	−0.617	0.78	0.70	0.59
(e) Maintenance grants in 17th year $\eta = 0$	0.079202	−0.011	0	0.075807	−0.014	0	0.070656	−0.009	0	0.31	0.27	0.21
$\eta = 1$(I)	0.079191	−0.010	−0.160	0.075788	−0.012	−0.120	0.070618	−0.005	−0.034	0.45	0.39	0.32
(II)	0.079037	+0.007	−0.662	0.075630	+0.005	−0.619	0.070453	+0.013	−0.529	0.45	0.39	0.32
(f) Maintenance grants in 18th year $\eta = 0$	0.079216	−0.012	0	0.075833	−0.017	0	0.070725	−0.016	0	0.23	0.20	0.15
$\eta = 1$(I)	0.079210	−0.012	−0.116	0.075819	−0.015	−0.091	0.070686	−0.012	−0.038	0.31	0.27	0.21
(II)	0.079126	−0.003	−0.462	0.075670	+0.001	−0.426	0.070415	+0.017	−0.355	0.31	0.27	0.21
(g) Fees in higher education $\eta = 0$	0.078909	+0.021	0	0.075464	+0.023	0	0.070562	+0.001	0	−0.15	−0.13	−0.10
$\eta = 1$(I)	0.078900	+0.022	+0.082	0.075435	+0.026	+0.027	0.070465	+0.012	−0.078	−0.11	−0.09	−0.07
(II)	0.079271	−0.104	+0.480	0.076878	−0.130	+0.421	0.072419	−1.198	+0.312	−0.11	−0.09	−0.07

Note: On computation of parameters, see text.

Table 3.2 Net social benefits per person receiving additional education
(present values at age 15, pounds sterling, 1971 prices)

		$i = 0$	$i = 0.02$	$i = 0.05$
(a) Qualitative improvement in universal schooling +				
(b)	Change in after-tax earnings	233	157	100
	Change in taxes generated	100	67	43
	− New institutional subsidy	−200	−219	−251
(c) Raising minimum school leaving age				
	Change in after-tax earnings	3619	2014	959
	Change in taxes generated	1551	863	411
	− Existing institutional subsidy	−291	−285	−277
(d) Maintenance grants in 16th year				
$\eta = 1$ (I)	$\bar{B}$	131	128	125
	+ Change in taxes generated	1551	863	411
	− Existing institutional subsidy	−291	−285	−277
	− New cash subsidy	−300	−294	−285
(II)	Change in after-tax earnings	3619	2014	959
	+ Change in taxes generated	1551	863	411
	− Existing institutional subsidy	−291	−285	−277
(e) Maintenance grants in 17th year				
$\eta = 1$ (I)	$\bar{B}$	132	127	120
	+ Change in taxes generated	2347	1295	607
	− Existing institutional subsidy	−386	−371	−350
	− New cash subsidy	−300	−288	−272
(II)	Change in after-tax earnings	5477	3023	1417
	+ Change in taxes generated	2347	1295	607
	− Existing institutional subsidy	−386	−371	−350
(f) Maintenance grants in 18th year				
$\eta = 1$ (I)	$\bar{B}$	133	126	115
	+ Change in taxes generated	2798	1515	682
	− Existing institutional subsidy	−386	−363	−333
	− New cash subsidy	−300	−282	−259
(II)	Change in after-tax earnings	6528	3534	1592
	+ Change in taxes generated	2798	1515	682
	− Existing institutional subsidy	−386	−363	−333

Table 3.2   continued

		$i = 0$	$i = 0.02$	$i = 0.05$
(g) Fees in higher education[a]				
$\eta = 1$ (I) $\bar{B}$		−405	−367	−317
+ Change in taxes generated		−5715	−3113	−1442
+ Existing institutional subsidy		2172	1967	1703
+ Existing cash subsidy		1068	967	837
(II) Change in after-tax earnings		−13335	−7264	−3366
+ Change in taxes generated		−5715	−3113	−1442
+ Existing institutional subsidy		2172	1967	1703

Notes:

[a]In case (g) we show the social benefit that would result had each person who previously received higher education had not received it.

For policies (d)–(g) a uniform value for income changes was calculated for all persons affected, using mean values for all background variables (averaged over the whole sample). For policy (c) individual earnings estimates were used. However, to avoid confusion, the same 'uniform' values have been shown in this table under (c) as under (d).

school life. Unfortunately, we have no idea what the rate of return to this would be. Jencks, Coleman and others imply that in terms of measureable outcomes it is small, though Jencks stresses that children may enjoy qualitatively better schools more. Suppose, for illustration, that the social rate of return is 3 per cent and takes the form of a constant income stream from the year of the investment until retirement. (While the individual is still being educated, the benefit will be in the form of improved ability to learn plus psychic benefits.)[30] Then each individual's present value at 15 would rise by a constant depending on the discount rate. This appears as equalising, since a given absolute amount has been given to each person and a given proportional amount removed (in the language of section IV, $\beta = 1$, $\alpha < 1$). At a 2 per cent interest rate, the increase in equality is 0.04 per cent and there is no loss in total output. The policy is therefore desirable. On the other hand, at a 5 per cent rate of interest, the increase in equality is outweighed by the loss of output and the policy should not be pursued. This conflict of findings highlights the problem that arises when one wishes to use one (low) rate of interest to measure existing lifetime income in a way that correctly reflects inequality, and another (higher) rate of interest (or set of rates) to measure changes in income as experienced by those concerned. This problem really cannot be overcome until data on consumption streams become available.

Qualitative improvements of early leavers only ((b))

If the qualitative improvements could be restricted to less able children, they would of course be more equalising. Suppose, for example, that it were administratively possible to identify children who were going to leave at the minimum school-leaving age of 15 (for this cohort) and £20 per annum were then spent on each of these children. The rate of return is again uncertain; suppose it is 3 per cent. Then, at a 2 per cent rate of interest, this 'selective' policy appears as more equalising than the same policy applied to all children. At a 5 per cent rate of interest, there is already so much overlap in lifetime income among those who leave later that the selective policy is actually less equalising than the universal one.

Raising the compulsory minimum school-leaving age ((c))

Another policy that may benefit early leavers is the raising of the minimum compulsory school-leaving age, which was 15 for our cohort but was raised to 16 in 1972–3. Since the option of staying on was available without compulsion to do so, staying on was clearly judged undesirable by the family decision-makers, whoever they were. This may be because the costs of an extra year of schooling for a child may normally be borne mainly by the parents. A 16-year-old British male worker normally lives with his parents and pays them for board and lodging; a 16-year-old schoolboy pays them nothing. Unless his alternative wages were much higher than his board and lodging, he may lose little by staying on a year. If he bears none of the earnings forgone, he gains the present value of his increased earnings from 16 onwards. But this probably overstates the gain, as the individual may hate school. We therefore attribute the full cost of earnings forgone to the child, so that he is assessed as gaining only if the private present value of the differences in after-tax earnings is positive. In our calculations we should, of course, allow for the effects that more staying on will have upon the wages of stayers-on. But, throughout this analysis, we assume, instead, perfect substitution among different types of labour.[31] As a result, equality rises and, at interest rates of 5 per cent or below, so does output.

Changing cash support for students in post-compulsory education ((d)–(g))

An alternative policy for widening education opportunity is higher financial subsidies, such as cash maintenance grants to those who stay on at school.

Extremely little is known about the effects of variation in the price of
education upon quantity demanded. Suppose, first, that there is no effect
($\eta = 0$). Then, those affected gain the full value of the extra subsidy. Probably
the main people affected are the parents, who would otherwise have been
bearing that part of the cost of the child's education. The child may also
experience some increase in his living standard. Lacking data on parents, we
attribute the whole gain to the children.[32] The expenditure is pure transfer
and has no efficiency implications.

Suppose now that the subsidy did induce an increase in staying on. Handa
and Skolnik (1972) provide tenuous evidence that the demand elasticity may
be unitary, and we shall assume this. In this case,

$$q_1 = q_0 \frac{p_0}{p_1}$$

where q_0 and p_0 are the present numbers staying-on and present private costs,
and q_1 and p_1 are the values after the policy change. We assume that the
$(q_1 - q_0)$ new stayers-on are selected randomly from those who previously
took the next-lower level of education.

For those who already stay on, the benefits are, as before, $(p_0 - p_1)$. But what
are they for the new stayers-on? The normal approach (approach *I*) would be
to estimate their gain in consumer surplus. In this case, the average gain
is measured by the average value of $p(q) - p_1$, over the range q_0 to q_1, in
Figure 3.3, where $p(q)$ is the demand price. This, before discounting, is:[33]

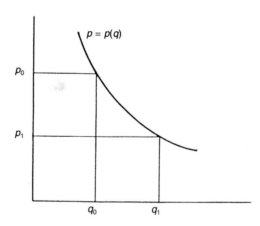

Figure 3.3 Welfare effects of an educational subsidy

$$\overline{B} = p_0 p_1 \frac{\log p_0 - \log p_1}{p_0 - p_1} - p_1$$

This assumes, of course, that education is available at each age for those who demand it at the going price; this is broadly true in Britain, though demanders may not be able to get the exact kind of education that they want. The gain so measured may be divided between parents and children, and may even include losses for parents. However, we again impute all of the effects to children. The resulting calculations for equality and output change are shown in Table 3.1 on the rows marked $\eta = 1$ (*I*).

However, this approach assumes that the marginal individual in each situation is not only indifferent about staying on or leaving, but that he would *ex post* get zero benefit from staying on. In other words, it assumes on his part a perfect knowledge of monetary income streams. If we adopt the alternative 'human capital' approach (*II*), we measure the benefits for him. In this approach, psychic benefits are omitted, since there is no way of inferring them. We now measure private benefits as the change in the present value of after-tax earnings plus the present value of any maintenance grant gained. This approach is adopted in the rows marked $\eta = 1$ (*II*).

Finally we should review the calculation of the social present value of the effect of educating one extra person (S), the elements of the calculations being shown in Table 3.2.[34] This is the sum of the present value of the items listed:[35]

Assumption I

Beneficiary

$\overline{B}$ Educated person

$\left.\begin{array}{l} + \text{ Change in taxes generated} \\ - \text{ Existing institutional subsidy} \\ - \text{ Existing cash subsidy} \\ - \text{ New cash subsidy} \end{array}\right\}$ Taxpayers

Assumption II

$\left.\begin{array}{l} \text{Change in after-tax earnings} \\ + \text{ Existing cash subsidy} \\ + \text{ New cash subsidy} \end{array}\right\}$ Educated person

$\left.\begin{array}{l} + \text{ Change in taxes generated} \\ - \text{ Existing institutional subsidy} \\ - \text{ Existing cash subsidy} \\ - \text{ New cash subsidy} \end{array}\right\}$ Taxpayers

There are no *a priori* remarks that one can make about the sum of these items (i.e. *S*). Under assumption *I*, we know that $\overline{B}$ < new cash subsidy, so that $S > 0$

only if additional taxes exceed the existing subsidies. Under assumption *II*, if capital markets were perfect and knowledge likewise, net private benefits without the new cash subsidy would be zero, so the same condition for social gain applies. However, in practice, net private benefits so computed are not zero.

Using this framework we now evaluate the following policies:[36]

(d)   maintenance grant for all children at school in the 16th year raised from zero to £300 ((d));
(e)   maintenance grant for all children at school in their 17th year raised from zero to £300 ((e));
(f)   maintenance grant for all children at school in their 18th year raised from zero to £300 ((f)); and
(g)   higher-education fees raised from zero to £300 ((g)).

The conclusions to be drawn differ with the assumptions made. This may be due in part to the small sample numbers used in this preliminary exercise.[37] It may also be due to the high degree of overlap in the income distributions of the different groups;[38] as suggested in section IV, this makes the inequality effects of different policies very sensitive to specific assumptions. I shall concentrate on the case of $i = 0.05$, $\eta = 1$ (*I*). In this case, grants to 16-year-olds in school would have been equalising, but would have induced some loss of output, making the policy of marginal social value at the chosen level of inequality aversion. Grants to 17- and 18-year-olds, though disequalising, may be justified by the induced gain in output, while fees in higher education may be equalising and efficient. These findings, though tentative, make quite good sense, bearing in mind the massive current subsidies to higher education and the strange form of the educational pyramid, whereby most people either end their education at 19 or over or at below 17.

I do not claim to have solved the discount rate problem which lies at the heart of all analyses of lifetime welfare, but I hope to have clarified some of the issues, and to have adopted a useful framework within which distributional and efficiency effects of policies can be simultaneously viewed.

Notes

1.   These correspond respectively to the United Kingdom Central Statistical Office's 'final' and 'original' distributions (f. 54).
2.   Weisbrod and Hansen were able to allow only for wealth and current earnings.
3.   Of course, in the full lifecycle model with perfect capital markets and perfect foresight, present consumption and potential future consumption will be related to past consumption. But the assumptions are rather stringent.

4. (a) V should be computed at the interest rate net of tax.
    (b) It is sometimes considered double-counting if bequests are treated as giving utility to donor and recipient. However, they clearly do just that.
    (c) Some people consider inequalities of inherited wealth more or less inequitable than inequalities in earnings. Such judgements are not easily handled in the present framework, but could be handled in a wider one where psychic (non-monetary) sources of satisfaction, especially leisure, were allowed for.

5. For a good discussion of the relation of discount rates to annual, rather than lifetime, earnings, see Becker (1967). See also Brainard (1974).

6. This can be seen geometrically by drawing a line through Y^{II}, parallel to $Y^I C^I$. The ratio of the horizontal intercepts of these two parallel lines measures the ratio of discounted incomes.

7. As predicted above, inequality is higher when $i = 0.02$ and still higher when $i = 0$ (see Table 3.1).

8. If they had no pure time preference, and given a positive interest rate, individuals would, choose a rising path of consumption. One might, therefore, prefer to compute for each individual a value A where the stream $A (1 + g)^t$ $(t = 1, \ldots, T)$ has the same present value as the actual income stream, g could be based on observed rates of growth or on the outcome of maximising some suitable utility function subject to a given perfect capital-market constraint. However, comparisons of A so computed might tend to understate the real incomes of those who live long.

9. For discussions of the problem in the single-year case see Musgrave (1964), Prest (1968), and Peacock and Shannon (1968). Prest (1968) is doubtful whether calculations so far made of the total effect of State expenditure and taxes are useful, while Musgrave (1964) thinks they are. There has also been considerable debate about how questions about these effects should be formulated. Peacock and Shannon (1968) suggest that the comparison should be put forward as one between a condition where government expenditure and taxes are as at present and one where government expenditure remained unchanged but everyone paid for his benefits. A more relevant alternative would seem to be one in which both the government expenditure and the corresponding taxes are abolished. The general equilibrium effect of such a change might well be less than that of the Peacock and Shannon alternative, and the question is more interesting.

10. On exogenous growth, the chief proposition is that, if the rate of growth exceeds the interest rate, an additional pension proportional to the wage will make each generation better off (Samuelson, 1958; Cass and Yaari, 1961; Aaron, 1966). By the same token, a youth endowment proportional to the wage will make everyone worse off. On steady-state growth with variable savings rates, Diamond (1965) has shown that, if the growth rate exceeds the rate of interest, an increase in the savings rate benefits all generations.

11. Nicholson (1964) does not take this *ex post* approach. He measures the National Health Service benefits to an individual not as the value of services rendered, but as their expected value. However, the benefits from the old-age pension are recorded at their actual current value, although the pension scheme is also an

insurance scheme providing a given expected value of benefits at each age (whether one is alive or dead), which is of course less than the actual old-age pension. This is less inconsistent than it might appear, since, for distributional purposes, the value of a given cover needs to be adjusted for the *ex post* length of life, as we have seen.

12. Gambling, of course, causes a problem here. If two gamblers start with the same incomes and voluntarily gamble so that they end up with different ones, we ought not necessarily to say that inequality has increased. However, if we used the Atkinson (1970b) approach (see section IV below), we should not necessarily say that it had. For the rationale of that approach is that the social welfare function is concave in individual utilities. If, in addition, utility is concave in income, the social welfare function is concave in individual incomes, as is generally assumed. But if we allowed increasing marginal utility of income, we might say that social welfare and 'equality' had increased *ex post* by permitting the gamble. So the *ex post* approach would still be preferable. The practical problem, however, is that we have to assume uniform tastes, and, therefore, assume diminishing marginal utility.

13. It is true that larger families often have higher incomes and pay higher taxes, but it would be most unusual for the average tax payments of families with X children to exceed, by a multiple X, those of families with one child. In addition, there is a transfer to families with children from families with none.

14. As Sen (1973b) implies, the Gini coefficient implies the same trade-off, since, in the Atkinson terminology (see below):

$$V_{EDE} = \overline{V}(1 - G)$$

where G is the Gini coefficient. But the welfare function corresponding to the Gini coefficient is less appealing than that used by Atkinson.

15. For a proof that this implies non-intersecting Lorenz curves, see Sen (1973a). If we drop the assumption of zero efficiency effects and allow for some losses, such that $\Sigma B(V_i) - \Sigma C(V_i) < 0$, then no strict statement is possible, since total income changes. For people with incomes low enough to experience positive net benefits, the Lorenz curve rises, since they all gain and total income falls; so their relative income share rises. But the share of the richest man may rise if his proportional loss is less than the proportional loss in the economy as a whole. However if there is some income V^* such that for all incomes greater than V^* the proportional loss exceeds that for the economy as a whole, then the Lorenz curve will rise for all incomes above V^*. And, if the proportional loss in the whole economy is not great, then V^* will lie close to the income for which net benefits are zero, and the Lorenz curve is likely to lie above its old level throughout its range.

16. Again, if condition (3.3) does not hold, this does not strictly follow.

17. It is perhaps a more convenient one than the traditional two-person classroom illustration that is sometimes used. In this, person 1 is richer than person 2 and therefore bears more costs. We then show that redistribution occurs if the project is efficient and $B_1/B_2 < C_1/C_2$. The proof is

$$B_1 - C_1 = C_2 - B_2 \qquad \text{(the efficiency condition)}$$

Therefore $$C_1\left(\frac{B_1}{C_1}-1\right)=C_2\left(1-\frac{B_2}{C_2}\right)$$

Therefore $$\left(1-\frac{B_2}{C_2}\right)\left(\frac{B_1}{C_1}-1\right)=\frac{C_1}{C_2}>1$$

Therefore $$2>\frac{B_1}{C_1}+\frac{B_2}{C_2}$$

But $$\frac{B_1}{C_1}<\frac{B_2}{C_2}$$

Therefore $$\frac{B_1}{C_1}<1$$

One can also show that an inefficient project hurts person 1 proportionately more than person 2 if $C_1/V_1 > C_2/V_2$.

18. An example occurs in Table 3.1 ($i = 0.05$), where a given benefit to early leavers raises equality by 0.050 per cent, and extending the benefit to all raises equality by a further 0.005 per cent.

19. Even taking into account the parents' income only, it is important to allow for lifetime income. The richest taxpayers in a given year may often be too old to have college-age children and the poorest taxpayers too young.

20. The correlation is the average of the correlation for different age groups. It is not, of course, a correlation of schooling and lifetime income, which would need to take into account the shorter working lives of those more schooled.

21. If lifetime income consists of a fraction of father's income and a fraction of own income so that $V = aV_F + bV_o$, then

$$\text{var}\,(V) = a^2\,\text{var}\,(V_F) + b^2\,\text{var}\,(V_O) + 2ab\,\text{cov}\,(V_F, V_O)$$

According to Bowles (1972, p.S247), the correlation of father's and son's incomes is 0.30.

22. Jencks (1972), using data on father's occupation, gets the reverse ranking. He finds that

r (father's occupation, son's schooling) $= 0.49$
r (son's occupation, son's schooling) $= 0.69$
and r (father's occupation, son's occupation) $= 0.44$

23. The General Household Survey is an annual national survey begun in 1971 (OPCAS, 1973). Different households are interviewed each year. The present preliminary analysis is confined to members of the labour force who when interviewed had worked at least one week in the last year, and who were interviewed in the last quarter of the year. There were 1868 such men aged 15–65. I am most grateful to the OPCAS for providing the survey tapes, and to Mrs Anne Thomas for help in understanding them.

24. See also Hill (1959).

25. Of course, in Mincer's model, if the (common) rate of return to education equals the private discount rate, all inequality of annual incomes due to educational differences disappears when discounted lifetime income is considered.

26. The sample included 213 individuals aged 25–29. Of these, six had error terms such that $| e | > 1$. These six were eliminated from the present preliminary analysis.

27. This figure, like all that follow, is based on a sample of 207 (see the previous foot-note). For the full 213, lifetime inequality is 0.116, compared with inequality of 1971 incomes of 0.157 (or 0.119 if variations in weeks worked are excluded). In the whole sample aged 15–65, cross-sectional inequality is 0.264.

28. For the detailed calculations, see a note available, on request, from the author.

29. It is right to relate the total effects of the project to the present value of one cohort so long as one is only measuring inequality in one cohort. A more desirable approach would be to include all relevant cohorts, in which case the effects for each cohort would be measured in terms of present values when the members of that cohort were aged 15, and not when members of the cohort aged 25–29 in 1971 were aged 15.

30. For simplicity, I assume that this is taxable.

31. For evidence on elasticities of substitution see Dougherty (1972) and Fallon and Layard (1973).

32. This, and what follows, may not be entirely consistent with our treatment of the raising of the minimum school-leaving age, where the net gain of the family may be negative and yet we show gains.

33.

$$\text{If } p(q) = kq^{-1}, \int_{q_0}^{q_1} kq^{-1}dq = k(\log p_0 - \log p_1)$$

$$\text{Therefore, average surplus } = \frac{k(\log p_0 - \log p_1)}{k/p_1 - k/p_0} - p_1$$

$$\text{If } p \text{ rises, } \overline{B} = -p_0 p_1 \frac{\log p_1 - \log p_0}{p_1 - p_0} + p_0$$

34. We are, of course, omitting all external effects (other than taxes), including externalities connected with the so-called screening hypothesis. For evidence that this hypothesis may not be quantitatively important, see Layard and Psacharopoulos (1974).

35. The scheme is different when one less person is educated, see Table 3.2. In Britain, and except for students of 19 and over, existing cash subsidies are approximately zero.

36. At a later stage, further policies will be considered (for instance, differential grants related to father's occupation).

37. The work reported here is the first item in a collaborative programme of work on income distribution using the *General Household Survey* data. This will cover, *inter alia*, the supply of working hours, labour force participation, and the determinants of unemployment – all of which are ignored in the present paper.

38. At $i = 0.05$, $\overline{V}$ for those who completed full-time education at different ages (using the full sample of 213 rather than the 207 used in Table 3.1) is: 14, £30,421; 15, £28,114; 16, £27,057; 17, £26,649; 18, £35,602; 19+, £32,169; all groups, £28,752.

References

Aaron, H.J. (1966) 'The social insurance paradox', *Canadian Journal of Economic and Political Science* (August).

Arrow, K.J. (1963) 'Uncertainty and the welfare economics of medical care', *American Economic Review* (December).

Asimokopoulos, A. and J.C. Weldon (1968) 'On the theory of government pension plans', *Canadian Journal of Economics* (Nov, Vol 1, No 4).

Atkinson, A.B. (1970a) 'National superannuation: redistribution and values for money', *Bulletin of the Oxford University of Economics and Statistics* (August).

Atkinson, A.B. (1970b) 'On the measurement of inequality', *Journal of Economic Theory* (September, Vol. 2, No 3).

Becker, G.S. (1967) *Human Capital and the Personal Distribution of Income*, The Woytinsky Lecture (Ann Arbor: University of Michigan Press).

Bowles, S. (1972) 'Schooling and inequality from generation to generation', *Journal of Political Economy* (May–June), pt II.

Brainard, W. (1974) 'Private and Social Risk and Return to Education', in K.G. Lumsden (ed.), *Efficiency in Universities: The La Paz Papers* (New York: Elsevier), see also Chapter 17 in this volume.

Cass, D. and M.E. Yaari (1966) 'A re-examination of the pure consumption loan model', *Journal of Political Economy* (August).

Diamond, P.A. (1965) 'National debt in a neo-classical growth model', *American Economic Review* (December).

Dougherty, C.R.S. (1972) 'Estimates of labour aggregation functions', *Journal of Political Economy* (November).

Fallon, P. and R. Layard (1973) 'Capital-skill complementarity, income distribution and output accounting', Higher Education Research Unit, LSE, mimeo, see Chapter 10 in this volume.

Friedman, M. (1957) *A Theory of the Consumption Function* (Princeton: Princeton University Press).

Glennerster, H. (1972) 'Education and inequality', in P. Townsend and N. Bosanguet (eds), *Labour and Inequality* (London: Fabian Society).

Handa, M.L. and M.L. Skolnik (1972) 'Empirical analysis of the demand for education in Canada', in S. Ostroy (ed.), *Canadian Higher Education in the Seventies* (Ottowa: Economic Council of Canada) (May).

Hansen, E.L. and B.A. Weisbrod (1969) 'The distribution of costs and benefits of higher education: the case of California', *Journal of Human Resources* (Spring).

Hansen, W.L. and B.A. Weisbrod (1970) 'On the distribution of costs and benefits of public higher education: reply', *Journal of Human Resources* (Summer).

Hartmann, R. (1970) 'A comment on the Pechman–Hansen–Weisbrod controversy', *Journal of Human Resources* (Fall).

Hill, T.P. (1959) 'An analysis of the distribution of wages and salaries in Great Britain', *Econometrica* (July).

Jencks, C. *et al.* (1972) *Inequality: A Reassessment of the Effect of Family and Schooling in America* (New York: Basic Books).

Jorgensen, D.W. and Z. Griliches (1967) 'The explanation of productivity change', *Review of Economic Studies*, Vol. XXXIV (3), no 99.

Kaldor, N. (1964) 'An expenditure tax', in R. Bird and O. Oldman, *Readings on Taxation in Developing Countries* (Baltimore: Johns Hopkins University Press).

Layard, R. and G. Psacharopoulos (1974) 'The screening hypothesis and the social returns to education', *Journal of Political Economy* (September–October), Chapter 9 in this volume.

Meade, J.E. (1956) *The Theory of International and Economic Policy, Vol. II: Trade and Welfare* (Oxford: Oxford University Press).

Mincer, J. (1974) 'Schooling, experience, and earnings', National Bureau of Economic Research. *Human Behavior and Social Institutions*, 2 (New York and London: Columbia University Press).

Musgrave, R.A. (1964) 'Estimating the distribution of the tax burden', in C. Clark and G. Stuvel (eds), *Income Redistribution and the Statistical Foundations of Economic Policy* (London: Bowes & Bowes).

Nicholson, J.L. (1964) 'Redistribution of income in the UK in 1959, 1957 and 1953', in C. Clark and G. Stuvel (eds), *Income Redistribution and the Statistical Foundations of Economic Policy* (London: Bowes & Bowes).

Office of Population Censuses and Surveys (OPCAS) (1973) Social Survey Division, *The General Household Survey, Introductory Report* (London: HMSO).

Peacock, A. and R. Shannon (1968) 'The welfare state and the redistribution of income', *Westminster Bank Review* (August).

Pechman, J. (1970) 'The distribution effects of public higher education in California', *Journal of Human Resources* (Summer).

Prest, A.R. (1968) 'The budget and interpersonal distribution', *Public Finance*, 1–2.

Prest, A.R. (1970) 'Some redistributional aspects of the National Superannuation Fund', *Three Banks Review* (June).

Samuelson, P.A. (1958) 'An exact consumption–loan model of interest with and without the social contrivance of money', *Journal of Political Economy* (December).

Sen, A.K. (1973a) *On Economic Inequality* (Oxford: Oxford University Press).

Sen, A.K. (1973b) 'Aggregation and income distribution', paper presented the International Seminar on Public Economics (Siena) (September).

Stiglitz, J. (1973) 'Education and inequality', *Annals of the American Academy of Political and Social Science*, 159 (September).

Verry, D. and R. Layard (1973) 'Costs functions for university teaching and research', *Economic Journal*, March.

Weisbroad, B.A. and W.L. Hansen (1969) 'An income–net–worth approach to measuring economic welfare', *American Economic Review* (December).

4 Family Income Distribution: Explanation and Policy Evaluation (1979)*

with A. Zabalza

Most people live in families, and their standard of living depends upon the family's income rather than on their own. So, if one is interested in income distribution from a welfare motivation one should study the distribution of family rather than individual income. Yet this has been studied surprisingly little. One obvious issue is: Can family income be more easily explained than individual income? The question is interesting in itself, and it has also been argued by Jencks *et al.* (1972) that it has policy relevance. For, they argue, if schooling explains little of the variance of income, then eliminating differences in schooling will have little impact on inequality. The argument is correct but of little relevance to policy since nobody has ever proposed eliminating all differences in schooling. So we prefer to think of the business of explanation (in section I of the paper) as motivated by positive concerns. If one wants to think about policy the questions have to be more specifically formulated, and in section II we attempt to show how the effects of policy changes on the distribution of family income can be analyzed most fruitfully.

A crucial question is, of course, how income should be measured. In section I we use in turn four measures. Beginning with annual money income, we show first how the variance of this is accounted for by the husband's earnings, the wife's earnings, and unearned income. Then we show how the earnings differences are accounted for by differences in hours, weeks, and hourly wage rates. Next, using family labor supply functions to explain hours, we show how much of the earnings variance can be accounted for by wage rates and unearned income alone. And finally we go behind wage rates to the personal characteristics that determine them and find that, due to assortative mating,

* *Journal of Political Economy*, 87(5), pt 2 (1979), pp. S133–S161, © 1979 by The University of Chicago. This paper was prepared jointly with Margaret Barton and Tony Cornford who together did the computing with great efficiency. We should also like to thank O. Ashenfelter, R. Freeman, S. Nickell, D. Piachaud, S. Rosen, A. Shorrocks, and J. Smith for helpful suggestions; the OPCAS for providing the General Household Survey tapes; and the Ford Foundation and the Social Science Research Council for financing the study.

schooling differences do indeed explain more of the variation of family income than of individual income.

After a brief look at annual money income *per head*, we then turn to a measure of annual 'welfare', which, we argue, is best measured not by 'full income' but by a measure in which the wage rates of husbands and wives are weighted by their average hours. Finally we turn to *lifetime* welfare, which we consider the most relevant measure of fundamental inequality. It is this which we use in section II, where we show how to analyze the equity and efficiency implications of various policy options, using the Atkinson equality measure which embodies an explicit equity–efficiency trade-off.

The main results of the study are summarized in section III. They relate to Great Britain and are based on the General Household Survey for 1975, which provided usable data on 4027 couples where the husband was under 65 and not self-employed nor permanently disabled (OPCAS, 1978).

I   EXPLANATION

Annual money income

We begin by trying to explain the gross money income of the family over a year (F).[1] We measure its inequality by the coefficient of variation (C_F). This is more intuitively interesting than the standard deviation. It is also more readily decomposable than the standard deviation of the log, since money income is a sum of incomes of different types, some of which are often zero. The coefficient of variation of family income is 0.51.[2] This compares with the inequality of the individual components of family income as follows: husband's earnings (Y_1), 0.48; wife's earnings (Y_2), 1.24; unearned income[3] (I), 5.03. So family income is a bit more unequal than men's earnings but much less unequal than women's earnings or unearned income.

Sources of income

How much do the various components contribute to the overall inequality? The decomposition proceeds as follows: $F = Y_1 + Y_2 + I$, so $F/\bar{F} = (\bar{Y}_1/\bar{F})(Y_1/\bar{Y}_1) + (\bar{Y}_2/\bar{F})(Y_2/\bar{Y}_2) + (\bar{I}/\bar{F})(I/\bar{I})$ or $f = a_1 y_1 + a_2 y_2 + a_3 i$ where lower case letters denote variables relative to their means and a_1, a_2, and a_3 are the shares of each component in the average.[4] In our case $f = 0.784 y_1 + 0.179 y_2 + 0.037 i$. It follows that var (f) = var $(0.784 y_1 + 0.179 y_2 + 0.037 i)$. In other words, the squared coefficient of variation of family income (c_F^2) equals the sum of all the terms in the variance/covariance matrix shown in Table 4.1.[5] It is easy to check that all the terms in the table sum to 0.263 which is $(0.513)^2$.[6]

Table 4.1 Variance–covariance matrix explaining family income (f)
(The sum of the entries is 0.263 and the variance of f is 0.263)

	$0.784y_1$	$0.179y_2$	$0.037i$
$0.784y_1$	0.143	−0.001	0.020
$0.179y_2$	−0.001	0.050	−0.001
$0.037i$	0.020	−0.001	0.034

Thus, of the squared coefficient of variation of family income, about 50 per cent comes from the husband's income on its own, about 20 per cent from the wife's income on its own, and 15 per cent each from unearned income on its own and from the covariance between husband's income and unearned income. Interestingly, there is almost no correlation between husband's and wife's earnings. The reason, as we shall shortly see, is that, although husband's and wife's wages are positively correlated,[7] the effect of this is offset by the negative correlation between husband's wages and wife's annual hours ($r = -0.10$).

Wages, hours and weeks

This emerges clearly if we now look separately at the role of wages (W = gross hourly earnings), hours (H), and weeks (N). For simplicity we do not in the case of women look separately at the effect of hours and weeks but only at their product (HN). The reason is that, whereas for men the variation in weeks is mainly due to differential demand constraints, for women the variation in weeks mainly reflects choice, and annual hours are as easy to explain as weekly hours – which is not true for men. However, there is an obvious problem about women's wages: if the woman does not work we do not observe her potential wage. However, we have an approximate method of handling this problem which we believe brings us pretty near to the truth.[8]

The decomposition now involves an approximation. By definition, $F = W_1 H_1 N_1 + W_2 (HN)_2 + I$ where 1 and 2 relate to husband and wife. Taking a first-order expansion about the means:

$$\frac{F}{\overline{F}} = \text{const} + \frac{\overline{W}_1\overline{H}_1\overline{N}_1}{\overline{F}}\left(\frac{W_1}{\overline{W}_1} + \frac{H_1}{\overline{H}_1} + \frac{N_1}{\overline{N}_1}\right)$$

$$+ \frac{\overline{W}_2\overline{(HN)}_2}{\overline{F}}\left[\frac{W_2}{\overline{W}_2} + \frac{(HN)_2}{\overline{(HN)}_2}\right] + \frac{\overline{I}}{\overline{F}}\left(\frac{I}{\overline{I}}\right)$$

Table 4.2   Variance–covariance matrix explaining family income (f)
(The sum of the entries is 0.268 and the variance of f is 0.263)

	$0.784w_1$	$0.784h_1$	$0.784n_1$	$0.179w_2$	$0.179(hn)_2$	$0.037i$
$0.784w_1$	0.152	−0.016	0.003	0.009	−0.007	0.020
$0.784h_1$	−0.016	0.019	−0.001	−0.001	−0.001	−0.001
$0.784n_1$	0.003	−0.001	0.006	. . .	. . .	. . .
$0.179w_2$	0.009	−0.001	. . .	0.010	. . .	0.001
$0.179(hn)_2$	−0.007	−0.001	. . .	. . .	0.038	−0.002
$0.037i$	0.020	−0.001	. . .	0.001	−0.002	0.034

or

$$f = \text{const} + 0.784(w_1 + h_1 + n_1) + 0.179[w_2 + (hn)_2] + 0.037i \qquad (1)$$

The coefficients of variation of these terms are husband's wages (W_1), 0.50; wife's wage (W_2), 0.56; husband's hours (H_1), 0.18; husband's weeks (N_1), 0.10; wife's annual hours $(HN)_2$, 1.08. The variance of the right-hand side of the equation equals the sum of the entries in Table 4.2. Happily these entries sum to 0.268, as compared with the actual var (f) of 0.263, which provides some support for this method of decomposition.

Let us look at the table by parts. The dashed lines divide the table into nine parts corresponding to the nine entries in Table 4.1. Among men, wage inequality is slightly greater than the inequality of annual earnings, which is not surprising since hours are so negatively correlated with wages $(r = -0.30)$. A striking finding is the small role of weeks worked in the inequality of men's annual earnings: the squared coefficient of variation of weeks worked is only 4 per cent of the squared coefficient of variation of earnings. This contrasts sharply with the importance of the logarithm of weeks in explaining log annual earnings:[9] in our male sample (excluding men with less than 1 week of work in the year) the variance of log weeks equals about 20 per cent of the variance of log annual earnings.[10] Which analysis is the more relevant? Clearly the variance of log annual earnings can be exactly decomposed between log weeks and log weekly earnings. But such a decomposition will be dominated by the small number of people who have very few weeks and very low annual earnings. Whether this is sensible is unclear. For one thing, the analysis has to exclude arbitrarily those who have been out of work for over a year and have therefore zero earnings and log earnings of minus infinity. Moreover, very low earnings due to very low weeks may not be especially interesting from an income point of view, since the people concerned will be mainly living on non-labor income (social security). So the standard deviation of the log of annual earnings (excluding zero earnings) may not measure anything very interesting. We therefore think that our focus on the variation of absolute annual earnings is justified, even in relation to the role of weeks.

Turning to women, the main variation in annual earnings comes from annual hours rather than wages (four-fifths of it does). Finally, it is interesting to look at the components of the covariance of men's and women's earnings and confirm that, although husband's and wife's wages are positively correlated, the effect of this is offset mainly by the negative correlation of husband's wages and wife's annual hours.

Labor supply

This correlation of course reflects the labor supply decision of the family. (2) and (3) show very simple labor supply functions for the husband and wife, estimated in a form that is consistent with our present framework (*SEs* in parentheses):

$$H_1 = 50.5 - 2.68\hat{W}_1 - 2.35\hat{W}_2 - 0.000139I \qquad R^2 = 0.023 \qquad (2)$$
$$ (0.43) \quad (0.75) \qquad (0.000166)$$

$$(HN)_2 = 743.7 - 74.0\hat{W}_1 + 154.4\hat{W}_2 - 0.067I \qquad R^2 = 0.005 \qquad (3)$$
$$ (46.0) \quad (80.0) \qquad (0.018)$$

Both wages are predicted from the wage equations (6) and (7) given later in order to avoid problems of measurement error due to wages being measured as earnings divided by hours. The low R^2 is of course due to the use of these predicted wages. The elasticities implied here are[11]

$$\epsilon_{11} = -0.09 \qquad \epsilon_{12} = -0.05 \qquad \epsilon_{13} = 0.00$$
$$\epsilon_{21} = -0.14 \qquad \epsilon_{22} = 0.18 \qquad \epsilon_{23} = -0.01$$

We can see now in behavioral terms why there is no correlation between husband's and wife's earnings. Let us ignore the variation in men's weeks which is not closely related to wages[12] and let us use h_2 to denote $(hn)_2$. Then the covariance of husband's and wife's earnings (each measured relative to its mean) is cov $(y_1, y_2) \simeq$ cov $(w_1 + h_1, w_2 + h_2) =$ cov $(w_1 + \epsilon_{11}w_1 + \epsilon_{12}w_2, w_2 + \epsilon_{21}w_1 + \epsilon_{22}w_2) =$ cov $(0.89w_1 - 0.05w_2, 1.18w_2 - 0.14w_1) = 0.01$. Thus the negative cross-elasticities (-0.05 and -0.14) are just sufficient to offset the effect of the positive correlation ($r = 0.23$) between husband's and wife's

Table 4.3   Variance–covariance matrix explaining family income (f)
(The sum of the entries is 0.213 and the variance of f is 0.263)

	$0.703w_1$	$0.178w_2$	$0.035i$
$0.703w_1$	0.122	0.008	0.017
$0.178w_2$	0.008	0.010	0.001
$0.035i$	0.017	0.001	0.029

wages. The most important of the two turns out to be the negative effect of husband's wages on wife's hours.

Going on, we can now express the whole variance of income in terms of W_1, W_2, and I. Substituting (2)–(4) into (1), we obtain, after some massaging,[13]

$$f = \text{const} + 0.703\,w_1 + 0.178\,w_2 + 0.035i \tag{5}$$

Owing to the negative effect of the husband's wage on both spouses' hours, the coefficient 0.703 is considerably less than the value of 0.784 in (1). By contrast the effect of women's wages is similar to what it was in (1), since the wife's own labor supply responds just enough to her own wage to offset the negative effect of her wage on her husband's labor supply.

The variance of the right-hand side of (5) equals the sum of the terms in Table 4.3 – wages and unearned income explain about 80 per cent of the total variance of family income. Once again the striking feature is the small contribution of wife's wage to the overall inequality.

Personal characteristics

We can now turn to the personal characteristics lying behind these wage and income differences. (6) and (7) are wage equations for husbands and participating wives, estimated in the natural values for consistency with our general framework. Here S_1 is the husband's terminal age of full-time education, P_1 his father's occupation, and X_1 his experience (age $- S_1$); similarly for the wife. For P we use transformations derived from previous estimates of the equations[14]

$$W_1 = -2.59 + 0.212S_1 + 2.26P_1 + 0.051X_1 - 0.000748X_1^2 \tag{6}$$
$$ (0.008) \quad (0.25) \quad (0.004) \quad (0.000070)$$
$$R^2 = 0.21$$

$$W_2 = -1.49 + 0.142S_2 + 0.83P_2 + 0.015X_2 - 0.000221X_2^2 \tag{7}$$
$$(0.008) \quad (0.28) \quad (0.003) \quad (0.000069)$$
$$R^2 = 0.14$$

These equations are consistent with earlier work on British wage functions. The slope coefficients indicate a flatter wage profile, but that is only to be expected since young single people are omitted and the regression line consequently need not be forced through some very low observations in early youth.[15] The R^2s are of course lower than are obtained when single people are also included, since it is experience in the first few years of working life which contributes so much to the human capital explanation of earnings.[16] We also estimate an equation for unearned income:

$$I = -2275 + 58S_1 + 730P_1 + 11.6X_1 - 0.27X_1^2$$
$$(10) \quad (294) \quad (8.4) \quad (0.13)$$
$$+ 70S_2 + 201P_2 + 9.5X_2 - 0.10X_2^2 \quad R^2 = 0.06 \tag{8}$$
$$(11) \quad (235) \quad (7.9) \quad (0.13)$$

Substituting (6), (7), and (8) into (5) would give us family income as a function of characteristics.[17] Alternatively, one can estimate the same function directly. The coefficients are fairly similar and we shall concentrate on the direct regression

$$f = \text{const} + 1.502s_1 + 1.224s_2 + 0.045p_1 + 0.017p_2$$
$$+ 0.351x_1^* + 0.585x_2^* \quad R^2 = 0.21 \tag{9}$$

where for presentational purposes we write x_1^* for $(x_1 - 0.266\,x_1^2)$ and x_2^* for $(x_2 - 0.555\,x_2^2)$.

It turns out that the characteristics of husband and wife are better at explaining family income ($R^2 = 0.21$) than are the characteristics of husband at explaining husband's earnings ($R^2 = 0.18$) or the characteristics of wife at explaining wife's earnings ($R^2 = 0.04$). This is not surprising. For suppose family income depended without error on husband's and wife's wages. Then if the productivity-augmenting traits of husbands and wives were positively correlated, the R^2 for the family equation would have to exceed the weighted average of the separate R^2 for the husband's and wife's equation.[18] And the correlation is in fact remarkably high as cross-sectional correlations go across individuals. So strong is the assortative mating that husband's and wife's schooling has a correlation of $r = 0.56$.[19] So an equalization of productivity traits across the population would lead to a greater equalization of family income than of husband's earnings (which is the effect that is normally considered).

Table 4.4 Variance–covariance matrix explaining family income (f)
(The sum of the entries is 0.056 and the variance of f is 0.263)

	$1.502s_1$	$1.224s_2$	$0.045p_1$	$0.017p_2$	$0.351x_1^*$	$0.585x_2^*$
$1.502s_1$	0.022	0.009	0.002	0.001	−0.007	−0.002
$1.224s_2$	0.009	0.012	0.001	0.001	−0.005	−0.002
$0.045p_1$	0.002	0.001	0.003	. . .	−0.001	−0.001
$0.017p_2$	0.001	0.001	. . .	0.001	. . .	. . .
$0.351x_1^*$	−0.007	−0.005	−0.001	. . .	0.009	0.004
$0.585x_2^*$	−0.002	−0.002	−0.001	. . .	0.004	0.005

Table 4.4 shows the role of the different characteristics in the variance of the right-hand side of (9). Nearly all of the 'explanation' comes from the four entries at the top left-hand corner of the table, for work experience is negatively correlated with schooling and its total effect on inequality is negligible. So it is most instructive to ignore all terms including x^*. This leaves us with an experience-constant variance of about 0.26, of which 0.052 (or about 20 per cent) is due to education. This is much more than the share of individual earnings, at given experience, that can be explained by education, which for men is about 13 per cent.

The effect of family background is a good deal less. If this were somehow equalized, the variance of f would, ignoring the covariance of background and work experience, fall by 0.014 points. Turning to work experience, its effect on inequality is much less among married couples than among the labor force as a whole since the main effect of experience on log earnings, stressed by Mincer and others, comes from the sharp rise in earnings in the first 10 years of working life. And the majority of those in these first 10 years are unmarried.

Family size and income per head

So far we have ignored the family size. If one assumes that people choose their family size this may be a reasonable approach to the welfare of adults, but it is hardly a reasonable approach to the welfare of children, who did not choose to be born. So it is also interesting to look at the distribution of income per 'head'. We measure family size in single adult equivalents as 1.6 *plus* half the number of children. The 'smallness' of the family (B) is the reciprocal of family size, and income per head (Z) is FB. This has a coefficient of variation equal to 0.587 (compared with 0.513 for income). A procedure similar to that used to obtain (1) yields the following approximate expression for

Table 4.5 Variance–covariance matrix explaining family income per head (z)
(The sum of the entries is 0.327 and the variance of z is 0.345)

	$0.779y_1$	$0.178y_2$	$0.035i$	$0.993b$
$0.779y_1$	0.140	−0.001	0.018	−0.011
$0.178y_2$	−0.001	0.049	−0.001	0.016
$0.035i$	0.018	−0.001	0.034	0.002
$0.993b$	−0.011	0.016	0.002	0.058

$z : z = (0.784y_1 + 0.179y_2 + 0.037i + b)(0.993)$ where b measures the smallness of the family.[20] So the squared coefficient of variation of income per head should equal the sum of the terms in Table 4.5. In fact the entries sum to 0.327, compared with a squared coefficient of variation of 0.345.

There is a small positive correlation between income and the smallness of the family, so that the squared 'inequality' of family income per head is slightly greater than the squared inequality of family income *plus* the squared inequality of family size. For, although husband's earnings fall as family size falls, this is more than offset by the fact that wife's earnings rise as family size falls.

To investigate these relationships further, we now undertake a very simple analysis of fertility. For this purpose we concentrate on the 470 families where the wife is aged 35–39, since such families are likely to have completed their childbearing but still have most of their live children living at home.[21] Table 4.6 repeats Table 4.5 but for this cohort only. As one would expect, there is less

Table 4.6 Variance–covariance matrix explaining family income per head (z),
families with mothers aged 35–39
(The sum of the entries is 0.338 and the variance of z is 0.420)

	$0.791y_1$	$0.156y_2$	$0.036i$	$0.983b$
$0.791y_1$	0.124	0.001	0.024	−0.001
$0.156y_2$	0.001	0.041	−0.004	0.015
$0.036i$	0.024	−0.004	0.047	0.002
$0.983b$	−0.001	0.015	0.002	0.052

Table 4.7 Variance–covariance matrix explaining family income per head (z), families with mothers aged 35–39
(The sum of the entries is 0.292 and the variance of z is 0.420)

	$0.791w_1$	$0.791h_1$	$0.791n_1$	$0.156w_2$	$0.156(hn)_2$	$0.036i$	$0.983b$
$0.791w_1$	0.129	−0.015	0.003	0.010	−0.007	0.026	...
$0.791h_1$	−0.015	0.021	...	0.004	...	−0.001	...
$0.791n_1$	0.003	...	0.006	...	...	0.001	...
$0.156w_2$	0.010	0.004	...	0.009	−0.001	0.001	0.001
$0.156(hn)_2$	−0.007	...	...	−0.001	0.025	−0.003	0.003
$0.036i$	0.026	−0.001	0.001	0.001	−0.003	0.047	0.001
$0.983b$	...	...	...	0.001	0.003	0.001	0.009

variation in the number of children within a narrowly defined cohort and hence less inequality arising from that source. Otherwise the figures in the two tables are similar. Once again the wife's earnings rise as family size falls. As Table 4.7 shows, this is partly because women with higher wages have fewer children (presumably due to the opportunity cost of their time),[22] but mainly it is because women with more children work fewer hours.[23] By contrast, men's wages have an insignificant effect on the number of children, and within this cohort the number of children is unrelated to men's hours.[24] This is all we shall say about income per head until we revert to it at the end of the paper.

A leisure-inclusive measure of welfare

Hitherto we have focused on money income. But if people work different hours, differences in money income are not appropriate measures of differences in welfare. Only differences in earnings opportunities and in unearned income matter.[25] But how can these best be summarized? The kind of question one would like to answer is, What is the ratio between the real incomes of families A and B? The traditional Hicksian measures of welfare difference are clearly not well suited to answering such questions. In the Hicksian framework one would typically ask, How much unearned income would family A need, given its wage levels, to achieve the same utility as family B? If the answer was £α and actual unearned income was £β, one might go on to say that family A was better off than family B by a multiple β/α.[26] But this would obviously not be a good way of answering the original question. For example if family A's wages were high enough, α (and β/α.) could be negative. Equally, if β was 0, family A would have no welfare.

An alternative, and more straightforward, approach would be to calculate the full income of each family – that is, the income the family would have if all members worked all the time (Taussig, 1973). In other words, real income is given by $Q = W_1 T_1 + W_2 T_2 + I$ where T_1 and T_2 indicate the total time available to husband and wife. However, this measure is misleading since it does not reflect the fact that, of two families with the same full income, the one with the higher wage rates will have to pay more for its leisure and is therefore worse off.[27]

A more sensible approach is to compute the family's money income as it would be if all members worked average hours:[28] $R = W_1\overline{HN}_1 + W_2\overline{HN}_2 + I$. This gives more appropriate relative weights to the different elements – wages are no longer overweighted relative to unearned income, nor are wives' wages overweighted relative to husbands'. Despite one reservation, we shall use this index in the following form:

$$\frac{R}{\overline{R}} = \left(\frac{\overline{W_1 HN}_1}{\overline{R}}\right)\frac{W_1}{\overline{W}_1} + \left(\frac{\overline{W_2 HN}_2}{\overline{R}}\right)\frac{W_2}{\overline{W}_2} + \left(\frac{\overline{I}}{\overline{R}}\right)\frac{I}{\overline{I}}$$

or

$$r = 0.787\,w_1 + 0.163\,w_2 + 0.036\,i$$

Our reservation concerns not the relative weights attaching to w_1, w_2 and I, but the excessive size of the resulting measure of inequality. To illustrate this, consider a simple world inhabited by single people with no unearned income and having Cobb–Douglas utility functions. If person A has a wage which exceeds B's by a fraction γ, he will work the same hours and earn $(1 + \gamma)$ times as much. Our index will record him as being $(1 + \gamma)$ times as well off. But in fact, though he *has* $(1 + \gamma)$ times as much money income, he has the *same* leisure and cannot be as much as $(1 + \gamma)$ times as well off. The ratio of A's utility to B's utility using a constant returns to scale Cobb–Douglas function would be $(1 + \gamma)^{HN/T} \simeq 1 + \gamma(HN/T)$, where (HN/T) is probably around a third. To deal with this problem we propose an alternative index in the Appendix, but we do not use it in the main paper since it is somewhat contentious and non-homogeneous with the rest of the paper. However, it also serves to support the system of *relative* weights used in our index r.

So let use see what we find by using this index. The weights are of course virtually the same as in (1), and the weights attaching to w_2 and i are very similar to those in (5) which explained money income. But the weight attaching to w_1 is 0.79 rather than 0.70 as in (5). Thus the welfare index attaches more relative weight to husband's wages than does the index aimed at explaining money income. This is because the man's labor supply curve bends back and the wife's is forward rising. But the difference in weights is not large enough to warrant showing another variance/covariance table.

The coefficient of variation of r is 0.49, nearly as high as that of money income. The reason for this similarity is that, although wives' wages are much less unequal than wives' earnings, husbands' wages are slightly more unequal than husband's earnings due to their backward-bending labor supply curve. A striking point here, as before, is how little women's earning power contributes to the explanation of family welfare. This simply reflects the fact that still in the 1970s women's earnings only account for 18 per cent of money income.

Lifetime welfare

Finally we turn to a lifetime welfare approach. This is of course necessary if one wants to exclude that part of inequality which is due to differential experience and does not therefore reflect any persistent inequality between people. It is also necessary to look at lifetime income if one wants to allow for differences in the age when people begin work caused, for example, by differences in schooling.

We construct our index of lifetime welfare for one particular cohort as follows. We take the cohort of families with husbands aged 25–29. To construct the lifetime wage profile of each spouse we use the experience effects from equations like (6) and (7) to project individual hourly wage rates backward and forward through time–back to the end of schooling and forward to age 65.[29] In other words, we assume that the error term on the individual's hourly earnings (averaged over a year) is mainly a permanent personal effect rather than transitory.[30] We then compute the present value of the lifetime earning power of the family, evaluated at age 15, as $V = V_1 + V_2 +$ present value of any student maintenance grants received where $V_1 = \Sigma_{A=S_1+1}^{65}$ $[W_{1A}\overline{HN}_1(0.65) + (0.35)955](1 + i)^{-(A-15)}$ and $V_2 = \Sigma_{A=S_2+1}^{65}[W_{2A}\overline{HN}_2(0.65) + (0.35)675](1 + i)^{-(A-15)}$. Thus we continue to use average hours as the basis for weighting earning power. For use in the second part of the paper, we measure earnings net of tax. Nearly all men pay tax according to a more or less linear tax with a £955 exemption limit and a marginal rate of 0.35. The appropriate tax treatment of women's earning power is less clear, since if they worked $\overline{HN}_2$ hours only about half would pay tax. We treat all as though they paid a proportional tax and received a grant of £(0.35)675, £675 being the tax exemption limit.

The choice of a common discount rate for money income is difficult in an imperfect capital market where individuals in fact have different discount rates. There is a good case here for using a quite low discount rate. For suppose two borrowers have the same human capital investment opportunities but one has a lower borrowing rate than the other. Then the present value of the income of the better-off person (having the lower borrowing rate) will be calculated as lower than that of the worse-off person, unless the common discount rate used is below the higher of the two rates.[31] And an even lower discount rate is needed to reflect the relative welfare levels of the two individuals. We therefore use discount rates of 0 and 5 per cent.

This gives us a value V for each family. The coefficient of variation of V is 0.286 (for $i = 0$) or 0.232 (for $i = 0.05$). Lifetime welfare is thus less unequal than annual money income ($c_F = 0.513$) or annual welfare ($c_R = 0.494$). Also, as one would expect, there is less inequality when a higher discount rate is used, since those with higher undiscounted lifetime incomes have more of their income coming later in life.

The variation in lifetime welfare derives in part, of course, from the variation in schooling and to a very small extent from the variation in family background. For $i = 0$,

$$v = \text{const} + 0.881 s_1 + 0.442 s_2 + 0.016 p_1 + 0.021 p_2 \qquad R^2 = 0.20$$
$$\phantom{v = \text{const} +} (0.127) \quad (0.142) \quad (0.011) \quad (0.009)$$

and for $i = 0.05$,

$$v = \text{const} + 0.436 s_1 + 0.136 s_2 + 0.014 p_1 + 0.018 p_2 \qquad R^2 = 0.08$$
$$\phantom{v = \text{const} +} (0.111) \quad (0.125) \quad (0.070) \quad (0.008)$$

where v is lifetime welfare divided by its mean. One should not necessarily expect schooling to explain a high proportion of discounted lifetime inequality. For, if all men were equal in ability and opportunity, there could be a wide dispersion of schooling with no associated variation in lifetime welfare.

II POLICY EVALUATION

We turn now to consider policies for changing the income distribution – in our case educational policy changes or changes in tax and transfers. One can of course look at the effect of educational policy changes on the distribution of *annual* income, but this does not really capture the main features of their effects. For example, raising the minimum school leaving age forces many low-paid young people out of the labor force. It thereby equalizes annual earnings, but a more important issue is how it affects the lifetime income of those who are now forced to stay on. The case for evaluating educational policies within a lifetime context and the difficulties of doing so were discussed at length in Layard (1977b). The questions for now are, What happens when the effects of educational reforms are analyzed in a family context? How does the use of education as a redistributive device compare with the use of ordinary cash redistribution? To answer such questions we concern ourselves from now on with net income, or net earning power.

To evaluate policies we need an inequality index that is explicitly related to a social welfare function. A convenient index is the Atkinson (1970) equality measure, defined as $E = V_E/\overline{V}$ where V_E (equally distributed equivalent income) is defined by $W(V_1, \ldots, V_n) = W(V_E, \ldots, V_E)$. For then it follows that W increases whenever $E\overline{V}$ increases. In evaluating policy changes we therefore always evaluate $\Delta \ln E + \Delta \ln V$ and consider the policy desirable if this is positive, that is, if the equity change plus the efficiency change is positive. To compute E, some specific social welfare function needs to be assumed. We use the function $W = (1/\alpha) \Sigma_i V_i^\alpha$ and perform the calculations for two commonly used values of α. One is where $\alpha = -1$, which gives us the equality measure we call E_1; the other is where α tends to 0,[32] which gives us the less egalitarian equality measure E_0. For the cohort the equality measures have the following values, as things are (with no policy change): for $i = 0$, $E_0 = 0.969$ and $E_1 = 0.942$; for $i = 0.05$, $E_0 = 0.979$ and $E_1 = 0.962$. Once again, there is more inequality at lower discount rates.

Educational policy changes

But how does all this change if we change educational policy? In evaluating the various policy changes we make life easy for ourselves by assuming that the policy is paid for by a tax proportional to net income. (The British tax system is roughly proportional.) As a result the tax financing additional education has no effect on income distribution. For each policy we therefore compute, for each family, $V + \Delta V$, where ΔV represents the impact of the policy (ignoring the tax changes that finance it). We then recompute our equality measure for the new distribution of $(V + \Delta V)$. The resulting change in *equality* ($\Delta \ln E$) is shown in Table 4.8 for each of the policy changes a–h which we are about to discuss.

The table also shows the proportional change in *efficiency* ($\Delta \ln \overline{V}$). This consists not only of the changes in the individual V's but also of the changes in the net present value of the national tax bill resulting from the policy change.[33] The calculation is as follows. First we estimate D, the social present value of the policy per person whose quantity of education was affected by the policy. Table 4.9 shows the constituent elements of this for each policy for men (i.e. D_1). Then we multiply this number by the proportion of men (π_1) whose quantity of education is in fact affected by the policy. We do the same for women. We then have $\Delta \ln \overline{V} = (D_1\pi_1 + D_2\pi_2)/\overline{V}$. We do all our calculations for $i = 0$ and $i = 0.05$, but we shall only discuss the calculations for $i = 0.05$. We regard all the calculations at this stage as largely illustrative until better data become available.

Table 4.8 Effect of various policy changes

	$i = 0$			$i = 0.05$		
	$\Delta \ln E_0$ $\times 100$	$\Delta \ln E_1$ $\times 100$	$\Delta \ln \bar{V}$ $\times 100$	$\Delta \ln E_0$ $\times 100$	$\Delta \ln E_1$ $\times 100$	$\Delta \ln \bar{V}$ $\times 100$
(a) Qualitative improvement in universal schooling:						
$\rho = 0.03$	0.026	0.049	0.119	0.020	0.034	−0.455
$\rho = 0.06$	0.051	0.097	0.541	0.040	0.075	0.113
(b) Qualitative improvement for early leavers:						
$\rho = 0.03$	0.032	0.063	0.067	0.022	0.042	−0.255
$\rho = 0.06$	0.064	0.124	0.304	0.043	0.083	0.063
(c) Raising minimum school leaving age:						
Method A	0.182	0.335	3.029	−0.007	−0.016	0.685
Method B	−0.016	−0.031	0.964	−0.024	−0.046	−0.351
(d) Maintenance grants at 16	−0.002	−0.003	0.096	−0.001	−0.002	0.004
(e) Maintenance grants at 17	−0.003	−0.006	0.037	−0.003	−0.005	0.005
(f) Maintenance grants at 18	−0.003	−0.006	0.030	−0.003	−0.006	0.007
(g) Raising maintenance grants in higher education	−0.009	−0.017	−0.001	−0.010	−0.019	−0.180
(h) Increase in linear income tax	0.186	0.368	−0.242	0.150	0.295	−0.242

Table 4.9 Net social benefit per male receiving additional education
(Present values at age 15 in 1975 pounds sterling)

	$i = 0$	$i = 0.05$
(a) Qualitative improvement in universal schooling $\rho = 0.03$ and		
(b) Qualitative improvement for early leavers $\rho = 0.03$:		
Change in after-tax earnings	293	147
Change in taxes generated	178	90
−Subsidy	−339	−426
(a) Qualitative improvement in universal schooling $\rho = 0.06$ and		
(b) Qualitative improvement for early leavers $\rho = 0.06$:		
Change in after-tax earnings	585	294
Change in taxes generated	356	179
−Subsidy	−339	−426
(c) Raising minimum school leaving age, method A:		
Change in after-tax earnings	6794	1213
Change in taxes generated	4870	1129
−Subsidy	−572	−545
(c) Raising minimum school leaving age, method B:		
$\bar{B}$	−360	−360
Change in taxes generated	4870	1129
−Subsidy	−572	−545
(d) Maintenance grant in 16th year:		
$\bar{B}$	48	48
Change in taxes generated	4870	1129
−Subsidy	−672	−640
(e) Maintenance grant in 17th year:		
$\bar{B}$	48	48
Change in taxes generated	3580	1128
−Subsidy	−753	−638
(f) Maintenance grant in 18th year:		
$\bar{B}$	49	49
Change in taxes generated	4071	1239
−Subsidy	−753	−650
(g) Raising grants in higher education:		
$\bar{B}$	144	113
Change in taxes generated	9379	1549
−Subsidy	−7292	−5718

Qualitative improvements in compulsory schooling ((a))

An obvious egalitarian policy is to improve universal schooling. We therefore ask what the effect would be of investing an extra £30 per annum on each child's education throughout his compulsory school life. Unfortunately we have little idea what the rate of return to this would be, and we suppose for illustration that the social rate of return (ρ) would be either 3 or 6 per cent, in the form of a constant income stream from the year of the investment until retirement. (While the individual was still being educated the benefit would be in the form of improved ability to learn plus psychic benefits.)[34] Thus each individual's present value at 15 would rise by a constant, depending on the discount rate. This appears as equalizing, since a given absolute amount has been given to each person and a given proportional amount removed (in tax). But if the rate of return is only 3 per cent, the increase in equality is outweighed by the loss of output and the policy should not be pursued (see Table 4.8).

Qualitative improvement for early leavers only ((b))

If the qualitative improvement could be restricted to less able children, it would be more equalizing. Suppose, for example, that it were administratively possible to identify children who were going to leave at the minimum school leaving age of 15 (for this cohort) and £30 per annum were then spent on each of these children. This 'selective' policy is more equalizing than the same policy applied to all children but still undesirable if the rate of return is 3 per cent.

Raising the compulsory minimum school leaving age ((c))

Another policy that *may* benefit early leavers is the raising of the minimum compulsory school leaving age. This was 15 for our cohort but has since been raised to 16. This poses a problem. It would now be most interesting to evaluate a further raising to 17, to which the British government is committed at some unspecified date. But we cannot calculate the inequality effects of this within our sample, since the main distinction in our sample is between those who left at 15 and at 16 or over. So instead we ask, What would have happened to incomes in our cohort if the leaving age had been 16 rather than 15? This captures much of the essence of the problem.[35]

Evaluating increases in compulsory schooling is a controversial business. Revealed preference theory tells us that, if a child who could stay on leaves school, he cannot gain if he is forced to stay on. On the other hand the children may not be deciding their own fate, or those who do so may be misinformed about the benefits of extra education. We therefore evaluate in two ways the effect of compulsory staying on upon those forced to stay on. Method *A*, we assume the individual gains by the amount that the present value of his net lifetime income changes. On the basis of earnings functions estimated for a number of recent years[36] we assume that (after allowing for general equilibrium effects) spending the sixteenth year of life in school will raise each person's gross earnings by 10 per cent. On this basis, the raising of the minimum school leaving age is mildly disequalizing but efficient enough for this to be ignored.[37] In method *B*, if one follows the revealed preference approach, the individual loses (net) an amount equal to the private cost of education *minus* his evaluation of the gains as measured by the demand price. There is some evidence in the United States that the demand elasticity for higher education is around 1, or rather more (Freeman, 1976).[38] There is little evidence for earlier years of education, or for Britain at all. But we shall assume a unit elasticity of demand. If p_0 is the private cost (including earnings foregone), q_0 the number demanding schooling at that price, and q_1 the total number staying voluntarily and involuntarily, then the average net loss for those involuntarily staying is $p_0 - [p_0 q_0 \ln (q_1/q_0)/(q_1 - q_0)]$. On this basis the policy is inefficient and disequalizing.

Maintenance grants for postcompulsory school ((d–g))

Of course an alternative way of inducing people to stay on is by bribery. We therefore evaluate next the effects of a maintenance grant to pupils staying on. First we suppose £100 is given to all at school in their sixteenth year, then (separately) to all at school in their seventeenth year, and then to all at school in their eighteenth year. This of course involves a transfer to those who would have stayed on anyway. It also confers an average net benefit to each individual induced to stay on (on the revealed preference basis) of around £50.[39] The efficiency effects consist of this net benefit, plus the change in tax receipts induced by the higher earnings produced by extra schooling,[40] *minus* the subsidy toward the individual's schooling, including any maintenance grant. It turns out that all these policies are both disequalizing and efficient, but they pass the social welfare test at our assumed levels of inequality aversion.

Finally we look at increased maintenance grants in higher education. These are already substantial, but we assume they go up by £100 per year for the 3-year course. Not surprisingly, in the lifetime context this appears as disequalizing and inefficient. This does not mean that a better system of student finance is not needed. A rational solution would, however, support the level of students' consumption in return for some repayment in later life when earnings are much above the national average.

Redistribution in cash

By contrast, what are the effects of cash redistribution? We assume that a lump-sum handout of £100 per annum per family is financed by an increased proportional tax on gross income (policy (h), analyzed in Table 4.10). The

Table 4.10   Effect of various policies on annual net family income

	$\frac{\Delta \ln E_0 \times 100}{F}$		$\frac{\Delta \ln E_1 \times 100}{F}$		$\Delta \ln \bar{V} \times 100$
	F	F/B	F	F/B	
(h) Increase in linear income tax	0.490	0.562	1.014	1.099	–0.242
(i) As (h) but with handout related to number of children	0.539	1.470	1.062	3.510	–0.269
(c) Raising of school leaving age:					
Method A	1.850	1.768	3.106	2.995	0.685 (for $i = 0.05$)
Method B	0.469	0.456	0.912	0.873	–0.351 (for $i = 0.05$)

efficiency cost of this comes from the substitution effect in labor supply. We assume an excess burden of £0.13 per marginal £ of tax revenue.[41] The efficiency cost, equal to 0.24 per cent of GNP, has then to be compared with the equality gain. On the more egalitarian criterion (E_1) the equality gain outweighs the efficiency loss, but this is not the case with the less egalitarian welfare measure (E_0).

The annual income approach

Finally we look at this same policy, and some others, in the more familiar context of the distribution of annual incomes among families of all ages (under 65). The equality of family annual income is as follows (with the equality of lifetime income at $i = 0.05$ in parentheses): $E_0 = 0.907$ (0.979), $E_1 = 0.835$ (0.962). As one would suppose, annual incomes are markedly less equal, partly because we allow them to reflect variations in women's participation. In the annual income context it is also meaningful to look at income per head, and here the equality measures are even less equal: $E_0 = 0.872$, $E_1 = 0.767$.

If we now look at the effect of our linear income tax change (£100 handout to every family financed by a proportional tax), it appears as much more equalizing than in the lifetime context (cf. Table 4.10 compared with Table 4.8). The reason is that, with more inequality around, a lump-sum handout represents a more variable fraction of family income.

We now consider a handout of £100 times the number of children in the family – something akin to the new British child benefit scheme (policy (i)). This again is financed by a proportional tax. Clearly such a policy has a more equalizing effect on family income per head than the previous policy. Its efficiency cost is similar, since the total revenue needed to pay for it is only slightly higher (there being on average 1.1 children per family).

Finally, we revert to our basic concern with education. Most of the work on education and income distribution done by others has focused on the role of education in explaining annual earnings. We have already queried whether this is indeed the most relevant framework for asking policy questions. However, in Table 4.10 we show the effect on the distribution of annual family income which results from assuming that each individual who left school below 16 had 1 more year of education. This we assume would raise his hourly wage by 10 per cent and have the same effect on his gross earnings. In measuring the effect on equality in table 10, we do not allow for the costs which the raising of the school leaving age would impose on those affected during their fifteenth year of life. So we are allowing only for the private benefits and not the private costs. This makes the policy appear much more equalizing than it does in the whole-lifetime context and makes it appear acceptable (even though we include all social costs and benefits in the efficiency calculation). We do not agree with the annual income approach to educational policy evaluation and only show its results in order to illustrate the difficulties it gives rise to.

III SUMMARY

We can now highlight our main findings. As measured by its coefficient of variation of 0.5, annual family income is about as unequal as husband's earnings, but much less unequal than wife's earnings or unearned income. Yet, of its variance, rather over a half comes from the variance of husband's earnings and the rest comes roughly equally from the variance of wife's earnings, the variance of unearned income, and the covariance of husband's earnings and unearned income. There is *no* covariance between husband's and wife's earnings.

When earnings are broken down into wages, hours, and weeks, it turns out that for men the variation of weeks explains a tiny fraction of the variance of annual earnings, even though in the more traditional analysis (which we query) the variance of log weeks explains a high fraction of the variance of log annual earnings. The variance of wages is all important for men, whereas for women the main variation comes from the variation of annual hours.

When these variations in hours and weeks are traced back through the labor supply response to variations in ages and unearned income, we can understand the zero covariance of husband's and wife's earnings. The positive effect of the correlation of husband's and wife's wages ($r \simeq 0.2$) is just offset by the negative effect of the husband's wage on the wife's hours (an elasticity of -0.14) and, to a lesser extent, by the negative effect of the wife's wage on the husband's hours (an elasticity of -0.05). Altogether wages and unearned income explain about 80 per cent of the variation of family income.

So what really matter are the characteristics determining wage rates. The spouses' schooling, father's occupation, and work experience explain altogether 21 per cent of family income. Given the positive correlation between husband's and wife's productivity traits (the correlation between their schooling is 0.56), it follows that this R^2 of 0.21 for family income is higher than a weighted average of the R^2s for husband's and wife's income, which are in fact 0.18 and 0.04, respectively. The role of father's occupation in directly explaining family income is much less than that of schooling, which explains no less than 20 per cent of experience-constant family income.

If we turn to annual money income per head as the income measure, we now have an additional source of inequality (family size), but one that is not much explained by schooling or wage rates. In any case, one could argue that from the parents' point of view it is wage rates rather than income (or income per head) that correctly measure welfare. We therefore evaluate various possible ways of aggregating wage rates and unearned income into a measure of *family annual welfare*. The Hicksian approach to welfare differences is unsuited to measuring inequality, and so, we argue, is the full-income measure, which ignores the fact that the higher wage rates make leisure more expensive at a given level of full income. Instead we measure welfare by weighting the wage rates of husbands and wives by their average hours worked. It turns out that husbands' wages play a more important role, relative to wives' wages, in determining welfare than in determining money income – though even with money income wives' wages only explain 10 per cent of the variation, after including all covariance terms involving wives' wages.

Annual welfare inequality, of course, includes some inequality arising from differences in work experience. Since this is less ethically disturbing than more persistent elements in inequality, *lifetime welfare* is in many ways the most interesting measure of welfare. We measure this by the present value of the hourly earnings streams of the husband and wife, weighted by their average hours. The coefficient of variation of lifetime welfare (around 0.30) is of course much less than the coefficient of variation of annual welfare (0.49). The schooling of husband and wife explains about 10 per cent of lifetime welfare inequality (at $i = 0.05$) – one would not necessarily expect schooling to explain any higher fraction of lifetime than of annual inequality.

How relevant is any of this to educational *policy*? In our view such aggregative analyses throw limited light on real policy issues. For one never really asks what happens if all educational inequality is abolished (which is the question variance analysis helps one to answer). Instead one is interested in a whole set of fairly limited policy options, and one wants a framework in which to analyze them. In our view the lifetime framework provides the right setting (Layard, 1977b). One then asks, in relation to each policy change, what its effects are on equality and on efficiency (i.e. on the present value of GNP). For this purpose one needs an equality measure that embodies an explicit welfare trade-off between equality and efficiency, and the Atkinson measure provides one.

In Britain the major policy options at present include better-quality universal education, further extension of compulsory schooling, and bribery to induce more staying on (especially at ages 17 and 18, for which there is now much public support). Better-quality universal education is of course equalizing – especially if confined to disadvantaged children. Its efficiency depends on its rate of return, where we make a variety of assumptions. The compulsory raising of the school leaving age 16, recently completed, was (at a 5 per cent discount rate) mildly disequalizing but efficient, if returns are measured without allowing for psychic costs. If we evaluate the returns on a revealed preference basis, the policy is both disequalizing and inefficient.

Policies of bribery operate differently, since they subsidize not only those induced to stay on but also those already staying on who tend to have high lifetime income prospects. As a result they are disequalizing. However, during the later years of secondary schooling, the present value of the extra taxes generated by educating an extra child would exceed the public expenditure cost of educating and subsidizing the child. So a policy to induce more staying on would be efficient, and at the assumed levels of inequality-aversion this efficiency gain outweighs the loss of equality. In higher education, more grants would be not only inequitable but inefficient, due to the huge public expenditure cost.

What, by contrast, can one say about cash redistribution? Using our preceding cost-benefit framework, one cannot of course say whether cash redistribution is better or worse than those educational policies we have found to be desirable. For the policies are not mutually exclusive. If we decide each policy on its own, and we have a convex economy, we get led toward the optimum. However, as an example of cash redistribution we take a cash handout of £100 per family, financed by a proportional tax on gross income (the tax base being our annual index of earning power). Assuming a marginal excess burden of £0.13 per £ of tax raised by the proportional tax, such a step would be warranted by its equalizing effects only when using the more egalitarian measure of welfare. Finally, we evaluate a policy of child support (within an annual income context) and find this acceptable, especially if equality is measured in relation to income per head. We also show the pointlessness of evaluating educational policy changes in an annual income context.

If any one lesson emerges from this paper, it is that different questions produce different answers. If one is concerned with explaining annual family income, one finds that schooling explains a fairly small fraction of the variation. Thus excessive claims about the income-equalizing effects of educational equalization are unwarranted. But particular educational policies have to be judged on their individual merits. Some induced educational expansion may be efficient as well as equalizing. But since there are bound to be diminishing returns to education in the efficiency dimension, one would always expect cash transfers to be the main instrument of redistribution.

Appendix: A New Measure of Leisure-Adjusted Real Income

It is convenient to think of the budget line as being defined by full income (Q) and the wages of husband and wife (W_1 and W_2). Here $Q = W_1 T_1 + W_2 T_2 + I$ where T_i is the available time of the ith partner. The indirect utility function is therefore $U = U(W_1, W_2, Q)$, $U_1 < 0$; $U_2 < 0$; $U_Q > 0$ and, totally differentiating and dividing by U_Q,

$$\frac{dU}{U_Q} = \frac{U_1}{U_Q} dW_1 + \frac{U_2}{U_Q} dW_2 + dQ \tag{A1}$$

Now comes a crucial assumption – that the direct utility function displays constant returns to scale with respect to husband's and wife's leisure and money income. This is partly a normalization assumption, analogous to the assumption that someone with £2,000 is twice as 'rich' as someone with £1,000. But the assumption of homotheticity is also a behavioral assumption, which can in principle be checked. As regards the normalization aspect of the assumption, we are *not* saying that cardinal utility is a constant returns function of our utility index (we believe it to be a concave function). We are saying that our index is the best first step in combining leisure and money income into a utility index.

Given constant returns, $U_Q = U/Q$, by Roy's Identity we also have $U_1/U_Q = -(T_1 - H_1)$ and $U_2/U_Q = -(T_2 - H_2)$ where H indicates annual hours. Substituting all these expressions into ($A1$) and noting that $dQ = T_1 dW_1 + T_1 dW_2 + dI$, we find that $dU/U = (H_1 W_1/Q)(dW_1/W_1) + (H_2 W_2/Q)(dW_2/W_2) + (I/Q)(dI/I)$. Measuring differences about the mean, it follows that, approximately

$$\frac{U}{\overline{U}} = d + \left(\frac{\overline{W_1 H_1}}{\overline{Q}}\right)\frac{W_1}{\overline{W_1}} + \left(\frac{\overline{W_2 H_2}}{\overline{Q}}\right)\frac{W_2}{\overline{W_2}} + \left(\frac{\overline{I}}{\overline{Q}}\right) \cdot \frac{I}{\overline{I}}$$

where $d = [\overline{W}_1(T_1 - \overline{H}_1) + \overline{W}_2(T_2 - \overline{H}_2)]/\overline{Q}$ = average share of leisure in full income. The weights on w_1, w_2, and i now sum to the share of money income in full income, rather than to approximately unity as is the case with the index $R/\overline{R}$. Thus

$$\frac{U}{\overline{U}} \simeq d + \frac{R}{\overline{R}}\left(\frac{\text{average money income}}{\text{average full income}}\right) \tag{A2}$$

As a result, the coefficient of variation of $U/\overline{U}$ is about one-third of the coefficient of variation of $R/\overline{R}$, depending on the values assigned to T_1 and T_2. Thus the coefficient of

Table 4.A1 Correlation coefficients, coefficients of variation and means: whole sample

	F	Y_1	Y_2	I	W_1	H_1	N_1	W_2	$(HN)_2$	S_1	P_1	X_1	X_1^2	S_2	P_2	X_2	X_2^2	B	Z	Coefficient of Variation	Mean
F	1	0.83	0.42	0.56	0.78	−0.04	0.20	0.45	0.24	0.34	0.21	−0.01	−0.03	0.31	0.17	−0.01	−0.05	0.06	0.89	0.513	4 061.641
Y_1	0.83	1	−0.01	0.28	0.92	0.03	0.24	0.21	−0.11	0.35	0.22	−0.05	−0.08	0.26	0.16	−0.05	−0.08	−0.12	0.64	0.482	3 179.803
Y_2	0.42	−0.01	1	−0.02	0.02	−0.09	0.03	0.06	0.78	0.11	0.05	−0.03	−0.03	0.18	0.07	−0.05	−0.06	0.29	0.52	1.242	732.992
I	0.56	0.28	−0.02	1	0.27	−0.04	0.03	0.07	−0.06	0.09	0.08	0.13	0.12	0.10	0.06	0.12	0.11	0.05	0.51	5.026	148.846
W_1	0.78	0.92	0.02	0.27	1	−0.30	0.08	0.23	−0.10	0.39	0.23	−0.04	−0.06	0.29	0.18	−0.03	−0.06	−0.09	0.62	0.497	1.438
H_1	−0.04	0.03	−0.09	−0.04	−0.30	1	−0.04	−0.08	−0.05	−0.12	−0.06	−0.07	−0.08	−0.09	−0.06	−0.07	−0.08	−0.11	−0.08	0.177	44.503
N_1	0.20	0.24	0.03	0.03	0.08	−0.04	1	0.03	..	0.04	0.03	0.04	0.03	0.05	0.04	0.04	0.03	0.02	0.18	0.099	50.861
W_2	0.45	0.21	0.06	0.07	0.23	−0.08	0.03	1	..	0.27	0.10	−0.09	−0.10	0.36	0.17	−0.09	−0.10	0.04	0.45	0.555	0.906
$(HN)_2$	0.24	−0.11	0.78	−0.06	−0.10	−0.05	..	..	1	−0.03	−0.01	0.03	0.03	..	−0.02	0.01	..	0.31	0.35	1.076	766.897
S_1	0.34	0.35	0.11	0.09	0.39	−0.12	0.04	0.27	−0.03	1	0.30	−0.47	−0.46	0.56	0.24	−0.41	−0.40	−0.15	0.23	0.098	15.280
P_1	0.21	0.22	0.05	0.08	0.23	−0.06	0.03	0.10	−0.01	0.30	1	−0.12	−0.11	0.17	0.25	−0.11	−0.10	−0.01	0.18	1.128	0.037
X_1	−0.01	−0.05	−0.03	0.13	−0.04	−0.07	0.04	−0.09	0.03	−0.47	−0.12	1	0.98	−0.44	−0.11	0.95	0.94	0.47	0.14	0.486	26.167
X_1^2	−0.03	−0.08	−0.03	0.12	−0.06	−0.08	0.03	−0.10	0.03	−0.46	−0.11	0.98	1	−0.46	−0.09	0.93	0.94	0.47	0.13	0.834	846.534
S_2	0.31	0.26	0.18	0.10	0.29	−0.09	0.05	0.36	..	0.56	0.17	−0.44	−0.46	1	0.29	−0.46	−0.44	−0.13	0.23	0.0896	15.254
P_2	0.17	0.16	0.07	0.06	0.18	−0.06	0.04	0.17	−0.02	0.24	0.25	−0.11	−0.09	0.29	1	−0.10	−0.10	..	0.15	1.427	0.025
X_2	−0.01	−0.05	−0.05	0.12	−0.03	−0.07	0.04	−0.09	0.01	−0.41	−0.11	0.95	0.93	−0.46	−0.10	1	0.98	0.49	0.13	0.532	24.007
X_2^2	−0.05	−0.08	−0.06	0.11	−0.06	−0.08	0.03	−0.10	..	−0.40	−0.10	0.94	0.94	−0.44	−0.10	0.98	1	..	0.13	0.911	739.168
B	0.06	−0.12	0.29	0.05	−0.09	−0.11	0.02	0.04	0.31	−0.15	−0.01	0.47	0.47	−0.13	..	0.49	..	1	0.46	0.250	0.490
Z	0.89	0.64	0.52	0.51	0.62	−0.08	0.18	0.45	0.35	0.23	0.18	0.14	0.13	0.23	0.15	0.13	0.13	0.46	1	0.587	2 016.850

variation is recorded as smaller by using $U/\bar{U}$ than $R/\bar{R}$, but the share of each source in explaining inequality is exactly the same.

By contrast, if one is concerned with the Atkinson measure of inequality used in section II of the paper, one can note the following. (A2) can be approximated by $u = r^{(1-d)}$. If the social welfare function is $W = (1/\gamma) \Sigma u_i^\gamma$ ($\gamma < 1$), we then have $W = (1/\gamma) \Sigma r^{\gamma(1-d)}$. So whatever value is assumed for α in section II, it can be taken as being intended to measure $\gamma(1 - d)$.

Notes

1. A family is defined as a married couple with the man under 65, plus their dependent children. From a welfare point of view their net income is more interesting than gross income. But we wish to decompose income into its sources, and whereas, for given wage rates, gross earnings vary proportionately with hours, net earnings vary in a strictly non-linear way with hours.

2. Table 4.A1 (p. 75) gives coefficients of variation, means, and correlations for all variables.

3. Rent dividends and interest (multiplied by 2.36 to allow for underreporting; see Layard, Piachaud and Stewart, 1978, Appendix 4), *plus* imputed rent *less* gross mortgage interest. We do not include social security income.

4. An alternative formulation is that used in 'path analysis', where in our case we should have

$$\frac{F}{\sigma_F} = \left(0.784 \frac{c_{Y_1}}{c_F}\right) \frac{Y_1}{\sigma_{Y_1}} + \left(0.179 \frac{c_{Y_2}}{c_F}\right) \frac{Y_2}{\sigma_{Y_2}} + \left(0.037 \frac{c_I}{c_F}\right) \frac{I}{\sigma_I}$$

The variance of F/σ_F (like every other standardized variable) is unity and equals the variance of the right-hand-side expression. We have not used this approach since we are interested in the size of the variance of F and not only in the fraction of it attributable to each source.

5. To understand how the table works, note that the diagonal term (0.143) equals $0.784^2 \, c_{Y_1}^2$, the off-diagonal element (-0.001) equals $(0.784)(0.179) c_{Y_1} c_{Y_2} r_{Y_1 Y_2}$, and so on.

6. Note that the coefficient of variation of a sum is always less than the weighted average of the coefficients of variation of the parts, unless the parts are perfectly positively correlated. For example, if we had only two components of income, Y_1 and Y_2, we should have var $f = \text{var}(a_1 y_1 + a_2 y_2) = a_1^2 \text{var}(y_1) + a_2^2 \text{var}(y_2) + 2a_1 a_2 \text{cov}(y_1, y_2) = a_1^2 c_1^2 + a_2^2 c_2^2 + 2a_1 a_2 c_1 c_2 r_{12} < a_1^2 c_1^2 + a_2^2 c_2^2 + 2a_1 a_2 c_1 c_2 = (a_1 c_1 + a_2 c_2)^2$. The property stated in fact applies to any strictly convex inequality measure (Shorrocks, 1978).

7. $r = 0.23$ (the method of computation is explained below).

8. If P indicates participant women and N indicates non-participant women, and $\alpha = N/(P + N)$, we use the following approximations: var $(W_2)_{P+N} = $ var $(W_2)_P + \alpha[\text{var}(\hat{W}_2)_N - \text{var}(\hat{W}_2)_P] + \alpha(1 - \alpha) [\text{mean }(W_2)_P - \text{mean }(\hat{W}_2)_N]^2$ and cov$(W_2, X)_{P+N} = \text{cov}(W_2, X)_P + \alpha[\text{cov}(\hat{W}_2, X)_N - \text{cov}(W_2, X)_P] + \alpha(1 - \alpha)$

[mean$(W_2)_P$ − mean$(\hat{W}_2)_N$][mean$(X)_P$ − mean$(X)_N$] where W_2 is the wife's wage, $\hat{W}_2$ is the wife's wage predicted by (7) below, and X is any other variable. Since $W_2 = \hat{W}_2 + e_2$, the assumptions here are that var $(e_2)_N =$ var $(e_2)_P$, cov $(e_2, X)_N =$ cov $(e_2, X)_P$, and mean $(e_2)_N =$ mean $(e_2)_P = 0$. Other assumptions make very little difference to our substantive findings. For a more rigorous procedure based on a complete model of labor supply, see Smith (1979).

9. Mincer (1974) and Psacharopoulos and Layard (1979).
10. This difference is due to the strong skew in the distribution of weeks worked, with some workers working a tiny fraction of the average. The percentages of men are shown in parentheses following the number of weeks worked: 0 (1.0), 1–13 (0.4), 14–26 (1.4), 27–39 (2.5), 40–47 (4.5), 47–51 (6.1), 52 (84.1). This contrasts with the approximate log normality of annual earnings. (Among married men under 65 the variance of log weeks is 0.031 and of log annual earnings 0.162.)
11. There are some problems with these results. (i) The own wage substitution effect for men is negative and the cross-substitution effect in the women's equation is positive, though it is negative in the men's equation. We have tried other formulations in the hope of overcoming these problems. In particular we have constructed a fuller model which allows for male overtime (Layard 1977a) and includes age of youngest child. We have estimated this model simultaneously for men and women using the Ashenfelter/Heckman (1974) formulation so as to generate direct estimates of substitution effects. The results were essentially the same. We have also estimated both equations in the form indicated by the linear expenditure system, again with similar results. (ii) For women the absolute sizes of the own and husband's wage elasticities are very low and their sizes very similar. In other work (Layard, Barton and Zabalza, 1980) we have found that if age of youngest child and age of mother are included, the elasticities are $\epsilon_{21} = -0.29, \epsilon_{22} = 0.41$. However, we wished to minimize the number of variables included in the present analysis.
12. The equation for men's weeks (*SEs* in parentheses) is

$$N_1 = 49.9 + 0.539W_1 + 0.190W_2 + 0.0000499I \qquad R^2 = 0.0071 \qquad (4)$$
$$(0.118) \qquad (0.177) \qquad (0.0001100)$$

13. Here the coefficients correspond essentially to the following combinations of elasticities. (We ignore the effects via weeks which are negligible, though included in the final value of the coefficient.)

$$0.703 \simeq a_1(1 + \epsilon_{11}) + a_2\epsilon_{21} = 0.784(1 - 0.09) + 0.179(-0.14)$$
$$0.178 \simeq a_1\epsilon_{12} + a_2(1 + \epsilon_{22}) = 0.784(-0.05) + 0.179(1 + 0.18)$$
$$0.035 \simeq a_1\epsilon_{13} + a_2\epsilon_{23} + a_3 = 0.784(0.00) + 0.179(-0.01) + 0.037$$

Thus, e.g., the effect of husband's wages on family income depends not only on the direct effect of wages on husband's income but also on the influence of his wage on his own labor supply (and weeks) and on his wife's labor supply.

14. The actual P values are, *for men*: professional and managerial 0.098, other non-manual 0.106, skilled manual 0.041, semi-skilled manual −0.018; *for women*: professional and managerial 0.088, other non-manual 0.090, skilled manual 0.021, semi-skilled manual −0.010.

15. There is of course the standard problem of selectivity bias in the women's wage equation (Heckman, 1980). We doubt whether this is serious.
16. The R^2s for the same equations run in semi-log form were no better.
17. The fraction of variance explained by this substituted function is 0.16.
18. For illustration, consider the following simplified version of (5), where the units of W_1 and W_2 are different and have been chosen to make the equation hold, apart from the omitted unearned income and error terms:

$$F = W_1 + W_2 \qquad (5')$$

Suppose also that W_1 is determined by X_1, and W_2 by X_2, with units chosen so that

$$W_1 = X_1 + \epsilon_1 \quad (R^2 = R_1^2) \qquad\qquad W_2 = X_2 + \epsilon_2 \quad (R^2 = R_2^2)$$
$$\mathrm{cov}(\epsilon_1, \epsilon_2) = 0 \qquad\qquad\qquad\quad \mathrm{cov}(\epsilon_i, X_j) = 0 \quad \text{all } i,j$$
$$\mathrm{var}(W_1) = \sigma_1^2 \qquad\qquad\qquad\quad\ \mathrm{var}(W_2) = \sigma_2^2$$

Then if F were regressed on X_1 and X_2 we should find $R_F^2 = [(\sigma_1^2 R_1^2 + \sigma_2^2 R_2^2 + 2r_{X_1 X_2}\sigma_{X_1}\sigma_{X_2})/(\sigma_1^2 + \sigma_2^2 + 2r_{X_1 X_2}\sigma_{X_1}\sigma_{X_2})]$. If $r_{X_1 X_2} = 0$, R_F^2 is a weighted average of R_1^2 and R_2^2, and if $r_{X_1 X_2} > 0$, R_F^2 exceeds the weighted average. If, however, $(5')$ held with error, this inequality need not necessarily hold.

19. This correlation is partly due to intercohort differences. Within the cohort with wives aged 35–39, the correlation was 0.45.
20. $b = B/\bar{B}$. The Taylor series expansion about the means of the right-hand variables yields the expression $z = (a_1 y_1 + a_2 y_2 + a_3 i + b) \cdot \overline{FB}/\overline{FB}$.
21. The survey provides no data on the number of children who have left home.
22. A very simple fertility equation for this cohort gives the following results:

$$1/B = 2.70 + 0.051\, W_1 - 0.196\, \hat{W}_2 - 0.000028\, I \qquad R^2 = 0.028$$
$$\quad\ \ (0.036) \quad\ \ (0.055) \qquad (0.000026)$$

The elasticity of children with respect to men's wages is 0.06 and with respect to women's wages is −0.18. We experimented with quadratic terms, with no good results. We also experimented with a fertility function in terms of personal characteristics, but neither schooling nor parental background of either partner showed a significant effect.
23. For a more detailed study of the effect of children on hours, see Layard *et al.* (1980).
24. Other work (Layard 1977a) has shown that in a multicohort sample children increase men's hours, but this presumably reflects intertemporal substitution of time.
25. This abstracts from differences in utility functions. Since people with the same opportunities often choose different hours, we know that utility functions vary. But to make interpersonal comparisons, we need to assume that all people have the same utility functions with respect to those variables we can measure.
26. For an application of this procedure to the calculation of real wages in the presence of differences in prices and unearned income, see Pencavel (1977).
27. Of course it is possible that people with higher wage rates also have proportionately greater power to enjoy leisure. In this case one could write

the utility function of a single consumer as $u[Y + I, W(T - H)]$, from which it would follow that the cost of wage-adjusted leisure $[W \cdot (T - H)]$ in terms of goods was the same (unity) for all consumers. This would justify the use of full income as the appropriate income measure. This assumption is made in Heckman (1976), but there is at present little evidence of any close association between wage rates and the power to enjoy leisure. Since the association between education and wage rates is low, the established association between education and nonmarket productivity (Michael, 1973) does not take us very far. A more general approach to the problem under discussion would be to assume that $u = u[Y + I, W^\beta(T - H)]$, and we shall explore this in future work.

28. See, e.g., Blinder (1974) and Eckhaus, Safty, and Norman (1974). For this purpose (and later for constructing V) we use W_2 for non-participant women.

29. If W_A^* is a man's actual wage rate at his current age A^*, then his imputed wage at age A is

$$W_A = W_A^* e^{a_1(A - A^*) + a_2[(A - S)^2 - (A^* - S)^2]}$$

and similarly for women. The a_1 and a_2 were estimated from semi-log versions of (6) and (7) and had the following values: for men, $a_1 = 0.025$ and $a_2 = -0.00039$; for women, $a_1 = 0.017$ and $a_2 = -0.00035$.

30. According to Lillard (1977) just over half of the variance of the unexplained residual in annual male earnings is due to permanent individual components and just under half to transitory components. However, our figure relates to hourly earnings, and the residuals in equations for log hourly earnings have a standard error two-thirds that for log annual earnings. This is largely because they exclude unexplained transitory variations in log weeks. Even so, our figures must somewhat exaggerate the inequality in lifetime earning power. But they may not exaggerate the inequality in lifetime wealth, since this also includes inherited wealth.

31. Figure 4.1 illustrates the problem (see Layard 1977b): $PV(Y^A | i_B) < PV(Y^B | i_B)$.

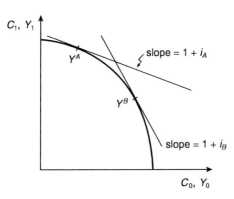

Figure 4.1

32. In this case $W = \Sigma_i \ln V_i$. Taking two values of α is enough to indicate the sensitivity of our results to different values of α.
33. This has been multiplied by $(1 + e')$ where e' is the marginal excess burden per pound of tax revenue. We assume $e' = 0.13$ (see below).
34. For simplicity we assume this is taxable.
35. Unless rates of return to the next year's extension of education would have been very different.
36. See Psacharopoulos and Layard (1979); Layard, Piachaud and Stewart (1978), etc.
37. The disequalizing effect arises because for women the net present value (both private and social) appears as negative, making the net private value for a family negative.
38. Willis and Rosen (1979) find figures a good deal higher, but we suspect this may be due to negative correlation between personal discount rates and personal rates of return.
39. $[(p_0 p_1)/(p_0 - p_1)] \ln (p_o/p_1) - p_1$ where p_0 is the cost before the subsidy and p_1 is $(p_0 - 100)$.
40. Again on the basis of earnings functions for a number of years, we assume that the rate of return to each year of schooling beyond 16 is 6 per cent. For staying onto 16 we again assume a figure of 10 per cent, though strictly this figure should be higher if fewer additional people stay on than in the case where the school leaving age is compulsorily raised.
41. We assume that most marginal tax receipts come from husband's earnings. The excess burden per marginal £ is then approximately $\epsilon t/(1 - t)$ where ϵ is the substitution wage elasticity of husband's hours. We assume $t = 0.4$ and $\epsilon = 0.2$ (Brown, Levin and Ulph 1976). For evaluating the equality effects of the tax we ignore the fact that labor supply will respond to the tax, since this is a second-order effect and allowing for it would barely alter the measured change in equality.

References

Ashenfelter, O. and J.J. Heckman (1974) 'The estimation of income and substitution effects in a model of family labour supply', *Econometrica*, 42 (January), 73–85.

Atkinson, A.B. (1970) 'On the measurement of inequality', *Journal of Economic Theory*, 2 No 3 (September), 244–63.

Blinder, A.S. (1974) *Towards an Economic Theory of Income Distribution* (Boston: MIT Press).

Brown, C.V., E. Levin and D.T.Ulph (1976) 'Estimates of labour hours supplied by married male workers in Great Britain', *Scottish Journal of Political Economy*, 23 (November), 261–77.

Eckhaus, R.S., A.E. Safty and V.D. Norman (1974) 'An appraisal of the calculations of rates of return to higher education', in M.S.

Gordon (ed.), *Higher Education and the Labour Market* (New York: McGraw-Hill).

Freeman, R.B. (1976) *The Overeducated American* (New York: Academic Press).

Heckman, J.J. (1976) 'A life-cycle model of earnings, learning, and consumption', *Journal of Political Economy*, 84(4), pt 2 (August), S11–S44.

Heckman, J.J. (1980) 'Sample selection bias as a specification error', in J.P. Smith (ed.), *Female Labor Supply: Theory and Estimation* (Princeton: Princeton University Press).

Jencks, C. *et al.* (1972) *Inequality: A Reassessment of the Effect of Family and Schooling in America* (New York: Basic Books).

Layard, R. (1977a) 'Hours supplied by British married men with endogenous overtime', *Discussion Paper*, 30, Centre for Labour Economics, LSE.

Layard, R. (1977b) 'On measuring the redistribution of lifetime income', in M.S. Feldstein and R.P. Inman (eds), *The Economics of Public Services* (London: Macmillan), Chapter 3 in this volume.

Layard, R., M. Barton and A. Zabalza (1980) 'Married women's participation and hours, *Economica* (February), Chapter 11 in this volume.

Layard, R., D. Piachaud and M. Stewart (1978) *The Causes of Poverty*, Background Paper 5, Royal Commission on the Distribution of Income and Wealth (London: HMSO).

Lillard, L.A. (1977) 'Inequality: earnings vs human wealth', *American Economic Review*, 67 (March), 42–53.

Michael, R.T. (1973) *The Effect of Education on Efficiency in Consumption* (New York: National Bureau for Economic Research).

Mincer, J. (1974) 'Schooling, experience and earnings, National Bureau of Economic Research, *Human Behavior and Local Institutions*, 2 (New York and London: Columbia University Press).

Office of Population Censuses and Surveys (OPACS) (1978) *General Household Survey, 1975* (London: HMSO).

Pencavel, J.H. (1977) 'Constant-utility index numbers of real wages', *American Economic Review*, 67 (March), 91–100.

Pscharopoulos, G. and R. Layard (1979) 'Human capital and earnings: British evidence and a critique', *Review of Economic Studies* (July), Chapter 8 in this volume.

Shorrocks, A.A. (1978) 'Income inequality and income mobility' (London: LSE), mimeo.

Smith, J.P. (1979) 'The distribution of family earnings', *Journal of Political Economy*, 87 (5), Pt 2.

Taussing, M.K. (1973) *Alternative Measures of the Distribution of Economic Welfare* (Princeton: Princeton University, Industrial Relations Section).

Willis, R.J. and S. Rosen (1979) 'Education and self-selection', *Journal of Political Economy*, 87 (5), Pt 2.

5 Education versus Cash Redistribution: The Lifetime Context (1979)*

1 INTRODUCTION AND SUMMARY

In what ways should the public allocation of educational resources be influenced by distributional considerations? Jencks (1972) argued that, since the correlation between education and experience-specific earnings was so low (around 0.3), education should not be considered an important instrument of redistribution. For even if all men had the same education, the variance of log earnings (within experience groups) would be reduced by only around 10 per cent.[1] Therefore, he argued, the main emphasis should be on redistri-bution by means of cash.

However the Jencks analysis was focused on the distribution of annual income and there are at least two other income distributions which may be more relevant: (1) lifetime income from, say, age 16 onwards; (2) lifetime income from birth onwards. I shall suggest that, as one moves from considering annual income to considering (1) and even perhaps (2), the redistributive power of education relative to cash redistribution may rise. In the case of (1), this is because cash redistribution in a year responds to transitory variations in income and family size, which may be of little consequence in the lifetime context. In the case of (2), it is because, whereas it is very difficult to direct compensatory education at children who will be low-earning adults, it is easy to direct it at children who are currently poor.[2]

In order to do this kind of analysis one has to find a way of comparing the amount of redistribution which occurs within two distributions which start off with different amounts of inequality. This is a quite general problem which often arises in discussing the power of other policies (such as minimum wages) in different contexts. I propose a solution based on the Atkinson equality measure (Atkinson, 1970).

In what follows I first develop the general case for moving to a lifetime perspective (section 2). I then do a formal analysis of the lifetime case from age 16 (section 3), followed by the whole-lifetime case (section 4).

* *Journal of Public Economics*, 12 (3) (1979), pp. 377–85. © *North–Holland Publishing Company*. I am most grateful to Richard Freeman, Tony Shorrocks and the referee for helpful comments, and to the Ford Foundation for financial support.

2   THE CASE FOR LIFETIME INCOME

Whether the lifetime approach is right is of course a philosophical question. If one were a straight utilitarian, then one would not be bothered about how utility levels in different periods were linked together within individuals.[3] However one *ought* to be bothered about this. For example consider the following two societies (*I* and *II*). In each of them there are *n* people of type *A* and *n* people of type *B*. Each person lives for two periods (youth and age). In society *I* each person has the same consumption in both periods (2 units if he is an *A*-person and 1 unit if he is a *B*-person), while in society II consumption levels alternate, thus:

	Society I		Society II	
	Youth	Age	Youth	Age
Type *A* person	2	2	2	1
Type *B* person	1	1	1	2

In both societies the annual distribution of consumption is the same, but in most peoples' eyes society *II* is the more equal. For those of us who think like this, the social welfare function must be concave in individual aggregate lifetime utilities.

So I am going to assume that the lifetime approach is what is relevant to welfare. The question now is: How much difference does this make to the Jencks conclusion? To answer this we need to distinguish between two kinds of annual income distributions. The first is that which includes in the distribution all workers at all stages of work experience (see for example Mincer, 1974 or Psacharopoulos and Layard, 1979). This is of very limited interest from a welfare point of view. It excludes some people (students) of the same age as others who are included. And it includes a massive amount of income variation due to varying levels of work-experience.

To get around these problems, one can confine oneself to workers with a given level of work-experience. This was essentially what Jencks did, though he held age, not experience, constant. In doing this he had taken a big step in the direction of lifetime income. However experience-specific earnings are by no means equivalent to lifetime income, for two reasons. First they include only the benefits of education. They do not take into account the costs – in particular the way in which the length of working life varies with education. It is extremely difficult to generalise about the effects of allowing for this – only a detailed empirical analysis will do (see for example Layard, 1977 and Layard and Zabalza, 1979). The second problem with taking experience-specific income is that it includes transitory income and also, if one is concerned with income per head, transitory elements associated with transitory family size. These problems *can* be examined on an a priori basis and we shall take them in turn in the next section.

3   ADULT-LIFETIME INCOME VERSUS ANNUAL INCOME

In each case we shall conclude that, using our chosen measure of 'equalising power', the equalising power of education is the same in the lifetime as in the annual context, but the equalising power of cash redistribution is less. So the relative role for education is greater in the lifetime context.

Suppose that annual earnings (Y) consist of a part related to schooling ($a + bS$) plus a permanent error (u_p) plus a transitory error (u_t),[4] independent of S and u_p. Then i's annual earnings are

$$Y_{it} = a + bS_i + u_{pi} + u_{ti}$$

If life lasts long enough, his average annual earnings over his working life (Y_i^*) will be approximately[5]

$$Y_i^* = a + bS_i + u_{pi}$$

So schooling (S) explains a higher fraction of the variance of lifetime income (Y^*) than of annual income (Y). Thus if we equalise S the proportionate reduction in var (Y^*) will be greater than the proportionate reduction in var (Y).

But does this mean that educational equalisation is more likely to pass the cost-benefit test when evaluated in a lifetime than in an annual context? The answer is not obvious, since lifetime income was already less unequal than annual income. So how can one say whether one equalisation, starting from one level of inequality, appears more desirable than another, starting from another level of inequality? Like all normative questions, the question can only be answered within an explicit framework of welfare economics. We always want to measure changes in inequality in a way that enables us to compare them with efficiency changes measured in some standard way (e.g. as proportions of GNP). The Atkinson measure of equality (E) provides one such measure,[6] since it is defined in such a way that social welfare improves if

$$\Delta \ln E + \Delta \ln \overline{Y} > 0$$

where $\Delta \ln \overline{Y}$ is the proportional change in GNP. To evaluate $\Delta \ln E$ we note that, if Y is log-normal,

$$\ln E = -\frac{1}{2}\varepsilon \ln\left(\frac{\text{var } Y}{\mu^2} + 1\right) \simeq -\frac{1}{2}\varepsilon \frac{\text{var } Y}{\mu^2} \tag{1}$$

where ε is the coefficient of inequality aversion ($\varepsilon > 0$) (see Shorrocks, 1974). So the gain in equality if we move from the distribution Y to the distribution $(Y + \Delta)$ with the same mean is approximately[7]

$$\Delta \ln E = \frac{1}{2}\frac{\varepsilon}{\mu^2}(\text{var } (Y) - \text{var } (Y + \Delta))$$

Thus, if we equalise *schooling*, the rise in equality in the annual income perspective is approximately

$$\Delta \ln E = \frac{1}{2}\frac{\varepsilon}{\mu^2}(\text{var } (bS + u_p + u_t) - \text{var } (u_p + u_t))$$

$$= \frac{1}{2}\frac{\varepsilon}{\mu^2}\text{var } (bS)$$

In the lifetime perspective the gain in equality is approximately

$$\Delta \ln E = \frac{1}{2}\frac{\varepsilon}{\mu^2}(\text{var } (bS + u_p) - \text{var } (u_p))$$

which has the same value.

But the gains from *cash redistribution* are less in the lifetime than the annual perspective. Suppose, starting with no taxes, we introduce a linear income tax based on annual incomes, so that after-tax income Q is

$$Q = a + (1 - t)Y = a + (1 - t)(bS + u_p + u_t)$$

Then in the annual income perspective

$$\Delta \ln E = \frac{1}{2}\frac{\varepsilon}{\mu^2}\text{var } (bS + u_p + u_t)(1 - (1 - t)^2)$$

and in the lifetime perspective

$$\Delta \ln E = \frac{1}{2}\frac{\varepsilon}{\mu^2}\text{var } (bS + u_p)(1 - (1 - t^2))$$

The latter is smaller, because we are not allowing the equalisation related to transitory income differences to 'count'. So the comparison between education and cash redistribution becomes a lot more favourable towards education when viewed over a longer time period.

This argument is further reinforced if one takes *income per head* as the measure of annual welfare. To see this we now ignore transitory income, and show again that education has the same effect on the inequality of welfare in both contexts, but cash redistribution is more powerful when viewed in the annual context.

Suppose that individual i earns the same income (Y_i) in every period of his life. Suppose also that every individual has family size F^0 in 'year' 0, and F^1 in 'year' 1. Then i's income per head in one particular year t is (in the absence of taxes)

$$Z_{it} = Y_i/F_{it}$$

and his average income per head over a lifetime of two years is

$$Z_i^* = \frac{Y_i}{2}\left(\frac{1}{F^0} + \frac{1}{F^1}\right)$$

It is now convenient to use the following formulation for ln E, which again applies to any log-normal distribution of Z^*,

$$\ln E = -\frac{1}{2}\varepsilon \operatorname{var} \ln(Z^*) \tag{2}$$

Given the definition of Z^*, var ln (Z^*) equals var ln (Y). Hence in a lifetime context if we equalise *schooling*

$$\Delta \ln E = \frac{1}{2}\varepsilon(\operatorname{var} \ln(Y) - \operatorname{var} \ln(Y + \Delta))$$

and in the annual income context the effect is exactly the same.

However, *cash redistribution* is less effective in a lifetime than in an annual context. We can see this by first considering a tax where the handout is unrelated to family size, i.e. after-tax income equals $a + (1 - t)Y$. This has the following effect in the annual context,

$$\Delta \ln E = \frac{1}{2}\varepsilon(\operatorname{var} \ln(Y) - \operatorname{var} \ln(a + (1 - t)Y)$$

and the effect is the same in the lifetime context. But here the handout was unrelated to family size. It follows that if it were related to family size, the policy would be more equalising in the annual than in the lifetime context. This result comes about of course simply because, though income is now held constant, family size is transitory. But once again we have established that educational policy is relatively more effective in the lifetime context.

Before going on, it may be worth pointing out that the argument we have just mounted in relation to education applies equally to any policy designed to influence the distribution of gross wages. Consider for example an effective minimum wage policy with no employment effects. This could appear relatively more favourable compared to cash redistribution when viewed in a lifetime than an annual context. Suppose for example that everybody had the same wage in each year of his life. Then the effect of a minimum wage on the variance of log income per head is the same in the annual and the lifetime context. However, this conclusion is modified if we allow for transitory income components of annual income: a minimum wage would reduce the spread of these and would thus have a greater effect on annual income variation than on lifetime income variation.

There is one final comment on the conclusions so far. We have not allowed for capital market imperfections in our concept of welfare. But in fact one reason why taxes are based on current income (and family size) is that the capital market is imperfect, and welfare can be improved if current taxes take into account current income and family size more than past or future income and family size. Thus the general argument so far, while it shifts the balance towards education, shifts it less than the formal argument might suggest.

4 FULL-LIFETIME INCOME VERSUS ADULT-LIFETIME INCOME

The balance may shift further towards education if we cease to confine a lifetime to the years of adulthood, as is customary, and instead run together the periods of childhood and adulthood. This, as I understand it, is a major reason why economists ought to be interested in social mobility. A person's real income as a child is based on his father's income, and his real income as an adult is based on his own income. For given dispersions of fathers' and sons' incomes, the dispersion of lifetime income will be less the lower the correlation of father's and son's income – that is, the higher the degree of social mobility.[8]

How does the full-lifetime perspective affect our view of educational policy. It may lead to an altogether different evaluation of compensatory education from that normally arrived at. The standard criticism of compensatory education is that, even if we concentrate educational resources on slum schools, there are many children in those schools who will end up rich anyway. So the equalising effect of the policy is small. This is true as regards adult income. But it is not so true of lifetime income. For the extra education (and the resulting extra income as adults) is being given to people whose income *as children* is low. So we have to evaluate the following changes in income distribution, where 1 indicates child and 2 adult, and life consists of two equally-long halves.

Under the adult-life perspective $\begin{cases} \text{Original income} & = Y_2 \\ \text{Final income} & = Y_2 + \Delta \end{cases}$

Under the full-life perspective $\begin{cases} \text{Original income} & = Y_1 + Y_2 \\ \text{Final income} & = Y_1 + Y_2 + \Delta \end{cases}$

Under the adult-life perspective, the gain in equality is (using (1)) approximately[9]

$$\Delta \ln E = \frac{1}{2} \frac{\varepsilon}{\mu_2^2} (\sigma_1^2 - \sigma_2^2 - \sigma_\Delta^2 - 2\sigma_{2\Delta}) = \frac{1}{2} \frac{\varepsilon}{\mu_2^2} (-\sigma_\Delta^2 - 2\sigma_{2\Delta})$$

where σ_j^2 is var (Y_j) and $\sigma_{2\Delta}$ is cov (Y_2, Δ). Under the full-life perspective, the gain in equality is approximately (assuming $\mu_1 = \mu_2 = \mu$)

$$\Delta \ln E = \frac{1}{2} \frac{\varepsilon}{4\mu^2} (\sigma_1^2 + \sigma_2^2 + 2\sigma_{12} - \sigma_1^2 - \sigma_2^2 - \sigma_\Delta^2 - 2\sigma_{12} - 2\sigma_{1\Delta} - 2\sigma_{2\Delta})$$

$$= \frac{1}{2} \frac{\varepsilon}{4\mu^2} (-\sigma_\Delta^2 - 2\sigma_{1\Delta} - 2\sigma_{2\Delta})$$

Assuming $\sigma_2 = \sigma_1$ the full-life gain in equality exceeds the adult-life gain if

$$(-r_{1\Delta}) > 3(-r_{2\Delta}) - \frac{3}{2} \frac{\sigma_\Delta}{\sigma_1}$$

The last term is small; so what is needed is that the negative correlation between the income effect of the policy (Δ) and childhood income is big enough relative to the negative correlation between the income effect (Δ) and adult income. One can easily imagine policies where this was true, and in such cases the policy appears more desirable in a full-life perspective than in an adult-life perspective. If one also added in the psychic gains to slum children from spending their childhood in better schools, then the case for compensatory education is of course further strengthened.

Turning to the other end of the educational system, the case against higher education subsidies will be stronger in the full-life than in the adult-life perspective, if the disequalising effects are greater in the full-life perspective. This would require that

$$r_{1\Delta} > 3r_{2\Delta} + \frac{3}{2} \frac{\sigma_\Delta}{\sigma_1}.$$

In other words, the positive correlation of the income effect with childhood income must be sufficiently large relative to its correlation with adult income. This again seems possible, and the effect could be strengthened if one added in the enjoyment derived from being a student.[10]

Notes

1. This assumes that the equalisation of education did not reduce the disequalising effect of ability differences. There is no obvious reason why it would, though it would probably matter at what level education was equalised (Tinbergen, 1975).
2. To be fair to Jencks, he notices this but fails to unify it with his general analysis. Note also that adult training can be given to adults who are currently poor.
3. I am assuming that intertemporal utility is additive. So, even if social welfare *is* a function of lifetime incomes, utilitarianism means that it is then a sum of individual annual utilities.
4. If we interpret u_t to include the effects of experience, the exercise which follows will also reflect the effect of moving from the overall earnings distribution to the experience-specific distribution, which is of course one step towards focusing on lifetime income.
5. This ignores discounting and differences in length of working life.
6. $E = Y_E/\bar{Y}$ where equally-distributed-equivalent income, Y_E, is defined by $nY_E^{1-\varepsilon} = \Sigma Y_i^{1-\varepsilon}$. The social welfare function is $\Sigma Y_i^{1-\varepsilon}/(1-\varepsilon)$.
7. The approximation is acceptable since (var $Y)/\mu^2$ is of the order of 0.25. The formula implies that if all predicted variance is eliminated from a distribution

$$\Delta \ln E = \frac{1}{2}\varepsilon R^2 \frac{\text{var }(Y)}{\mu^2}$$

   where var (Y) is the original variation and R^2 the fraction of it explained by the right-hand variables.

8. If Y_1 is income as child and Y_2 income as adult and life has two equal halves, the inequality of lifetime income is (using (1)) given by

$$\ln E = -\frac{1}{2}\varepsilon \text{ var}\left(\frac{Y_1 + Y_2}{\mu_1 + \mu_2}\right) = -\frac{1}{2}\varepsilon \text{ var}\left(\frac{Y_1}{\mu_1}\cdot\frac{\mu_1}{\mu_1 + \mu_2} + \frac{Y_2}{\mu_2}\cdot\frac{\mu_2}{\mu_1 + \mu_2}\right)$$

$$= -\frac{1}{2}\varepsilon\left(\frac{\mu_1^2}{(\mu_1 + \mu_2)^2}\cdot\frac{\sigma_1^2}{\mu_1^2} + \frac{\mu_2^2}{(\mu_1 + \mu_2)^2}\cdot\frac{\sigma_2^2}{\mu_2^2} + \frac{2\mu_1\mu_2}{(\mu_1 + \mu_2)^2}\cdot\frac{\sigma_1}{\mu_1}\cdot\frac{\sigma_2}{\mu_2}\cdot r_{12}\right)$$

   This is smaller the smaller r_{12}. It is also less than a weighted average of the inequality measures for Y_1 and Y_2 (provided $r_{12} < 1$).

9. I am now assuming that lifetime income (rather than annual income) is log-normally distributed. Creedy (1977) assumes, instead, that annual income is log-normal, and derives expressions for the variance of lifetime income using various assumptions about the process by which individual incomes evolve over life. I also assume $\Sigma \Delta = 0$.

10. One might think it right to go on at this stage to introduce differences in family size. However, unless it were possible to give more education to children who were poor because they were in large families (which it is generally not), more educational spending would simply add a constant to each lifetime income. It is only in the context of a distribution of *annual* income per head that educational expenditure appears as highly equalising, since the subsidy is so closely related to the size of family.

References

Creedy, J. (1977) 'The distribution of lifetime earnings', *Oxford Economic Papers* (November).

Jencks, C. *et al* (1972) *Inequality: A Reassessment of the Effect of Family and Schooling in America* (New York: Basic Books).

Layard, R. (1977) 'On measuring the distribution of lifetime income', in M.S. Feldstein and R.P. Inman (eds), *The Economics of Public Services* (London: Macmillan), Chapter 3 in this volume.

Layard, R. and A. Zabalza (1979) 'Family income distribution: explanation and policy evaluation', *Journal of Political Economy*, 87 (5), Pt 2, Chapter 4 in this volume.

Mincer, J. (1974) 'Schooling, Experience, and Earnings National Bureau of Economic Research, *Human Behavior and Social Institutions*, 2 (New York and London: Columbia University Press).

Psacharopoulos, G. and R. Layard (1979) 'Human capital and earnings: British evidence and a critique', *Review of Economic Studies* (July), Chapter 8 in this volume.

Shorrocks, A. (1974) 'A note on the computation of Atkinson's inequality measure' (London: LSE), mimeo.

Tinbergen, J. (1975) *Income Distribution: Analysis and Policies* (Amsterdam: North-Holland).

6 The Causes of Poverty (1979)*

with D. Piachaud and M. Stewart

Why are some people poor, and what can be done about it? Since incomes come mainly from earnings or from social security, the question turns on the role of each of these. Most, but not all, of the poorest people have little or no earnings, and they are poorer than others because social security incomes are lower than normal earnings. Such people include pensioners, the unemployed and single-parent families. But there are also some poor families where the father is in work but his earnings do not provide much more than social security – even after the addition of Child Benefit, rate and rent rebates and Family Income Supplement. The size and importance of these various groups of people we shall document in a moment, using our analysis of the 1975 General Household Survey.

However the question then arises of what, if anything, should be done to change things? We shall begin with a brief survey of the issues, before presenting whatever relevant evidence we have been able to put together. There are two basic questions:

- Should the government try to influence earnings (and if so, how); or should it rely only on redistribution via social security and taxation?
- How redistributive should the tax and social security system be and how should different groups be treated?

WAGES POLICY

Earnings depend both on hourly wages and hours worked. Women's hours of work vary a lot and have an important influence on whether a family is poor. Men's hours per week also vary, but a more important issue is the variation in annual hours due to differential unemployment. There is clearly scope for policies which make it easier for women to work (day nurseries, etc.) and for

* *National Westminster Bank Quarterly Review* (February 1979), pp. 30–42. This article is based on work reported more fully in R. Layard, D. Piachaud and M. Stewart, *The Causes of Poverty*, Background Paper, 5, Royal Commission on the Distribution of Income and Wealth (London: HMSO, 1978). We should stress that we alone (and not the Commission) are responsible both for that paper and for this article. The work was financed by the commission and by the Esmée Fairbairn Charitable Trust.

policies which either reduce unemployment or spread it around more evenly. But the main issue about earnings has always concerned the hourly wage. Ought the state to try to influence the wage distribution as a way of reducing poverty among working families?

Clearly the first point to establish is the extent to which low hourly wages are associated with low income relative to need. It is not obvious that (among working families) the lowest paid people come from the poorest families. For the lowest paid people are mostly women, and the poorest working families are mostly those with only the husband at work and with lots of children at home. So the social security system has a major role to play in relation to poverty, even among working families. There is of course the problem of the stigmatizing or demoralizing effect of handouts. But these could be largely eliminated by a serious attempt to make the transfer system automatic, so that employed people did not need to claim in order to receive benefits. Wages do, however remain an important source of inequality: they are especially important, in explaining the inequality of lifetime income, since completed family size varies less than does the number of children at home in a particular year.

If the state wants to affect the wage structure, it has essentially two options. First it can accept the way in which wages are currently determined, but try to alter the outcome by altering supply or demand or by encouraging wider coverage of collective bargaining. The most obvious supply-side policy, much advocated in the United States, is to reduce the spread of educational differences between workers. This would tend to reduce the dispersion of wages, but as we shall show it might not reduce it by very much: policies on adult training might be likely to have more effect. Demand-side policies include regional policy (which works mainly through the level of unemployment), employment subsidies, public employment programmes and the like. Those who believe in the 'dual labour market' often argue that steps to improve the characteristics of low-paid workers will have no effect on their pay, and that only measures to improve the demand for their services can have any effect. We shall review some evidence on dualism.

A more radical approach to wages is to remove all or some of wage determination from the market, either by a comprehensive incomes policy (job evaluation scheme) or a minimum wage. Here two questions arise: can such policies actually be enforced; and if they can, what will their effects be? Some discouraging evidence on the first comes from the effects of the incomes policies of 1972–4 and 1975–7. In each year the formula was strongly equalizing, yet in each year there was no appreciable reduction in inequality. And this happened even though few overtly infringed the policies. This suggests that without a different political system a detailed wages policy is very difficult to enforce. However a minimum wage may be more enforceable, especially if it is not too high.[1] But the main success of institutional intervention in the labour market relates to women. Equal pay legislation largely explains the fact that the average hourly wage of full-time women relative to men has risen by 15 per cent over three years (1973–6). This brings us to the second question: What effect, if any, will a successful wages policy have on employment? The US research on the employment effects of minimum wage legislation is inconclusive. In the United Kingdom equal pay has not been accompanied by a decline in the relative employment of women. But this may be due to the simultaneous introduction of 'equal opportunities' for women to be employed, and women can of course more easily be identified in law than many other disadvantaged groups with less visible characteristics. Our conclusion is that while wages policy can help to equalize wages these effects are probably limited. Taxes and transfers are more important.

POLICY ON TAX AND TRANSFERS

The fundamental issue here is what degree of equalization is to be aimed at. Most people would probably favour a high degree of equality, were it not for the problem of incentive. At the extreme, a policy of total equality would guarantee everybody the same income, regardless of their effort. Those with less than the average income would have their actual income topped up by the whole amount by which it fell short of average income. And those with more than average income should have the whole of the excess taken away. In such a regime we would have 100 per cent marginal tax rates, not only for the rich but also for the poor, since they would lose £1 of benefit for every extra £1 they earned. By comparison with this, the 'poverty trap' would seem mild indeed. Under perfect equality a person would be completely unable to affect his income, and this would be bound to deter effort.

How does this difficulty arise? The problem is one of identification: the state identifies the fortunate by the fact that they actually earn a lot, rather than that they have high earnings potential. So if people are taxed on their earnings, they naturally work less than they would if they could pay the same tax (or receive the same transfer) as an unconditional lump sum, and then pay no tax on their earnings. If only the state could behave like Robin Hood, descending unexpectedly on the rich and giving windfalls to the poor. But it has to announce its rules in advance. So the crucial thing is how far people respond to these marginal tax rates on earnings.

We therefore have to examine the evidence of labour supply responses. This suggests that the disincentive effects of high marginal tax rates on hours of work of men are less than is sometimes supposed. But women do appear to be more responsive to financial incentives, at any rate as far as their decisions to work are concerned. So the efficiency cost per additional £1 of tax collected from women must be much higher than the comparable cost for men.

A related issue is: how far does the existence of unemployment benefit encourage unemployment? Here again it is impossible to believe that, if there were no unemployment benefit, there would be the same amount of unemployment at a given level of shortage in the labour market. The evidence we shall present suggests that the level of unemployment does respond to the level of benefit, but this response is nothing like sufficient to account for the increased unemployment over the last twelve years. As we have already said, one expects redistribution to have efficiency costs. The question is always whether these are more undesirable ethically than the benefits of greater equality.

WHO ARE THE POOREST?

After these preliminaries, it is time to review the evidence in a systematic way. To identify which families are poorer than which we need to measure income relative to needs. If two couples have the same income but family A is childless and family B has three children, family B is worse off because it has greater needs. To measure needs is difficult, though economic research on expenditure patterns is beginning to provide relevant evidence. In any event we have chosen to assume that a family's needs are proportional to the income it would receive on the long-term Supplementary Benefit (SB) scale. Thus our measure of a family's 'real' income is its actual income expressed as a percentage of its long-term SB entitlement.[2] Housing costs are deducted from actual income and not included in the basic SB rates which we use. The data relate to annual net money income and, though they are subject to some margin of error, we believe the broad picture of inequality they give is correct.

Table 6.1 shows the estimated number of people living at each level of income in 1975. Thus $4\frac{1}{2}$ million people live on annual incomes at or below the long-term Supplementary Benefit rate and another $4\frac{1}{2}$ million are below an income level equal to 120 per cent of SB. A further 5 million are below 140 per cent of SB. Taking these three groups together, we have nearly 14 million people, or 26 per cent of the population, living below 140 per cent of SB. The average level of living was, interestingly enough, exactly double the SB level and about 1.5 per cent of people lived at over five times the SB level.

So who were the poor? If we focus on those at or below the SB level, about a half are pensioners, mostly women. One quarter (over a million) are children and of these over a third are in single-parent families. The remaining quarter were non-elderly adults. Moving up to include all those below 140 per cent of SB, we find that pensioners and children in single-parent families are a smaller proportion, though still important, and children in 'ordinary' families a greater part of the problem.

So far we have looked at how the poorer are divided between types of family. An alternative way of viewing the matter is to ask which groups are most likely

Table 6.1   Distribution of individuals (including children) by income relative to
SB and by type of family (000's) (Great Britain, 1975)

Income as percentage of SB

Type of family	100 or less	100-	120-	140-	200-	250-	Over 500	All
Elderly couple	620	860	710	1090	350	320	40	3990
" man	200	160	110	180	70	50	10	770
" woman	1370	680	410	620	230	160	10	3490
Other couple + no child	230	160	310	1840	1950	4720	400	9590
" 1 "	120	280	450	2660	1900	1820	110	7330
" 2 "	350	590	980	4960	2860	2040	140	11 920
" 3 "	280	440	780	2340	980	730	40	5600
" 4 "	230	360	280	880	130	160	10	2040
" 5+ "	220	280	260	340	–	20	–	1120
Singe parent + child(ren)	670	340	210	410	140	130	–	1910
Other single man	140	110	140	870	790	760	30	2840
Other single woman	160	160	230	750	500	390	20	2210
All	4580	4410	4890	16 930	9880	11 270	810	52 790

Source: General Household Survey tapes, kindly provided by the Office of
Population Censuses and Surveys. The number of families in the final sample
analysed was 10 067. Elderly indicates of pensionable age.

to experience poverty? Again there is no magic attached to the 140 per cent
standard but if we continue with it, we can examine the percentage of families
living below the standard. This is shown graphically in the 'poverty-tree' in
Figure 6.1 which summarizes our key findings. Using this poverty level (or any
other) old people are the most prone to poverty. This is especially so if the
family head is not working and has no occupational pension, when 79 per cent
fall below the chosen standard. Among families where the head is of 'working-
age', the single-parent families are the most exposed, since there is only one
potential earner in the family and there are children to feed and look after.
Once again it is crucial whether the parent works.

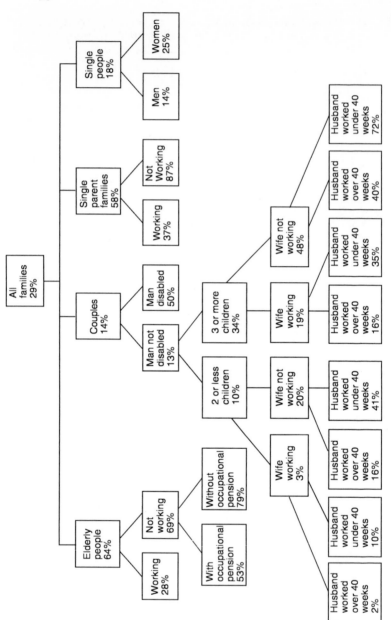

Figure 6.1 Percentage of families in each category having income below 140 per cent of SB
Note: *The* number given in each box gives the percentage of that group of families defined by the corresponding 'branch' of the tree who have an income of below 140 per cent of SB.

Turning to non-elderly couples, only a small proportion of the total are poor. However poverty is much more common where there are many children and if the wife is not working. It is even more common if the husband is not working, as well. For example, in large families where the wife is not working and where the husband has worked less than 40 weeks in the year, no less than 72 per cent of families fall below our poverty line. Thus in general we can summarize the poverty problem as affecting mainly (in order of age):

(a) children in large families or with a lone parent,
(b) disabled, sick and unemployed adults, and
(c) the elderly.

LOW PAY AND POVERTY

This brings us to the point where we can begin to investigate the issues we laid out earlier. The first question is just how closely are low hourly wages related to poverty. This is crucial information if one wants to know how far a national minimum wage would reduce poverty. A minimum wage would have to be specified in terms of hourly earnings. There is no reason why the minimum should not be different for adults and young people, but it could not be differentiated by sex. It would also be difficult to have a lower minimum for part-time work, since this might lead employers to offer less full-time work. So in Table 6.2 we look to see how far adults (over 21) on low hourly wages are in poor families, and vice versa.

The results are rather striking. In 1975 nearly 10 per cent of all employees earned under 62.5 pence an hour. Of these only 22 per cent were in households with incomes below 140 per cent of SB (20 out of 93). All workers with less than 140 per cent of SB comprised just over 10 per cent of adult workers. So of workers in the lowest 10 per cent of wages, only one in five was in the lowest 10 per cent of relative incomes. And by the same token, of workers in the bottom 10 per cent of incomes only one in five was in the bottom 10 per cent of hourly wage-earners. The reason is of course that most of those on low hourly wages are married women, and married women workers are not usually poor–although they might have been poor if they did not work.

Taking a broader definition of low pay and poverty, just under 30 per cent of workers earned under 87.5 pence an hour. Of these about 40 per cent were in the bottom 30 per cent of relative incomes, and vice versa. Clearly the wider we cast the definition of low pay and poverty, the closer the two concepts will coincide. But it is remarkable that when we cast the definition as widely as the bottom 30 per cent of each, we find that under a half of the low paid are at the bottom end of the income scale and vice versa. This lack of

Table 6.2   Distribution of 1000 typical employees by income relative to SB and
by individual hourly earnings (Great Britain, 1975)

	Income as percentage of SB			All
Hourly earnings (pence)				
Under 62.5	20	34	39	93
62.5 to 87.5	28	64	95	187
87.5 and over	58	194	468	720
All	106	292	602	1000

Notes:
1.   People under 21 or over pensionable age are excluded.
2.   Income relative to SB measures the income of the household to which the
employee belongs relative to the household's SB entitlement.
Source: See Table 6.1.

overlap means that minimum wage policies cannot provide any comprehensive remedy to poverty among the employed population, for there are so
many poor who are not low-paid. Moreover even if a minimum wage of £*x*
were introduced it would not necessarily eliminate poverty among those now
paid less than £*x* per hour.

However we do not wish to under-emphasize the importance of low pay. For
though a minimum wage would have a limited impact on the inequality of
annual income per head, it would have a greater impact on the inequality of
lifetime income per head. One can see this by imagining an artificial world
where everybody had the same number of children and only the husband
worked, receiving the same wage every year of his life. Thus a family's position
in the scale of lifetime income would be exactly the same as the husband's
position on the wage scale. But the family's position in any one year would not
necessarily be the same – it would also depend on how many children were
dependent in that particular year. However, even in terms of lifetime income
the position is not in practice that clear. For wages fluctuate from year to year,
so that a minimum wage would have a less sharp impact on lifetime inequality
than if wages were stationary. So while wage inequality matters, it is not the
whole story about inequality.

SUPPLY AND DEMAND FACTORS IN WAGE DISPERSION

What, in any case, can be done about it? To answer this we need to understand what causes the inequality in the first place. Our approach here is to estimate a 'multiple regression' equation which predicts a person's hourly earnings from his education, family background, and work experience and from whether he is covered by a collective bargaining procedure. Other things equal, an extra year of education adds about 9 per cent to a man's hourly earnings, according to the equation. But this estimate may be biased upwards due to the fact that ability is not included in the equation. Our best guess of the true figure is between 5 and 10 per cent. But how much would male wage inequality be reduced if all men had the same education? Surprisingly little. The standard deviation of the logarithm of wages would fall by at most 7 per cent of itself. This is due to the very wide spread of earnings among men with the same education. For the same reason it may not be easy to identify in school those children who will have low earnings in later life, and then to prevent future poverty by practising positive discrimination in their favour. Positive discrimination is much easier to practise in the training and retraining of adults, after those who have low earning power have demonstrated the fact.

Earnings are also affected by father's occupation. But the direct effect on earnings is much smaller (in terms of explanatory power) than the direct effect of education. The main influence of father's occupation is indirect – through education. Studies of American twins show that over a half of the variance of earnings can be explained by factors correlated with family background and genes. However this has no clear relevance for policy, since the level of the association is itself a product of policies relating for example to who gets what educational resources. Nor is it possible to separate out the effect of genes alone on earnings, without making highly arbitrary assumptions.

So supply-side policies may have some effect on the wage distribution, but the question is whether this is enough. In particular are there some people (in a 'secondary' labour market) who are in dead-end jobs and could perhaps not be helped except by intervention on the demand side? To answer this question it would help to have longitudinal data in which we could trace the year-to-year progression of earnings for different people. The General Household Survey does not provide these data and all we can do is to examine the average profile of earnings in relation to age for different broadly-defined groups. It turns out that earnings rise over life at roughly similar rates for the different groups. Most manual workers have little further increase in earnings (except from general economic growth) after the first 10 years experience, and most non-manual workers gain little after 15 years. Within the manual group the unskilled start rather higher than the semi-skilled and thus have flatter profiles, but apart from that there is no marked difference.

INSTITUTIONAL FACTORS IN WAGE DISPERSION

What about the influence of institutional factors upon wage dispersion? Collective bargaining raises the relative wages of men covered by it and can raise them by up to a quarter. The estimates are subject to many econometric problems but suggest that, if the small fraction of low-paid workers not now covered by collective bargaining were to become covered, this would be likely to raise their wages.

But there remains the question of the role of the state. It is widely believed that the incomes policies of recent years have had strongly equalizing effects. This applies particularly to the £1 + 4 per cent which operated from April 1973, the £4.40 'threshold' which operated from April 1974, and the £6 which operated from August 1975. Yet little of this shows up in the figures (Table 6.3). Between April 1975 and April 1977 there was almost no change in the ratio of upper and lower deciles to the median. Instead at each point on the earnings distribution, wage increases occurred which were roughly proportional to the

Table 6.3   Dispersion of gross male weekly earnings; 1970–78

	£ per week					As percentage of the corresponding median			
Year	Lowest decile	Lowest quartile	Median	Highest quartile	Highest decile	Lowest decile	Lowest quartile	Highest quartile	Highest decile
1970	18	22	27	35	44	65	80	127	161
1971	20	24	30	38	48	66	80	127	161
1972	22	27	33	42	54	66	80	126	161
1973	25	31	38	48	61	66	80	125	159
1974	29	35	44	55	69	67	81	125	157
1975	38	45	60	70	88	67	81	125	158
1976	45	54	66	83	105	68	81	126	160
1977	49	59	72	91	114	68	81	126	158
1978	55	66	82	103	130	67	81	125	158

Note:
The lowest decile means the man 10 per cent from the bottom the lowest quartile the man 25 per cent up, and the median the man half-way up.
Source: 'New Earnings Survey', *Department of Employment Gazette* (October 1978).

existing wage. For example, according to the policies the maximum increase between April 1975 and April 1977 should have been not much more than £10; but in the event those at the lowest decile secured £12 while those at the top decile secured £26. And this despite the fact that virtually all pay settlements kept to the norms. An institutional view of the labour market would surely lead one to expect a good deal of equalization to result. But it did not happen. This seems to us to indicate the strength of demand and supply forces in explaining the pattern of wages.

However intervention does seem to have had a striking effect on the pay of women relative to men. The following figures show women's hourly earnings as a percentage of men's (full-time workers only, men over 21, women over 18):

1970	1971	1972	1973	1974	1975	1976	1977	1978
63	64	64	64	66	70	74	74	73

However the difference is still striking. What explains it? Women's starting wages (on leaving school or college) are not much lower than those of comparably-educated men. But thereafter they rise much less fast. This is especially true of married women, but this can be partly explained by their intermittent labour force participation. The striking point is the relatively flat profile of single women. The following figures show the average hourly earnings of women as a percentage of those of comparably-educated men, at different numbers of years after leaving school or college.[4]

	5 years after	10 years after	20 years after
Single women	91	79	71
Married women	92	74	60

This indicates that single women, who presumably work more regularly also fall behind. It is difficult to know how far these figures reflect differential payment for the same work, as opposed to different work opportunities, or different attitudes to work. But the figures indicate an important field for further investigation, and perhaps further intervention on the wages front.

INCENTIVES AND LABOUR SUPPLY

However, as we have stressed, the social security and tax system must always be the main engine of redistribution. The present system is considerably redistributive. For example, if inequality is measured by the coefficient of variation of family income relative to SB, this is 0.55 for net income, compared with 0.93 for income before taxes and transfers. Redistribution between family types accounts for one-third of the reduced variance, and redistribution within family types (between richer and poorer families) for two-thirds.

But the question remains whether more or less redistribution is desirable. This depends partly on ethical judgments but partly on the factual evidence about the disincentive effects of taxation and handouts. Here we have only been able to study the effects of net wages and income upon hours of work, and not upon effort at work, willingness to take risk and so on. Here the evidence is quite clear. Married men work longer hours, the lower their hourly net pay, holding constant the wife's hourly pay and unearned income. A 10 per cent fall in the man's hourly pay causes a 1 per cent rise in hours. Thus a cut in income tax would be likely to reduce hours worked.

For women the incentive effects are sharper. Married women's work responds positively to wages. A 10 per cent rise in women's hourly pay will raise the participation rate by some 4 per cent of its original level. But a rise in the husband's hourly pay will reduce the likelihood of a woman working – a 10 per cent rise causing a fall of roughly 2 per cent. Thus wives are more likely to work in families that would otherwise be poor.

Children also matter, of course. Other things equal, women are nearly 70 per cent less likely to work if they have a young child under 3 than if they have no children. Women whose husbands are unemployed are 33 per cent less likely to work than otherwise-similar women, possibly due partly to the workings of the Supplementary Benefit system.

UNEMPLOYMENT

This brings us to the related question of the effect of unemployment benefit upon the level of unemployment, where we report the work on male unemployment done by our colleague Stephen Nickell. The key statistic is the 'replacement ratio' (the ratio between the net income a family would get if the man is out of work and the corresponding income if he is in work). For the unemployed this ratio is on average about 75 per cent, compared with about 70 per cent for those who are employed. In other words the probability of being unemployed is related to the level of the replacement ratio. But does this mean that the replacement ratio is affecting the level of unemployment? After all, the unskilled are much more likely to be unemployed than the skilled, and they have higher replacement ratios because of the way the benefit system works. In fact the unemployment rate for unskilled men is about four times as high as the average unemployment rate, and for professional men it is about half the average rate.

So we need to separate out the demand-side reasons for unemployment (no jobs) from the supply-side reasons (lack of incentive to take the first job that comes along). The evidence suggests that if, holding constant the availability of jobs, the replacement ratio rises by 10 per cent, the unemployment rate is likely to rise by about 5 per cent. However this effect comes entirely from the effect on people who have been unemployed for less than six months. The replacement ratio seems to have no effect on the probability that a person who has been out for over six months will become employed. So there is no clear incentive argument in favour of paying a lower level of unemployment benefit after six months, as is now done.

Moreover in terms of equity, it is relevant that the average annual income relative to SB of men that have been unemployed for over twelve months is 104 per cent, compared with 171 per cent for men unemployed for one to six months (and 200 per cent for society as a whole). It is obviously easier to raise benefits for the long-term unemployed than for the short-term unemployed since their replacement ratios are now so much lower. And if there are difficulties arising from high replacement ratios, there are always two ways out. One is not to raise unemployment benefits (which is hard on the unemployed); the other is to raise unemployment benefit and at the same time to raise the incomes of the working poor (especially those with children) by some form of improved income support programme.

Any realistic approach to unemployment policy must bear in mind that unemployment means loss of psychic income as well as money income. Presumably the psychic hardships as well as the financial hardships of unemployment grow with duration. The average spell which the unemployed in 1975 had already experienced was around 28 weeks. And duration is longer for the unskilled than for the average unemployed worker. For all types of workers the chances of getting back to work fall progressively after the first few weeks of unemployment. This poses a real challenge to the Employment Services, and raises the issue of whether the long-term unemployed can be adequately helped without specific measures to encourage employers to take them on.

CONCLUSION

Thus there is no one cause of poverty. But two basic facts emerge. Most of the poorest families have little or no earnings. In some cases they lack earnings because they cannot work, as for example with many old people and with the sick and the disabled. In other cases it is difficult for them to work because of

Education and Inequality

the need to look after children – this is most likely to lead to poverty when there is only one parent. And finally there is the case of the unemployed, who cannot find work. Since the social security system provides a basic level of support that is lower than normal earnings in work, it is the presence or absence of earnings rather than the level of pay in work that mainly determines which families are the poorest.

Our second fact is a consequence of the first. It is social security which determines the level at which the poorest members of our community live. It may be reasonable that benefits for those without earnings should be set below incomes in work. But this does not of itself mean that real benefits for those without earnings could not be raised. For there is already a parallel social security system for the working poor (Child Benefit, FIS, rent and rate rebate, free school meals). Particularly if this could be made automatic, so that the curse of claiming was abolished, the living standards of the working poor, and also of the non-working poor, could within limits be set at whatever level society chose. How much income equality is desirable depends on the facts about income distribution and incentives, and on ethical judgments about the relative importance of equity and efficiency.

Notes

1. Not all Wages Council orders are complied with.
2. We in fact use the income relative to SB of the whole 'household' to which the 'family' belongs, in order to allow for income pooling between families, e.g. between an elderly widow and her married son's family.
3. The figures are got from multiple regression equations and relate to persons who left school at 15, except for the last column which relates to people who left at 19+.

7 The Effect of Collective Bargaining on Relative and Absolute Wages (1978)*

with David Metcalf and Stephen Nickell

This paper is concerned with two questions. First, how do unions affect relative wages in Britain? Second, how has the effect varied over time, and what, if anything, does this tell us about the role of unions in wage inflation?

There has by now been a good deal of work on the first question, using group data.[1] But the fundamental problem in all estimates of union wage effects is to ensure that quality is being held constant when the wages of 'covered' and 'uncovered' workers are being compared. This is particularly difficult using group data, since not many quality variables are available at group level. However the General Household Survey (GHS) provides individual data on a whole range of quality variables, for large numbers of individuals. Thus both the wider range of quality variables and the greater number of observations make it possible to control for quality in a more efficient manner.

In Section 1 we use the individual GHS data to estimate for male manual workers the wage differential between those who are covered by collective agreements and those who are not. Unfortunately we do not have data on whether each individual in the sample is covered, but we do know the proportion of workers in his 3 digit occupation who are covered.[2] And we argue that this enables us to arrive at relatively reliable results. We conclude that workers of a given quality get paid some 25 per cent more if they are in a wholly covered occupation than if they are in one that is not covered at all.[3]

* British Journal of Industrial Relations, 16 (1) (March 1978), pp. 287–302. The authors are extremely grateful to Roger Cooley, Tony Cornford and Kathy Pick for first-rate computing and research assistance. We have had very helpful discussions of the paper with Orley Ashenfelter, Jim Heckman, Marcus Miller, Richard Freeman and the members of the University of Chicago Labor Workshop. We are also grateful to the Esmée Fairbairn Charitable Trust, the Department of Employment and the Nuffield Foundation for financing the various parts of the study. An earlier version of the paper was presented to the International Economic Association Conference on Personal Income Distribution in April 1977; see A. Shorrocks and W. Krelle (eds), The Economics of Income Distribution (Amsterdam: North-Holland, 1978).

In other words, an individual worker of given quality is on average paid 25 per cent more if he personally receives a collectively bargained wage than if he does not. We stress, however, the very approximate nature of the finding. Among non-manual workers we find no reliable evidence of an effect of collective bargaining on relative wages.

Some writers have argued that unions increase inequality among manual workers. However, whether this is so depends on the relationship of coverage to personal characteristics, and on the relation between the mark-up and personal characteristics. Coverage is roughly independent of skill, but there is evidence that the mark-up is higher the lower the skill level. So one cannot infer that unions have increased inequality.

The preceding remarks relate to 1973. But how long has this state of affairs existed? According to the evidence of Section 2, for male manual workers in manufacturing the effect of coverage rose sharply by about half of itself between 1968 and 1972. This change was accompanied by a rise in the share of wages in manufacturing, a fall in relative employment in covered industries and a rise in unemployment. All of this is consistent with a model of a cost-push inflationary episode which we put forward. The whole paper is confined to males.

1   THE EFFECTS OF UNIONS ON RELATIVE WAGES IN 1973

Theory

We first want to know how collective bargaining has changed the inequality of hourly wages from what it would otherwise have been. This does not require any information about how collective bargaining has altered the mean level of real wages, which clearly cannot be discovered from any cross-sectional study of individuals. It does require us to know how collective bargaining has altered the level of each individual's wage relative to the mean.

The simplest model is one in which, after collective bargaining is introduced, all individuals with given characteristics are paid the same except for those who are covered by a collective agreement. The latter receive $W e^m$ where W is the uncovered wage and m is the proportional mark-up (for small m). Hence, for the *ith* individual,

$$\ln W_i = a + bX_i + m T_i \tag{1}$$

where W is hourly wages, X is a vector of personal characteristics and T is a dummy variable indicating whether the individual receives the union wage. Two possible complications suggest themselves. First, the wage of the uncovered workers in a sector of the economy might be affected by the degree of coverage due to the threat effect. However, this does not seem likely.

For any effect of unionisation on the wages of non-union workers is already reflected in the fact that many non-union workers are paid the covered (union) wage – while 57 per cent of men are union members, 75 per cent are covered by collective agreements.[4] Second, the mark-up may well vary across sectors and in particular might be affected by the coverage in the sector. So

$$m = m' + c\,U_j$$

where U_j refers to coverage in the *j*th bargaining group.
Thus

$$\ln W_{ij} = a + bX_{ij} + m'T_{ij} + c\,U_j\,T_{ij} \tag{2}$$

where i_j refers to the *i*th individual in the *j*th bargaining group.

These effects comprise about as much of the effects of collective bargaining as one could possibly hope to identify. As Lewis has pointed out,[5] there may well be others. In particular, forcible changes in unionised wages will affect the labour supply available to the uncovered sector, and this may alter the pattern of relative values which are placed on the different personal characteristics in the uncovered sector. For example, if uneducated workers become particularly heavily unionised, this could depress the relative wages of uneducated workers in the uncovered sector.[6] But there is little hope of measuring these effects.

Estimation

For Britain there is a further limitation. We have no comprehensive survey data that show whether an individual belongs to a union, nor whether he receives the union wage. But data are available which show the proportions of workers covered by the union wage in different groups (U_j). So two alternatives are open. (i) One can run inter-group regressions using group means of all variables. (ii) One can run regressions for individuals, using individual data for all variables, except for coverage where the group mean would be used. Method (i) leads to unbiased estimates. But due to the small number of observations much information is wasted. Method (ii) is in that sense more efficient, but leads to biased estimates.

Thus, suppose we accept model (1). If we use group data to run

$$\ln W_j = a_0 + a_1 X_j + a_2 U_j$$

a_2 gives us an unbiased estimate of *m*. But if we use individual data to run

$$\ln W_{ij} = a_0 + a_1 X_{ij} + a_2 U_j$$

the estimated value a_2 is

$$a_2 = b_{TU/X} \cdot m$$

Table 7.1 Regression equations explaining individual log hourly earnings (1973, males)

Type of occ: Sector:	All All	Manual All	Manual All excl. primary	Manual Manufacturing	Non-manual All
Variables					
Coverage	−0.25(8.3)	0.56(10.9)	0.33(5.3)	0.27(2.7)	−0.32(6.4)
Schooling yrs	0.05(10.6)	0.04(4.7)	0.04(4.6)	0.04(1.1)	0.05(7.8)
Degree	0.41(9.1)	0.05(0.2)	0.04(0.5)	0.04(0.1)	0.38(6.6)
Advanced	0.40(16.6)	0.30(5.4)	0.32(5.6)	0.31(3.8)	0.35(10.6)
A level	0.21(9.2)	0.13(4.7)	0.14(4.7)	0.06(1.6)	0.22(6.0)
O level	0.16(8.5)	0.10(4.7)	0.11(4.6)	0.09(2.8)	0.14(4.3)
Other qual.	0.08(3.2)	0.03(0.9)	0.04(1.1)	0.03(0.6)	0.10(2.6)
No quals	–	–	–	–	–
Sel. school	0.13(8.9)	0.07(3.4)	0.07(3.4)	0.10(3.5)	0.12(5.2)
Ex-apprent.	0.03(2.1)	0.05(3.5)	0.06(3.9)	0.06(2.7)	0.01(0.4)
Aim qual.	−0.08(3.4)	−0.06(2.2)	−0.05(1.9)	−0.10(2.4)	−0.08(2.1)
Exp. 0–5	0.14(16.6)	0.15(16.2)	0.16(16.1)	0.15(11.1)	0.11(7.4)
6–10	0.04(7.2)	0.03(5.1)	0.03(4.9)	0.04(4.0)	0.06(5.4)
11–20	0.01(4.4)	0.01(2.8)	0.01(2.9)	0.01(1.3)	0.01(2.4)
21–30	0.00(0.9)	0.00(1.7)	0.00(1.7)	0.00(0)	0.00(0.5)
31–40	0.0(0.1)	0.00(0.5)	0.00(0.9)	0.00(0.4)	0.00(0.2)
41+	−0.01(4.1)	−0.01(3.0)	−0.01(3.0)	−0.01(2.3)	−0.01(2.1)
Father 1	0.10(5.0)	0.04(1.6)	0.03(1.0)	0.09(2.9)	0.14(2.8)
Father 2	0.07(3.6)	0.02(0.7)	0.01(0.6)	0.06(1.9)	0.12(2.5)
Father 3	0.09(5.3)	0.05(3.0)	0.03(1.8)	0.05(1.8)	0.11(2.5)
Father 4	–	–	–	–	–
W. Indies	−0.11(2.4)	−0.07(1.5)	−0.07(1.5)	−0.13(2.1)	−0.14(1.2)
Other coloured	−0.05(1.8)	0 (0.2)	−0.01(0.7)	−0.05(1.4)	−0.06(1.3)
Eire	0.07(1.3)	0.09(1.6)	0.08(1.3)	0.05(0.5)	0.18(1.1)
Other white	–	–	–	–	–
Sick	−0.09(5.8)	−0.08(4.8)	−0.09(5.0)	−0.04(1.6)	−0.10(3.2)
Married	0.09(6.3)	0.07(4.4)	0.07(4.4)	0.07(3.2)	0.14(4.6)
S. East	0.13(9.4)	0.08(5.6)	0.09(6.0)	0.08(3.4)	0.15(5.9)
Urban	0.00(0)	−0.13(2.5)	−0.15(3.0)	−0.30(4.3)	0.25(2.6)
Public	0.06(4.4)	0.04(2.6)	0.01(0.7)	NA	0.03(1.1)
Non manuf.	−0.01(0.5)	−0.02(0.6)	−0.01(0.2)	NA	−0.11(1.5)
Plant size	0.00(0.3)	0.00(0.1)	0.00(0.1)	0.00(0.1)	0.00(0.6)
Conc. ratio	0.14(1.2)	0.19(1.7)	0.18(1.5)	0.19(1.6)	0.18(0.6)
Constant	−1.87(22.8)	−2.29(19.5)	−2.11(16.7)	−0.197(11.6)	−1.86(12.6)
R^2	0.510	0.429	0.426	0.410	0.512
S.E.	0.32	0.29	0.27	0.27	0.36
N	4306	2829	2598	1385	1476

Notes: 1. *t*-statistic in brackets.
2. The population covered included male employees normally working 30 hours a week or more, in non-seasonal and non-military employment, aged under 65.
3. For definition of variables, see Appendix 1.

Source: GHS tapes.

where $b_{TU/X}$ is the regression coefficient of T on U holding X constant. However, there is good reason to think that $b_{TU/X}$ is not substantially different from unity.[7] So we believe that, if model (1) is correct, our individual regressions ought to provide a reasonable estimate of m. If model (2) is correct, this could be estimated from group data by

$$\ln W_j = b_0 + b_1 X_j + b_2 U_j + b_3 U_j^2$$

However at no stage in our work was the squared term ever significant.[8]

There are other notorious estimation problems in this area. Suppose high wages encourage low turnover and thus provide an incentive to unionisation. Then an OLS regression of wages on unionisation cannot identify the causal effect of unions on wages, even if the wage-determining equation is properly specified.[9] This problem is less serious when we are measuring the effect of coverage rather than unionisation. And in any case previous work suffers at least as seriously from inadequate specification of the wage equation to allow for quality differences between workers and for non-pecuniary differences between jobs. These are problems on which we focus.

Individual regressions

We shall begin with the individual regressions (see Table 7.1). These are based on the GHS (1973),[10] and are incidentally the first male hourly wage equations run for Britain. The variables for which we control are described in full in Appendix 1. They include, first, various educational variables: qualification, length of full-time schooling, type of school, apprenticeship completed and current educational activity. Next comes work experience. All these variables normally take the expected signs. So does father's occupation. Interestingly, of our two variables for colour (West Indian and 'other') the West Indian dummy has a coefficient of around minus 10 per cent, but with a standard error making it hardly significantly different from zero. 'Other' (mainly Asian) is insignificantly different from zero, as is the variable for Irish-born (Eire). As expected, long-standing illness reduces wages. Marital status is included mainly as a quality variable, and appears to perform as such.

The next set of variables are somewhat inadequate for their purpose. They are two variables intended to pick up the fact that wages are higher for people working in large city centres, and consequently faced with higher rents for any given travel costs, or with higher travel costs for given rents. Unfortunately, we have no information on where people work. We only know the region where they live. When we included the full set of regional dummies, we found that all regions had very similar coefficients except for the South-East. So the only dummy we include is for the South-East. However, following the previous line of argument we have also included as a continuous variable the percentage of the population living in the region who live in urban areas. This proved to have a positive effect for white-collar workers, but (surprisingly) a negative effect for manual workers.

Finally, we come to variables connected with the 2-digit industry in which the person works. In the light of recent debate in Britain, it is interesting to find that whether the industry is predominantly public seems to make little difference to wages ('on average'). For manufacturing industries we also examine the effect of plant size and concentration ratio, but neither has an effect which is significantly different from zero.

We have deliberately commented on the effects of other variables so that we can henceforth concentrate on the effect of coverage. The available data on coverage come in two forms.[11] One statistic shows the percentage of workers in each 'occupation' (3-digit level) who are covered. The other shows the percentage of workers in each 'industry' (3-digit level) who are covered (separately for manual and non-manual workers). But unfortunately our data on individual wages and characteristics only identify the person's 2-digit industry. So in the individual regressions there is no problem of choice: we measure coverage by its level in the person's 3-digit occupation.[12]

Before looking at the multiple regressions it is a good idea to look at the simple regression of log hourly wages on coverage for different groups of the population (see Table 7.2). As this shows, if all workers, manual and non-manual together, are considered, there is a negative correlation of coverage and wages. However this chiefly reflects the fact that manual workers are more highly covered and get lower wages. Within the working class, coverage and wages are positively correlated, particularly when the highly paid and highly unionised miners are included as well as the low paid and little unionised agricultural workers. Among non-manual workers there is once again a negative correlation between coverage and wages.

Turning to the multiple regressions in Table 7.1, among manual workers coverage works wonders if all sectors are included. However if coverage is excluded and residuals are grouped by occupation, much the largest deviations are among miners (positive) and agricultural workers (negative). Non-pecuniary factors must also be important in both these cases, and neither of these groups form part of the ordinary urban labour market, for which alone it is probably feasible to assess union wage effects. So we shall henceforth concentrate on estimates excluding agriculture and mining. Coverage now seems to raise wages by some 33 per cent for manual workers.[13]

In Table 7.3 this figure is confirmed by regressions run on occupational group data, which, for manual workers yield very similar estimates to the individual regressions. Many of the individual quality variables do not in this case acquire significant coefficients, presumably due to multicollinearity and lack of degrees of freedom.

Table 7.2 Simple regressions of log hourly wages on 'coverage'
(1973, male employees)

Occupation: Sector:	All All	Manual All	Manual All excl. primary	Manual manufacturing	Non-manual All
Individual data					
Coefficient (*t*)	−0.56(16)	0.67(11)	0.40(5)	0.34(3.1)	−0.34(5.7)
R^2	0.046	0.038	0.009	0.005	0.020
N	4307	2830	2593	1386	1477
Group data					
(occupations)					
Coefficient (*t*)	0.22(1.4)	0.64(4.4)	0.26(1.5)		
R^2	0.030	0.240	0.040		
N	79	65	61		
Group data					
(industries)					
Coefficient (*t*)				0.19(2.9)	
R^2				0.013	
N					
Standard					
deviation of					
'coverage'	0.176	0.107	0.088	0.075	0.212

Note: *t*-statistic in brackets.
Sources: Coverage: Department of Employment, *New Earnings Survey, 1973*,
Tables 110 and 112. Wages: Individual data: GHS. Group data on occupations;
New Earnings Survey, 1973, Table 80. Group data on industries: see Table 7.5.

In Table 7.4 we present another similar analysis, this time using group data
on 3-digit manufacturing industries. The coverage effect is somewhat less.

An obvious issue is: If data are to be grouped, which grouping is preferable:
occupation or industry? If we believe Model 1, it ought to be possible to
partition the population into groups in any way one likes and obtain unbiased
estimates of *m*. However, if Model 2 were true, the sample ought to be
partitioned into groups such that the U_j measured the relevant influences on
the union mark-up. This points to the use of data on occupations, for the
following reason. The normal bargain relates to an occupation within an

Table 7.3 Regression equations explaining occupational group log hourly earnings (1973, male employees)

Type of occ:	All	Manual	Manual
Sector:	All	All	All excl. primary
Variables			
Coverage	0.16(1.2)	0.49(2.6)	0.28(1.4)
Schooling yrs	0.10(0.7)	–0.00(0.0)	–0.29(1.2)
Degree	0.00(2.6)	–0.43(0.1)	1.06(0.2)
Advanced	–0.08(0.1)	0.66(0.6)	2.15(1.8)
A level	0.12(0.2)	–0.24(0.2)	–0.14(0.2)
O level	0.07(0.3)	0.17(0.4)	0.37(0.8)
Other qual.	–0.33(0.8)	–0.25(0.4)	1.09(1.5)
No quals	–	–	–
Sel. school	0.26(0.7)	0.16(0.3)	0.43(0.9)
Ex-apprent	0.28(1.8)	0.20(1.1)	0.17(1.0)
Exp. 0–5	0.01(0.0)	–0.11(0.3)	–0.20(0.5)
6–10	0.11(0.4)	0.05(0.2)	0.22(0.7)
11–20	0.00(0.0)	0.03(0.2)	0.06(0.3)
21–30	–0.16(0.8)	–0.24(1.0)	–0.44(1.6)
31–40	–0.23(1.5)	–0.23(1.2)	–0.30(1.5)
41 +	–	–	–
Father 1	0.08(0.3)	–0.00(0.0)	–0.52(1.6)
Father 2	0.12(0.3)	–0.41(1.0)	1.13(2.4)
Father 3	0.55(3.5)	0.30(1.6)	–0.31(1.2)
Father 4	–	–	–
Sick	–0.47(1.5)	–0.39(1.2)	–0.20(0.6)
Married	0.11(0.6)	0.17(0.9)	0.02(0.1)
Urban	–0.01(0.9)	–0.00(0.0)	–0.1(1.2)
Constant	3.06(2.2)	3.66(1.6)	8.10(3.2)
R^2	0.77	0.73	0.69
S.E.	0.11	0.10	0.09
N	79	65	61

Notes: 1. *t*-statistic in brackets.
2. The experience variables measure the proporations in each experience category.
Source: Wages: *New Earnings Survey, 1973*, Table 80. Coverage: *New Earnings Survey, 1973*, Table 112. Other variables: GHS, 1973.

Table 7.4   Regression equation explaining industrial group log hourly earnings
(3-digit manufacturing industries, 1973, male, manual employees)

Coverage	0.19(3.0)
Proportion skilled	0.15(2.2)
Proportion unskilled	−0.08(0.5)
Proportion 20–24	−0.93(2.4)
Proportion 25–54	1.20(6.4)
Proportion in S.E. and midlands	0.02(0.4)
Proportion in conurbations	0.04(0.7)
Constant	3.50(22.9)
R^2	0.39
S.E.	0.089
N	121

Definition of variables
Skilled: proportion of male manual workers in SEC 8 and 9 (foremen and skilled)
– Census 1971.
Unskilled: proportion of male manual workers in SEC 11 (unskilled) – Census
1971.
Age 20–24: proportion of male manual workers aged 20–24 – Census 1971.
Age 25–54: proportion of male manual workers aged 25–54 – Census 1971.
S.E. and Midlands: proportion of male workers in the industry working in the
S.E. and Midlands – Census 1971.
Conurbation: proportion of male workers in the industry working in a conurbation
(Census definition) – Census 1971.
Note: *t*-statistics in brackets.

industry. This is so, even though it may be contained within an industry
settlement (e.g. the engineering industry manual workers' settlement). And the
influence which affects the union mark-up is the level of coverage (or
unionisation) in the occupation within the industry. But unfortunately we have
no data on coverage within the occupation within the industry. So which
variable will be a better proxy for this: unionisation within the occupation or
unionisation within the industry? Fairly clearly the latter, since the variation of
coverage across industries within occupations is likely to be less than the
variation of coverage across occupations within industries. As regards the
individual regressions, similar arguments apply. For this reason we are
somewhat more inclined to accept the results of regressions where coverage is
measured at the level of the occupation.

This would leave one with an estimate of around 30 per cent for the mark-
up. But one is bound to worry about whether in fact this reflects the influence

of unmeasured quality differences. After all, a rational employer, if he had to pay covered workers more than uncovered workers would, provided he could select his own workers, choose the highest quality. So that in the end, although unions had affected the wage structure, this would not show up as a wage difference among workers of a given quality. Clearly one would not expect a complete equilibration of this kind, but this line of thought leads us to think that 30 per cent is too high an estimate.[14] Moreover, the crude difference between covered and uncovered male manual workers in 1973 was only 12 per cent.[15] So we think that 25 per cent is an upper limit for the quality-constant mark-up.

What does this imply for the effect of unions on inequality among manual males? One would have to conclude that inequality was increased if (a) coverage were independent of skill *and* (b) the mark-up were independent of skill. The first is roughly true. Coverage is 85 per cent for skilled workers, 80 per cent for semi-skilled and 87 per cent for unskilled. It is also very poorly correlated with the personal characteristics determining wages. But the second proposition is not true. When regressions are done separately for the three groups of workers the mark-up is higher, the lower the skill group.[16] Similar results have been found for the USA.[17] Given that coverage is independent of skill, it is therefore not surprising that there is less inequality among covered manual workers than among uncovered. For example, if we measure inequality by the difference between the top and bottom decile divided by the median, in 1973 this was 0.87 for uncovered workers, 0.77 for those covered by national agreements only, 0.71 for those covered by national and supplementary agreements and 0.75 for those covered by company and local agreements only.[18] Nor has the rise in the union mark-up, which we document in the next section, been accompanied by a growth in manual workers' wage dispersion.[19] So one cannot infer that unions have increased inequality among manual workers – still less among all workers.[20]

2   CHANGES IN UNION EFFECTS OVER TIME

We now ask: Have unions always had these effects or is this something new? Phelps-Brown[21] and others have suggested that the events of Paris 1968 heralded a new era of union militancy. They argue in support of this that the share of wages has risen in a number of countries. But there is of course no reason why the mechanism of recent inflation need be the same in all countries and we shall confine our remarks to Britain.

The only units of observation for which one can estimate a long time-series of coverage effects are 3-digit manufacturing industries (manual workers). In Table 7.5 we present two such time-series. Both use coverage data for 1973. The first series is comparable with the data presented in Table 7.4. It is based on the 1968 Standard Industrial Classification (SIC) and uses independent variables relating to the 1970s, the same values of these independent variables being used in all years, while the dependent variable (wages) changes from year to year. The second series is based on the 1958 Standard Industrial Classification and uses independent variables relating to the mid-1960s, the same values of the independent variables being again used in all years. For each series we show the partial regression coefficient of log average hourly earnings on coverage, holding constant the variables listed in Table 7.4.

As the table shows, the effect of coverage grew sharply between 1968 and 1972.[22] In column (2) the difference in effects from 1968 to 1972 is significant.[23] Lest this might be due to increasing measurement error in the coverage series as we go back from 1973, we repeated the analysis using as independent variable the level of unionisation in 1966. The coefficient again rose by one half of itself between the late 1960s and the early 1970s.[24] A final partial check on our findings is provided by a recent analysis of the New Earning Survey. This shows the crude ratio between the median hourly earnings of male manual workers covered by 'listed' collective agreements and those of workers not so covered nor covered by Wages Boards:[25]

1970	1971	1972	1973	1974	1975	1976	1977
0.97	0.99	1.00	1.01	1.01	1.03	1.04	1.03

The data do not hold 'other things' constant, but the distribution of 'other things' is not likely to change greatly over a short period of years. So the data should reflect changes in the covered mark-up for workers of given quality, even if they do not reflect its level. *However*, it is important to remember that the data do not include among those covered the growing proportion of workers covered by company and local-only agreements. Moreover the data do not unfortunately reach back into the late 1960s when the rise in the mark-up appears to have begun. Nevertheless the data do confirm the impression of a rising mark-up.[26]

This only tells us that the effect of unions on relative wages has changed. Does it tell us anything about the effect on absolute wages? Taken on its own this evidence does not. However, we begin to have a set of data that is highly consistent with the notion of cost-push inflation, at any rate in the period 1968–72, when we combine this evidence with evidence on the time path of unemployment, of the employment pattern and of the share of wages.

Let us take the *unemployment* series first. At the same time that the union mark-up increased, unemployment also increased (see Table 7.5). This is what

Table 7.5 Time series: 1961–75

	Partial regression coefficient of ln W on U 1968 SIC industries (1)	1958 SIC Industries (2)	Unemployment (%) (3)	Covered employment ÷ uncovered employment (4)	Share of wages (%) (5)	% change in hourly earnings (annual rate) (6)
1961 April		0.17(2.5)	1.5		75.0	7.3
October		0.17(2.5)	1.6			7.0
1962 April		0.15(2.2)	1.9		75.4	5.1
October		0.19(2.8)	2.2			4.1
1963 April		0.19(2.7)	2.6		74.7	3.6
October		0.15(2.2)	2.1			4.1
1964 April		0.17(2.5)	1.8		73.4	7.4
October		0.16(2.3)	1.5			8.2
1965 April		0.20(3.0)	1.5		74.9	8.4
October		0.19(2.6)	1.4			10.1
1966 April		0.21(3.1)	1.2		76.7	9.8
October		0.17(2.4)	1.7			6.2
1967 April		0.17(2.4)	2.2		76.4	2.8
October		0.17(2.5)	2.3			5.3
1968 April		0.18(2.5)	2.4		77.0	8.1
October		0.20(2.8)	2.3			7.2
1969 April		0.21(2.8)	2.3		80.2	7.1
October	0.14(2.3)	0.21(2.9)	2.4			8.0
1970 October	0.16(2.5)	0.26(3.4)	2.5	2.30	84.2	15.3
1971 October	0.17(2.5)	0.26(3.1)	3.7	2.31	83.4	12.9
1972 October	0.19(2.9)	0.31(3.8)	3.4	2.25	82.9	15.0

Table 7.5 continued

	Partial regression coefficient of ln W on U 1968 SIC industries (1)	1958 SIC Industries (2)	Unemployment (%) (3)	Covered employment ÷ uncovered employment (4)	Share of wages (%) (5)	% change in hourly earnings (annual rate) (6)
1973 October	0.19(2.9)	0.31(3.7)	2.2	2.27	83.1	14.1
1974 October	0.19(3.3)	0.25(3.2)	2.8	2.26		21.4
1975 October	0.26(4.0)	0.31(3.3)	4.7	2.26		26.9
Sample size (N)	121	96				

Note: *t*-statistics in brackets.
Sources: Cols. (1) and (2). See text. Based on group data on 3-digit manufacturing industries, male manual employees. Hourly earnings data from *Department of Employment (DE) Gazette*, articles on 'Earnings and Hours of Manual Workers in April or October' (only October after 1969). April data are usually published in the following August; October data are usually published in the following February. Coverage data from Department of Employment, *New Earnings Survey, 1973*, Table 110.
Col. (3). *DE Gazette* and Department of Employment, *British Labour Statistics: Historical Abstract 1886–1968*. When possible school-leavers and adult students are excluded.
Col. (4). *DE Gazette*. June Census of Employment. See n. 28 below.
Col. (5). M. King, 'The UK Profits Crisis: Myth or Reality', *Economic Journal* (March 1975), Table II. The data relate to the calendar year. They show labour costs as a percentage of labour costs plus pre-tax profit less capital consumption and stock appreciation, in manufacturing.
Col. (6). *DE Gazette*. Data relate to percentage changes since previous period (annual rate).

any normal model of cost-push inflation would predict. For example, consider the following simple model. The only input is one type of labour, which can be employed in a unionised industry (U workers) or in a non-unionised industry (N workers). In each industry one worker produces one unit of output. The economy is closed, and the output mix is determined according to a social utility function $u(U, N)$ such that the relative marginal utility of the two outputs equals their relative prices, which equals the relative wages in the two sectors.

$$\frac{u_U(U, N)}{u_N(U, N)} = \frac{W_U}{W_N} \tag{1}$$

The system is completed by an equation which equates monetary demand (Y) to the wage bill

$$Y = W_U U + W_N N \tag{2}$$

Suppose we begin with $W_U = W_N$ and $Y = Y^0$ such that there is full employment:[27]

$$U + N = L$$

This is illustrated at point P in Figure 7.1.

Now the unions push up their wages by a factor λ to W'_U. Monetary demand remains unchanged. So consumption moves to say P'. Unemployment emerges. To relieve this the government starts to 'validate' the wage increase by expanding monetary demand. How far monetary demand has to be expanded depends on the behaviour of unionised workers. If unionised workers who lose their jobs are willing to take non-unionised jobs at less than the union rate, the government will only have to expand monetary demand by somewhat less than λ times the original share of unionised workers. In this case the mark-up is maintained (as in Table 7.5), and employment in high-coverage industries falls permanently relative to employment in low-coverage industries (as also happens in Table 7.5).[28] The alternative is that previously covered workers refuse to move into the uncovered sector and remain unemployed. To restore full employment the government must then raise Y by the full multiple λ. In this case the mark-up gets eliminated. We see no evidence of that in our time series.

We have just given a cost-push interpretation of the positive relationship between the mark-up and the level of unemployment.[29] However such a relationship is found since the First World War in the USA[30]. Lewis offers a different explanation. He says that union wages are sticky, so they rise less fast in the boom and fall less fast in the slump. This may do for periods when there was not sustained inflation. But in Britain over the last ten years inflation has been sustained. It is not clear how stickiness of union wages can lead to higher union wage increases in a slump (rather than smaller union wage decreases).

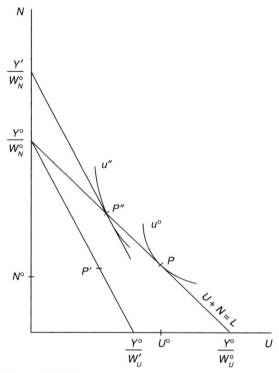

Figure 7.1   Cost-push inflation

In our preceding account there was only one push (e.g. in 1968–72). However the model is also consistent with further pushes, offset by a simultaneous bidding-up of the uncovered wage. According to our evidence this may or may not have been happening since 1972.[31] However the picture since 1972 is exceptionally difficult to interpret, since, apart from 1974–5, there has been a continuous sequence of incomes policies. By contrast there were none between 1969 and 1972.

The final piece of evidence in Table 7.5 concerns the time path of the share of wages, again in manufacturing. This rose sharply between 1968 and 1970 and remained at the new high level till the end of our series. Without developing a model, it seems intuitively reasonable that the share of wages should go up in a period of cost-push, and unreasonable that it should go up in a period of demand-pull.

The picture of a continuing mark-up from 1973 to 1975 is confirmed by group regressions on 3-digit occupations for manual males (excluding agriculture and mining). These yield the following simple regression coefficients and partial regression coefficients (using the same independent variables as Table 7.4) (*t*-statistics in brackets).

	Simple regression coefficient	Partial regression coefficient
1973 Apr.	0.26 (1.4)	0.28 (1.5)
1974 Apr.	0.24 (1.4)	0.32 (1.8)
1975 Apr.	0.32 (2.1)	0.47 (2.9)

These provide some support for the view that the 1975 increase in unemployment may have been connected with a further round of cost-push (see also Table 7.5).

Appendix 1

List of variables used in regressions using individual data

Coverage	Proportion of workers in the 3-digit occupation covered by any collective agreement.
Schooling years	Years of full-time education (measured by age on completing full-time education minus 5).[32]
Degree	First or higher degree (dummy).
Advanced	Non-graduate qualification above the standard of GCE Advanced Level (dummy).
A level	One or more passes at GCE Advanced Level (typically taken at age eighteen or equivalent technical qualification (dummy).
O level	One or more passes at GCE Ordinary Level (typically taken at age sixteen) or City and Guilds craft/ordinary technical qualification (dummy).
Other qual.	Some other qualification (dummy).
No quals	No qualifications (excluded category).
Sel. School	Selective school (grammar or fee-paying) (dummy).
Ex-apprent.	Successfully completed apprenticeship (dummy).
Aim qual.	Currently apprenticed or studying for a qualification (dummy).
Exp. 0–5	Age minus years of schooling minus 5.
6–10	
11–20	(The coefficients indicate the effect of *one* additional year within each experience category.)
21–30	
31–40	
41 +	
Father 1	Father professional or managerial (dummy).
Father 2	Father other white-collar (dummy).
Father 3	Father skilled or semi-skilled manual (dummy).
Father 4	Father unskilled (excluded category).
W. Indies	Coloured and born in British West Indies (dummy).
Other coloured	Other coloured (inteviewer's classification) (dummy).
Eire	Born in Eire (dummy).
Other white	Other white (excluded category).
Married	married (dummy).
Sick	Suffers from a long-standing illness, disability or infirmity which limits activities compared with most people of the same age (dummy).
S. East	Living in South-East region (dummy).
Urban	Proportion of residents in the region living in conurbations or urban areas (as defined in GHS).
Public	Working in a 2-digit industry in which majority of employment is public sector, including nationalised industries.

Non-manuf.	Working manufacturing (dummy).
Plant size	Average number of employees in each plant in the individual's 2-digit industry (manufacturing only) (zero in non-manuf.).
Conc. Ratio	proportion of employment in 2-digit industry accounted for by largest five firms (manufacturing only) (zero in non-manuf.).

Sources: All variables except the four defined immediately below are from Office of Population Censuses and Surveys (OPCS) *General Household Survey, 1973* (data tapes). Urban variable is from GHS 1972. Plant size and concentration ratio from Department of Trade and Industry, *Census of Production, 1968*, Summary Table 158. Coverage data from the *New Earnings Survey, 1973*, Table 112.

Notes and References

1. J. Pencavel, 'Relative wages and trade unions in the UK', *Economica* (May 1974); C. Mulvey, 'Collective agreements and relative earnings in UK Manufacturing in 1973', *Economica* (November 1976); C. Mulvey and J. Foster, 'Occupational earnings in the UK and the effects of collective agreements', *Manchester School* (September 1976); S. Nickell, 'Trade unions and the position of women in the industrial wage structure', *British Journal of Industrial Relations* (July 1977); and D. Metcalf, 'Unions, incomes policy and relative wages in Britain', *British Journal of Industrial Relations* (July 1977).

2. The only source which does use such data is A.W.J. Thompson, C. Mulvey and M. Farbman, 'Bargaining structure and relative earnings in Great Britain', *British Journal of Industrial Relations*, 15(2) (July 1977), which relies on special tabulations of the New Earnings Survey done by the Department of Employment.

3. This estimate is based on regressions excluding agriculture and mining, where non-pecuniary factors play a special role. For US estimates, see O. Ashenfelter, 'Union relative wage effects: new evidence and a survey of their implications for wage inflation', Industrial Relations Section, Princeton University, *Working Paper*, 89 (1976).

4. See New Earnings Survey and P. Price and G.S. Bain, 'Union growth revisited: 1948–1974 in perspective', *British Journal of Industrial Relations*, 14 (3) (1976). For manual workers the figures are 65 per cent and 83 per cent respectively.

5. H. Gregg Lewis, *Unionism and Relative Wages in the US*, Chicago: University of Chicago Press (1963).

6. This effect could be reversed if they mainly became unionised in sectors not intensive in their services.

7. If X is a single variable

$$b_{TU/x} = \frac{\sigma_T}{\sigma_U} \left(\frac{r_{TU} - r_{TX}r_{UX}}{1 - r_{UX^2}} \right)$$ where the r's are simple correlations.

If we assume $r_{TX} = r_{UX}$, we can estimate the degree of bias. The bias must on that assumption be downward since

$$\frac{\sigma_T}{\sigma_U} \cdot r_{TU} = 1$$

and $\sigma_T > \sigma_U$. To get a feel for orders of magnitude, a typical correlation between U and an important variable like years of schooling is 0.1. Let us assume the correlation between U and the relevant product $b\,X$ would also be 0.1. For manual workers σ_U is just under 0.1 and $\sigma_T = \sqrt{p(1-p)} \simeq \sqrt{0.8(.2)} = 0.4$, p being the probability of being covered. So

$$b_{TU/X} = \frac{0.4}{0.1}\left(\frac{0.25 - 0.1^2}{1 - 0.1^2}\right) \simeq 1$$

8. According to C. Mulvey ('Estimating the Union/non-union Wage Differential: a Statistical Issue', Industrial Relations Section, Princeton University, *Working Paper*, 108, 1978) the mark-up within an industry (not holding quality constant) is positively related to the coverage in the industry. But we find no evidence of a linear relationship between the quality-constant mark-up and coverage within industries or occupations.

9. G.E. Johnson, 'Economic Analysis of Trade Unionism', *American Economic Review* (May 1975).

10. See Office of Population Censuses and Surveys (OPCAS), *General Household Survey, 1973*, (London: HMSO, 1976). The GHS is an annual survey of some 10 000 households throughout Britain. We are extremely grateful to the OPCAS for making the tapes available to us. Other related papers that have used these data are R. Layard, 'On measuring the redistribution of lifetime income', in M.S. Feldstein and R.P. Inman (eds.), *The Economics of Public Services*. (London: Macmillan, 1977, Chapter 3 in this volume); G. Psacharopoulos and R. Layard, 'Human capital and earnings: British evidence and a critique', *Review of Economic Studies* (July 1979, Chapter 8 in this volume); G. Psacharopoulos, 'Family background, education and achievement: a path model of earnings determinants in the UK and some alternatives', *British Journal of Sociology* (September 1977); M. Stewart, 'The determinants of earnings in Britain: an occupation-specific approach', Centre for Labour Economics, LSE, *Discussion Paper*, 4 (1977); C. Greenhalgh, 'Is marriage and equal opportunity?' Centre for Labour Economics, LSE, *Discussion Paper*, 14 (1977) and R. Layard, D. Piachaud and M. Stewart, *The Causes of Poverty*, Background Paper, 5, Royal Commission on the Distribution of Income and Wealth (London: HMSO, 1978, Chapter 6 in this volume).

11. The data are from the *New Earnings Survey*, 1973, which is a roughly 1 per cent sample of all employees.

    The survey asks the employer in respect of each member of the sample:
    'Please indicate the type of negotiated collective agreement, if any, which affects the pay and conditions of employment of this employee, either directly or indirectly: 1. National agreement and supplementary company/district/local agreement; 2. National agreement only; 3. Company/district/local agreement only; 4. No collective agreement.' The survey report comments, 'Even though an employee may have more favourable terms and conditions from those in an agreement, or may be employed by an employer who is not a member of an

association which is a party to the agreement, the employee's pay and/or conditions of employment may nevertheless be affected by an agreement' (p. 291). We interpret this to mean that any employer, whether a party to an agreement or not (by membership of an employer's federation), is covered if he is basing his pay on the agreement. We are grateful to Dave Winchester for advice on this and other points. This analysis has not been repeated in subsequent Surveys.

12. The overall proportions covered are as follows (1973, males)

	Manufacturing	Non-manufacturing	All
White-collar	0.46	0.67	0.60
Manual	0.84	0.83	0.83
All	0.74	0.76	0.75

13. The standard deviation of coverage in this group is 0.088. We looked for interaction between coverage and other variables without success except in the case of skill group, reported later.

14. As Phelps Brown has pointed out in private correspondence, the estimates essentially reflect wage differences between occupations rather than differences within occupations, which were mainly used by Lewis (1963).

15. See Thompson, Mulvey and Farbman (1977); Mulvey (1978) argues in favour of a 13 per cent quality-constant mark-up, but the method of quality control is very limited.

16. The analysis was done on 1975 individual GHS data. Fewer variables were controlled for than in Table 7.1 (plant size and concentration ratio in particular being omitted). As a result the coefficients on coverage were much higher than in Table 7.1: for skilled 0.48, for semi-skilled 0.58 and for unskilled 1.34.

17. Ashenfelter (1976); R. Freeman, 'Unionism and the distribution of labour income', Harvard University (September 1977), mimeo.

18. Thompson, Mulvey and Farbman (1977).

19. See *New Earnings Survey, 1977*, Part A, Table 16.

20. For manual workers a crude simulation was undertaken in which it was assumed that a randomly selected 85 per cent of skilled workers had their wages reduced by 20 per cent, a randomly selected 80 per cent of semi-skilled had their wages reduced by 25 per cent and a randomly selected 87 per cent of unskilled had their wages reduced by 40 per cent. This simulation assumed that the structure of uncovered wages remained the same in the absence of collective bargaining. It was found that in such a world the variance of log wages was not substantially different from that actually prevailing.

21. E.H. Phelps Brown, 'A Non-monetarist View of the Pay Explosion', *The Three Banks Review* (March 1975).

22. We also tried adjusting the coverage data to reflect known changes in unionisation. This led to very sharp increases in the measured effect of coverage between 1968 and 1972 but we suspect that these are artifacts of the method of adjustment used.

23. We have

$$\ln W_{72} = a_0 + a_1 X + a_2 U$$
$$\ln W_{68} = b_0 = b_1 X + b_2 U$$
$$\text{So } \Delta \ln W = (a_0 - b_0) + (a_1 - b_1)X + (a_2 - b_2)U$$

where X is the other independent variable. In this regression the coefficient on U turns out to be significant.

24. The coefficients on the proportion unionised comparable with those in column (2) were as follows: 0.08, 0.09, 0.09, 0.09, 0.09, 0.08, 0.08, 0.09, 0.09, 0.08, 0.08, 0.06, 0.05, 0.07, 0.08, 0.06, 0.06, 0.07, 0.11, 0.13, 0.11, 0.11, 0.11, 0.11. (Most t-values were around 2.5.) The data on unionisation were kindly provided by Dr Byron Eastman, and relate to men and women.

25. The same story emerges using average hourly earnings. We are grateful to the Department of Employment for providing these data. The numbers in the sample in 1977 were: covered by listed agreement 27 233, not so covered nor covered by wages council 18 539. The number covered by wages councils was 2215.

26. Why this should have happened lies beyond the subject of this paper. It may have been a delayed response to prolonged employment at higher levels than before the Second World War, which led unions to become less worried at the employment effects of wage push.

27. As will appear later, we could have full-employment with $W_u \neq W_N$. But this initial assumption simplifies the exposition without altering the structure of the argument.

28. In column (4) the coverage level in each industry has been assumed constant at its 1973 level throughout. This is deliberately done so that this measure is not confounded with one that is affected by union recruitment.

29. By a cost-push process of wage setting, we mean one where the wage is set above the market-clearing level.

30. Lewis (1963).

31. At a later stage we intend to test a more formal time-series model of cost-push inflation, in which nominal demand will be explicitly included, as well as unemployment analysed by industry.

32. In about 3 per cent of cases the reported value of this figure was so large relative to the person's qualifications that the person had clearly re-entered education and a number was assigned based on the individual's qualifications.

8 Human Capital and Earnings: British Evidence and a Critique (1979)*

with G. Psacharopoulos

INTRODUCTION AND SUMMARY

What is the private rate of return to schooling and to on-the-job training? And how far does human capital explain the inequality of earnings? We try to answer these questions for Britain for a random sample of about 7000 employed males. Basically, we use the framework of Mincer (1974), but at some important points we find this unsatisfactory, and offer our own critique.[1] In Mincer's regression approach log earnings are regressed on schooling, work experience and experience squared. (The effects of experience are held to reflect the influence of costly investment in on-the-job training.) But this method only yields valid estimates of the direct effects of schooling on earnings if there is no relationship between schooling and the amount of post-school investment and its profitability. A necessary (though not sufficient) condition for this to be true is that the profiles of log-earnings, as experience varies, are vertically parallel for all schooling groups. Casual inspection is not sufficient to verify whether this is so. So the obvious approach is to specify a model in which the pattern of post-school investment and its profitability are allowed to depend on schooling. Such a model also allows one to estimate the rate of return to on-the-job training.

When we estimate the model, we do indeed find a strong relation between schooling and post-school training. The rate of return to training grows with schooling and is much higher than the rate of return to schooling. As in the United States, the estimated direct rate of return to schooling is around

* *Review of Economic Studies*, 46 (3) (July 1979), pp. 485–503.
We are most grateful to Louise Hamshere for intelligent and efficient programming, to Stephen Nickell for suggesting the model of *equation* (3), to the journal's reviewers for helpful comments, to Mark Stewart for helpful discussions, to the Office of Population Censuses and Surveys for making the data available and to the Esmée Fairbairn Charitable Trust for making the money available.

126

10 per cent. The fraction of the variance of log annual earnings of men under 65 that is explained by the simple regression model is about a third, as in the USA – though there is much more inequality to be explained in the USA.

However, this approach does not capture all the effect of human capital on earnings, since there are unmeasured differences between people in human capital investment. If there are periods of life when people vary less in the net effect of post-school investment than they do at other times, then we can learn something by confining our measure of the unexplained variation in earnings to its level in those periods of life. But when are those periods? According to Mincer they are likely to occur at the 'overtaking year', when individuals are actually just earning as much as they could have earned when they left full-time education, had they taken the highest-paying job available (and consequently the job with the lowest learning opportunities). But according to our estimates this overtaking year comes quite quickly, rather than 7–9 years after leaving full-time education as Mincer argues. More importantly, there is no reason why those people on steep earnings profiles and those on flatter profiles should have their profiles cross in the same year that they are 'overtaking'. So we think it is quite reasonable that 'cross-over' should occur 9–11 years after the end of education, as British evidence tends to suggest. Taking the unexplained variance in that year as the true measure of unexplained variance, we estimate that human capital (meaning schooling and on-the-job training) explains about a half the variance of earnings – again as in the USA. However we think this is an overestimate, since it assumes that all the increased variance of log earnings in later life is due to human capital, that costless learning from work experience is impossible and that schooling is uncorrelated with ability, opportunity and other determinants of earnings. Despite Mincer's claim that human capital (as defined) explains 'close to two-thirds' of annual earnings inequality (p. 96), we should be surprised if it really explained more than a third. This does not mean that human capital is unimportant, but only that the more complex models of human capital need to be applied (Becker, 1975, pp. 94ff).

After indicating the fallacy in Mincer's so-called 'short-cut' approach to the rate of return to schooling, we estimate a model of weekly earnings and weeks worked. One extra year of schooling raises weekly earnings by about 8.5 per cent. If we assume (rather extremely) that all the unexplained variance in weeks is transitory, we can then obtain an estimate of the share of permanent income explained by human capital.

We end by examining special features of the British educational system – in particular the importance of part-time education, which is not measured by our years of full-time schooling variable. This leads to more detailed rates of return. Earnings are rather better explained by educational qualifications than by years of full-time education, but this is not evidence in favour of the screening hypothesis. Rather it reflects the importance of part-time qualifications.

1 THEORY

We can start with Mincer's model. A man with no schooling and no training is assumed to earn E_0 in each year of his life. If a man receives one year's education this raises these earnings by a fraction r, the rate of return to schooling. Let us use E_s to denote the level of the flat earnings profile of an untrained man with S years of schooling. So[2]

$$E_S = E_0 e^{rS}$$

For each person, there is thus assumed to be some job in which he would not acquire any new marketable skill. He receives training if he takes a job where he produces less net output now than his current maximum, in order to raise his maximum in the next period. If the training is general, the trainee bears the cost in reduced earnings and reaps the returns in increased future potential earnings. Thus the potential earnings of the ith person with t years of work experience are given by

$$\ln E_{it} = \ln E_0 + rS_i + \Sigma_{j=0}^{t-1} q_i k_{ij}$$

where q_i is the rate of return to training for this individual and k_{ij} is the fraction of his potential earnings which he has foregone in his jth year of experience. It follows that observed earnings are given by

$$\ln Y_{it} = \ln E_0 + rS_i + \Sigma_{j=0}^{t-1} (q_i k_{ij}) - k_{it}$$

For simplicity we shall confine ourselves to the case where the investment ratio k_{it} falls linearly with years of experience (t_i) so that

$$k_{it} = k_{i0} - b_i \cdot t_i$$

where k_{i0} and b_i are parameters.[3] So, integrating and adding an error term,

$$\ln Y_{it} = \ln E_0 - k_{i0} + rS_i + (q_i k_{i0} + b_i + \tfrac{1}{2}q_i b_i)t_i - \tfrac{1}{2}q_i b_i t_i^2 + u_{1it} \tag{1}$$

This is Mincer's quadratic earnings function. Alternatively we can rewrite the function as if everyone had the same values of k_0, b, and q – in which case we are pushing the effects of any individual variation in these parameters into the error term u_{2it}

$$\ln Y_{it} = \ln E_0 - k_0 + rS_i + (qk_0 + b + \tfrac{1}{2}qb)t_i - \tfrac{1}{2}qbt_i^2 + u_{2it} \tag{2}$$

It follows that var (u_2) exceeds var (u_1).

1.1 Can the returns to schooling be identified?

We are now ready to ask: Can the rate of return to schooling in this model be identified? Mincer offers three approaches. What we shall call Method 1 is a regression of the form of (2). But is it true that in such a regression the coefficient on S_i is an unbiased estimator of the rate of return to schooling (r)? Clearly it must be if in (1) k_{0i}, b_i and q_i are independent of schooling (and experience). But there is no reason why they should be independent of schooling. If they were independent, then the profile of log earnings against experience would, of course, look the same for each schooling group except for a vertical shift. It is sometimes suggested that this independence can be inferred from the alleged fact that the profiles of log earnings against experience, when drawn for different schooling groups, are roughly parallel. But casual inspection is not really enough. The obvious procedure is to set up the model explicitly in a way that does not assume independence. In this context the simplest assumption is that, for all individuals in the S_ith schooling group,[4]

$$q_i = q_1 + q_2 S_i$$
$$k_{0i} = k_1 + k_2 S_i$$
$$b_i = b_1 + b_2 S_i$$

Substituting in, we get an expression which looks unwieldy, but, when estimated for Britain, yields extremely sensible results:

$$\ln Y_{it} = \ln E_0 - k_1 + (r - k_2)S_i + (k_1 q_1 + b_1 + \tfrac{1}{2} q_1 b_1) t_i - \tfrac{1}{2} q_1 b_1 t_1^2$$
$$+ (k_1 q_2 + q_1 k_2 + b_2 + \tfrac{1}{2} q_1 b_2 + \tfrac{1}{2} q_2 b_1) S_i t_i + (k_2 q_2 + \tfrac{1}{2} b_2 q_2) S_i^2 t_i$$
$$- \tfrac{1}{2}(q_1 b_2 + q_2 b_1) S_i t_i^2 - \tfrac{1}{2} q_2 b_2 S_i^2 t_i^2 + u_{3it} \quad (3)$$

This is our basic estimating equation and its results do not support the hypothesis that k_0, q or b are independent of schooling. Nor do they support the notion that the rate of return to training is the same as that to schooling – a point to which we return later.

We turn next to Mincer's Method 2. This is designed to cut through the difficulties connected with the shape of age–earnings profiles, by using data only for one year of experience. It tries to get at E_S directly by only looking at earnings in that year $\hat{j}_S$ when actual current earnings ($Y_{S\hat{j}_S}$) equal potential earnings with no training ($\hat{E}_S$). Thus, if we knew the 'overtaking' year $\hat{j}$ for each schooling group, we could readily compute the rate of return to any particular level of schooling S by simply taking $\ln Y_{S\hat{j}_S} - \ln Y_{S-1,\hat{j}_{S-1}}$. However, unless we know the rate of return to training we cannot compute the overtaking year for each group.

We might of course assume the overtaking years were the same $(\hat{j})$ for each individual. In this case, from (1),

$$-k_{i0} + (q_ik_{i0} + b_i + \tfrac{1}{2}q_ib_i)\hat{j} - \tfrac{1}{2}q_ib_i\hat{j}^2 = 0 \quad \text{(all } i)$$

So we have

$$\ln Y_{\hat{ij}} = \ln E_0 + rS_i + u_{1\hat{ij}} \tag{1'}$$

This would enable us to identify r by multiple regression, using only data for the year $\hat{j}$.

But the assumption of uniform $\hat{j}$ is very stringent. Suppose it were not true. In the early years of life, earnings grow rapidly with experience – often by up to 10 per cent per annum. Suppose those with S years of schooling 'overtake' one-half year later than those with $S - 1$ years of schooling. The rate of return to schooling will be underestimated by up to 5 percentage points, and vice versa. How likely is it that $\hat{j}$ will be identical for all schooling groups? If all groups have parallel profiles, and q is the same for each group, then $\hat{j}$ must be the same for each group.[5] But there is no reason why these assumptions should hold.

However, suppose $\hat{j}$ is the same for all groups. How can it be identified? If one knew the rate of return to training there would of course be no problem, but we do not, using this method, have any method of computing it. Instead Mincer offers an approach which involves an essentially independent idea, which we shall call the 'cross-over' year. As (1) indicates, two individuals A and B in any particular schooling group (say with no schooling) may have different earnings streams. But ignoring non-pecuniary factors, information problems and capital market imperfections, the present value of the two expected streams must be the same. So the two streams must cross over. We shall call the cross-over year $\hat{t}$ (see Figure 8.1). There is no logical reason why crossing over should occur at the overtaking year. So in Figure 8.1 we have assumed that cross-over in fact occurs before the overtaking year of either A or B. Now suppose that the profiles of C and D, each with one year of education, cross over at the same number of years of experience as the profiles of A and B. We now estimate for year of experience $(\hat{t})$

$$\ln Y_{\hat{u}} = a_0 + a_1S_i + u_{1\hat{u}} \tag{1''}$$

Is a_1 an unbiased estimator of r? Not necessarily, for as we have drawn it, the overtaking year for C and D comes before $\hat{t}$ and that for A and B after $\hat{t}$. So

$$\ln \hat{Y}_{C\hat{t}} - \ln \hat{Y}_{A\hat{t}} > \ln \hat{E}_1 - \ln \hat{E}_0$$

However, if the average profiles of both groups are parallel and q is the same for both groups, then for *any* experience group the difference in log earnings is a good measure of the rate of return to schooling. $\hat{t}$ is a good age at which to

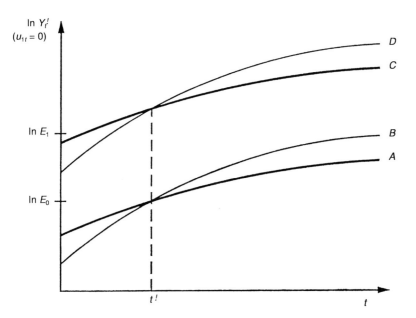

Figure 8.1   The cross-over year

run regressions because at that level of experience the residual variance due to differences in individual profiles is much less. This also makes the cross-over year regressions especially relevant to the question of the explanatory power of human capital, to which we shall shortly return.

However first we must refer to Mincer's Method 3. This 'short-cut method'[6] involves using the conventionally-calculated rate of return to compute estimates of E_S for each level of schooling (S). The rate of return to the Sth year of schooling is then $(\hat{E}_S/\hat{E}_{S-1}) - 1$, where $\hat{E}_S$ is the estimate of E_S. The method is only correct if the rate of return to training equals the rate of return to schooling. Mincer claims that the method can be used to check that this is so. However, as Note 2 demonstrates (p. 148), this claim is incorrect and the method, which is now being used in many countries, ought to be discarded.[7]

1.2   How much does human capital explain?

Instead we can concentrate on Methods 1 and 2 and ask: How much of the variance in log earnings is due to human capital?[8] The most obvious approach is to examine the residual variance in (2) – or better still (3). Concentrating for the moment on (2), if var (ln Y) is the variance of log earnings for the whole population (including people with all years of experience), the fraction of it explained by human capital is

$$1 - \frac{\text{var}(u_2)}{\text{var}(\ln Y)}$$

Using this approach Mincer explains 0.31 of earnings inequality. However a glance at Figure 8.1 shows that there is far less inequality at $\hat{t}$ years of experience than there is before or after this. This is because the difference in earnings due to differences in k_0, b and q are not present at that stage of working life. So the only unexplained variance is that due to the variation of u_1, whereas if the whole working population is analysed the unexplained variance will also include that part of u_2 due to the assumption that all individuals with a given schooling have the same k_0, b and q. So Mincer argues that a better measure of the overall unexplained variance is the unexplained variance in the cross-over year. Indeed if all cross-overs were at exactly the same year, and this were the overtake year, the unexplained variance in that year would correspond exactly to var (u_1) in (1), which is the true measure of variance not explained by human capital. So, if we now ran (1″) and computed var $(u_{1\hat{t}})$, the fraction of overall variance among people with all years of experience that is explained by human capital would be

$$1 - \frac{\text{var}(u_{1\hat{t}})}{\text{var}(\ln Y)}$$

To find the cross-over year, Mincer runs (1″) for different years of experience and picks that year $(\hat{t})$ when the R^2 is highest. R^2 rises (though rather slightly) up to 7–9 years of experience, and then falls (his Table 3.4). It also turns out that overtaking, as he calculates it, occurs within this range of years.[9] On the assumption that the model is correct, human capital now explains 0.50 of earnings inequality in the USA.[10]

But apart from doubts about the assumptions, there are some major arguments against accepting so high a figure.

(i)   It involves attributing the growth in residual variance in later life entirely to unrecorded differences in earlier human capital investments. But this growth must in part reflect the growing ability of employers to discriminate between more and less productive workers and hence to pay them a more individually-tailored wage.

(ii) Human capital is earning power acquired at a cost. Is it true that every time earning power increases with work experience this is because a cost has been incurred? Is costless learning impossible? For this to be the case there must always exist a job at which no learning occurs and at which we could currently produce more (net) than in any job where we can learn anything. There need not actually be anybody doing this job, though in a perfect market it would be surprising if someone were not doing it, since the present values of all jobs are equalized. We have spent some years trying to think what this job is for us, since it would be much easier to persuade students to accept the theory if one could illustrate it. But we have found it impossible to think of any such job for us or for most professional people one can imagine. It seems that costless learning may be possible. But of course the crucial question is how fast earnings rise with experience in the job where the least learning occurs. For any *additional* growth of earnings with experience could then be attributed to human capital. Perhaps most of the growth of earnings with experience is due to human capital, but not, we think, all of it.

(iii) A person's productivity is affected by dimensions of ability, acquired without cost. Most studies have been relatively unsuccessful at isolating the effects of this, but this does not mean it is not there. Since this is correlated with schooling, we continue to believe that the coefficients on schooling are biased upwards.

We therefore conclude that a half is an over-estimate of the fraction of annual earnings variance due to human capital.

1.3 Treatment of weeks worked

This completes what in our view can be sensibly said about the variation of annual earnings. Those of Mincer's findings that we have reported so far are recorded in the first row of Table 8.1. But these all ignore the variation of

Table 8.1 Proportion of variance of log annual earnings explained by schooling and experience (earnings of full-time male employees who worked at least 1 week)

	USA 1959	Britain 1972
Using residual variance from regressions for:		
All years of experience	0.31	0.32
Cross-over year	0.50	0.48

Sources:

For USA (all from Mincer, 1974)
0.31: Table 5.1 eq. P(2);
0.50: Table 3.3 Top Row, var ln Y = 0.668.

For UK
0.32: Table 3;
0.48: 0.206/0.436 (see Table 6).

weeks worked. These are of interest from two points of view. In the first place a good part of the variance of annual earnings is associated with variation in weeks worked, and a part of the variation of weeks worked is transitory. For this reason the variance of 'permanent' annual earnings is less than the variance of annual earnings in any one year. The following model seems to capture the essence of the system. If R_{it} is weekly earnings and Z_{it} is the vector (S_i, t_i, t_i^2) and W_{it} is weeks worked,

$$\ln R_{it} = b_0 + b_1 Z_{it} + u_{4it} \tag{4}$$

$$\ln W_{it} = c_0 + c_1 Z_{it} + c_2 \ln R_{it} + u_{5it} \tag{5}$$

$$\ln Y_{it} \equiv \ln W_{it} + \ln R_{it} \tag{6}$$

(2) is the reduced form of this system.[11] Clearly (5) is also a reduced form of some other system. There are many demand and supply influences that could make weeks vary positively with weekly earnings. On the demand side, employers vary their demand for skilled manpower less than for unskilled when product demand varies – hence higher unemployment of the unskilled. On the supply side, workers may concentrate their lifetime labour supply towards periods when their earnings are high (Ghez and Becker, 1975).

If we now want a measure of permanent earnings (Y_p) we might assume that u_{5it} measures the transitory component of log annual income.[12] Thus

$$\ln Y_{i\hat{p}} = \ln Y - u_{5it}$$

So the fraction of the variance of permanent income explained by the model is

$$\frac{\text{var}(\ln \hat{Y})}{\text{var}(\ln Y) - \text{var}(u_5)} \tag{7}$$

The preceding model is also interesting from a second point of view: it shows the role of human capital in explaining weekly earnings. Of course, once variation in weeks is taken into account, the ordinary human capital model ought in principle to be expanded, assuming that weeks worked in the past affect present earnings potential. This applies equally to the explanation of annual and weekly earnings. But in any case weekly earnings is a more accurate measure than annual earnings of current productivity and thus it is of interest.

2   BRITISH EVIDENCE

The study is based on the General Household Survey, using data for 1972 (see OPCAS, 1973, 1975).[13] The survey covers over 10 000 different households, interviews being spread evenly over the year. Our analysis is for 6873 men aged

Table 8.2a   Variances of key variables in Britain (and the USA)

Variable	Definition	Britain	(USA)
ln Y	Annual earnings	0.436	(0.668)
S	Years of schooling	4.805	(12.250)
t	Years of experience	207	
ln W	Weeks	0.128	(0.106)
ln Y/W	Weekly earnings	0.235	

Source: USA–Mincer (1974, pp. 60, 96).

Table 8.2b   Correlation coefficients, Britain

	ln Y	S	t	ln W	ln (Y/W)
ln Y	1.000	0.176	0.216	0.697	0.849
S	0.176	1.000	–0.404	0.001	0.239
t	0.216	–0.404	1.000	0.140	0.191
ln W	0.697	0.001	0.140	1.000	0.212
ln (Y/W)	0.849	0.239	0.191	0.212	1.000

15–64 who in their main occupation were 'employees' and had worked at least 1 week in the 52 weeks before the interview, people with Scottish educational qualifications being excluded.

We use the following variables:

Y Annual real earnings[14] in the previous year
S Years of full-time education[15]
t Years of work experience (= Age − Years of full-time education − 5)
W Weeks worked in the previous year.

Table 8.2a shows the relevant variances and Table 8.2b the correlation coefficients. As Table 8.2a shows, the inequality of schooling is much less in Britain than in the USA. Figure 8.2 shows the mean annual earnings for some key levels of education, measured for groups with different numbers of years of experience (1–10 years, 11–20 years, and so on).

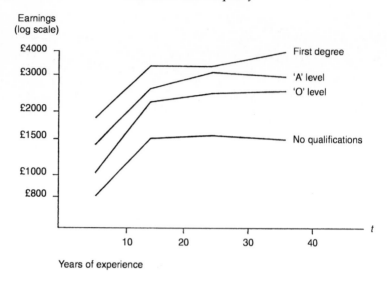

Figure 8.2   Experience profiles of annual earnings
Notes: 'A' level is normally taken at the end of secondary schooling (after 13 years of schooling). 'O' level is normally taken 2 years earlier.

2.1   Annual earnings: the basic analysis

Moving to the regression analysis, we begin with annual earnings (see Table 8.3). We can start with simpler functions, before looking at our general form. In Regression (3.1), log earnings are simply regressed on schooling. The coefficient on schooling is quite low and the explanatory power negligible. In Regression (3.2), however, experience (and its square) is added. The coefficient on education nearly doubles – in Regression (3.1) it was held down due to the negative correlation of schooling and experience. The private rate of return to an additional year's schooling is now estimated at about 10 per cent. The explanatory power of schooling and experience taken together is 32 per cent (31 per cent for the comparable analysis for the USA). According to this regression, maximum earnings are reached after about 30 years' experience and are equal to about four times initial earnings.

Before proceeding further, we need to allow for the possibility that the marginal rate of return may differ according to the level of schooling. This is done in Regression (3.3) by introducing separate dummies for each number of

Table 8.3 Regression of log annual earnings on schooling (S) and experience (t)

	(3.1)	(3.2)	(3.3)	(3.4)	(3.5)	(3.6)	(3.7)
Constant term	6.604	5.199	5.917	5.790	5.824	6.010	5.143
S	0.053	0.097					0.094
	(0.004)	(0.003)					(0.008)
t		0.091	0.093	0.113	0.065	-0.212	-0.166
		(0.002)	(0.002)	(0.004)	(0.009)	(0.030)	(0.019)
t^2		-0.0015	-0.0015	-0.0016	-0.00041	0.0053	0.0047
		(0.00004)	(0.00004)	(0.00004)	(0.00020)	(0.0007)	(0.0005)
St				-0.0018	0.0033	0.0476	0.041
				(0.0003)	(0.0008)	(0.0047)	(0.003)
St^2					-0.00012	-0.0011	-0.00098
					(0.00002)	(0.0001)	(0.00009)
S^2t						-0.0017	-0.0014
						(0.0002)	(0.0001)
S^2t^2						0.00004	0.000033
						(0.000004)	(0.000004)
$S = 10$			0.225	0.303	0.277	0.100	
11			0.333	0.438	0.391	0.144	
12			0.539	0.666	0.590	0.289	
13			0.501	0.647	0.541	0.215	
14			0.642	0.808	0.684	0.363	
15			0.726	0.909	0.752	0.446	
16			0.770	0.987	0.801	0.527	
17			0.878	1.09	0.873	0.676	
18+			1.003	1.29	0.980	1.144	
R^2	0.031	0.316	0.324	0.327	0.331	0.339	0.337
var (u)	0.422	0.298	0.295	0.294	0.293	0.288	0.289

Notes: 1. Standard errors are in brackets.
2. The omitted schooling dummy is 9 years or less. All the schooling dummies have highly significant coefficients. The standard errors rise from 0.03 for $S = 10$ to 0.09 for $S = 18+$.

years of education. As regards explanatory power there is little increase over the previous equation. But we can now see more clearly the pattern of incremental returns from one year to the next. The return is very high for the first few years and then fluctuates sharply. However in the British educational system there is a sharp distinction between those who leave at the minimum school leaving age and those who go on: until recently the only children who had more than 10 years of schooling were drawn from those who at 11 were judged to be above the top quartile of ability. For this reason one should not focus too sharply on the distinction between the earlier rates of return and the later ones, as we think the earlier ones are more biased upwards by ability factors.[16]

In Regression (3.4) we allow the level of schooling to influence the slope of the log earnings profile (but not its rate of change). As in the USA schooling appears to reduce the slope but the effect is one-third of its value in the USA (0.0018 compared with 0.0043).[17] In Regression (3.5) we also allow the rate of change of the slope to be affected by schooling.

But neither of these specifications is consistent with our basic model, which is estimated in Regression (3.6). Here the coefficients on all the various interaction terms are highly significant. From them we can compute the values of the underlying parameters in the functions determining k_0, b and q.[18] These are

$$q = -0.313 + 0.0491S$$
$$k_0 = 0.767 - 0.0330S$$
$$b = 0.0337 - 0.00145S$$

The most interesting result of course concerns the rate of return to training. For someone with 10 years' education this is 18 per cent and for someone with 16 years' education nearly 50 per cent. This is much higher than the rate of return to schooling. The rest of the results make good sense. The investment ratio in the first year of work is 44 per cent for people with 10 years' education and rather less for more educated people (in Britain apprenticed manual workers receive very low relative pay). The investment ratio falls each year for someone with 10 years' education by 1.9 per cent and more slowly for more educated people. The peak of earnings is reached after 29 years for people with 10 years' education and rather earlier for the more educated groups. But the overall rise from starting salary to peak earnings is slightly higher for the more educated. The ratio of peak to starting salary is about 4.2 for those who left school after 10 years and 4.9 for those who had 16 years' education. Since the overtaking year is approximately $1/q$, overtaking occurs a good deal earlier than the 7–9 years normally assumed; the shorter period is more consistent with what many of us suppose about ourselves.[19]

2.2 Weekly earnings and weeks

We can now repeat the basic analysis for weekly earnings (see Table 8.4). If we use the simple model of Regression (4.2) the rate of return to schooling compared with that in Regression (3.2) is now reduced by just over 1 percentage point, to 8.5 per cent. This is to be expected, for people with higher weekly earnings work for more weeks.[20] If variations in weeks reflect private choice, then 8.5 per cent would be the relevant private rate of return, but if not the more relevant figure comes from the annual earnings function.[21]

Regression (4.6) shows our basic model but applying it to weekly earnings. The results are quite similar to those for annual earnings. The implicit equations for q, k_0 and b are

$$q = -0.217 + 0.0389S$$
$$k_0 = 0.592 - 0.0247S$$
$$b = 0.0266 - 0.00113S$$

Again the rate of return to training is much higher than the rate of return to schooling. The profiles for weekly earnings are less steep than for annual earnings, since over much of the range weeks rise with experience. So the ratio of peak to initial earnings is 3 for people with 10 years schooling and 3.4 for people with 16 years schooling.

As regards explanatory power, human capital is slightly better at explaining weekly than annual earnings. There is no logical necessity for this. It depends on the size of the coefficients in (4) and (5) and on the relative size of the variances of u_4 and u_5. (5) is estimated in Table 8.5. As can be seen the power of human capital to explain weeks is not large, which helps to explain the limited power of human capital to explain annual earnings, given the fact that the variance of log weeks is over a quarter the total variance of log annual earnings.

We can now use Table 8.5 to provide an estimate of the fraction of the variance of permanent income explained by human capital. If we assume that var (u_5) reflects only transitory income variation (which must be an exaggeration) we find that the share of permanent income explained by human capital is 0.46.[22]

2.3 The cross-over year of experience

We turn now to Mincer's method 2, based on the cross-over year. As Mincer explains, regressions using all years of experience will tend to understate the explanatory power of human capital because they wrongly assume that all

Table 8.4 Regression of log weekly earnings on schooling (S) and experience (t)

	(4.1)	(4.2)	(4.3)	(4.4)	(4.5)	(4.6)	(4.7)
Constant term	2.751	1.692	2.337	2.251	2.271	2.373	1.627
S	0.053	0.085					0.086
	(0.003)	(0.002)					(0.005)
t		0.070	0.072	0.085	0.058	−0.105	−0.115
		(0.001)	(0.001)	(0.003)	(0.006)	(0.021)	(0.014)
t^2		−0.0012	−0.0012	−0.0012	−0.0006	0.0029	0.0034
		(0.00002)	(0.00003)	(0.00002)	(0.0001)	(0.0005)	(0.0004)
St				−0.0010	0.0018	0.0279	0.030
				(0.0002)	(0.0006)	(0.0033)	(0.002)
St^2					−0.00007	−0.0006	−0.00073
					(0.00001)	(0.00008)	(0.00006)
S^2t						−0.0010	−0.0011
						(0.0001)	(0.0001)
S^2t^2						0.00002	0.000026
						(0.000003)	(0.000003)
$S = 10$			0.183	0.234	0.220	0.121	
11			0.279	0.348	0.322	0.184	
12			0.456	0.541	0.497	0.329	
13			0.460	0.558	0.496	0.319	
14			0.567	0.678	0.607	0.427	
15			0.679	0.800	0.710	0.540	
16			0.695	0.839	0.732	0.580	
17			0.726	0.869	0.743	0.637	
18+			0.873	1.066	0.886	0.989	
R^2	0.057	0.366	0.377	0.379	0.382	0.387	0.385
$\widehat{\text{var}}(u)$	0.222	0.149	0.147	0.146	0.146	0.144	0.145

Notes: See notes to Table 8.3.

Table 8.5 Regression of log weeks worked on schooling (S), experience (t) and log weekly earnings (Y/W)

	(5.1)	(5.2)	(5.3)
Constant	3.331	3.272	4.107
S	−0.00081	0.048	−0.112
	(0.00222)	(0.015)	(0.041)
S^2		−0.0014	0.0042
		(0.0006)	(0.0015)
t	0.0025	0.0211	−0.095
	(0.0003)	(0.0012)	(0.023)
t^2		−0.00034	0.0019
		(0.00002)	(0.0005)
St			0.017
			(0.004)
St^2			−0.00032
			(0.00008)
S^2t			−0.00059
			(0.00014)
S^2t^2			0.000011
			(0.000000)
ln (Y/W)	0.143		0.085
	(0.009)		(0.011)
R^2	0.055	0.056	0.071
vâr (u)	0.121	0.121	0.119

individuals have the same investment profile. According to the cross-over theory, if we estimate

$$\ln Y_i = a + a_1 S_i + u_{1i} \tag{1''}$$

within groups which differ by years of experience, we should find that var (u_1) falls as we approach the cross-over year from either side. As Table 8.6 shows, var (u_1) does indeed fall monotonically with experience up to 12–17 years of experience and then fluctuates about a somewhat higher level.[23] By the same token var (ln Y) falls up to those years of experience and then fluctuates around a somewhat higher level. One would expect that R^2 would follow the same pattern – indeed Mincer only presents the data on R^2 and var (ln Y). But in fact R^2 fluctuates completely erratically and never reaches the high level of 0.33 which Mincer finds for 7–9 years of experience (his Table 3.4). This is partly

Table 8.6   Regression of annual earnings on schooling: within experience groups

t	a_1	R^2	var (u_1)	var S	var (ln Y)	N
0–2	0.166	0.161	0.946	6.60	1.127	448
3–5	0.114	0.236	0.273	6.50	0.357	455
6–8	0.064	0.068	0.263	4.67	0.282	475
9–11	0.068	0.105	0.206	5.24	0.230	518
12–14	0.078	0.151	0.138	4.04	0.162	476
15–17	0.079	0.182	0.135	4.75	0.165	444
18–20	0.069	0.092	0.224	4.80	0.247	428
21–23	0.084	0.158	0.194	5.20	0.230	396
24–26	0.103	0.254	0.206	6.50	0.276	306
27–29	0.104	0.150	0.191	3.20	0.225	366
30–32	0.108	0.103	0.274	2.72	0.306	421
33–35	0.093	0.137	0.185	3.39	0.214	442
36–38	0.093	0.110	0.182	2.62	0.204	445
39–41	0.117	0.120	0.278	2.79	0.316	331

Note:
The data relate to the equation ln $Y = a_0 + a_1 S + u_1$.

because var (S) varies unsystematically, while a_1 also varies substantially. If we had concentrated on Mincer's R^2 approach, we should have been led to completely reject the cross-over hypothesis for Britain. However the movements of var (u_1) do lend some support to it, and we shall therefore pursue its implications. One cannot, as we have argued earlier, have confidence that it yields unbiased estimates of the rate of return to schooling. But it may still give us a reasonable feel for the variance in log earnings that cannot be explained by human capital. A crucial issue here is where we take the cross-over year to occur. Var (u) is at its lowest from 12–17 years after beginning work, but this seems implausibly late for crossing-over. (It is clearly too late for the overtake year, but as we have explained, there is no logical connection between 'overtaking' and 'crossing-over'.) So we shall take the variance unexplained by human capital to equal var (u) at 9–11 years of experience. Thus we would compute that human capital explains just under a half the variance of annual income. But, for the general reasons we have already given, we believe this is an overestimate.

2.4 The rate of return to educational qualifications

Finally to learn more about the effects of schooling we turn to an altogether different line of thought. The British education system is in many ways more varied than the American. In particular, part-time education is much more highly developed,[24] and many of those who reach degree-level qualifications as engineers, accountants or the like have had only 10 years' full-time schooling. An analysis based entirely on years of full-time schooling therefore fails to capture a good part of reality. In Table 8.7 we show the main qualifications in what is generally considered to be ascending order.[25] Individuals are classified according to their single highest qualification (be it part-time or full-time). There are two columns according to whether the qualification is mainly obtained by full-time or part-time study. As can be seen, *within* each column the average years of full-time schooling rise with level but there are many part-time qualifications with lower years of schooling than a full-time qualification to which they are superior (e.g. Higher National Certificate compared with 'A-level' of the General Certificate of Education).

The interesting questions are: How much of earnings inequality does this battery of qualifications explain, and does the pecking order of qualifications correspond to an order of earnings? Table 8.8 shows regressions comparable to Regressions (3.2) and (4.2) but with years of education replaced by qualifications. The comparable R^2s are as follows

	Annual earnings	Weekly earnings
Years of schooling (dummies)	0.339	0.387
Qualifications	0.365	0.420

The difference of about 3 per cent may not appear large in relation to the original figure (of over 30 per cent). But it is more relevant to relate it to a figure such as 0.097^2. Var (S) ($= 4.5$ per cent), which measures the contribution of schooling, holding experience constant, in (3.2). Even so, it is small in relation to the overall R^2, which is why our earlier discussion of the *share* of earnings inequality explained by human capital remains valid.

But to understand the *effect* of education on earnings it is clearly better to look at qualifications than years of schooling. As Table 8.8 shows, the established pecking order seems to correspond remarkably to the order of earnings. The one exception is non-graduate school-teaching qualifications. Holders of these take a 3-year course (2 years till 1960) and about half of them

Table 8.7 Average years of schooling by highest educational qualification

Full-time qualification	Part-time qualification	S		N	
		FT	PT	FT	PT
None	None	9.7		4872	
1–4 'O' levels		11.3		317	
	C and G craft/ordinary		10.5		359
5+ 'O' levels		11.9		283	
	C and G advanced/final		10.8		134
	Ordinary Nat. Cert./Dip.		11.3		117
1+ 'A' levels		13.4		132	
	C and G tech. and prof. Level C		12.5		142
	Higher Nat. Cert./Dip.		12.5		139
	Prof. Level B		14.0		140
Non-graduate teaching cert.		15.8		66	
First degree		17.7		145	
Higher degree		18.7		27	

Notes:
'O' level is the Ordinary Level of the General Certificate of Education and 'A' level is the Advanced level.
C and G qualifications are issued by the City and Guilds of London Institute and are mainly in technical subjects or skills, as are the Ordinary and Higher National Certificates.
Professional qualifications shown separately are mainly in engineering or commercial fields, level B being treated as of degree-equivalent status for purposes of schoolteachers' pay.

Table 8.8 Annual earnings: using highest educational qualification

Variable	Annual earnings		Weekly earnings	
	FT	PT	FT	PT
Constant	6.144		2.536	
t	0.087		0.067	
t^2	−0.0015		−0.0012	
No qualification*	0.000		0.000	
1–4 'O' levels	0.180		0.138	
C and G craft/ordinary		0.298		0.193
5+ 'O' levels	0.286		0.298	
C and G advanced/final		0.362		0.234
Ordinary Nat. Cert./Dip.		0.369		0.272
1+ 'A' levels	0.462		0.436	
C and G tech. and prof. Level C		0.546		0.461
Higher Nat. Cert./Dip.		0.555		0.454
Prof. Level B		0.763		0.676
Non-graduate teaching cert.	0.506		0.421	
First degree	0.876	0.76	0.769	
Higher degree	1.097		0.990	
R^2	0.339		0.393	

Notes: All coefficients are significantly different from zero at 1 per cent level.
*'No qualification' is the omitted category in the regression.

have 'A' level and half 'O' level qualifications. They end up earning barely more than those with 'A' level only – partly presumably due to the length of their paid holidays. But, this case apart, the rise of earnings with educational 'level' is remarkably smooth.

We can look first at the full-time qualifications, using annual earnings data. To compute the rate of return to each course we need to know the entry qualification to it: roughly speaking, 'A' level requires five or more 'O' levels, and a first degree requires 'A' level. We also need to know the corresponding period of study (ΔS). We take this from Table 8.7.[26] The resulting rates of return are shown in Table 8.9, columns (1) and (2). In columns (3) and (4) we do the same thing, but estimating an earnings function confined to people with

Table 8.9   Rate of return of 'A' level and degree (percentage)

	Using general earnings function		Using specific earnings function	
	Annual earnings	Weekly earnings	Annual earnings	Weekly earnings
	(1)	(2)	(3)	(4)
'A' level	11.7	9.2	17.3	12.2
First degree	9.6	7.7	9.2	7.4

the two qualifications being compared. Thus in comparing degree graduates with 'A' level holders we run the equation

$$\ln Y_i = a_0 + a_1 D_i + a_2 t_i + a_3 t_i^2$$

for these two groups where D is a dummy variable (= 1 for degree graduates and = 0 for 'A' level holders). We then report the coefficient a_1 divided by the relevant number of years. Given the roughness of the data on which they are based, we would only conclude that the rates of return to 'A' level and degrees are broadly similar – and similar to the average rate of return to schooling. (The rates to 'A' level appear to be higher but the relative number of years taken to obtain the qualification may be underestimated.)

As part-time qualifications increase, earnings also increase sharply. For example, people with Higher National Certificate earn nearly 20 per cent more than those with Ordinary National Certificate. They only have one extra year of full-time schooling but in addition a good deal of part-time schooling, which would need to be taken into account before a valid rate of return could be calculated.

NOTE 1

Parallel experience–earnings profiles do not prove q, k and b independent of S

In the following example experience-log-earnings profiles are parallel even though q and k vary with S. As a result any regression estimate of r would be biased.

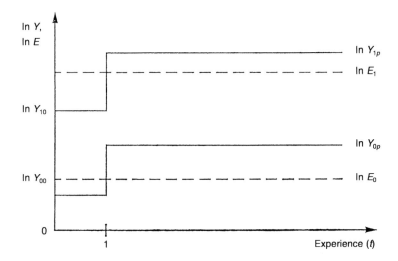

Figure 8.3 The logic of parallel profiles

In Figure 8.3 we draw two profiles – one for people with no schooling ($\ln Y_0$) and one for people with one year of schooling ($\ln Y_1$). For simplicity, the profiles have been drawn with only one step in them: training occurs in one period only. The profiles are parallel: ($\ln Y_{1t} - \ln Y_{0t}$) is the same (Δ) for all years of experience (t). Thus if $\ln Y$ is regressed on schooling and experience the coefficient on schooling will equal Δ. Δ is also approximately the conventionally-calculated rate of return.[27] But we cannot infer that Δ is the true rate of return ($\ln E_1 - \ln E_0$). It might or it might not be. For example suppose that people with 1 year of schooling invest more than people with no schooling but get a proportionately lower rate of return to training. Then, as the diagram shows, ($\ln E_1 - \ln E_0$) exceeds ($\ln Y_{1t} - \ln Y_{0t}$). Yet the profiles are parallel. This happens because for each educational group i

$$\ln Y_{ip} = \ln E_i + k_{0i} \cdot q_i$$

and

$$\ln Y_{i0} = \ln E_i - k_{0i}$$

so that

$$\ln Y_{ip} - \ln Y_{i0} = k_{0i}(q_i + 1)$$

and in our particular case $k_{0i}(q_i + 1)$ is the same for both educational groups. But the investment rate (k_0) is higher for the more educated group and the rate of return (q) is lower.

So, even if profiles are parallel, nothing can be inferred about rates of return to schooling from vertical differences between earnings profiles.

NOTE 2

Mincer's short-cut method[28]

Description

Let Y_{Sx} be the average earnings of people with S years of schooling at age x. The short-cut method then proceeds as follows:

(i) *Estimate* the internal rate of return to education (conventionally-calculated), by solving for ρ_S in

$$\Sigma_{x=p+S+1}^{T} Y_{Sx}(1+\rho_S)^{-x} = \Sigma_{x=p+S}^{T} Y_{S-1,x}(1+\rho_S)^{-x} \tag{A.1}$$

where p is the number of pre-school years and T the age of retirement.

(ii) *Assume* initially that the rate of return to training (q) is the same as the true rate of return to schooling (r_S). This implies that each of the two is equal to the conventionally-calculated rate of return to education (ρ_S), since the latter is a weighted average of the first two. Now, from the definition of the rate of return to training (q)

$$E_S \Sigma_{x=p+S+1}^{T}(1+q)^{-x} = \Sigma_{x=p+S+1}^{T} Y_{Sx}(1+q)^{-x}$$

So, approximately

$$E_S = q(1+q)^{p+S} \Sigma_{x=p+S+1}^{T} Y_{Sx}(1+q)^{-x}$$

If we assume $q = \rho_S$ we obtain an estimate of E_S from

$$\hat{E}_S = \rho_S(1+\rho_S)^{p+S} \Sigma_{x=p+S+1}^{T} Y_{Sx}(1+\rho_S)^{-x} \tag{A.2}$$

and of E_{S-1} from

$$\hat{E}_{S-1} = \rho_{S-1}(1+\rho_{S-1})^{p+S-1} \Sigma_{x=p+S}^{T} Y_{S-1,x}(1+\rho_{S-1})^{-x} \tag{A.3}$$

The estimate of the true rate of return to schooling is now

$$\hat{r}_S = \frac{\hat{E}_S}{\hat{E}_{S-1}} - 1$$

(iii) However, this estimate is only correct if $q = \rho_S$. Therefore, says Mincer, now *check whether the assumption was correct* by checking whether

$$\hat{r}_S = \rho_S$$

If the true rate of return to schooling ($\hat{r}_S$), computed on the assumption that the rate of return to training (q) equalled itself ($\hat{r}_S$), turns out to be equal to a weighted average of the two represented by ρ_S, then the assumption has, he claims, been verified.

Critique

This is not, however, the case. In fact, subject to one minor assumption, $\hat{r}_S$ must always equal ρ_S, as a tautology. For, from (A.1), (A.2) and (A.3),

$$\hat{r}_S = \frac{\hat{E}_S}{\hat{E}_{S-1}} - 1 = \frac{\rho_S(1 + \rho_S)^{p+S}}{\rho_{S-1}(1 + \rho_{S-1})^{p+S-1}} \frac{\Sigma_{x=p+S}^{T} Y_{S-1,x}(1 + \rho_S)^{-x}}{\Sigma_{x=p+S}^{T} Y_{S-1,x}(1 + \rho_{S-1})^{-x}} - 1$$

Now suppose that $\rho_S = \rho_{S-1}$. This is certainly logically possible (and in equilibrium to be expected from human capital theory). In that case

$$\hat{r}_S = (1 + \rho_S) - 1 = \rho_S.$$

But ρ_S is definitely an average of the rate of return to schooling and training and so therefore is $\hat{r}_S$. So the computation cannot in general tell us anything about the rate of return to training. Moreover even if $\rho_S \neq \rho_{S-1}$, it is not obvious which discount rate should be used to convert the profile $Y_{S-1,x}$ into an equivalent annuity. One could equally well argue in favour of using ρ_{S-1} and ρ_S – the one is the rate of return to additional education ending at age $S-1$ and the other is the rate to additional education beginning at age $S-1$. If ρ_S were used to discount $Y_{S-1,x}$ and also to discount $Y_{Sx,}$ we are back with $\hat{r}_S = \rho_S$. So the ratio of annuities method cannot check whether the rates of return to schooling and training are the same. For this reason neither ρ_S nor $\hat{r}_S$ can be used as estimates of the true rate of return to education. And the computation of $\hat{r}_S$ adds nothing to knowledge, once ρ_S has been computed.

Finally it may be useful to use the preceding framework to demonstrate in what sense the calculated rate ρ_S is a weighted average of the true rate of return to schooling (r_S) and the rate of return to training (q), assuming the latter is the same for people with S and $S-1$ years of schooling. From the definition of the rate of return to training, the true E_S is

$$E_S = q(1 + q)^{p+S} \Sigma_{x=p+S+1}^{T} Y_{Sx}(1 + q)^{-x}$$

and

$$E_{S-1} = q(1 + q)^{p+S-1} \Sigma_{x=p+S}^{T} Y_{S-1,x}(1 + q)^{-x}$$

Now

$$r_S = \frac{E_S}{E_{S-1}} - 1 = (1+q)\frac{\Sigma Y_{Sx}(1+q)^{-x}}{\Sigma Y_{S-1,x}(1+q)^{-x}} - 1$$

$$\therefore \quad \frac{1+r_S}{1+q} = \frac{\Sigma Y_{Sx}(1+q)^{-x}}{\Sigma Y_{S-1,x}(1+q)^{-x}} \tag{A.4}$$

But by the definition of the conventionally-calculated rate of return (ρ_S), the right-hand side of this equation equals unity if $q = \rho_S$ and exceeds unity if $q < \rho_S$. Therefore if $q < r_S$, $q < \rho_S$. This is not the same as saying that, if $q < r_S$, then $q < \rho_S < r_S$, which is the normal definition of a weighted average.

In fact one can image some curious situations. For example suppose that the profiles are parallel, so that

$$Y_{S,x} = Y_{S-1,x-1}(1+d) \quad \text{all } S, x$$

Then

$$\rho_S = d$$

And, if q is the same for both groups,

$$r_S = \frac{E_S}{E_{S-1}} - 1 = d$$

So $r_S = \rho_S$ whatever the value of q. One can only loosely say that ρ_S is a weighted average of r_S and q.

Notes

1. For other recent evaluations of the Mincer model see Blinder (1976) and Klevmarken and Quigley (1976). These are chiefly concerned with the relative roles of experience and age, not discussed in the present paper. See also Hanushek and Quigley (1978a/b).
2. The true private rate of return to one year's education is

    $$(E_S - E_{S-1})(1-t)/(E_{S-1}(1-\bar{\imath}) + T - G)$$

    where t is the marginal tax rate, $\bar{\imath}$ the average tax rate, T tuition fees and G scholarship. Only if the relevant items balance each other is the private rate of return equal to $(E_S - E_{S-1})/E_{S-1}$ as is assumed in this paper. In Britain $\bar{\imath} < t$, but $T - G < 0$, since nearly all students have no fees or have fees paid out of scholarships.
3. What follows is based on Mincer (1974, pp. 85–6, 90 and 97–8).
4. Note that even if the profiles were parallel, this would not rule out the possibility that q, k and b depend on S. An example is given in Note 1 (p. 146). However there is no way in which the data normally available could be used to investigate

such occurrences. Our approach (below) uses functional forms that could hope to pick up some but not all cases where q, k and b depend on S.

5. For any group S, $\hat{j}$ is given by the following relations. From the definition of q

$$E_S = q\Sigma_{t=0}^{L} Y_{St}(1+q)^{-t}$$

where L is the length of working life; and from the definition of $\hat{j}$

$$Y_{S\hat{j}} = E_S$$

If for another group M, $Y_{Mt} = \lambda\, Y_{St}$ (all t), $\hat{j}$ for that group must be the same as for group S.

6. Mincer (1974), pp. 49–50.
7. Mincer offers one other approach which we have not so far mentioned. If the investment ratio is assumed to decay exponentially (so that $k = k_0 e^{-\beta t}$) then, if β can be identified, so can q. Mincer gives only a partial reporting on his estimates here (pp. 93–4). For Britain we have found it impossible to obtain sensible estimates using this form of function, and so has Riboud (1975) for France.
8. See Mincer (1974, pp. 85–6, 90 and 97–8).
9. The evidence for the cross-over model, as presented by Mincer, is not in fact overwhelming. For example on p. 105 he shows the pattern of variance of weekly earnings in relation to experience. One would expect this to fall up to $\hat{t}$ and then rise. But for people with 16 years' schooling it tends to rise continuously, while for people with 8 years' schooling it falls up to $\hat{t} = 8$ and is then level. Only for people with 12 years' schooling is the predicted U-shape found.
10. Table 3.3 (top row) gives var $(u) = 0.333$; $0.50 = 0.333/0.668$.
11. By contrast Mincer runs the equation

$$\ln Y_{it} = d_0 + d_1 Z_{it} + d_2 \ln W + u$$

and finds (as we do) that the coefficient on d_2 exceeds unity. However this is probably due to misspecification (Hall, 1975). If the correct specification is as in the text, the estimate of d_2 in Mincer's equation is biased upwards, i.e. it is biased to exceed unity.

12. Mincer makes two assumptions. (i) All variation in weeks worked is transitory. But if this is so, weeks worked would not be partially related to human capital in the way we find them to be. (ii) There is no transitory variation in weeks worked and all the (permanent) variation in weeks worked is due to human capital. This is equally extreme in the opposite direction. Using residuals for the cross-over year, Mincer finds the functions of variance explained by human capital to be 0.62 (Assumption (i)) and 0.70 (Assumption (ii)) (his p. 96). This is the basis of his claim that human capital explains 'close to two-thirds of the inequality of adult, white urban men in the US in 1959'.

13. For previous annual earnings functions using these data see Layard (1977), Psacharopoulos (1977) and Stewart (1977). An hourly earnings function appears in Layard, Metcalf and Nickell (1978), and in Layard, Piachaud and Stewart (1978).

14. Earnings in the year preceding the interview divided by the monthly index of earnings in the month of interview (CSO, 1973, Table 16) to reduce the effects

of inflation. Self-employment earnings are included where they occur (the average value is £6 for the year).

15.   This is computed as the age on completing full-time education minus 5, subject to one proviso. For each qualification we constructed a maximum such age that was possible if the individual had had no gap in his full-time education. If the reported age exceeded this age we replaced it by this maximum age. About 3.5 per cent of the sample were affected by this adjustment. The mean years of schooling are 10.5 years compared with 10.9 in the USA (Mincer, 1974, p. 60): compulsory schooling in Britain begins on the 5th birthday.

16.   The numbers in each schooling group are:

9 or less	2464
10	2322
11	963
12	336
13	249
14	65
15	86
16	119
17	135
18+	134

17.   If St is added to Regression (3.2) it only attracts a coefficient of -0.00046.

18.   There are two algebraic solutions of which only one makes sense. The same exercise was also repeated treating S as a continuous variable rather than using a set of dummies (Regression (3.7)). The resulting values were

$$q = -0.23 + 0.039S; \quad k_0 = 0.86 - 0.035S; \quad b = 0.040 - 0.0011S.$$

Interestingly the coefficient on schooling was 0.094 – almost the same as in Regression (3.2).

19.   However this highlights the fact that the rate of return to training may be overestimated if not all the upwards slope in earnings profiles is due to human capital.

20.   Note that weekly earnings vary less than annual earnings.

$$\text{var}(\ln Y) = \text{var}\,\ln(Y/W) + \text{var}(\ln W) + 2\,\text{cov}(\ln Y/W, \ln W)$$

In our case the corresponding figures are

$$0.436 = 0.235 + 0.128 + 0.073$$

21.   If work is preferred *per se* to non-employment, one ought even to reduce the measured earnings of those who work shorter weeks to allow for the disvalue of non-work. This would raise the rate of return to education above 10 per cent. If we were concerned with the *social* returns to education we should use weekly earnings. For it is not very plausible to suppose that for males the average level of schooling affects the average level of weeks worked very much, even though individual schooling affects who works which number of weeks.

22. $0.46 = 0.436(0.339)/(0.436 - 0.119)$. The relevant figures are taken from Regressions (3.6) and (5.3).
23. The size of the sample does not permit an analysis of the pattern of experience-specific earnings variation *within* schooling groups, comparable with Mincer's (pp. 104–105).
24. Successful part-time students most commonly attend college one full weekday and 1–3 evenings a week.
25. See Robbins Committee (1963), Appendix Two B and Appendix One, pp. 192–6.
26. This gives 1.5 years for 'A' level and 4.3 years for a first degree, as compared with the conventional stereotype of 2 and 3 years respectively. However, one needs to remember that 'A' level can be taken in one year, whereas some first degrees involve four-year courses. The essential point is that earnings differences must be related to the actual schooling differences which generate them.
27. ρ_1 is defined by

$$(0 - Y_{00}) + \frac{(Y_{10} - Y_{0p})}{1 + \rho_1} + \frac{(Y_{1p} - Y_{0p})}{\rho_1(1 + \rho_1)} = 0$$

But $Y_{10} = Y_{00} (1 + d)$ and $Y_{1p} = Y_{0p} (1 + d)$. If these expressions are substituted in and ρ_1 is set equal to d, the equation still holds. $\Delta \simeq d$.
28. See his pp. 49–50.

References

Becker, G.S. (1975) *Human Capital*, 2nd edn (New York: Columbia University Press for the National Bureau of Economic Research).
Blinder, A.S. (1976) 'On dogmatism in human capital theory', *Journal of Human Resources* (Winter).
Central Statistical Office (1973) *Annual Abstract of Statistics* (London: HMSO).
Ghez, G.R. and G.S. Becker (1975) *The Allocation of Time and Goods over the Life Cycle* (New York: National Bureau of Economic Research).
Hall, R.E. (1975) 'Review of Mincer (1974)', *Journal of Political Economy* (April).
Hanushek, E. and J.M. Quigley (1978a) 'Implicit investment profiles and intertemporal adjustments of relative wages', *American Economic Review* (March).
Hanushek, E. and J.M. Quigley (1978b) 'More exacting tests of the OJT investment model', paper presented at the UK–US Conference on Human Capital and Income Distribution (Cambridge) (March).
Klevmarken, A. and J.M. Quigley (1976) 'Age, experience, earnings and investments in human capital', *Journal of Political Economy* (February).
Layard, R. (1977) 'On measuring the redistribution of lifetime income', in M.S. Feldstein and R.P. Inman (eds), *The Economics of Public Services* (London: Macmillan), Chapter 3 in this volume.
Layard, R., D. Metcalf and S. Nickell (1978) 'The effects of collective bargaining on relative and absolute wages', in A. Shorrocks and W. Krelle (eds), *The Economics of Income Distribution* (Amsterdam: North-Holland), Chapter 7 in this volume.

Layard, R., D. Piachaud and M. Stewart (1978) *The Causes of Poverty*, Background Paper, 5, Royal Commission on the Distribution of Income and Wealth (London: HMSO).

Mincer, J. (1974) 'Schooling, experience, and earnings', National Bureau of Economic Research, *Human Behavior and Social Institutions*, 2 (New York and London: Columbia University Press).

Office of Population Censuses and Surveys (OPCAS) (1973) *The General Household Survey. An Introductory Report* (London: HMSO).

Office of Population Censuses and Surveys (OPCAS) (1975) *The General Household Survey, 1972* (London: HMSO).

Psacharopoulos, G. (1977) 'Family background, education and achievement: a path model of earnings determinants in the UK and some alternatives', *British Journal of Sociology* (September).

Riboud, M. (1975) 'An analysis of the earnings distribution in France', paper presented to the Workshop in the Economics of Education (London: LSE).

Robbins Committee on Higher Education (1963) *Higher Education*, Appendix One: The Demand for Places in Higher Education and Appendix Two B: Students and their education, Cmnd. 2154 I and II–I (London: HMSO).

Stewart, M. (1977) 'The determinants of earnings in Britain: an occupation-specific approach', Centre for Labour Economics, LSE, *Discussion Paper*, 4.

9 The Screening Hypothesis and the Returns to Education (1974)*

with G. Psacharopoulos

The productive role of education has been questioned before, but is now under unusually heavy attack from the 'screening hypothesis.' If true, this hypothesis has quite devastating implications for educational policy and research. Broadly, it says that the earnings differentials associated with education do not mainly reflect improvements in individual productive capacity caused by education but, rather, employers' use of education to identify preexisting differences in talents. If education has any social value, it is as a signaling device which helps to place the right man in the right job. But even in this case, too much education is likely to be sought, with the private returns to education exceeding the social returns.

THE HYPOTHESIS

The most rigorous version of the hypothesis is by Arrow (1973) who assumes for purposes of argument that individual productive ability is completely unaffected by education. Employers have no information about employees except their education, so education is used as the sole basis of pay. If the marginal product of graduates (treated as a class) is higher than that of nongraduates, due to their higher initial ability, graduates get paid more than nongraduates. So it pays someone with a good chance of graduation to go to college, as long as the private returns exceed the cost. We now distinguish two cases, one where different qualities of labor are perfect substitutes in production and the second where their productivity depends on what job they are in. In the first case, all education is socially valueless, since the productive contribution of the individual is not affected by what job he does and there is

* *Journal of Political Economy*, 82 (5) (1974), pp. 985–98.
 We are grateful to K. Arrow, M. Blaug, H.G. Johnson, W. McMahon, D. Metcalf, and P.J. Wiles for helpful comments on an earlier draft.

155

thus no return to improving employers' information about individual abilities. As a result, everybody could be better off if the more able would agree not to seek education in an attempt to signal their ability to employers. In the second case, education has social value up to a point by improving the allocation of people between jobs, but, depending on its cost, there may well be overinvestment such that no screening would be better for everyone than the amount provided at competitive equilibrium.

Other leading exponents of the screening hypothesis, such as Berg (1971), Taubman and Wales (1973), and Wiles (1974), put forward similar though less sharply delineated models, so we shall concentrate on Arrow's.[1] The problem is how to test it.

THE PRODUCTION FUNCTION APPROACH

If there were perfect substitution between different categories of labor (which there is not), the screening hypothesis could in principle be tested by production functions fitted across regions where labor forces differed only with respect to education. Interregional production functions which make this assumption have indeed been fitted by Griliches (1970) and others and show an effect of education on production similar to that indicated by wage differentials between people with different levels of education. However, within one country it is not correct to assume that the educational level of the labor force varies across states without any associated variation in non-educational labor force quality. More seriously, insofar as the labor force in one state is drawn disproportionately from those brought up in the same state, there is a simultaneity problem in that people who are richer may wish to 'consume' more education even if it does not raise their output. This problem has not yet been fully tackled (but see Johnson, 1970; Tolley and Olson, 1971; Fallon and Layard, 1975). Until more work has been done, one cannot claim production function results as very clear evidence against the screening hypothesis.

THE EARNINGS FUNCTION APPROACH

One therefore turns naturally to earnings functions, where individuals provide the observations. Unfortunately, no simple answer can be found here either. If P is the individual's marginal contribution to output, S his schooling, and A a vector of ability and other relevant attributes not caused by education, we may suppose

$$P = f(S, A) \tag{1}$$

We wish to know f_S, the effect of schooling on productivity.

For purposes of an earnings function, however, research workers observe income Y and a different vector of ability variables A^R. They then estimate a function

$$Y = g(S, A^R) + u \tag{2}$$

The question is whether f_S and g_S are the same.

Until recently, the main controversy concerned the problem of whether A^R sufficiently approximated A for g_S not to be biased upward owing to positive correlation between S and elements of A not included in A^R. The general finding of research, summarized in Appendix 1, has been that the partial regression coefficient of earnings on education (g_S) is a high fraction of the simple regression coefficient where no attempt is made to control for ability.

But the screening hypothesis has added a quite new problem. Suppose schooling really has no effect on productivity ($f_S = 0$), but employers do not know the full vector A for their employees. Suppose also that the productivity of an individual cannot be directly measured, so that employers cannot pay a person his marginal product (P). They can, however, statistically predict it from a production relation

$$P = h(S, A^E) + v \tag{3}$$

where A^E is the set of ability data available to employers.[2] If A^E is not the same as A, h_S may easily be positive even if f_S is zero. If the employer now paid an income (Y) equal to $\hat{P}$, the researcher's earnings function could show a positive effect of education ($g_S > 0$), even if he included in it the set of non-educational variables which exactly determine productivity ($A^R = A$).[3] Thus, education might wrongly appear to effect productivity whereas in fact it only affects earnings. *The issue is thus no longer whether education has an effect in a properly specified earnings function, but why it has an effect, if it does.*

Clearly, such an issue cannot be solved without data on A^E as well as A, A^R, and P. This is the fundamental problem with the pioneering study by Taubman and Wales (1973). Essentially they estimated function (2) for each occupational group, finding substantial education effects in each. They then hypothesized that in the absence of screening each individual would enter that occupation in which he could obtain the highest wage, given his schooling and other attributes. Hence, they produced a 'free-entry' occupational distribution for each educational group, which is broadly compared with the actual distribution in Table 9.1. As this shows, college-educated people achieved almost exactly the free-entry distribution, while those with only high school did far worse than under free entry. Taubman and Wales conclude that this was due to screening and that, under free entry, the private returns to

Table 9.1   Actual and free-entry distribution of educational
groups between occupations (males)

	Percentage		
	High-pay occupation[a]	Low-pay occupation[b]	Total
Education			
High school:			
Actual	61	39	100
Free entry	96	4	100
College:			
Actual	96	4	100
Free entry	98	2	100

Source: Taubman and Wales (1973), Table 5.
[a] High-pay occupations are 'professional, managerial, technical, and sales workers'.
[b] Low-pay occupations are 'blue collar, white collar, and service workers'.

education would have been one-half to two-thirds what they actually are. If screening is unproductive, the true social return to education is then a third to a half of that indicated by earnings differentials.

This ingenious analysis raises many problems. First, it is not clear what information employers are meant to have, except for *S*. We are told that, once in an occupation, people are paid their marginal product,[4] so there is presumably no screening problem of the kind described by Arrow and most other writers. This kind of problem only arises if an employer may end up paying a worker an amount different from his marginal product. Taubman and Wales assume that employers have no difficulty in paying people appropriately once they employ them. So screening presumably reflects not some objective difficulty of selection, but a taste for discrimination.

However, this leaves one crucial problem with their analysis. Why, if employers are willing to offer a given 'high' wage to some high school graduates of a given quality, are they not willing to pay it to all high school graduates of that quality? It is surely not 'screening' to discriminate between identical non-graduates who are, according to the model, able to produce the same output in the high-paying occupation. The truth of the matter is that the non-graduates who enter the top occupations are not the same (in terms of *A* variables, like motivation) as those with the same A^R who fail to enter them, and employers know this.

A quite different test of the screening hypothesis has been propounded by Berg (1971), who points to the rise over time in the educational qualifications found in each occupation. However, the nature of occupations changes over time, and such a test is no evidence of anything.

THREE UNVERIFIED PREDICTIONS OF THE SCREENING HYPOTHESIS

So what can one say, or should one say nothing? Unfortunately, the matter is of such importance that we have to operate with some provisional view of the significance of screening. No one, least of all Arrow, would maintain that all earnings differentials are in fact due to screening, so a test of his pure hypothesis, could it be devised, would not be very informative. Equally, no sane person would deny that the idea had some truth in it. What is needed is an estimate of the share of differentials due to it. Pending further empirical work, we shall examine three predictions which are in the spirit of the screening hypothesis and show that they are at variance with the evidence, including that of Taubman and Wales.

Private returns are to certificates and not to years of schooling

The screening hypothesis implies that some aspects of a person's educational record are more useful to an employer than others. In particular, graduation from a course should provide more evidence of ability and staying power than mere attendance for a number of years. This is the basis for the 'sheepskin' version of the screening hypothesis according to which wages will rise faster with extra years of education when the extra year also conveys a certificate.

To test this, we compare the rates of return obtained by dropouts and by those who completed their courses.[5] The main available data are shown in Table 9.2. In both the studies which allowed for the differential ability of dropouts, the rate of return to dropout exceeded that to completion. Taubman and Wales, though 'surprised' at the finding, failed to note that it is in the least damaging to the screening hypothesis. In fact, it is devastating, unless the hypothesis says that employers use years of education rather than certificates as the screen.[6]

Two other studies explicitly claim to throw light on the role of certificates as compared with educational experience. The first concerns the effect of graduate study on earnings about 7 years after obtaining a bachelor's degree and uses a sample of 1300 Woodrow Wilson fellows (Ashenfelter and Mooney, 1968). The authors conclude that variables such as profession, degree level,

Table 9.2 Private rates of return to dropouts and to those completing courses, males (United States)

Course	Rate of return		Source	Sample	Main variables controlled for by earnings functions
	Dropout	Completed course			
BA	15	11	Taubman and Wales (1973)	NBER sample of World War II veterans	Ability, father's education
BA + MA	8[a]	8	Rogers (1969)	Eighth graders in certain Connecticut schools, 1935	IQ, parental class, religion, marital status, number of jobs
High school	7	6			
BA	12	8	Hanoch (1967)	Census 1959, whites, North[b]	Place of residence, hours worked, marital status, family size, region of birth
High school	16.3	16.1			
BA	7.1	9.6	Hansen (1963)	Census 1949	None
High school	12.3	14.5			
BA	5.1	10.1	Becker (1964)	Census 1939, urban whites	None
BA	9.5	14.5			

Notes:
a This figure is the rate of return on BA + MA courses for those who dropped out during the MA course.
b A further recent analysis of the 1959 census (Eckaus, 1973) gives the following private rates of return for white males, North and South, adjusted for hours of work but not controlled for other variables by earnings functions.

	Dropout	Completed Course
High school	3.5	4.0
BA	11.5	12.0

and field of graduate study always explained more of the variance in earnings than years of graduate study and that this casts doubt on the 'application of traditional rate of return analysis to the area of graduate education'. However, the effect of graduate degree level (when compared with the effects of a bachelor's degree) consists of the positive effect of the Ph D (with t-statistic = 2.5) and the negative effects of the master's ($t = -0.9$) and of other higher degrees in law and the like ($t = -1.6$). Such strange effects can hardly be adduced in support of the screening hypothesis.

At the other end of the educational scale, Hansen, Weisbrod and Scanlon (1970) claim to have cast doubt on the screening effect of high school graduation. They regress earnings of 2400 low achievers rejected for the draft in 1963 on years of schooling, Armed Forces Qualification Test results, and age. They show that, holding AFQT and age constant, high school graduation does not significantly affect earnings. This, they claim, rejects the 'sheepskin' hypothesis at the high school level, but the finding must be viewed with great caution for technical reasons pointed out by Chiswick (1972) and Masters and Ribich (1972).[7] Nevertheless, the opposite view – that certificates are crucial to the effect of education on earnings – is certainly not supported by the evidence.

Private returns to education fall with work experience

A second prediction in the spirit of the screening hypothesis is that the partial effect of education on earnings, A^R held constant, will fall with experience as employers come to have better information about their employees' real productivity. (At the same time, the effect of A^R would rise.) Of course, one could proffer a screening hypothesis in which employers never learn, but this is not plausible. So we look to see whether the effect of education on earnings falls with experience, either absolutely or relatively.

If we ignore the problems caused by on-the-job training, we can at once reject the prediction of falling returns from Taubman and Wales's own findings, reproduced in Table 9.3. This shows the earnings of those with each level of post-high school education, holding A^R constant, expressed as a percentage of average high school earnings, first when the sample was 33 and then when it was 47. As the table shows, the education effects rise both proportionately and absolutely with age. As one would expect, the proportional effect of measured ability also rises, but this does not reduce the effect of education, as the screening hypothesis would suggest. A similar pattern emerges from Hanoch's cross-sectional study based on census returns, reproduced in Table 9.4, though in this case A^R is not held constant.

However, some would argue that the labor market is like a set of escalators. People are selected for a given escalator when they join the labor force and cannot thereafter easily jump from one escalator onto another. People with credentials are selected for escalators that rise rapidly and others for ones that

Table 9.3 Standardized earnings of those with higher
education as a percentage of earnings of those
with completed high school: by age (males)

	Average age		Increase in differential
	33	47	
Some college	111	117	6
BA	112	131	19
Some graduate work	115	126	11
MA	110	132	22
PhD	102	127	25
MD	172	206	34
LLB	119	184	65

Source: Based on Taubman and Wales (1973, Table 1). Data relate
to NBEr–TH sample of World War II veterans.

move more slowly. People may of course walk at different speeds up their own
escalator, but earnings differences between groups with different credentials
are basically determined by the speeds at which their escalators are traveling.

However, the notion of rigidly separated escalators is not borne out by most
studies of the relation of education and occupation, which reveal a wide variety

Table 9.4 Standardized earnings: by age (males, United States, 1959)

Education	Age				
	22	27	37	47	57
Secondary (12 years) as % of elementary (8 years)	127	128	126	126	134
BA (16 years) as % of secondary (12 years)	. . .	126	144	161	161

Source: Hanoch (1967, p. 316).

of educational backgrounds among those in similar occupations (OECD, 1969; Layard *et al.*, 1971). Some occupations, like teaching, are of course more rigid than others; and there is unfortunately as yet little evidence on the correlation of starting salaries and lifetime incomes. However, our impression is that the correlation is far from perfect.

An alternative, and less institutional, explanation of why earnings differentials rise with age might attribute this to differential training (Mincer, 1972). Suppose for example that training is employee financed and that graduates forgo a higher proportion of their potential starting salaries than non-graduates for this purpose. Then if workers were paid their marginal product, proportional earnings differentials between graduates and non-graduates would rise with experience. Now introduce screening so that earnings differentials are artificially raised in the early years of working life but not later. We might still find that proportional earnings differentials rise with experience, provided the difference in training is great enough. There is no conclusive answer to this argument, since the exact form of function relating training costs to experience is exceedingly difficult to determine empirically, even in the absence of the screening hypothesis. It is however up to the 'screenists' to provide direct evidence of the importance of screening when there is *prima facie* evidence that casts doubt on it.

Education will not be demanded if (privately) cheaper screening methods exist

We turn now from earnings data to consider the institutional implications of the screening hypothesis. According to the hypothesis, employers are willing to take on graduates at a substantial earnings differential because they consider this more profitable than employing non-graduates at a lower wage. This is simply because, although able non-graduates exist, graduates are on average abler, for reasons not connected with their studies. The hypothesis therefore implies that the cost of discovering non-graduate talent by suitably devised tests is at least as great as the observed discounted earnings differential between graduates and non-graduates of the same real ability.

Is this really plausible? One 'screenist' (Wiles) believes it is not: 'In all non-vocational cases a good one-day test of docility, perseverance and ability, costing about £20 instead of £2,000, would do as well [in revealing talent].' If this is so, why don't employers use it? Wiles's answer consists of two main points.

Educational subsidies

First he draws attention to the public subsidy to higher education. However, this is irrelevant if, despite subsidies, employers still have to pay graduates a great deal more than non-graduates of the same measured ability – as the rates of return in Table 9.2 indicate. True, measured ability is not the same as real ability, but casual observation confirms that employers do pay a good deal more for graduates than for non-graduates considered of equal natural ability. So why do they hire graduates if they could find equally able non-graduates at a lower wage? Wiles's answer is that the costs of finding able non-graduates, which could be small in a well-organized world, are in fact large.

Unexploited economies of scale

He offers as an example a hypothetical table in which the total cost to employers of finding one able non-graduate is £600 as against £60 for a graduate. This difference occurs mainly because graduates have been pretested by the universities while non-graduates have not. But in this case, one must ask why no one private agency has established itself as a non-graduate testing body making its results available to all. The Educational Testing Service and American College Testing Program do this for academic abilities. If, as Wiles believes, similar tests can also pry out other abilities, there seems no reason why such a service has not developed – monopoly legislation is certainly not the reason why it has not.[8] We would not ourselves wish to decry the possibility of a disequilibrium in this market and the urgent need for government support for vocational guidance. But it is impossible to believe that a graduate differential as large as it is (holding ability constant) could be mainly explained by a failure to market some very cheap tests, plus a subsidy to a more expensive test.[9]

CONCLUSION

The screening hypothesis challenges the view that earnings differentials, standardized for differences due to other factors, measure the social returns to education. As formulated by Arrow (1973) the hypothesis is very difficult to test. If there are no social returns to the screening function of education, it could in principle be tested by production functions, but these are in practice beset with simultaneity problems. Nor do earnings functions for individuals provide a clear test, since the question is not *whether* education explains earnings, but *why* it does.

Most people would agree that screening is a part of the explanation, but how much of a part? The Taubman and Wales (1973) measure is not satisfactory. But three pieces of evidence suggest that screening is not a major part of the explanation. First, rates of return to dropouts are as high as to those who complete a course, which refutes the sheepskin version of the screening hypothesis. Second, standardized educational differentials rise with age, while a reasonable version of the screening hypothesis would lead one to expect a fall. Third, if screening is the main function of education, it could probably be done more cheaply by testing and other means, and agencies would have developed to reap the very large profits that could be made by doing this. Pending further work, we conclude that the theory of human capital is not after all in ruins.

Appendix 1: The Proportion of Educational Earnings Differentials Due to Education

The Appendix Table 9A.1 shows what proportion of crude intereducational earnings differentials survive after extracting the effects on earnings of other variables correlated with education but not caused by it. We do not allow here for any effect of screening, which constitutes round 2 of the debate referred to above; instead, we summarize the results of round 1. In each case, we compare the coefficient (b) obtained when an earnings variable is regressed on education and a minimum number of other 'original' variables with the coefficient (b') obtained when earnings are regressed on education, the original variables, and a number of 'additional' variables not caused by education. The table gives the values of b'/b. Where the earnings function includes interaction effects, the values of b'/b are shown for some representative group of people.

The striking finding is that the ratio is rarely less than Denison's (1964) assumed value of 3/5 and often higher. One must, however, recognize that many relevant variables such as motivation are not allowed for. If this is a major determinant of both earnings and educational choice, the figures in the table must greatly overstate the true position (*pace* Griliches, 1970). We would not therefore consider that any figure approaching 100 per cent of the crude age-standardized differentials is likely to be relevant to educational policy or to the analysis of the effects of education on growth.

Table 9.A1 Proportion (b'/b) of earnings differentials due to education (males, United States)

Course	b'/b	Main variables controlled for		Source	Sample
		Original	Additional		
Higher education	0.65	Age	Ability, family background, marital status, health	Taubman and Wales (1973)	NBER sampel of World War II veterans
BA	0.97	Age	Ability	Hause (1972)	NBER sample
BA	0.87	Age	Ability	Hause (1972)	Rogers (1969) (see below)
Years of schooling after military service	0.88	Age, schooling before service, color, length of military service	Ability, father's status, place of schooling	Griliches and Mason (1972)	Bureau of the Census sample of postwar veterans
Years of schooling	0.56	Age	Family size, father's occupation and income	Bowles (1972)	Mainly US Census survey data
Years of schooling	0.57	Age	IQ, father's occupation, and portion of ability and occupation not due to education	Jencks (1972)	Mainly March 1962 Current Population Survey data
BA	0.86	Age	IQ, parental class, religion, marital status, no. of jobs	Rogers (1969)	Eighth graders in certain Connecticut schools, 1935
High school	0.73	Age			
BA	0.82	Age, race, region	Place of residence, hours worked, marital status, family size, region of birth	Hanoch (1965)	Census 1959

Appendix 2: Interpreting the Coefficient on Schooling in an Earnings Function

This Appendix illustrates how the researcher's earnings function could show a positive effect of education ($g_S > 0$), even if he included in it the set of non-educational variables (A) which exactly determine productivity and if f_S is zero. For convenience we assume that A and A^E are each single variables (rather than vectors of attributes), positively but imperfectly correlated, and that all functions are linear. We then have the following representation of the general model outlined in the text (the general expression being shown in brackets):

Productivity relation:

$$P = a_0 + a_1 A \qquad [P = f(S, A)] \tag{A.1}$$

researcher's estimating relation:

$$Y = b_0 + b_1 S + b_2 A^R + u_2 \qquad [Y = g(S, A^R) + u] \tag{A.2}$$

employer's estimating relation:

$$P = c_0 + c_1 S + c_2 A^E + u_3 \qquad [P = h(S, A^E) + v] \tag{A.3}$$

employer's method of pay:

$$Y = \hat{P} = \hat{c}_0 + \hat{c}_1 S + \hat{c}_2 A^E \tag{A.4}$$

Although schooling does not affect productivity ($f_s = 0$), it will affect income positively in the researcher's estimating equation ($b_1 > 0$) if ($\hat{c}_1 S + \hat{c}_2 A^E$) is positively correlated with S, A held constant. If $\hat{c}_1$ and $\hat{c}_2$ are positive, sufficient conditions are that A^E be positively correlated with S, A held constant; in other words,

$$r_{SA^E} > r_{A^E A} r_{AS}$$

Needless to say, the necessary conditions are more elaborate and less strong than this.

Notes

1. See also Spence (1973) and Stiglitz (1975). For another discussion of this issue in a different vein but a similar spirit, see Blaug (1972).
2. Alternatively, assume that, although individual productivity can be directly measured, hiring arrangements make it necessary to fix a person's wage before his productivity is known.
3. Sufficient conditions for this are shown in Appendix 2.
4. If people are paid their marginal product and screening is and will be practiced, then graduation does raise a person's productivity partly by pushing him through the screen, and this is a genuine social return (*pace* Taubman and Wales 1973, p. 50).
5. We would have preferred to show the earnings gain associated with each year of the course, including the year when it was successfully completed. Unfortunately, the data are not generally available in this form. They also generally show the rate of return to completion of one course over completion of the next lowest course rather than over non-completion of the same course (see Table 9.2).
6. If the analysis is confined to students who are not 'business owners', the rates of return to dropouts and graduates are the same. This is presumably because business owners have more earnings opportunities not directly dependent on their educational qualifications. The striking point is, however, the high rate of return to non-business-owning dropouts. In addition Taubman and Wales did an analysis which distinguished those who finished 1, 2, and 3 years of college. This showed a substantial earnings gain in the first year with none in the second or third, which might support a screening hypothesis which included college entry in the screen.
7. The study also implies that education has virtually no effect (sheepskin or other) unless one is willing to accept Hansen, Weisbrod, and Scanlon's view that the correlation of AFQT and education arises mainly from an effect of education on AFQT, which seems unlikely.
8. Wiles suggests that his screening hypothesis (or what he calls external-test-not-content hypothesis) be checked by comparing the incomes of graduates in a given field of work having degrees in subjects more or less relevant to that field. The lower the correlation between income and relevance of degree subject, the more likely the hypothesis. Such an examination of incomes at a microlevel is certainly of high priority.
9. Needless to say, even if screening were done by tests rather than education, the competitive equilibrium could well involve overinvestment. If types of labor were perfect substitutes (and ignoring the problem of incentives), it unquestionably would be.

References

Arrow, K. (1973) 'Higher education as a filter', *Journal of Public Economics*, 2(3) (July), 193–216.

Ashenfelter, O. and J.D. Mooney (1968) 'Graduate education, ability, and earnings', *Review of Economics and Statistics*, 50 (February), 78–86.

Becker, G.S. (1964) *Human Capital* (New York: Columbia University Press for the National Bureau of Economic Research).

Berg, I. (1971) *Education and Jobs: The Great Training Robbery* (Boston: Beacon).

Blaug, M. (1972) 'The correlation between education and earnings: what does it signify?', *Higher Education*, 1(1), 53–76.

Bowles, S. (1972) 'Schooling and inequality from generation to generation', *Journal of Political Economy*, 80(3), Supplement (May–June), S219–S251.

Chiswick, B.R. (1972) 'Schooling and earnings of low achievers: comment', *American Economic Review*, 62 (September), 752–4.

Denison, E.F. (1964) 'Proportion of income differentials among education groups 'due to' additional education: the evidence from the Wolfe–Smith survey', in J. Vaisey (ed.), *The Residual Factor and Economic Growth* (Paris: OECD).

Eckhaus, R. (1973) 'Returns to education with standardised incomes', *Quarterly Journal of Economics*, 87 (February), 121–31.

Fallon, P. and R. Layard (1975) 'Capital–skill complementarity, income distribution and output accounting', *Journal of Political Economy* 83(2), Chapter 10 in this volume.

Griliches, Z. (1970) 'Notes on the role of education in production functions and growth accounting', in W.L. Hansen (ed.), *Education, Income, and Human Capital* (New York: Columbia University Press for the National Bureau of Economic Research).

Griliches, A. and W. Mason (1972) 'Education, income, and ability', *Journal of Political Economy*, 80(3), Supplement (May–June), S74–S103.

Hanoch, G. (1965) 'Personal earnings and investment in schooling', PhD dissertation, University of Chicago.

Hanoch, G. (1967) 'An economic analysis of earnings and schooling', *Journal of Human Resources*, 2 (Summer), 310–29.

Hansen, W.L. (1963) 'Rates of return to investment in schooling in the United States', *Journal of Political Economy*, 81(2) (April), 128–41.

Hansen, W.L., B.A. Weisbrod and W.J. Scanlon (1970) 'Schooling and earnings of low achievers', *American Economic Review*, 60 (June), 409–18.

Hause, J.C. (1972) 'Earnings profile: ability and schooling', *Journal of Political Economy*, 80 (3), Supplement (May–June), S108–S138.

Jencks, C. *et al*. (1972) *Inequality: A Reassessment of the Effect of Family and Schooling America* (New York: Basic Books).

Johnson, G.E. (1970) 'The demand for labor by educational category', *Southern Economic Journal*, 37(2) (October), 190–204.

Layard, R., D. Sargan, M. Ager and D. Jones (1971) *Qualified Manpower and Economic Performance: An Inter-plant Study in the Electrical Engineering Industry* (London: Allen Lane, The Penguin Press).

Master, S. and T. Ribich (1972) 'Schooling and earnings of low achievers', *American Economic Review*, 62 (September), 755–9.

Mincer, J. (1972) 'Schooling, experience, and earnings' (New York: National Bureau of Economic Research), mimeo.

OECD (1969) *Statistics of the Occupational and Educational Structure of the Labour Force in 53 Countries* (Paris: OECD).

Rogers, D.C. (1969) 'Private rates of return to education in the United States: a case study', *Yale Economic Essays*, 9 (Spring), 89–134.

Spence, D. (1973) 'Job market signaling', *Quarterly Journal of Economics*, 87(3) (August), 355–74.

Stiglitz, J. (1975) 'The theory of screening, education, and the distribution of income', *American Economic Review*, Vol. LXV, No. 3, June.

Taubman, P.J. and T.J. Wales (1973) 'Higher education, mental ability, and screening', *Journal of Political Economy*, 81 (January–February), 460–80.

Tolley, G.S. and E. Olson (1971) 'The interdependence between income and education', *Journal of Political Economy*, 79 (May–June), 460–80.

Wiles, P. (1974) 'The correlation between education and earnings: the external-test-not-content hypothesis (ETNC)', *Higher Education*, 3(1).

10 Capital–Skill Complementarity, Income Distribution, and Output Accounting (1975)*

with P. Fallon*

INTRODUCTION AND SUMMARY

How quickly do the returns to education fall when the number of educated people rises? This has been a crucial question for the philosophy of educational planning, since the case for manpower forecasting and planning is stronger the less easy the process of substituting educated for less educated people.

In answer to the questioning, Blaug (1967) and others pointed out that US rates of return to education had been remarkably constant over time despite a vast increase in the educated labor force. This suggested that substitution was relatively easy. Likewise, cross-sectional data on countries (Bowles, 1970) and on US states (Dougherty, 1972) showed that the relative wages of the educated tend to vary with their relative numbers by only small amounts – evidence again, it was claimed, of easy substitution.

However, the inference, whether from time series or cross-section, may not be valid if other things are varying at the same time. And the relative use of physical capital always varies, the ratio of physical capital to raw labour generally rising with the ratio of educated to raw labor. If physical capital is more complementary to educated than to raw labor, this could then explain why the relative wages of the educated are not much lower when their relative numbers are much higher.[1] Equally, if this is the explanation, planners should avoid excessive educational expansion not accompanied by physical investment, since this could produce a rapid fall in relative wages.

* *Journal of Political Economy*, 83(2) (1975), pp. 279–301.
We are grateful for financial support to the UK Social Science Research Council, and to C. R. S. Dougherty and G. Pyatt for helpful comments. For further discussion of many of the topics see Fallon (1974).

This 'capital–skill complementary hypothesis' has been advanced by Griliches (1969, 1970) and partially confirmed on a cross-section of US states. Because of lack of data, he assumed constancy across states in the absolute wage of educated manpower and in the rate of return on physical capital in any given industry. The present study relies instead on international data on 23 countries, including detailed information on national education-specific wages and data on physical capital stocks and rentals at the national, though not at the sectoral, level. The data have the advantages of wide variation but obvious problems of comparability. As regards the form of the relationships involved, Griliches restricted these by assuming constant own- and cross-elasticities of demand in each factor demand equation, while we restrict them by assuming an explicit form of production function – the two-level CES function.[2] This has the advantage, apart from yielding meaningful results, that we can use the explicit function to account for income differences between countries and for differences in the functional distribution of income.

The paper is constructed as follows. Section I examines capital-skill complementarity and the ease of substitution between types of labor at the level of the whole economy. The problem here is that factor prices affect educational choices as well as vice versa, and a complete model is therefore specified. Section II examines the same question at the sectoral level, factor prices being taken here as exogenous. Both sections I and II confirm the capital–skill complementarity hypothesis and suggest much lower elasticities of substitution between educated and raw labor than either Bowles or Dougherty. Sections III and IV revert to the whole-economy model. Section III illustrates how the production function, together with the relation determining the supply of educated people, determines the evolving pattern of income distribution as countries get richer (as measured by their total capital per head). If the supply of educated people is always such that the rates of return to education and to human capital are in fixed proportion, the parameters of the production function correctly predict that as economic progress occurs, human capital per head will grow faster than physical capital per head and the share of physical capital in national income will fall. In section IV we examine the relative importance of physical and human capital in explaining income differences between countries and conclude (contrary to the claims of Krueger, 1968) that physical capital is generally the more important.

I THE PATTERN OF SUBSTITUTION: WHOLE-ECONOMY LEVEL

The problem

Suppose there are only three factors of production, physical capital (K), skill (S – to be defined), and other labor (N – to be defined), and output (Y) is determined by: $Y = f(K, S, N)$. Then the capital–skill complementarity hypothesis, in the form in which we are interested, states that:

$$\frac{\partial}{\partial K}\left(\frac{f_S}{f_N}\right) > 0$$

which implies

$$\frac{f_{SK}}{f_S} > \frac{f_{NK}}{f_N}$$

By contrast, the production function used by Bowles and Dougherty assumes that physical capital has no effect on the relative marginal products of skill and other labor, the function having the form

$$Y = f(K, [bS^\theta + (1 - b)N^\theta])$$

To examine the capital–skill complementarity hypothesis we need to use a form of function which permits it to be confirmed or rejected. The Cobb–Douglas does not, and the simplest form which does is the two-level CES function,

$$Y = A[aQ^\rho + (1 - a)X_1^\rho]^{1/\rho} \qquad (\rho \leq 1)$$

where

$$Q = [bX_2^\theta + (1 - b)X_3^\theta]^{1/\theta} \qquad (\theta \leq 1)$$

and X_1, X_2, and X_3 are any permutation of K, S and N.[3] The Bowles function would correspond to the version where K played the role of X_1 ('the odd man out') and was equally complementary to skill and other labor. Only if S or N played the role of X_1 could capital be more (or less) complementary to skill than to other labor. We have tested all three permutations of the two-level function using the two-stage least-square models developed later and found that the production function estimates where N played the role of X_1 were the most satisfactory on a number of criteria.[4]

Our preferred function form is thus

$$Y = A[aQ^\rho + (1 - a)N^\rho]^{1/\rho} \qquad (\rho \leq 1)$$

where   (1)

$$Q = [bK^\theta + (1 - b)S^\theta]^{1/\theta} \qquad (\theta \leq 1)$$

If the capital-complementarity hypothesis is true, $\rho > \theta$, and vice versa.[5] In other words, the direct elasticity of substitution between N and Q (i.e.,

$1/[1 - \rho])$ must exceed the direct elasticity of substitution, within the 'nest', between K and S (i.e. $1/[1 - \theta]$). This is really all that needs to be said about the capital–skill complementarity hypothesis given the two-level CES function. However, it may be useful to relate the condition $\rho > \theta$ to the other elasticities used in general discussions of the issue. Of these, the most relevant is the elasticity of complementarity (Hicks, 1970). This is defined for a constant-returns production function $f(X_1, \ldots, X_n)$ as

$$c_{ij} = \frac{1}{v_j} \frac{\partial \log f_i}{\partial \log X_j} \left(= \frac{1}{v_i} \frac{\partial \log f_j}{\partial \log X_i} = c_{ji} \right)$$

where v_j is the share of the jth factor in output, and $\partial \log f_i / \partial \log X_j$ indicates the proportional effect on the marginal product of the ith factor of a change in the quantity of the jth factor, holding all other input quantities constant. Clearly

$$c_{SK} = \frac{1}{v_K} \cdot \frac{f_{SK}}{f_S} \cdot K$$

and

$$c_{NK} = \frac{1}{v_K} \cdot \frac{f_{NK}}{f_N} \cdot K$$

so that our form of the capital–skill complementarity hypothesis is fulfilled if $c_{SK} > c_{NK}$. In the case of our two-level CES function,[6]

$$c_{SK} = 1 - \rho + \frac{1}{v_Q}(\rho - \theta)$$

and

$$c_{NK} = c_{SN} = 1 - \rho$$

This confirms that the capital–skill complementarity hypothesis requires that $\rho > \theta$. We may also note that, in Hicks's language, the pairs N, K and N, S are q-complements whatever the value of ρ (< 1), while capital and skill (K and S) may or may not be q-complements but must be if $\rho > \theta$.

From our point of view, the elasticity of complementarity is a more useful concept than the better-known Allen elasticity of substitution, used in the Griliches (1969) analysis. The reason is that the former deals with the effect of a factor quantity change on factor prices (other factor quantities and output price constant), while the latter deals with the effect of a factor price change on factor quantities (other factor prices and output quantity constant). The Allen elasticity of substitution is defined as

$$\sigma_{ij} = \frac{1}{v_j} \cdot \frac{\partial \log X_i}{\partial \log p_j} \left(= \frac{1}{v_i} \cdot \frac{\partial \log X_j}{\partial \log p_i} = \sigma_{ji} \right)$$

However, under constant returns to scale it can be shown that, even in the n-factor case,[7] $c_{SK} > c_{NK}$ implies and is implied by $\sigma_{SK} < \sigma_{NK}$. In our two-level CES function

$$\sigma_{SK} = \frac{1}{1-\rho} + \frac{1}{v_Q} \left(\frac{1}{1-\theta} - \frac{1}{1-\rho} \right)$$

and

$$\sigma_{NK} = \sigma_{SN} = \frac{1}{1-\rho}$$

This confirms again that the capital–skill complementarity hypothesis requires $\rho > \theta$. In addition we may note that, in Hicks's language, the pairs N, K and N, S must be p-substitutes, while capital and skill (K and S) may or may not be p-substitutes but must be if $\rho < \theta$.

So much for capital–skill complementarity – that is, the effect of changes in *capital* on rates of return to education. Turning to the effect of *education* on rates of return to education, the measure normally used is the direct elasticity of substitution, defined as

$$d_{ij} = -\frac{\partial \log (X_i/X_j)}{\partial \log (f_i/f_j)} \left(= -\frac{\partial \log (X_j/X_i)}{\partial \log (f_j/f_i)} = d_{ji} \right)$$

that is, the proportional change in the relative quantities of the ith and jth factors for a given change in their relative marginal products, all other factors and output being held constant. To measure the rate at which the returns to education will fall as the relative number of educated people rises, we take the inverse

$$\frac{1}{d_{SN}} = -\frac{\partial \log(f_S/f_N)}{\partial \log(S/N)}$$

In the case of our function,[8]

$$\frac{1}{d_{SN}} = \frac{v_S v_N}{v_S + v_N} (2c_{SN} - c_{SS} - c_{NN})$$

Like all direct elasticities, this is positive and lies between $1/(1 - \theta)$ and $1/(1 - \rho)$. It may not be strictly what is needed from a planning point of view, since, if the number of skilled people is increased in a country, the number of unskilled is constrained to decline by the same number. So output rises and substitution does not occur along an isoquant. Thus, unless the production function is homothetic in skilled and unskilled labor, the proportional change in f_S/f_N for a change in S/N such that, $dS + dN = 0$ slightly exceeds $1/d_{SN}$ (provided $f_S > f_N$). However, in our estimated function the difference is small for most countries,[9] and we shall simply quote the direct elasticities of substitution as the occasion arises.

The model with more educated and less educated labor

In order to estimate the parameters of the production function (1), we must specify the model generating our observations. It is convenient to begin with some definitions:

Quantity	Price (1963 $)	Definition of quantity
K	r	Physical capital ($000, 1963 prices)
S	z	Workers with 8 or more years of education (000)
N	w	Workers with 7 or less years of education (000)
Q	q	$(bK^\theta + (1-b)S^\theta)^{1/\theta}$
Y		Output ($000, 1963 prices)
P		Population (000)

The following two basic estimating equations follow from the condition that price equals marginal product.

$$\log \frac{r}{z} = \log \frac{b}{1-b} + (\theta - 1)\log \frac{K}{S} \tag{2}$$

$$\log \frac{q}{w} = \log \frac{a}{1-a} + (\rho - 1)\log \frac{Q}{N} \tag{3}$$

Clearly (2) has to be estimated before (3), since it provides the parameters needed to construct the variables Q and q.

However, ordinary least-square estimates of these equations could be seriously biased if relatively more people get educated in countries where the private rate of return to education is high relative to the rate of return on physical capital. We therefore need an equation for the supply of educated labor, relating this to the relative rate of return and (owing to the consumption aspects of education) to income per head. The private rate of return to education is approximately proportional to the ratio of more educated to less educated wages (z/w), so we have

$$\log \frac{S}{N} = \log c_0 + c_1 \log \frac{z/w}{r} + c_2 \log \frac{Y}{P} \tag{4}$$

Clearly S, N and P are not unrelated, since $S + N$ is the total labor force. There is, therefore a total labor supply equation,[10]

$$\log (S + N) = \log d_0 + d_1 \log P \tag{5}$$

and the model is completed by the product exhaustion condition

$$Y = rK + zS + wN \tag{6}$$

Treating Q and q not as separate variables but as weighted aggregates of K, S, r and w, we have six endogenous variables (Y, S, N, r, z, w) and two exogenous variables (K and P). If the system were linear, we should conclude that (2), which includes six linear restrictions, was overidentified. The same holds for (3), as can be seen by explicitly adding two equations defining $\log Q$ and $\log q$. (4) would be just identified. However, the system is not linear; but Fisher (1966, p. 149) has shown that, in general, non-linear systems are not less identified than the corresponding linear systems. We therefore estimate equations (2), (3) and (4) using two-stage least squares, $\log K$ and $\log P$ being the exogenous variables.

The model with human capital and raw labor

The preceding model is rather crude in the way it adds together all workers with higher education (L_H) and with secondary education (L_S) to form a single category for more educated workers (S), and all workers with primary education (L_P) and with no education (L_0) to form a single category of less educated workers (N).[11] If we want to take into account differences between countries in L_H/L_S and L_P/L_0 while continuing to work within a three-factor model, the natural approach is to differentiate between human capital (S') and raw labor (N'). The latter (N') consists simply of the number of workers in the labor force, irrespective of how much human capital, if any, each worker has; and its price (w') is the wage of workers with no education ($= w_o$). Human capital (S') is a weighted sum of the human capital formed by primary education (L_P, by secondary education (L_S), and by higher education (L_H). Since we are treating each type of human capital as a perfect substitute for each other, we need a constant set of weights, the natural weights being the average world price for the services of each type of capital. So

$$S' = (\bar{w}_H - \bar{w}_0)L_H + (\bar{w}_S - \bar{w}_0)L_S + (\bar{w}_P - \bar{w}_0)L_P$$

where $\bar{w}_H$ is the world average wage of higher-educated workers (the unweighted country average), and likewise for the other categories. The dimension of S' is units of skill. Its price (z') equals its income divided by its quantity and is a money flow per unit of time. Thus

$$z' = \frac{(w_H - w_0)L_H + (w_S - w_0)L_S + (w_P - w_0)L_P}{S'}$$

where w_H are the wages of higher-educated people in the country in question and likewise for the other categories. This price (z') is not the same as the private rate of return to education, which depends on the return to education (z') relative to its cost, which in turn is roughly proportional to the earnings of the uneducated (w'). Thus, if all educated workers had primary education only, the rate of return would be proportional to $(w_P - w_0)/w'$, which would be proportional to z'/w'. It is this latter expression which we take as our proxy for the rate of return to education.[12]

We can now set up our model. The key feature is that now total capital (C), both human and physical, is taken as exogenous rather than physical capital (K) only, as in our first model. Physical capital is measured in the same way as before under the assumption that the price of a capital good is equalized across the sample by international trade. On the other hand, human capital must be measured in units of domestic value rather than, as S', in physical units. Since the monetary rate of return on education is influenced by its non-monetary returns, it seems reasonable to take the rate of return on physical capital (r) as the rate of time preference, so that the value of human capital is $z'S'/r$. The total capital identity is then

$$C = K + \frac{z'S'}{r} \tag{7}$$

The balance between human and non-human capital is determined as before by relative rates of return and income per head:

$$\log \frac{z'S'/r}{K} = \log c_0 + c_1 \log \frac{z'/w'}{r} + c_2 \log \frac{Y}{P} \tag{4'}$$

The total labor force (N) is related to the total population (P) by

$$\log N' = \log d_0 + d_1 \log P \tag{5'}$$

and the model is completed by equations $(1')$, $(2')$, $(3')$, and $(6')$, which are identical with (1), (2), (3), and (6) except that N', w', S', z', Q', and q' replace the corresponding variables. This model has one equation more than the first and one additional variable (C). The identification of $(2')$, $(3')$, and $(4')$ is thus the same as for (2), (3), and (4). Estimation is by two-stage least squares, log C and log P being the exogenous variables.

Estimates

The data used relate to 1963 and are described in Appendix B, while the countries included are shown in Table 10.4. Broadly the wage data are based on the sources used in the rate-of-return studies summarized in Psacharopoulos (1973),[13] while the employment data are based on the 1961 Censuses. The capital measure is the sum of gross fixed capital formation from 1949 to 1963 inclusive, at 1963 prices, and capital rental is the ratio of estimated capital income to capital so measured.

Table 10.1 shows the estimates of θ and ρ provided by (2) and (3) and (2′) and (3′). The regressions are done for the whole sample and for the richer and poorer countries separately. We thus have six estimates of $\rho - \theta$, all but one positive, as predicted by the capital–skill complementarity hypothesis. To measure the significance of the differences between $\hat{\rho}$ and $\hat{\theta}$, Table 10.1 assumes that they are independent. The t-statistics shown in the third column

Table 10.1 Substitution parameters: whole economy

	(2), (2′) $\theta - 1$	(3), (3′) $\rho - 1$	$\rho - \theta$	No. of observations
All countries:				
Using S, N	−3.45	−0.67	2.78	22
	(−1.8)	(−11.0)	(1.5)	
Using S', N'	−1.72	−0.96	0.76	22
	(−4.3)	(−8.5)	(1.8)	
Richer countries:				
Using S, N	−1.81	−0.54	1.27	9
	(−2.1)	(−3.8)	(1.4)	
Using S', N'	−0.94	−1.27	−0.33	9
	(−4.6)	(−5.7)	(−1.1)	
Poorer countries:				
Using S, N	−1.50	−0.47	1.03	13
	(−1.2)	(−4.1)	(0.8)	
Using S', N'	−2.03	−0.41	1.62	13
	(−1.6)	(−2.0)	(1.3)	

Note: Figures in parentheses are t-statistics (see text re: third column).

are computed on this assumption, but a sensitivity analysis has suggested that a weak positive relation exists between $\hat{\rho}$ and $\hat{\theta}$, in which case these t-statistics are (absolutely) too low. At the crude aggregate level there is thus some mild confirmation of the capital–skill complementarity hypothesis.

As for the substitutability of more and less educated people, for the whole sample the direct elasticity of substitution is 0.61, much less than the values of 6–8 found by Bowles. This is partly due to differences in data and partly due to differences in specification. If on our data we use the two-level function with K taking the role of X_1, which is analogous to Bowles's procedure, we find an elasticity of 3.54.[14]

II THE PATTERN OF SUBSTITUTION: SECTORAL LEVEL

Estimating approach

Economy-wide functions are, however, necessarily crude and we turn now to the sectoral level. Apart from the advantage of disaggregation, we can also drop the simultaneous model, treating each sector as a price taker. However, we lack data on physical capital stocks and rentals at the sectoral level and have therefore to estimate our marginal productivity equations in their absolute rather than relative price form. This time we begin by estimating ρ from the condition that

$$\frac{\partial Y}{\partial N} = w = (1 - a)A^\rho \left(\frac{Y}{N}\right)^{1-\rho}$$

or, in its estimating form,

$$\log \frac{Y}{N} = -\frac{1}{1 - \rho} \log[(1 - a)A^\rho] + \frac{1}{1 - \rho} \log w \tag{8}$$

We then need to estimate θ. This requires some tedious manipulations. Our remaining marginal productivity condition is for S, since we have no data on K or r. This gives

$$\frac{\partial Y}{\partial S} = z = aA^\rho \left(\frac{Y}{Q}\right)^{1-\rho} (1 - b)\left(\frac{Q}{S}\right)^{1-\theta}$$

This cannot be estimated, since Q depends on θ. To eliminate Q we use Euler's theorem:[15]

$$Y = wN + \frac{\partial Y}{\partial Q} \cdot Q$$

Now

$$\frac{\partial Y}{\partial Q} = aA^\rho \left(\frac{Y}{Q}\right)^{1-\rho}$$

$$\therefore Q = a^{-(1/\rho)}A^{-1}(Y - wN)^{1/\rho}Y^{(\rho-1)/\rho}$$

$$= a^{-(1/\rho)}A^{-1}X$$

where X is defined by

$$X = (Y - wN)^{1/\rho}Y^{(\rho-1)/\rho}$$

We now substitute for Q in the marginal productivity condition above and rearrange to obtain

$$\log \frac{X}{S} = -\frac{1}{1-\theta}\log\left[(1-b)a^{\theta/\rho}A^\theta\right]$$

$$+\frac{1}{1-\theta}\log\left(\frac{z}{X^{\rho-1}Y^{1-\rho}}\right) \tag{9}$$

As long as A (the 'efficiency parameter') is regarded as a constant across countries, (8) and (9) provide our basic estimating equations, the first term on the right-hand side being in each case a constant. If, however, A is considered variable, then the estimates of ρ and θ will in general be biased. Two ways were used for dealing with this. First, a *dummy variable* was included distinguishing the poorer from the richer countries. Second, an *efficiency variable* (A_i) was calculated from the whole-economy regression of section I as follows:[16]

$$A_i = \frac{Y_i}{[aQ_i^\rho + (1-a)N_i^\rho]^{1/\rho}}$$

We then assumed that in each sector, the ratio of the efficiency parameters of the different countries was the same as in the whole economy (as in Arrow *et al.*, 1961). The estimating equations are got by rearranging (8) so that $1/(1-\rho)$ is the regression coefficient of $\log Y/NA$ on $\log w/A$, and by rearranging (9) so that $1/(1-\theta)$ is the regression coefficient of $\log X/SA$ on $\log z/X^{\rho-1}Y^{1-\rho}A$.

Estimates

Owing to the lack of data, we do not at the sectoral level distinguish between richer and poorer countries. So for each sector we have four estimates of the parameters, one pair using the dummy variables and the efficiency variable (A) on (8) and (9) and another pair using them on equations (8') and (9'), in which S' (human capital) and N' (raw labor) appear. Since we are studying four sectors, this gives 16 estimates altogether of $[1/(1 - \rho)] - [1/(1 - \theta)]$, which must be positive if $\rho > \theta$. Of these 16 estimates, 15 are positive and seven significantly so at at least the 90 per cent level (see Table 10.2). The negative estimate is not significant. A sensitivity analysis again suggested that our t-statistics for $[1/(1 - \hat{\rho})] - [1/(1 - \hat{\theta})]$ are downward biased. Thus the capital-skill complementarity hypothesis receives strong support at the sectoral level.

As regards the direct elasticities of substitution between skill and other labor, these lie between $1(1 - \rho)$ and $1/(1 - \theta)$ and are generally not above unity.

III INCOME DISTRIBUTION IN THE WHOLE-ECONOMY MODEL

Some stylized facts

We now revert to the whole-economy model in its human capital version, and look at some of its implications. First we set out some stylized facts from the data and then show how the model helps to explain them. The stylized facts can be usefully summarized by stating how our key variables change when a country gets richer in terms of total capital per man (see Table 10.3). (1) The prices of skill (z') and of raw labor (w') rise, but the price of raw labor rises faster. This reduced wage differential (z'/w') does not of itself, of course, guarantee that inequality of earnings as measured by the Gini coefficient is reduced,[17] but taken with the actual changes in relative numbers it does in fact have the effect of reducing inequality so measured.[18] This is consistent with the findings of others (Lydall, 1968). It also, of course, implies a reduction in the rate of return to investing in skill. (2) The rate of return to physical capital (r) also falls absolutely, but remains roughly proportional to the rate of return on skill. (3) The ratio of physical capital relative to skill measured in physical units (K/S) rises. But the ratio of physical capital to the value of human capital ($rK/z'S'$) falls. (4) The share of raw labor in national income does not change in any systematic way, while the share of physical capital falls and that of human capital rises.

An explanation

Let us now see how our model relates to these facts. The estimated production function taking all countries together is

$$Y = A(0.87K^{-0.72} + 0.13S'^{-0.72})^{0.62/-0.72}N'^{0.38} \tag{1'}$$

As can be seen, this is a Cobb–Douglas function in Q' and N', the reason being that the estimate of ρ is 0.04 (see Table 10.1), which is not significantly

Table 10.2 Substitution parameters: sectoral level

	Using dummy			Using variable A			
	(8), (8') $\frac{1}{1-\rho}$	(9), (9') $\frac{1}{1-\theta}$	$\frac{1}{1-\rho} - \frac{1}{1-\theta}$	(8), (8') $\frac{1}{1-\rho}$	(9), (9') $\frac{1}{1-\theta}$	$\frac{1}{1-\rho} - \frac{1}{1-\theta}$	No. of observations
Mining:							
Using S, N	1.45	0.76	0.69	0.84	0.54	0.30	15
	(7.1)	(3.9)	(2.9)	(4.0)	(3.1)	(1.1)	
Using S', N'	0.93	0.84	0.09	0.48	−0.09	0.57	15
	(5.2)	(9.6)	(0.8)	(2.8)	(−0.6)	(2.5)	
Manufacturing:							
Using S, N	1.66	0.74	0.92	1.11	0.85	0.26	16
	(7.9)	(3.2)	(2.4)	(6.7)	(8.3)	(1.3)	
Using S', N'	1.16	0.91	0.25	0.63	0.40	0.23	16
	(4.2)	(8.6)	(0.4)	(3.8)	(2.6)	(1.03)	
Construction:							
Using S, N	0.90	0.25	0.65	0.89	0.66	0.23	14
	(3.5)	(1.3)	(2.0)	(3.6)	(5.3)	(0.8)	
Using S', N'	0.70	0.08	0.62	0.44	−0.44	0.88	14
	(5.4)	(0.6)	(3.4)	(2.7)	(−2.09)	(3.29)	
Electricity, gas, water:							
Using S, N	1.03	1.06	−0.03	1.09	1.01	0.08	16
	(3.6)	(39.6)	(−0.10)	(6.1)	(8.3)	(0.4)	
Using S', N'	0.63	0.23	0.40	0.69	0.22	0.47	16
	(3.2)	(1.66)	(1.66)	(4.1)	(1.4)	(2.0)	

Note: Figures in parentheses are *t*-statistics (see text). The sample of countries for the *mining* sector consists of United States, Sweden, Canada, New Zealand, France, Norway, United Kingdom, Japan, Greece, Israel, Puerto Rico, Chile, Philippines, Ghana, and Thailand. The samples for the other sectors are identical except that *manufacturing* excludes Greece and includes India and Korea; *construction* excludes Greece and Ghana and includes India and Korea; *electricity and gas* includes India and Korea. The last column shows the number of observations for regressions using the dummy variable. In the regressions using variable *A*, Israel was excluded.

Table 10.3 Correlation coefficents between C/N' and the variables shown

Variable	Coefficient	Variable	Coefficient
w'	0.86	S'/N'	0.83
r	–0.79	K/N'	0.96
z'	0.70	K/S'	0.76
z'/w'	–0.45	$rK/z'S'$	–0.39
r/w'	–0.54	rK/Y	–0.36
r/z'	–0.52	$z'S'/Y$	0.26
$z'/w'r$	0.00	$w'N'/Y$	0.06

different from zero ($t = 0.4$). This function therefore implies that w' rises proportionately to Y/N' and that the share of raw labor is constant.

To go further than this we need to know how growth in total capital per man is allocated between growth in physical and human capital. In our model this is determined in (4′), but before turning to this it is instructive to look at the implication of a simpler model in which the rates of return on human and non-human capital are constrained to a fixed ratio (m).[19] So

$$\frac{z'/w'}{r} = m \tag{4″}$$

or $(z'/r) = mw'$. Given this, increased wealth per head must raise not only w' but also z'/r. And since Q is homothetic in K and S', this must raise K/S'. However, we know from Table 10.1 that the direct elasticity of substitution between K and S' is less than unity ($1/1.72$), so that when K/S' rises, the ratio $rK/z'S'$ falls. In this way our production function, together with one simple behavioral constraint, predicts that the relative share of physical capital will fall with economic progress and that the share of human capital and earnings will rise (fact 4). It also predicts that the value of human capital will rise faster than physical capital (fact 3).

As for the absolute rate of return on physical capital (r), this is bound to fall, provided A is constant, since both K/S' and K/N' are rising (fact 2). And by the same token the rate of return on human capital also falls (fact 1). However, as we have seen, the efficiency parameter A is not constant, and r falls with total capital per head only because the effects of changing factor proportions outweigh those of changes in efficiency.

The preceding discussion has used an exceedingly crude behavioral equation (4″) in order mainly to highlight some features of the production function. We now simulate the behavior of our key variables as C/N' changes, applying equations (1), (2'), (3'), (4'), (6'), and (7) to a country having a participation rate (N'/P) of 0.34. The supply equation estimated by two-stage least squares is

$$\log \frac{z'S'}{rK} = -0.21 + \underset{(t=0.89)}{0.51} \log \frac{z'}{w'r} + \underset{(t=3.4)}{0.36} \log \frac{Y}{P} \tag{4'}$$

As can be seen, more of total capital is allocated to human capital the higher the rate of return to human capital relative to physical capital, though the estimated effect is not highly significant. Likewise, for given relative profitabilities of human and physical capital, relatively more human capital is chosen the richer the country. This reflects the psychic value attaching to human capital as such.

To see how (4') brings about the rise of K/S' as C/N' rises (fact 3), we need simply combine it with (2') to obtain

$$\log \frac{z'S'}{rK} = -3.17 + 2.22 \log w' - 1.57 \log \frac{Y}{N'}$$

Since when Y/N' rises, w' rises at the same rate, the dependent variable rises also $(2.22 - 1.57 > 0)$.

As for the fall in the absolute magnitude of r, this follows from the estimation of one further efficiency-determining equation which can be added to the model.[20]

$$\log A = 0.83 + \underset{(t=5.84)}{0.20} \log \frac{C}{N'} \tag{10}$$

IV   ACCOUNTING FOR VARIATIONS IN OUTPUT PER HEAD

Finally, we can use our production function to analyze the sources of differences between countries in their income per head. Unfortunately a substantial part of this remains unexplained, except insofar as we choose to attribute it to efficiency differences. However, the unexplained part is a great deal less than if the role of human capital had been ignored, as columns ((1)–(3)) of Table 10.4 show. Column (1) shows the actual income per head of each country relative to that of the United States. For column (2) we have estimated a simple CES function using capital and raw labor only,[21] and then shown the efficiency of each ith country relative to that of the United States (A_i/A_{US}), where

$$A_i = \frac{Y_i}{[aK_i^\rho + (1-a)N_i'^\rho]^{1/\rho}}$$

Table 10.4 Sources of differences in income per head

Country	$(Y/P)_i$ $(Y/P)_{us}$ (1)	A_i/A_{us} 2-factor model (2)	A_i/A_{us} 3-factor model (3)	D^K (4)	D^S (5)	D^N (6)	D^A (7)	ΣD (8)
Richer:								
United States	1.00	1.00	1.00	...	...	...	...	...
Sweden	0.70	0.73	0.63	0.28	−0.47	−0.28	1.27	0.80
Canada	0.66	0.77	0.75	0.16	0.21	0.04	0.72	1.13
New Zealand	0.57	0.52	0.50	−0.39	0.05	−0.04	1.19	0.81
France	0.52	0.59	0.60	0.35	0.03	−0.13	0.85	1.10
Norway	0.50	0.58	0.60	0.16	0.26	−0.06	0.81	1.17
United Kingdom	0.49	0.59	0.61	0.52	0.03	−0.18	0.76	1.13
Japan	0.23	0.32	0.38	0.58	0.06	−0.18	0.81	1.27
Greece	0.17	0.33	0.37	0.64	0.24	−0.08	0.75	1.55
Poorer:								
Puerto Rico	0.32	0.66	0.61	0.53	0.17	0.07	0.61	1.38
Mexico	0.13	0.46	0.61	0.75	0.64	0.20	0.44	2.03
Chile	0.10	0.40	0.46	0.72	0.50	0.21	0.61	2.04
Columbia	0.09	0.29	0.33	0.72	0.38	0.12	0.73	1.95
Brazil	0.08	0.31	0.45	0.75	0.66	0.18	0.60	2.19
Turkey	0.08	0.26	0.38	0.84	0.52	−0.07	0.67	1.96
Philippines	0.08	0.37	0.47	0.86	0.38	0.26	0.57	2.07
Ghana	0.07	0.20	0.37	0.70	0.76	0.01	0.68	2.15
S. Korea	0.05	0.27	0.37	0.88	0.51	0.04	0.66	2.09
Thailand	0.04	0.16	0.23	0.84	0.43	−0.06	0.80	2.01
Kenya	0.03	0.18	0.28	0.85	0.74	0.13	0.74	2.46
India	0.03	0.11	0.22	0.85	0.74	−0.05	0.81	2.35
Uganda	0.02	0.12	0.19	0.88	0.60	−0.02	0.83	2.29

Column (3) shows the relative efficiencies we have already used in sections II and III. As can be seen, the differences in income per head in column (1) are greater than the efficiency differences in column (2), which in turn are greater than the efficiency differences in column (3). This pattern can be summarized by the coefficients of variation for each column which are 1.03, 0.56, and 0.40, respectively.

But although differences in factor endowments leave much unexplained, it is still useful to summarize their effects. Following Krueger (1968), we focus on the differences in income per head in each ith country from that in the United

States. For each factor in turn we ask how much the US income per head would fall if the endowment per head of that factor were reduced to its level in the ith country, all other US factor endowments held constant. This fall is then expressed as a proportion of the total gap in income per head between the two countries, so as to yield a measure D^j_i indicating the relative fall due to reducing the jth factor to its level in the ith country. If the production function is written as

$$\frac{Y}{P} = Af\left[\frac{K}{P}, \frac{S'}{P}, \frac{N'}{P}\right]$$

we have, for example, that

$$D^K_i = \frac{(Y/P)_{US} - A_{US}f[(K/P)_i, (S'/P)_{US}, (N'/P)_{US}]}{(Y/P)_{US} - (Y/P)_i}$$

D^S_i and D^N_i are calculated analogously. In addition, we have

$$D^A_i = \frac{(Y/P)_{US} - A_i f[(K/P)_{US}, (S'/P)_{US}, (N'/P)_{US}]}{(Y/P)_{US} - (Y/P)_i}$$

Clearly the statistics D do not account for income differences in the sense that they generally sum to unity. In fact, for any country less well endowed in all factors than the United States and less efficient,[22] $D^K_i + D^{S'}_i + D^{N'}_i + D^A_i \geq 1$. Nevertheless, the relative magnitudes of the D terms do provide as good an indication as any of the 'importance' of different factors in explaining income difference. Physical capital is more 'important' than human capital in five out of eight richer countries, and in 12 out of the 13 poorer ones.[23] This finding was already implicit in section III, which showed that the proportional differences between rich and poor countries are much greater for physical capital per head than for the skill input per head measured in physical units. Since the distribution parameter in the production function is much higher for physical capital than for skill, it follows that differences in physical capital per head account for a greater proportion of differences in output per head.

This finding conflicts with that of Krueger, who offered 'minimum estimates' of $D^{S'}$ higher than our own for more than half the countries covered in both our studies. In most countries her estimate exceeded one-half, on the strength of which she claimed that human capital was more important than all other factors put together (including efficiency) in explaining differences in income per head. However, she appears to have calculated the statistic

$$\frac{\Sigma_j w^j_{US}(L_j/N')_i}{\Sigma_j w^j_{US}(L_j/N')_{US}}$$

the labor force being divided into a large number of age-education-sector categories. This statistic is then presented as a minimum estimate of the income per head that would obtain in country *i* relative to that of the United States if country *i* had the US endowment of physical capital per head but its own labor-force composition. If this is a correct interpretation of the statistic (in Krueger, 1968, Table 2, col. 2), it overestimates the amount by which output per head would in fact be reduced.[24] For assuming with Krueger that all types of labor are perfect substitutes and can be combined into a measure (*E*) of efficiency units per head of labor, it follows that if the elasticity of output per head with respect to *E* is a constant *e* (< 1) over the relevant range, the relevant ratios of income will be[25]

$$\left(\frac{E_i}{E_{US}}\right)^e > \frac{E_i}{E_{US}}$$

Our conclusion about the greater relative importance of physical than human capital therefore stands.

Appendix A: Alternative Forms of Nested CES Function

The three alternative forms of nested CES production functions using K, S, and N are:

$$Y = A[aQ^\rho + (1-a)N^\rho]^{1/\rho}, \quad \text{where} \quad Q = [bK^\theta + (1-b)S^\theta]^{1/\theta} \quad \text{(A.1)}$$

$$Y = A[aQ^\rho + (1-a)K^\rho]^{1/\rho}, \quad \text{where} \quad Q = [bN^\theta + (1-b)S^\theta]^{1/\theta} \quad \text{(A.2)}$$

$$Y = A[aQ^\rho + (1-a)S^\rho]^{1/\rho}, \quad \text{where} \quad Q = [bK^\theta + (1-b)N^\theta]^{1/\theta} \quad \text{(A.3)}$$

Another three functions (1′)–(3′) correspond to the permutations on K, S', and N'. We use the following criteria to distinguish between functions (1)–(3) and between functions (1′)–(3′).

(a) How well does the function, when estimated using the two-stage least-square model in section I, explain output? To answer this we use (A1) to compute for each country i

$$A_i = \frac{Y_i}{[aQ_i^\rho + (1-a)N_i^\rho]^{1/\rho}}$$

and then compute the coefficient of variation $\sqrt{\Sigma(A_i - \bar{A})^2/\bar{A}}$. An analogous computation is also made using equations (A2) and (A3). The results are as follows.

	(A1), (A1′)	(A2), (A2′)	(A3), (A3′)
Using S, N	0.41	0.49	0.80
Using S', N'	0.41	0.44	0.43

Functions (A1) and (A1′) perform best.

(b) How stable is the estimate of the effect of X_2/X_3 on p_2/p_3 when we also let X_1 influence p_2/p_3? To answer this, we first assume X_1 separable and estimate

$$\log \frac{p_2}{p_3} = e + f \log \frac{X_2}{X_3} \quad \text{(A.4)}$$

We then assume that this is a misspecification and estimate each of the two alternative specifications, the first with X_2 separable and the second with X_3 separable:

$$\log \frac{p_2}{p_3} = e + f \log \frac{X_2}{X_3} + g \log \frac{Q^{13}}{X_3}, \quad \text{where} \quad Q^{13} = [bX_1^\theta + (1-b)X_3]^{1/\theta} \quad \text{(A5)}$$

$$\log \frac{P_2}{P_3} = e + f \log \frac{X_2}{X_3} + g \log \frac{Q^{12}}{X_3}, \quad \text{where} \quad Q^{12} = [bX_1^\theta + (1-b)X_2]^{1/\theta} \quad \text{(A6)}$$

To estimate functions (A5) and (A6), we used prior estimates of b and θ obtained from the corresponding fully estimated model. The resulting estimate of f are shown in Table 10.A1. For each pair (p_2, p_3) the results of the three equations (A4)–(A6) are shown on a given row. There are three rows corresponding to the three pairs (p_2, p_3) among r, z, and w, and another three rows corresponding to the three pairs among r, z', w'. As the table shows, the estimates of f are far more stable (along a row) for the pair r/z than for its two rivals, and for r/z' than for its two rivals. This provides strong support for the corresponding functions (A1) and (A1′).

(c) How sensible are the estimates of $(\theta - 1)$ and $(\rho - 1)$, and how consistent are they between rich and poor countries? This is a trickier criterion. Clearly there is no reason why $(\theta - 1)$ should be the same in both groups of countries, though one might be surprised if it differed by a multiple of 10 or if it were significantly different from zero in one group and not in the other. The same applies to $(\rho - 1)$. The estimates for (A1) and (A1′) are in Table 10.1. For (A2) and (A2′), $(\theta - 1)$ was significant when all countries were pooled, but both very different and insignificant in rich countries and poor countries taken separately. The same applies to $(\rho - 1)$. (A3) and (A3′) performed even worse; $(\theta - 1)$ was significant for all countries and for rich and poor on their own; but $(\rho - 1)$ varied wildly and was often positive – implying isoquants in Q, S space that are concave to the origin.

Table 10A.1 Estimates of f from (A4), (A5), and (A6)

| p_2/p_3 | Additional variable other than X_2/X_3 | | | |
	None	$Q^{KS}, Q^{KS'}$	$Q^{SN}, Q^{S'N'}$	$Q^{KN}, Q^{KN'}$
Using S, N:				
r/z	−3.45	N.A.	−1.56	−2.48
z/w	−0.28	−1.50	N.A.	−1.38
r/w	−0.81	−∞	−37.07	N.A.
Using S', N':				
r/z'	−1.72	N.A.	−4.41	−1.02
z'/w'	−0.60	693.44	N.A.	−11.82
r/w'	−1.07	1.93	0.45	N.A.

Note:
N.A. = not applicable.

Appendix B: Data Sources

A) WAGES AND LABOUR FORCE

The wage data came from Psacharopoulos (1973) except for New Zealand, where they are taken from the 1966 Census. For Japan, France, and Puerto Rico only relative wages are available; absolute wages are generated from estimates of total labor income (see below). Wage data are converted into US dollars using free market exchange rates where these are available, or, otherwise, official exchange rates. They are adjusted to 1963 levels by multiplying them by the ratio of monetary GDP in 1963 to monetary GDP in the year to which the data relate (these dates vary from 1959 to 1968).

The labor force data come from Psacharopoulos (1973) or OECD (1969). For most countries the sectoral breakdown is taken from the 'Education by Branch of Economic Activity' tables in OECD (1969). However, this breakdown has to be generated indirectly for Canada, France, Greece, the United Kingdom, Chile, Ghana, Korea, and Puerto Rico. The method is as follows. Let A be the occupation-by-sector matrix with n rows for occupations and m columns for sectors. Let B be the occupation-by-education matrix with each element expressing the proportion of those in a given occupation having a given level of education attainment; B consists of k rows for educational levels and n columns for occupations. Then $BA = C$ gives us a $k \times m$ matrix C, which is our estimate of the 'Education by Branch of Economic Activity' table. To examine the validity of this method, we have also applied it to some of those countries for which an 'Education by Branch of Economic Activity' table is given in OECD (1969). A comparison of the elements in the actual and estimated tables tends to confirm the validity of the method.

A final problem is the treatment of age. As workers get older their earnings rise, and presumably they become more productive. We therefore subdivide each educational category, such as the higher-educated, into five age classes, $L_{H1}, \ldots, L_{H5}$. We then assume that the age classes are perfect substitutes for each other, and estimate the labor input, for example, from higher-educated people as

$$L_H = \frac{\bar{W}_{H1}L_{H1} + \cdots + \bar{W}_{H5}L_{H5}}{\frac{1}{5}(\bar{W}_{H1} + \cdots + \bar{W}_{H5})}$$

where $\bar{W}_{Hi}$ refers to the world average wage of the higher-educated in the ith age class (strictly the unweighted intercountry average of the country average wages). The choice of denominator is of course immaterial, but the one chosen has the effect that L_H is of the same order of magnitude as the crude number of higher-educated people in a country. The corresponding wage per unit of higher-educated labor is

$$W_H = \frac{W_{H1}L_{H1} + \cdots + W_HL_H}{L_H}$$

where W_{Hi} is the wage of higher-educated people in the ith age class in the country in question. The age distributions are obtained either from the United Nations (1964, 1965) or from the original samples on which the various rate-of-return studies in Psacharopoulos (1973) were based. In many cases, data are lacking on the labor force as such, and total population statistics have to be used. We assume that the proportion of workers in each age group is the same in each sector. For illiterates however, the paucity of age data for either wages or labor force made the above procedures impossible; no age adjustment was therefore made – a justifiable procedure if age–earnings profiles are roughly flat. No data on L_0 and W_0 exist for several of the richer countries. In these cases L_0 can be safely set at zero; W_0 is approximated by an average of unskilled wage rates in various sectors of the economy, as quoted in the International Labour Office, *Bulletin of Labour Statistics*.

B) OUTPUT, CAPITAL STOCK AND CAPITAL RENTAL

On output (value added), United Nations (1966) provides a convenient source for mining, manufacturing and electricity, gas, and water, while the United Nations, *Yearbook of National Accounts Statistics* provides the remaining data. Physical capital is measured as the simple sum of gross fixed capital formation from 1949 to 1963 inclusive, measured always at 1963 prices. Most of the data on capital formation come from various editions of the United Nations, *Yearbook of National Accounts Statistics*, although for some countries national sources are also used to obtain figures for the earlier years (especially before 1953). Data given at current year prices are converted to 1963 prices using wholesale price indices from either the united Nations, *Monthly Bulletin of Statistics*, or from local country sources. To compute the total income of capital, GDP at factor cost is divided into employee income, income from unincorporated enterprises, and 'other'. Income from unincorporated enterprises is then divided between labor and capital in the ratio of employee to 'other' income, and total capital income is the capital share of unincorporated income plus 'other' income. Labor income is the labor share of unincorporated income plus employee income. Capital rental (per unit of capital) is total capital income divided by total capital.

Notes

1. Other possible hypotheses explaining the constancy of relative wages over time include the following: (a) Luxuries are more education-intensive than necessities. Here Folger and Nam (1967) show that shifts in the sectoral composition of the labor force account for a negligible proportion of the over-all rise in relative proportions of educated people in the United States. (b) Technical progress is biased (in the Hicksian sense) toward educated rather than raw labor. (c) Technical progress is fastest in education-intensive industries having demand elasticities greater than unity. Both (b) and (c) are extremely difficult to study. Other possible hypotheses explaining the cross-sectional

stability of relative wages are: (a) as above; here Fallon (1974, Chapter 8) shows the same as Folger and Nam's time series; (b) the factor-price equalization theorem; however, this implies identical factor proportions in all countries in any one industry, which is inconsistent with the data used in our section II.

2. We also tried the Griliches approach (modified so that prices are the dependent variables and quantities the independent variables), but found that the results for the richer and poorer countries taken separately were grossly inconsistent with each other and with the results for the pooled sample, whether judged by F-tests or by consistency of the signs of the coefficients.

3. Another function which does is the log-quadratic, but this does not enable one to take advantage of data on relative prices.

4. The evidence is presented in Appendix A.

5. Taking derivatives in (1), if $(f_{SK}/f_S) > (f_{NK}/f_N)$,

$$a(1 - a)b(1 - b)A^{2\rho}Y^{2(1-\rho)}K^{\theta-1}S^{\theta-1}N^{\rho-1}Q^{\rho-2\theta}(\rho - \theta) > 0$$

6. $c_{SS} = 1 - \rho + \dfrac{1}{v_Q}(\rho - \theta) + \dfrac{1}{v_S}(\theta - 1) < 0$ (and analogously for c_{KK});

$$c_{NN} = 1 - \rho + \frac{1}{v_N}(\rho - 1) < 0$$

7. On the relationship between elasticities of complementarity and substitution, see Sato and Koizumi (1973).

8. The expression for $1/d_{KN}$ is analogous, while $1/d_{SK} = 1 - \theta$.

9. If S' is defined as human capital (see below) and N' as the total labor force, there is no constraint of the form $dS' + dN' = 0$, and the rate at which the returns to education fall is given by

$$-\frac{d \log (f_{S'}/f_{N'})}{d \log S'}$$

which exceeds $1/d_{S'N'}$.

10. In many ways it would have been simpler to treat the total labor supply as exogenous, but we should then have had to explain S/N in (4) by income per worker rather than by income per head; the latter seems more plausible. Fortunately, the estimated value of d_1 for the whole sample was 1.03, making the solution values of real prices and quantity ratios approximately independent of the size of country and dependent only on the ratio of the two exogenous variables K and P.

11. $L_H = 13 +$ years of education, $L_s = 8-12$, $L_p = 1 - 7$, $L_0 =$ less than 1.

12. In the case of more than one type of education, if the relative prices of the different types of human capital are constant, as assumed in constructing S', then the relative rates of return on the different types of human capital vary. Thus suppose there are two levels of education, secondary and primary, each lasting 1 year. By assumption,

$$\frac{w_S - w_0}{w_P - w_0} = k = \frac{\bar{w}_S - \bar{w}_0}{\bar{w}_P - \bar{w}_0}$$

By definition

$$r_P = \frac{w_P - w_0}{w_0} = \frac{w_P}{w_0} - 1$$

$$r_S = \frac{w_S - w_0}{w_P} = \frac{k(w_P - w_0)}{w_P} = k - \frac{kw_0}{w_P} = k - \frac{k}{r_P + 1}$$

Thus r_s and r_p vary positively, r_p/r_s rising as r_p rises (an observation confirmed by Psacharopoulos, 1973). Therefore

$$\frac{z'}{w'} = \frac{(w_S - w_0)L_S + (w_P - w_0)L_P}{(\bar{w}_S - \bar{w}_0)L_S + (\bar{w}_P - \bar{w}_0)L_P} \cdot \frac{1}{w_0} = \left(\frac{w_P - w_0}{\bar{w}_P - \bar{w}_0}\right)\frac{1}{w_0} = \frac{r_P}{\bar{w}_P - \bar{w}_0}$$

So z'/w' is proportional to r_p and varies positively with r_s.

13. We are very grateful to the author for making the data available to us.
14. The comparable estimates using human capital and raw labor are 1.09 in our formulation and 1.67 where K takes the role of X_1.
15. An alternative approach is to obtain Q from the production function relationship.

$$aQ^\rho = \left(\frac{Y}{A}\right)^\rho - (1 - a)N^\rho$$

This leads to a different estimating equation from (9) which, unlike (9), uses the constant-term estimate from (8) and does not use wage data. However, the estimated values of $1(1 - \theta)$ are similar to those given by (9).
16. The relative values are shown in Table 10.4 (p. 187). Since A varies between countries but is not directly observable, the model in section I should strictly be completed by a function explaining A. In section III we assume in a model with S' and N' that

$$\log A = \log e_0 + e_1 \log \frac{C}{N'} \tag{10}$$

This alters the model by adding one variable and one equation and does not change the identifiability of (2'), (3'), and (4').
17. For example, if there are two categories of labor and the poorer category grows in relative number, then the Gini coefficient can easily rise even if wage differentials are reduced.
18. The Gini coefficient used takes no account of variation in wages within educational categories. It is simply measured as

$$\frac{1}{2}\frac{1}{(L_H + L_S + L_P + L_0)^2}\frac{1}{\bar{w}}\sum_i \sum_j L_i L_j |w_i - w_j| \qquad (i, j = H, S, P, 0)$$

19. In our sample the rate of return (z'/w') is positively correlated with r, the correlation coefficient, being 0.41. The ratio of z'/w' to r is completely uncorrelated with C/N'.

20. The function was actually estimated in the form $\log A = \log_{e0} + e_1 \log (C/P)$, and (10) is obtained by substituting $N' = 0.34\ P$.
21. The regression equation was

$$\log \frac{r}{w''} = 0.06 - \underset{(t = -13.75)}{1.07} \log \left(\frac{K}{N'}\right)$$

where w'' is the average wage of all workers irrespective of skill. From these parameter values, A was computed for each country.
22. First there is the problem of the multiplicative relation of A and f.

$$A_{US}(f_{US} - f_i) + (A_{US} - A_i)f_{US}$$
$$= A_{US}f_{US} - A_{US}f_i + A_{US}f_{US} - A_i f_{US} - A_i f_i + A_i f_i$$
$$= A_{US}f_{US} - A_i f_i + (A_{US} - A_i)(f_{US} - f_i)$$
$$> A_{US}f_{US} - A_i f_i$$

Second, consider the interaction effects within f. To simplify, suppose f a function of two variables only, $f(K, N)$. Then, since N raises the marginal product of K,

$$f(K_{US}, N_{US}) - f(K_i, N_{US}) > f(K_{US}, N_i) - f(K_i, N_i)$$

Therefore, adding $f(K_{US}, N_{US})$ to both sides and rearranging,

$$[f(K_{US}, N_{US}) - f(K_i, N_{US})] + [f(K_{US}, N_{US}) - f(K_{US}, N_i)]$$
$$> f(K_{US}, N_{US}) - f(K_i, N_i)$$

So the sum of the differences got by varying one factor at a time exceeds the overall difference $f_{US} - f_i$.
23. Exactly the same result is obtained when we start with the lower country's endowment and calculate, for example,

$$D_i^K = \frac{A_i f[(K/P)_{US}, (S/P)_i, (N/P)_i] - (Y/P)_i}{(Y/P)_{US} - (Y/P)_i}$$

24. We are grateful to C.R.S. Dougherty for discussion on this subject; see also Dougherty (1974).
25. The only type of measure which would definitely underestimate the share of human capital in accounting for income differences in a constant-returns production function $Y/N' = f(K/N', E)$ would be

$$\frac{(E_{US} - E_i) \cdot f_E[(K/N)_{US}, E_{US}]}{(Y/N')_{US} - (Y/N')_i}$$

This would be an underestimate in the sense that, if added to a similar measure for the share of K/N', the sum would be less than unity. For a proof, see Krueger (1968, p. 644, note).

References

Arrow, K.J., H.B. Chenery, B.S. Minhas and R.M. Solow (1961) 'Capital-labor Substitution and Economic Efficiency', *Review of Economics and Statistics* (August).

Blaug, M. (1967) 'Approaches to educational planning', *Economic Journal* (June).

Bowles, S. (1970) 'Aggregation of labour inputs in the economics of growth and planning: experiments with a two-level CES function', *Journal of Political Economy*, 78(1) (January–February), 68–81.

Denison, E. (1967) *Why Growth Rates Differ* (Washington, DC: Brookings Institution).

Dougherty, C.R.S. (1972) 'Estimates of labour aggregation functions', *Journal of Political Economy*, 80(6) (November–December), 1101–19.

Dougherty, C.R.S. (1974) 'Factor endowments and *per capita* income differences among countries: a note' (London: LSE), mimeo.

Fallon, P.R. (1974) 'The productive roles of workers with different levels of education: an international cross-section study', PhD thesis, University of London.

Fisher, F.M. (1966) *The Identification Problem in Econometrics* (New York: McGraw-Hill).

Folger, J.K. and C.B. Nam (1967) *Education of the American Population: A 1960 Census Monograph* (Washington, DC: US Government Printing Office).

Griliches, Z. (1969) 'Capital–skill complementarity', *Review of Economics and Statistics* (November).

Griliches, Z. (1970) 'Notes on the role of education in production functions and growth accounting', in W.L. Hansen (ed.), *Education, Income, and Human Capital* (New York: Columbia University Press for the National Bureau of Economic Research).

Hicks, J.R. (1970) 'Elasticity of substitution again: substitutes and complements', *Oxford Economic Papers* (November).

Krueger, A.O. (1968) 'Factor endowments and *per capita* income differences among countries', *The Economic Journal* (September).

Lydall, H. (1968) *The Structure of Earnings* (Oxford: Clarendon). Organization for Economic Cooperation and Development (OECD) (1969) *Educational Characteristics of the Labour Force* (Washington, DC: OECD).

Psacharopoulos, G. (1973) *Returns to Education: An International Comparison* (Amsterdam: Elsevier).

Sato, R. and T. Koizumi (1973) 'On the elasticities of substitution and complementarity', *Oxford Economic Papers* (March).

United Nations (1964, 1965) *Demographic Yearbook* (New York: UN).

United Nations (1966) *Growth in World Industry* (New York: UN).

11 Married Women's Participation and Hours

(1980)*

with M. Barton and A. Zabalza

INTRODUCTION

Since 1950 the proportion of wives under 60 who work has risen from 25 to 60 per cent. Although this is one of the major transformations of our time, its causes are little understood. Many people, if asked, would attribute the change to the falling birth rate. Yet, as Figure 11.1 shows, the fertility rate rose during much of the period when female participation also rose. And participation rose sharply among women aged 25–34 as well as among older women.[1] Another possible explanation is the rising real wage of husbands and wives. While one might expect the income effect of these improvements to discourage work, the positive substitution effect of better opportunities for women is likely to outweigh any negative cross-substitution effect of the husband's wage increase. So one asks whether wage changes, among other things, can help to explain the transformation in the working role of women.

This question is intrinsically interesting but is also important for two practical reasons. First, one wants to be able to forecast the future size of the labour force, possibly as a step towards predicting unemployment. Second, one wants to know the strength of labour supply responses in order to evaluate the efficiency cost of various tax and social security policies. It is commonly believed that women's labour supply response is more elastic than men's and may thus be an important possible source of welfare cost.

To explain the evolution of participation using only time series data is clearly going to be very difficult, for husbands' and wives' wages are highly collinear.

* *Economica*, 47 (February 1980), pp. 51–72

This paper arises from work done jointly with Tony Cornford who constructed the basic computer files with great efficiency. We are grateful to O. Ashenfelter, C. Greenhalgh, J. Heckman, D. Metcalf and S. Nickell for hours of instructive discussion on this topic, to OPCS for providing the GHS data, and to the Department of Employment and the Social Science Research Council for financing the study.

Cross-sectional evidence is crucial, and we use data on 3877 families from the 1974 General Household Survey. This means that the study has also a third motivation – to explain which women work and how long they work.

After surveying the theory of participation and hours, we present in section II logit estimates of the factors influencing the participation decision. These suggest that the probability of participating responds with an elasticity of about

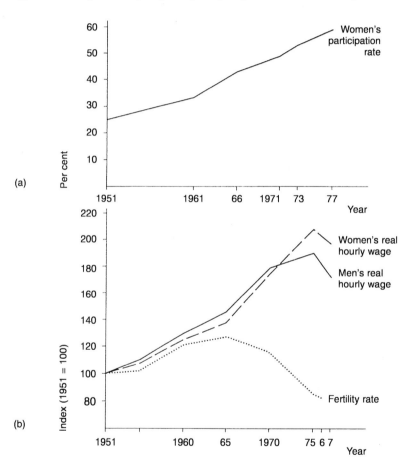

Figure 11.1 (a) Participation rate of married women (20–59); (b) Some possible influences. The participation rates in (a) are those shown in note 1 (p. 223). Real hourly earnings are defined for full-time manual workers (18 and over for women, 21 and over for men) in all industries, excluding extra pay for overtime hours. The fertility rate is defined as total births per 1000 women aged 15–44 in Great Britain. (*Sources*: *Annual Abstract of Statistics 1976, British Labour Statistics Historical Abstract 1886–1968, British Labour Statistics Yearbook 1975, 1976* and *1977*, and *Department of Employment Gazette*.)

Education and Inequality

0.5 to the wife's own wage, and with a negative elasticity of -0.3 to the husband's wage. The estimated income effect is very low. These elasticities explain about a third of the growth of participation up to 1973. However, they may explain most of the growth from 1973 to 1977, since husbands' real wages fell somewhat over that period while wives' real wages rose substantially. But the elasticities we have quoted are about a half of those found in the United States, suggesting a smaller responsiveness here to monetary incentives and a smaller welfare cost of distortions. However, the estimates are necessarily tentative.

The age of the youngest child is another fundamental influence on participation, and the recent fall in family size helps to explain the recent increase in the participation of younger, but not of older, women. Regional differences in participation rates are, other things equal, small. If a wife's husband is unemployed she is much less likely to be found working, but it is difficult to be sure how far this is due to the disincentive effects of the social security system and how far it reflects local labour market conditions.

In sections III and IV we use ordinary least squares (OLS) to analyse the hours of work of those women who do work and the hours of participants and non-participants taken together. The hours of participants appear to be weakly related to wages of husband or wife, and the effect of wages on overall hours (of participants and non-participants) seems to come mainly through their effects on participation. In section V we impose the Tobit framework on the analysis, in order to explain participation and hours by the same fundamental supply relation. This leads to very similar estimates of the effects on overall hours to those got by OLS, but with a more even split between effects via participation and via hours of workers.

Even though the influences we are able to measure account for only a part of the long-term rise in women's participation, we believe they can be used to improve forecasting methods. And they also help us in evaluating the welfare cost of tax and social security policies.

I THEORY

First, some theory. We assume that each woman faces a given wage rate at which she can choose to work any number of hours, or none. Suppose she is unwilling to work at all for less than some wage W^*. If W rises above W^*, the hours that the woman works will, at least initially, rise as W rises, provided the utility function is strictly quasi-concave and twice differentiable.[2] We shall assume the supply function is linear. Thus for $H > 0$ the supply function is

$$H = a_0 + a_1 X + \varepsilon \qquad (1)$$

where H is annual hours, X is a vector of measured variables, including wages, which affect work effort, and ε is a random variable independent of X and with mean zero.

Let us use $\hat{H}$ to describe $(a_0 + a_1 X)$, recognizing that $\hat{H}$ may well be negative for someone whose measured characteristics do not dispose them to work:

$$\hat{H} = a_0 + a_1 X$$

So actual hours are $(\hat{H} + \varepsilon)$ *provided* $(\hat{H} + \varepsilon)$ is positive. If $(\hat{H} + \varepsilon)$ is negative, the person does not work:

$$H = \hat{H} + \varepsilon \qquad \text{if } \hat{H} + \varepsilon > 0$$
$$H = 0 \qquad \text{if } \hat{H} + \varepsilon \leq 0$$

The participation decision

It follows that for a person with given $\hat{H}$, the probability of working is

$$P = \Pr(\hat{H} + \varepsilon > 0)$$
$$= \Pr(\varepsilon > -\hat{H})$$
$$= 1 - F(-\hat{H})$$

where F is the cumulative distribution function of ε. Figure 11.2 illustrates this. If $\hat{H}$ was, for example, 500 hours a year, the probability that the person would participate is the shaded area $(1 - F(-500))$. If the distribution is symmetrical, as we shall assume, this is also equal to $F(\hat{H})$:

$$P = F(\hat{H})$$

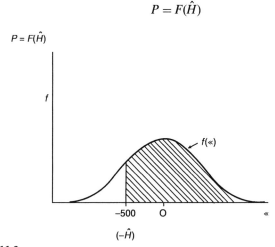

Figure 11.2

The higher $\hat{H}$, the higher the probability of participating. Or, in terms of participation rates, if we compare groups with different values of $\hat{H}$, their expected participation rates will be measured by $F(\hat{H})$. In our particular study we use individual data on participation. We assume that F is the logistic distribution and thus use Logit to explain the participation decision.[3]

Hours of participants

Let us look now at the hours of work of those who are working. Can we estimate a_1 by ordinary least squares regressions for those who participate? Unfortunately not. For participants are a self-selected group and their errors are not a random drawing from the population at large. In fact the expected value of ε for a given participant is clearly related to her $\hat{H}$, thus:[4]

$$E(H \mid H > 0) = E(\hat{H} + \varepsilon \mid \varepsilon > -\hat{H})$$
$$= \hat{H} + E(\varepsilon \mid \varepsilon > -\hat{H})$$
$$= \hat{H} + \frac{1}{1 - F(-\hat{H})} \int_{-\hat{H}}^{\infty} \varepsilon f(\varepsilon) d\varepsilon$$
$$= \hat{H} + \frac{f(-\hat{H})}{1 - F(-\hat{H})} \text{(if } \varepsilon \text{ is normal)}$$

Clearly the unexpected error $E(\varepsilon/\varepsilon > -\hat{H})$ rises steadily as $(-\hat{H})$ rises, and by the same token it falls steadily as $\hat{H}$ rises. Suppose we compare two people, one of whom has measured characteristics (X) that make her less likely to work than the other. Then, if *both* of them are working, it follows that the person with the lower $\hat{H}$ is likely to have a more hard-working nature as indicated by the expected value of her unmeasurable ε.

This is shown in Figure 11.3. For simplicity of exposition we assume for the moment that the distribution of ε is rectangular. The line EBF shows the $\hat{H}$-function ($\hat{H} = a_0 + a_1 X$), while the two lines parallel to it show the range of possible values of H that could be observed with any particular X (treated as a scalar). The diagram implies that no woman for whom X is less than OA will participate, and all of those for whom X is more than OG will participate.[5] The locus of expected hours for participants is $ACBF$. The mean ε for participants is as follows:

If $X =$	$E(\varepsilon \mid H > 0) =$
OA	ε_{max}
OE	$\frac{1}{2}\varepsilon_{max}$
OG	0

The expected value of ε among participants falls monotonically with X.

It follows that if one tried to estimate (1) by an ordinary least squares regression run on a sample of participants, the estimate of a_1 would be biased down owing to the negative correlation between X and ε. We therefore estimate (1) not only by a (biased) OLS regression run on participants, but also by an unbiased Tobit analysis which we shall explain shortly.

Hours of all women

Finally, we may be interested in predicting how the average number of hours worked by participants *and* non-participants will vary with X. This unconditional expectation of hours is given by the expected hours of participants times the probability of participation:

$$E(H) = E(H \mid H > 0).\Pr(H > 0)$$

$$= \left\{ \hat{H} + \frac{1}{1 - F(-\hat{H})} \int_{-\hat{H}}^{\infty} \varepsilon f(\varepsilon) d\varepsilon \right\} F(\hat{H})$$

$$= \left\{ \hat{H} + \frac{f(-\hat{H})}{1 - F(-\hat{H})} \right\} F(\hat{H})$$

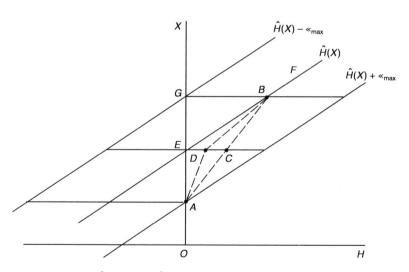

Figure 11.3 The $\hat{H}$-function $\hat{H} = a_0 + a_1 X$ is given by *OEBF*. The predicted hours of participants are given by *ACBF*. The predicted hours of all the sample are given by *OADBF*.

Hours at $X = OE$ are measured by ED $(= \frac{1}{2}\varepsilon_{max} \cdot \frac{1}{2})$. Thus, the locus of unconditional expected hours is the non-linear locus $OADBF$. Note that the elasticity of expected hours with respect to X is simply the sum of the separate elasticities for participation and for hours of participants:

$$\frac{d \log E(H)}{d \log X} = \frac{d \log \Pr(H > 0)}{d \log X} + \frac{d \log E(H/H > 0)}{d \log X}$$

To estimate the expected hours function for all women, one could use an OLS regression of H on X. But this would involve forcing a linear pattern on a relationship that is non-linear owing to the fact that H cannot be less than zero. Once again a better approach is via the Tobit method, though we also show the OLS results.

Tobit analysis

Tobin's problem (1958) was to estimate the demand (or supply) function for a good, from a sample of individuals some of whom did not demand (or supply) any of it. In our case we are concerned with the supply of hours, which cannot be negative. The aim is to estimate the parameters of the $\hat{H}$-function:

$$\hat{H} = a_0 + a_1 X$$

using both the data on hours supplied by participants and the information about those individuals who choose not to participate. To derive the likelihood function, let us first consider non-participants. The likelihood that individual i is not participating is $\Pr(\hat{H}_i + \varepsilon_i < 0)$ which equals $F(-\hat{H}_i)$. The likelihood that individual j is supplying positive hours H_j is $\Pr(\hat{H}_j + \varepsilon_j = H_j)$ which equals $f(H_j - \hat{H}_j)$. Thus, if there are I non-participants and J participants, the likelihood of observing our set of sample values is

$$L = \prod_{i=1}^{I} F(-\hat{H}_i) \prod_{j=1}^{J} f(H_j - \hat{H}_j)$$

$$= \prod_{i=1}^{I} F(-a_0 - a_1 X_i) \prod_{j=1}^{J} f(H_j - a_0 - a_1 X_j)$$

Parameter estimates are obtained by maximizing this likelihood function with respect to the parameters; these estimates are unbiased as the problem of negative correlation between X and ε has been avoided.

We are now ready to look in turn at[6]

(a) participation (logit and OLS estimates);
(b) hours of participants (OLS estimates);

(c) hours of participants and non-participants (OLS estimates);
(d) Tobit estimates of (a)–(c).

II PARTICIPATION

The analysis is based on the 1974 General Household Survey, using data on 3877 married women aged 60 or under (OPCS, 1974). The variables (X) that we use to explain participation are as follows.[7]

(1) *Predicted log gross hourly earnings of wife.* We must use the predicted gross hourly earnings of the wife since for women who do not work we do not know what wage they would be paid. Thus we assume that

$$\ln W = b_0 + b_1 S + u$$

where W is hourly earnings[8] and S is a vector of characteristics relevant to productivity. We estimate this equation using observations for participants only. There are some problems with this since participants are a self-selected group and an individual's u may affect whether she works. For example, an individual with an unfavourable S may work only if she has a positive u. Thus among participants u will not be independent of S. Heckman (1980) has proposed a method of dealing with this problem, but his own work showed that the wage equation estimated on participants only was not seriously biased. The estimated wage equation is shown in the Appendix, Table 11.1.

We use the predicted *log* gross hourly earnings since the appropriate earnings function is in the logs and it is econometrically preferable to use the predicted value from the estimated equation rather than to transform it to its antilog, unless there is a behavioural presumption that it is the natural value that affects hours. There is no obvious presumption that this is so. We shall often for simplicity of speech refer to a person's hourly earnings as her wage.

(2) *Gross hourly earnings of husband.* We use actual recorded hourly earnings except when the husband is unemployed or self-employed, where we use the hourly earnings predicted from an equation run on employed men. We catch the effect of husband's unemployment through a separate dummy variable (see below), but even where the husband is temporarily unemployed, we expect the husband's wage (if in work) to affect the wife's current labour supply.[9] To examine whether the hybrid variable used for men was causing problems, we also ran all estimations using predicted wages throughout. The results were very similar.

(3) *Net annual unearned income.* This is rent, dividends and interest multiplied by 0.67 (to allow for tax) and multiplied by 2.36 (to allow for the average level of under reporting), *plus* family allowance net of tax, *plus* owner-occupier's imputed rent *minus* net mortgage interest.[10] Since over 95 per cent

Table 11.1   Analyses to explain participation, hours of participants and hours of participants and non-participants

	Participation		Hours of participants		Hours of participants and non-participants	The 'Tobit' line
	Logit (1)[a]	OLS (2)	Net wage (3)	Gross wage (4)	Gross wage (5)	Gross wage (6)[c]
Own log wage	0.26	0.20	74	99	315	576
(predicted £ per hr)	(0.04)[b]	(0.04)	(72)	(65)	(58)	(90)
Husband's wage	−0.13	−0.10	−116	−121	−179	−335
(£ per hr)	(0.02)	(0.01)	(31)	(31)	(23)	(42)
Net unearned income	−0.12	−0.09		−27	−84	−271
(£ 000 p.a.)	(0.03)	(0.02)		(47)	(35)	(69)
Intercept			−13			
(£ 000 p.a.)			(46)			
Unemployed husband	−0.34	−0.27	76	77	−301	−748
	(0.05)	(0.04)	(92)	(92)	(62)	(121)
Youngest child 0–2	−0.81	−0.67	−1053	−1036	−1306	−2393
	(0.03)	(0.03)	(74)	(71)	(49)	(66)
3–5	−0.49	−0.41	−793	−779	−1003	−1515
	(0.03)	(0.03)	(66)	(65)	(52)	(64)
6–10	−0.24	−0.19	−522	−513	−600	−840
	(0.03)	(0.03)	(57)	(57)	(49)	(60)
11–13	−0.13	−0.10	−327	−321	−338	−509
	(0.04)	(0.03)	(60)	(60)	(54)	(81)
14–15	0.04	0.02	−250	−243	−142	−132
	(0.05)	(0.04)	(61)	(61)	(59)	(95)
16–17	0.01	−0.02	−238	−237	−232	−162
	(0.09)	(0.07)	(114)	(114)	(109)	(182)
18+	−0.06	−0.07	−314	−310	−335	−341
	(0.12)	(0.10)	(170)	(170)	(148)	(256)
No. of children	0.04	0.03	−3	−2	26	86
	(0.01)	(0.01)	(20)	(20)	(15)	(28)
Coloured, West Indies	0.24	0.19	438	426	527	725
	(0.13)	(0.09)	(143)	(143)	(143)	(235)
Other coloured	−0.08	−0.06	327	316	79	52
	(0.08)	(0.06)	(125)	(125)	(99)	(179)
Irish-born	0.14	0.11	−2	−5	115	252
	(0.06)	(0.05)	(78)	(78)	(71)	(125)
Long-standing illness	−0.07	−0.06	−54	−51	−124	−174
	(0.02)	(0.02)	(35)	(35)	(30)	(52)
Age: under 25	0.05	0.03	105	100	100	148
	(0.03)	(0.03)	(54)	(54)	(46)	(67)
25–34	0.04	0.03	58	54	77	118
	(0.02)	(0.02)	(38)	(38)	(34)	(46)
45–54	−0.12	−0.09	−131	−126	−244	−314
	(0.02)	(0.02)	(40)	(40)	(37)	(52)
55–60	−0.24	−0.21	−266	−256	−514	−668
	(0.03)	(0.03)	(59)	(59)	(52)	(79)

Table 11.1 continued

	Participation		Hours of participants		Hours of participants and non-participants	The 'Tobit' line
	Logit (1)[a]	OLS (2)	Net wage (3)	Gross wage (4)	Gross wage (5)	Gross wage (6)[c]
North	−0.01	0.01	12	12	13	−15
	(0.03)	(0.03)	(63)	(63)	(54)	(78)
Yorkshire and Humberside	−0.06	−0.05	−82	−83	−83	−173
	(0.03)	(0.03)	(60)	(60)	(51)	(73)
North West	0.04	0.03	82	83	88	141
	(0.03)	(0.03)	(54)	(54)	(47)	(62)
East Midlands	−0.04	−0.03	63	64	−18	−62
	(0.04)	(0.03)	(65)	(65)	(54)	(6)
West Midlands	0.07	0.06	86	87	111	181
	(0.03)	(0.03)	(55)	(55)	(49)	(67)
East Anglia	−0.05	−0.04	−95	−95	−115	−165
	(0.05)	(0.04)	(82)	(82)	(698)	(112)
South East (excl. GLC)[d]	0.03	0.03	−79	−79	−13	4
	(0.03)	(0.03)	(49)	(49)	(43)	(59)
South West	0.01	0.01	−55	−54	−45	−29
	(0.04)	(0.04)	(64)	(64)	(55)	(88)
Wales	−0.11	−0.08	142	142	−46	−187
	(0.04)	(0.04)	(72)	(71)	(58)	(98)
Scotland	−0.01	−0.002	101	100	48	35
	(0.04)	(0.03)	(58)	(58)	(49)	(7)
Constant	0.60	0.99	1820	1812	1668	1820
		(0.05)				
R^2		0.20	0.23	0.23	0.27	
log likelihood	−2200					−18 287

Notes:
[a] The logit coefficients shown are $\partial P/\partial X = \gamma a_1 P(1 - P)$ evaluated at the mean of P.
[b] Standard errors are in parentheses.
[c] The Tobit values have been rescaled by the estimated value for $1/\sigma$ of 0.000903.
[d] The omitted region is the Greater London Council area. The net wage and intercept variables are defined in section III.

of families in the sample were paying the standard rate of tax, little bias is introduced by taking the standard tax rate as exogenous and as applying to the whole range of income from rent, dividends, interest and Family Allowance. Any alternative approach would be enormously more complicated. Note that the alternative of using gross unearned income is not open, unless imputed rent and rent, interest and dividends are entered separately, since imputed rent is not taxable.

(4) *Age of youngest child* (7 dummies). These dummies, along with the total number of children, have more explanatory power as judged by $\bar{R}^2$ than the numbers of children in each of the age groups shown. The omitted category is 'No child'.

(5)–(10) *Number of children*; *Ethnic background* (3 dummies); *Has long standing illness* (dummy); *Age* (4 dummies); *Region* (10 dummies); *Husband currently unemployed* (dummy).

Results

The first column of Table 11.1 shows the results of the logit analysis. The statistic shown is the effect of each variable on participation evaluated at the mean of P (i.e., γa_1 $(0.54)(0.46))$.[11] For continuous variables or for dummy variables having only small effects, there is no difficulty in interpreting the statistic; but for dummy variables with large coefficients, the effect, as we shall show, requires some further computation. The second column of the table gives the corresponding OLS estimates. The results of the two exercises are similar, and we shall comment only on the logit results. The elasticities are in Table 11.2.

Table 11.2 Elasticities

	Independent variable		
Dependent variables	Own wage[a]	Husband's wage	Income
Participation			
Logit	0.49	−0.28	−0.04
OLS	0.37	−0.21	−0.03
Hours of participants			
OLS	0.08	−0.10	−0.003
Hours of participants and non-participants			
OLS	0.44	−0.28	−0.02
Tobit	0.49	−0.32	−0.04

Note:
[a] All own wage elasticities are calculated on the basis of gross wages.

Wage and income effects

The own wage elasticity is 0.49 and the husband's wage elasticity −0.28. The income elasticity is very low, −0.04. These wage elasticities are rather lower than those typically found from individual data in the United States, but the low income elasticity is echoed there. The equation implies that a simultaneous doubling of husbands' and wives' real wages from their 1951 levels while holding other factors constant would increase the participation rate of wives by 11 percentage points. Between 1951 and 1973 both husbands' and wives' wages roughly doubled, and income rose by rather less. Yet the participation rate of married women under 60 rose by 29 percentage points. So our estimates of income and wage effects explain less than half of the long-term rise in women's labour force participation. This is consistent with some US analyses of individual data which do not suggest that much of the growth of women's participation can be explained by the growth of real wages and real income (Schultz, 1976).

Turning to the more recent past, between 1973 and 1977, the real weekly wages of women rose by about 10 per cent while the gross real wages of men fell by nearly as much, and real unearned income (including the real value of tax allowances) fell substantially. Statistically this explains most of the increase in women's participation since 1973, though in fact our elasticities should not really be applied slavishly to short-run changes since other long-run forces must also have been at work in the recent past. An additional explanation must be the much greater uncertainty affecting all families, which would make them feel poorer even if their average income had not changed. It can hardly be a coincidence that in this recession both personal savings *and* wives' work have increased markedly.[12]

However at this point we should enter a caveat. Our results depend heavily on the functional form used: linear in the log of wife's wage and in the natural value of the husband's wage. We adopted this form because it fitted slightly better than the function where both wages were entered in log form. In the latter case the difference between wife's and husband's wage elasticity was somewhat less, but more important is the fact that a projection of the function back through time would account for a much smaller part of the growth in women's participation.[13] We therefore regard our findings in this section as fairly tentative.

Effect of young children

We can now look at other influences on participation. The most important of these is of course the family responsibilities of the wife.[14] Suppose we take a woman who has average own and husband's wage and average income, a working husband, and is white, not born in Ireland, in good health, aged 25–34, and living in Greater London. If she has one child and that child is under three, she has a probability of participation that is about 65 percentage points less than someone with the same characteristics but no children.[15] If her youngest child is between three and six, her probability of participation is about 41 percentage points less, and if the youngest child is between six and ten, only 16 percentage points less. If the child is above fourteen, its effect on participation is either measured as positive or is insignificant. On top of this, the number of children has a positive effect on participation. Since larger families have lower real income than smaller families with the same wage and income opportunities, the mother may be driven out to work.

Since only children under six have any major effect on participation, changes in family size cannot have a very large direct effect on participation. For example, if children are born three years apart and every women decides to have two children in her lifetime instead of three, then within six years the participation rate of women under 60 (assuming the same number of women in each group from 20 to 60) will have risen by 5 per cent.[16] This change will be concentrated among women aged 25–34. But as an earlier footnote shows, the increased participation has been spread across all ages. Moreover, all ages were increasing their participation during the period 1951–66 when the fertility rate rose by about a quarter.[17] Since 1966 the fertility rate has fallen by over a third,[18] yet the rate of labour force participation has been growing at a slightly lower rate of growth. So, while fertility levels must be having an effect, it is difficult to suppose that this effect is the main force at work.

Ethnic background, health and age

Wives born in the West Indies or in Ireland are more likely to go out to work. If the woman is ill, she is somewhat less likely to work. The older a woman is (holding family responsibilities constant), the less likely she is to work. It is unfortunately not possible to say from one year's cross-section to what extent this is an effect of age and to what extent it reflects different lifetime behaviour patterns by different cohorts.

Regional differences

The literature on participation has often pointed to the differences between regions. However, when other things are held constant, the differences are less than is sometimes supposed. Taking Greater London as the standard, the main differences are that participation is some 7 percentage points higher in the West Midlands and 3 points higher in the rest of South East; while it is 11 percentage points lower in Wales, 6 points lower in Yorkshire and Humberside, and 5 points lower in East Anglia.[19]

Clearly these differences in part reflect differences in the degree of urbanization between regions.[20] Unfortunately the 1974 GHS tapes do not allow one to identify the type of urban or rural area in which each household was situated. The 1971 tapes did separate individual households into those in conurbations, other urban areas, semi-rural areas and rural areas. Greenhalgh (1977a) then did an OLS regression of participation on this variable and also on the set of regional dummies. The coefficients on the locational dummies for the individual household were:

Conurbation	Other urban	Semi-rural	Rural
+0.031	–	–0.033	–0.160

The coefficients on the regional dummies were jointly insignificant at the 95 per cent level. We can now take the estimated effects of household location and see to what extent they explain the estimated regional effect in Table 11.1. Taking Greater London as the standard and using Census data on the residential structure in each region, we find the predicted differences shown in column (1) below. Next to these we list the differences estimated in Table 11.1. Residential structure goes a long way to explaining the low participation rate in Wales, Yorkshire and Humberside, East Anglia, and East Midlands, though it does not explain the high rates in the West Midlands and the South East.

	Predicted from residential structure (1)	From Table 11.1 (2)
North	–0.039	–0.006
Yorkshire and Humberside	–0.027	–0.063
North West	–0.017	0.041
East Midlands	–0.040	–0.041
West Midlands	–0.026	0.069
East Anglia	–0.067	–0.045
South East (excluding GLC)	–0.064	0.034
South West	–0.054	0.006
Wales	–0.060	–0.111
Scotland	–0.046	–0.007

Unemployed husband

Wives with unemployed husbands are 31 percentage points less likely to work than otherwise similar wives with husbands at work.[21] This is a striking finding. The gross difference has often been observed, but we have now confirmed that it exists holding other things constant.

What does it mean? One possibility is that it reflects the working of the Supplementary Benefit system. About half of the families of unemployed men receive Supplementary Benefit, which, after the disregards, is reduced pound for pound for any earnings of the wife. This creates an incentive for wives to stop work when their husbands become unemployed, and cases have been observed where this happens. However, a wife presumably would do this only if she expected her husband to remain unemployed for some time, as it is not always easy to go back to work the moment you want to do so. As the average expected duration of unemployment among men becoming unemployed was under 20 weeks, many wives might consider it a bit risky to stop work for such a comparatively short period of time.

On another interpretation, wives who have unemployed husbands are less likely to participate than others because they live in local areas where there is less work for husbands as well as wives. In time series analysis it has been found in Britain (Corry and Roberts, 1974) and the United States (Mincer, 1966) that female participation typically falls when employment opportunities deteriorate, the substitution (discouraged worker) effect outweighing the income (added worker) effect of husbands losing their jobs.[22] If so, the same phenomenon could explain differences between local (rather than regional) areas in participation. Unfortunately the data do not enable us to separate the 'area' from the 'person' effect, and one must suppose that our result reflects a mixture of both of these.

III HOURS WORKED BY PARTICIPANTS

We now turn to the hours worked by those who participate. This raises a problem we have not so far needed to face; for the wage that determines whether a woman works at all is the net wage she would be paid on her first few hours of work. And in Britain that wage is her gross wage.[23] However, once tax comes into the picture, a wife's hours are determined by her marginal *net* wage (which determines the relevant slope of the budget line) and by the location of the budget line. Ignoring for the moment the husband's wages and unearned income, the wife's budget line is as shown in Figure 11.4.[24] Y^0 is the wife's earned income allowance. As long as $H < Y^0/W$, the wife can increase Y at the rate W for each hour worked. After that point has been reached income can be increased only at a rate $W(1 - t^0)$, where t^0 is the standard rate of tax.

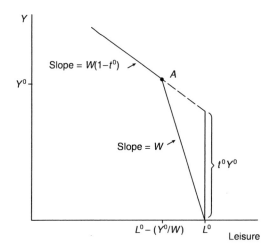

Figure 11.4

Thus the first segment of the budget line has the equation

$$Y = WH \qquad H < Y^0/W$$

and the second segment has the equation

$$Y = WH - t^0(WH - Y^0)$$
$$= W(1 - t^0)H + t^0 Y^0 \qquad H > Y^0/W$$

Or, more generally, we can write the budget constraint as

$$Y = W(1 - t)H + tY^0$$
$$\text{where } t = 0 \qquad H < Y^0/W$$
$$t = t^0 \qquad H > Y^0/W$$

Individuals may choose one of four general alternatives:

(a) do not work (corner solution);
(b) work $H < Y^0/W$ (interior solution);
(c) work $H = Y^0/W$ (corner solution);
(d) work $H > Y^0/W$ (interior solution).

Inspection of the data reveal that few individuals work $H = Y^0/W$. In Britain in 1974 Y^0 was £625 per year, and the distribution of women's annual earnings was as shown in the Appendix, Table 11A.2. The density is somewhat higher in the neighbourhood £625 than elsewhere, and the fact that few people earn exactly £625 must presumably be due to the fact that individuals cannot choose their hours with the necessary precision. One could of course assume that people with hours within $\pm \alpha$ hours of Y^0/W were in fact at corner solutions and use maximum likelihood methods to estimate the structure of the utility function. However, in the present paper we simply assume that all individuals were at interior solutions.[25]

There remains however one serious problem: the tax rate is endogenous.[26] For the complete model is as follows:

$$H = a_0 + a_1 \ln\{W(1-t)\} + a_2(tY^0 + I) + a_3 Z + \varepsilon \tag{2}$$

$$\begin{cases} t = 0 & H < Y^0/W \\ t = t^0 & H > Y^0/W \end{cases} \tag{3}$$

where I is net unearned income and Z is a vector of other relevant variables. The more hard-working people (with higher ε) are more likely to be taxpayers. Thus, if (2) were estimated by ordinary least squares, the coefficient on $W(1-t)$ would be biased down and the coefficient on tY^0 would be biased up. To deal with this problem we use two-stage least squares.[27] In the first stage we regress a dummy variable t, where $t = t^0$ for taxpayers and $t = 0$ for non-taxpayers, on $\ln W$, I and Z. Then we estimate (2), using predicted t instead of actual t. We continue to measure $\ln W$ by the predicted log wage, even though we know the actual wage of every participant. The reason is that wage is measured by annual earnings divided by (weeks times usual weekly hours). If hours are mis-measured, this introduces a spurious element of negative correlation between W and H. The dependent variable is annual hours, which have generally been found a more appropriate variable than weekly hours, given that married women's weeks vary largely owing to voluntary choice. The results are given in Table 11.1, column (3).

Wage and income effects

The own wage effect is estimated to be very small and not significantly different from zero, but we have already explained that it is biased down relative to the slope of the true supply function (2). The result is similar to US results (Schultz, 1976). The estimate of the net wage elasticity is 0.06. The husband's wage elasticity is -0.10 and the income elasticity negligible. Thus a simultaneous equi-proportional increase in husband's and wife's wage would

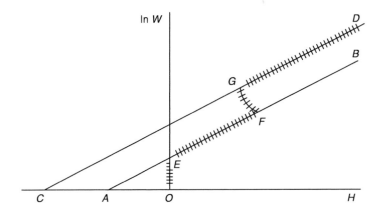

Figure 11.5

lead to little change in hours. This may or may not help to explain why the number of part-time women workers in the labour force has grown so sharply since 1961, while the number of full-time women workers has slightly fallen.[28]

In case we are suffering from some econometric bias associated with the use of $\hat{t}$, we also estimate the reduced form of (2) and (3) imposing on it the incorrect linear form

$$H = b_0 + b_1 \ln W + b_2 I + b_3 Z + v \qquad (4)$$

The true shape is illustrated in Figure 11.5. The line AB represents (2) given $t = 0$. The line CD represents (2) given that $t = t^0$. (Remember that $b_1 > 0$ and probably $b_2 < 0$.) The individual participates if $\ln W$ exceeds OE. As the wage increases she expands her labour supply along EB. But when she reaches point F, $HW = Y^0$. If the wage rises further, she will for a while continue to earn the same income by working less and her labour supply will fall along the line FG. Throughout this range she is at a corner solution like that at point A in Figure 11.4. (with the corner moving horizontally to the right). Once G is reached, the individual is again at an interior solution and, as the wage increases, she moves out along GD. Thus the true supply function consists of the locus $OEFGD$ (as hatched). Though this function is non-linear, it is still interesting to examine the results of forcing a line through the points from E onwards. One would expect that, relative to the net wage supply function, the gross wage function would be biased to have a steeper slope (i.e. a lower $dH/d \ln W$). In fact there is no significant difference.

Other effects

Very young children affect the hours of participants much as they do the participation decision. People with a young child under three will work 1000 hours a year less than those without children. But even if their children are older, mothers will still tend to work rather less. The number of children seems to have little effect on hours.

If they go out to work, coloured women are likely to work longer. Older women are more likely to work part-time, but this effect is not as strong as one might expect. The only significant regional difference in hours is in Wales, where working women spend about 140 more hours a year at work than in Greater London.

IV   HOURS WORKED BY PARTICIPANTS AND NON-PARTICIPANTS

We can next look at hours worked including all the zero hours worked by non-participants. If we can explain this, we can explain the total labour input from married women. We give in column (5) our OLS estimate, even though a linear estimate is incorrect since the relationship between expected hours and X is nonlinear. We use wife's gross wage and net unearned income, the same variables as in the participation equation.[29]

The own wage elasticity is 0.44, which is about equal to the sum of the OLS wage elasticity of participation plus the wage elasticity of hours for participants. The husband's wage elasticity is -0.28, which is also roughly consistent with the estimates from the participation and hours equation. Once again the income elasticity is small. The other effects are consistent with the estimates we have already obtained.

V   THE TOBIT ANALYSIS

Finally we come to our Tobit results. Again we use the wife's gross wage, since the gross wage is also the marginal wage for three-quarters of all women and using the predicted marginal tax rate would not correctly represent the structure of the participation decision.[30] Column (6) shows the coefficients of the 'Tobit line':

$$\hat{H} = a_0 + a_1 X$$

These are not of course the coefficients of an expected hours equation for participants, since, as Figure 11.1 shows, this is also affected by the average

Table 11.3   Tobit estimates: effects of varying wife's predicted log wage

Wife's predicted log wage	$\hat{H}$ (1)	Predicted participation rate (2)	Average hours of participants (3)	Average hours of participants and non-participants (4) = (2).(3)
(μ = −0.46) (σ = 0.22)				
−0.7	94.8	0.534	918.1	490.3
−0.5	210.1	0.595	965.1	554.9
−0.3	325.4	0.616	1012.1	623.5
−0.1	440.7	0.655	1064.6	697.3
+0.1	555.9	0.692	1119.2	774.5

Notes:
(a) $\hat{H} = 498.3 + 576.4 \ln \hat{W}$ where the constant has been corrected to include the sum of the means of all excluded variables times their coefficients.
(b) The predicted participation rate equals $F(H/\sigma)$ where $\sigma = 1107.4$ and where F is the cumulative of the standard normal distribution.
(c) The average hours of participants and non-participations are given by the Tobit expected value locus, $E(H|\hat{H}) = \{\hat{H}F(\hat{H}/\sigma) + \sigma f(\hat{H}/\sigma)\}$.

positive error term for participants and its joint distribution with the X variables. Nor are they the coefficients of an expected hours equation for participants and non-participants, which is affected not only by the errors among participants but also by the implied probabilities of participation.

The meaning and power of the Tobit approach can be brought out by taking the main variables of interest and constructing for each of them tables like Table 11.3. In this table all variables except own predicted log wage are set at their mean and we now trace out the effect of varying own wage upon

(a) $\hat{H}$;
(b)   the probability of participation;
(c)   the expected hours of participants;
(d)   the expected hours of participants and non-participants.

As the wife's wage rises, both the probability of participating and the expected hours if working rise. The overall effect is to raise unconditional expected hours. The estimated elasticity (0.49) is very similar to that obtained by

OLS.[31] We can also do the same exercise for the other variables and the results are shown in Table 11.2. For participants, the elasticities along the Tobit line are of course much greater than those we have quoted, and they provide the proper basis for calculating the welfare costs of distortions among participants.[32]

VI CONCLUDING COMMENTS

We have explained a good deal of the differences in labour supply among the women of today. We have also obtained estimates of wage and income effects which explain between a third and a half of the postwar increase in participation. More work is needed to explain the time series. For example, there may have been a reduction in job rationing (especially of part-time jobs), which requires the simultaneous estimation of a model of supply and demand for female labour on which we are now embarking. But the effects we have measured (assuming they are correct) can already help to improve forecasting, by proceeding as follows:

(a)   Use our estimates to isolate the 'unexplained growth' in participation, and make assumptions about the future course of this 'unexplained growth'.

(b)   Forecast the value of those variables whose effects we do measure, and use our estimates to predict the consequential changes in participation.

(c)   Adding (a) and (b) will give a forecast total change in participation.

This should be better than crude extrapolation of trends.

Appendix

Table 11A.1 Regression to predict wife's log hourly earnings

Constant	−1.07	Experience (years)	
Left full-time education at		Under 5	0.09
15	0.05		(0.03)
	(0.03)	5–9	0.01
16	0.14		(0.01)
	(0.03)	10–19	−0.01
17	0.22		(0.00)
	(0.05)	20–29	0.00
18	0.33		(0.00)
	(0.06)	30–39	−0.00
19+	0.75		(0.00)
	(0.04)	40+	−0.02
Father's occupation[a]			(0.01)
Professional and managerial	0.16	Coloured, West Indies	0.04
	(0.04)		(0.10)
Other manual	0.08	Other coloured	−0.12
	(0.04)		(0.09)
Skilled	0.06	Irish-born	−0.00
	(0.04)		(0.05)
Semi-skilled	−0.03	Long-standing illness	−0.02
	(0.04)		(0.02)
Non-professional self-employed	0.05		
	(0.05)	R^2	0.22
Other	0.11	N	2206
	(0.06)		

Note:
[a] Father's occupation is classified according to the Registrar-General's Socioeconomic Groups as follows:

Professional and managerial	1–6	Unskilled	14
Other non-manual	7–9	Non-professional self-employed	15–17
Skilled manual	11–12	Others	19, Y
Semi-skilled	10, 13, 18		

The omitted category is unskilled.

219

Table 11A.2   Annual earnings of married
women under 60

Earnings (£ p.a.)	Percentage	
Under 12	41.1	
12–112	3.9	
112–212	4.5	
212–312	3.8	
312–412	4.1	
412–512	4.2	
512–537	1.1	
537–562	1.3	4.5
562–587	0.9	
587–612	1.2	
612–637	1.1	
637–662	1.3	4.7
662–687	1.1	
687–712	1.2	
712–812	3.4	
812–912	3.1	
912–1012	3.1	
1012–1112	2.4	
1112–1212	3.0	
1212–1312	2.2	
1312–1412	2.1	
1412–1512	1.3	
1512–1612	1.5	
1612 and above	6.0	
All	100.0	
N (=100.0%)	4321	

Table 11A.3 Means and standard deviations of all variables (excluding wives of unemployed husbands)

	Participants and non-participants		Participants	
	Mean	S.D.	Mean	S.D.
Participation	0.56	0.50	NA	NA
Annual hours	739	817	1317	655
Own log wage (predicted) (gross) (log £ per hr)	−0.46	0.22	−0.45	0.23
Own log wage (predicted) (net) (log £ per hr)	−0.66	0.21	−0.68	0.21
Husband's wage (£ per hr)	1.13	0.56	1.10	0.48
Net unearned income (£ p.a.)	157	305	146	273
Intercept (£ p.a.)	269	314	272	279
Youngest child: 0–2	0.20	0.40	0.07	0.26
3–5	0.15	0.35	0.12	0.32
6–10	0.17	0.37	0.19	0.40
11–13	0.07	0.26	0.09	0.28
14–15	0.05	0.21	0.06	0.25
16–17	0.01	0.11	0.01	0.12
18+	0.01	0.08	0.01	0.08
No. of children	1.29	1.24	1.11	1.24
Coloured, West Indies	0.01	0.08	0.01	0.09
Other coloured	0.01	0.11	0.01	0.10
Irish-born	0.03	0.16	0.03	0.17
Long-standing illness	0.18	0.39	0.17	0.38
Age: under 25	0.12	0.33	0.10	0.30
25–34	0.32	0.47	0.27	0.44
45–54	0.24	0.43	0.27	0.45
55–60	0.08	0.27	0.08	0.27

Table 11A.4 Correlations

	Participation	Annual hours	Own log wage (predicted) (gross)	Own log wage (predicted) (net)	Husband's wage	Net unearned income	Intercept	Unemployed husband
Participants and non-participants								
Participation	–							-0.09
Annual hours	0.02	–						-0.06
Own log wage (predicted) (gross)	0.02	0.02	–					-0.04
Own log wage (predicted) (net)	-0.17	-0.17	0.93	–				-0.03
Husband's wage	0.07	-0.09	0.38	0.35	–			-0.09
Net unearned income	-0.06	-0.06	0.24	0.19	0.33	–		0.00
Intercept	-0.00	-0.00	0.25	0.17	0.33	0.99	–	-0.00
Unemployed husband	-0.09	-0.06	-0.04	-0.03	-0.09	0.00	-0.00	–
Participants								
Annual hours		–						0.04
Own log wage (predicted) (gross)		0.01	–					0.00
Own log wage (predicted) (net)		-0.15	0.93	–				0.00
Husband's wage		-0.09	0.40	0.38	–			-0.07
Net unearned income		-0.04	0.20	0.18	0.28	–		0.01
Intercept		0.03	0.24	0.17	0.29	0.99	–	0.01
Unemployed husband		0.04	0.00	0.00	-0.07	0.01	0.01	–

Notes

1. The participation rates by age were:

	20–24	25–34	35–44	45–54	55–59	All aged 20–59
1951	36.6	24.4	25.7	23.7	15.6	25.0
1961	41.4	29.5	36.4	35.3	26.0	33.7
1966	43.9	34.3	48.6	49.8	38.4	43.5
1971	46.7	38.4	54.5	57.0	45.5	49.0
1973	51.3	43.6	60.1	62.6	47.6	53.9
1977	54.9	48.8	68.0	68.1	50.8	59.4

See *Department of Employment Gazette.*

2. For an illustration of this using the Stone–Geary utility function, see Barzel and McDonald (1973).

3. Thus we assume that the probability (P) of participation is given by

$$P = \frac{1}{1 + e^{-\gamma\hat{H}}} = \frac{1}{1 + e^{-y(a_0 + a_1X)}}.$$

Maximizing the likelihood of the observed decisions, given the Xs, yields estimates of γa_0 and γa_1, from which we derive the estimated effects of the X's shown in Table 11.1, column (1). We also used OLS and obtained very similar results, as did Schultz (1976) for the United States. (If $F(.)$ followed the cumulative normal distribution we should instead use probit analysis, but in fact the logistic and the cumulative normal distributions have very similar shapes.)

4. For the normal distribution

$$\int_{-\hat{H}}^{\infty} \varepsilon f(\varepsilon) d\varepsilon = f(-\hat{H})$$

since, if z is the standard normal variable,

$$\frac{d}{dz}f(z) = \frac{d}{dz}\frac{1}{\sqrt{2\pi}}e^{-(\frac{1}{2}Z^2)} = -zf(z)$$

and hence

$$\int_{z^0}^{\infty} f(z)dz = f(z^0)$$

5. Using the rectangular distribution one can easily see the relationship between the participation response and the hours response (a_1). For X between OA and OG, $dP/dX = 1/AG = a_1/2\varepsilon_{max}$. Thus the response is greater the greater a_1 and

the smaller the spread of individual tastes. (All elasticities are greater the less the spread of tastes.)
6. For an analysis of US data on similar lines see Schultz (1976).
7. The small number of self-employed women are treated as non-participants since for the subsequent analysis we do not know their annual weeks worked. This did not affect our results on participation.
8. Hourly earnings equal annual earnings divided by annual weeks times weekly hours. The same measure is used for husbands.
9. We also ran all our regressions excluding families where the husband was unemployed. The results were very similar to those reported below.
10. For the figure of 2.36, see Layard *et al.* (1978), Appendix 4, Table 1. Imputed rent is measured by gross value since, for tenants, average rent $\simeq$ average gross value, and the elasticity of rent with respect to gross value is approximately unity. Net mortgage interest is based on gross payment to building societies times 0.67 times the fraction of the payment that is interest, predicted by the husband's age.
11. Since

$$P = \frac{1}{1 + e^{-\nu(a_0 + a_1 X)}}$$

$$\frac{\partial P}{\partial X} = \gamma \frac{e^{-\nu(a_0 + a_1 X)}}{\left\{1 + e^{-\nu(a_0 + a_1 X)}\right\}^2} a_1$$

$$= \gamma a_1 P(1 - P)$$

12. As we point out later on, one might have expected participation to fall in the current recession, so powerful forces must have been at work to increase it.
13. The values were

	R^2	Own wage elasticity	Husband's wage elasticity
(a) Function using husband's absolute wage	0.219	0.37	−0.21
(b) Function using log husband's wage	0.213	0.32	−0.21

Using formulation (a) the *de facto* husband's wage elasticity has been more or less constant over time since participation and husbands' wages have risen at about the same rate. Using formulation (b) the *de facto* husband's wage elasticity was much larger in absolute size in the past, since

$$\varepsilon_H(\text{evaluated at 1950}) = \varepsilon_H(\text{evaluated at 1974})\frac{P_{74}}{P_{50}}$$

where ε_H is the husband's elasticity, and P_{74} and P_{50} are the participation rates in 1974 and 1950 respectively.

14. One could of course argue that these are affected by the earning opportunities of the wife, high wages leading to fewer children. If this were so, the estimates of Table 11.1 would underestimate the total effects of wage changes on participation. However, if Table 11.1 is estimated without the children variables, the wage and income effects are practically unaffected.

15. To obtain this number, one computes

$$P = \frac{1}{1 + e^{-va1X}}$$

for the two relevant X vectors. The result is very similar to the figure of $(-0.67 + 0.03)$ read off the OLS analysis.

16. This is $0.65 \ (3/40) = 0.05$. Suppose we call the age at which a woman i has her first child T_i. Then initially all women aged between T_i and $T_i + 9$ have youngest child aged under three (assuming one child born every three years and three children per completed family). In addition all women aged $T_i + 9$ to $T_i + 12$ have youngest child aged between three and five. If instead the completed family size is two, then in the new steady state (reached after six years) all women aged T_i to $T_i + 6$ have youngest child aged under three and all aged $T_i + 6$ to $T_i + 9$ have youngest child aged between three and five. So the net effect is to 'free' three cohorts of mothers from having youngest child under three. This raises participation by 0.65 over a three-year period. If this effect is averaged over the 40 years for which we are calculating the aggregate participation rate, this aggregate rate rises by $0.65 \ (3/40)$. During the transition the effect is of course less. For example, after three years all women aged T_i to $T_i + 6$ have youngest child under three and all women aged $T_i + 6$ to $T_i + 12$ have youngest child aged between three and five. The example is artificial because reductions in the size of completed family may be accompanied by a greater spacing between children. If so, this reduces the effect on participation.

17. Central Statistical Office, *Social Trends* (1976), p. 64.

18. From 2.77 to 1.77: OPCS (1977), p. 44.

19. The hypothesis that all the regional coefficients are simultaneously zero can be rejected at the 5 per cent level, though it is just acceptable at the 2 per cent level.

20. Unemployment does not show up as a clearly important influence. The correlation between the set of dummy coefficients and the unemployment rate is 0.28 (*t*-statistic $= 0.8$); the result is the same whether the total unemployment rate is taken or the unemployment rate for females.

21. -0.31 differs from -0.34 shown in Table 11.1, column (1), owing to the logit formulation.

22. In the present recession women's participation has not fallen, presumably owing to the factors discussed above.

23. In 1974, the tax (if any) paid by a family not paying higher rate tax or investment income surcharge was

    0.33   (husband's income–husband's allowances)
   +0.33   (wife's earnings–wife's allowance);

if the latter term were positive, and if the latter term were negative, it was

    0.33   (husband's income–husband's allowances).

So the marginal tax rate on the wife's earnings was zero if she earned less than her allowance, and in a few families it was zero for even higher levels of earnings, when the husband had not exhausted his allowances.

24. Figure 11.4 ignores higher rates of tax and the effect of means-tested benefits.

25. In similar works, Greenhalgh (1977b) has found that omitting individuals with earnings within £50 of the allowance makes little differences to the estimated coefficients.

26. Approximately half the women who work pay tax on their earnings.

27. Unfortunately the structure of the model is not linear since t is a function of HW, rather than a weighted sum of H and W. It is not clear how much this matters.

28. *Social Trends* (1976), p. 96: *Department of Employment Gazette* (November 1973). Note that one cannot infer from the conditional supply function for an individual how average aggregate hours of workers will change in response to a wage change. For example, let us suppose that the Tobit model is correct and that a simultaneous doubling of husband's and wife's wages would lead to an increase in the individual probability of participation *and* in conditional expected hours. Even so, a doubling of all husband's and wife's wages in the population could lead to a fall in average hours worked by participants if it induced large numbers of people to participate who were almost indifferent between working and not working and so had small conditional expected hours. It all depends on how the independent variables are distributed in the population.

29. We also did the analysis with wife's net wages and intercept, with almost identical results.

30. One could attempt a full maximum-likelihood analysis in which choices between all parts of the budget constraint are treated symmetrically.

31. A similar result was obtained by Schultz (1976) for the United States. For participation, our elasticities are rather less than those from the logit analysis, and for hours of participants our elasticities are higher than those from the OLS exercise.

32. Calculating the welfare costs of distortions affecting participation is somewhat more complicated. For the essential tools see Ashenfelter (1977, Appendix).

References

Ashenfelter, O. (1977) 'The labour supply response of wage earners in the rural negative income tax experiment', Centre for Labour Economics, LSE, *Discussion Paper*, 17.

Barzel, Y. and R.J. McDonald (1973) 'Assets, subsistence and the supply curve of labour', *American Economic Review*, 63, 621–33.

Corry, B.A. and J.A. Roberts (1974) 'Activity rates and unemployment: the UK experience – some further results', *Applied Economics*, 6, 1–21.

Greenhalgh, C. (1977a) 'Participation and hours of work for married women in Great Britain', Centre for Labour Economics, LSE, *Discussion Paper*, 25.

Greenhalgh, C. (1977b) 'Estimating labour supply functions with progressive taxation of earnings', Centre for Labour Economics, LSE, *Discussion Paper*, 13.

Heckman, J.J. (1980) 'Sample selection bias as a specification error', in *Female Labour Supply: Theory and Estimation*, ed. J.P. Smith (Princeton University Press).

Layard, R., D. Piachaud and M. Stewart (1978), *The Causes of Poverty*, Background Paper, 5, Royal Commission on the Distribution of Income and Wealth (London: HMSO).

Mincer, J. (1962) 'Labour force participation of married women', in H.G. Lewis (ed.), *Aspects of Labour Economics* (Washington, DC: National Bureau of Economic Research).

Mincer, J. (1966) 'Labour force participation and unemployment', in A. Gordon and M.S. Gordon (eds), *Prosperity and Unemployment* (New York: John Wiley).

Office of Population Censuses and Surveys (OPCAS) (1974) *General Household Survey, 1974* (London: HMSO).

Office of Population Censuses and Surveys (OPCAS) (1977) *Population Trends*, 9 (London: HMSO).

Schultz, T.P. (1976) 'Estimation of labour supply of married women', Rand, Mimeo.

Tobin, J. (1958) 'Estimation of relationships for limited dependent variables', *Econometrica*, 26, 24–36.

12 Why are More Women Working in Britain? (1985)*

with H. Joshi and S. Owen

I INTRODUCTION AND SUMMARY

The increasing number of women at work is one of the most striking phenomena in the history of postwar Britain. In 1931 only 32 per cent of women aged 20–64 were in the labor force; by 1981 the proportion had risen to 58 per cent. Why is this? There is clearly a demand side as well as a supply side to the story. After laying out the facts in section II of this paper, we concentrate on a supply model in section III and conclude in section IV with some reflections on the largely unresolved problems relating to the demand side.

Female participation rose steadily from the Second World War until 1977, from which time it has been static. Until the 1970s the main increase was among married women aged over 35. Most of the extra workers have been part time.

To explain the increase in labor supply we estimate a pooled time-series, cross-section supply function for single-year age groups of women from 1950 to 1974. This function is estimated in two steps, for reasons to do with the pattern of serial correlation. In the first step, the proportion of women working in each age group is explained by the number of children they have of different ages, by age itself, by the state of the business cycle, and by a dummy for each individual birth cohort. As one might expect, the cohort dummies pick up most of the secular increase in participation, while the children and age variables map out the lifecycle pattern of participation. To understand the secular rise in participation we need to explain the coefficients on the cohort dummies, the second stage of the estimation process. We do this by various measures of early work experience, as well as by time and by the real wage levels prevailing at certain stages of life.

A key issue is the role of real wages. It is impossible to separate the influence of male and female wages, since the relativity between them was almost

* *Journal of Labour Economics*, 3(1) (1985), pp. S147–S176.

constant from 1950 to 1974. But we can examine the effect of the general wage level. We concentrate on the level of wages when the cohort was aged 35. If this variable is included but the time trend is excluded, the implied elasticity of participation with respect to the real wage level is about 0.4, while if the time trend is included the elasticity falls to 0.3, with a t-statistic of 2.4. However, we do not want to claim too much for this estimate, given some of the other less satisfactory experiments reported below.

It is interesting to compare these elasticities with those obtained from cross-section estimates on individual data relating to married women. These are based mostly on the General Household Survey(GHS) (a continuous survey of households in Great Britain published annually by the Office of Population Censuses and Surveys) and they differ according to which year's data set is used and which model. The GHS estimates of the effect of an equiproportional rise in all wages and incomes range from 0.34 to zero.

So what does explain the postwar rise in participation? It is certainly not explained by demographic trends, since up to the end of the 1960s the number of young children at home was growing. It could be the growth in real wages, but the evidence here is suggestive rather than conclusive.

One would like to have an explanation that accounted also for the earlier trends in women's work. From the mid-nineteenth century up till the Second World War there was no trend at all. At the same time there was a fairly steady rise in real wages and from the 1880s a fairly steady fall in the number of young children at home. There was also increased schooling keeping children out of the home. It is hard to see why these influences did not produce an increase in women's paid work over that period.

Three possible explanations suggest themselves. First, job rationing in the interwar period may have discouraged female labor supply. In particular, employers may have had little incentive to provide part-time jobs, which have proved particularly attractive to women in the postwar period. One can well imagine that even with no change in hourly wages many women would be willing to take part-time jobs if these became available, even if they were not willing to take the equivalent full-time job.[1]

Second, the postwar period witnessed two major developments, which we have not documented and which affected the supply side. First were dramatic falls in the real prices of domestic appliances (especially of refrigerators, gas and electric cookers, noncoal heating appliances, vacuum cleaners, and washing machines) and the prices of processed foods and easy-care fabrics. This drastically reduced the time required to feed a family to a given standard, to keep a house clean, and to wash the clothes and linen. Theory does not enable one to sign the effect of such price changes, but on balance one would expect them to reduce the supply of housework. Second was a major fall in the morbidity of children, which made it much easier for women to offer a reliable supply of labor outside the home.

Finally, we offer the tentative thought that changes in women's labor supply may not be easy to explain in terms of recent values of any variable. Rather they may reflect long-term changes in the roles women see for themselves in life. The basic exogenous change here could be the reduction in the late nineteenth and early twentieth centuries in the mortality of children and young adults. This lowered the number of children needed in order to generate a given number of adult survivors. Again, theory does not predict the effect on fertility, but what actually happens is that people choose to have fewer children. At the same time the life expectancy of adult women rises, so that the fraction of her adult life a woman spends rearing children falls dramatically. This releases the woman for other roles. But it could easily take decades for labor supply behavior to react fully to this opportunity.

In section IV we turn to the demand side. The puzzle here is that the relative hourly earnings of women (compared with men) rose by 15% from 1973 to 1976 because of the Equal Pay Act, but apparently with no effect on relative employment. Indeed, in the typical private-sector industry the employment of women relative to men increased sharply. What can explain this? One possible explanation is the Sex Discrimination Act, which outlawed discrimination in employment (rather than in pay). But most observers believe this law to have been too weak to account for what happened. The alternative explanation is simply that employers began to realize the true worth of female labor.

II TRENDS IN WOMEN'S WORK, PAY AND FERTILITY

The growth in women's work is a relatively modern phenomenon. The proportion of adult women who were economically active remained at around one-third from the mid-nineteenth century until the Second World War (see Table 12.1). Except briefly during the First World War things began to change only after the Second World War. Between 1931 and 1981 the economic activity rate of women aged 20–64 rose from 32 per cent to 60 per cent.

Until the 1970s the main increase was among women over 35. This shows clearly in Table 12.2. Until the 1970s there was little increase among women in their childbearing twenties. But in the early 1970s, when the birthrate was falling, this group participated much more, while for women in mid-life the trend continued strongly upward. However, from around 1977 both trends stopped dead in their tracks, despite the economic recovery in 1978–79.

The main growth has been among married women (see Table 12.3). Between 1951 and 1981 their participation rate more than doubled, and for mothers of dependent children the rise was proportionately more.[2] However, at the same time, the proportion of women who were married rose sharply, so that the overall participation rate of women rose less than it otherwise would have done.

Table 12.1   Activity rates: women aged 20–64 (%)

	All	Married	Single, widowed, and divorced
Census years:			
1851	34.5	n.a.	n.a.
1861	35.2	n.a.	n.a.
1871	34.5	n.a.	n.a.
1881	33.1	n.a.	n.a.
1891	33.5	n.a.	n.a.
1901	33.9	13.0	65.6
1911	32.5	10.5	66.4
1921	30.6	9.4	65.2
1931	31.6	10.9	66.7
1941	n.a.	n.a.	n.a.
1951	36.3	23.2	70.0
1961	41.0	31.6	73.3
1966	48.3	41.8	72.0
1971	51.5	45.9	72.7
1981	57.7	54.0	68.9
Recent years:			
1971	52.0	46.8	72.9
1972	52.7	47.6	72.4
1973	55.6	51.4	72.3
1974	57.3	53.4	72.5
1975	57.4	54.0	72.2
1976	58.6	55.3	71.7
1977	60.0	57.0	71.4
1978	59.9	56.7	71.7
1979	59.8	56.5	72.4
1980	59.7	56.2	72.0
1981	59.9	56.5	72.2

Sources: Census years: Original census reports. Data for 1861–1931, England and Wales only: otherwise Great Britain; 1851–71 are obtained as follows. The census in 1871 and earlier uses a different concept of the occupied population from the census of 1881 and after. But a consistent series of the occupied population has been estimated in Department of Employment and Productivity (1971), table 102. We compute the ratio of this to the population ages 20–64 in 1851–81. For 1851–71 we divide this ratio by the ratio of its value in 1881 to the actual proportion of women ages 20–64 occupied in 1881. Recent years: *Department of Employment Gazette* (April 1981) adjusted to exclude students from numerator and denominator. The Department of Employment series is based on a variety of sources, especially the *Labour Force Survey*.

Table 12.2 Age-specific activity rates (%)

	Age					
	20–24	25–34	35–44	45–54	55–64	20–64
Census years:						
1851	59.1	41.3	35.5	36.8	37.0	42.1
1861	. . .	. . .	. . .	. . .	. . .	. . .
1871	60.0	40.4	36.3	38.4	39.5	42.5
1881	55.9		29.0		26.1	33.1
1891	58.1	33.0	25.1	25.4	24.4	33.5
1901	56.5	31.5	25.8	28.2	29.2	33.9
1911	62.0	33.8	24.1	23.0	20.4	32.5
1921	62.2	33.5	22.9	21.0	19.3	30.6
1931	65.1	36.3	24.5	21.1	17.8	31.6
1941	. . .	. . .	. . .	. . .	. . .	. . .
1951	65.4	40.5 33.5	35.2	34.4	27.6 15.0	36.3
1961	62.3	39.5 36.6	42.4	43.3	36.9 20.4	41.0
1966	61.6	40.4 41.5	52.7	54.8	46.3 27.0	48.3
1971	60.2	43.1 45.0	57.2	60.4	51.0 28.0	51.5
1981	69.2	55.4 53.4	65.5	66.0	52.3 22.4	57.7

	Age						
	20–24	25–34	35–44	45–54	55–59	60–64	20–64
Recent years:							
1971	64.1	44.0	57.4	60.6	51.1	28.2	52.0
1972	65.6	44.9	58.0	61.2	51.3	28.2	52.7
1973	66.8	48.7	62.3	65.2	52.6	28.2	55.6
1974	68.4	51.2	65.3	66.1	53.3	28.2	57.3
1975	68.8	52.0	65.9	66.3	53.3	28.2	57.4
1976	70.9	53.8	67.5	66.9	55.0	26.8	58.6
1977	72.4	56.5	68.7	67.1	57.3	25.0	60.0
1978	73.4	56.2	69.0	67.2	56.0	22.8	59.9
1979	73.3	56.2	68.5	67.5	54.9	21.3	59.8
1980	73.8	56.3	68.3	67.8	54.9	20.5	59.7
1981	73.2	56.2	68.2	68.4	54.6	19.2	59.9

Sources: See Table 12.1. In Table 12.2 there is a break in the series between 1871 and 1881 for which we have not attempted to adjust, whereas we did attempt an adjustment in Table 12.1.

Table 12.3 Activity rates by marital status and age: marriage rates, female non-students, Great Britain (%)

Marital status	Year	Under 20	20–24	25–34	35–44	45–54	55–59	60–64	65–69	70 and Over	All Ages	20–59
Single	1951	94.9	92.4	87.1	79.8	74.5	66.4	35.0	21.6	6.8	76.4	76.7
	1961	94.3	91.9	89.5	85.1	81.7	75.1	39.2	19.6	6.3	76.1	86.1
	1971	90.3	93.6	85.8	85.1	82.6	76.4	33.3	16.6	4.4	71.1	87.5
Married	1951	38.3	37.1	24.5	24.9	23.4	15.6	6.7	3.6	1.5	21.5	24.2
	1961	41.8	41.8	29.5	36.4	33.9	26.0	12.7	5.2	1.5	29.4	33.7
	1971	41.5	45.8	38.4	54.2	56.8	45.1	24.8	10.0	2.6	42.0	48.8
	1981	45.7	55.1	48.6	64.0	64.4	49.7	22.3	6.9	2.0	47.3	57.2
Widowed and divorced	1951	100.0	64.4	67.6	66.2	53.9	38.1	18.4	10.1	2.9	20.9	52.4
	1961	75.0	62.7	68.4	71.7	67.7	51.8	28.2	13.4	3.0	22.9	62.3
	1971	38.9	52.4	60.2	70.9	73.9	62.2	33.7	15.0	2.8	23.1	66.8
All	1951	92.0	66.7	37.1	34.7	34.0	27.7	14.4	9.0	3.2	35.0	42.4
	1961	91.8	63.9	39.5	36.6	42.0	36.9	20.4	10.3	3.1	38.3	43.4
	1971	88.3	63.6	44.0	57.1	60.6	50.9	28.0	12.7	3.0	43.9	54.6
	1981	91.8	74.5	54.9	65.7	66.1	52.3	22.4	7.6	2.0	47.4	62.3
Percentage of women never married	1951	95.7	52.7	18.8	13.9	15.6	15.9	15.9	16.8	16.6	24.5	26.6
	1961	93.7	43.0	13.5	10.0	11.3	14.2	14.8	15.3	16.0	20.8	15.5
	1971	82.8	36.7	10.7	7.4	8.4	10.0	11.8	13.9	15.4	17.5	12.6

Sources: Census reports on occupation, economic activity, and education. In the adjustment to exclude students all students were assumed to be single (approximately true in 1971).

Table 12.4 Full- and part-time work among women aged 20–64 (%)

	Full-time workers	Part-time workers	Unemployed	All active
1951	30.3	5.2	0.8	36.3
1961	29.8	10.2	1.0	41.0
1966	31.7	15.2	1.4	48.3
1971	29.0	20.2	2.3	51.5
1981	31.6	22.4	3.7	57.7

Note:
Full-time means worked more than 30 hours normally (or 24 for teachers).
Source: Census reports, for Great Britain. In 1951, 13 out of 15 of self-employed were assumed full time. The percentages of all women aged 20–64 who were self-employed in the 5 years were 1.5, 1.7, 1.9, 2.0, and 2.6.

Remarkably, there has been no growth at all in the propensity to work full time. The whole growth has been in part-time work (see Table 12.4).[3]

As Table 12.5 shows, there has been a big increase in female unemployment (using survey definitions). In the early postwar years, unemployment was low, about the same for women and men. Since the early 1970s it has risen sharply, but rather less for women than men.

Wages

We can now look at two main variables that might explain the trends in female labor supply: real wages and fertility. Real wages of women and men have been rising ever since the eighteenth century, and though the rate of growth has been most rapid since the Second World War, the proportional increase from, say, 1850 to 1950 was greater than that since 1950. As Figures 12.1 and 12.2 and Table 12.6 show, women's wages rose relative to men's during the Second World War, and the relativity rose again sharply between 1973 and 1975, by around 15 per cent. This 15 per cent rise happened both for manual workers, shown in the table, and for nonmanual workers. It was due to the Equal Pay Act of 1970, which outlawed the use of separate rates of pay for men and women from January 1976 onward.[4] Two main pieces of evidence are sufficient to establish this causality. First, there is the timing: the rise corresponds exactly to the last possible moment allowed by the law, and the relativity has remained fairly stable ever since. Second, if one looks at wage rates negotiated in

Table 12.5 Unemployment rates (%)

	Census data (survey definition)		Department of Employment (Registered unemployment rate)	
	Women	Men	Women	Men
Census years:				
1951	1.9	2.2	0.9	0.9
1961	2.5	3.0	0.9	1.3
1966	3.2	2.8	0.6	1.4
1971	4.8	5.4	1.2	4.2
1981	7.4	11.4	7.7	13.3

	General Household Survey (survey definition)		Department of Employment (Registered unemployment rate)	
Recent years:				
1971	3.6	3.3	1.2	4.2
1972			1.4	4.6
1973	3.3	3.2	1.0	3.3
1974	2.0	3.2	0.8	3.2
1975	3.2	4.3	1.6	4.9
1976	3.6	5.6	3.3	6.9
1977	4.8	5.4	4.0	7.2
1978	4.4	5.1	4.2	6.9
1979	4.7	5.4	4.1	6.3
1980	6.2	6.7	5.2	7.8
1981	9.4	11.1	7.7	13.3
1982	9.4	12.4	8.9	15.2

Note:
Covers all ages, except for General Household Survey, which relates to women under 60 and men under 65.
Sources: Census reports, data for Great Britain, Registered unemployment, annual average: *Department of Employment Gazette.*

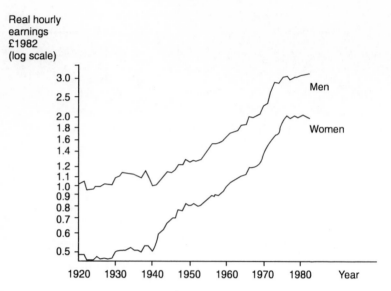

Figure 12.1   Real hourly earnings of men and women, Great Britain, 1920–82

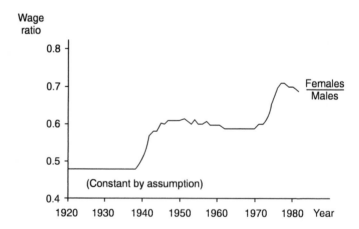

Figure 12.2   Ratio of female to male hourly earnings, Great Britain, 1920–82

Table 12.6 Average hourly real earnings of adult full-time manual workers
(1982 prices in £ = 1)

Year	Women over 18	Men over 21	Women as proportion of Men	Year	Women over 18	Men over 21	Women as proportion of Men
1920	0.47	1.01	0.47	1950	0.79	1.29	0.61
1921	0.48	1.05	0.47	1951	0.80	1.30	0.62
1922	0.43	0.95	0.47	1952	0.78	1.28	0.61
1923	0.44	0.96	0.47	1953	0.79	1.31	0.60
1924	0.45	0.96	0.47	1954	0.84	1.37	0.61
1925	0.47	0.99	0.47	1955	0.86	1.44	0.60
1926	0.46	0.97	0.47	1956	0.89	1.50	0.60
1927	0.47	1.01	0.47	1957	0.90	1.48	0.61
1928	0.46	1.01	0.47	1958	0.92	1.52	0.60
1929	0.46	1.01	0.47	1959	0.94	1.58	0.60
1930	0.50	1.09	0.47	1960	0.99	1.66	0.60
1931	0.51	1.10	0.47	1961	1.04	1.73	0.60
1932	0.51	1.13	0.47	1962	1.05	1.77	0.59
1933	0.51	1.13	0.47	1963	1.07	1.80	0.59
1934	0.52	1.12	0.47	1964	1.11	1.88	0.59
1935	0.51	1.12	0.47	1965	1.13	1.92	0.59
1936	0.51	1.11	0.47	1966	1.20	2.03	0.59
1937	0.50	1.10	0.47	1967	1.20	2.03	0.59
1938	0.53	1.15	0.47	1968	1.22	2.10	0.58
1939	0.53	1.09	0.49	1969	1.29	2.20	0.59
1940	0.51	1.00	0.51	1970	1.41	2.38	0.59
1941	0.55	1.01	0.54	1971	1.48	2.46	0.60
1942	0.60	1.06	0.57	1972	1.60	2.65	0.60
1943	0.64	1.10	0.58	1973	1.69	2.78	0.61
1944	0.67	1.15	0.58	1974	1.74	2.76	0.63
1945	0.69	1.15	0.60	1975	1.95	2.92	0.67
1946	0.70	1.17	0.60	1976	2.06	2.94	0.70
1947	0.76	1.25	0.61	1977	1.97	2.77	0.71
1948	0.76	1.25	0.61	1978	2.05	2.87	0.71
1949	0.80	1.31	0.61	1979	2.02	2.90	0.70
				1980	2.10	3.00	0.70
				1981	2.07	3.01	0.69
				1982	2.05	3.02	0.68

Note:
Weekly earnings of women relative to men did not change between 1886 and the interwar period (Department of Employment and Productivity, 1971).
Source: Data relate to April. Wages (£): 1938–82; Department of Employment and Productivity (1971), tables 46–48; and comparable *Department of Employment Gazette* thereafter ('April survey' grafted backward onto New Earnings Survey). Earlier: The *Abstract* agives data for male/female weekly wage ratios in 1935. It also gives data on average hourly wages (for men and women combined) back to 1920. We assumed that the male–female ratio for 1920–35 was constant. Prices; *Abstract* Tables 89–93 and *Department of Employment Gazette* thereafter (1982 prices = 1).

national collective bargaining agreements, the rates of women relative to men moved in almost exactly the same pattern as for earnings – though, as one would expect, relative earnings rose slightly less.[5]

There is little reason to think that human capital accounts for the recent narrowing of the male–female wage gap. The educational attainment of women relative to men was constant or declining for cohorts entering the labor force up to the 1960s, as attested by the *Education Tables* of the 1961 census and the *Qualified Manpower Tables* of the 1971 census. It is true that since then women have increased their educational activity rather more rapidly than men, but the quantitative effect of this on the human capital in the labor force has been small.[6] Moreover, most of the newly educated are still quite young, and for young adults extra education directly raises earnings but also indirectly reduces earnings by reducing work experience.[7]

Fertility

Fertility fell from around the 1880s, when the total period fertility rate was about 4.5, until the 1930s when it was under 2 (see Figure 12.3 and Table 12.7). It rose briefly after each world war, but there was a sustained rise from the mid-1950s to the mid-1960s. From the late 1960s there was a precipitate fall

Figure 12.3 Total period fertility rate, England and Wales, 1920–82

Table 12.7 Total period fertility rate

Year	Total period fertility rate	Year	Total period fertility rate
1841–5	4.59	1951	2.14
1851–5	4.62	1952	2.16
1860–5	4.66	1953	2.21
1871–5	4.81	1954	2.20
1881–5	4.58	1955	2.22
1891–5	4.01	1956	2.35
1901–5	3.46	1957	2.45
1911–15	2.83	1958	2.51
1916–20	2.42	1959	2.53
1921–5	2.39	1960	2.66
1926–30	2.00	1961	2.77
1930	1.94	1962	2.84
1931	1.89	1963	2.88
1932	1.82	1964	2.94
1933	1.72	1965	2.84
1934	1.75	1966	2.76
1935	1.75	1967	2.66
1936	1.77	1968	2.58
1937	1.79	1969	2.48
1938	1.83	1970	2.41
1939	1.83	1971	2.38
1940	1.74	1972	2.19
1941	1.71	1973	2.02
1942	1.92	1974	1.90
1943	2.02	1975	1.79
1944	2.24	1976	1.73
1945	2.04	1977	1.68
1946	2.46	1978	1.75
1947	2.69	1979	1.86
1948	2.38	1980	1.90
1949	2.26	1981	1.82
1950	2.18	1982	1.77

Note:
Fertility rate $= \Sigma_i(B_i/P_i)$, where i is age $15 \leq i \geq 44$,
B is births, and P is female population.
Sources: Office of Population Censuses and Surveys, *Birth Statistics* (1980), Table 1.4., and *Population Trends* (Spring 1983).

until 1978, when a slight recovery began. Thus fertility, unlike wages, has been anything but trended.

III   THE SUPPLY MODEL

We turn now to the problem of explanation. For this purpose we use as dependent variable the proportion of women of each age who worked as employees in each year from 1950 to 1974.[8] There are clearly two main features to be explained: the lifecycle pattern of participation and the difference in pattern between the different cohorts.

These two features are illustrated in Figure 12.4. This shows the work history of six selected cohorts of women over the period 1950–74. Each cohort is labeled by the date at which it was age 20. Thus for the cohort age 20 in 1962 we see an early fall in participation, followed by the beginning of a return to work. For those age 20 in 1954, we see more of this pattern of reentry. Indeed, we can see how steep it is and how misleading it would be to infer lifecycle behavior from the evidence of the cross-section. The cross-section of work in 1974 can be obtained by joining up the loose ends of each cohort profile. This suggests that participation is falling between ages 48 and 56, whereas the profile for the 1938 cohort rose over those ages. The apparent drop is due to differences in the behavior of the different cohorts, rather than an effect of aging. Figure 12.4 also makes it clear that the main increase in women's work has been in midlife. However, the graph does not bring out the full increase in participation at younger ages that happened in the 1970s.

The age-specific employment rates are explained by three kinds of variables:

(i)   those whose values change from year to year and are age specific (e.g. number of children under 5) – we call these lifecycle variables;
(ii)   those whose values change from year to year but affect all ages equally (e.g., the state of the economy) – we call these calendar-time variables; and
(iii) those that differ between cohorts but do not change over the lifecycle (e.g. year of birth) – we call these cohort variables.

If t denotes date and j denotes cohort, we can refer to these three sets of variables as L_{tj}, B_t and C_j respectively. Hence if E_{tj} is the proportion of non-student women at work as employees, $E_{tj} = f(L_{tj}, B_t, C_j)$. The particular variables we consider are (i) lifecycle variables: children of different ages, wages, and age; (ii) calendar-time variables: business cycle (vacancies); and (iii) cohort variables: completed family size, male and female wages at specified ages, education, unemployment experience early in working life, experience of wartime working, and trend.[9]

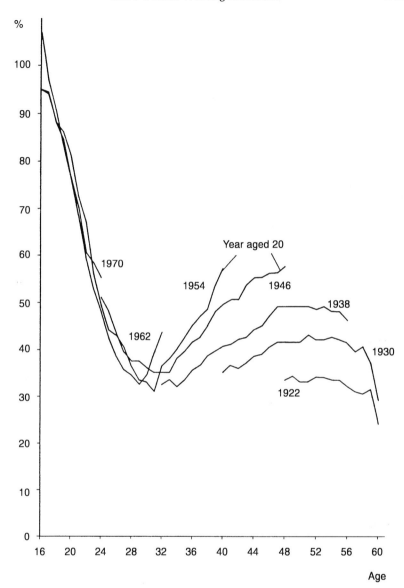

Figure 12.4   Percentage of women in employment as employees: selected cohorts, 1950–74

Our aim is to estimate a supply function for female labor (in terms of numbers of workers rather than woman-hours). There is an obvious problem of identification, since for data reasons the dependent variable has to be age-specific employment, not labor force.[10] However, there is a relationship among employment (E), labor supply (S), and vacancies (V) given by the U/V curve; $E = S + \gamma V + $ constant. There is also a supply relation, in which supply may respond to vacancies as well as to other variables (Z): $S = Z\beta + \alpha V + $ constant. Hence, eliminating S, $E = Z\beta + (\alpha + \gamma)V + $ constant. This means that all is well, provided we include vacancies in our equation.

Our estimation proceeds in two steps. First, in (1), we estimate the effect of all variables that are not purely cohort variables. We estimate their effect simultaneously with a vector of coefficients (**a**) on the vector of cohort dummies (**D**$_j$). Thus we estimate

$$E_{tj} = \mathbf{L}_{tj}b + \mathbf{B}_t c + \mathbf{D}_j \mathbf{a} + u_{tj} \tag{1}$$

Then as a second stage we estimate the effects of the cohort variables by regressing the $\hat{a}_j$s estimated in (1) on the purely cohort variables (**C**$_j$):

$$\hat{a}_j = \mathbf{C}_j c + v_j \tag{2}$$

This two-stage approach is necessary if we are to handle problems of autocorrelation in a satisfactory manner.[11] There are two dimensions in which we found important serial correlation. One is serial correlation in the unexplained behavior of a given cohort over its life-cycle (i.e. between adjacent ages for the same people). This is captured in the error terms of (1).[12] The second is serial correlation in the unexplained behavior of adjacent cohorts, captured in the error term of (2). For both equations, ρ was estimated by grid search.

The equations are estimated for ages 20–59 for the 43 cohorts on which there were at least 10 observations at these ages during the period 1951–74.[13]

Results

Table 12.8 shows estimates of (1) and Table 12.9 shows estimates of (2). Let us look at these one by one. Table 12.8 enables us to look at the effect of the lifecycle and calendar-time variables, while Table 12.9 turns to the cohort variables. As we go through the variables, we shall first describe them and then document their effects.

Life-cycle and calendar-time variables

Children

Children are not exogenous if chosen jointly with work decisions. Thus a reduced-form supply function of work would have in it the cost of children

Table 12.8 Estimates of (1)

Explanatory variables (other than cohort dummies)	Regression coefficients (with t-statistics)			
	(1)	(2)	(3)	(4)
Age	−0.0052	−0.0058	−0.0047	−0.0064
	(19.98)	(13.86)	(12.38)	(8.45)
$(\text{Age} - 39.5)^2$	−0.00013	−0.000079	−0.00013	−0.000089
	(7.29)	(2.53)	(7.34)	(3.24)
Children ages 0–4 per woman	−0.346	−0.339	−0.350	−0.336
	(38.17)	(34.65)	(37.75)	(31.64)
Children ages 5–10 per woman	−0.141	−0.134	−0.140	−0.128
	(28.72)	(22.37)	(28.68)	(14.39)
Children ages 11–14 per woman	−0.072	−0.0707	−0.0735	−0.066
	(8.78)	(8.62)	(8.94)	(7.47)
(Children ages 11–14 per woman) × (cohort birth year − 1925)	0.0030	0.0032	0.0032	0.0031
	(4.47)	(4.71)	(4.67)	(4.57)
Vacancies × 10^{-6} × dummy (age 20–39)	0.058	0.0578	0.0615	0.0579
	(12.07)	(11.89)	(12.07)	(11.92)
Vacancies × 10^{-6} × dummy (age 40–59)	0.040	0.0412	0.0434	0.0412
	(8.36)	(8.49)	(8.53)	(8.54)
Age-specific wage ratio males to females, 1968		0.306		
		(1.81)		
Current real wage of women			−0.00045	
			(1.82)	
(Cohort birth year − 1000) × age spline[a]				0.0000023
				(1.73)
Dependent variable: proportion of nonstudent women employed				
$\hat{\rho}$	0.6	0.6	0.6	0.6
$D - W$	2.13	2.13	2.14	2.15
$\bar{R}^2$	0.997	0.997	0.997	0.997
SSE	0.07415	0.07385	0.07383	0.07388
df	799	798	798	798
N	850	850	850	850

Note:
[a] Age spline = (age − 30) × dummy (30–59) − (age − 50) × dummy (50–59). For full definition of variables see Joshi *et al.* (1981), Annex C.

Table 12.9 Estimates of (2)

Explanatory variables	Regression coefficients (with t-statistics)							
	(1)	(2)	(3)	(4)	(5)	(6)	(7)	(8)
Cohort birth year	0.0057 (8.50)		0.0011 (0.51)	0.0023 (1.22)	0.0013 (0.68)	0.0052 (10.73)	0.0084 (4.59)	0.0082 (6.14)
Years at ages 20–29 during World War II	0.0031 (1.46)	0.0040 (2.00)	0.0038 (1.87)	0.0048 (3.13)	0.0041 (2.77)	0.0036 (2.62)	0.000024 (0.0079)	0.00040 (0.68)
Average unemployment rate at age 15–24 (%)	−0.0046 (1.97)	−0.0080 (4.38)	−0.0072 (2.95)	−0.0042 (1.91)	−0.0012 (0.40)	0.0028 (1.11)	−0.0045 (1.66)	0.0043 (1.73)
Log average real wages of men and women at age 35		0.166 (9.40)	0.138 (2.39)	0.153 (2.90)	0.119 (2.25)			
Log male wage–log female wage at age 35				0.190 (2.37)				
Log average real wages of men and women at age 20					−0.309 (2.37)	−0.395 (3.18)	−0.120 (1.76)	−0.134 (2.34)
Log male wage–log female wage at age 20								−0.480 (3.91)
Constant	−2.221 (7.4)	0.121 (3.33)	−0.314 (0.37)	−1.379 (1.23)	−0.425 (0.40)	−3.046 (7.74)	−2.601 (4.36)	−4.806 (5.73)
(Dependent variable: cohort coefficient $\hat{a}_i$)								
$\hat{\rho}$	0.5	0.5	0.5	0.3	0.3	0.2	0.6	0.2
D–W	2.28	2.29	2.32	2.28	2.14	1.98	2.40	2.03
$\bar{R}^2$	0.887	0.902	0.899	0.952	0.952	0.959	0.836	0.964
SSE	0.00809	0.00706	0.00701	0.00640	0.00639	0.00725	0.00753	0.00629
df	38	38	37	36	36	37	37	36
N	42	42	42	42	42	42	42	42

Note: For full definition of variables, see Joshi *et al.* (1981), Annex C.

rather than their number. However, we can eliminate the cost variable by substituting in from the demand function for children, to get a relationship between work and children.[14] This is the only practicable procedure if we want to trace out the lifecycle pattern of work.

Cross-sectional work on micro data makes it clear that the effect of children is best measured by the presence of any child, interacted with the age of the youngest child.[15] However, no time-series evidence is available for this. Instead we use three variables: (i) children under age 5 (preschool) per woman, (ii) children 5–10 (primary school age) per woman, and (iii) children 11–14 per woman (15 being the minimum school-leaving age till 1973). Each variable measures the number of children (born to the cohort) per woman (married and unmarried) in the cohort.[16]

Turning to the results, the final column of Table 12.8 shows our preferred equation. Each preschool child lowers participation by 35 per cent, each primary school child by 14 per cent, and each secondary school child by 7 per cent (for the cohort age 20 in 1945).

It is interesting to see how children affect the fraction of a woman's life that she works as an employee. Each child reduces the years a mother works by about 2.9, so that if mothers averaged 2.5 children they would work about 7 fewer years than childless women. Put another way, these average mothers would work 44 per cent of the years between ages 20 and 59, while the average childless woman would work 62 per cent of that time.

We can next examine how far fertility changes explain the evolution of postwar female employment. Table 12.10 shows on the left-hand side the changes in the number of children over each decade and on the right-hand side the predicted effect of these changes on female employment. The changes in the number of children between 1951 and 1971 seem to have depressed female activity to a relatively small extent, whereas the sharp decline in the number of young children between 1971 and 1981 would produce, given these coefficients, a marked rise (of almost half a million workers). Thus, of the actual intercensal changes in female employment (shown at the bottom of the right-hand panel), the increases observed between 1951 and 1971 occur *despite* increased numbers of children and must be explained by other factors. On the other hand, most of the estimated increase between 1971 and 1981 *is* attributable to falling numbers of children.

One puzzle is why participation has increased more over time at older rather than at younger ages. We have in part picked this up by finding that the deterrent effect of secondary school children declined over time.[17]

Real wages

We do not have time-series data on age-specific wages. Instead we use data on age-specific wages for 1 year and on aggregate wages for all years. The former could explain a part of the lifecycle pattern of participation (see Smith, 1973;

Table 12.10   Hypothetical effect on female employment of changes in the child
population, 1951–81, Great Britain (000)

Children	Change in population			Effect on employment		
	1951–61	1961–71	1971–81	1951–61	1961–71	1971–81
0– 4 years	–76	238	–1044	26	–82	361
5–10 years	212	998	–964	–30	–141	134
11–14 years	801	–112	215	–58[a]	5[a]	–3[a]
Total	937	1124	–1793	–62	–218	492
Actual change in employment of women aged 20–59				564	1149	687

Notes:
Estimated effect on employment calculated using coefficinets from Table 12.8, (1).
a Change in population of ages 11–14 times the coefficient on children 11–14 at
end year (reflecting effect of the interaction with cohort).
Source: Census reports.

Becker and Ghez, 1975), while the latter could explain time-series variation.
We take them in that order.

The cross-sectional ratio of hourly earnings of women relative to men in
1968 was as follows:

Age					
18–20	21–24	25–29	30–39	40–49	50–59
0.81	0.73	0.70	0.62	0.58	0.63

Source: New Earnings Survey, 1968 (described in App. B), Table 40B.

The relative earnings of women are highest early in life, which may help to
explain why they participate most then; but the data do not suggest that there

is any relative wage incentive for women to return to work in midlife. It is therefore not surprising that the variable attracts the wrong sign (col. (2) of Table 12.8).

Turning to the time-series wage variables for men and women (hourly earnings of adult full-time manual workers), these are almost perfectly collinear, since there was no appreciable change in the male/female wage ratio between 1950 and 1974. We therefore included only the female real wage. This too attracted the wrong sign (see col. (3) of Table 12.8). Note that this result is obtained in the presence of a vector of cohort dummies that are picking up the positive trend in participation.

Age

Age itself could have an effect in two ways. The waning of vitality later in life, particularly if anticipated, suggests that work should be done earlier rather than later. But even apart from this, it will make sense to concentrate work earlier in life if the return to savings sufficiently compensates for the postponed enjoyment of consumption and time at home.[18] This pattern will be further reinforced if retirement and pension arrangements lead to higher consumption in old age than would be freely chosen. The sample is restricted to ages below 60 to exclude any impact of the formal retirement age.

We include as variables not only age but age squared. It appears that age leads to a decline in participation at an increasing rate, so that between 20 and 59 it reduces participation by 20 percentage points. In order to try to allow for the fact that the main growth in participation is at older ages, we included an interaction term between cohort birth year and an age spline (col. (4)). This had a positive but very small effect and was not highly significant.[19]

Vacancies

Vacancies (for men and women) registered at employment exchanges are more or less untrended between 1950 and 1974. We tried them, as well as two other indices of the business cycle – the male unemployment rate and a Wharton index of excess capacity – both of which yielded less stable estimates. We had reason to expect a differential impact of demand on the employment of women at different ages (Joshi, 1981), and after experimentation discovered a different effect above and below 40. However, the vacancy effects are rather low.

To conclude our analysis of (1), various tests suggested that results were extremely similar when the sample was confined to cohorts having a full 25 observations, or to ages over 30. Splitting the sample over calendar time (into three equal periods) significantly improved the fit, but not strongly so ($F_{90/709}$ = 2.12), the main differences from the overall estimates being rather minor ones during the period 1951–8. If the equation was estimated separately for the age group 20–29, it became somewhat less stable.

In a separate analysis we investigated whether it is better to specify (1) only with an autoregressive error, as above, or also with a lagged dependent variable (which might reflect state dependence in work behavior). We concluded that the choice makes little difference to any of our other results and that it is intrinsically difficult to determine the issue.

Differences between cohorts

The coefficients on the cohort dummies generated by the preferred version of (1) $(\hat{a}_j)$ show a fairly linear trend up to the cohort at age 20 in 1955. After that the trend flattens off, though one should note that for these later cohorts most of our data are on participation in their twenties only.[20] If these cohorts should in fact conform to the rising trend only when they reach mid-life, we would not have enough evidence to detect this from participation early in life.

Table 12.9 shows the results of fitting (2) to explain the cohort coefficients. Before discussing the results, we shall review all the variables considered for the analysis, some of which were eventually rejected.

Completed family size

We have already allowed for the influence of children at the time when they are at home. However, we also want to know whether family size has an effect at times other than when the children are young. For example, if a woman has been out of the labor force for a long time with children, she may be less likely to work when they are grown up. She may also be less likely to work before she has a family if she expects to have a large one (though this could go the other way if the need to accumulate savings was strong enough). We therefore look at the effect of *completed* family size as proxied by numbers of children born by age 36. This grew steadily from the cohort aged 20 in 1928 to that aged 20 in 1958. We also experimented with the proportion of women who ever had children by age 36. This also grew very sharply: comparing the 1928 and 1958 cohorts, we have the following approximate changes: fertility (cumulated to age 36), +60 per cent; percentage who ever had children (by age 36), +20 per cent; children per mother (by age 36), +30 per cent. However, as our data come from a period dominated by an upswing in fertility, it is not surprising that completed fertility attracted a perverse sign in our regressions, and we therefore rejected it as an explanatory variable.

Education

Another factor possibly affecting women's work is education, which may act directly as well as through its effect on wage levels. If we look at the crude differences in participation between different educational groups we see the joint effect of these forces. Table 12.11 shows how in 1961 better-educated

Table 12.11 Female economic activity rates, by terminal education age, 1961
(%)

| | Terminal education age | | | | |
Age	Under 15	15	16	17–19	20 and over
15–19	(83)	93	95	94	. . .
20–24	(57)	59	78	78	87
25–44	40	39	42	43	56
45 and over	26	29	31	29	46
All	31	56	49	45	56

Note:
Parentheses indicate small base numbers.
Sources: Data for Great Britain constructed from census of England and Wales, 1961, *Education Tables*, and census of Scotland, 1961, *Terminal Education Age Tables*.

women were more likely to work than less-educated women, holding age constant. However, the difference between the different groups is so small that, even if all women had moved from the lowest to the highest educational group, it would only account for a fraction of the actual increase in women's participation since the Second World War.

To isolate the direct effect of education on women's work (rather than its effects via wages), we included in our regressions a variable that reflected the minimum compulsory school-leaving age for the cohort in question. We also included as an alternative the proportion of the cohort with A-level standard qualifications or above (higher secondary) (from the *Qualified Manpower Tables* of the 1971 census). Both were highly correlated with the trend, and it proved impossible to detect a distinct education effect.

Early unemployment and wartime work experience

Past job rationing may influence present activity. If a cohort experiences severe job rationing early in life, it fails to acquire human capital in a way that our wage series (which are not age specific) fail to identify. In addition, the cohort's perception of job opportunities may be permanently affected, even if actual job opportunities are not. We therefore include as a variable the average percentage unemployment rate during the years when the cohort was age 15–24.

The Second World War enormously increased women's participation in all kinds of work. Female employment rose by about 45 per cent between 1938 and 1943, and then after the war returned to about halfway between its prewar and wartime levels. The experience of warwork led many women (especially in their twenties) to acquire skills they would not otherwise have acquired. This must have made many of them more willing to work later. We therefore include as a cohort variable the number of wartime years experienced by cohorts when they were between 20 and 29.

Real wages

The variables mentioned so far are not going to do very much to explain the strong trend in the coefficients on the cohort dummies. An obvious candidate for this job is real wages. From cross-sectional work we have some *a priori* expectations about the effects of wage changes. If the man's wage increases, the wife's labor supply will fall. But if the wife's wage increases, her labor supply will increase, and this effect is usually found to be sufficiently strong to ensure that an equiproportional increase in husband's and wife's wage will lead to a net increase in the wife's labor supply. It may of course be the case that labor supply depends in part at least on individual wages relative to the general average. If this is so, the cross-section estimates of wage effects will exceed in absolute magnitude the time-series effects.

In time series, men's wages and women's wages are highly correlated (for 1950–74, $r = 0.99$, and each is nearly as highly correlated with time). Thus it is not easy to distinguish their separate effects, although one may still be able to estimate the net effect of a rise in the *general* level of real wages.

In our regressions we experimented with earnings when the cohorts were age 20 and again when they were 35. We also included the level of men's pay relative to women's at both ages.

Trends

Finally there may be omitted trended variables that help to explain the upward tendency in participation (e.g. social attitudes, better health). The natural way to allow for this is to include a time trend: the date of birth of the cohort. There are many other variables we would have liked to include that may or may not be adequately proxied by a time trend. Notable among these are child-care facilities and the prevalence of family breakup, both of which involve several elements that are not systematically recorded.[21]

Results of analysis of cohort dummies

We can now turn to Table 12.9, which is estimated with an autoregressive error. Column (1) shows a simple time trend, plus the effects of the war and of early unemployment, which are as expected. The time trend is 0.57 per cent per year. Column (2) drops the time trend and replaces it by the wage level when the cohort was 35. This highly trended series implies a wage elasticity (at average participation) of 0.36, which compares with the cross-sectional elasticity computed by Layard, Barton and Zabalza (1980) of 0.21 for an equiproportional increase in husband's and wife's wages. Thus one might say that the cross-sectional estimate 'explains' roughly half the time-series changes. The next step, however, is to see whether the time series can yield their own estimate of wage elasticities when some reasonable allowance has been made for the effect of other trended variables. Thus in column (3) we include both a time trend and the wage variable and let them fight it out. The result is that the wage effect falls by about one-fifth of itself, and the time trend is correspondingly about one-fifth of 0.57 per cent per year. However, we do not want to put too much weight on these results, given the high correlation of this wage variable and the trend.

In the rest of the table we explore other variants. Column (4) adds the wage of men relative to women at age 35 – with significant effects of a perverse sign. However, the wage ratio at age 20 – reflecting the big differences between the wage ratio for cohorts beginning work before and after the Second World War – does yield a negative sign, shown in column (5). This variable is highly correlated with the unemployment level in early life and greatly reduces the measured impact of the latter. The *t*-value is higher on the wage ratio at 20, but one cannot be very confident about which variable is playing the greater role. The remaining columns of the table show perverse signs on the level of the wage at 20.

IV SOME DEMAND-SIDE ISSUES

We turn now to the demand side. There is a major puzzle here for economic theory, which we feel is worth airing. As a result of the Equal Pay Act, between 1973 and 1976 the relative wage of women rose by 15 per cent and stayed there. Most economists would have predicted that in the private sector at least this would reduce the relative employment of women. But no such result occurred. Why was this?[22]

A possible explanation is that two acts were passed in 1970: the Equal Pay Act and the Sex Discrimination Act. The latter outlawed any discrimination in employment practices (especially hiring and firing) on grounds of sex or marital status. If there had formerly been massive discrimination in employment, which was suddenly reduced in 1976 when the Sex Discrimination Act became operative, this could have offset the effect of the Equal Pay Act, as it was intended to. However, the impact of the Sex Discrimination Act is not generally believed to have been large, and the number of cases brought to tribunals has been quite small.[23] The number of cases under the Equal Pay Act has also been fairly small,[24] but then one should bear in mind that collectively bargained pay is more visible and any one case will affect more people.

To investigate these issues, we first calculate the relative employment of women and men in man-hours (see Table 12.12). The results of this exercise will surprise many people. They indicate that the proportion of hours contributed by women fell somewhat from 1951 to the mid-1960s and rose sharply only during the 1970s when the rise was continuous (see Table 12.12, column 1). The reason is that the number of full-time women workers fell slightly, while the number of male workers rose sharply and more than enough to offset the rise in part-time workers.

Turning to the explanation of labor demand, the most obvious influence to examine first is the effect of changes in the pattern of employment between more and less female-intensive industries. We do this by means of an index in which the female/male ratio in each industry (assumed constant) is weighted by the (changing) fraction of all males working in that industry.[25] This index is shown in Table 12.12, column (2). There was a steady rise in the female intensity of the structure of the economy, but at a much more rapid pace in the 1970s than earlier. During the 1970s the index rose by 4.5 percentage points, reflecting the vast expansion of service industries. But the actual ratio of woman-hours to man-hours rose twice as much as this, by nine points. Thus there were also sharp increases in the proportion of women workers within each industry, in spite of the sharp rises in women's pay.

One might not perhaps be surprised by this if it happened in the public sector. So let us see what happened in the private sector (columns (5), (6)). The structure of demand index for the private sector rose very little, reflecting only a mild shift toward private rather than public services. But the actual ratio of female to male employment rose quite sharply. So our puzzle holds even when we confine our gaze to the private sector.

To see whether we could resolve the puzzle we did some very crude regressions for the private sector, shown in Table 12.13. In the first of these we regressed the employment ratio on the structure of demand, vacancies, time, and the wage ratio. The coefficient on the wage ratio was highly significant but of the wrong sign. This confirmed the results of earlier work in which it proved possible to estimate a sensible demand system for labor in manufacturing up to 1969 (Layard, 1982) but impossible to extend the work into the 1970s. The only way to save the situation is to introduce dummies to represent the effect of the Sex Discrimination Act. This is done in column (2). The dummy allows for anticipatory effects and takes the value 1/6, 2/6, 3/6, 4/6, 5/6, and 1,

Table 12.12   The composition of employment (employees only)

	Whole economy				Private sector	
Year	Female hours / Male hours (1)	Demand index (2)	Proportion of women in private sector (3)	Proportion of men in private sector (4)	Female hours / Male hours (5)	Demand index (6)
1950	0.412	0.377	0.762	0.688	0.457	0.408
1951	0.413	0.379	0.763	0.691	0.456	0.408
1952	0.405	0.375	0.757	0.687	0.446	0.402
1953	0.409	0.378	0.760	0.689	0.452	0.405
1954	0.409	0.379	0.761	0.692	0.450	0.404
1955	0.404	0.377	0.762	0.698	0.441	0.399
1956	0.403	0.378	0.757	0.698	0.437	0.398
1957	0.400	0.383	0.754	0.703	0.428	0.401
1958	0.396	0.383	0.747	0.698	0.424	0.401
1959	0.393	0.387	0.743	0.701	0.416	0.403
1960	0.393	0.388	0.745	0.711	0.412	0.400
1961	0.392	0.390	0.739	0.712	0.407	0.399
1962	0.392	0.394	0.734	0.711	0.405	0.402
1963	0.388	0.397	0.728	0.710	0.398	0.403
1964	0.386	0.399	0.728	0.717	0.392	0.402
1965	0.388	0.401	0.723	0.719	0.390	0.400
1966	0.398	0.404	0.715	0.720	0.395	0.400
1967	0.398	0.405	0.699	0.712	0.391	0.398
1968	0.403	0.410	0.700	0.713	0.395	0.399
1969	0.405	0.412	0.691	0.712	0.393	0.398
1970	0.415	0.415	0.682	0.712	0.397	0.397
1971	0.412	0.420	0.667	0.713	0.398	0.394
1972	0.432	0.428	0.668	0.710	0.406	0.401
1973	0.435	0.427	0.662	0.713	0.404	0.397
1974	0.449	0.420	0.686	0.725	0.425	0.396
1975	0.469	0.428	0.642	0.699	0.431	0.393
1976	0.470	0.445	0.618	0.700	0.415	0.407
1977	0.476	0.444	0.619	0.704	0.419	0.406
1978	0.482	0.450	0.622	0.704	0.426	0.413
1979	0.492	0.451	0.619	0.699	0.435	0.414
1980	0.505	0.456	0.612	0.688	0.443	0.418

Sources: Column (1): total employment: *Department of Employment Gazette*. Percentage part-time, census year 1951: census; 1961–6: Department of Employment and Productivity (1971); 1971: census, assuming those with hours not stated are self-emloyed; and 1981: census; intercensal years to 1971: linear interpolation; *General Household Survey* used to interpolate between 1971 and 1981. Hours per person, to 1970, April survey of manual workers grafted onto *New Earnings Survey* (1970–81) manual workers. Column (2): $\Sigma_i(F_i/M_i)_{70}(M_{it}/M_t)$, where M_i is male employment in the ith industry, and F_i is female employment, the resulting measure being standardized to equal column (1) in 1970. Columns (3) and (4); *Department of Employment Gazette*, employment by industry tables (private sector = agriculture, manufacturing, construction, distributive trades, insurance, etc. and miscellaneous services). Column (5): columns (1), (3), and (4). Column (6): as column 2 but for the restricted range of industries.

Table 12.13 Regressions to explain log female–male
employment ratio in private sector

	(1)	(2)
Constant	0.59	–0.29
	(1.41)	(0.92)
Log demand structure index	0.63	0.49
	(1.25)	(1.46)
Log vacancies	0.04	–0.01
	(1.93)	(0.60)
Time	–0.01	–0.01
	(5.16)	(9.09)
Log female/male hourly earnings	0.80	–0.76
	(4.59)	(2.62)
Dummy for Sex Discrimination Act		0.28
		(5.85)
$\bar{R}^2$	0.70	0.87
D–W	0.66	1.32

Note:
t-statistics in parentheses. Vacancies are vacancies/
employment, where vacancies have been adjusted from 1974
onward using the Confederation of British Industry series on
labor shortages. The dummy is described in the text.
Dependent variable is log of Table 12.12, column (5).

respectively, in each year from 1971 to 1976, and 1 thereafter. The result is that
the wage becomes significantly negative, but a huge and implausible effect has
been attributed to the Sex Discrimination Act.

Notes

1. This proposition depends simply on the quasi-concavity of the utility function.
2. Nowadays nearly all women return to work at some point after childbearing – a
    practice that was formerly rare. For data on work histories see Martin and
    Roberts (1984).
3. Trends in part-time work during the 1970s differ according to the data source.
    Details available on request.

4. In addition to requiring equal pay for equal work (i.e., the same work), it insisted that where job evaluation was in force there should be equal pay for work of equal value. However, the general principle of equal pay for work of equal value was only being introduced in 1983.

5. *Department of Employment Gazette.* The data relate to manual workers. The question how women's pay is determined is examined at length in Zabalza and Tzannatos (1983), who show that conventional demand-side factors explain very little of the rise. They also show that among workers covered by collective bargaining agreements, the relative rise occurred entirely through changes within bargaining groups with no change in men's relative pay between groups.

6. See the various reports of the General Household Survey (GHS) published by the Office of Population Censuses and Surveys (OPCS).

7. At older ages this would not matter so much if the effect of experience on earnings is concave. Note that the available evidence does not enable one to calculate trends in the work experience of women currently working. The work of Zabalza and Arrufat (1983) argues that human capital explains most of the female-male wage gap in the late 1970s. Whereas the actual hourly earnings of married women were 62 per cent of males' earnings, they would have been between 67 per cent and 73 per cent if they had been determined by the male rather than the female earnings function. On this issue see also Stewart and Greenhalgh (1984).

8. There is no annual series on labor force participation. The employment series we use is based on a survey of one-half of 1 per cent of all employees covered by National Insurance. This was discontinued in 1975 and no subsequent time-series data exist on age-specific employment (except from surveys with large sampling error).

9. For exact definitions of variables see Joshi *et al.* (*1981*), Annexes A, C; or Joshi and Owen (1981), Annexes A, B.

10. The National Insurance Card data also give, separately by age, data on those not employed but receiving 'credits.' But these exclude unregistered unemployed and include the sick.

11. As an estimation strategy, this is a standard procedure for pooled time series. It resembles the procedure adopted by Heckman and MaCurdy (1980) for their micro-panel data: they specify fixed effects, to capture 'permanent' variables among individuals, analogous to our a_j.

12. Once cohort dummies were included there was little serial correlation in the error terms of adjacent time periods holding age constant, or adjacent age groups holding time constant. (ρ was 0.16 and 0.20, respectively, in regression 1 of Table 12.9).

13. We restrict our analysis to ages 20–59 to avoid specific questions associated with women's retirement age and educational enrolment. There was some doubt about the National Insurance data on teenage employment, but data for ages below 20 are used where necessary to allow for lags.

14. We are assuming that between cohorts those with a high 'taste' for work have on average a normal 'taste' for children.

15. The number of children also has a minor, non-linear effect (Joshi and Owen, 1981, sec. 4(i)).

16. The numbers are derived from data on births and therefore ignore mortality and migration. Joshi and Owen also experimented with other variables such as marital status and the existence of any child, some of which marginally improved the fit.
17. There is no evidence for a changing deterrent effect of younger children.
18. If the interest rate exceeds the pure rate of time preference, individuals will consume more later in life, and hence, if the price of home time in terms of goods is constant, they will also consume more home time later in life. For models of life-cycle planning see Smith (1973) and Heckman and MaCurdy (1980).
19. The effect of age *per se* disappears at ages below 40 when family structure is specified in more detail (see Joshi and Owen, 1981).
20. The coefficients for cohorts aged 20 in 1922 to 1964 were 0.64, 0.67, 0.67, 0.66, 0.70, 0.70, 0.71, 0.73, 0.72, 0.74, 0.74, 0.77, 0.75, 0.78, 0.78, 0.78, 0.79, 0.79, 0.83, 0.81, 0.82, 0.82, 0.84, 0.84, 0.85, 0.87, 0.88, 0.89, 0.89, 0.88, 0.90, 0.89, 0.91, 0.94, 0.92, 0.93, 0.92, 0.92, 0.91, 0.93, 0.93, 0.93, 0.92.
21. For broken families we only know the proportion of women *currently* divorced or widowed. The former was still quite small in 1974, reaching a maximum of 3.8 per cent in the 32–36 age bracket. The number of widows has been falling and in 1974 was 5 per cent at 48 years and 12 per cent at 56. There are no good time series on the proportion of lone women with children, but in any case they are a small proportion of all mothers (7 per cent in the 1975 General Household Survey). If they were to be adequately treated, we should also have to bring in their income maintenance opportunities (see Horton, 1979).
22. For a further discussion of this issue see Zabalza and Tzannatos (1983).
23. On average, the annual number of applications has been around 200, the number of cases actually heard around 80, and the number of cases upheld around 15. For this reason we reject the approach of Landes (1968), which argues that if employers are faced with a cost if they discriminate against women this will raise their demand price for women.
24. In the first year (1976), there were 1742 applications, 709 cases heard, and 213 upheld; in 1982 these numbers had fallen to 39, 13, and 2, respectively.
25. The index is thus $\Sigma_i(F_{it}/M_i)_0(M_{it}/M_t)$. The rationale is as follows. Suppose the demand function in each sector is $(F_{it}/M_{it}) = a_i f(R_t)$, where R_t is relative wages. Hence $(F_{it}/M_{it}) = (f(R_t)/f(R_0))(F_i/M_i)_0$ and $(F_t/M_t) = \Sigma(F_{it}/M_{it})(M_{it}/M_t) = (f(R_t)/f(R_0)) \Sigma(F_i/M_i)_0(M_{it}/M_t)$.

References

Arrufat, J.L. and A. Zabalza (1983) 'Female labour supply with taxation, random preferences and optimization errors', Centre for Labour Economics, LSE, *Discussion Paper*, 174.

Becker, G.S. and G. Ghez (1975) *The Allocation of Goods and Time over the Life Cycle* (New York: Columbia University Press for the National Bureau of Economic Research).

Blundell, R. and I. Walker (1982) 'Modelling the joint determination of household labour supplies and commodity demands', *Economic Journal*, 92, 361–64.

Department of Employment and Productivity (1971) *British Labour Statistics: Historical Abstract 1886–1968* (London: HMSO).

Greenhalgh, C. (1977) 'A labour supply function for married women in Great Britain', *Economica*, 44 (August), 249–65.

Greenhalgh, C. (1980) 'Participation and hours of work for married women in Great Britain', *Oxford Economic Papers*, 32 (July), 296–318.

Heckman, J. and T. McCurdy (1980) 'A life-cycle model of female labour supply', *Review of Economic Studies*, 47 (January), 47–74.

Horton, R. (1979) 'Work and the single parent', Centre for Labour Economics, LSE, *Working Paper*, 131.

Joshi, H. (1981) 'Secondary workers in the employment cycle, Great Britain, 1961–74', *Economica*, 48 (February), 29–44.

Joshi, H. (1984) 'Women's participation in paid work', Department of Employment, *Research Paper*, 45.

Joshi, H. and S. Owen (1981) 'Demographic predictors of women's work participation in post-war Britain', Centre for Population Studies, London School of Hygiene and Tropical Medicine, *Discussion Paper*, 81–3.

Joshi, H., R. Layard and S. Owen (1981) 'Female labour supply in post-war Britain: a cohort approach', Centre for Labour Economics, LSE, *Discussion Paper*, 79.

Joshi, H., R. Layard and S. Owen (1983) 'Why are more women working in Britain?', Centre for Labour Economics, LSE, *Discussion Paper*, 162.

Landes, W.M. (1968) 'The economics of fair employment laws', *Journal of Political Economy*, 76 (July–August), 507–22.

Layard, R. (1982) 'Youth unemployment in Britain and the US compared', in R. Freeman and D. Wise (eds), *The Youth Labor Market Problem* (Chicago: University of Chicago Press).

Layard, R., M. Barton and A. Zabalza (1980) 'Married women's participation and hours', *Economica* (February), 51–72, Chapter 11 in this volume.

Martin, J. and C. Roberts (1984) *Women and Employment: A Lifetime Perspective* (London: HMSO).

Smith, J.P. (1984) 'Family decision-making over the life-cycle', R-1121-EDA (Santa Monica: Rand).

Stewart, M. and C. Greenhalgh (1984) 'Work history patterns and occupational attainment of women', *Economic Journal*, 94 (September).

Zabalza, A. (1980) 'The 1974/75 GHS comparison exercise', Centre for Labour Economics, LSE, *Working Paper*, 203.

Zabalza, A. (1983) 'The CES utility function non-linear budget constraints and labour supply: results on female participation and hours', *Economic Journal*, 93 (June), 312–30.

Zabalza, A. and J.L. Arrufat (1983) 'Wage differentials between married men and women in Great Britain: the depreciation effect of non-participation', Centre for Labour Economics, LSE, *Discussion Paper*, 151.

Zabalza, A. and Z. Tzannatos (1983) 'The effect of Britain's anti-discriminatory legislation on relative pay and employment', Centre for Labour Economics, LSE, *Discussion Paper*, 155.

13 On the Use of Distributional Weights in Social Cost-Benefit Analysis (1980)*

Harberger (1978b) argues against using distributional weights on two grounds.[1] (1) If the weights differ too much between people, they could be used to justify excessively inefficient projects. (2) Even so, the distributional-weights approach can lead to regressive marginal tax rates, which the public considers inequitable. This is Morton's Fork indeed.[2] I shall consider the two prongs in sequence.

HOW WIDE A SPREAD IN WEIGHTS SHOULD WE EXPECT?

Harberger's basic argument against accepting too wide a spread of weights consists of two propositions.

1 *A logical proposition* – Suppose R is richer than P, and it costs c dollars deadweight efficiency loss at the margin to transfer one dollar from R to P (c is of course endogenous). Let w_i be i's distributional 'weight', that is, the social or ethical value of a dollar accruing to i. Then, so long as

$$-w_R + w_P(1 - c) > 0$$

we should continue transferring dollars from R to P. Thus, at an optimum we would never observe w_R less than w_p by more than the factor c:

$$\frac{w_R}{w_P} \geq 1 - c. \tag{1}$$

2 *An empirical proposition* – The cost of redistribution is fairly small: 'most beginning graduate students could in one afternoon invent a hundred ways of bringing about major transfers at an efficiency cost of less than 20 percent of the amounts involved' (p. 115).

---

* *Journal of Political Economy*, 88(5) (1980), pp. 1041–7.

258

Proposition 1 is standard, so the issue is essentially empirical and revolves around proposition 2. I wish to argue that the costs of any significant redistribution are a lot higher than Harberger and others imply.[3] The measure of c that is normally quoted in discussions of these issues is the marginal excess burden per unit change in *tax revenue*, somehow defined (see, e.g., Musgrave, 1969).[4] But this is not the relevant measure. What matters is the marginal excess burden per unit change in the *net transfer* from richer to poorer. The second measure of cost is much larger than the first.

As an example consider a self-balancing linear income tax, where individual i makes positive or negative net transfers to the government equal to $T_i = tn_i - t\bar{n}$ where n_i is his gross income and $\bar{n}$ is average income. The marginal excess burden per unit change in 'tax revenue' (tn_i) is $\eta t/(1 - t - \eta t)$, where η is the compensated elasticity of supply.[5] Empirical estimates of η for married men's supply of hours are around 0.2,[6] so this measure of the efficiency cost could not be over 20 per cent, unless tax rates were nearing 50 per cent. But the proper measure of c is the marginal excess burden per dollar of net transfer, not per dollar of tax revenue. And the amount of net transfer is much less than the amount of tax revenue. Let me first illustrate this with a simple two-person example and then show how it is that n-person optimal income tax calculations regularly end up with widely spread distributional weights.

Suppose R has a gross income of unity, while P's income is α (< 1). Then the 'tax proceeds' are $t(1 + \alpha)$. But the net transfer is only $\frac{1}{2}t$ $(1 - \alpha)$, since, although the rich man pays t in tax, he gets back $\frac{1}{2}t$ $(1 + \alpha)$ in handout. Thus the net transfer is $(1 - \alpha)/2(1 + \alpha)$ times the tax proceeds. Suppose, for example, that P has half the income of R.[7] The net transfer is then *one-sixth* of the tax proceeds. So the cost per marginal dollar of transfer (c) is *six times* the cost per marginal dollar of tax revenue. Thus even quite low taxes may involve high efficiency costs per unit of net transfer.

But what levels of tax are desirable? Clearly if taxes are very low the income distribution will remain unequal and the distributional weights will be far enough apart to justify the costs of further redistribution via higher tax rates. At the optimum (1) will hold as an equality. We shall suppose that the marginal social value of a dollar for a person with net income y is $y^{-\epsilon}$ ($\epsilon > 0$). We therefore require that

$$\left(\frac{y_P}{y_R}\right)^\epsilon = 1 - c = 1 - \frac{\eta t}{1 - t - \eta t} 2\frac{1 + \alpha}{1 - \alpha}$$

or, substituting in for y, that

$$\left[\frac{\alpha(1 - t) + \frac{1}{2}t(1 + \alpha)}{1(1 - t) + \frac{1}{2}t(1 + \alpha)}\right]^\epsilon = 1 - \frac{\eta t}{1 - t - \eta t} 2\frac{1 + \alpha}{1 - \alpha} \tag{2}$$

Suppose, for example, $\alpha = 0.5$ (as before), $\eta = 0.2$, and $\epsilon = 1$. The optimal tax rate is then 24 per cent. And the excess burden per dollar of net transfer is no less than 40 per cent. The amount of redistribution that has occurred is quite small; P still has only 60 per cent of R's net income.

This little calculation illustrates three points. First (as above), even quite low tax rates involve quite high efficiency costs of net transfer. Second, any major redistribution requires quite high tax rates. Hence, third, optimality involves a balance where distributional weights are likely to be quite widely spread, reflecting simultaneously the high cost of further redistribution and the considerable amount of remaining inequality.[8]

The argument is further reinforced if we introduce a requirement for some form of government expenditure which cannot be allocated to individual net income (e.g., defense, law and order).[9] The reader can try varying the parameter values used in these calculations, but I suspect he will end up with a marginal cost per dollar of net transfer that is higher than 20 per cent.

However, the argument so far is oversimplified in two ways. First it is artificially restricted to two people.[10] Turning to the n-person case, an optimal linear income tax requires that at the margin the social cost from the tax levied on all individuals ($\Sigma t n_i$) equals the social benefit of the handout ($t\bar{n}$).

So suppose the tax rate is raised by Δt. Individual i pays approximately $\Delta t n_i$ more in taxes. He also receives an additional handout which consists of the total increase in tax revenue averaged over all taxpayers. This, after allowing for the deadweight loss, is

$$\Delta t \bar{n}[1 - (\eta t / 1 - t - \eta t)]$$

At the optimum the social value of these two changes must be the same when summed over all individuals. To compute social value we need to weight each individual by the weight appropriate to his net income, $w_i = w(y_i) = w[n_i(1 - t) + \bar{n}t]$. So optimality requires that

$$\Delta t \int_0^\infty n \cdot w[n(1 - t) + \bar{n}t]f(n)dn$$

$$= \Delta t \bar{n}\left(1 - \frac{\eta t}{1 - t - \eta t}\right) \int_0^\infty w[n(1 - t) + \bar{n}_t]f(n)dn$$

Suppose we assume that $w(y) = y^{-1}$ and n is lognormal with var ln $n = 0.36$. There is no simple analytical solution to the problem, but one can check that the solution $t = 0.5$ approximately satisfies the equation.[11] Such a tax rate will leave us with quite widely spread distributional weights. Stern has examined similar problems using explicit utility functions and programming methods to solve the problems; he reports quite widely spread distributional weights (Stern, 1976, 1977).[12]

This leads to the second issue: Would the optimal tax be linear? Mirrlees (1971) found results in which it did not diverge markedly from linearity except at the extreme ends. However, this is a matter explicitly studied in Harberger's paper, where he claims that one can end up with marginal tax rates that fall with income. I shall therefore turn to his method of calculating the optimal income tax.

HARBERGER'S METHOD OF COMPUTING THE OPTIMAL INCOME TAX

There seems to be one basic omission in his argument. He assumes that the tax schedule can be completely described by the set of marginal tax rates for the different income brackets. In fact, however, one more parameter is needed – to fix the level of the tax. Harberger implicitly assumes that the tax paid by a man with zero income is zero. He then develops his argument as follows. If we raise the marginal tax on a low bracket of income, this also brings in revenue from the higher-income groups, while, if we raise the marginal tax on a high-income bracket, there is no analogous advantage. Since similar efficiency costs are involved in both exercises, this constitutes a case for raising marginal tax rates at the bottom. However, once we let the level of tax at zero income be a parameter to be determined, we can quite easily reduce the marginal tax paid by lower-income groups without affecting the taxes paid by higher-income groups. For example, in Figure 13.1 if the marginal tax rate for the bracket 0–1000 were reduced from 30 per cent to zero, this would not affect the taxes paid by higher-income groups if at the same time the net tax paid by a man with zero income were raised by $300.

In fact there is in the net-tax system no asymmetry of the kind which Harberger assumes. The tax system could be just as well described by the total tax at *any* income plus the set of marginal tax rates. Suppose we define the tax system by the intercept at income n_{max} and the set of marginal tax rates. Then the marginal tax rate on the *top* incomes affects *all* income groups, while the marginal tax on the lowest incomes only affects the poorest groups. If we now repeat Harberger's method of calculation, but calculating marginal tax rates from the top downward, the optimal marginal tax rate for the top income group now turns out to be about 165 per cent,[13] rather than the 28 per cent which Harberger found starting from the bottom up.

This result stems from Harberger's particular numbers, which do not allow for the possibility of any endogenous determination of the level of taxes at zero income. If the level of tax at zero income were allowed to be freely determined, it turns out that it ought to be increased.[14] If the tax at zero income were set endogenously and Harberger's weights represented a consistent set of equilibrium values, they would need to have an average value equal to the shadow price of public revenue.

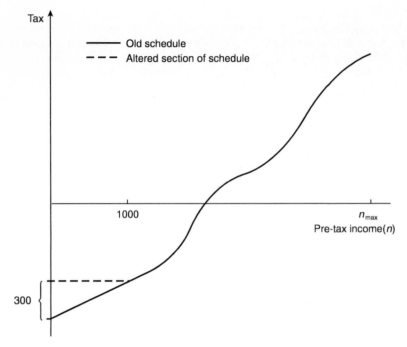

Figure 13.1

There is a second numerical curiosity. Harberger does not have a preassigned net government revenue requirement (for public goods) but lets government revenue be determined *ex post* by, among other things, its shadow price (of unity). In the upshot, government revenue equals 40 per cent of GNP. This is very high for public expenditure on goods and services. To allow part of it to be given back to households as income-related subsidies is contrary to the spirit of optimum income tax exercises. However, it would be possible within Harberger's framework to alter net tax receipts by altering the shadow price of government expenditure. But it is easy to verify that quite minor changes in the shadow price lead to markedly different tax structures from those he reports.

Despite these criticisms it is true that generalized calculations of the optimal income tax will produce lower marginal tax rates at the extremes of the distribution than over its main range, for reasons analogous to those which Harberger adduces. It is easy to confirm this by imagining an (optimal) tax structure defined by a set of marginal rates and a level parameter (located at *any* given point of gross income) and then varying each parameter marginally, one at a time. However, once we have freed up the level parameter, we normally find that the *average* tax rates rise with income except at the very top, and this is the basic point for which there is surely a democratic consensus. In particular, average tax rates at the bottom are generally negative – a possibility for which Harberger's analysis makes no allowance.

Thus, the distributional-weights approach cannot be faulted for inconsistency with the evidence about actual social preference. Moreover, using income taxation, the marginal cost of redistribution is high even for quite small redistributions. So, unless other methods of redistribution can be shown to be feasible, one would expect quite widely dispersed distributional weights at the social optimum.[15]

Notes

1. See esp. p. S113. The argument is spelled out further in Harberger (1978a), and my description of it draws on that paper as well. I am grateful to Harberger for a helpful discussion of this note and to N. Stern for extensive comments.
2. Morton was Chancellor to King Henry VII. If a nobleman was spending a lot Morton concluded that he could afford high taxes, and if he was spending a little Morton also concluded that he could afford high taxes.
3. This is implicit in the outcome of fully specified optimal income tax models (see Mirrlees, 1971 and Stern, 1976). However, the relation of those results to those which would be obtained using the more old-fashioned concept of excess burden has not been made explicit. The first part of this note aims to show this relation.
4. Musgrave in fact uses the *average* excess burden per unit of tax revenue.
5. I assume all factors of production are perfect substitutes. Suppose an individual has a fixed gross wage, w, per hour and pays a constant marginal tax of wt for each hour he works. This marginal tax is now raised by one unit. The efficiency loss is wt $(\partial H / \partial w^*)$ where w^* is the net wage. The tax revenue increases by $H - wt(\partial H / \partial w^*)$. So the excess burden per marginal dollar of revenue is

$$\frac{(wt/H)(\partial H/\partial w^*)}{1 - (wt/H)(\partial H/\partial w^*)} = \frac{\eta t/(1-t)}{1 - [\eta t/(1-t)]}$$

   For further discussion of the concept of deadweight loss (= excess burden = efficiency cost), see Harberger (1973, *passim*).
6. Ashenfelter and Heckman (1973) and Brown *et al.* (1976).
7. This income distribution gives a Gini coefficient of 0.166 and is therefore less unequal than observed distributions. In general, optimal taxes are lower the lower the dispersion of gross incomes.
8. Of course, how much redistribution is desirable depends on ϵ. E.g. if $\epsilon = \frac{1}{2}$, the optimal tax rate would be only 17 per cent. The marginal cost per dollar of net transfer would be 25 per cent. But very little redistribution would have occurred: P's net income is still only 56 per cent of R's.

9. Let this requirement, elsewhere determined, be a fraction g of national income. So optimality requires that

$$\left[\frac{\alpha(1-t)+\frac{1}{2}(t-g)(1+\alpha)}{1(1-t)+\frac{1}{2}(t-g)(1+\alpha)}\right]^{\epsilon} = 1 - \frac{\eta t}{1-t-\eta t}2\frac{1+\alpha}{1-\alpha}$$

10. If there were only two people one would hardly choose a linear tax to redistribute income between them. This was done in order to illustrate clearly a more general principle.

11. If $t = 0.5$ and z is the standard normal variable, the left-hand side simplifies to $\Delta t \int 2/(1 + e^{-\sigma z + \sigma^2/2}) f(z) dz = 0.91\Delta t$. The right-hand side simplifies to $\Delta t \int 1.6/ (1 + e^{\sigma z - \sigma^2/2}) f(z) dz = 0.87\Delta t$. The integrals are evaluated using Table 8 and (55) of Johnson (1949). I am grateful to Jim Heckman for showing me this source.

12. E.g. with a constant-returns utility function implying η equals about 0.2, and with a social welfare function of $(-\sum_i 1/U_i)$ and with a government revenue requirement equal to about 20 per cent of GNP, he ends up with the weight at the eighty-fifth percentile equal to 40 per cent of the weight at the fifteenth percentile.

13. $1875 t = $ own group benefit + intramarginal benefit $= -525 + 3640$.

14. The social value of a dollar of lump-sum tax paid by each person is $29.5 - (0.4)(120) < 0$ (see his Table 2); so the social value of a dollar of lump-sum subsidy is positive.

15. It is unlikely that differential commodity taxes will help a very great deal, but if it proved possible to distribute lump-sum subsidies related to hourly wage rates, this could greatly reduce the cost of subsidizing some low incomes.

References

Ashenfelter, O. and J.J. Heckman (1973) 'Estimating labor supply functions', in G. Cain and H.W. Watts (eds), *Income Maintenance and Labor Supply* (Chicago: Rand McNally).

Brown, C.V., E. Levin and D. Ulph (1976) 'Estimates of hours supplied by married male workers in Great Britain', *Scottish Journal of Political Economy*, 23 (November), 261–77.

Harberger, A.C. (1973) *Taxation and Welfare* (Boston: Little, Brown).

Harberger, A.C. (1978a) 'Basic needs versus distributional weights in social cost-benefit analysis', University of Chicago, mimeo.

Harberger, A.C. (1978b) 'On the use of distributional weights in social cost-benefit analysis', *Journal of Political Economy*, 86(2), pt 2 (April), S87–S120.

Johnson, N.L. (1949) 'Systems of frequency curves generated by methods of translation', *Biometrika*, 36 (June), 149–76.

Mirrlees, J.A. (1971) 'An exploration in the theory of optimum income taxation', *Review of Economic Studies*, 33 (April), 175–208.

Musgrave, R.A. (1969) 'A cost-benefit analysis and the theory of public finance', *Journal of Economic Literature*, 7 (September), S797–S806.

Stern, N.H. (1976) 'On the specification of models of optimum taxation', *Journal of Public Economy*, 6 (July–August), 123–62.
Stern, N.H. (1977) 'Welfare weights and the elasticity of the marginal valuation of income', in M.J. Artis and A.R. Nobay (eds), *Studies in Modern Economic Analysis* (Oxford: Blackwell).

14 Human Satisfactions and Public Policy (1980)*

HUMAN SATISFACTIONS AND PUBLIC POLICY

There is much casual evidence that people in the West are not becoming happier, despite economic growth. There is also some systematic evidence.[1] Opinion polls reveal no increase in self-rated happiness in the United States since the War. And, more slippery evidence this, rich countries appear to be no happier than poorer ones – at any rate among the advanced countries.[2] But if growth has not brought happiness, the important question is what policy conclusions follow.

That depends, of course, on why growth has not produced the answer. Why, one might ask, do people seek to be rich if riches do not bring happiness? The answer is that riches do bring happiness, provided you are richer than other people. Thus a basic finding of happiness surveys is that, though richer societies are not happier than poorer ones, within any society happiness and riches go together.[3] I shall therefore assume as my *first* basic proposition that happiness depends, *inter alia*, on position in some *status ranking*. This explains for example why people are often quite willing to make sacrifices if they are sure everybody else is going to do the same.[4]

However, other factors may also be at work. An obvious problem with high income is that you get used to it, take it for granted and cannot do without it. The same is true of status. So I shall take as my *second* basic fact that happiness also depends on income and status relative to what you *expected* it to be. This explains why people fight much harder against cuts in their income than they fight for increases. It also explains the havoc caused by inflation, which continually reorders people in the status ranking.

Our two psychological facts are well supported by the research on relative deprivation (Runciman, 1966)[5] and must help to explain why happiness has not increased with growth. However, from now on I am simply concerned with the policy implications of these facts, which are only now beginning to become clear.[6] The first fact is particularly relevant to the efficiency branch of government and is discussed in section I of this paper; and the second is

The Economic Journal, 90 (December 1980), pp. 737–50.
I am grateful to D. de Meza. H. Gintis, D. Grubb, J. Margolis. J. Mirrlees, P. Mueser, S. Nickell, M. Reder, S. Streiter and P. Wiles for helpful comments.

particularly relevant to equity questions, and is discussed in section II. The conclusions are summarised at the end.

I THE PURSUIT OF STATUS

If status is defined by rank order, the pursuit of status is a zero-sum game – one man's gain in rank is another man's loss. It is not quite the same as Hirsch's example of the situation where everyone stands on tiptoe to see better, and all end up seeing the same but straining to keep on tiptoe. For the status game can lead to changes of view (i.e. of rank order). There might sometimes be an equity case for wanting some of these changes. But, if not, a major task of public policy is to counteract the effects of the desire for status upon human behaviour.[7] For, though individuals are willing to make sacrifices to improve their individual position, the net result of status-motivated action will be no increase in status satisfaction but an increase in sacrifice. So how can the government offset the individual drive for status? As usual, there are three methods – fiscal, institutional and moral.

Taxation

If it could identify the actions that improve status, the government could tax them. For example, if income confers status, it can and should be taxed on efficiency grounds. Thus it may be that the income tax is a lot less inefficient than is sometimes supposed.[8]

The matter is not easy to investigate. The simplest approach is to assume that status depends on income relative to the mean. If in addition we begin with the extreme assumption that net income (y) is not valued for its own sake at all, then

$$u^i = u\left(\frac{y_i}{\bar{y}}, h_i\right) \tag{1}$$

where h_i is work effort. In order to concentrate on efficiency issues, let us assume that all men have the same wage rate. In this case the optimal tax rate is unity.[9]

However, this assumes that people do not value income at all for its own sake. This does not seem reasonable. All over the world there is net migration towards richer areas. This does not prove that additional income actually makes people happier. For people may move due to misinformation – they may not realise it is the status which income confers rather than its intrinsic worth which leads them to want it. However, many migrants do not return. Here again one could argue that a person who has migrated would be involved in money cost and loss of face if he returned and is not therefore necessarily better off after moving than he would have been had he never moved in the first place. But for the sake of generality I shall from now on assume that income is partly valued for its own sake.[10]

To allow for this we could assume that

$$u^i = u(y_i, \bar{y}, h_i) \tag{2}$$

We now represent the status problem by the negative effect of the average income level upon individual utility ($\partial u / \partial \bar{y} < 0$). In this case the additional tax paid by an individual who does an extra hour of work (wt) should equal the money value of the harm done to others.[11]

$$wt \simeq -n \frac{\partial u}{\partial \bar{y}} \left(\frac{w}{n} \bigg/ \frac{\partial u}{\partial y_i} \right)$$

where w is the gross hourly wage and n is population. In other words, the optimum marginal tax rate equals approximately the ratio of the marginal disutility of average income ($\bar{y}$) to the marginal utility of individual income (y_i).

This formulation may begin to catch some elements of the tax problem. But it is probably not very realistic. For the evidence is that people are mainly bothered about the incomes of people close to them in the income distribution and do not suffer greatly from the riches of the rich (or of the poor), unless they happen to be nearly rich (or poor) themselves (Runciman, 1966). Thus one cannot really assume that status is determined by a person's income relative to mean income. Instead it is more realistic to revert to our basic initial concept that what matters is a person's percentile rank-order (R) in the earnings distribution.

It is expositionally convenient to assume an additive form of utility function so that[12]

$$u_i = aR_i + v_i(h_i)$$

Social utility is now given by a $\sum R_i + \sum v_i(h_i)$. Since the first term cannot be altered, the social optimum once more requires a tax rate of unity, so that people only work for its own sake.

If, by contrast, people also value income as such, we can, again for simplicity of exposition, write

$$u_i = aR_i + v_i(y_i h_i)$$

To produce an optimum we ensure that the additional tax paid by an individual who does an extra hour of work (wt) equals the money value of the harm which others suffer from their consequential loss of rank.[13]

$$wt = -a \sum_{j \neq i} \frac{\partial R_j}{\partial h_i} \bigg/ \frac{\partial v_i}{\partial y_i}$$

Since the total value which people derive from rank is constant, this tax per hour is also equal to the money value of the benefit to the individual from *his* gain in rank: we tax away all his gains from doing better in the zero-sum game.

There is an apparent worry about the rank-order model that is worth defusing at this point. One might be tempted to argue as follows. If a tax system reduces the money gain from extra work, it will not necessarily affect work choice. For status may depend on gross earnings; or, even if it depends on net earnings, the tax will reduce the money gap between individuals so that the gain in rank order resulting from an extra hour of work may not be reduced by the tax. However, this argument overlooks the fact that the tax does reduce the private return to work via its effect on the enjoyment of income *per se*. Hence (assuming the tax proceeds are distributed) the tax *will* reduce effort and thus offset the tendency towards excessive work induced by status-seeking. Thus, whether we use the relative income model or the rank-order approach, we find a case for government intervention to reduce the private return to work.

As usual in discussions of pollution, there will be people who argue that intervention is also needed to reduce the rate of growth of market output. But, as usual, this does not follow, and it is worth a brief digression to prove it. For simplicity we shall assume that intertemporal utility (U^i) equals the sum of the utilities in two periods (o and 1), each of which depends on current individual consumption (y_i) and current average consumption ($\bar{y}$).

$$U^i = u^0(y_i^0, \bar{y}^0) + u^1(y_i^1, \bar{y}^1) \tag{3}$$

The sacrifice of consumption in period o can raise consumption in period 1 (we are for simplicity assuming no capital market). It follows that there will only be too much sacrifice if the marginal disutility of average consumption in period 1 (relative to personal consumption) exceeds the marginal disutility of average consumption in period o (relative to personal consumption).[14]

For there is an external benefit from the lowered consumption in the first period which has to be more than offset by the external disbenefit from the higher consumption in the second period. There is no obvious reason why this should happen and thus in general there does not seem to be any status argument against productive investment.

So far we have assumed that status is conferred only by income. But suppose, for example, that status is conferred directly by effort. This will lead to too much effort.[15] Or, suppose education as such confers status. This leads to over-investment in education. Much has been made of the external benefits of education, and some extraordinary claims made. For example, people have pointed out what fun it will be for the existing graduates to have more other graduates to talk to. I have never seen it pointed out that by the same token the non-graduates will have fewer non-graduates to talk to. In fact there must surely be many perverse incentives encouraging extra education, which all boil down to the reason that other people are getting it.

Likewise, in a poor society a man proves to his wife that he loves her by giving her a rose but in a rich society he must give a dozen roses. A poor family can entertain graciously on beer but a rich one must give champagne. It is not nice to assert that many of the strivings of modern man (to educate himself, to migrate, to entertain well and so on) are in part self-defeating in terms of collective satisfaction, but to pretend otherwise is to ignore the evidence that human satisfaction is not expanding as the economic model without externalities suggests it should be. And many of these externalities can be dealt with by fiscal policy.[16]

Institutions

The scope for status competition is also of course affected by institutions. It may be true that human nature is intrinsically competitive (see, for example, Russell, 1949). But the extent to which the competitive motive dominates his behaviour depends upon the number of competitions that are open to him. Every organiser knows this, and when he worries about insufficient motivation among those for whom he is responsible he is tempted to invent a competition. Parents organise races, school teachers publish form orders,[17] Stalin appoints model workers, the Chinese government encourages 'socialist emulation', the Nobel committee offers prizes whose chief value is non-monetary, and the British government offers titles (Sir, Lord). There is no doubt that these devices do motivate.[18] The question is whether they add to or subtract from human welfare.

This is a difficult question. Some competition is enjoyable even for the loser, though most tennis-players choose to play with people they occasionally beat – an option less open to those who have to earn their living. There is also the problem of anomie, if there are insufficient external goals to keep the mind occupied.[19] Competition is also enjoyable to those looking on from outside – as Lucretius said, 'when the sea is tossed with great winds, it is delightful to be on land and watch others sweating it out'. But since the institutions of the world are mainly devised by those who have succeeded in the competitive struggle, one cannot assume that the social cost of competition (to the loser) has been fully taken into account.

To think about the optimum structure of institutions, one can perhaps consider the utility function as follows. There are some rank-orders which are unavoidable and which people will always care about (money, in particular). Call this R^1. But there are other rank-orders which may or may not be made available by the society. For example, the rank-order on an exam (R^2) can only matter to people if a rank-order is published. If there is no rank order in a particular possible dimension, we can proceed as though on that particular variable (t) everyone had $R_i{}^t = 0.5$ (the median). So, if there are T technically possible rank-orders, we can write the utility function as

$$u_i = \sum_{t=1}^{T} a_t[R_i^t - 0.5] + v_i(y_i, h_i)$$

The question is then what is the optimum degree of differentiation by the non-monetary characteristics 2 up to T.

The answer is that we want people to work until the value of their marginal product equals the marginal disutility of work. If we have a competitive (or other) market that pays gross wages equal to the value of the marginal product, and if we need no taxes for other purposes, then we want as little non-monetary differentiation as possible and some taxes to offset the effects of the rank-order differentiation that is inevitable.[20] But if we are prevented (for example by school-teacher unions or Maoist ideology) from paying people for their efforts, then we may need to use other methods of motivation.

Sometimes it is not easy to pay people at the time for their effort – for example, to pay properly the inventors of public goods (such as modern microeconomic theory). In this case any *ex post* money payment almost inevitably brings with it an enormous amount of non-monetary reward.[21] Whether these prizes are a good thing depends on the value of the resulting gains to knowledge compared to the strains induced among the competitors.[22]

An interesting competitive institution that is much hated is the examination system. This has a number of functions. First it provides information to employers, so that good performance leads to higher income. This means that, if the examination can be prepared for, it will motivate study. Moreover, if the examination results are given wide publicity, good performance will also confer status (directly rather than through income) and this further motivates students.

However, students can be over-motivated and, if too much hangs on the results, failure can be very painful. Hence Mao's attack on exams. The Chinese reforms of the late 1960s were designed to remove the anxieties associated with the exam system – and, even wider, with the system by which the individual rather than the bureaucracy takes the initiative in charting his educational and occupational destiny. But the Chinese discovered the inefficiency of the alternative system for mobilising talent, and in 1977–8 restored the system of open examinations for university entry. They thus reinstated just about the most individualistic activity open to man, except perhaps for solo competitive sports and solo writing. This gives us some indication of the productive cost of a system that prevents the individual running in the rat-race.

Yet the rat-race also has its costs. Interestingly the American examination system, which consists of a large number of small hurdles, is probably less costly than the British system, which consists of a small number of 7-footers. The clearest indication of a bad selection system is the extent to which its victims are obsessed by the process of selection. For the costs of education are not just direct costs and earnings foregone, but also the anxieties which students experience. And institutional arrangements like exam systems do affect these anxieties.[23]

Changing human nature

Of course the Chinese must be hoping that their new exam system will not have as bad effects as the old one because they have 'changed human nature' in the meantime. At this point we have to distinguish between two forms of moral change. First, there is the argument (stressed by Sen, 1973 and Hirsch, 1977) that where there is an externality problem that cannot easily be handled by fiscal policy or regulation it is in the interest of all that all should exercise restraint rather than that none should do so. This does not require a change in people's utility functions – but only in the actions they take in pursuit of utility. Clearly such restraint can happen. Politicians do not always do everything possible to further their cause; they prefer to preserve the political fabric itself. But Hirsch is not at all specific about how private restraint could effectively overcome the externality problem of status competition, if people really do value status. He argues that modern men have been encouraged to think they have a moral duty to do the best for themselves, since this will help out the invisible hand. And he believes that if they were disabused of this fallacy, things would improve. One hopes so. But the problem of status competition is much less clear-cut than the problem of litter, and it is not clear just how a person observing the social contract would know when to stop work.

This brings one to the second possibility: that the utility function could itself be changed by education, so that people got more pleasure from the welfare of others and less from the feeling of being better off than others are.[24] This seems to be a much surer approach. One wants people to work not in order to excel over others (a game against persons) but in order to do the job well (a game against nature). This is not pie in the sky – most people who do crossword puzzles are not competing against other people. But the problem is that every stage of life is littered with institutions that reinforce the competitive value system. To do our work we need to know whose articles are worth reading, who is worth asking for a seminar, and who is worth appointing to a job. If we spend so much time putting people in order, can we really expect ourselves to work for motives unconnected with rank-order? Yet if we cannot, it is not going to be easy to improve human welfare (at any rate once a modicum of physical comfort has been achieved). If personality is largely constructed in the first six years of life, perhaps the best hope lies in a moral code which forbids all comparisons between children until they are, say, six.[25]

II. THE ROLE OF EXPECTED INCOME AND EXPECTED STATUS

I now need to bring in another consideration – the role of expectations. Happiness depends not only on status and income (*per se*), but also on what a person expected his income and status to be.

Expected income

Let us begin with the role of expected income and ignore questions of status for the moment. One obvious reason why higher income has not brought more happiness is that expected income has risen.[26] (By expected income in year *t*, I mean the income which in some earlier year a person expected to have in year *t*.)

Even if public policy cannot easily influence expectations, it has to take their existence into account. This means that the ordinary cardinal utility function, $u(y)$, used in public economics is inadequate, and may also be the reason why $u(y)$ has never so far had any impact on practical affairs. A more satisfactory approach would recognise the following:

(a) Utility depends negatively on expected income.
(b) The marginal utility of a given income depends positively on expected income.
(c) Expected income is an increasing function of past income.
(d) Marginal utility is much lower for an increase in income than for a fall, if one starts out from the expected level of income.[27]

I suspect that politicians believe many of these propositions, especially (d), which explains their unwillingness ever to make anybody worse off. But let us take the propositions in turn and explore their implications.

Suppose social welfare is given by

$$W = \Sigma u^i$$

where[28]

$$u^i = u(y_i, e_i)$$

and e is expected income. Then the just division of a cake of given size requires

$$\partial u / \partial y_i = u_1(y_i, e_i) = \lambda \quad \text{(all } i)$$

We can compare the implied optimal incomes of people with different expected incomes by totally differentiating:

$$u_{11} \, dy + u_{12} \, de = 0$$

therefore

$$dy/de = u_{12}/-u_{11}$$

One would normally assume that $u_{11} < 0$, and our proposition (b) says that $u_{12} > 0$. So someone with higher expectations should have higher income. Yesterday's rich should have higher net incomes than if all had the same expectations.[29]

This is clearly a rather conservative outcome. It becomes less so if we allow for the fact that expectations adjust over time towards the level of income actually experienced. Thus there is an optimal time path of the income distribution. If there were no time discounting and a constant cake, the income distribution should eventually become equal.[30] Equality would be approached faster, the faster expectations adjust to actual income experienced.

The psychological postulates used so far can be summarised graphically in Figure 14.1. The utility function for someone with expectations of e_1 is above that for someone with expectations of e_2, but flatter. If, in the long run,

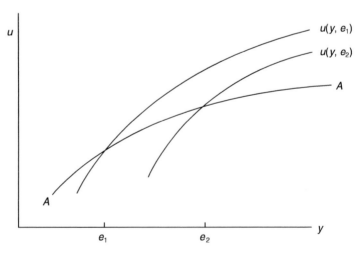

Figure 14.1

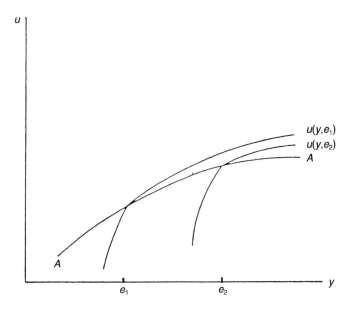

Figure 14.2

expectations tend to actual income, we have a *long-run* utility function, $u^*(y)$, shown by the line AA. Nothing we have assumed so far requires that AA slope up, but it would certainly be odd if it sloped down, so that someone who had got used to a high income was more miserable than someone who had got used to a low income. In fact, there is some not very rigorous evidence that the long-run utility function does slope up.[31]

I now come to assumption (d). People seem to fight against cuts in their living standards much more energetically than they fight for increases.[32] This suggests that the marginal utility of income for decreases in income below what is expected is much greater than the marginal utility for increases in income. In other words, the short-run utility function should be redrawn with a kink as in Figure 14.2. This again has rather conservative implications, since the gain to a poorer man from an income transfer can quite easily be less than the loss to a richer man. A feeling that this is so explains the understandable unwillingness of politicians to make rationalisations of, for example, social security, in which almost inevitably a few people lose. It also explains their willingness to protect even quite well-off people from the effects of economic change.[33] But if the long-run curve AA is concave, the optimal long-run goal is still equality. In order to achieve this goal it is at first necessary to reduce social welfare by disappointing the expectations of the rich, which then alters appropriately. It is asking a lot of politicians to ask them to embark on this process.

The point I have been making about expectations bears some relation to Scitovsky's argument about novelty. We need to be surprised, and this is a difficult thing for the individual to contrive for himself. Clearly he will be better off if his income is always running ahead of his expectations. This argues in favour of public policies to encourage low expectations[34] and, perhaps, low juvenile wages. One argument for economic growth is that, at any rate in the 1950s, it surprised people. But people can have expectations of a constant level of income or a constant first derivative, second derivative, or any higher derivative. The trouble with the 1960s may have been that people had become adjusted to expecting constant growth and they got no more than that. This may explain why the Gallup Poll results quoted by Easterlin (1972) suggest an increase in happiness in the United States up to 1965 followed by a decrease.

Expected status

However, another reason is inflation, which has brought about much more frequent rearrangements of people in the status hierarchy.[35] Once again we may suppose that increases in status above the level expected produce smaller gains in happiness than the loss of happiness caused by a shortfall in status below the level expected. Given this we have a good partial explanation of why inflation reduces social welfare, even when real incomes are rising. For in Britain at least the non-synchronised nature of pay settlements means that, of two groups whose real incomes over a year are equal and rising smoothly, each spend half of the year resenting that the other group is way ahead of them in the ladder of pay.[36]

The importance of expected status is not of course an argument against the redistribution of income. The fact that the poor do not resent the riches of the wealthy does not mean that their happiness could not be increased by a bigger cut. But it does again argue in favour of preserving relative rankings, unless there is some good reason to the contrary.

III CONCLUSION

Somehow, policy-makers need to take into account all the factors we have reviewed, as well as many others. Clearly the job cannot be done perfectly. But if status and expectations are as important determinants of human satisfaction as they seem to be, it will not do for economists to tell policy-makers to ignore them. There is little virtue in tidy solutions that ignore major elements in a situation. However, the arguments in this paper only begin to nibble at the problems.

Two features of human nature are considered. The first is the desire for status. Since status depends on rank order, the total amount of status available is given. So if people work partly to improve their status, they will work too hard (assuming no other distortions to exist). This can be corrected by taxing the proceeds of work. It can also be affected by institutional reform. The extent to which people work for status depends on the number of status competitions which are being run. If there are already a number of distortions in an economy discouraging effort, it may be necessary to invent competition to motivate people. But if there are not already large distortions, there may be a presumption against having too many competitions, except perhaps to reward the inventors of public goods. Finally, one can attempt to change human nature. One approach is to accept existing utility functions, but persuade people that the collective interest requires individual restraint in the quest for status. The other, more hopeful, approach is to try to alter utility functions in order to reduce status-consciousness by getting adults to spend less time comparing the performances of young children.

The second feature we investigate is the effect of expected income and expected status on satisfaction. As regards income, this suggests a more conservative approach to income redistribution than follows if the role of expected income is ignored. However, expectations respond to actual income experienced, with a lag. So the case for long-term income redistribution remains, with the speed of equalisation depending on the speed at which expectations adjust. But there is a further problem. In the short run, the marginal utility for increases in income is much less than for decreases, starting from a given level of expected income. This means that, in the short run, redistribution may be very unpopular and reduce welfare, even though it may be justified within a long-term context over which expectations adjust. People also have expectations about status. This indicates the importance of avoiding unintended rearrangements in the status hierarchy, such as those often produced by inflation.

These conclusions are piecemeal and not integrated into an overall model. However, it is important that economists should continue, with other social scientists, to work on these problems, if their advice is to be taken seriously by politicians, who often know a good deal about what makes people tick.

Notes

1. For general discussions see Scitovsky (1976), Hirsch (1977), Mishan (1977) and Akerlof (1976). For specific evidence see Easterlin (1972), who cites US time series and provides cross-country comparisons, and Duncan (1975), who reports a time-series for Detroit wives.

2.   The evidence is slippery because the word 'happy' cannot easily be translated and because cultures may differ in their honesty about these questions. Within the United States richer states are not self-reported as happier than poorer ones, but migration between states could be expected to equalise real income anyway.

3.   Easterlin (1972), Duncan (1975), and National Opinion Research Centre surveys.

4.   Keynes had this in mind when he said that real wages could more easily fall through a price rise than through wage cuts, which are likely to affect different people differently. On the role of envy see Schoeck (1966).

5.   The book is an invaluable source on the positive study of relative deprivation, but the concept is surprisingly little used in the normative part of the book.

6.   See in particular Hirsch (1977). Scitovsky (1976) also discusses the facts in an illuminating way but without pursuing the policy implications.

7.   I am ignoring problems of administrative cost, which may be quite severe, especially allowing for the costs of information.

8.   This point was well made by Duesenberry (1949, Chapter 6), but lost sight of as alternative theories of consumption developed.

9.   (i) Since $y_i/\bar{y}$ cannot be altered, the social optimum requires h_i be chosen so that $\partial u/\partial h_i = 0$. If w is the gross hourly wage and we tax income at a marginal rate t, the private optimum will be where

$$\frac{\partial u}{\partial(y_i/\bar{y})}\frac{w(1-t)}{\bar{y}} + \frac{\partial u}{\partial h_i} = 0$$

So we require $t = 1$.

(ii) If $\bar{y}$ includes foreign incomes, the optimal tax would be less than unity, assuming the domestic government does not care about negative externalities affecting foreigners. Provided foreign income is not too large relative to domestic income, an increase in foreign income will increase the socially optimal amount of work in the home country, and thus decrease the optimum tax rate. To see this, suppose for simplicity that $w = 1$ and $u = u[h/(\bar{h} + x), h]$, where x represents foreign income times the weight it assumes in the function. For society $h = \bar{h}$. Now suppose x rises from zero by a small amount. We are worse off and there is a positive return to work which was not there before. If leisure is a normal good we should work more. However, as x rises, the time price of relative income will eventually rise, and the effect of further rises of x upon optimal hours of work will become ambiguous. If, by contrast, $u = u[(h-x)/h, h]$ the time price of relative income falls continuously, and higher foreign income always implies higher optimal hours of work.

(iii) David Grubb has suggested to me that a better model would have $u^i = u(y_i/\bar{y}, h_i/\bar{h})$, i.e. effort has as much of a social dimension as the income earned. But I doubt whether most peasants would not feel better off if they all worked less for the same income.

10.   If growth has not increased happiness, this must therefore be due to some other offsetting losses.

11.   The social optimum requires h_i be chosen so that

$$\frac{\partial u}{\partial y_i}w + n\frac{\partial u}{\partial y}\frac{w}{n} + \frac{\partial u}{\partial h_i} = 0$$

The private optimum will be where

$$\frac{\partial u}{\partial y_i} w(\mathrm{I} - t) + \frac{\partial u}{\partial h_i} \simeq 0, \quad \text{since} \quad \frac{\partial u}{\partial y} \frac{w}{n} \quad \text{is small.}$$

Boskin and Sheshinski (1978) pursue much more fully the implications of a utility function like (2) in the context of an optimal income tax model in which wages differ between people. They show how the optimum tax rate rises as the weight attaching to *y* rises. I became aware of their paper only after writing this one, but as the next paragraph explains, I do not consider this approach fully adequate.

12.   To avoid equity problems, we continue to assume that all men have the same wage rates, and this means that we have to assume they have different utility functions. For, if not, there could be no equilibrium: an infinitesimal increase in hours by one individual would involve him in an infinitesimally small cost and raise his rank from the (tied) median to the top – a non-infinitesimal gain.

13.   The social optimum requires

$$a \frac{\partial R_i}{\partial h_i} + a \sum_{j \neq i} \frac{\partial R_i}{\partial h_i} + \frac{\partial v_i}{\partial y_i} w + \frac{\partial v_i}{\partial h_i} = 0$$

where the first two terms sum to zero. The private optimum produces

$$a \frac{\partial R_i}{\partial h_i} + \frac{\partial v_i}{\partial y_i} w(\mathrm{I} - t) + \frac{\partial v_i}{\partial h_i} = 0. \quad \text{Hence} \quad wt = -a \sum_{j \neq i} \frac{\partial R_j}{\partial h_i} \bigg/ \frac{\partial v_i}{\partial y_i}$$

14.   If *r* is the physical rate of return on investment plus unity, the social optimum then requires

$$-u_1^0 - nu_2^0 \frac{\mathrm{I}}{n} + u_1^1 r + nu_2^1 \frac{\mathrm{I}}{n} r = 0$$

The private optimum with no taxes will lead to

$$-u_1^0 + u_1^1 r = 0$$

Hence if $-u_2^0 + u_2^1 r < \mathrm{o}$, a tax is needed on the investment yield, with no tax deductibility for investment cost. Substituting for *r* gives as an equivalent condition: $-u_2^0/u_1^0 < -u_2^1/u_1^1$.

15.   The simplest way of representing this would be by assuming that status depends on one's own work relative to the means. So we are back to the model of (I) with uniform $w : u^i = u(h_i/\bar{h}, h_i)$.

16.   A major difficulty in fixing the correct tax/subsidy levels for education and migration is that so often these seem to be information problems making for too little of the activity, and these have to be offset against the negative externalities making for too much of the activity. (ii) The liberal argument that equalising taxes would produce a dull uniformity is remarkably at variance with the correct liberal emphasis on the remarkable variety of human nature.

17.   In at least one English public school the place where you pray in chapel has been determined by your exam results, and likewise the place where you sit for your meals and your lessons.

18. It is of course possible for an incentive to be set at such a high level that the organism seizes up and less productive work is done. But this is not that common. The main problem with incentives is the cost of the effort they bring forth.

19. As Durkheim (1951) pointed out, humans need an adequate external challenge, but not too great a challenge, in order to enjoy life.

20. If we allow for differences between people, then we would want to introduce a tax for equity reasons. If this was sufficient of a disincentive to work, the interesting question then arises of whether we should want to restore incentives partially by introducing (disequalising) competitions for non-monetary prizes. The answer seems to be 'yes'.

21. It may also be appropriate to pay producers of private goods on an *ex post* basis, but this is unlikely to generate large non-monetary rewards.

22. The question of the optimal reward to invention is of course plagued in addition by two further problems: (i) the fact that the winner takes all and removes all return to the losers' inputs and (ii) problems of uncertainty about when and whether the invention will occur.

23. I have not mentioned the screening argument, which also implies that the private return to education (Δy_i) exceeds the productive social return ($\sum \Delta y_j$), since there is no strong evidence that the screening argument is correct. I disagree with Hirsch here. The main problem is that status competition encourages people to put more effort (and anxiety) into raising income and status via exams than is optimal.

24. As Weisbrod (1977) has pointed out, it may be possible even in an ordinalist framework to compare economic states A and B in which utility functions are different. For if the outcome in state B is preferred whether we use the utility function of state A or state B, then the utility function of state B can be said to be better.

25. Margaret Mead (1937) and others have shown the wide variations in the degree of competitiveness as between different societies. *Pace* Lynn (1971), these differences are probably socially determined.

26. Rainwater (1975) has shown how people's views of the income needed for an adequate life have risen almost as fast as incomes generally (using answers to Gallup Poll questions).

27. This is an instance of the 'endowment effect' discussed by Thaler (1980), according to which people have a strong emotional attachment to the *status quo*.

28. u_i here is not utility but a concave transformation of it.

29. (i) The exact difference in income that is appropriate depends of course on the form of function. For example, if $u = u(y - \alpha e)$, then $dy/de = \alpha$. The stronger the negative influence of expectations, the bigger the income difference. (ii) If expected income equals current income, redistribution will be from rich to poor if $dy/de <$ I. So $u_{12} < -u_{11}$.

30. This assumes that the long-run curve AA discussed below is concave. In other words, $u_{12} < -(u_{11} + u_{22})/2$, since $d^2u = (u_{11} + u_{12} + u_{21} + u_{22}) \, dy^2$.

31. See Van Praag (1978). However, the question that was asked in this survey was not well adjusted to the task of eliciting the utility of income function. A better approach might be to ask questions of the following kind: (a) 'Imagine a £100

increase in your income. Having had this increase, how much more would you need to induce an equal further increase in happiness?' And so on up and down the income scale. *(b)* 'How much income would you say you needed to be neither very happy nor unhappy but just happy?'

32. Of course one has to distinguish between expressed discontent and actual discontent. For example Runciman (1966, p. 78) reports that in the 1930s there was much more agitation over the proposed standardisation of unemployment benefit in 1934 than there was over unemployment as such. This was because the public believed the government could do nothing about unemployment. But the unemployment benefit reform (though it made most people better off) made some people worse off, and this was not considered inevitable. All the cases of proposed reduction had to be abandoned. Having said this, it may be the case that *actual* discontent in fact depends not only on objective circumstances but also on whether these are thought to be inevitable or due to other peoples' freely chosen actions. For example, I dislike an identical banging at night much less if it is due to the wind than to my neighbours.

33. I am not implying that politicians are only concerned with maximising an ethical social welfare function regardless of votes.

34. I do not know quite how to relate this argument to another basic human need – for hope. I have also been deliberately vague about whether by 'expected' income I mean 'forecast' income or income which one 'requires' as a result of habit. If habit is the problem, then no indoctrination about what is going to happen will ease the blow.

35. Using the General Household Survey, one finds that a male log weekly wage equation that had an R^2 of 0.50 in 1971 had an R^2 of only 0.41 in 1975, although the variance of log earnings had not changed. Apparently, random factors had taken over in part the role of systematic factors in the ranking. For a fuller discussion of the argument in relation to inflation, see Layard (1980).

36. In addition high price inflation with annual wage settlements means that real wages fall fairly steeply for 364 days a year. If *e* adjusts up on each settlement day, this provides another explanation of the discontents generated by inflation.

References

Akerlof, G (1976) 'The economics of caste and of the rat race and other woeful tales', *Quarterly Journal of Economics*, 90 (November), 599–618.
Boskin, M.J. and E. Sheshinski (1978) 'Optimal redistributive taxation when individual welfare depends upon relative income', *Quarterly Journal of Economics*, 92 (November).
Duesenberry, J.S. (1949) *Income, Saving and the Theory of Consumer Behaviour* (Cambridge: Harvard University Press).
Duncan, O.D. (1975) 'Does money buy satisfaction?', *Social Indicators Research*, 2(3) (December), 267–74.
Durkheim, E. (1951) *Suicide*, English edn (London: Routledge & Kegan Paul).
Easterlin, R.A. (1972) 'Does economic growth improve the human lot?', in P.A. David and M.W. Reder (eds), *Nations and Households in Economic Growth* (New York Academic Press).

Hirsch, F. (1977) *Social Limits to Growth* (London: Routledge & Kegan Paul).
Layard, R. (1980) 'Wages policy and the redistribution of income', The Colston Research Society Annual Lecture, in D. Collard, R. Lecomber and M. Slater (eds), *The Limits to Redistribution* (Bristol: Colston Society).
Lynn, R. (1971) *Personality and National Culture* (Oxford: Pergamon Press).
Mead, M. (1937) *Cooperation and Competition among Primitive Peoples* (New York: McGraw-Hill).
Mishan, E.J. (1977) *The Economic Growth Debate* (London: Allen & Unwin).
Rainwater, L. (1975) *What Money Buys: Inequality and the social meanings of income* (New York, Basic Book).
Runciman, W.G. (1966) *Relative Deprivation and Social Justice* (Harmondsworth: Penguin).
Russell, B. (1949) *Authority and the Individual* (London: Allen & Unwin).
Schoek, H. (1966) *Envy* (London: Secker & Warburg).
Scitovsky, T. (1976) *The Joyless Economy* (Oxford: Oxford University Press) .
Sen, A.K. (1973) 'Behaviour and the concept of preference', *Economica* (August) .
Thaler, R.H. (1980) 'Towards a positive theory of consumer choice', *Journal of Economic Behaviour and Organisation*, March, Vol. 1 No.1
Van Praag, B. (1978) 'The Perception of Income Inequality', in A. Shorrocks and W. Krelle (eds), *The Economics of Income Distribution* (Amsterdam: North-Holland).
Weisbrod, B.A. (1977) 'Comparing utility functions in efficiency terms or what kind of utility functions do we want?', *American Economic Review*, 67 (December).

15 Economic Theories of Educational Planning
(1972)*

There are two main schools of thought on educational planning. One says that education should adjust to the demand for manpower in the labour market; the other that it should satisfy the private demand for education *per se*. Each school is again divided. Manpower specialists differ on whether to do rate-of-return analysis or manpower forecasting; while those who believe in satisfying the private demand for education disagree about criteria for financing, on which the private demand depends.

Much has been written on these issues.[1] The aim here is to help in developing an integrated framework for resolving them. Part I deals with the relation between cross-sectional social rate-of-return analysis and manpower forecasting, within the framework of a general cost-benefit approach. It first considers the case for using the rate of return on its own – as a signal variable in a control system where the student intake is the controlled variable; but this is rejected owing to the lead time between policy decisions and their effects in the labour market.

The next step is to examine what affects the relative importance of the cross-sectional rate of return and the manpower forecast, for policy purposes. The former shows how graduate numbers need changing due to current imbalances of supply and demand, while the latter deals with shifts in demand. The change indicated by the rate of return increases with the difference between the rate of return and the social discount rate and with the elasticity of demand for graduates; while the change indicated by the manpower forecast increases with the growth rate of demand and with the lead time. The planner's research priorities should thus depend on the elasticity of demand and on the lead time, and on the costs of getting better estimates of rates of return and growth rates of demand. Psychic benefits and external effects may make it difficult to interpret the absolute level of the calculated rate of return, but trends in the rate can be valuable for avoiding echo effects and for reducing the inadequacy of the coefficients used in manpower forecasts.

***Part I** in M. Peston and B. Corry (eds), *Essays in Honour of Lord Robbins* (London: Weidenfeld & Nicolson, 1972), pp. 118–49. I should like to thank M. Blaug, H.G. Jonson, G.R.J. Richardson and G.L. Williams for most useful comments on an earlier draft and L.P. Foldes for some very helpful suggestions.

Finally, two practical arguments are considered in favour of forecasting. A high proportion of educated people are employed in public services, where rates of return are peculiarly difficult to interpret and where the government, as the future employer, may be able to make a more reliable estimate of the future demand than it can for the private sector. In addition, there may be substantial cost-savings when educational decisions are made not marginally from year to year, but as part of an integrated though flexible longer-term strategy.

However, most educational systems are not planned on cost-benefit grounds, but are regulated by the private demand for education. In section II of the paper, therefore, we ask: What are the cost-benefit implications of meeting this private demand? We assume that individuals pursue education until the private rate of return to the marginal graduate equals the private discount rate. If so, the difference between the actual stock of graduates and that required on cost-benefit grounds depends on the proportion of the social cost of education that is subsidised and on the share of the social returns that goes in taxes and external effects, as well as on the private and social discount rates and the elasticity of demand for graduates.

However, if these are constant, the proportional divergence of the stock from its desirable level will not alter through time, if the educational system expands as directed by private demands. Thus if the stock is satisfactory now, it will remain so in future. But this assumes that we have got the subsidies right, which requires information on social rates of return, and it ignores the short-term problems of leads and lags, which are the main argument for forecasting.

We finally consider some alternative sociological explanations of how educational systems grow, and find them stimulating but somewhat lacking in explanatory power.

I   SOCIAL RATE OF RETURN ANALYSIS VERSUS MANPOWER FORECASTING

The cost-benefit objective

Assume a world in which education is publicly provided: not all worlds are like this but we are not discussing here the question of how education should be supplied. Assume too, for this part of the paper, that the government decides how many places to provide by setting its own targets rather than by responding to the private demand for education. The question is: How should it arrive at its decisions? What weight should it give to evidence on cross-sectional rates of return and how much to attempts at manpower forecasting?

Despite the general disarray on methods, most economists would agree on the *objective* of expanding the numbers who receive each type of education to

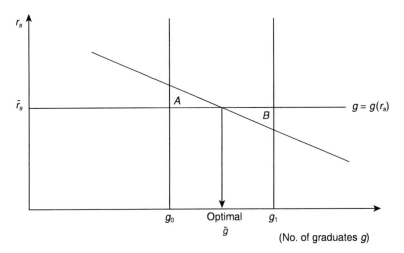

Figure 15.1

the point where, taking into account all social costs and benefits, the present value of the education of the last man educated falls to zero. Since the net return stream to education has only one sign-reversal and different types of educational provision can in practice be varied independently, the same result is obtained by following the more convenient rate-of-return criterion: Expand the numbers educated until the marginal social rate of return of education (r_s) falls to equality with the social discount rate $(\bar{r}_s)$[2].

The basic idea is that education, like most other things, yields diminishing returns and hence, assuming costs fall less steeply, a falling rate of return. If the number of graduates is not expanded enough (e.g. only to g_0 in Figure 15.1), there is a loss corresponding roughly to triangle A.[3] Each extra unit of resources used in producing graduates would have yielded r_s, whereas society would have been indifferent between an investment yielding only $\bar{r}_s$ and no extra investment. There would thus be a surplus on each extra unit invested in education. Conversely if the number of graduates is too great (e.g. g_1) there is a loss corresponding roughly to triangle B.

But what is the rate of return on education? Most people would agree on some broad listing of the social returns and costs of an individual's education, along the lines of the left-hand column of the following table. (The right-hand column becomes relevant in section II.)

	To society	To the individual
Returns	Direct gains in production	Gains in earnings (post-tax)
	+ Psychic benefits	+ Psychic benefits
	+ External economies (net)	
Costs	Loss of student's production	Loss of earnings (post-tax)
	+ Cost of tuition	+ Fees
		− Grants to student

The rate of return is the discount rate which equates the return to the cost. It will help to use a simplified way of representing it. Psychic benefits and external economies are notoriously difficult to estimate, and, though attempts have been made to do so (Becker, 1964, p. 119; Weisbrod, 1964), we shall ignore them for the time being. As regards wages we shall assume that all graduates are paid the same (W_G), and likewise for non-graduates (W_N) and that wages measure the marginal private product. If all costs are treated as incurred in one year, including tuition costs (C), the cross-sectional social rate of return on undergraduate education becomes approximately[4]

$$r_s = \frac{W_G - W_N}{C + W_N}$$

It is a marginal rate of return because the wages that it uses reflect marginal products.

Now this rate of return is the government's target variable and its aim is to maintain $r_s = \bar{r}_s$. The instrument variable is the number of graduates, which the government aims to regulate by its pattern of educational provision.[5] The relation between instrument and target comes through the demand for graduates. Suppose that this depends on the relative wages of graduates and on time. Then $g = g^1(W_G/W_N, t)$. But $r_s = (W_G - W_N)/(C + W_N)$, and therefore $g = g^2(r_s, W_N, C, t)$ or more simply, taking W_N and C as depending on time, $g = g^3(r_s, t)$. The desired equilibrium stock of graduates is $\bar{g} = g^3(\bar{r}_s, t)$. One can, if one likes, call this number the nation's manpower 'need', provided this is understood to mean the optimal from a set of possible numbers.

The optimal number changes over time in response to shifts in demand. In general it seems likely that the demand for graduates relative to non-graduates rises with time, capital being more complementary to graduates than to non-graduates, and technical progress likewise raising their relative marginal product. Provided the consequent rise in W_G/W_N (for given g) is not completely offset by simultaneous changes in W_N and C, the result will be a rise in the rate-of-return function $g = g^3(r_s, t)$ as time passes.[6] Thus, unless $\bar{r}_s$ varies significantly over time, the desired stock of graduates rises.

Granted this general framework for looking at the problem, the argument should be one about *methods* of achieving the desired stock and not about objectives. The issue is: How much can we learn for policy purposes from studying the cross-sectional rate of return and how important is the forecasting of shifts in demand?[7]

What does the social rate of return indicate for policy?

In principle there might be general agreement about the desirability of forecasting, if it were possible. In the ordinary cost-benefit analysis of a project, for example, it is standard practice to estimate the future demand for its product and thus to forecast the price which the public would be willing to pay for the proposed increase in supply. Applying this approach to education, one might for example be considering the admission of an extra 500 engineering students. The problem is then to estimate the future demand for engineers and thus the wage which the extra 500 graduates could command, taking uncertainty into account if possible. Since the future wages of those who graduate today depend also on the future output of graduates, we are in principle involved in a problem of the simultaneous optimisation of investment over all points of time.

However, daunted by the obvious perils of forecasting, a school of thought has developed which argues that educational planning should devote its main research effort to the study of the current cross-sectional rates of return. But the way in which policy conclusions should be drawn have not been very fully examined, and some rate-of-return practitioners seem to have been rather incautious in their approach to this. For example W. Lee Hansen (1963, p. 148) found that the rates of return on college graduation over each other level of education were greater than 10 per cent – college education over 'no education' yielded for example 12.1 per cent. In his view these facts, using a 10 per cent alternative rate of return, 'suggest the obvious advantages of seeing to it that everyone completes college'. If the rate of return had been under 10 per cent, would this have suggested the obvious advantage of giving no-one higher education? The approach seems to ignore the possibility of diminishing returns or, in the reverse example, of growth in the demand for graduates. It seems more appropriate to think of responding to rates of return by marginal variations in current flows than by such discontinuous changes.

This is the approach advocated by Mark Blaug: 'Rate of return analysis merely provides a signal of direction: invest more or less. But how much more or less? A little more or less is the answer and then recalculate the rate of return' (Blaug, 1967, p. 268). This argument may be couched in terms of a control system. Deviations of the signal variable (the rate of return) from its desired level should produce automatic variations in the controlled variable (the student intake) such that the signal variable never strays far from its optimum.

The problem, of course, as with all control systems, lies in the lag between the change in the controlled variable and its effect on the signal variable. In education a change in student intake has no effect on labour supply for at least two or three years (the length of course) and the relevant lead time may be even longer if we allow for the time needed for buildings to go up and institutions to adapt. Therefore, in general, it may or may not be appropriate to act on the signal of the rate of return, depending on what happens in the period between action and its effects in the labour market. However, since action is needed, it is of practical importance to ask: In what qualitative circumstances will acting on the basis of the rate of return lead to a policy change in the right direction?

We have to distinguish between the case where rate of return data are available for the current year only, as for example in Hansen's early study referred to above, and that where we have time series data, as would be the case with Blaugh's control system. In most countries except the USA policy makers using rates of return have in fact as yet only one year's data to go on.[8]

The problems of using such data are illustrated in Figure 15.2. This shows the rate of return function $g = g^3(r_s, t)$ for three years, the curve being labelled D to indicate that it reflects the demand side of the labour market. At the current (t_o) balance between demand and supply the rate of return is too low. Does this definitely suggest that we should reduce the rate of growth of supply?

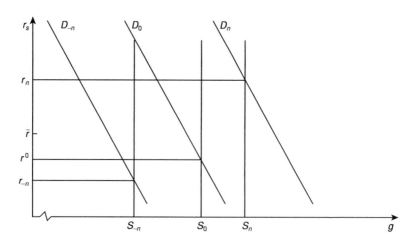

Figure 15.2

The problem is one of adjustment from a non-optimal capital stock to an optimal stock that is growing over time. In principle the adjustment path should of course be optimised over all points of time but this aspect is not considered in the preliminary thoughts put forward in the present paper. Instead we assume that for practical purposes policy should simply aim at reducing the gap $|r_s - \bar{r}_s|$ between now (t_0) and the first year (t_n) in which the number of graduates can be affected by this year's decisions.

As Figure 15.2 shows, the policy of reducing growth rates ($S_n - S_0 < S_0 - S_{-n}$) will not necessarily lead to a smaller gap between r_s and $\bar{r}_s$ than if growth rates had been left unchanged ($S_n - S_0 = S_0 - S_{-n}$). The reason is that demand has been assumed to grow faster in future than in the past and that it was already growing faster than supply. We can however be sure of improving things by acting on the signal of a low rate of return when (a) demand is not expected to grow faster in future than in the past and (b) past demand did not grow faster than past supply.[9] The same is true of a high rate of return, with the inequality conditions reversed. If these conditions are not met the rate of return signal could lead to a policy step in the wrong direction.

If we have time series data we do not have to make assumptions about past trends in rates of return: we know them. We can then see whether low rates of return are in process of correcting themselves, as may often happen when poor social returns correspond to poor private incentives. In this way it should be relatively easy to dampen any major echo effect.[10]

But there remains the problem of guessing at future trends in demand. How likely is it that they will resemble trends in the past? In general this assumption seems more reasonable in developed than in underdeveloped countries and in large countries than in small ones. In developed countries there is of course the major discontinuity of technological change, but this is in any case very difficult to forecast. In underdeveloped countries this problem is much less acute, making forecasting easier, while discontinuous changes in the structure of the economy may be more common; making forecasting more necessary.

Consider, for example, Indian engineering education in 1955, before the Second Five Year Plan. Rates of return were probably fairly near to the relevant discount rate. But a massive surge of demand was in sight. A conservative expansion policy based on rate of return calculations would have led for some years to an excessive rate of return. Happily, from that point of view and at that time, policy was in the hands of forecasters.

The relative role of rate of return analysis and manpower forecasting

But how serious is it if future trends in demand are not foreseen? This depends mainly on two variables: the lead time, already mentioned, and the elasticity of demand. If the elasticity of demand for graduates is high, their marginal

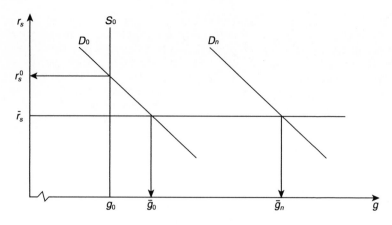

Figure 15.3

product will rise little when demand rises. Equally, if the rate of return is inappropriate, it will take massive changes in the number of graduates to correct it; and these changes will dwarf in importance those required by changing demand conditions.

This point is crudely illustrated in Figure 15.3. Here we assume that the social discount rate is the same at t_0 and t_n and that in t_n we wish to have the desired stock of graduates $\bar{g}_n$. At present we have a suboptimal stock g_0. Thus the desired increase in supply between t_0 and t_n is $(\bar{g}_n - g_0)$, which can conveniently be broken down into $(\bar{g}_n - \bar{g}_0)$ and $(\bar{g}_0 - g_0)$.[11] The first is the increase due to growth of demand and the second is that due to the unsatisfactory balance of present demand and supply, as revealed in the current rate-of-return calculation. In this sense, rate-of-return analysis is a method of evaluating the base from which a forecast is made and adjusting it to eliminate the effect of current imbalance. Once this important task is done – and so often it is not – forecasting is acceptable.

The magnitudes of the two adjustments are approximately $\bar{g}_0 - g_0 = \bar{g}_0 \eta (r_s^0 - \bar{r}_s)/\bar{r}_s$, where η is the elasticity of demand, and $\bar{g}_n - \bar{g}_0 = \bar{g}_0 (\dot{D}/D) t$, where $\dot{D}/D$ is the annual rate of growth in the optimal number and t is the number of years for which the forecast is needed (the lead time).

The relative size of the effects thus depends on $\eta (r_s^0 - \bar{r}_s)/\bar{r}_s$ and $(\dot{D}/D)t$. Thus research strategy should concentrate more on rate of return analysis (relative to forecasting) the higher (η) and the lower t, and the cheaper an improved estimate of r_s and the more expensive an improved estimate of $\dot{D}/D$. As for the magnitudes, lead times (t) vary between levels and specialities of education and between countries. On the elasticities (η) there is deplorably little information and research here has perhaps the highest priority in all the economics of education.[12] The lower the elasticity, the stronger the case for forecasting. Advocates of flexible planning urge steps such as later specialisation, which would shorten lead times and might also improve the substitutability of manpower and hence raise demand elasticities.

As regards accuracy, estimates of $\dot{D}/D$ and r_s are both difficult, but the real question is the cost of improving them. If $\dot{D}/D$ is quite likely to be the same as in the recent past and to make any better estimate is very expensive, then there is little case for manpower-forecasting research – though still a need for explicit guesses about future growth rates of demand. Equally it may be hard to ascertain the true social rate of return, which must include external effects and psychic benefits as well as allowing for divergencies between wages and marginal private product and for the effects on wages of determinants other than education. Thus in some cases one may not be able to improve on a judgement, based perhaps on job analysis or international comparisons, as to whether the present stock is optimal. Since externalities and psychic benefits are likely to be positive, especially for general education as opposed to training, rate-of-return analysis may be more useful when the rate of return is suspected of being too high than too low. Neither rate-of-return analysis nor forecasting are free of the danger of substantial error, but both can hopefully, with proper attention and loving care, be improved.

This is not the place to pursue this point, except to remark that the best way to improve manpower forecasting seems to be to combine it ever more closely with rate-of-return analysis. The forms of manpower forecasting are many and varied,[13] but the simplest and most useful form is based on input/output coefficients indicating numbers of educated people per unit of output (G/Y). The two standard problems with these coefficients are, first, that their present level may be non-optimal and, second, that their trends (which might be extrapolated) are also non-optimal. Both these points can be checked by rate-of-return analysis, and suitable adjustments made. For example in Figure 15.4 the input coefficients have been falling and at the same time the rate of return has been rising to an unacceptably high level. The first step is to adjust up the level of the input coefficient to eliminate the current imbalance, using some assumption about elasticities of demand as suggested earlier. This is a standard use of rate-of-return analysis. But the next step is to adjust upwards the trend in the coefficient, which was evidently too steeply downward, since it led to a rising rate of return. This adjustment could again be done using standard elasticity assumptions. The suggestion is made, however, largely to illustrate the point that rate-of-return analysis may be as valuable in what it tells us about trends in the manpower balance as in what it says about the optimality of the current position. The snags are a good deal less in the former than the latter.

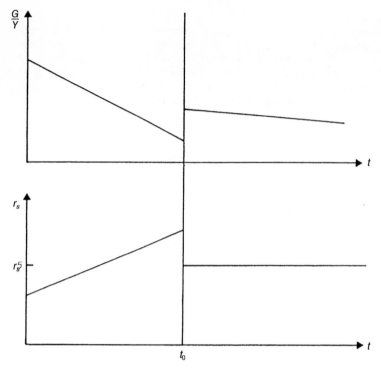

Figure 15.4

Two cheers for manpower forecasting

The preceding discussion has been less than concrete about the practical problems of planning, and it is time to make two points which justify a great deal of the forecasting work which is actually done. First, a very high proportion of the more educated people in most countries are, for better or worse, employed in the public sector. In Britain and India for example the proportions are about two-thirds of graduates and a similar proportion of those with completed secondary education.

This has two implications. Public sector wages are administered and it is therefore particularly difficult to interpret the calculated rates of return. Even if the public sector has no monopsony power but operates in the labour market on the same footing as the private sector, this only tells us that public sector wages correspond to the marginal product of labour in the private sector. We have no way of knowing whether the public sector is operating on its own 'true' demand curve – corresponding to its curve of marginal social productivity. There is certainly no market discipline which could ensure that it did. Thus it seems impossible to avoid the need for some elements of judgement in settling such questions as: What is the right number of teachers, given the school population and the costs of training teachers and of diverting their services from other employments? There is also the second point that over time the government should be better placed to foresee changes in its own demands than in those of the private sector. In any case it seems only natural that the government, which we have assumed plans education under one hat, should also put on its other hat and count up its demands as a future employer. When governments fail to foresee future demands for, say, teachers and doctors, they are not always forgiven by their electorates.

Making such forecasts need not imply that their results get mechanically translated into plans for educational provision. With some forecasts, such as the British forecasts of demand for school teachers, this is made quite explicit and the forecasts merely aim to show what the number of teachers would be, given various pupil – teacher ratios, so that the resulting numbers can be compared with supply forecasts on various policy assumptions. The forecasts are made, not to commit the future, but simply to add another dimension to thinking about it. The fact that forecasts of this, and any other, kind are bound to be wrong to some extent, provides no logical reason for supposing that things would have been better without them. Decisions are bound to be taken on some implicit or explicit assumption about the future and a wrong forecast may well be more realistic than the assumption that would otherwise prevail.

The second argument for forecasting concerns the length of the planning period. Our earlier discussion assumed that this need only be as long as the lead time between educational policy decisions, say to expand the student intake, and their impact on the labour market. But this implies that efficient educational decisions can always be marginal. This is not so. Many educational investments are lumpy, and a new university, for example, can be built much more cheaply if its early development is based on some general idea of its subsequent growth.

If foresight of this kind can save costs, what is there against it? There is the danger that long-term plans once made cannot be changed. But long-term plans can quite well be rolling plans, so that what ultimately happens is the short-term parts of a series of long-term plans. The aim of including the long-term part of the plan is to reduce the ultimate cost of the sequence of short-term plans – by allowing for the cost reductions made possible when decisions about interdependent projects are taken jointly.[14] Efficient spending requires that spenders have definite ideas about how much they are likely to be spending over a period of time. This applies not only to education but to health, defence and the rest; and the resources they get depend in part on how much goes to education.

There are two remaining criticisms of forecasting (in Blaug, 1967) that call for comment. The first is that it encourages excessive specialisation. In Britain this is causally not so – our deplorable specialisation began long before forecasting was dreamed of. And if one looks at other countries, one finds that some countries that are more planned than Britain have less specialisation (e.g. France) and others (e.g. in higher education, Russia) have more. The correlation between specialisation and planning appears to be low.

The second criticism of manpower demand forecasts is that there may be no way of telling whether they turn out right or not. According to Blaug the only case in which a forecast can be falsified is if the GDP target from which it comes is hit but manpower falls short of the forecast demand. This implies that the forecasters believe that manpower, say graduates, and all other factors of production are so complementary that a certain GDP can only be produced with the specified number of graduates. Perhaps some forecasters have implied this, but it is not the point of view put forward in this paper. A forecast of the demand for, say, graduates should be an estimate of the optimal number of graduates over a series of future years; that is, the number for which the rate of return would be right. It should thus take into account the facts both of substitutability, ignored by rigid manpower forecasters, and of diminishing returns, ignored by pure rate-of-return advocates. And the test of the forecast is this: Would the rate of return have been suitable if the projected number of graduates had been educated? The answer can be got from the actual number and the actual rate of return in the target year, together with an estimated elasticity of demand.

II   COST-BENEFIT IMPLICATIONS OF MEETING THE PRIVATE DEMAND FOR EDUCATION

Educational planning as it actually happens

Partly because of the difficulties of evaluating manpower demand, no country outside the centrally planned economies uses this as its main criterion for educational planning. For particular forms of specialised manpower – doctors, teachers, engineers and trained craftsmen – manpower assessment is certainly used. But in nearly all countries the broad structure of the educational system is determined quite otherwise. In general, the minimum level of compulsory schooling is based on a mixture of general reasoning about human rights (enabling the poor to protect themselves against money-lenders, politicians and the like) and about income distribution (giving to each individual the capital source of a minimum income stream), as well as unquantified reasoning about rates of return to universal literacy, externalities being often invoked. Needless to say at compulsory levels of education it often proves necessary to force the people to come in.

At post-compulsory levels, there is a different story. Most governments simply respond to the private demand for places. This is often described as bowing to political or social pressure, but this pressure after all transmits the demands of individuals. In Britain the most obvious examples of provision adjusted to private demand are in post-compulsory schooling and in 'further education'. In universities we do not, as on the continent, have an open door policy, even for arts and science places. But the Robbins Committee put forward the principle that 'courses of higher education should be available for all those who are qualified by ability and attainment to pursue them and who wish to do so'. This is not of course the same as providing higher education to all who want it, since places are to be rationed to those 'qualified'. But it does mean that the number of places in higher education should grow as fast as the numbers who get the qualifications. For higher education as a whole, but not for the university sector, the government have acted on this policy. And the result has been a steady rise in student numbers.[15]

Some might question whether an approach like this can be dignified with the title of 'educational planning'. But there seems to be no real problem. The government simply sets the terms on which education is available, and then plans to provide for the number of students who, using their own foresight, demand it on these terms. The remarks which follow are addressed mainly to this case but would be equally relevant where education is privately supplied at constant cost but the state provides subsidies and maintenance grants.

These kinds of arrangement, where education responds to the private demand, are often contrasted with a system that expands in relation to manpower 'need'. But how sharp in fact is the contrast? How does the pattern of manpower thrown up by a system of this kind compare with the pattern that is optimal on cost-benefit grounds?

What determines the private demand for education?

To answer this we need a theory of what determines the private demand for education. The proposed theory is that individuals weigh up the benefits and the costs, and decide whether to seek education by comparing its internal rate of return with their own private discount rate $(\bar{r}_p)$.[16] If we imagine the individual to form his picture of his own expected rate of return by looking at current wage differentials and costs, and if we ignore psychic benefits until later, we can construct a simplified theory of the demand for undergraduate education.[17]

As before, we use a model of the labour market, so that the demand for undergraduate education is not shown directly but corresponds to changes in the supply of graduates (plus replacement of those who retire). On the vertical axis we again have the rate of return, but this time it is the private rate (r_p), where (from the table on p. 286)

$$r_p = \frac{(W_G - W_N)(1 - T)}{W_N(1 - T) + F - M}$$

and T is the average tax rate, assumed the same for graduates and others, F is the fee and M is the maintenance grant per student. As before the rate of return is related to the number of graduates. The demand function is $g = g^1 \, (W_G/W_N, t)$, and thus $g = g^4(r_p, W_N, t, T, F - M)$. If all the independent variables except r_p vary with time, we have a series of simple rate-of-return functions $g = g^5 \, (r_p, t)$, of which two are illustrated in Figure 15.5. They are again labelled D to show that they reflect the demand side of the labour market. We assume that the demand curve rises over time, and hence likewise the rate-of-return curve, provided the effect is not offset by changes in fees, maintenance grants or tax rates.[18]

What of the supply of graduates? We could of course draw the normal upward-sloping curve. However we have not so far introduced any source of individual differences which would account for the upward sloping character of the supply curve, and it seems helpful to start with the simplest possible model. Accordingly we assume a capital market so perfect that the private discount rate of all individuals becomes equal, and we also assume that it remains constant over time at $\bar{r}_p$. Thus any rise of r_p above this level leads to an automatic increase in the number of graduates.

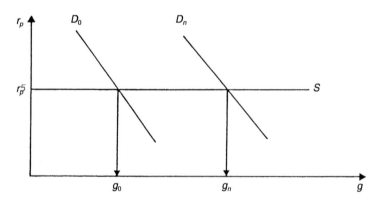

Figure 15.5

We now have a very simple explanation of the growth in the stock of graduates. The demand for them grows and the supply is at once forthcoming. Provided the absolute growth in demand increases each year, the demand for entry to higher educational will also grow.

What is the relation of private supply to manpower need?

But how optimal is this? There is clearly no automatic mechanism whereby the privately-determined supply of graduates will equal numbers 'needed' on manpower grounds. How nearly this happens depends on the relation first between r_p and r_s, and second between $\bar{r}_p$ and $\bar{r}_s$. In most countries private rates of return exceed the calculated social rates, as the high levels of subsidy outweigh the effect of taxes in reducing private returns. The optimal level of subsidy can be readily derived from our model (ignoring psychic and external effects and questions of income distribution). The aim at any time is that $g = g^2(\bar{r}_S, W_N, C, t)$. The instruments available, assuming costs and tax rates cannot be varied, are fees and maintenance grants. And the behavioural assumption is that $g = g^4(\bar{r}_p, W_N, t, T, F - M)$. We then have a relation $g^2(\bar{r}_S, W_N, C, t) = g^4(\bar{r}_p, W_N, t, T, F - M)$ which determines $F - M$.

Another way of looking at this is shown in Figure 15.6. On the left-hand side are the social and private discount rates. Either of these might be the larger, but

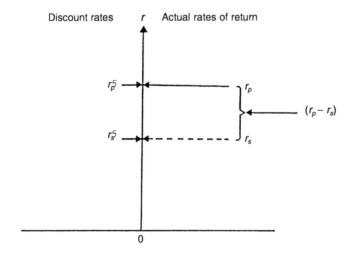

Figure 15.6

the private rate is shown here as higher.[19] On the right-hand side are the actual rates of return. It is desired that $r_s = \bar{r}_s$. But private behaviour will only ensure that $r_p = \bar{r}_p$. Public policy should therefore contrive a pattern of subsidy such that $r_p - r_s = \bar{r}_p - \bar{r}_s$. When this happens, the number of graduates will be optimal.

But it may not happen. Actual subsidies may be set at the wrong level and thus produce the wrong number of graduates. How far the actual number differs from the desirable level is a matter for empirical research and for judgement. However, regardless of whether the level is right, it is also relevant to ask: Do *changes* in the private demand for education correspond to *changes* in manpower 'need'?

As before we assume,

$$r_p = \frac{(W_G - W_N)(1 - T)}{W_N(1 - T) + F - M} = \bar{r}_p = \text{constant}$$

Now if average tax rates stay constant and likewise the proportion of the total social cost carried by public funds,[20] it follows that

$$\frac{W_G - W_N}{W_N + C} = \text{constant}$$

so that the social rate of return is constant. Its (constant) level will probably not equal the social discount rate. But their proportional difference $(r_s - \bar{r}_s)/\bar{r}_s$ will remain the same if $\bar{r}_s$ is constant, and so, given a constant elasticity of demand for graduates, will the proportional divergence of the stock of graduates from its desirable level. Thus, on these assumptions, the policy of expanding in step with private demand will not worsen the proportional waste of resources. Implicitly, those, like the Robbins Committee, who have advocated this policy are saying that in their judgement the current equilibrium is about right and a policy to maintain it is therefore sound.

However, the assumptions are important. If the degree of subsidy were altered it would no longer be true that an increase in the graduate stock which held r_p constant would do the same for r_s. If the subsidy rate were reduced the social rate of return would rise, and vice versa. In British higher education it seems most unlikely that maintenance grants will rise as fast as the forgone earnings of youth – a policy decision which *ceteris paribus* is justified only if the present social rate of return on education is too low.

Introducing psychic benefits, external effects and individual difference

The reason why we have so far omitted psychic benefits is not because they are unimportant. Indeed in a society where hundreds of millions of pounds are privately spent on the arts, gramophone records, books, travel to centres of culture, and so on, it would be very odd if people did not attach a positive value to having been educated *per se*. For education is complementary to many of the most characteristic forms of modern consumption. And, just as people value (and pay for) the driving lesson which enables them to enjoy a car, they value the (often free) education which enables them to enjoy the Choral Symphony or the Parthenon. In this sense the nation's stock of educational experience is not only an input which helps to produce the standard of living, but is itself a part of the standard of living. The pleasures of having been educated are not however the only psychic benefits which flow from education, and there are three other forms which, though probably less important and possibly negative, should also be considered. First there is the pleasure of acquiring education, as opposed to having acquired it. Secondly, there are the different non-pecuniary advantages of the jobs to which higher education gives access. Third, there is the satisfaction parents may derive from educating their children.

There can be little doubt that the prospect of some of these psychic benefits materially affects the private demand for education. In other words psychic benefits enter into the *ex ante* private rate of return.[21] In full equilibrium we should therefore be able to measure the non-pecuniary benefits of education by the difference between the real rate of return on financial assets (assuming these to convey no psychic benefit) and the financial rate of return on education, which would be lower. Unfortunately, as Becker points out (1964, p. 122), we are not normally in full equilibrium and financial rates of return on education often exceed those on other capital. This may be due to capital rationing or other reasons, and only means that the psychic benefits of education are peculiarly difficult to measure, not that they do not exist.

From the policy point of view, cost-benefit reasoning requires psychic benefits to be included also in social rates of return. Blaug argues that to include them involves a political choice (Blaug, 1965, p. 230), but as a matter of principle this cannot be right. Here are benefits which are in principle no less objective than the benefits flowing from the enhanced productivity of educated people. But in practice they are different – they are less measurable. In this sense only, the politicians may have as much to say about their importance as the economists.[22] How far does including them modify our analysis?

Since psychic benefits appear in both private and social rates of return at the same (untaxed) value, their inclusion may not radically alter the relationship between the two rates. However, both numerator and denominator are lower for the private than for the social rate, so that, when psychic benefits are added to the numerators of both rates, the private rate will rise more than the social rate, both absolutely and proportionately. And the greater the psychic benefits are, the greater of course is the proportion of the total social benefit that is unequivocally appropriated by the educated person.

We can now, briefly, reformulate the model, including psychic benefits (P), as valued by the man who marginally chooses to be educated, and the net external benefits (E) resulting from his education. Now

$$r_p = \frac{(W_G - W_N)(1 - T) + P}{W_N(1 - T) + F - M} = \bar{r}_p = \text{constant}$$

and

$$r_s = \frac{(W_G - W_N) + P + E}{W_N + C}$$

Provided the share of external effects and of taxes in the marginal social return remains constant, and likewise the ratio of subsidy to cost, then the social rate of return will remain constant.

However, this depends on the assumption of a constant private discount rate common to all men. Once this is dropped we need to reformulate our explanation of educational growth. This is done in Figure 15.7. As before we measure the private financial rate of return on the vertical scale. But now the supply curve of graduates slopes upward, for three main reasons. People differ in the relative value they put upon the psychic aspects of education; thus when a small financial return would be enough to induce one man to get educated, another will require something more attractive, even if they both have the same discount rate. Similarly, they may vary in the disutility attaching to the risks of educational investment. And finally they may, due to capital rationing, have different discount rates. The supply curve slopes upwards more sharply in the short run than in the long term, due to the limited number of people with

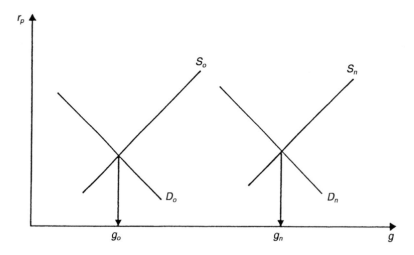

Figure 15.7

qualifications within striking distance of entry to higher education over any one period of time.

As incomes rise the long-run supply curve shifts to the right. The financial rate of return which an individual requires of education falls, since with growing income he puts an increasing value on its psychic benefits. This is one source of the income elasticity of demand for education observed at the economy level.

Equally, or more, important is the effect of income growth in raising the demand for educated people as factors of production. Economic growth increases the number of graduates through both these income effects. To disentangle them is one of the largely unsolved problems of research.[23] But enough has already been said to dispose of the old examination chestnut: Does economic growth produce educational growth or vice versa? Any investment, like education, having a positive rate of return, produces economic growth. But likewise economic growth, however caused, raises the demand for education, both as a financially productive investment and for its psychic benefits.

Some sociological objections to the theory of private demand

Finally we must consider some of the main sociological objections to the kind of theory of private demand that has been proposed. One argument, often put forward by people with educated parents, is that people who get higher education have never decided to do so. Once on a certain escalator they get carried on upwards without choosing. To explain their behaviour by a theory of choice is thus said to be impossible.

Now much of human behaviour is certainly a matter of habit. Were it not so, the economic system could be subject to violent fluctuations. A tiny excess of actual private rates of return over their required level could produce a sudden flood of new graduates; this could drive down the rate too low and another equally violent cut-back could occur. It is the frictions produced by habit – in other words the sluggishness of the dynamic adjustment functions – which stabilise the system. But the fact is that habits change and people do step off the escalator in varying numbers at each level. Our theory only requires that these marginal choices be substantially influenced by an assessment of costs and benefits.[24]

A second argument relates to the decision-making unit. In the model this is implicitly the family rather than the individual. For other family members, as well as the student, reduce their current consumption in order to allow him to study, and therefore they normally participate in his decision. Yet the benefits accrue very largely to the graduate alone, especially where the institution of the nuclear family has heavily eroded the graduate's economic responsibility for his parents or siblings. To the individual who gets educated the private rate of return is, strictly, a good deal higher than we have said, because while studying he is subsidised not only by the state but by his family.[25] This gives rise in some families to conflicts between parents and child as to whether the individual should continue his education. In other families the satisfactions which parents get from educating their children may be the main form of benefit, and in these cases there may also be conflicts – with the roles reversed. The fact of such conflicts of interest clearly calls for a more sophisticated theory but should not however undermine our general conclusions.

A third line of criticism comes from those who propose essentially different models for explaining the growth of education. All of these can be broadly termed 'snowball' models, that is they invoke some self-sustaining process of growth.[26] A common idea, for which there is some evidence, is that parents' educational level is a major determinant of the educational level of their children.[27] Provided parents make sure their children become better educated than themselves, education must grow. Another suggestion is that information about higher education is a major determinant of the demand for it. The more educated people there are around, the easier is access to such information, not only by direct contact with graduates but also because graduates form an increasing proportion of workers in the mass media and of the mass media's public. Both these two models operate by changing the taste for education, which in our economic model is assumed unchanged. Another model works through the demand for educated people and alleges that graduates like employing graduates. Hence any increase in the supply of graduates leads to an increase in demand for them. In each of these models education is regarded as infectious, and it has been suggested that the time path of its expansion might have the sigmoid form of an epidemic process 'in which changes in the demand for places depend, in part, on the number infected and so liable to infect others and, in part, on the number not yet infected and so available to catch the infection' (Stone, 1965, pp. 179–81).

None of these models purports to be based on a theory of rational individual choice nor to aim at evaluating whether the expansion of education has been desirable. There is however a type of 'Hobbesian snowball' model which has a strong hold over the man in the street and over some academics, and which, to them, both explains the growth of higher education in terms of rational individual choice and shows why it has been a social disaster. As before there is a supply and a demand side variant of the model. On the supply side it is said that people seek higher education for status. Since status is purely relative, the more people have higher education the more others have to have it, simply in order to maintain their relative position. On the demand side the argument is that employers do not fundamentally care about a person's education but only his ability. If the ranking of people by education corresponds broadly to that by ability, then employers can use a person's education as a proxy for his ability. The role of the educational system is thus that of a selective device. But this function could in principle be performed as well if the general educational level were low as if it were high, provided in each case there was a reasonable spread of education in the population. The Hobbesian character of the situation is that, to attract employers' favours, individuals try to rise in the educational scale, but they thus force other individuals of their level of ability to do the same in self-defence. To get a person of given ability employers have to take, say, a graduate, where before a man with School Certificate would have done.

The wasteful feature of both these Hobbesian situations is that, if only the individuals concerned could get together and agree not to raise the educational requirement for a given status or job, they could all be as well off as before. Then much of the educational growth which has historically occurred would have been unnecessary. Each individual acting singly (as a free rider) can improve his welfare by gaining extra education, either through consumption benefits in the form of higher status or through higher earnings from a better job. But society cannot improve its welfare this way because the education of others adversely affects the welfare of each individual. There are strong external diseconomies from educational expansion, which offset the internal benefits to each of the individuals involved.

What are we to make of these alternative models? They have been crudely stated, but, if suitably modified and combined with other forms of explanation, they each undoubtedly contain seeds of truth. For example a country with a weak educational tradition may be so unaware of the potentialities of education that not all the opportunities for privately fruitful investment in education get taken up. To allow for this we could subject our own model to a 'parental education' constraint, which said that education expands on the lines outlined in the paper provided there are enough children around with adequately educated parents. Alternatively the parental education model could have a rate of return constraint. One hopes that one day really sophisticated models of educational growth will be developed. However at the present stage it seems important to establish which lines of approach promise to yield the greatest explanatory power. The question to be answered is: What causes the number of students to be what it is and to change as it does?[28]

The most obvious criticism of the non-economic models is that they do not seem to explain at all adequately the timing of educational development, which ought according to them to have been happening continuously and without interruption.[29] Yet educational development has not been like that. Since the Second World War there has been an unprecedented educational expansion, accompanied by unprecedented economic growth, in almost every country in the world. Between the wars on the other hand higher education barely grew in Britain and in many other countries – and economies slumped. This is indirect evidence for the economic interpretation in this essay. But there is also direct evidence in that private rates of return (not including consumption benefits) seem in many countries to be surprisingly similar to alternative rates of interest

(Psacharopoulos, 1971), and in the USA for which we have time series they have remained astonishingly stable since before the War despite many-fold increases in student numbers. Unless the elasticity of demand for graduates is very high, we do seem to have here an explanation after a fashion of why the number of students is what it is, whereas the other theories would be compatible with its being any number. And if the other theories held, the rates of return would be most unlikely to be what they are.

We must however exempt from this general attack the Hobbesian model which describes education as a selective device. The theory says, after all, that students are each singly pursuing their own advantage which may well be largely financial. What it denies is that the financial return to the student corresponds in any way to a social return deriving from the higher productivity of graduates. The argument is that only ability is productive but that employers cannot tell who is able. So, knowing there is a high correlation (though no causal link) between education and ability, they give educated people the better-paid jobs. In this crude form the hypothesis is contradicted by the evidence of marked pay differences between ability groups within given educational groups (Becker, 1964, pp. 79–88; Denison, 1964, pp. 86–100). A milder version of the theory says that employers know something, but not everything, about employees' abilities. However, they must surely know more, the longer they have been employing a person. So the effect of education on income (holding ability constant) should diminish with age; but in fact it increases. We must also count against the theory the tentative evidence from production functions that the marginal productivity of educated people is broadly in line with their pay.[30]

The theory is also weak in explaining the timing of educational development, since the process of self-defeating expansion could have proceeded indefinitely from any moment of initial disturbance. But a peculiarly subtle version of the theory (Wiles, 1969, p. 195) attempts to pin this disturbance into the post-war period by linking it to the demand for education as consumption. We are now told that education was originally demanded for its psychic benefits, with a high income elasticity of demand, but this then led employers to upgrade jobs thereby raising the financial pay-off to education. Of course the more the theory stresses the psychic benefits of education the harder it becomes to explain the observed level of the financial return, but one must allow that this version broadly passes the historical test. However, as argued above, it does not seem to portray adequately the rationale of graduate pay.

In due course we shall hopefully have complex and validated explanations of educational growth. In the meantime striking things are happening, with surprisingly similar patterns in different countries. It seems appropriate to begin with simple models of explanation. A clear merit of the theory of this essay is that its predictions are reasonably clear, and it can therefore be tested and refined by research.

But we are also interested in affecting change, as well as explaining it. The general argument in section II has been that, given the right level of subsidy, a system driven by the private demand for education will produce an outcome broadly in line with what is needed on cost-benefit grounds. The Robbins approach is not as uneconomic as many letters to *The Times* would have us think. But does this mean that the arguments in section I are redundant? The answer is No, for section II has ignored what for short-run policy purposes may be of great importance – the leads and lags in the system.

In a state of steady growth we could with luck find a steadily-changing level of subsidy which equated the social rate of return to its desired level.[31] But in a world of irregular change, private choices under this system might not lead, as we have assumed they would, to stable social rates of return. Unheralded changes in the demand for graduates would, unless demand elasticities are very high, disturb the rate of return. Even if students responded at once to altered private returns, the rate of return would only revert to its proper level after the responding cohort had worked itself through the system. And the chances are that students would respond with a lag. How important these problems are is an empirical matter and varies between fields.

Some forecasting, however, is inevitable and desirable, and should be done both by governments and individuals. The government can use its forecasts to influence individual choice through variable subsidies and by vocational guidance; but also, where it provides education, it may use the pattern of provision as an instrument of policy.[32] There may, in the present state of knowledge, be relatively few forecasts inspiring enough confidence for use, but we should use these and try to improve the others.

Notes

1. I have in mind particularly the writings of Mark Blaug which have provoked many of the ideas in this paper, see Blaug (1965, 1966 and, especially, 1967).
2. For an explanation of why it is more convenient to deal with rates of return than present values in educational planning see Blaug, Layard and Woodhall (1969, p. 26). The most convenient formulation is to take as $\bar{r}_s$ the rate of social time preference, provided the costs of education are measured to allow for their social opportunity cost (Marglin, 1963b). It is somewhat arbitrary to take the rate of social time preference as independent of the investment decision but this may not be serious, at least with reference to investment in one small sector (Feldstein, 1964). The whole cost-benefit approach is naturally subject to certain reservations about the income distribution effects of the way in which education is provided and financed.
3. For an investment yielding a permanent income stream the present value per £ invested is $£(r_s - \bar{r}_s)/\bar{r}_s$, and this measures the gain from spending one more £ on such an investment. For investments yielding other than permanent income

streams or single-period returns, there is no strict relation between $r_s, \bar{r}_s$ and the present value per £ invested.

4. The income stream generated by education is not of course perpetual but ends after about forty years. However, at a 10 per cent discount rate, 98 per cent of the present value of a perpetual income stream is accounted for by the income over the first forty years; the approximation is thus quite close. The assumption of a one-year course is simply to reduce the number of symbols, and the denominator can be multiplied by an appropriate number without significantly affecting the argument at any point. The relevant wage differential is between what the same man would be paid as a graduate as a non-graduate: if we use the wages of actual graduates and non-graduates, it needs to be reduced to allow for the non-educational determinants of income.

5. As section II brings out, the government has also to ensure by subsidies or other means that the places are taken up.

6. A sufficient condition for r_s to rise as W_G/W_N rises is that C does not rise relative to W_G since $r_s = \dfrac{1 - W_N/W_G}{C/W_G + W_N/W_G}$

7. Blaug (1967, pp. 285–6) proposes a different framework for considering the question, in which the role of the social discount rate as the target variable is less explicit. His model predicts what will happen and then evaluates it; our model is explicitly prescriptive.

8. This is so, for example, in India where an attempt to draw policy conclusions from rates of return is made in Blaug, Layard and Woodhall, 1969.

9. The demand functions referred to here are the demand-derived rate of return functions $g = g^3 (r_s, t)$. The argument is as follows. We can only be certain that a marginal reduction in the growth of supply will help if the neutral policy of setting $\dot{S}$ *(future)* $= \dot{S}$ *(past)* would reduce r_s still further. Sufficient conditions for this are that $\dot{S}$ *(past)* $> \dot{D}$ *(past)* $> \dot{D}$ *(future)*, since in this case $\dot{S}$ *(future)* $> \dot{D}$ *(future)*. If $\dot{S}$ *(future)* $< \dot{S}$ *(past)*, r_s will fall less and may rise. If on the other hand $\dot{S}$ *(past)* $< \dot{D}$ *(past)* $< \dot{D}$ *(future)*, as in Figure 15.2, the neutral policy will raise r_s and may raise it too far, in which case we need to increase the growth of supply. The whole argument here and in the text could of course be presented in terms of growth rates $(\dot{D}/D$ and $\dot{S}/S)$ which for some purposes would be more useful.

10. Trends in earnings of new entrants to the labour market are particularly sensitive to changes in the balance of supply and demand and deserve special study.

11. Note that $(\bar{g}_0 - g_0)$ could be negative if $r_s < \bar{r}_s$.

12. Bowles (1969) argues that it is very high and uses this as an argument for assuming non-declining marginal productivity of educated people. For a fuller explanation of the relevance of elasticities of demand (or, more accurately, of substitution) in educational planning, see Dougherty (1971).

13. For a fair sample of methods of manpower forecasting see Blaug (ed.), (1968, pp. 263–348).

14. The rate-of-return approach, despite the boldness of many if its supporters, thus implies a serious risk of overcaution. It has another conservative aspect in that it can only be used to evaluate courses already in existence and long-enough established to yield data on earnings by age. But this does not imply that all manpower forecasters are paragons of innovatory thinking.

15. For a more discriminating analysis of the degree to which British higher education responds to the private demand for places see Layard, King and Moser (1969, pp. 21–5). In teacher training of course the plans have been based on forecasts of demand for school teachers.

16. Strictly the rate-of-return criterion is inappropriate for private choices in education, since different types of education may be mutually exclusive while differing in cost. When there is no capital rationing, the rate-of-return rule can thus lead to the wrong decision, but it is still true that in general equilibrium, given diminishing returns and ignoring psychic benefits and risk, the rate of return on each type of education will become equal to the interest rate. The assumption in the text may thus be adequate for describing the general equilibrium position. Under capital rationing, the market outcome depends on the pattern of access to capital.

17. A number of objections to the theory will be raised and discussed at the end of the paper.

18. Sufficient conditions for r_p to rise as W_G/W_N rises are as follows: if $F > M$, that $(F - M)/(1 - T)$ rises no faster than W_G; and if $F < M$ that $(M - F)/(1 - T)$ rises no less fast than W_G.

19. The optimal level of $F - M$ in our simplified model is in fact $[W_N(\bar{r}_s - \bar{r}_p) + \bar{r}_s C](1 - T)/\bar{r}_p$ but the approach in the text illustrates the kind of framework that would be needed if one were going to make r_s include external effects and psychic benefits. One may also note that in our simplified model the condition for $r_p > r_s$ is that $(C - F + M)/C > T$, i.e. that public expenditure as a proportion of tuition costs exceed the average tax rate. In this case, of course, the rate of return to public funds $r_f < r_s$, since

$$r_f = \frac{(W_g - W_N)T}{W_N T + C - F + M} < \frac{(W_G - W_N)T}{W_N T + CT} = r_s$$

20. A sufficient condition for this would be for F/C, C/W_N and M/W_N to remain constant.

21. Blaug (1965, p. 229), suggests that the *ex ante* evaluation of these benefits may be less than their *ex post* value to people who are already educated. The reverse is also possible: that some people are disappointed by education and do not feel that as such it has made them happier. On this point agnosticism may be the best course.

22. It is sometimes said that allowing for psychic benefits is all right for advanced but not for developing countries. This argument is clearly wrong unless linked to issues of income distribution, which are not discussed in this paper.

23. Campbell and Seigel (1967, pp. 482–94), for example, estimate the income elasticity of demand for US education, but are unable to differentiate these two effects.

24. An example of the force of social habit is provided by recent experience in Britain as the population bulge passed through the higher education age group. Presumably the demand for new graduates did not expand abnormally fast in those years, yet the number of new graduates expanded tremendously – at the rate predicted by the trend in the proportion of the age group graduating (Layard, King and Moser, 1969, pp. 35–6).

25. If he had been earning, the student would in some cases have been subsidising the rest of the family. This further reduces the cost to him of studying.
26. We omit *ad hoc* institutional explanations, such as the structural reform of school systems, since there remains the question of why these reforms came about.
27. See, for example, Committee on Higher Education (1963), Appendix One, pp. 54–61, 69–70.
28. Note that we are not trying to explain *which* people get educated. Economists may have something but not a lot to say on this.
29. The 'infection' models can also be criticised because they ignore the cost of education but this is only to say that they differ from the present theory. What is needed is an external test.
30. See for example Griliches (1964). This reports an inter-state production function so that, unless there are great ability differences between states, differences in educational level must be taken at their face value.
31. In principle this could be done without calculating rates of return, by simply allowing for external effects; taxation and the differences between social and private discount rates. But in practice we know little about effective private discount rates and might need to experiment directly with different subsidies and observe the variation in social rates of return.
32. In strict logic there is an asymmetry here – the provision of places can only reduce the number of students below what it would be, given free choice on the terms offered. However a liberal supply of places does also seem to increase the demand for entry.

References

Becker, G.S. (1964) *Human Capital* (New York: Columbia University Press for the National Bureau of Economic Research).

Blaug, M. (1965) 'The rate of return on investment in education in Great Britain', *Manchester School* (September); reprinted in Blaug (ed.) (1968), to which page nos refer.

Blaug, M. (1966) 'An economic interpretation of the private demand for education', *Economica* (May).

Blaug, M. (1967) 'Approaches to educational planning', *Economic Journal* (June).

Blaug, M. (ed.) (1968) *Penguin Modern Economics. Economics of Education I* (Harmondsworth: Penguin).

Blaug, M., R. Layard and M. Woodhall (1969) *The Causes of Graduate Unemployment in India* (London: Allen Lane: The Penguin Press, 1998). Chapter 11 in R. Layard, *Tackling Unemployment* (London: Macmillan, 1999).

Bowles, S. (1969) *Planning Education for Economic Growth* (Cambridge, Mass.: Harvard University Press).

Campbell, R. and B.N. Seigel (1967) 'The demand for higher education in the United States 1919–1964', *American Economic Review* (June).

Committee on Higher Education (1963) *Higher Education: Report of the Robbins Committee*, Appendix One: The Demand for Places in Higher Education, Cmnd. 2154–I (London: HMSO).

Denison, E. (1964) 'Proportion of income differentials among education groups "due to" additional education: the evidence of the Wolfe–Smith survey', in J. Vaisey (ed.), *The Residual Factor and Economic Growth* (Paris: OECD).

Dougherty, C.R.S. (1971) 'The optimal allocation of investment in education', in H.B. Chenery (ed.), *Studies in Development Planning* (Cambridge, Mass.: Harvard University Press).

Feldstein, M.S. (1964) 'The social time preference rate in cost benefit analysis', *Economic Journal* (June).

Griliches, Z. (1964) 'Research expenditures, education and the aggregate agricultural production function', *American Economic Review* (December).

Hansen, W.L. (1963) 'Total and private rates of return to investment in schooling', *Journal of Political Economy* (April); reprinted in Blaug (ed.) (1968), to which page nos refer.

Layard, R., J. King and C. Moser (1969) *The Impact of Robbins: Expansion in Higher Education* (Harmondsworth: Penguin).

Marglin, S.A. (1963a) 'The social rate of discount and the optimal rate of investment', *Quarterly Journal of Economics* (February).

Marglin, S.A. (1963b) 'The opportunity costs of public investment', *Quarterly Journal of Economics* (May).

Psacharopoulos, G. (1972) 'The economic returns to higher education in 25 countries', *Higher Education*, vol. 1, No. 2: 141–58.

Stone, R. (1965) 'A model of the educational system', *Minerva* (Winter).

Weisbrod, B.A. (1964) External Benefits of Public Education: *An Economic Analysis* (Princeton: Princeton University, Industrial Relations Section).

Wiles, P. (1969) 'Die Bauchschmerzen eines Factidioten', in D. Martin (ed.), *Anarchy and Culture* (Routledge and Keegan Paul, London).

16 University Efficiency and University Finance (1973)*

with R. Jackman

Universities are often inefficient. In section 1 we quote some examples of this, especially their failure to exploit the new media of communications. But the question is why the inefficiency occurs and how it can be reduced. It seems mainly caused by the difficulty of measuring the output of individual teachers and of institutions, and thus of paying them appropriately. We therefore explore the efficiency effects of different ways of paying teachers (section 2) and of financing institutions (in section 3). The analysis assumes that universities are labour-managed enterprises, and leads to some piecemeal policy conclusions.

1 UNIVERSITY EFFICIENCY

When people complain of university inefficiency, they may mean that the choice of techniques is inappropriate (e.g. too high a staff–capital ratio) or they may mean that the wrong outputs are being produced (e.g. too much research). Though these issues are interrelated it is important to distinguish between them. If we knew the university production function, efficient allocation would of course generally require us to secure three sets of equalities: the marginal rates of substitution between factors should equal their relative marginal social costs; the marginal rates of transformation between products should equal their relative marginal social benefits; and the social value of the marginal product of each factor should equal its marginal social cost. Unfortunately, little is known so far about the university production function, though a good deal is known about the school production function (Hanushek, 1971; US Department of Health, Education and Welfare, 1970) and work is afoot on universities.[1] Equally, not much is known about the shadow prices of many of

* Chapter 10 in M. Parkin (ed.) *Essays in Modern Economics*, Longmans, 1973 (with R. Jackman) The authors are grateful to L.P. Foldes, H.G. Johnson, A.K. Sen, B.A. Weisbrod amd G.L. Williams for useful comments and suggestions. Richard Layard is grateful to the Nuffield Foundation for a Small Grant which financed a visit to the USA in 1971 during which he began thinking about this subject.

the main outputs, particularly research (Byatt and Cohen, 1969) so that remarks such as 'we need not double research by 1980 but we must double teaching output' are little more than assertions of value judgement. However, rather more is known about the prices of the main inputs such as student time, staff time, and non-staff inputs, and this makes it easier to think about questions of the choice of techniques provided one is willing to guess at marginal rates of factor substitution.

Before coming to the new media, we shall give a few examples of apparent inefficiency in the use of the old. One class of these concerns the use of student time, which teachers tend to treat as a free good although it accounts for about half the total real cost of universities. A small example illustrates this point. Suppose one is teaching a course where a book on the reading list will be read in the library by, on average, n students. One can either put the catalogue numbers on the reading list or leave each student to look them up individually. Efficiency requires the former, unless n is less than the ratio between the price of one's own (or one's secretary's) time and the price of students' time.[2] Yet how often do we do it? Moreover, the provision of books and articles often seems inadequate relative to the provision of teachers. If, as undergraduates in some institutions allege, they spend two hours a week looking for books and articles, the cost of this search will normally exceed the cost of all the materials which their library provides for them.[3]

Turning to the use of staff time, one is struck by the passion for small teaching groups and the proliferation of optional courses.[4] Yet all the evidence suggests that students' gains in cognitive understanding are independent of class size over a wide range of class sizes (Dubin and Taveggia, 1968; Mckeachie, 1963). The psychic benefits to students may of course be higher in smaller classes, since the possibility of personal contact between teachers and students is higher. However there is no reason to suppose that these contacts, which are clearly an important means whereby students discover their talents, are best produced jointly with cognitive learning, rather than by separate arrangements in which teachers participate, but with personal guidance rather than exposition as the goal. So there must be many cases where classes are inefficiently divided into sections, and there is an excessive input of teaching time and an inadequate input of guidance.

Against this point of view it may be argued that, although the inputs of teaching time are unnecessary for producing teaching output, they are important for research; they train researchers and keep them abreast of current knowledge. This argument is particularly strong when applied to the proliferation of options, which, though it reduces class sizes, enables people to teach the subject areas of their research. If this is true, the joint-product nature of the university justifies what seems inefficient from the teaching point of view; and the choice of techniques may be efficient, in the sense that the university is producing on its research/teaching production possibility frontier.

However, when the new media are introduced into the production set, this argument becomes implausible. The issue here is complex and we shall only sketch a basic argument: a fuller treatment appears elsewhere (see Layard, 1973). Television, film, programmed texts, and computer-assisted learning are clearly most suited to teaching well-structured bodies of knowledge. Here they offer clear scope for reducing costs per student-hour without loss of quality, if used on a large enough scale. In fact many of the advocates of the new media believe that quality would be improved – by individualising the process of instruction (students pacing themselves, and so on); by disseminating more widely the influence of the few outstanding teachers; and by making economic the allocation of more preparation time to any particular hour's worth of teaching materials. Against this, others argue that quality per student-hour is bound to fall, owing to the absence of direct human contact, lack of personal feedback and external pacing, and the like. In fact, however, the finding of the available surveys of empirical evidence (Dubin and Hedley, 1969; Chu and Schramm, 1987; Tickton, 1970; Schramm, 1964) is that student achievement is fairly similar whatever teaching medium is used – neither better nor worse. Moreover, the new media seem to be as successful in teaching problem-solving ability as in teaching concepts and facts. Attiyeh, Bach and Lumsden (1969) found that students who spent twelve hours reading one of their programmed introductory economics texts without any live teaching did as well on questions testing the application of economic theory to real problems as students who had taken twenty-one hours' coursework and read the associated textbook.

As regards student attitudes to the new media, these are sometimes favourable and sometimes unfavourable, depending on the exact circumstances of the change. Moreover a new medium is almost always liked more by those who have experienced it than by those who have not (Dubin and Hedley, 1969). Just as there are televised and computer-based courses which have failed to attract students to whom live instruction was also available for the course, there are others where, even in competition with a popular instructor, the new medium has swept the field (Suppes and Morningstar, 1969). At the State University of New York at Oneonta, the introductory economics course is now taught to all students, except one undersubscribed live section, by two hours a week of prerecorded television and one hour of informal discussion sections with faculty members; the new system is preferred to the old, and is cheaper (Office of Educational Communications, 1970; Gordon, 1969). The general conclusion must be, as before, that students want and need contact with staff, but it is unlikely that this is produced most efficiently as a complementary output with the learning of formally structured material, and it may not be produced at all by large lecture courses.

On the cost side the basic argument for the new media derives from the large overhead costs involved in the preparation of any teaching material. Effective teaching requires not only the preparation of exposition and of exercises, but also an evaluation of each component part. If these overhead costs are incurred in each teaching institution, there is a degree of duplication that has become quite unnecessary now that the new media are available. Of course, if there were only one university teaching introductory economics, it would almost certainly be cheaper to teach the subject by live instruction only – probably even without a printed textbook. But there are in this country, say, a hundred introductory economics courses, each taught by a different live instructor who works out his own course. In general university teachers are conscientious and devote much time to devising what they consider makes the best course. And yet, in the event, most of the courses will be very similar, most could be improved if more time were devoted to the preparation of better problems and expositional sequence, and many of them are taught by people who lack a talent for teaching. Such a situation seems highly irrational when we now have the means to devise a few competing packages which could do much of the job a great deal better and more cheaply.

Space precludes giving detailed statistics of cost. But the following comparison of videotape with live lectures may give some impression of the issues. Whereas the cost of lectures is roughly proportional to the number of presentations, videotape involves substantial fixed costs of two kinds. First, there is the cost of producing the master tape, which depends on the complexity of the production. The cost of this per presentation falls directly with the number of institutions using the material. Second, there is the cost of the equipment needed to present the material (videotape recorders and TV sets). The cost of this per presentation again falls directly with the number of presentations for which it is used. However, provided the production is of the simplest kind, it will be cheaper than live lecturing, even if used in only two institutions, provided those institutions are using their equipment for at least sixty-five presentations a year. The more complex the production the larger the number of participating institutions (or of presentations per institution) needed to make it economic.[5]

So it seems that there are well-established possibilities of reducing costs per unit of output by the selective use of new media, provided these are adopted on a sufficiently large scale. In the immediate future the best bet appears to be the use of programmed texts and videotape to replace much live exposition. The materials currently available are often of poor quality; but even those that are good are rarely used outside the institution where they were prepared, even though they are sometimes made available free of charge. Thus the potential scale economies of the media are wasted and their use fails to expand. The question is: Why are institutions unwilling to use materials they have not themselves produced, when these could be used to reduce their own teaching commitments, liberating time for research or other teaching? It cannot be due to an objection in principle to other people's materials, for on that principle each university should provide its own textbooks. Can it be due to the infant industries, chicken and egg, problem? Until there is a reasonable market the incentive to produce is small and quality may be poor; but equally until the quality is good, the market remains small. All one can say is that this problem has not prevented the spread of a whole host of new commercially produced items, especially in the communications industry. Of course, the universities are not in business to make a profit and may therefore lack the incentives affecting commercial manufacturers. But textbooks are not produced by universities, but by publishers and authors, and neither publishers nor computer firms have ventured far into the new media. The reason is that they do not trust the market; they doubt the demand.

So can there be some feature of universities (either intrinsic or due to their methods of financing) which makes them likely to reject efficient techniques of producing the teaching and research that society wants? A casual glance at the main users of bought-in materials suggests that there may be. The main users are private firms and the armed services. There are now in the USA many schemes whereby local firms buy televised Master's courses in engineering for their employees and pay at least the full incremental media costs.[6] But there are very few cases of one university buying such facilities from another. Similarly the new media are widely used for training, both by firms and the Army. Though the material here may be more clearcut than much of what is taught in universities, it is idle to pretend that there are no routine manipulations which university students must master.

So we need to look closely at the non-profit nature of the university and its objective function to see whether these provide any explanation of university inefficiency. But we also need to look at the internal processes of universities and examine whether it is within their power to be efficient even in achieving their own objectives.[7]

2 PROBLEMS OF INTERNAL PRICING

Universities as labour-managed enterprises

First, we have to identify the university's process of decision-making. Most universities in this country are formally governed by mainly lay councils, but most of the effective decisions are probably taken by academics, some of them *ex officio* and others elected by other academics. So the most relevant simple model seems to be that of the labour-managed enterprise, the relevant labourers being in this case only the academic staff. The objective of the enterprise is then to maximise the welfare of its members subject to the production functions, the budget constraint and any other externally imposed constraints.

Why are universities run in this way unlike most other enterprises? The answer seems to lie in the difficulty of measuring their output. If teaching and research could be readily measured, students or governments would be willing to pay for defined quantities and the form of organisation would probably be autonomous hierarchically organised units, whether privately or publicly owned. But given the problem of output measurement there are two obvious possible methods of providing for quality control: internal democratic self-government or external bureaucratic management (e.g. as in France). Each has obvious dangers, as Adam Smith pointed out (Smith, 1776):

> If the authority to which the teacher is subject resides in the body corporate, the college, or university, of which he himself is a member, and in which the greater part of the other members are, like himself, persons who either are, or ought to be teachers; they are likely to make a common cause, to be all very indulgent to one another, and every man to consent that his neighbour may neglect his duty, provided he himself is allowed to neglect his own. In the University of Oxford, the greater part of the public professors have, for these many years, given up altogether even the pretence of teaching.
>
> If the authority to which he is subject resides, not so much in the body corporate of which he is a member, as in some other extraneous persons, in the bishop of the diocese for example; in the governor of the province; or, perhaps, in some minister of state; it is not indeed in this case very likely that he will be suffered to neglect his duty altogether. All that such superiors, however, can force him to do, is to attend upon his pupils a certain number of hours, that is, to give a certain number of lectures in the week or in the year. ... From the insolence of office too they are frequently indifferent how they exercise it, and are very apt to ensure or deprive him of his office wantonly, and without any just cause. The person subject to such jurisdiction is necessarily degraded by it, and, instead of being one of the most respectable, is rendered one of the meanest and most contemptible persons in the society.

There are it seems some who think this latter model describes our present situation. But we shall assume that our universities do have at least sufficient discretion to be regarded as labour-managed.

But because they are not paid for their outputs, there is no automatic mechanism such as that which ensures that classical labour-managed enterprises in perfectly competitive industries free of external effects will in long-run equilibrium be allocatively efficient (Meade, 1972). Instead universities may receive their incomes in a block grant, or in the form of a per student fee or in many other ways. This inevitably makes possible a divergence between the university choice of inputs and outputs and what the rest of society would like, since in a labour-managed enterprise the preferences of the teachers will play a preponderant role. We shall discuss this problem in section 3 and ask how different forms of external finance are likely to affect university behaviour. But first we consider the internal problem that arises because universities are unable to measure the output of their own staff. This makes it difficult for universities to achieve even their own objectives.

The objective function and the ideal pricing of output

We can best think about this by imagining what the university would do if it could pay teachers for their output. Suppose that all teachers have the same utility function and that the university aims to maximise the average level of utility of its members. The key question is: What affects individual utility? Clearly, the teacher values his wage, the way he spends his time, the products of his labour and also the quality of the university where he works. While he values the use of his time for its own intrinsic satisfaction, he may value his outputs for other reasons also – for example a good research reputation may raise his future earnings from outside work. The reputation of the university is valued for similar reasons and also because it attracts good students and colleagues. This reputation depends on the teaching and research outputs of the institution, which teachers may also value as goods in themselves. They differ from the other sources of individual satisfaction in that they are collective goods which affect the welfare of all. For this reason each teacher cannot be left to do what he likes; for, unless motivated to do so, he will not take into account the effect of his decision on the welfare of his colleagues. Instead he should be paid for each unit of output an amount equal to the sum of its marginal value to all individuals.[8] In this way, the university could achieve its objective of maximising average welfare if individual outputs were measurable.

The actual payment of teachers and the problem of information

But unfortunately, measurement is difficult. One alternative now open is to pay for inputs, just as Oxford and Cambridge pay for tutorial supervision and many universities for examining. The scope for this approach seems wider than is currently practised. In principle, if production functions were fully known, it could achieve exactly the same results as paying for output. The same is true of the policy most commonly followed, namely regulation, by which certain dimensions of the teacher's inputs are laid down, in return for which the teacher gets his wage in the form of a block grant.

The difficulty with regulation is that not many dimensions of work can in fact be effectively policed: one can require so many hours of teaching of such and such type, residence in the UK, and the like, but control over quality is inevitably poor. Moreover, regulation makes it difficult to take advantage of the different teaching and research talents of different individuals, and all tend to be given the same teaching load whether or not their comparative advantage is in that line.

Pricing problems also seem to explain many of the problems referred to in section 1 of this paper. First, there is the alleged lack of concern about the quantity and quality of teaching output as opposed to research. A possible explanation is as follows. The university will wish to pay its members on the basis of their expected productivity. But how is this to be assessed? It is widely believed that teaching capacity is more difficult to evaluate than research capacity and that an academic's accumulated research is often used as a proxy measure of the potential value of his current teaching and research output. This may be particularly the case when he moves from one university to another. If this is so, it introduces an extraneous element into the individual teacher's utility function, for he now values his current research output more highly relative to his teaching output, purely because of the higher command over future income which it gives him. This in turn will affect the level of teaching load for which he is willing to vote.[9]

Given this it might well be asked why even the current amount of teaching is done. Three possible explanations can be offered. The first, and most charitable, is that teachers obtain direct utility from their own and their colleagues' teaching output. A second is that they enjoy the teaching input (holding forth), even if they are not especially concerned with whether anything is learnt. A third, and perhaps important, explanation is that certain forms of teaching activity are an important input into research, which in this sense is produced jointly with the teaching output. Most people believe that, at any rate in theoretical subjects, there is a high degree of complementarity between research and teaching (especially lecturing or other forms of systematic exposition), and this must certainly be one important source of resistance to replacing live instruction by effective teaching.

Thus, pricing problems affect the university's ability to achieve its own true objectives. However, these need only be accepted if the cost of improved information on the teaching performance of individual teachers exceeds its benefit. The most obvious source of better information is the use of systematic student questionnaires, which could provide direct information to the teacher himself as well as relevant data to those who set his pay (National Board for Prices and Incomes, 1968). There would be costs – of administration and lost ease – but the potential benefits seem in the context of this paper to be great.

Similar arguments apply to the problem of organising desirable innovations in teaching methods. Teachers when they leave a university carry as a claim to future income only their past research, and someone who is likely to move in the near future has little incentive to devote time to innovations which will benefit others but not himself. A similar problem arises in the determination of the rate of reinvestment in the classic labour-managed enterprise where workers have no property rights in the assets of the enterprise (Neuberger and James, 1970). It is therefore not surprising that innovations in teaching methods are as often made by the older as the younger staff – a situation not paralleled in manufacturing enterprises, where a reputation for profitable investment decisions provides an excellent claim to future income. The Prices and Incomes Board's proposal to formalise payments for innovation in teaching therefore deserves strong support (National Board for Prices and Incomes, 1968).

Pricing problems also arise over the teachers' use of students' time. This is clearly an input into the production function of each university teacher but he does not pay for it. This would create no problem if the teacher were paid for his net output, but he is not. He therefore has little incentive to economise in the use of his students' time. This is one of the main reasons why syllabuses become overloaded, the other reason being that teachers are using their students as stimuli to their own research. There are of course limits to this process given that students are free agents. They can often opt out of excessively overloaded courses or refuse to do the full volume of reading and writing expected. But the problem of effectively coordinating the institution's use of students' time remains a severe one.

The teacher as entrepreneur

At this stage someone might point out that these kinds of incentive problem arise in any organisation. This is true. But the difficulty is probably more acute in universities, because the problem of policing the individual worker is greater due to the individualistic and non-cooperative nature of the basic production process, which at present depends critically on the face-to-face interaction between the lone teacher and his students.

However, this suggests one obvious general solution for our problems, which is for universities to be 'deschooled' and teachers to be self-employed. In this scheme we replace the university as the entrepreneur hiring services from the teacher, by the teacher as the entrepreneur hiring services, where necessary, from the university. All payments for teaching services would be made directly by the consumers to the teachers, who would rent their rooms from the university. The function of the university would be to provide capital facilities, to certify the teachers and to provide the necessary informational and administrative services to establish effective contacts between students and teachers. If a coordinated teaching programme were felt to be necessary, teachers could bid for the right to give particular courses but they would collect their fee at the door. Such a Smithian scheme has many attractions. It brings the customers' evaluation of teaching output directly on the teacher, and so overcomes the problem of teachers being paid on the basis of past research rather than current teaching.[10] It also makes it more likely that student time will be economically used. But its main defects are the classic ones adduced by Coase in his explanation of the existence of the firm (1937). These are the transaction costs involved in using the market to organise a process in which there is a degree of interdependence between the outputs of many different agents.[11] The higher the ratio of non-teacher inputs to teachers, the more important the coordinating role of the university organisation becomes; and if the arguments about new media and innovation are accepted, more non-teacher inputs may be what are needed at the moment. There is also the obvious danger of teachers exploiting their monopoly of their own differentiated product.

A final and less radical proposal for expanding the role of prices in achieving university efficiency is to give a greater entrepreneurial role to departments, who would receive a general budget out of which they would pay for the factors they employ. This type of limited internal pricing is now becoming more prevalent and could further encourage efficiency if departmental incomes were in some degree related to the department's output (Breneman, 1971a, 1971b). But the more important internal reform involves the deliberate and costly gathering of more information about teaching performance.

3 PROBLEMS OF EXTERNAL FINANCE

This brings us to the question of the optimum method of financing institutions, as opposed to individuals. There are a number of ways in which governments can alter the conditions in which universities make their decisions and we shall try to discover how some of these affect the staff–student ratio and the output mix. Specifically we shall examine the effects of salary regulation and grant levels, the question of block versus *per capita* finance, and the wisdom of separate finance for research and innovation. We shall start by assuming bureaucratic financing (viz. fixed income and student numbers for each university).

The regulation of salaries and the size of grant

In the classic labour-managed enterprise the workers determine their own average level of pay, but in universities the government may, as in Britain, restrict this freedom by imposing salary scales and maximum senior/junior staff ratios.[12] The purpose of this is presumably to prevent university teachers feathering their own nests and paying themselves more than their supply price out of public money. In a full-blooded socialist market economy with free entry this problem does not of course arise; for, if one enterprise is paying more than the going wage, others are set up in that industry until the product price has fallen sufficiently to eliminate the wage differential. But in a state-financed system free entry may not be possible. So a system of unregulated wages may involve inequitable transfers of income. It may also be allocatively inefficient.

The allocative problem arises because, when deciding on the number of colleagues to hire, university teachers realise that each additional teacher reduces their own income. This cost they balance against the value to them of the extra teacher's output, be it his research performance, his contribution to reduced teaching loads or whatever. The resulting equilibrium could well be inefficient. Suppose for example that teachers were only interested in the level of output per teacher and in their own wage. Equilibrium would then require that the average product per teacher be increasing with the number of teachers, so as to offset the monetary loss to existing teachers involved in hiring a new one.[13]

A more general problem is that, whereas under regulated wages the government can always bring about any desired staff–student ratio by varying the grant paid to the university, this may not be possible under unregulated wages. For the higher the level of grant the greater the cost of an extra teacher to those already employed. This is analogous to the problem in labour-managed factories that a remission of rent may reduce output and employment in the firm (Meade, 1972). On the other hand, higher incomes may raise the marginal value which teachers place on their colleagues' output so that an increase in the grant leads to an increase in employment. But there may still be some maximum number of teachers beyond which no variation of grant can induce the university to go.[14]

If, however, wages are fixed, the existing teachers experience no monetary cost from an expansion in their number, and employment expands till the subjective value of the output of the additional teacher falls to zero, or, as is more likely, until the budget is exhausted. If the wage is fixed at the supply price, the number of teachers employed for a given grant will be larger than if the wage is either unregulated or regulated above its supply price. By varying the grant it should always be possible to achieve the desired staff–student ratio, and at minimum cost to the taxpayer.[15]

The staff–student ratio and the output mix

The staff–student ratio will of course be simultaneously determined with the balance between teaching and research, and if an increase in grant raises the staff–student ratio, it can be expected to alter the output mix. The direction of the change will depend on the precise form of the teachers' utility function. Suppose that teachers value research output per teacher (R) and teaching

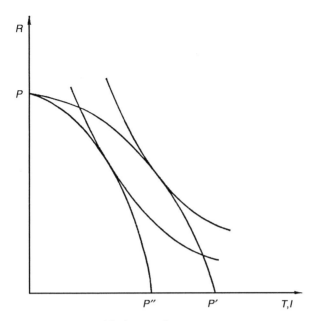

Figure 16.1   *Per capita* versus block grant finance

output per teacher (T) and that the marginal rate of substitution between these is independent of their wage. Suppose too, that the production function of R depends only on the way each teacher uses his time, while the production function of T depends on this and on the staff–student ratio. An increase in the staff–student ratio reduces the maximum teaching output per teacher (T), as each teacher has fewer students with whom to work; but it leaves his maximum research output unchanged.[16] It therefore shifts the production possibility curve in from PP' to PP'' in Figure 16.1. Given homotheticity in the utility function this increases R/T, and hence the share of research in university output. Conversely a cut in grant would be expected to cut research output relative to teaching, as common belief suggests.

However, it is equally possible that teachers, while valuing research output per teacher (R), value teaching output per *student* (I). With this new variable measured on the horizontal axis, a rise in the staff-student ratio (n/s) shifts the production possibility curve out from PP'' to PP' and decreases R/I. However, the change in the university's balance of output (R/T) is indeterminate, since $R/T = (R/I).(n/s)$ and the fall in R/I may be proportionately less than the rise in n/s.

Thus neither of two widely different utility functions suggests that increasing the staff–student ratio will definitely raise the share of teaching in output, while one of them leads to the view that this share will be reduced.

We turn now to the effects of replacing a block grant conditional on fixed student numbers by a system of *per capita* finance with the university free to take as many students as it wants. This has been widely advocated as a remedy for university inefficiency and in particular as a method of increasing the emphasis on teaching relative to research (Peacock and Wiseman, 1964; Prest, 1966).

However, a first look at the question suggests that this conclusion is by no means obvious. For instance suppose the outputs which teachers value depend only on the ratios between the various inputs, as we assumed in our recent example. Then if a block grant is replaced by a *per capita* grant of equal size, as has been suggested (Peacock and Wiseman, 1964), the university's choice of staff–student ratio and output mix would be unaffected.[17] The only difference is that the scale of university becomes indeterminate. This is true whether or not wages are regulated.

If there are not constant returns to scale, a university receiving a *per capita* grant can choose its own size, whilst under bureaucratic finance this choice is constrained. It can be shown that under *per capita* finance if the university values its outputs in the same way as society it will choose to operate at the socially most efficient scale. But nothing can be said *a priori* about the balance of outputs at this scale as opposed to any other.[18]

We have however so far ignored one of the main arguments put forward in support of the view that *per capita* financing would tilt the output mix towards teaching. The argument is this. Under *per capita* finance universities can no longer count on having any students unless they can attract them, whereas under the bureaucratic system they are sure of receiving their quota. The number of students wanting to go to a university depends on its teaching and research, but primarily on its teaching. Therefore, teaching output will rise relative to research if a block grant system is replaced by a *per capita* system.

There are severe problems in finding a convincing formulation of this argument. Let us begin with a world of perfect competition between identical universities. It then follows that, if under bureaucratic finance there is no excess demand for places from students, universities are already under pressure to maintain the standard of their teaching – any relaxation would lead to a loss of students from the system. If on the other hand there is excess demand universities can, under *per capita* finance, expand, if they wish, without improving teaching standards. In this case, the final situation depends on whether the total number of students is allowed to grow. The government could presumably limit this by selecting those students for whom it was willing to provide *per capita* finance. But if it did not and instead accepted an open-ended commitment, the movement to equilibrium would be likely to involve an increased pressure towards higher standards of teaching.

Should total student numbers remain constant, there will only be an increase in teaching if universities wish to expand because they have been constrained at less than their perceived optimum scale, and if there are intrinsic *differences* in production arrangements between universities or they face a rising supply curve of students. If there were intrinsic differences in efficiency or if some universities had a greater taste for teaching, they would attract all the students from the other universities, which would be forced to close unless they retaliated by improving their teaching. Equally if the supply curve of students facing a particular university were rising, in the sense that more teaching per student was needed to attract more students, some universities might find it worth their while to pinch from others by raising their offering. In the British case one might question whether universities offer such a differentiated product that they are in this situation. Moreover, to the extent that they are, this already applies to each category of student quality and may influence university behaviour even under the block grant.

Finally, students may in fact have great difficulty in assessing teaching and, like universities in paying staff, may make their assessment on the basis of research reputations. For all these reasons the line of argument expressed at the beginning of this section seems fraught with question marks.

Paying separately for research and innovation

One other suggestion is sometimes made for effecting a shift to teaching (National Board for Prices and Incomes, 1968). This is to offer universities a separate payment for research, in the hope that the reduced block grant would be used for teaching. But it seems unlikely that this would in fact happen. If the university receives a given income in the form of a block grant plus a payment related to its research output, this seems bound to lead to a higher research output (and less teaching) than if the same sum were given as a single unconditional grant. For while this system provides an additional motivation for research, it does not remove any of the incentives that were there before. Administrative controls to ensure that the research grant is spent only on research could not help. Likewise administrative controls to ensure that the block grant was spent on teaching would be difficult to enforce, but if enforceable could be used equally with undifferentiated grants.

However, if paying for things the universities will do anyway is ill-advised, it may be well worth while to pay them for things they would not do but which are socially desirable. As we have seen, innovation falls into this category. The University Grants Committee has followed just such a policy, giving earmarked money to individual universities for use on new media. However, this has typically had little or no effect on the teaching methods of the universities because good teachers have not believed that the materials they developed would ever reach a wider market, such as that reached by their textbooks. The answer seems to be for media development to be sponsored by the central government either on its own or through consortia of universities or professional associations. These methods should ensure a sufficient market for the materials. A consortia of northern universities have successfully developed a packaged course in computer science that is used in each university. But this type of development is still more important in the bread and butter subjects, such as economics, where the real costs arise. If the natural sponsor for such an enterprise is the professional association, we would urge that the Association of University Teachers in Economics take this role upon itself.

4 SUMMARY

In sum, the universities seem to be inefficient in their choice of techniques and may be inefficient in their choice of outputs. The main reason for these problems is the difficulty of measuring the outputs of individuals and of institutions.

Mainly because of this difficulty, universities in Anglo-Saxon countries are constituted as labour-managed enterprises, and the utility functions of individual teachers thus affect the universities' input and output mix. It may or may not be true that teachers value the research output of their university relatively more highly than society does. But in any case the difficulty of measuring individual teaching output leads to teachers being paid largely for their past research. This greatly raises the value to them of their own current research output, and in turn reduces the incentive to introduce new teaching methods and materials, since the institution gains more from these than the individual teacher. Teachers will also value highly those kinds of teaching activity, like lecturing, which are most complementary to research but can be most efficiently replaced by packaged materials.

One proposed solution is to transfer the entrepreneurial role to the individual teacher who would be paid directly by students or research councils, according to their judgement of his output. But in fact the degree of interdependence between different university activities seems to make it worth while to preserve the university as a 'firm'. However, there may be more scope for pricing in the relation between universities and their constituent departments and for more piecework payment of individual teachers. A more fundamental need, however, is to improve information about teaching output, and this provides a strong case for the use of student questionnaires on individual courses.

Another approach is to alter the external stimuli to which universities are exposed. Here we have examined a number of proposals that have been put forward for raising the output of teaching relative to research. The first, a cut in university income for a given number of students, seems likely to have this effect. The second would replace the existing block grant to universities (with student numbers fixed) by an equivalent grant per student, with the university free to determine its own size. However, it is not clear that this would have the desired result. If the outputs that teachers value are produced by processes subject to constant returns to scale, there might be no change, and, if they are not, the direction of change is unpredictable. However, this argument assumes that an individual university faces an infinitely elastic 'supply curve' of students. But if institutions can only attract more students by raising their teaching output per student and they wish to expand, then a move to *per capita* finance may indeed raise the output of teaching relative to research. Better information on the teaching outputs of individual institutions might also have this effect. A third suggestion has been that universities should receive separate earmarked payments for research and teaching. But as it is not administratively easy to earmark money for teaching, earmarking might well raise relative research output rather than lowering it. However, separate payments for development work on teaching materials would have the desired effect, and are best organised on an interuniversity basis, perhaps through professional associations.

NOTE I

Assume

$$U_i = U\left(W_i, L_i, X_i, Q\left[\sum_{j=1}^{n} X_i\right]\right)$$

where U_i, W_i, L_i and X_i are respectively the utility, wage, labour input vector and output vector of the representative ith teacher, n is the number of teachers, and Q is some function of the university output vector. Assume too a separate and identical production function relating the inputs and output of each teacher and having a unique inverse function $L(X_i)$. The university now has to select a wage function which, when presented to individual teachers, will lead them to maximise collective welfare. Suppose this linear. Then

$$W_i = a + p_x X_i$$

where p_x is a price vector. If the university has fixed income (Y^0) and staff (n) and no other inputs, the budget constraint may be written

$$a = (Y^0 - p_x \sum X_i)/n$$

To maximise average welfare we require

$$\frac{\partial\left(\sum\limits_{i=1}^{n} U_i\right)}{\partial X_j} = \frac{\partial U_j}{\partial X_j} + \sum_{i \neq j} \frac{\partial U_i}{\partial X_j} = 0$$

However, the maximising individual will set $\partial U_j / \partial X_j = 0$, so we require

$$\sum_{i \neq j} \frac{\partial U_i}{\partial X_j} = \sum_{i \neq j}\left(U_{W_i}\left[-\frac{p_x}{n}\right] + U_Q Q_{X_j}\right) = 0$$

$$\therefore \quad p_x = n \frac{U_Q}{U_{W_i}} \cdot Q_{X_j}$$

where U_Q, Q_{X_j} and U_{W_i} indicate partial derivatives. Since all individuals have the same utility functions and production functions, U_W and Q_X will be the same for all individuals.

NOTE II

In what follows we confirm that

(a) the output mix is the same under block and *per capita* finance, given constant returns and unregulated wages,
(b) the same is true, given regulated wages,
(c) the size of university under *per capita* finance is optimal if teachers value outputs as society does.

We shall assume throughout that labour is the only input (it can be shown that introducing other inputs makes no difference). We shall also assume a utility function involving wages (W), research per teacher (R) and teaching per teacher (T). The results would not be affected if teaching per student (I) were used instead, provided both T and I depend only on ratios such as the proportion of time (r) which teachers spend on research and the staff-student ratio (n/s).

Unregulated wages

$$U = U(W, R, T)$$
$$R = R(r)$$
$$T = T\left(r, \frac{n}{s}\right)$$

(a) Block grant finance: $Y^0 = nW; s = s^0$
1st order conditions are

$$\frac{\partial U}{\partial n} = -U_W \frac{Y^0}{n^2} + U_T T_{n/s} \frac{1}{s^0} = 0$$

$$\frac{\partial U}{\partial r} = U_R R_r + U_T T_r = 0$$

(b) *Per capita* finance: $g^0 s = nW$
1st order conditions are

$$\frac{\partial U}{\partial n} = -U_W \frac{g^0 s}{n^2} + U_T T_{n/s} \frac{1}{s} = 0$$

$$\frac{\partial U}{\partial s} = U_W \frac{g^0}{n} - U_T T_{n/s} \frac{n}{s^2} = 0$$

$$\frac{\partial U}{\partial r} = U_R R_r + U_T T_r = 0$$

The first two equations are identical to each other, and, with the third, are identical to those in (a) if $g^0 = Y^0/s^0$.

Regulated wages

(a) Block grant finance: $Y^0 = nW^0; s = s^0$
1st order conditions are

$$n = \frac{Y^0}{W^0}$$

$$\frac{\partial U}{\partial r} = U_R R_r + U_T T_r = 0$$

(b) *Per capita* finance: $g^0 s = nW^0$
1st order conditions are

$$\frac{n}{s} = \frac{g^0}{W^0}$$

$$\frac{\partial U}{\partial r} = U_R R_r + U_T T_r = 0$$

As before, these equations are identical to those in (a) if $g^0 = Y^0/s^0$.

Optimum scale under *per capita* finance

(The result is the same under regulated and unregulated wages; regulated wages are assumed. Thus $g^0 s = W^0 n$.) With non-constant returns assume

$$U = U(W, R, T)$$
$$R = R(r) h(n)$$
$$T = T\left(r, \frac{n}{s}\right) \cdot f(s)$$

1st order conditions are

$$\frac{\partial U}{\partial n} = U_R R(r) h'(n) + U_T T_{n/s} f(s) \frac{1}{s} = 0$$
$$\frac{\partial U}{\partial r} = U_R R_r h(n) + U_T T_r f(s) = 0$$
$$\frac{\partial U}{\partial s} = -T_{n/s} \cdot \frac{n}{s^2} f(s) + T\left(r, \frac{n}{s}\right) f'(s) = 0$$

Combining the first and third equations to eliminate $T_{n/s}$

$$U_R R(r) h'(n) + U_T T\left(r, \frac{n}{s}\right) f'(s) \frac{s}{n} = 0$$

As n is increased by 1 unit, its effect on utility via research plus its effect on utility via teaching (s/n being instantaneously constant) is zero. Under normal assumptions about the utility function, it is sufficient for such a maximum that $h(n)$ and $f(s)$ are convex upwards.

Notes

1. The Higher Education Research Unit, LSE, is currently estimating cross-sectional production functions in five subject-groups in the UK.
2. Once a student is enrolled in a college the price of his time in the Catalogue Room is of course equal to the present value of the returns to time used in its next best use. Normally this is some alternative type of study. If it is efficient for him to be studying, then the present value of returns to study must at least equal the value of the earnings he could (given no indivisibilities) command with the same time. The reader should note that we are not attributing inefficiency to the fact that the university does not pay for its students: we are saying that it misuses the time of students having enrolled them.
3. These remarks assume that students' time is worth £0.50 per hour, so the cost per student per year is £30. The average number of bound volumes per student in university libraries in the UK in 1968–9 was about 115, but less than half of

these were probably used by undergraduates, say 50. If these books cost on average just over £2 and depreciate over two years at a 10 per cent interest rate, the annual cost of these 50 books is £20.

4. For a good discussion of the economies to be had from controlling these phenomena, see Bowen and Douglass (1971).
5. For a fuller discussion see Layard (1973).
6. The most celebrated examples are at Stanford, Florida State University, University of Colorado and Southern Methodist University.
7. For interesting discussions of utility-maximising non-profit institutions see Newhouse (1970) and Culyer (1970).
8. For a more formal exposition see Note I (p. 325 below).
9. Owing to the public goods characteristics of university outputs, teachers would always be willing to vote for higher required outputs than they would themselves voluntarily deliver. But this is particularly so of teaching, owing to its low private monetary reward. For evidence that teachers would on average prefer to do less teaching relative to research see Williams, Blackstone and Metcalf (1973).
10. According to Calvin and Lumsden (1970) there is no prospect of progress unless teachers are paid directly for their output.
11. The same considerations may explain why teachers are not paid in relation to their teaching hours.
12. There are obvious difficulties in enforcing any particular level of salaries, given that institutions can decide where to place individual teachers on the scale, and when to promote them (Metcalf, 1972). Likewise, they can always vary non-wage benefits and the quality of recruits. The actual system must therefore lie somewhere between the regulated and unregulated extremes.
13. An illustrative example is given in Note II, which is however mainly concerned with points coming later in the text.
14. The government, by varying the grant, could always reduce the number of teachers to any desired number.
15. A further argument in favour of payment at the supply price is that any other price would distort the choice between teachers and other factors of production.
16. More realistically, of course, we should allow for the influence of other inputs. Both maximum R and T would change, but their rate of transformation would probably change as shown in Figure 16.1.
17. The same would be true of its wage if this was unregulated.
18. The points made in this section are formally illustrated in Note II (p. 326).

References

Attiyeh, R.E., G.L. Bach and K.G. Lumsden (1969) 'The efficiency of programmed learning in teaching economics: the results of a nationwide experiment, *American Economic Review* (May).

Bowen, H.R. and G.K. Douglass (1971) *Efficiency in Liberal Education* (New York: McGraw-Hill).

Breneman, D.W. (1971) 'The PhD production process', paper presented to the National Bureau for Economic Research Conference on Education as an Industry.

Breneman, D.W. (ed.) (1971) *Internal Pricing Within the University – A Conference Report*, Office of the Vice-President (Planning), University of California (December).

Byatt, I.C.R. and A.V. Cohen (1969) *An Attempt to Quantify the Economic Benefits of Scientific Research*, Department of Education and Science (London: HMSO).

Calvin, A.D. (1970) A Psychologist Looks at the 'Teaching' of Economics at the Undergraduate Level, in K.G. Lumsden (ed.), *Recent Research in Economics Education* (New York: Prentice-Hall).

Chu, G.C. and W. Schramm (1967) *Learning from Television: What the Research Says*, Institute for Communications Research, Stanford University.

Coase, R.H. (1937) 'The nature of the firm', *Economica*, Nov, Vol IV, No. 16.

Culyer, A.J. (1970) 'A utility-maximising view of universities', *Scottish Journal of Political Economy* (November).

Dubin, R. and R.A. Hedley (1969) *The Medium may be Related to the Message: College Instruction* (Eugene, OR.: University of Oregon Press).

Dubin, R. and T.C. Taveggia (1968) *The Teaching–Learning Paradox* (Eugene, OR.: University of Oregon Press).

Gordon, S.D. (1969) 'Optimising the use of televised instruction', *Journal of Economic Education* (Autumn).

Hanushek, E. (1971) 'Teacher characteristics and gains in student achievement: estimation using micro data', *American Economic Review* (May).

Layard, R. (1974) 'The cost-effectiveness of new media in higher education', in K.G. Lumsden (ed.), *Efficiency in Universities. The La Paz Papers* (New York: Elsevier), Chapter 17 in this volume.

McKeachie, W.J. (1963) 'Research on teaching at the college and university level', in N.L. Gage (ed.), *Handbook on Research and Training* (Chicago: Rand McNally).

Meade, J.E. (1972) 'The theory of labour-managed firms and of profit-sharing', *Economic Journal*, Supplement (March).

Metcalf, D. (1972) 'Some aspects of the UK university teachers' labour market', paper presented at the AUTE Conference (Aberystwyth) (March).

National Board for Prices and Incomes (1968), Report 98, *Standing Reference on the Pay of University Teachers in Great Britain* – First Report, Cmnd. 3866 (December) (London: HMSO).

Neuberger, E. and E. James (1970) 'The Yugoslav self-managed enterprise: a systematic approach', Economic Research Bureau, State University of New York, Stony Brook, *Working Paper*, 26.

Newhouse, J.P. (1970) 'Towards a theory of non-profit institutions: an economic model of a hospital', *American Economic Review* (March).

Office of Educational Communications, 'Assembling the revolution', State University of New York, mimeo.

Peacock, A.T. and J. Wiseman (1964) 'Education for democrats', Institute of Economic Affairs, *Hobart Paper*, 25.

Prest, A.R. (1966) 'Financing university education', Institute of Economic Affairs.

Schramm, A. (1964) *The Research on Programmed Instruction: An Annotated Bibliography* (Washington, DC: US Government Printing Office).

Smith, A. (1776) *The Wealth of Nations*, Book V, Chapter 1.

Suppes, R. and M. Morningstar (1969) 'Computer-assisted instruction', *Science*, 17 (October).

Tickton, S. (ed.) (1970) *To Improve Learning. An Evaluation of Educational Technology*, vols i and ii (R.R. Bowker & Co.).

US Department of Health, Education and Welfare (1970) *Do Teachers Make a Difference?* (Washington, DC: US Government Printing Office).

Williams, G., T. Blackstone and D. Metcalf (1973) *The Academic Labour Market* (New York: Elsevier).

17 The Cost-effectiveness of the New Media in Higher Education (1974)*

with M. Oatey

If industries are ranked by their rate of technical progress, communication comes high and higher education low. This seems surprising, since to a large extent higher education is communication. However, it is less surprising when one considers the differing views of the educational technologists about what precise advantages they have to offer.

There are broadly two schools of thought. One considers that the new media are bound to cost more per student-hour; the gain lies in the still higher increment to output. The Congressional (McManus) Commission on Instructional Technology (1970) took this view, as have a number of other experts.[1] By contrast others believe that the real strength of the media is their ability to reduce costs per student-hour, while holding outputs constant. According to this view, educational technology so far has been mostly, though not always, used as an 'add-on' to existing inputs, whereas its chief use should be as a substitute for existing inputs, especially teachers. This substitution is presumably easiest in higher education, where teachers are not needed to keep order in class.

This paper takes the latter point of view. It begins by reviewing the available evidence on benefits. It next presents a framework for thinking about costs, which shows how the media can indeed be economic if used on a wide enough scale. This then raises the final organizational question of how this scale is to be reached.

But first there is the problem of definition. Rather like economics, educational technology can be defined by its objective matter or its intellectual method. The common approach has been in terms of objective matter (hardware). So educational technology consists of TV (live and video), film, radio, slide-tape, computer-assisted instruction (CAI) and so on. But it has now become more fashionable to talk in terms of intellectual method

---

* Chapter 7 in K. Lumsden (ed.), *Efficiency in Universities. The La Paz Papers* (New York: Elsevier, 1974), pp. 166–76.

(software). Educational technology then consists of a systematic approach to instruction, where the objectives are defined, the logical blocks in the argument worked out, and students tested for their ability to absorb the blocks at different rates, in different sequences and so on. According to this definition a good textbook is an example of educational technology, especially if it happens to verge on a programmed text.

But for the purposes of this paper, and for policy generally, definitions are unnecessary. The question is: Do the new forms of activity, be they programmed texts or more electronic devices, offer a better way of providing any of what we now provide than the mode of live instruction by which it would otherwise be provided? No one is suggesting that live instructors should disappear altogether – even Britain's Open University spends a good deal of its income on them. What we are asking is: Can a significant *part* of the live teacher's work of exposition, testing students' understanding and answering their questions be usefully substituted by capital?

BENEFITS

Some say the outputs per student-hour would be increased, others that they would fall. The arguments for expecting higher outputs depend of course on the medium in question, but there are some common elements.

Individualized instruction

Most of the media in principle permit students to study more at their own pace than is possible under live instruction. Some of them (though not all) can also provide the student with more immediate awareness of whether he understands what has been presented to him. Moreover, if different students learn best in different ways, a multi-media system could allow each to work where his comparative advantage lay.

Against these theoretical advantages, Oettinger (1969) has forcibly pointed out the administrative difficulties of permitting greater individualization of timetables and work schedules. He quotes with relish the instructions in the Watertown Language Laboratory Procedures, 1966: 'No one is an individual in the laboratory. Do nothing and touch nothing until instructions are given by the teacher.' These difficulties may be less in higher education than at the school level, but they still exist. Then there are the motivational problems of individualized learning. The optimal level of external pacing is clearly not zero, though it may be lower than the amount we now provide. Finally one should not overlook the versatility of all media of instruction (Gagné, 1970). A live lecturer can pause in a lecture and ask each student to write out their answer to a question, before revealing his own. However, programmed texts and computer-assisted instruction may be more intrinsically suited to this method of proceeding, and even televised lectures, which are the least flexible of the new media, can be repeated for the benefit of one student, which live lecturers cannot.

Better-prepared materials

The second alleged advantage of the new media derives from their ability to carry the same material to many more students than can be reached by one live instructor. This means that the potential returns from additional work in preparing the material are that much higher. If as a result more preparation is done, output per student-hour will be higher.

Educational technologists regularly urge that up to 100 hours of teacher time should be devoted to preparing material which will take 1 hour to present to the students using it (Bright, 1970). This excludes time spent by the teacher mastering the subject matter and refers only to the time he spends in designing the content of what is presented. For television, teachers often allow less than 100 hours, but still a great deal more than one would consider justified in the case of a live lecture, even if it was going to be repeated for some years. Textbook writers may well, of course, spend 100 hours preparing 1 hour's worth of reading, for books reap the economies of scale. But the new media may be able to replace some of the functions of the live instructor better than the textbook can.

Fuller use of outstanding talent

They also offer the possibility of replacing bad instructors by good ones. Teaching talent is after all in quite limited supply, and it is wasteful and inegalitarian to exclude from access to the finest teachers those who cannot get into the institutions where they happen to teach. Textbooks have hitherto been the students' main protection against bad teaching and have disseminated the works of the masters. But television in particular offers further possibilities.

Reducing the optimum size of institution

There are of course internal economies of scale within individual institutions using live instruction. These arise mainly from the low marginal costs of expanding lecture audiences, though the savings are often obscured by the tendency of large institutions to offer more options and thus a higher quality of output. If the purely instructional economies of scale were fully exploited, they would probably require very large institutions – say, 20 000 students in a university teaching all the main branches of knowledge. But, with the new media the costs per student-hour may be less dependent on the size of institutions. If large institutions are felt to involve psychic loss, one advantage of the new media may be in making more economical the smaller institution.

Against all these advantages are the alleged *disadvantages* of loss of human contact between teacher and student, which some consider the central element in higher education. If this is significantly reduced, some believe that the mental development of students and their motivation to learn will be seriously impaired. It is therefore time to turn from a priori theorising to evidence.

Evidence of student attainment

There have been two major surveys of the effects of television, compared with live instruction, on student attainment as measured by normal final examination results.[2] Chu and Schramm (1967) surveyed 202 comparisons in higher education and concluded that though television on balance performed as well as live instruction, the case for this was not as clear in higher education as in schools. However, Dubin and Hedley (1969), applying more sophisticated statistical tests to 42 studies involving 193 independent comparisons showed that, as far as standard one-way television was concerned, there was no significant difference in performance. This was so for all the major subject groups.

In the majority of cases there was no significant difference between the two media, and the cases of significant difference were evenly balanced between the two. Paradoxically two-way television, with talkback, performed less well, presumably because the technology and use of the medium is less well developed.

The cumulative evidence of many studies is more relevant than the quoting of particular instances. However, the finding of indifference between the media is confirmed by more recent experiments in teaching elementary economics at the Universities of Nebraska and Illinois (Urbana) and the State University of New York (Oneonta) (McConnell, 1968; Paden and Moyer, 1969; Gordon, 1969).

For programmed learning the balance of the survey evidence is the same – results are similar to those for live instruction plus textbook (Schramm, 1964). In economics the results obtained by students who read Lumsden, Attiyeh and Bach's microeconomics text for an average of 12 hours, were as good as those of students taught live for 21 hours who also used a textbook (Attiyeh, Bach and Lumsden, 1969). This evaluation study differed from most in collecting data on study time, which is unfortunately treated as a free good in most of the psychological literature. Its results imply of course a higher output per student-hour (including private study) than under predominantly live instruction, but strong conclusions should not be drawn from a single study.

At this point one should perhaps sound a note of caution. For it appears that live instruction can be effectively replaced not only by TV and programmed learning but by unaided self-instruction from the textbook alone. This has been shown in a number of studies surveyed by McKeachie (1963) and Dubin and Taveggia (1968), and in economics by an experiment of McConnell and Lamphear (1969). The surveys also show that for live teaching large lectures are as effective as small tutorial groups. These findings are of course deeply disturbing, for they seem to suggest that all our teaching institutions could be disbanded without loss of teaching output. But this conclusion is misplaced. For the experiments surveyed normally represent a small part of the total experience of the students concerned. In this sense they show the effects of a marginal adjustment, against the background of a campus life involving regular meetings of staff and students. However, from a policy point of view it is marginal adjustments that interest us, and if the marginal benefits of the new media are similar to those of the old, it is clearly essential to compare their costs to see if fruitful adjustments are possible. It may also be well worth considering a simple reduction in the amount of organized teaching combined with an increase in reading.

Evidence on attitudes

However, what changes are desirable, and even feasible, depend not only on their effects on students' attainments but also on their attitudes. Here the evidence on television is that students prefer it to large lectures but rate it lower than live teaching in small groups (Dubin and Hedley, 1969). However, students who have actually experienced television have more favourable attitudes to it than those who have not, and the same is true of teachers. People like what they know. In general students attach more importance to the quality of teaching than to the medium, and the great majority of students say they would prefer an 'excellent teacher' on television to the probability distribution of live instructors which they would alternatively face. They also believe that they will do as well in their examinations if taught by TV as live – a correct view, as we have seen, although teachers tend to expect them to perform worse and exaggerate the degree of student opposition to TV.

When individual experiments are examined, there are of course stories of success and failure. Gordon (1969) claims that at Oneonta 'the one section of the introductory course offered in a traditional way by one of the most popular instructors and limited to 30 had 7 empty spaces, while 300 students had enrolled in the TV sections'. In addition, the proportion of all social science students who read economics increased when the TV course was introduced. By contrast Paden and Moyer (1969) suspect that economics on TV discouraged some students who might have continued the subject. Their experience was not unique and the amount of teaching by TV fell sharply during the later 1960s at Urbana and some other campuses due to student aversion to it, especially when it was inappropriately shown in large lecture theatres. In computer-aided instruction success stories are reported from

Stanford where the computer-assisted course in Russian in its first year kept 73 per cent of its students throughout the course, as against 32 per cent for the live course (Suppes and Morningstar, 1969). The computer-assisted students also performed better in the final examination, and the course has since steadily attracted a growing proportion of students. The fact that the media fail to provide human contact between staff and students evidently does not rule them out as expository and testing devices, provided contact occurs in other (more suitable?) ways.

COSTS

We can therefore concentrate our attention on cost differences between the media provided we confine ourselves to cases where there is no good reason for expecting different outputs. For example, if pictorial motion is necessary for achieving some particular objective, it is meaningless to compare the costs of slides and videotape. Even so the problems are formidable. The only correct procedure is of course to cost separately all the alternatives being considered and one can imagine various fascinating programming problems which could arise.[3] Marginal substitutions in one institution will have different cost implications from non-marginal ones; simultaneous changes in more than one institution will offer advantages that are not available to one institution acting on its own. Nevertheless, from a public point of view, it is important to get some idea of the orders of magnitude involved, and in particular to see at what scale of operation the new media show signs of becoming competitive.

Sources of scale economies

The costs of any medium can usefully be looked at in 3 parts:

a. the preparation of a master copy of the material involving content design as well as production (master costs);
b. the making available of the material to presentation points either by duplicate copies or other forms of transmission (duplication costs);
c. the presentation of the material at the presentation points (presentation costs).

The lines of division are often rather arbitrary but Table 17.1 indicates the broad idea.

Table 17.1 shows at once the fundamental difference between most of the media and the live instructor. Most of the other media have high master costs and fixed presentation costs, while for the live lecturer it is the variable presentation cost which is crucial. We shall explore the implications of this first in general

Table 17.1 The main costs of different media

	Master[a]	Duplication	Presentation[a]	
			Fixed	Variable per presentation
Live lecturer	-	-	-	Lectures
Videotape	Recording and photography	Duplicate copies	VTR + TV set	Equipment and duplicate wear
Film	"	"	Projector + screen	"
Slide-tape	"	"	Projector, screen + tape-recorder	"
Broadcast TV	"	Transmission	TV set	"
Computer-assisted instruction	Programme production	Computer	Terminal + cable	"
Books/programmed texts	Compositing	Printing	-	-

Note:
[a] All master costs also include the costs of designing the content of the material.
All presentation costs also include the cost of student time and space used.

terms and then specifically for videotape and computer-assisted instruction. At this stage we shall be very unspecific about the extent to which live instruction is being replaced in any one institution, i.e. how marginal the change is. The 'presentation-hour' is the natural unit of output with which to begin cost comparisons between media where students are taught in groups (e.g. live lectures, communally-viewed videotape, TV, slide-tape, film, etc.). For live instruction the costs may be crudely regarded as constant (say £v) per 'presentation-hour'. By contrast the cost per presentation using a new medium depends on its master costs and its fixed presentation costs. The master costs per presentation are the annual cost of the 'course-hour' of material being presented (say, £m) divided by the number of times it is presented per year, which we initially assume would correspond to the number of institutions (I) using the material. A course-hour of material might for example be a film of Harry Johnson exposing the liquidity trap. Should each institution wish to show a repeat performance the master cost per presentation would naturally be halved. The relevant fixed presentation costs per presentation are the annual value of the set of presentational facilities used (e.g. film projector and screen) (say £p) divided by the average annual number of presentation hours for which the equipment is used (P). Thus the new medium is cheaper than live instruction if

$$v > \frac{m}{I} + \frac{p}{P}$$

This becomes increasingly likely as the number of institutions using the material grows and as the rate of utilization of the presentation equipment expands – in other words, as the external and internal economies of scale in the media are exploited. Of course this approach is irrelevant to marginal decisions where materials may already exist and the issue is whether they should be more widely used, or where equipment already exists and the issue is whether to put more courses onto it. But in the present context we shall concentrate on changes from scratch. We shall also in due course have to bring in student-hours rather than presentations as the unit of output, but this is best done in terms of specific cases.

Videotape versus the live lecturer

We can begin by comparing the costs of substituting some videotape teaching for teaching by a live lecturer. Throughout the comparison we omit the cost of student time and space, assumed the same for each medium. We assume that lectures and videotape programmes are rewritten every 7 years (perhaps it should be more often) and that their once-for-all content design takes 10 hours. This, together with a rather lavish allowance for variable presentation costs, makes a cost of £10 per live lecture.[4]

Table 17.2 Costs per presentation-hour of videotape and live lecturer

	Master	Duplication	Presentation	
			Fixed	Variable
	£	£	£	£
Live lecturer	2.5	–	–	7.5
Videotape	$\underline{13.5}$	0.8	$\underline{138}$	0.2
	I		P	

For videotape the master-costs include the same 10 hours content design time, plus production costs which can vary fantastically with the complexity of the production. A simple tape of a live lecture recorded with fully-utilized equipment could have a (capital) production cost of about £50 per course-hour, while a sophisticated and professional production might cost about £10 000 and a full spectacular as much as £250 000.[5] For the purpose of the current exercise we shall assume the bare minimum of about £65 production costs. This includes 10 hours' extra work by the lecturer per course-hour.[6] As for duplication costs, these are mainly the costs of tape and we shall assume that with effective planning our tape can be shared between three institutions. Presentation costs at each presentation point consist mainly of the cost of the videotape-recorder and TV set and their maintenance.

The resulting costs per presentation are summarized in Table 17.2.

Figure 17.1 shows the combinations of institutions and hours of usage at which videotape is as economic as live teaching. Whatever the number of institutions, videotape can never justify its fixed presentation costs unless the equipment is used for at least 15 hours, as can be seen by writing the break-even equation in the form:

$$P = \frac{138I}{9I - 13.5}$$

Similarly, whatever the number of hours' usage, it can never justify its master costs unless each course-hour is used by at least two institutions, as can be seen by writing the equation in the form:

$$I = \frac{13.5P}{9P - 138}$$

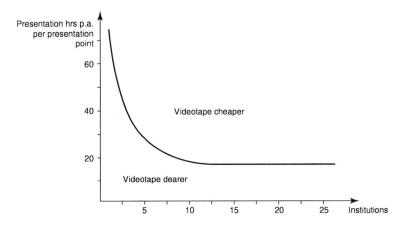

Figure 17.1

However, even with only two institutions the equipment only has to be used for about 60 hours a year – say for 15 hours a year on each of 4 courses. This is of course for a very simple production, and if the master-costs of the production are doubled the number of locations needed is doubled too.

So much for the cost per presentation. But if we are choosing between the media, can we assume that the number of presentations needed to present a given body of subject matter to a given set of students is the same for both media? Clearly not. For videotape, the maximum number of students who can watch a 23 inch TV set is about 20. Suppose every institution has 30 students taking each of the courses we are concerned with. It can either introduce an extra TV set or show each programme twice. If the number of programmes per year for which the videotape-recorder is used is less than about 100, it is cheapest to repeat the presentation.[7] As can be seen from Table 17.2, this simply raises costs per programme shown by £0.2. So, if the two media were to cost the same if there were less than 20 students taking each course at each institution, the media would also cost almost the same if there were 30 students doing so. But this of course assumes that the live course would not be sectionalized once it grew beyond 20. If this did happen, the videotape method would become progressively more favourable the more students were taking each course. These points are illustrated in Table 17.3 which shows the costs per student-hour, assuming that for up to 20 students the two media cost the same.

If sectionalization of live courses is common, therefore, videotape can become economical even if used in one institution only. An example comes

Table 17.3   Cost per student-hour where videotape and live lectures cost the
same for less than 21 students per institution per course

Students per institution per course	Videotape	Live	
		One section	All sections less than 21
	£	£	£
1	10	10	10
.	.	.	.
19	0.525	0.525	0.525
20	0.500	0.500	0.500
21	0.485	0.475	0.952
.	.	.	.
40	0.255	0.250	0.500

from Oneonta where the cost per student credit-hour in economics taught
using videotape to 476 students was, in 1967, $5.40 per student credit-hour
compared with $22.30 per student credit-hour in 'equivalent courses at other
Colleges of Arts and Science' in the State University of New York. These
figures are equivalent to about £0.14 and £0.65 respectively per student-hour.[8]
The cost-accounting conventions used are not explained, but the explanation
seems to be that the live lecturing is much more expensive than it would be if all
the students were taught in one group. In Britain the average size of lectures is
about 25 (see Table 17.4) making a cost per student-hour of just under £0.5.

Computer-assisted Instruction

If the total costs of communally viewed videotape vary little with student
numbers per location, the opposite is true of computer-assisted instruction,
since this is a completely individualized method of instruction. Its costs depend
very heavily on the number of terminals, and thus, assuming full utilization of
terminals, on the number of student-hours. The technology of CAI is probably
changing faster than that of any other medium and cost-estimates are
correspondingly more tendentious. The most flexible system so far developed
is the PLATO system at the University of Illinois, Urbana. The plans for the
new PLATO IV system envisage 4000 terminals spread over a wide area, and
its projected annual costs (with amortization over five years) are:

Table 17.4 Projected costs of PLATO IV CAI system

	$m p.a.
Central management services	0.2
Computer systems software	0.1
Central computer facility	0.9
Communication channels to consoles (at $18–50 per console p.a.)	0.1–0.2
Student consoles (at $360–1000 per console p.a.)	1.5–4.1
Total	2.8–5.5

Source: British Computer Society (1971–2) (this presents a survey of 17 leading CAI project).

If each console is used 44 hours a week for 45 weeks a year the cost per student-hour is $0.34–0.68 or £0.13–0.27. Of this, between a half and three-quarters is directly dependent on the number of student hours. Though however one should point out that the PLATO IV project is not yet in operation and the costs of most existing systems are a good deal higher, it is interesting to compare these costs with those of around £0.5 per student-hour in live lectures in Britain.[9]

Live instruction

This figure is got by dividing our national cost of £10 a lecture by the average lecture attendance in 1961–2 of around 20 students (see Table 17.5). However, it is time to define rather more closely what we mean by the cost of live instruction. The universities are joint product enterprises and the question we are asking is 'Can their existing outputs be produced at less cost?' To find the marginal cost of a lecture under the existing system we therefore ask how much money we could save if we produced our existing outputs minus, say, x lectures; the cost per lecture is this saving divided by x. Now if x were at all significant, the number of teachers would fall and each remaining teacher would do more research and less teaching. We should save not just the short-run cost of the lectures but the long-run cost involved in apprenticing the extra teachers and improving their knowledge of the subject over their working lives.

There is, of course, no fully defensible way of estimating the marginal cost implied in this approach. However, suppose that every teacher needed to spend a certain amount of time on private study and other activities, but that

Table 17.5   Teaching arrangements in universities Great Britain 1961–2

	Average hours a week given per teacher			Average hours a week received per student	Student–staff ratio	Average size of class (students per teacher)
	Given by teachers (1)	Given by post-graduates (2)	Total (3)	(4)	(5)	(6)
Lectures	2.3	0.2	2.5	7.1	8.0	23.0
Discussion periods	3.2	0.3	3.5	1.5	8.0	3.6
Practicals	2.4	0.9	3.2	3.4	8.0	8.4
Written exercise classes	0.4	0.1	0.5	0.4	8.0	7.3
All teaching	8.2	1.4	9.7	12.5	8.0	10.4

Note:
Col.(6) = Col.(5) × Col.(4) ÷ Col.(3).
Source: Committee on Higher Education (Robbins Report) (1963A) p. 351.

over the range of change with which we are concerned, his research output could be considered proportional to the time he spent on research and his teaching output proportional to the time he spent on teaching. If the teaching output of live teachers is reduced, the cost saving per unit of teaching output is then the annual cost of a teacher *times* the proportion of his total annual time spent on teaching and research which it takes to produce one unit of teaching output.[10] Becoming specific, the cost of a lecture is the annual cost of a teacher *times* the proportion of his annual time on teaching and research spent on teaching *times* the proportion of this attributable to one lecture. According to a recent survey (Committee of Vice-Chancellors, 1972) British teachers attribute about 60 per cent of their allocable working time at the university to teaching. (The actual proportions were: work for undergraduates 37 per cent, for graduate course-work students 5 per cent, for graduate research students 5 per cent, personal research 24 per cent, unallocable university work 18 per cent and outside work 11 per cent.) As regards the distribution of teaching time, Table 17.5, column (1) shows the latest available data. If one assumed that a lecture-hour requires twice as much preparation as any other teaching event and that teaching proceeds for 25 weeks a year, then each lecture represents 0.75 per cent of a teacher's annual teaching effort.[11] As for the university costs attributable to one teacher, these are clearly less than the total cost of the institution divided by the number of teachers, since costs of maintenance and so on are more dependent on the number of students than of teachers. If we include only the teacher and his share of secretaries and technicians, this might be about £4000 p.a. of which £2400 p.a. goes to teaching and £18 to each lecture. This is a little higher than our earlier estimate which may have been unduly biased against the new media. The new estimate implies an average cost per student-hour in lectures of around £0.8 and in all forms of teaching of nearly £1.[12]

The Open University

All of this is concerned with marginal changes in campus universities. However, higher education is possible without campus universities, as the Open University is already showing. Here the relevant cost comparison is of a different character, and as it is not the central theme of the paper, only a brief discussion is included (see Perry, 1972; Wagner, 1972). The Open University's teaching system depends on correspondence material, TV and radio broadcasts, and some class tuition at local study centres and summer schools. Most students have hitherto taken one course per year requiring in principle 10 hours work a week from January to November, including on average one half-hour TV programme and a half-hour radio programme. In fact students have worked on average something nearer 12 hours per course. This compares with an average for full-time students in campus universities of 38 hours a week (Committee on Higher Education, 1963, p. 277). Allowing for the different weeks worked each student could be considered to be about half a full-time student. The university regulations imply a similar approach in that six courses are normally required for a pass degree and eight for an honours degree. Working on this assumption we can now compare in terms of cost these two totally different learning systems.

The projected Open University budget for 1973 is reported by Wagner (1972) as shown in Table 17.6, though there have been some modifications since then. The student numbers associated with the budget were 36 500. Though the ultimate size of the university is still unsettled, the only basis for provisional analysis is to assume a steady state. The University intends to revise its materials continuously and thus its fixed outlays are likely to be maintained at a roughly constant rate: though many of them are intrinsically for capital formation they can for the present purposes be crudely treated as if they represented an annual flow of services. Thus, according to Table 17.6, the University's cost function is (in £, 1971 prices)

$$C = 6\,945\,000 + 61S$$

Education and Inequality

Table 17.6 Open University's budgetary estimates for 1973, £000 (1971 prices)

Fixed (independent of student numbers)	
BBC	1647
Academic staff and library	1588
Administration	
Central	1093
Regional	1244
Other (e.g. media production, ed. tech. etc.)	1373
	6945
Variable with student numbers	2232
Total	9177

where S is student numbers. For the planned number of students, which substantially fails to reap the full economies of scale, the average cost is £250 p.a. or £500 per full-time equivalent. In campus universities the total institutional expenditure divided by the number of full-time equivalent students (unadjusted for faculty mix and the like, but omitting expenditure financed by research grants and including notional rent) is about £1300 (again in 1971 prices). How much of each of the two figures should be attributed to research is clearly debatable, but any adjustment would reduce the Open University's relative advantage. On the other hand, adding in the resource cost of students' time (however one valued leisure) would enormously improve the relative efficiency of the Open University. Until these adjustments are made and more evidence collected on the outputs of the two systems, no sensible judgement can be made. Nor, from a policy point of view, is there any need for an all-or-nothing judgement, since a major aim of the Open University is in any case to provide for people such as housewives and workers for whom attendance at a campus university is not really practicable.

However, from the point of view of campus universities, the Open University may have much to contribute both in terms of actual teaching materials and in lessons about the cost-effectiveness of different media. This is being actively studied in the University's Institute of Educational Technology. At present television absorbs the main part of the University's BBC budget. Supposing it absorbs £1 500 000 and that the 36 500 students watch on average 25 half-hour programmes a year, the cost per student-hour is around £3 whereas for radio it is about one-tenth of this. The reason lies in the complexity of the TV programmes, which, if 300 are made per year, cost on average around £10 000 per programme hour. Clearly this is a quite different type of operation from the low quality videotape programme discussed earlier. While the latter may be adequate for substituting a portion of live teaching in a campus rich with social and cultural life, the TV programmes of the Open University may provide the main sense of institutional belonging and also act as important recruiting agencies for the Open University and the life of the intellect generally. These are questions on which work is proceeding. But perhaps the greatest single achievement of the Open University is that it has broken through the organizational obstacles which seem everywhere else to have inhibited a really large scale substitution of one system of learning for another.

ORGANISATION AND INCENTIVE

If the new media have so much to offer, the problem is how to bring about their introduction. What are the obstacles? These have been discussed at some length elsewhere (Layard and Jackman, 1973) and a few basic points will suffice here. There are difficulties on both the demand and the supply sides of the market. However, textbooks are fairly efficiently supplied by commercial publishers, who could equally well do the same for the new media. So it seems that the real problems lie on the side of demand.

The people who decide whether to demand the new media are the teachers, and the main things that teachers value are probably their income, the way they spend their time and the university's outputs of teaching and research. These provide us with a framework for analyzing the factors influencing demand.

The financial incentive to introduce new teaching methods are clearly extremely limited. There is no mechanism by which the members of a department can appropriate a share of its increased social profitability. Given the lack of financial competition between institutions, it may be as well that teachers are not as free as workers in the classic labour-managed corporation to set their own wages. However, it is highly unsatisfactory that, owing to the stress on research as the criterion for pay, individual teachers have no incentive to devote time to organizing the introduction of new teaching methods, especially when, as with the new media, this involves a considerable investment of time. In fact, there may in some cases be positive disincentives in that an individual teacher who mechanizes his course may not be considered to be pulling his weight in teaching. Unless positive recognition is given to the management of innovation, the prospects for change are bleak. It is also said that teachers fear technological unemployment. If this is used to explain the absence of labour-saving innovation, this implies a degree of collusive co-operation between teachers for which there is little evidence. However, innovation is obviously easiest in a period of expansion, when the capital–labour ratio can be raised without a reduction in the absolute number of teachers. For this reason the prospects for innovation in the 1970s may be brighter in the UK than the US. If expansion is accompanied by a reduction in university income per student, this might add to the pressures for labour-saving innovation.

Turning to the way teachers value their use of time, they may in general prefer exposition to other forms of staff–student contact, either because it best advances their own thinking or because they like holding forth. Yet this is the task most readily substituted by the media, none of which unfortunately can read a student's essay. Teachers are naturally unwilling to reduce the ratio of exposition to other teaching, as the majority of them would have to. The problem would be sharpened if the new order were organized on a hierarchical basis – with a group of superstars producing the media and a race of helots handling students' problems. Yet the new media are bound to add to the kind of division of labour which already occurs when many of us use one man's textbook. There are simply limits to the number of teachers who can efficiently be involved in supplying new media – or textbooks. But, subject to this, it is important from the demand point of view that as many teachers should be involved as possible.

Even so there is still a puzzle. For, as we have seen, if university outputs were held constant, each remaining teacher could do more research. Moreover, if the departmental or university budget remained unchanged during the period of innovation, it could offer its teachers many additional non-pecuniary perks – more secretarial assistance, equipment and so on. Yet innovation lags. A major reason seems to be the fear that if the department or university shows that it can save money it will lose the money it has saved. This is of course what happens ultimately in a perfectly competitive economy, but those who innovate have a period during which they experience quasi-rents before their profits are again eroded. The climate for innovation in universities would be much improved if the financing agencies would guarantee not to remove the non-pecuniary profits of innovation for a certain limited period of years. Otherwise there is a real danger that our semi-decentralized arrangement will turn out to be less efficient than either decentralized firms or the centralized armed forces, both of which use the new media a lot more than the universities.

This brings us to the teachers' concern for the teaching and research output of their institution. Many teachers fear that if they showed that teaching could be done more efficiently, research output would not in fact be held constant but would fall. If research has been financed covertly out of money that the donors thought was going on teaching, this is certainly a possibility. Whether or not the world would be poorer if it lost some of the research done in the weaker institutions is debatable, but if the teachers feel it would then this helps to explain their resistance.

Teachers are also legitimately concerned about the quality of teaching offered to their students. Most of the videotape programmes currently available are used only in the institutions where they were produced, simply because other institutions do not consider them suitable or good enough. If the market for materials is to become large enough for their production to be economic, one approach is for consortia of institutions to produce them. This involves at the minimum joint sponsorship and at the maximum sharing of the actual work, in such a way that a number of institutions stand morally committed to using the resulting materials. The seven regional 'co-operative learning-technology centres' proposed for the USA by the Carnegie Commission on Higher Education are an example of this approach.

Turning to the supply side, there are two main issues: first, whether firms or universities should be the entrepreneurs and, second, how to provide incentives to attract really good people into the field. Clearly there will be all kinds of entrepreneurs: publishing and information-processing firms, individual universities, consortia of universities, professional associations and governments. Given the past weakness on the side of demand, as well as copyright problems, one cannot expect firms to rush in yet, and heavy subsidies will be needed. Hitherto, these have mainly gone to individual university units of instructional technology. This strategy has not been very successful and more emphasis now will have to be placed on centralized sponsorship.

There remains the question of whether the aim should be to develop a separate academic career structure in the new media or whether people in the regular career structure should be tempted into the media on a short-term contract basis. The former has the virtue that it develops media expertise and might attract able people who, in the traditional career structure, would be inevitably attracted to research. On the other hand, it runs the risk of failing to bring into the new media men in touch with the best of current thought. It also involves fewer people in toto in the media and thus, while good for supply, may be bad for demand. The Open University is the leading example of an attempt to build up a semi-independent career structure, within which there would yet be substantial time for research. This new emphasis is timely, but the optional pattern of future recruitment to media activities remains hard to descry. As with the media generally, a thousand forms will bloom – most of them only once. But more and more will, one hopes, prove hardy perennials.

Appendix A

COSTS OF VIDEOTAPE AND LIVE LECTURES

Capital outlays are amortized over 7 years at 5 per cent per annum (Table 17A.1). In the case of master costs this is due to the assumption that course-hours are redesigned every 7 years. In addition, all equipment is assumed to have a life of 7 years due to obsolescence or 7000 hours due to wear and tear, whichever is the shorter: organizational factors will however normally prevent more than 1000 hours use per year, and 7 years is again assumed here.

Notes

1. See for example Committee for Economic Development (1968) and Bright (1970). Bright believes that the main advantage of the new media is that they should make possible a reduction in the length of course, but he goes on to say that the public is unlikely to accept such a reduction. However, if the media are as cost-effective as he suggests, a reduction in the period of study would probably mean foregoing a profitable investment in further learning. For a different view see Oatey (1972).
2. Some of the experiments reported in this section may be fouled up by Hawthorn effects and self-selection among the students. But most of them are not.
3. The classic study costing TV and CAI in certain well-defined school situations is that by Booz, Allen and Hamilton summarized by H.J. Kiesling in Tickton (1970).
4. For details of the cost, see Appendix A.
5. The programmes for *Sesame St* are said to cost £16 000 per hour, but this includes some cost of evaluation and revision of material.
6. Dubin and Hedley (1969) quote the findings of Macomber and Siegel at Miami University that open circuit TV lectures take a median of 9.6 hours compared with 1.7 hours for live lectures. Presumably the material was already partially designed.
7. The fixed presentation cost is unchanged and the variable presentation cost of £0.2 per presentation comes (for less than 100 presentations per year) to less than £20, which is about the annual cost of an extra TV set.
8. A student credit-hour normally involves one hour a week of teaching for 15 weeks.
9. Jamison, Suppes and Butler (1970) report that the cost of the New York City system of compensatory CAI in schools costs about $3.5 per student-hour, or ten times more than the PLATO IV system, partly because its utilization rate is only one-third of that assumed in the PLATO calculations. However, they also describe a mini-computer system, suited to school drill and practice and tutorial

Table 17A.1   Cost outlays

I. VIDEOTAPE

	£(1970 prices)	
	Capital cost	Annual cost

Master costs per course-hour.
Lecturer's time (at £1.5 per hour)

	Capital cost	Annual cost
Design of content (10 hours)	15	
Rehearsing, recording and checking (10hours)	15	
Technician's time (10 hours at £0.75 per hour)	8	
Master tape (1 inch)	28	
Rental value of equipment (1 videotape recorder (1 inch) costing £800, 2 cameras costing £600, and other items costing £700, used to produce 50 course-hours p.a.)	8	
Maintenance of equippment (at an annual cost of 10 per cent of the original cost of equipment)	4	
	78	13.5
Duplication costs per course-hour per institution		
$\frac{1}{3}$ duplicate tape ($\frac{1}{2}$ inch) at £12 each	4	0.7
Postage of duplicate to an institution		0.1
		0.8
Fixed presentation costs per presentation point		
1 videotape recorder (1/2 inch)	400	
1 TV set (23 inch)	100	
	500	88.0
Maintenance of equipment (at an annual cost of 10 per cent of the original cost of equipment)		50.0
		138.0
Variable presentation costs per presentation		
Wear on heads, etc. and variable maintenance		0.2

II LIVE LECTURER

	Capital cost	Annual cost
Master costs per course-hour		
Lecturer's time (at £1.5 per hour)		
Design of content (10 hours)	15	2.5
Variable presentation costs per presentation		
lecturer's time assuming a one-hour lecture needs four other hours of adaptation and organization)		7.5
		10.0

work in foreign languages, which will operate at half the cost of the New York system.

10. If the annual time per teacher spent on teaching is t and on research $k° - t$, the number of teachers is n, and the total annual teaching output (T) and research output (R) are measured in units such that each requires one hour of a teacher's time, then

$$T = tn$$
$$R° = (k° - t)n$$
$$\therefore T = kn - R°$$
$$\therefore \frac{dn}{dT} = \frac{1}{k}$$

11. Lectures represent 2(2.3)/(8.2 + 2.3) of his annual teaching load and he gives 25 × 2.3 lectures a year. So each lecture is 2/(8.2 + 2.3) 25 of his annual teaching.

12. £2400 ÷ (students per teacher × student hours per student per week × weeks per year) = £2400/8 (12.5)25.

References

Attiyeh, R.E., G.L. Bach and K.G. Lumdsen (1969).

Bottomley, J.A. *et al.* (1972) *Cost-effectiveness in Higher Education* (New York: OECD Centre for Educational Research and Development).

Bright, L. (1970) 'Educational technology – practical issues and implications', OECD, Committee for Scientific and Technical Personnel, Conference on Policies for Educational Growth.

British Computer Society (1972) *Educational Yearbook 1971–2* (London: British Computer Society).

Chu, C.G. and W. Schramm (1967) *Learning from Television: What the Research Says*, Institute for Communications Research, Stanford University.

Commission on Instructional Technology (1970) *To Improve Learning. A Report to the President and Congress of the US by the Commission* on Instructional Technology, Committee on Education and Labor, House of Representatives (March).

Committee for Economic Development (1968) *Innovation in Education: New Directions for the American School*, a statement on national policy by the Research and Policy Committee (July).

Committee of Vice-Chancellors and Principals of the Universities of the UK (1972) *Report of an Enquiry into the Use of Academic Staff Time*.

Committee on Higher Education (Robbins Report) (1963) *Higher Education*, Appendix Two (B), Students and their Education, Cmnd. 2154 II–I (London: HMSO).

Dubin, R. and R.A. Hedley (1969) *The Medium may be Related to the Message: College Instruction* (Eugene, OR: University of Oregon Press).

Dubin, R. and T.C. Taveggia (1968) *The Teaching-Learning Paradox* (Eugene, OR.: University of Oregon Press).

Gagné, R.M. (1970) *The Conditions of Learning*, 4th edn (New York, London: Holt, Rinehart).

Gordon, S.D. (1969) 'Optimising the use of televised instruction', *Journal of Economic Education* (Autumn).

Jamison, D., R. Suppes and C. Butler (1970) 'Estimated costs of CAI for compensatory education in urban areas', *Educational Technology* (September).

Layard, R. and R. Jackman (1973) 'University efficiency and university finance', in M. Parkin (ed.), *Essays in Modern Economics* (London: Longman), chapter 16 in this volume.

McConnell, C.R. (1968) 'An experiment with television in the elementary course', *American Economic Review* (May).

McConnell, C.R. and Lamphear, C. (1969) 'Teaching Principles of Economics without Lectures', *Journal of Economic Education* (Fall).

McKeachie, W.J. (1963) 'Research on teaching at the college and university level', in N.L. Gage (ed.) *Handbook on Research and Training* (Chicago: Rand McNally).

Oatey, M. (1972) *Effectiveness and Costs of Instructional Media*, Air Transport and Travel Industry Training Board.

Oettinger, A.P. (1969) *Run, Computer, Run. The Mythology of Educational Innovation* (New York: Collier-Macmillan).

Office of Educational Communications (1970).

Paden, D.W. and M.E. Moyer (1969) 'The relative effectiveness of three methods of teaching principles of economics', *Journal of Economic Education* (Fall).

Perry, W. (1972) *The Early Development of the Open University, Report of the Vice-Chancellor* (Milton Keynes: Open University).

Schramm, A. (1964) *The Research on Programmed Instruction: An Annotated Bibliography* (Washington, DC: US Government Printing Office).

Suppes, R. and M. Morningstar (1969) 'Computer-assisted instruction', *Science*, 17 (October).

Tickton, S. (ed.) (1970) *To Improved Learning. An Evaluation of Educational Technology*, vols i and ii (R.R. Bowker & Co).

Wagner, L. (1972) 'The economics of the Open University', *Higher Education*, 1(3).

18 The Pool of Ability (1963)*

INTRODUCTION

The crucial question is whether, within the next twenty years, the growth in the output of qualified school leavers is likely to be limited by a scarcity of inherited potential ability. This raises the fundamental issue of whether the pool of ability, as it is usually called, can be measured and, if so, how.

Is it possible to tell what proportion of the population are so constituted at birth that, growing up under the most favourable circumstances, they could reach a level of attainment suitable for entry to higher education?

The answer is 'no': that is to say, one cannot specify an upper limit. There is, however, a great deal of evidence which suggests that the reserve of untapped ability in this country is still very considerable and that, on present trends, it is most unlikely to be fully mobilised within the next twenty years. This evidence, which is summarised below, does not, however, help in predicting the rate at which untapped ability could, or will, be mobilised.

In talking about the pool of ability three terms are often used:

(a) *Innate potential*, biologically inherited.
(b) *Measured ability*, as estimated by the use of intelligence tests, and
(c) *Attainment* in a specific branch or branches of knowledge.

It is important to be as clear as possible about the nature of measured ability, and its relationship to innate potential, on the one hand, and attainment on the other.

Views of what is measured by intelligence tests have changed since they were first invented. Then, it was thought that measured intelligence depended mainly on heredity, and that in most western countries the influence of the environment on test scores was small. More recently, comparative studies in widely different social and cultural groups have modified this view.

Genetic factors are undoubtedly important, but the influence of the environment is great, and its extent cannot easily be determined.[1] For our present purposes it is enough to say that measured ability is a function of two

---

* Committee on Higher Education, Appendix One, Part III, *The Demand for Places in Higher Education*, Cmnd. 2154, III (1963), pp. 79–89.

variables, innate and environmental, and that the contribution of the latter increases with age.[2]

There has been another change in general ideas about ability (both actual and potential).[3] What was at one time assumed by scientists, as it still is by some laymen, to be a single trait has been gradually broken down, with the help of experimental evidence, into a number of distinguishable components, each requiring a measurement of its own. Some of these components are not even cognitive: and what is generally called 'intelligence' is partly dependent upon personality and motive.

Thus, while the distinction between measured ability and innate potential has been increasingly emphasised, the distinction between measured ability and attainment has tended to become less clear. Recent work has called in question the view that intelligence in some way comes prior to attainment and partly determines it. Nevertheless it is still true, that, because of early leaving or failure to enter higher education, there are many young adults of high measured ability, whose educational attainments are modest.

With all these considerations in mind, it is probably true to say that, at present, the best evidence we have on the pool of ability, so far as it is relevant to our discussion, comes from the different achievements of young people of the same measured ability, but differing in:

1 social class;
2 sex;
3 the local education authority in whose area they live;
4 the country in which they live; or
5 secondary schooling.

This evidence can be summarised so as to yield a series of different minimum estimates of potential numbers. It will, however, be apparent from the examples that are given that these estimates are extremely artificial, and can be most misleading if they are taken as anything more than illustrations of the fact that considerable reserves of untapped ability exist.

DIFFERENCES IN ATTAINMENT BETWEEN SOCIAL CLASSES

Differences that exist between social classes in the proportions of those of given ability who enter higher education. Before discussing these differences further, it should be said that, once in higher education, working class children do at least as well as children from middle class homes. Both in terms of degrees obtained and in terms of wastage, the performance of university students with fathers in manual occupations has been as good as that of students from other homes, where there is likely to have been a longer tradition of education. The details of this evidence are discussed elsewhere; but it suggests that there need be no fear of a decline in the ability of students if a growing proportion of them were to be 'new students' coming from working class homes.

The Crowther Report[4] provided some good evidence on the relation between the measured ability and the attainment of a complete cross-section of the (male) population. It showed that, of army recruits in the top 12 per cent of measured ability, the proportion obtaining entry qualifications to higher education[5] was 68 per cent for children whose fathers were in professional or managerial jobs, compared with 31 per cent for those whose fathers were semi- or un-skilled workers. There is, of course, no way of knowing what proportion of those in the top 12 per cent of measured ability could, in the most favourable circumstances, obtain entry qualifications. Moreover, logically, the most favourable circumstances could never be specified. A minimum estimate of potential numbers could, however, be made by assuming that, in the highest social group, talent is already fully mobilised and that, in the other groups, it could in time be mobilised to the same extent. Both the Dutch Central Planning Bureau and the Swedish Commission on Higher Education have worked on this type of hypothesis.[6] They have assumed that the proportion from each ability group who could achieve success is the same, irrespective of social class, as the proportion of upper middle class children who are already successful. If this assumption were made, it would show that, whereas 9 per cent of army recruits in 1956–7 had obtained entry qualifications, the proportion of men who could achieve this level is at least 16 per cent.

This approach is of course artificial, for, as was shown in Part II, there has in recent years been a rapid improvement in the achievement of children in the higher social groups, and only a small reduction in the differences between social groups. The recent educational upsurge appears to spring from general economic and social changes affecting all classes more or less equally. If this continues to be the case, a calculation made in a few years' time on the above lines would inevitably yield a much higher estimate of the minimum potential numbers. But it remains true that there is a greater proportionate reserve of untapped ability in working class than middle class families.

DIFFERENCES IN ATTAINMENT BETWEEN THE SEXES

Women who enter higher education do on average as well as men.[7] But, as was shown in Part I, a much lower proportion in fact enter.

It is generally held that no significant differences exist between the innate potential of men and women; there may be differences in kind – for example as between linguistic and mathematical aptitudes – but not differences in level. Indeed at some ages the test performance of girls is better than for boys. But many fewer girls than boys achieve 2 or more 'A' levels. It follows that there is here an important reserve of untapped ability. Whereas the proportion of all children achieving 2 or more 'A' levels is 6.9 per cent, the proportion for boys is 8.7 per cent. If girls did as well as boys there would at this level be a minimum potential of 8.7 per cent. But here again the assumption is unreal for, over the last seven years, the difference between proportions for boys and girls has been hardly reduced, while the proportions for boys as well as girls have risen steeply. Therefore a pool of ability calculation on these lines would soon require an upward revision. Nevertheless one should not forget that the reserve of untapped ability is greater among women than among men.

DIFFERENCES IN ATTAINMENT BETWEEN LEA AREAS

There are great differences between the proportions entering higher education from different local education authorities (LEAs). It can be shown that degree performance is slightly worse for undergraduates from authorities where a high proportion go to university, than for those where the proportion is low. But the differences in performance are far less than the differences in the proportions who reach university.[8] It follows that there is a source of untapped ability which could be mobilised by a levelling up of the less successful authorities to the standard of the best. Here again, however, though differences have been reduced in the past years, the reduction has been slight and a calculation based on the hypothesis of equality between LEAs would soon need to be revised upwards, as performance in the better LEA areas improved still further.

DIFFERENCES IN ATTAINMENT BETWEEN NATIONS

The most striking differences of all are perhaps those between countries. These are discussed in Appendix Five. They involve, of course, great difficulties of comparative standards. It would, however, be generally accepted that the Swedish studentexamen is roughly equivalent to British university entry qualifications. At present 13 per cent of the age group achieve the studentexamen. Unless the people of this country are of lower innate potential than the Swedes, it follows that at least 13 per cent could obtain university entry qualifications here. Nor do Swedish authorities believe that they have at all exhausted their reserves of talent. The calculations of Professor Härnquist (under the auspices of the Swedish Commission on Higher Education and based on the methods described above suggest that at least 28 per cent of young people could obtain the studentexamen.[9]

DIFFERENCES IN SECONDARY SCHOOLING

The evidence discussed so far compares the performance of people of the same measured ability but of different backgrounds or sex. There is another method of approach which relies much less on factors external to the educational system. Instead it examines the educational record of children of apparently the same capacity (in terms of tests or head teachers' opinions) but whose paths have diverged, either because some were not selected for academic secondary school courses, or because some left school before studying for the necessary examinations. It is then usually assumed that children who did not study for these examinations could have done as well as those of like capacity who did. There is a considerable tradition of Scottish studies based on this type of approach.[10] From 1935 to 1939, McClelland conducted a follow-up study of children to the end of their third year in secondary school. A pupil was judged to have been successful 'if his teacher considered he had a 50 per cent chance of obtaining a minimum group leaving certificate[11] in a suitable course within six years'. At the time, 11 per cent of the age-group were judged to be successful, but McClelland estimated that, if they had taken the right course of schooling, 17 per cent would actually have been successful. He also reckoned that, if disadvantages of background were ignored, 30 per cent had the capacity (in terms of measured ability and primary school attainment) to be successful. From 1950–7 McIntosh made a study of one year's secondary school intake in Fife. In this group, 6 per cent obtained a minimum group leaving certificate. But McIntosh estimated that, if secondary school selection were more effective and early leaving reduced, the proportion could have been 11 per cent, even if 'present conditions' remained in all other respects unchanged. Similarly, McPherson found that, of a group of children born in 1936, 6 per cent obtained university entrance qualifications. Basing himself on the results of the secondary school selection examination and the opinions of head teachers, he calculated that 9 per cent might be capable of achieving university entrance requirements.

An example of the use of head teachers' opinions is provided in a recent estimate by Furneaux.[12] This was largely based on the findings in the *Early Leaving* Report[13] of a survey conducted in 1953. For this survey, head teachers from a 10 per cent sample of grammar schools were asked what proportion of their children were capable of a course leading to 2 or more 'A' levels. Of the 1946 grammar school entry, 19 per cent in fact took this type of course; head teachers estimated that, if there were no early leaving, 33 per cent would have been suited to do so. By 1962, the proportions entering these courses were already well over 40 per cent[14] and 26 per cent of all grammar school leavers in 1960/1 had obtained 2 more 'A' levels. Furneaux's estimate was based on the assumption that the head teachers' estimates represented a maximum of the margin of waste to be taken up by early leaving. He concluded that only

24 per cent of grammar school children could obtain 2 or more 'A' levels. He did, however, assume that a considerably larger proportion of young people would be admitted to grammar school. From these assumptions he concluded that 'even at the most optimistic estimate, it seems unlikely that the proportion of those in a position to make an application (to a university) could rise beyond about 8 per cent of the population'. His computed estimate of the maximum proportion likely to obtain 2 or more 'A' level passes was in fact 6.6 per cent. It has to be noted that in 1961 the proportion of the age group obtaining these qualifications was 6.9 per cent. Pool of ability calculations are thus always in danger of being confounded by the speed of change.

PAST CHANGES IN THE QUALITY OF STUDENTS IN GREAT BRITAIN

The evidence up to this point demonstrates that, in terms of ability, 'more' need not mean 'worse'. There are, however, those who believe that 'more' has already meant 'worse'. Such evidence as exists does not support this view.

Standards at 'A' level

The problem here is the absence of standardised tests of student quality. Though the General Certificate of Education (GCE) Advanced Level qualifications of entrants to higher education have risen, there is no guarantee that GCE standards have remained constant from year to year. It is sometimes suggested that the upward trend in GCE performance is the arithmetical result of an increase in candidates, the percentage of candidates who pass being fixed. It is certainly true that, when the marks of examiners are being scaled in relation to the pass mark, consideration is often given, amongst other things, to the percentage of candidates who would pass as a result of the system of scaling adopted. Nevertheless, in the long term the pass percentages have altered considerably; as Table 18.1 shows, they tended to fall up to 1958, possibly owing to a decline in the average quality of candidates. But this change does not in itself indicate whether standards have been maintained, tightened or relaxed; on this opinions vary.[15]

Standards of reading ability

There is, however, a good deal of evidence on a standardised basis concerning the attainments of the school children of compulsory school age. Perhaps the most important relates to reading ages. There is a marked improvement in

Table 18.1   Successful entries as a percentage of all entries
at GCE Advanced level, Summer examination, %

1951	73.5
1952	71.9
1953	70.3
1954	70.6
1955	70.6
1956	69.9
1957	68.7
1958	68.0
1959	68.9
1960	67.5
1961	68.9
1962	67.6

Note:
Double mathematics is counted as two subjects in all years.
Source: Ministry of Education (see also *Statistics of Education*
1962, Pt 2, Table 6)

reading ages at eleven and fifteen, corresponding closely to the rising
proportion of the age group achieving 'A' level between 1954 and 1961. The
rise in GCE output is thus not only the product of more people staying on at
school, but also of improved standards of compulsory schooling. It remains
true, however, that there is no objective certainty about whether GCE
standards have remained constant.

The measured ability of students

There is, however, some objective evidence that the measured ability of
university students has remained at least as high as it was before the war,
despite the fact that the proportion of young people going to university has
doubled since then. Over the last thirty years, a verbal intelligence test[16] has
been regularly given to representative samples of arts and science undergraduates at Edinburgh, and of postgraduate Certificate of Education students
at Liverpool. At Edinburgh, the results show very little change in the ability of
students over this period, despite considerable expansion in their numbers (see
Table 18.2); in the last few years there has been a tendency towards a narrower
dispersion of the scores, but for the period as a whole there is no significant
change in this respect. At Liverpool, there has been a considerable
improvement in average measured ability.

Table 18.2   Average scores of university students in a verbal intelligence test,
pre-war and post-war performance

	Average score	Numbers tested
Undergraduates at Edinburgh		
1935–7	155.6	380
1945–8	157.0	619
1957–60	156.5	844
Cert. Ed. students at Liverpool		
1932–42	151.3	621
1943–50	156.3	262

Note:
Data for Edinburgh relate to a representative sample of undergraduates in arts and science.
Source: Edinburgh: Data supplied by Professor J. Drever
Liverpool: Tozer and Larwood (1953, pp. 347–58).

That this test is related to university performance is shown by Table 18.3, which compares the average scores of students obtaining different classes of degree.

The academic performance of students

The impression that the standard of those admitted to university has not been deteriorating since the war is confirmed by data on student performance and wastage. As Table 18.4 shows, the proportion of university entrants who leave without success has not risen with their growing numbers. In fact wastage in recent years has been considerably lower than in the early 1950s. This fact must be borne in mind in interpreting Table 18.5, which shows the class of degree obtained by those entrants who graduated. The proportion of graduates obtaining good honours degrees (1sts and 2nds) rose from 55 per cent in 1953 to 60 per cent in 1960. There was a similar (proportionate) rise in the percentage obtaining 1st or Upper 2nd class degrees only. There was a slight decline in the proportion of graduates obtaining 1st class degrees, but, if the decline in wastage is taken into account, there appears to have been a barely significant change in the proportion of entrants who achieve 1sts. In so far as degree results over the last decade offer a reliable picture of student quality, they indicate an improvement at all points of the scale except at the very top.

Table 18.3 Average scores in a verbal intelligence test, by class of degree

	Class of degree					Number tested
	1st	Upper 2nd	Lower 2nd	3rd	Pass/ Ordinary	
Liverpool: Cert. Ed. students 1932–50	157.1	155.3	153.7	151.4	147.8	*883*
Cambridge: Entrants to Newnham College 1930–33	157.3		155.1	151.4	..	*383*
St Andrews: All faculties 1930s		154.7			149.3	*778*

Source: Cambridge: Dale (1935), pp. 59–75.
St Andrews: Babington Smith (1940, pp. 184–97).
Liverpool: Tozer and Larwood (1953, pp. 347–58).

Table 18.4 Percentage of undergraduates (excluding medical subjects and agriculture) who left without success: by year of entry, Great Britain, %

	Percentage leaving without success	All entrants (=100%)
Year of entry		
1952	16.7	*15 300*
1955	13.9	*18 200*
1957	14.3	*21 800*

Source: University Grants Committee (U.G.C.) Returns 1960–1, paragraph 51 (base numbers supplied by UGC).

Table 18.5 Percentage of university graduates (excluding medical subjects) obtaining various classes of degree, Great Britain, %

	1sts	Upper 2nds	1sts or 2nds	All graduates (=100%)[b]
Year of graduation				
1953	8.0	27.2	55.3	*14 900*
1954	7.9	27.8	56.9	*14 300*
1958	7.3	28.2	59.0	*16 300*
1959	7.3	28.4	59.6	*17 600*
1960[a]	7.1	28.9	60.5	*19 400*

Notes:
[a] 1960 data are estimates based on changes between 1953 and 1960 at all universities other than Birmingham, Bristol, London and Newcastle.
[b] The numbers in the final column have been taken from the UGC Returns, Table 6.
Source: UGC.

PAST CHANGES IN THE QUALITY OF STUDENTS IN THE USA

It is also interesting to consider the experience of the USA, where the proportions entering higher education have grown since the war from a level that was already higher than the present level in Britain. A survey recently conducted by the Brookings Foundation investigated, amongst other points, the changes that have occurred since the war in the scores, on Scholastic Aptitude Tests, of entrants to a representative group of institutions of higher education.[17] These tests are designed by the College Entrance Examination Board to measure aptitude (both verbal and mathematical), but not attainment. The tests are not identical from year to year, but elaborate precautions are taken to ensure that the standard remains constant. Table 18.6 gives the results of the tests of verbal aptitude. It shows an improved standard in every institution surveyed. The tests of mathematical aptitude show a similar, though slightly less marked, trend. There is, however, the important caveat that coaching is known to affect performance in these (as in any other) tests, and coaching may have become more common in recent years. The apparent improvement may therefore be exaggerated in the figures. But the majority of the teachers in the institutions surveyed, when asked about the general quality of students, said they believed that it had definitely improved.

Table 18.6 Average scores on verbal Scholastic Aptitude Tests of entrants to certain American institutions, by year of entry

	1947	1953	1960
Institution			
A	490	..	550
B	430	460	500
C	..	570	650
D	..	590	640
E	..	420	500
F	510	520	620
G	..	440	570
H	590	580	640
I	530	520	640
J	530	510	610
K	600	620	630
L	640	640	680
M	..	450	580

Source: Orlans (1962).

Despite recent improvements in the quality of students, numerous American authorities argue that there are still many young people as talented as those entering higher education who do not enter.[18] Thus Wolfle estimated that in 1953 only about 40 per cent of those with measured ability equal to that of the upper half of current college graduates were entering college. This figure was probably rather too low, since it was based on an underestimate of the total college entry in that year. More recently, Bridgman estimated that in 1956 only about 60 per cent of those with ability equal to that of the upper half of college entrants were entering college. The data relate to ability as measured at about 18. It is therefore possible that the proportion of Americans going to college may still increase without a fall in quality.[19]

It is not suggested that the abilities of American college entrants are on average as high as those of United Kingdom entrants to full-time higher education. The American experience is merely an example of the fact that if, at any particular time, there are large numbers outside higher education who are as able as those inside, there is no logical reason why the expansion of higher education need necessarily mean a decline in the quality of students.

CONCLUSION

The main point is that there are considerable reserves of ability in our community. This is shown by many types of evidence – some of them quoted in earlier sections – which can be summarised to give a series of minimum estimates of potential numbers. An alternative procedure would be to bring all the evidence to bear upon a single estimate. This might assume, for instance, that all boys and girls of a given measured ability could reach the same level of attainment as boys of that ability from the 'best' homes, in favourable areas of the best-educated country, attending the leading schools, and completing a full secondary course. Merely to rehearse the steps is to show the extremely artificial character of pool of ability calculations. Yet it is also clear that, if this calculation were made, it would yield a far higher total than any of those presented earlier. Like these, however, it would remain a minimum estimate.[20]

In short, it is certain that, much untapped ability exists at present in this country. But little is known about ultimate human capacities. The levels of education already achieved would have surprised those alive a hundred or even fifty years ago, and it is impossible to circumscribe with a formula the potentialities of the future.

Moreover, pool of ability calculations have the further disadvantage that they give no indication of the speed at which existing untapped ability can be mobilised. For planning purposes this is the most important question, and an empirical scrutiny of existing trends seems to offer the best basis for action. The pace of change since the war has been considerable. Ten years ago there were few who foresaw how rapidly the numbers achieving university entrance qualifications would grow. But the variables affecting growth are complex, some tending to increase the rate of growth and others tending to retard it. But scarcities of inherited potential will not, as such, impose a limit on the growth in the output of qualified school leavers within the next twenty years.

Notes

1. For a review of the evidence see Vernon (1960).
2. Part II of Appendix One showed how the measured ability of children from favourable back-grounds improves progressively in relation to that of those whose background is less favourable. It also mentioned that the effect of environment appears to be stronger in the case of verbal than of non-verbal ability.
3. See Jenkins and Patterson (1961).
4. *15 to 18*, Report of the Central Advisory Council for Education – England (HMSO London: 1959).
5. The qualifications included were 2 or more 'A' Levels and the Ordinary National Certificate or its equivalent.

6. See de Wolff and Härnquist (1962).
7. See Appendix Two (A), Part IV.
8. See Little (1961).
9. de Wolff and Härnquist (1962).
10. McClelland (1942); McIntosh (1959); Macpherson (1958).
11. 2 highers and 3 lowers at Scottish Leaving Certificate.
12. Furneaux (1961).
13. *Early Leaving.* Report of the Central Advisory Council for Education – England (HMSO London: 1954).
14. Pupils engaged on the first year of this type of course (the majority of them aged 16) in January 1962 equalled 49 per cent of 13-year-olds in grammar schools in January 1959. They included some late transfers from secondary modern schools.
15. A further criticism sometimes made of reliance on 'A' level results is that an increasing proportion of the passes obtained are in 'non-academic' subjects (i.e. art, technical drawing, music, craft, handicraft and domestic subjects). In fact, the proportion has only risen from 2.8 per cent to 5.4 per cent – an insignificant change compared with the total rise in output. If religious knowledge is included (this being a subject not counted for matriculation in certain universities) the rise is from 3.3 per cent to 6.5 per cent.
16. *Group Test 33*, devised by Sir Cyril Burt.
17. 36 institutions were approached, but only 13 had reasonably comprehensive records of scores since the war.
18. See Wolfle (1954); Bridgman (1960, pp. 30–46).
19. This type of data was at one time used widely in pool of ability calculations, by assuming that, for example, all those with ability equal to that of the upper half of college entrants are capable of higher education. This approach is, however, even more artificial than that discussed earlier.
20. There are two reasons for this. First, it would implicitly assume that the performance of the most favoured group is already as good as it could ever be, whereas in fact it is always improving. Second, it would implicitly assume that measured ability directly reflects innate potential, whereas it is in part the product of environment.

References

Babington-Smith, B. (1940) 'The Conversion of Scores on Group Test 33 to Intelligence Quotients', *Occupational Psychology*, 14, 184–97.
Bridgman, D. (1960) *The Search for Talent* (Princeton: College Entrance Examination Board).
Dale, A.B. (1935) 'The Use of Mental Tests with University Women Students', *British Journal of Educational Psychology*, V, 59–75.
de Wolff, P. and Härnquist, K. (1962) 'Reserves of Ability', in *Ability and Educational Opportunity* (New York: OECD).
Furneaux, W.D. (1961) *The Chosen Few* (Oxford: Oxford University Press).
Jenkins, J.J. and Patterson, D.G. (eds) (1961) *Studies in Individual Differences: The Search for Intelligence* (London: Methuen).

Little. A. (1961) 'Will more mean worse? An Inquiry into the Effects of University Expansion', *British Journal of Sociology* (December).

McClelland, W. (1942) *Selection for Secondary Education* (London: ULP).

McIntosh, D. (1958) *Educational Guidance and the Pool of Ability* (London: ULP).

Macpherson, J. (1958) *11-year-olds Grow Up* (London: ULP).

Orlans, H. (1962) *The Effects of Federal Programs on Higher Education* (Washington, DC: Brookings Institution).

Tozer, A.H.D. and H.J.C. Larwood (1953) 'An analysis of intelligence test scores of students in a University Department of Education', *British Journal of Psychology*, 44, 347–58.

Vernon, P.E. (1960) *Intelligence and Attainment Tests* (London: ULP).

Wolfle, D. (1954) *America's Resources of Specialised Talent* (New York: Harper).

19 The Thatcher Miracle?

(1989)*

with S. Nickell

The ultimate criteria of economic achievement are productivity, unemployment, inflation, and income distribution. In section I we show Britain's record on these counts over the last nine years.

There are two main pluses. Productivity growth has improved relative to the European Community – but by little relative to the remainder of the OECD. And inflation has fallen more than elsewhere.

The minuses have been considerable. Unemployment performance has been poor compared with the non-EEC countries – and also when compared with Britain itself in the years after 1933. And inequality has greatly increased.

Those who believe in a Thatcher miracle must therefore (and do) consider that much of the harvest (in higher productivity growth and low inflation) is still to be reaped. They argue that Britain's improved productivity performance will continue for some years, since it results from a permanent shift in the balance of power at the workplace. To see whether this is likely, we investigate in section II the causes of the productivity turnaround. We conclude that, while further gains are likely, poor levels of training may be a serious drag.

The same hopeful conclusion does not apply to inflation (see section III). The level of unemployment needed to control inflation is now very much higher than in 1979. And we estimate that without the fortuitous blessing of North Sea oil (and the accompanying appreciation of sterling), inflation could now be as much as 10 per cent higher than it is – unless unemployment had been allowed to go still higher. Oil is now less help and the balance of payments weak.

* Issues Posed by High Unemployment in Europe, *American Economic Review*, *Papers and Proceedings*, 79(2) (May 1989), pp. 215–19.
We are grateful for help to A. Clark, P. Kong and M. Wall, as well as numerous commentators, and to the Economic and Social Research Council and the Esmeé Fairbairn Trust for financial support.

Table 19.1 Output per worker[a]

	1966–73	1973–9	1979–83	1983–8
United Kingdom	3.2	1.3	2.1	2.0
EEC (9)	4.2	2.2	1.2	2.2
OECD Other	3.0	1.1	1.3	1.8
United States	1.2	0.0	0.2	1.3
Japan	7.9	2.9	2.4	3.4
Sweden	2.8	0.5	0.9	1.9
OECD Total	3.5	1.5	1.3	1.9

Note:
All figures on output per worker, unemployment and inflation are annual averages, and growth rates are year on year.
[a] Per cent per annum.

I THE RECORD

Productivity growth

We begin with labor productivity growth (see Table 19.1). Throughout the period 1966–88, Britain has grown at slightly above the average for the non-EEC industrial countries. For most of these countries, including Britain, there was a dip in the late 1970s followed by a recovery. By contrast, the EEC, which was originally above the average, has now fallen to the average level.

The history of productivity is very similar whether we look at output per worker or total factor productivity (see OECD, 1987; Stephen Englander and Axel Mittelstädt, 1988). The story is told in level form in Figure 19.1 (where real output in 1980 is calculated using PPP exchange rates, and internal country growth rates are applied to calculate output in all other years). As this shows, the United States (at the technological frontier) has always grown more slowly than other countries since 1960. The diagram provides support for the 'catch-up' framework of analysis. Thus the EEC slowdown and the Japanese slowdown can both be explained to some extent by their approach to the technological frontier. But Britain's performance in the 1960s and 1970s was disappointing compared with Europe's. We are now so far behind that some relative improvement might have been expected. However, most observers feel

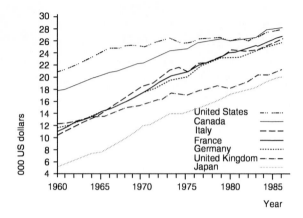

Figure 19.1 Labour productivity
Note: US $ (1980 prices and PPP exchange rates).
Source: OECD (1988, p. 52).

that something surprising has happened to British productivity, especially in manufacturing. Thus we shall assume that, without Mrs Thatcher, British productivity growth would have stayed near the same level that existed during the 1970s rather than recovering to the European average.

Unemployment

Thus the productivity record is good, if not miraculous. The unemployment record is terrible. Unemployment is nearly double that in 1979 (see Table 19.2). The same is also true in continental Europe but not in the remainder of the OECD (including Scandinavia). And, in Britain, unemployment is more heavily concentrated on 'primary' wage earners than in the rest of the EEC, with adult male unemployment above that in France, Germany, or Italy.

Since 1986, the official 'unemployment figures' have been falling quite sharply. But these are simply the number of people receiving benefits. Since 1986 the government has, for good or ill, made it more difficult to get benefits. Unemployed people now have to pass much more stringent tests that they are seeking work. Thus changes in the numbers on benefits are not an adequate proxy for changes in the number of people unemployed, on the standard survey-based (CPS-like) definition.

Unfortunately we currently have no survey estimates of UK unemployment after May 1987. In the year before that, the unemployment rate had fallen by only 0.3 percentage points, compared with 1.0 points for the percentage on benefits. Since May 1987, we have to use the government's figures for the numbers on benefit. These, with other evidence on vacancies and the like, suggest that unemployment did indeed fall substantially through 1987 and into 1988. But vacancies ceased rising in fall 1987, and whether unemployment has now ceased falling we shall not know for another year.

But, either way, the current level of unemployment is disappointing. The contrast with the 1930s is striking – by 1937 the unemployment rate had fallen right back to its level in 1929.

Inflation

Turning to inflation, in 1979 this was a good deal worse in Britain than elsewhere (see Table 19.2). Earnings growth was tending to rise, though the GDP deflator at factor cost in fact grew at the *same* rate in 1979 as in 1978 and 1977. However, upon election in May 1979, Mrs. Thatcher abolished the incomes policy and doubled VAT; inflation increased sharply in 1980. It then fell sharply in the two following years, and then again in 1986 (to 2.6 per cent). In the last two years it has risen back to 6 per cent.

Table 19.2

	Unemployment[a]		Inflationb[b]	
	1979	1988	1979	1988
United Kingdom	4.7	8.5	13.2	5.6
EEC (9)	4.7	8.7	8.9	3.1
OECD Other	5.7	6.7	8.0	3.7
United States	5.8	5.6	8.8	3.3
Japan	2.1	2.5	1.5	1.8
Sweden	2.1	1.7	8.3	5.8
OECD Total	5.4	7.5	8.3	3.5

Note:
See Table 19.1.
[a]Per cent, standardized.
[b]Per cent per annum, GDP deflator.

Inequality

Inequality has increased hugely for three main reasons. First, pre-tax earnings have become more unequal than in any previous data since records began. Second, average direct tax rates have been sharply reduced at the top of the earnings distribution but not at the bottom. In consequence, real post-tax earnings rose between 1979 and 1988 (post-budget) by the following amounts: top percentile, 73 per cent; bottom decile, 13 per cent. (The figures relate to males, taxed as single persons.)

Finally, the numbers dependent on social insurance grew sharply, due to high unemployment, while the basic level of social insurance (Supplementary Benefit) grew less fast than average earnings (though faster than prices). In the first six Thatcher years, the number of children living at or below this minimum level nearly doubled.

Clearly, government policy has a limited effect on the gross earnings distribution (via unemployment, the failure of skill training, and deregulation). But tax policy and social insurance are a direct government responsibility. In this connection we should note that the marginal tax rate of the average Briton is still the same as in 1979, so that tax changes do not explain productivity growth.

Intermediate objectives

This completes our review of the record so far, in terms of the ultimate policy objectives. However, since we are also interested in future prospects, we must also look at some intermediate objectives and see whether these are now in good shape or not.

First, the balance of payments. Despite the substantial contribution of North Sea oil, the current account in 1988 is likely to be in deficit by at least 3 per cent of GNP. This makes the inflation achievement distinctly insecure, since it is hard to see how a real depreciation can be avoided at some point unless unemployment is greatly increased.

Second, monetary growth. During the first Thatcher years, this was the prime intermediate objective. Due to a misunderstanding over the determination of M_3, interest rates were pushed so high that (due to this and North Sea oil) sterling appreciated in real terms by 44 per cent (1981 over 1978, relative unit labor costs). In consequence, in the first two Thatcher years, national output fell nearly as much as in the Great Depression (and manufacturing output only regained its 1979 level in 1987). However, since the mid-1980s, monetary targets have been largely replaced by exchange rate objectives, and short real rates are currently around 8 per cent, partly in order to sustain the exchange rate.

Third, the budget deficit. This has fallen from 4 1/2 per cent of national income in 1979 to a surplus of around 1 per cent this year. The big budget cuts were in 1980 and 1981, which together reduced the structural deficit by roughly 5 percentage points of GDP. Since then fiscal policy changes have been fairly neutral.

Fourth, company profitability. The rate of return on capital has recovered sharply, but the share of investment in GDP only climbed back to the level of the later 1970s during the last year. Thus our survey of the intermediate targets of policy adds little further ground for optimism. The key issues are how we interpret the record on productivity and inflation.

II PRODUCTIVITY GROWTH

Why has productivity growth improved relative to continental Europe? First, let us present some facts that rule out a number of obvious explanations. Capital stock growth has been lower in the 1980s than previously. The R&D expenditure has fallen relative to most EEC and OECD countries in the 1980s. In the manufacturing collapse of 1979–81, closures were not concentrated among the lowest productivity plants but among larger plants with higher than average productivity.

In the main, productivity growth has risen because production has been reorganized. Changes in work practices and reductions in manning levels have been proceeding more rapidly than previously and this has been accompanied by an increase in management grip in productivity-related areas.

Why has this happened in Britain? In 1979–81, the British economy was hit by a negative shock (as measured by the fall in output, say) that was far greater than that sustained by any other country. This was accompanied by a huge reduction in international competitiveness which gave workers *and* managers little alternative but to raise productivity or go under. So there was a massive shake-out of labor and, from 1981 on, productivity growth rose sharply. This improvement was sustained by a number of factors. Union and labor market legislation combined with continuing high unemployment shifted the balance of power at the workplace, enabling management to maintain the initiative. And productivity gains were readily available in the sense that, merely by moving manning levels and the organization of maintenance towards European best practice, tremendous improvements were forthcoming.

The importance of the shock and the change in the industrial relations situation, both consequences of Mrs Thatcher, are confirmed by the performance of UK companies. Productivity growth has been higher in more unionized firms and also higher in those that sustained a bigger shock in 1979–81.

What of the future? While there remains a considerable gap in productivity between British plants and similar European plants, this will start to become harder to close because of the low levels of training embodied in the British work force. As the work of Prais and his team at the National Institute makes clear, shortages of adequately trained workers are increasingly constraining productivity performance and this appears to be the most serious threat to the future.

III THE INFLATION-UNEMPLOYMENT TRADE-OFF AND THE BLESSINGS OF OIL

The most worrying feature of the British economy remains inflationary pressure. Despite high unemployment, the growth of average hourly earnings was almost constant at $7\frac{1}{2}$ per cent a year from 1982 to 1987, and (with the recent fall in unemployment) rose to over 9 per cent in 1988.

We attribute the alarming rise in the NAIRU to two main factors. First, there is now a huge mismatch between the skills demanded and the skills held by the unemployed. Second, the great buildup of unemployment in the early 1980s has left long-lasting scars. It has made unemployment into a way of life in many communities.

Thus inflation performance since 1982 has been very disappointing. Before that, however, there was the big disinflation. How did this come about?

The rise in unemployment was an important element in the story. But so was North Sea oil, which was not available to the other EEC countries. To evaluate the role of oil, we use the model we estimated earlier (1987a, 1987b). In simplified form, this has a price equation.

$$p - w = \alpha_0 - \alpha_1 u - \alpha_2 \Delta^2 w \qquad (1)$$

and a wage equation

$$w - p = \beta_0 - \beta_1 u + \beta_2 v(p^* - \bar{p}) - \beta_3 \Delta^2 p \qquad (2)$$

where p is (log) GDP deflator, w is (log) labor cost per worker-hour, u is the unemployment rate, $(p^* - \bar{p})$ is (log) competitiveness and v the share of imports. The current account of the balance of payments (CA) is determined by

$$CA = \gamma_0 + \gamma_1 u + \gamma_2 v(p^* - \bar{p}) + \gamma_3 \, OIL \qquad (3)$$

where OIL is the real value of U.K. oil production.

To use the model we begin with the observation that, over the Thatcher years, net exports have always been within ± 1 per cent of GDP (except for larger surpluses in 1980–2 and a larger deficit in 1988). Thus to get the broad picture, we shall assume that, without the North Sea oil, fiscal and monetary policy would have been such as to produce the same current account as actually arose. If we also assume that unemployment had been the same as actually arose, then inflationary pressure would have been much higher. For over the Thatcher years the real value of sterling would have averaged 12 per cent lower, and this would have raised the NAIRU implied by (1) and (2). If we set $\Delta^2 w \simeq \Delta^2 p$, we can cumulate the extra changes in inflation over the period and find that inflation would by now have been 11 per cent higher than in the presence of oil.

IV CONCLUSION

A miracle occurs when the facts are much better than might have been expected. We have not attempted to set up an explicit counterfactual situation. However, if pressed, we might hazard the following. Compared with a Callaghan–Healey government for the last ten years, Mrs Thatcher has raised unemployment and inequality, and reduced inflation. Though she has raised productivity, the verdict on output is uncertain.

Each reader will perform his or her own cost-benefit assessment. This will involve the record so far, the future prospects, and the set of value judgements used. Benefits there have certainly been, but there have also been major costs.

References

Englander, S. and A. Mittelstädt (1988) 'Total factor productivity: macroeconomic and structural aspects of the slowdown', *OECD Economic Studies*, 10 (Spring).

Layard, R. and S. Nickell (1987a) 'Unemployment in Britain', in C. Bean *et al.* (eds), *The Rise in Unemployment* (Oxford: Basil Blackwell).

Layard R. and S. Nickell (1987b) 'The labour market', in R. Dornbusch and R. Layard (eds), *The Performance of the British Economy* (Oxford: Clarendon Press).

OECD (1987) *Economic Outlook*, 42 (December), 39–49.

OECD (1988) *Economic Surveys, United Kingdom (1987–88)* (Paris: OECD).

20 Lifelong Learning (1995)*

with P. Robinson and H. Steedman

1 DIAGNOSIS

In a world where capital moves freely between countries, the main factor which determines the prosperity of a people is their skill. Countries which have higher levels of skill grow faster than other countries at the same level of income.[1] So our policy on skills cannot be passive – to wait until manifest shortages appear. It must be active – to improve skill levels and thus produce in advance a more flexible workforce, better-equipped to respond to and initiate change.

However, skill formation, like anything, has to be balanced against other priorities. The lower the existing levels of provision the stronger the case for expansion.

Britain's failure

Britain today is below the level of provision in other similar countries.[2] Our provision of higher education compares quite well with other countries. But the less academic the person, the worse a deal they receive.

As Figure 20.1 shows, the fraction of workers who have degrees in Britain is in line with our competitors. But as we move to lower levels the picture becomes steadily worse. At 16–18 we have fewer people studying than other countries (see Figure 20.2). In consequence many fewer obtain 'Level 3' qualifications, equivalent to 2 or more A Levels or their vocational equivalents (obtained full or part-time). In Northern Europe, the US and Japan 60 per cent or more of the labour force have these qualifications. In Britain the figure is 40 per cent. Indeed to reach the figure of 60 per cent we have to go down to Level 2 which includes GCSE (5 grades A–C) and equivalent part-time qualifications.

Even today 38 per cent of our youngsters fail to reach even Level 2 National Vocational Qualification (NVQ) – in itself a very low standard, which guarantees neither basic numeracy nor literacy. Thus we are starting from a highly distorted and unequal system, where the greatest weakness is at the bottom.

---

* Centre for Economic Performance, LSE, *Occasional Paper*, 9 (December 1995) pp. 1–27. The paper was submitted in evidence to the IPPR Committee on Public Policy and British Business. The authors are extremely grateful to Gerald Holtham, Simon Milner and Joshua Hillman for helpful discussions.

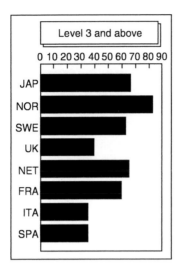

Figure 20.1a Percentage of the labour force who are qualified to level 3 and above, 1992

Notes: 'Level 3' is here defined as successful completion of a course of post-compulsory secondary education or training of at least two years duration or a higher qualification.

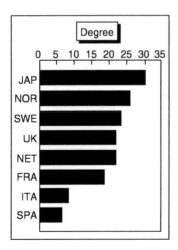

Figure 20.1b Percentage of the labour force holding degree level qualifications, 1992

Source: National publications (details on request).

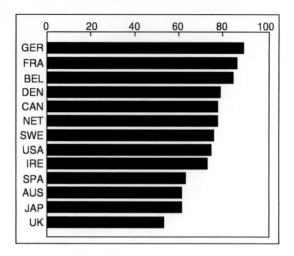

Figure 20.2   Educational participation, 16–19, 1991
Source: OECD, *Economic Surveys* (1995), UK figure adjusted to include part-time further education.

Priorities for new initiatives

In the context of current labour market trends, this is a most damaging situation. For the stark reality is that the demand for low-skilled labour is falling rapidly. Muscle-power has become largely useless and it is brain-power which is needed. This is perhaps the greatest problem facing industrial societies. The future of millions will depends on whether we can reduce the supply of unskilled people faster than the demand collapses. If we fail to do so, we shall face mass unemployment.

Thus the top priority is to ensure that every *young person* achieves a basic level of general education and skill, equivalent to at least the level of an upgraded NVQ Level 2. This is a necessary platform for any future learning or employment. A person must be able to read, understand and communicate instructions; work out costs, measurements and quantities accurately; and have some specialised professional knowledge. Other countries with which we compete have more people like that available to them, and their economies benefit from this.[3]

There is a parallel need to enable *adults* to upgrade themselves. This is particularly important for people with no basic skills. At least one European country, Denmark, has a declared policy of widespread training for unskilled adults – this is being achieved by government funding of off-the-job training. It is also important that people who have skills that have become obsolete should have the opportunity retool. The more rapid economic change, the more important this is.

Principles for state involvement

But how exactly should the state operate in this whole field? Should it pay for the whole cost of skill formation, including maintenance? Should it for example, pay for firm-specific training?

The answer is that the state's role in skill formation is to do those things that the market will not do properly – to remedy market failure. Where an employer provides to his own employees training that raises their productivity in his business (but much less elsewhere), he will be able to reap the return to this '*firm-specific*' training. So he will undertake the investment. This is just what British employers have been doing. They have provided ever more training to their workers – since 1984 the proportion of workers who 'got some training in the last four weeks' has risen from 9 to 16 per cent.[4] There is no reason why the state should concern itself at all with this sort of training, which is in fact mainly by short courses.

But most of this job-specific training goes to people who already have a platform for learning. In Spring 1994 the proportion who 'got some training in the last four weeks' was 24 per cent for graduates, 15 per cent for people with A or O level, 10 per cent for people with other qualifications and only 4 per cent for people with no qualification. This reinforces the point that the job of the state is to enhance peoples' *general* skills – those skills that will enhance their productivity wherever they work. This is a job that the market cannot do properly on its own: left to their own, individuals would invest much too little in their future skills, even if it became easier to borrow to finance educational investment.

The reasons are obvious. First, each individual investment is enormously risky, even though the average return to society is not. Second, individuals often underestimate the benefits; and anyway the tax system takes away a part of them. Third a large pool of educated workers provides major external benefits to firms. And fourth, a pool of uneducated workers imposes on the rest of society the cost of the unemployment benefits or in-work benefits which it generates.

These arguments provide a powerful argument for subsidies to 'general' education and to training that is not firm-specific. To generate the right amount of investment, the subsidy should in principle equal the value of the external benefit.[5] Such benefits are especially obvious from skill formation at the lower levels. Clearly it is irrelevant by what method of study a skill is obtained: a qualification obtained part-time should get a similar subsidy to one obtained full-time, and a qualification obtained in adult life should get a similar subsidy to one obtained earlier.

Thus for practical purposes we shall use the following guidelines:

(i)   Government policy should concentrate on general education and off-the-job training for general skills.
(ii)   The main new initiative must be to get every youngster up to at least an upgraded NVQ Level 2. The other main initiative is to promote upgrading of the adult workforce.
(iii) State subsidies should be provided on exactly the same principle for part-time as for full-time education, and for adults as for youngsters.

We can now summarise our proposals, as a preview to the rest of the report.

• All employed youngsters under 19 should be employed as trainees, with required off-the-job vocational education (section 2).
• Like full-time degree students, all other adults studying for recognised qualifications should have their fees paid from state money. Maintenance grants for full-time degree students should be progressively changed into loans (section 3).
• Costs where possible should be met from well defined sources (section 4).
• A Learning Bank should be established to provide loans to all students of 18 and above studying for degree and sub-degree qualifications (section 5).
• A University for Industry should be established to provide high-quality teaching materials for the new expansion of education, including distance learning (section 6).
• The teaching profession should be upgraded as a long-term contribution to skill formation in primary and secondary schools (section 7).

2   UNIVERSAL COVERAGE 16–19

Firms employing people under 19 would be required to employ them as trainees. This would require that they receive at least a day a week (or equivalent) of general vocational education.

This requirement implies a huge educational expansion with roughly half a million extra youngsters attending college part-time. It is an educational revolution not much smaller than the raising of the school leaving age to 16 in the early 1970s. To make it a success, answers are needed on many questions. What would the students study, how would they be motivated, how would the requirement be enforced, who would provide the tuition, and how could firms be induced to provide the traineeships?

Courses

For full-timers, Britain now has a reasonable set of vocational qualifications – the GNVQ (General National Vocational Qualifications), with separate courses relevant to 15 broad sectors of employment. All the courses include an element of Core Skills ie of Maths and Literacy. A Level 2 course for GNVQ lasts one year, and is equivalent to five GCSEs at Grade A–C. At Level 3 course lasts two years, and is equivalent to two or more A levels.

But, for part-timers, our set of qualifications is still not satisfactory. It is the system of National Vocational Qualifications (NVQ) – which are meant to have the same equivalences as the GNVQ. But unlike the GNVQ, the NVQ are purely competence-based (knowing how to do quite particular tasks); there is very little cognitive element (knowing why).

So the basic part-time qualification should be a part-time GNVQ. The part-time GNVQ would contain (like the full-time version) required and optional components, but in this case candidates could if they wished satisfy the optional requirement by taking a relevant NVQ. Even so the number of NVQs should be drastically reduced. At present there are separate NVQs in Fish (Salmon) and Fish (White), and there are altogether 160 'industry lead bodies' – these need cutting to 20.

On this basis we should set a *prime objective of policy as being to get everyone to a Level 2 qualification.*

Incentives

We want all youngsters to feel that they *have* to reach this basic level of attainment. This would also motivate children while they are still in school, which is very important. To provide this motivation, we could exempt from the traineeship requirement up to 19 any employee who already had a GNVQ qualification. (But they should still have the *right* to traineeship if they want to exercise it.)

The part-time education requirement should be an obligation on employers rather than youngsters. This will make youngsters feel that the education is more relevant to their work, and hopefully make it in fact more relevant.

Guidance and enforcement

But someone will have to police the requirement. The natural agent is the Careers Service (or possibly the Training and Enterprise Councils). In addition we still have some 10 per cent of 16–19 year olds doing nothing (neither studying, working, nor on Youth Training). These people include some of those at greatest risk of lifelong deprivation. There has to be an advisory service to help them equip themselves. This too must be the Careers Service.

Until recently only one third of youngsters ever saw the Careers Service. The new contracts with providers of the Careers Service now require that they see every youngster at 15, but to this should be added that they see them at 16 also and, if there is no job for them, encourage them to continue with full-time education.

Who would provide the extra tuition?

Most of the extra off-the-job tuition would be provided in public colleges of further education, but some could be in private colleges and some in firms' training centres. All of these should be eligible for reimbursement from the Further Education Funding Council (FEFC), which would cover the standard cost.

But in addition there has to be the element of on-the-job training. This requires the concept of a traineeship.

Traineeships

Every youngster employed under 19 should be employed as a trainee.[6] The employer would have to release the youngster for the equivalent of eight hours a week off-the-job vocational education. In addition the youngster would have a trainer at the workplace, who was responsible for practical skill development. Though the off-the-job education should be reimbursed directly by the FEFC, firms will need to be paid for providing the on-the-job traineeship element (say £1000 a year for two years).

Employers are not going to take on trainees if they cost too much. The traineeship wage could be laid down in a new Traineeship Act at say a half the Minimum Wage for a 32 hour week. This should ensure that employers who, currently employ youngsters at higher rates of pay but with no training requirement, would continue to employ them when there is a training requirement (plus a training subsidy).

The new traineeships would supersede Youth Training, which does not have a good name. The Training and Enterprise Councils (TECs) should be responsible for administering the new Traineeship scheme and the on-the-job training subsidy, but should be broadened by fusing them with Chambers of Commerce to which all local firms should belong. The finance of colleges should be concentrated in the Further Education Funding Council (FEFC), which currently provides the bulk of finance for vocational education and training. (TEC expenditure on tuition is under one tenth of FEFC expenditure.)

Our proposals are the opposite of 'letting bad employers off the hook'. All employers will have to participate. But we recognise that the cost of off-the-job training in general skills should be met by society as a whole.

Credit entitlements versus the 'Robbins principle'

A completely different approach to the finance of further education would be to expand training credits. At present these are confined to trainees on Youth Training. One could instead give them to every youngster aged 16–19. There are enormous difficulties with this. First, there is the problem of the units in which to define the entitlement. If they are in years of study, that is fine, but this can be achieved more easily by letting people choose the course, without paying for it. If they are in units of money, there is enormous difficulty because different subjects have different costs. If every training credit had the same monetary value, we should need very complicated systems for the more expensive courses – involving topping them up from other sources. This whole arrangement would not be likely to increase demand, but rather to discourage people through the unnecessary hassle and transactions costs.

The Further Education Funding Council only began work in 1993 and has done well to establish an effective system for funding further education. It would be wrong to subject the financing system to yet another major re-organisation unless there was an overwhelming case for doing so.

Instead we should have the simplest and most transparent system, based on the Robbins principle – that courses should be available free to all who are qualified and able to benefit. This principle should apply equally to adults as to those under 19, since the external benefits from their education are likely to be just as large.

3   FREE EDUCATION FOR ADULTS

For adults over 19, our present system is totally biased towards full-time degrees. People who take full-time degrees have their fees paid by the state, while those who study in further education or for part-time degrees have to pay the fees. Fees in further education amount to some £300 million.[7] Some £100 million is also paid in fees for part-time degree courses, including those at the Open University. By contrast, students on full-time degree courses not only have their fees paid but receive some £1300 million in maintenance grants and another £700 million net in student loans. With so distorted a system, it is not surprising that we are producing so few people with NVQ3-level qualifications.

The *outrageous discrimination* against sub-degree vocational education and part-time degrees reflects pure class interests. However a sense of respectability is given by the idea that for anything useful employers should pay 'since they benefit'. As we know, this is simply untrue for general skills – the individual employers has no way to trap the returns. Yet this wretched rhetoric has prevented the obvious efficiency and justice of an *equal treatment of academic and vocational education*. The anomaly must be rectified.

Tuition

The first need is for the state to pay all fees for (G)NVQ2 or 3 and for part-time degrees.[8] This would have the effect that all students taking major national vocational courses would at last be on the same footing as undergraduates in universities – which is the standard practice in France, Germany and Italy. By this method we should have established an entitlement for everybody to free education up to the level of a first degree. We should not abolish fees for either (i) recreational 'adult education', or (ii) postgraduate courses, or (iii) tailor-made courses put on at the request of firms. Nor could people repeat years for a given level of education free (any more than they can now take another first degree for free).

Clearly we want people to be able to get new skills throughout their life. When their new knowledge is firm-specific, the employer should pay. But, when it is not, the state must help. If people's skills have been eroded by economic change, they need to be able to take a second course at a 'level' at which they have already studied. This should probably be allowed after an interval of say 5 years between the two courses. But the exact process of rationing here may have to be developed through a process of trial and error. Equally, it is difficult to forecast accurately the general increase in take-up of education by adults. It may be wise to phase things in, starting with the younger adults.

Another possibility is to insist that students pay a (smallish) proportion of the fee. This would cause considerable uproar in universities where the replacement of maintenance grants will be a major political problem. Since it would be unjust to charge students elsewhere but not in universities, the issue of a student contribution to fees should probably be left as an option for the longer term only.

The aim of the new policy is the extension of opportunity. The method is to raise demand, with an obligation on the Further Education Funding Council to deliver the supply (subject to cost limits discussed in section 5). The FEFC should actively promote the supply of extra places – both in public colleges and through private suppliers, who are by law now treated on an equal footing. Colleges should be encouraged to enrol adults in all courses leading to recognised qualifications. Where necessary, they should put on separate courses for adults, provided student numbers warrant it.

Maintenance

One deterrent to adult enrolment has been fees. We have dealt with that. The other is living costs, when an adult stops work or goes part-time. This is a critical issue. But we should always keep separate the issue of tuition cost and the cost of maintenance. On maintenance we should increasingly expect all students to be self-sufficient, while at the same time making sure that the capital market works. All adult students should therefore have access to loans through the Learning Bank, even if they are studying below degree level or part-time. Access to loans should exist for people of all ages. Meantime the existing student grants for full-time degrees should be progressively phased out. This would not be a tax on anybody – certainly not parents (whose position would be unaffected), nor on students. The students would choose the size of their loan (up to a maximum) and would repay later in relation to their subsequent income until the loan was paid off.

The student maintenance grants currently cost around £1.3 billion a year and the existing loans (net) around £0.7 – adding £2 billion to the PSBR. Since the new loans would be privately financed, this would save the PSBR £2 billion – which should be redistributed to the education of those less privileged.

4 COSTS AND FINANCE

The programme described above would be a revolutionary improvement in our system and would put it on a proper basis to compete with our European rivals. The gross costs are shown in Table 20.1, which follows the order of presentation in the paper. The first is the cost of achieving universal coverage of all 16–19s. This involves, first, tuition on day release, which the FEFC believe can be provided at a marginal cost of £500 a year per person. Then there is the Training Rebate to employers of trainees. The employer would pay the wage, but receive £1000 a year to induce him to offer and administer the traineeship.[9] This is somewhat less than firms get on Youth Training but, even if we only allow a lowish traineeship wage, we should need to pay a reasonable amount to firms to compensate for other costs. In addition the Careers Service, which now costs around £180m, would need at least one third more funds, and the TECs would need funding to cover extra administration.

Turning to adults, existing fees paid to further education colleges and providers of part-time degree courses amount to some £480 million. These would become a public responsibility. In addition our drive to attract more adults would lead to a big increase in student numbers. We assume that 500 000 more adults would enrol in further education than would otherwise. This is an increase of 50 per cent on present numbers. The actual increase that occurs over the five year period would of course be more than this, because even on present policies the numbers will grow substantially (though there are no government projections beyond 1996/7).

Such an increase in student numbers is inevitably expensive. Since fees only cover one third of the cost, it would be expensive even if it could be achieved without abolishing fees (which it could not). In order to limit the extent of our financial commitment to adults, the correct strategy would be first to abolish fees for under 25s, then under 30s and so on, testing demand step by step.

Table 20.1   Additional public expenditure in 5th year (Britain, 1994 prices)

		£m
1 Universal coverage 16–19		
Tuition	230	
Training rebate to firms	460	
Careers Service	70	
TEC administration	40	
		800
2 Opportunities for adults		
Cost of abolishing fees		
Existing places	480	
New places	160	
Other cost of new places	320	
NI rebates for employers	100	
3 University for Industry		1060
		100
		1960

Notes:
1 Universal coverage 16–19
On the basis of the figures in the Annex, we assume that we have to provide extra part-time places as follows

16 year olds	17 year olds	18 year olds
10%	20%	30%

This means 460 000 places at £500 marginal cost for tuition and £1000 for Training Rebate to employers. In this calculation we have left intact all expenditure on existing programmes of youth training.

2 Free tuition for adults
We assume the same mix of full-time and part-time day students as now, and a marginal cost per fte student of £1500. We treat 3 part-timers as equal to 1 full-time, making 320 000 additional ftes.

3 Maintenance support
We assume that, of the 824 000+ part-time day students, 500 000 study for GNVQ2. At a wage of £10 000 the employers NI contribution on 1/5 of the wage bill would be £105 million.

We also have to assist the least well-educated to meet some of their maintenance cost. The proposal is that if any employee has less than GNVQ2 his employer can send him to get that qualification on day release while paying no employer's National Insurance contribution for the period of the absence. If this arrangement attracted 500 000 students a year, the cost in lost NI would be £100m.

Finally there is the University for Industry (discussed below). The Open University costs the government around £100m, and we have pencilled in a similar figure for the University for Industry.

On this basis the total cost would be nearly £2 billion a year by the end of the next Parliament. How would this be paid for?

(i)   The most natural method would be through a reallocation of the £2 billion which could be saved on student maintenance (if this could all be done within a Parliament). Certainly there are other important educational outlays, which have a claim on extra resources (nursery education and primary and secondary schools). Altogether new developments in education need more than £2 billion and therefore the issue arises of whether extra financing devices are needed for post-16 education.

(ii) One possibility is a Training Levy on firms. This would be a clear tax increase and would add to labour costs. Though employers would share in the benefits,[10] so would others and there is no clear reason why employers alone should pay.

(iii) Another possibility is to make individuals contribute some proportion of the fee. But, as we have suggested, this is only a longer term possibility if our initial aim is a major increase in participation by adults.

(iv) The other possibilities are general tax revenue, which will rise in real terms as the economy grows, and borrowing. It is important to stress that what we are proposing is an investment and could therefore justify some element of borrowing. There is surely some room for this, since the government can borrow at least £15 billion a year without increasing the ratio of debt to GDP.

5   THE LEARNING BANK

Turning to more detailed institutional issues, the Learning Bank should be the key instrument for dealing with the problem of *maintenance*. People should be able to borrow from it at reasonably low interest, and repay an appropriate fraction of their income until the loan was repaid (which in a few cases it would be never). Repayment should be by automatic surcharge on a person's National Insurance contribution.[11]

For some workers, especially those we are keenest to attract, the notion of losing earnings to acquire skill will not look great – even if loan finance is available. For people studying to get (G)NVQ2 we need a national campaign to persuade employers to release workers for day release on full pay. As we have suggested, such employers should be entitled to NI rebates for the period of study absence.

The second function of the Learning Bank should be to act as the channel whereby the state pays individual fees (the LEA offices will have lost their role once maintenance grants are abolished). Thus students could have Individual Learning Accounts (ILAs) through which their fees were paid from state funds and through which they borrowed to finance their maintenance.

Contribution-based individual learning accounts

We are not recommending the introduction of contribution-based individual learning accounts. These have been widely discussed.[12] The general idea is that individuals would accumulate educational entitlements over time, which they could then exercise when they wanted. The entitlements would derive from contributions by the employer, the individual and the state. These would then be used to pay for fees and, as desired, maintenance.

In the pure version of the proposal the Funding Councils would disappear and the whole state contribution would be funnelled through individuals. Sometimes the proposal is for ILAs from 16+ which raises enormous problems. Let us focus simply on the version which starts at 18+. There are four obvious problems with the proposal.

First, the money in the ILA accumulates gradually, while the greatest need is at the beginning between 18 and say 24. So individuals will have to borrow heavily at the beginning – not a great way to promote take-up. Even beyond 25 the money may not be there at the right time.

Second, there will be over 25 million accounts. As there are some 8 million job changes a year, it will be a major accounting exercise to record contributions and to supervise outlays.

Third, there would be serious difficulties for some colleges, if the Funding Council contribution was reduced and replaced by less certain fee income. Problems on the scale of the problems of the NHS could not be ruled out.

Fourth, many individuals and firms would resent contributing to the accounts, though of course they would be forced to do so. Remember that not all individuals would draw on them.

We should not therefore introduce contribution-based ILAs unless there are major gains to be had which cannot be secured in any other way. We think that all the gains can be got elsehow. The basic idea of entitlement can be secured by providing education free – in which case no further mechanism of entitlement to tuition is needed. It is much better for the state to provide support *when* it is needed than for it to pay into a fund.

By our system the state will of course end up providing more support to more able youngsters than to less able, because they will choose more education. Is this wrong? If we revert to the rationale for state finance, we see that it need not be wrong at all. For those who are more able to benefit from education are also more able to confer benefits on others when they study. However the existing student maintenance grant cannot be justified by this argument and should be abolished.

At the same time the biggest push should be on behalf of the least able. To really help them a major institutional effort is needed. Education is already free for 16–19s but they do not all take it up. Introducing fees and giving people an entitlement from which to pay them will change nothing. We need a new institution of universal traineeship. And, second, we need a new deal for sub-degree education beyond the basic level, and for part-time degrees. Our proposals will shift the balance of support away from the most able, without aiming at complete equality of treatment, for which there is no real argument. We believe that our proposals can achieve all the valid objectives of those who prefer contribution-based individual learning accounts, while avoiding the difficulties of that particular scheme.

6 THE UNIVERSITY FOR INDUSTRY

The University for Industry should draw on two basic ideas.

(i)   *There are vast economies of scale* to be reached from producing and disseminating good packages of teaching materials (books, videos, self-assessment programmes, computer-assisted instruction). The economies are greater the larger the market. If we want an educational revolution at a manageable cost we have to exploit these economies of scale. Clearly the savings will be greater the larger the scale, so that the initial focus will have to be on GNVQ2 and later GNVQ3.

(ii) *There are many adults who cannot or do not want to study by college-based methods.* For them the answer is to study at the workplace or at home. Again if we want to raise basic competence, we want to encourage people to take basic courses leading to recognised qualifications, and some organisation is needed to enrol the students and to assess them. This is a second function for the University for Industry.

The courses should not be yet another lot – they should be the GNVQs but superbly taught. The delivery method should be worked out with the technical experts. Probably the best approach would be to ask the Open University to propose a design concept.

7 OTHER REFORMS

We have focused on education and training after 16. Education before 16 is the essential foundation for this. But, once people are faced with the prospect of work, there is one more chance to motivate them to acquire the necessary basic foundation. We have focused on this stage because it comes closest to the world of work.

Even after 16 there is a vast range of other issues we have not covered. Clearly we need more basic business degrees at first degree level. We also need more management education at post-graduate level. At A level we need a broader curriculum, as recommended by the Higginson Committee, but there is no special gain in forcing A level and GNVQ into a single framework.

Throughout education we must encourage better professional standards among teachers in primary and secondary school: and a General Teaching Council is a good proposal. We should also make nursery education more generally available.

But we believe that our own proposals are at least as important as all of these. Further education is a neglected sector, lying in between the old Departments of Education and Employment. It is time we took really seriously the objective of skills for all.

8 CONCLUSIONS

The main proposals in this paper have a highly focussed aim: to prevent the continuation in Britain of an increasingly depressed group of under-skilled workers. The main intention is to ensure that all 16–19 year olds and as many adults as possible achieve at least Level 2 qualifications.

(i) For 16–19 we should require traineeships for all young people not in full-time education. Trainees would get at least one day a week off-the-job vocational education for a part-time GNVQ. The Further Education Funding Council which already organises and funds most of vocational education (over ten times more than the TECs) should be responsible for the delivery of this. The Careers Service should be strengthened to monitor and help all youngsters, and the TECs should supervise the delivery of traineeships in firms. Firms should receive tax rebates for taking on trainees, even if the trainee wage was controlled by law. This far-reaching change would require half a million extra places in colleges.

(ii) The vocational education of adults (for (G)NVQ2 and 3 or part-time first degrees) should, like full-time academic education up to first degree level, be free to the student. The state should pay the fees. This would stimulate uptake. But in addition employers should be offered tax rebates for the paid leave of workers studying for (G)NVQ2.

(iii) These proposals would cost around £2 billion. This could be funded by progressively replacing student maintenance grants by loans (repaid in relation to the student's subsequent income) and by shifting student loan finance outside the PSBR. Alternatively they could be financed by a Training Levy, by general taxation, or by borrowing, where up to £15 billion can be borrowed without increasing the ratio of public debt to GDP. At a later stage one could also consider requiring all students to pay some fraction of the fee.

(iv) The Learning Bank should provide loans to enable any adult to finance maintenance while studying.

(v) The University for Industry would develop teaching packages for use by colleges and by its own distance learning systems (mainly for adults). Its packages would help to ensure quality but also to control cost.

In sum our policy proposals would deliver (a) a skill for every youngster and (b) equal opportunities for all adults.

Appendix

THE CURRENT SITUATION IN POST-16 EDUCATION

Attainment

At 16+, 43 per cent get 5 GCSE Grades A–C (considered equivalent to NVQ2).[13] By the age of 19–21, 63 per cent have the equivalent of NVQ2 – the increase since 16+ coming mainly from vocational qualifications at level 2 got either full-time or part-time.[14] By the age of 21–23, 42 per cent have NVQ3 or equivalent, including 23 per cent who got 2 or more A levels. Enrolments are shown below in Table 20.2.

Table 20.2   Activity of 16–19 year olds, England, January 1994 (%)

	16–17	17–18	18–19
Full-time			
Higher education	0	0	18
A level	37	34	7
Vocational			
Level 3	8	12	7
Level 2	14	5	2
Level 1	6	4	3
GCSE	7	2	-
Total	72	57	37
Part-time further education	8	10	10
No education	20	33	53
	100	100	100
Full-time education	72	57	37
YT	13	16	47
Employed	7	17	
Unemployed	7	10	16
	100	100	100

Source: DfE Statistical Bulletin, 7/94 (July 1994) and other sources (on request).

The targets of the National Advisory Council on Education and Training Targets for the year 2000 are

Level 2   85 per cent (actually 63 per cent in 1994)
Level 3   60 per cent (actually 42 per cent in 1994).

The main conclusion is that the bottom 15 per cent have no target, and at present there is another 22 per cent who reach less than the minimum acceptable. In the labour force as a whole, there are some 40 per cent without this minimum.

Enrolments, expenditure and cost

Table 20.3 shows the pattern of enrolments by age and educational sector. Table 20.4 shows expenditure by educational sector, and Table 20.5 shows unit costs.

Table 20.3   Home students, UK, 1992–3 (000)

	16–19	19–21	21–25	25+	All 16+
Schools	558	5	–	–	563
Further education[a]					
FT	414	49	36	78	577
PT day	176	67	71	411	730
(PT evening only)	(49)	(45)	(97)	(540)	(733)
Degree-level					
FT	137	327	241	156	862
PT	8	30	71	350	459

Note:
[a] Sub-degree level. Excluding adult education centres, which are mainly non-vocational and not financed by FEFC.
Source: DfE, *Education UK* (1994).

Table 20.4 Public expenditure on education, main items, England, 1995–6
(£ million)

Schools		16 109
Further education	FEFC	3 022
	Payments by TECs	230
Higher education	HEFC	3 782
	Fees paid	993
	Maintenance grants	1 102
	Student loans (net)	644

Source: DfE, *Departmental Report* (March 1995) and (for TECs) FEFC. Data on schools and TECs are for 1993–4.

Table 20.5 Unit costs and home student numbers, England

	Unit costs per FTE 1992–3 £ p.a.	FTE students (000) 1993–4
Primary/nursery	1580	4125
Secondary	2260	2935
Further education	2970	993
Higher education tuition	4820[a]	921
grant	1610[b]	

Notes:
[a]1993–4.
[b]Average per award-holder, 1992–3.
Source: DfE *Department Report* (March 1995).

Notes

1. The evidence is explored fully in Barro and Sala-i-Martin (1995). Other factors conducive to growth include the freedom given to market forces.
2. A detailed analysis of our system is in the Appendix.
3. For general evidence see Barro and Sala-i-Martin (1995). For specific comparisons of Britain with continental Europe see Prais (1989) and elsewhere.
4. Employment Department, *Training Statistics*, (1994, p. 51).

5. For a discussion of all this see Layard (1994).
6. The traineeships would differ from the new Modern Apprenticeship scheme in requiring off-the-job training and more supervision by employers. (Modern Apprenticeships are aimed at NVQ3). Youngsters doing part-time jobs while studying full-time would of course be exempt.
7. Figures from FEFC, August 1994–July 1995. They exclude fees paid by TECs. Of the fees paid £130 million were for part-time courses (mainly paid by employers), £85 million for full-time and sandwich courses (usually paid by individuals) and £60 million were for HE (mostly individuals).
8. Overseas students would of course continue to pay.
9. We have applied the cost of £1500 to the *extra* number of trainees, assuming that the costs of 'Youth Training' are carried forward.
10. The advantages to firms include rebates: (i) for providing 16–19 traineeships (£0.5 billion); (ii) for financing study absence for adults (£0.1 billion). Firms would also receive the following other benefits: (iii) fees which they now pay for adults would be provided free (up to £0.2 billion); (iv) 1 000 000 extra employees would be receiving tuition (free), and (v) the University for Industry would be providing free tuition in basic skills at the workplace.
11. Barr and Glennerster (1993).
12. See Commission on Social Justice (1994), National Commission on Education (1993), Commission on Wealth Creation and Social Cohesion (1995).
13. 1994 data. 1993 was 41 per cent and 1989 was 33 per cent. (*DFE Statistical Bulletin*, 7/94, July 1994.) An extra 3 per cent reach this level through resits i.e., when older than 16+ (NACETT, *Report on Progress*, July 1995).
14. 1994 figures, NACETT, *Report on Progress*. 1993 only about 23 per cent of YT exiters achieved NVQ2, or above.

References

Barr, N. and H. Glennerster (1993) 'Funding a learning society', LSE, mimeo.
Barro, R. and X. Sala-i-Martin (1995) *Economic Growth* (New York: McGraw-Hill).
Commission on Social Justice (1994) *Social Justice* (London: Vintage).
Commission on Wealth Creation and Social Cohesion (1995) *Report*.
Higginson Committee (1988) *Advancing A Levels* (London: HMSO).
Layard, R. (1994) 'The welfare economics of training', in R. Layard, K. Mayhew and G. Owen, *Britain's Training Deficit* (Aldershot: Avebury).
National Commission on Education (1993) *Learning to Succeed* (London: Heinemann).
Prais, S. (ed.) (1989) *Productivity, Education and Training* (London: NIESR).

Part II
Economic Transition

21 Introduction

The biggest economic challenge today is how to rebuild the economies that rotted under Communism. Since 1990 I have been deeply involved in these issues. I have written every kind of piece from newspaper articles to a book on *The Coming Russian Boom*. I have also been responsible for the journal *Russian Economic Trends*. Much of what I have written has been highly topical,[1] and little of it academic. I am therefore including here only six short pieces.

PRIVATISATION

As everyone knows, the three key issues facing post-Communist governments are privatisation; stabilisation; and liberalisation. Chapter 22 deals with privatisation. In 1990 Olivier Blanchard and I visited Poland at the invitation of my colleague Stanislaw Gomulka, who was a major architect of the Polish reform programme. He invited our views on how to privatise. The problem was how to create a system of private ownership that would provide adequate incentives for managers to make the best use of their assets. Chapter 22 contains our proposals, which were not dissimilar to those being simultaneously developed by Gomulka, Sachs, Frydman and others. The idea was a 2-tier structure: citizens would own shares in funds and the funds would own shares in the companies 'out there'. The fund managers would be rewarded according to how their funds performed, and they would have sufficient stakes in individual companies to make those companies perform and restructure them. Eventually in 1996 a similar scheme was implemented in Poland.

STABILISATION

A second major issue in most countries emerging from Communism has been how to control inflation. In Poland there was near-hyperinflation in late 1989. Yet by mid-1990 inflation was down to 5 per cent a month. This was achieved by a combination of tight money and incomes policy. Chapter 23 (also written with Olivier Blanchard) analyses the process in some detail.

In Russia prices were freed on 1 January 1992, when prices rose overnight by 250 per cent. The difficulty thereafter was how to put the genie back in the bottle. Due to poor payment systems it was possible for the state to obtain seigniorage of over 30 per cent of national income. This of course caused a massive inflation, with an inflation tax of similar magnitude to the seigniorage obtained. Calculating the net impact of the seigniorage and the inflation tax is not easy, but Chapter 24 develops a methodology for doing this. This reveals clearly that enterprises gained massively from the inflationary process, and households lost.

Eventually inflation was tamed in 1995–7. In Chapter 25 I forecast that disinflation would probably happen gradually. It was widely doubted whether such an approach would work. It did – until financial stability was destroyed by the Asian contagion.

JOBS AND LIVING STANDARDS

But for ordinary citizens the key issue is jobs and living standards, both of which fell sharply after the first wave of liberalisation. In most of Eastern Europe, but not the Czech Republic, unemployment rose rapidly to 10–15 per cent and has stayed in that range. This looks therefore to be an equilibrium level of unemployment, that can be explained by the same principles as OECD unemployment, rather than a transitional phenomenon. In Russia the rise in unemployment was less than in Eastern Europe. As Chapter 26 explains, this was mainly due to Russia's remarkable wage flexibility and its weak or non-existent trade unions.

Even so, Russia has suffered much pain – even more than Eastern Europe: the fall in output and living standards has been greater. Many people now believe that the post-Soviet reform strategy has been a mistake and that Eastern Europe and Russia should have followed the Chinese model of gradual reform. I do not believe that. As Chapter 27 argues, that option was not in fact open. China was a rural country with a totalitarian state. The others were urban economies with massive state industry, and they had democracy, with all its strengths and weaknesses. Considering where they were coming from, I doubt whether they could have done much better. But life has been very hard for those who lived through it, and for those who died an early death.

Note

1.   See for example Ellam and Layard (1993); Illarionov, Layard and Orszag (1994).

References

Ellam, M. and R. Layard (1993) 'Prices, incomes and hardship', in A. Åslund and
    R. Layard (eds), *Changing the Economic System in Russia* (London: Pinter Publishers).
Illarionov, A., R. Layard and P. Orszag (1994) 'The conditions of life', in A. Åslund
    (ed.), *Economic Transformation in Russia* (London: Pinter Publishers).
Layard, R. (1992) *Russian Economic Trends* (London: Whurr).
Layard R. and J. Parwes (1996) *The Coming Russian Boom* (New York: Free Press).
Layard, R. (1997) *What Labour Can Do* (London: Warner Books).

22 How to Privatize (1991)*

with O. Blanchard

How to privatize? By now most sensible alternatives have been canvassed – as well as many that are senseless. But it is still useful to set out clearly the criteria that matter, and use these to arrive at a solution. Of course the detail must differ between countries, according to size and the degree of capitalist development. Therefore, our remarks are most relevant to the Soviet Union, which is the largest country (or countries) and the least capitalist. We shall discuss mainly the privatization of large enterprises, which constitute the bulk of existing socialist economies.

There is broad agreement about the ultimate goal – a mainly private economy. We want this because it is more responsive to consumer wants and better satisfies the need for efficient production and distribution. But we also want an economy that has a proper balance between efficiency and fairness. And indeed a major argument for capitalism is that it can lead to a major decentralization of power, conducive both to fairness and efficiency. The question is how to get there.

If one sets out the criteria that need to be satisfied, these suggest one model of privatization that is considerably better than most others. Therefore, we shall set out the criteria, one by one, building up our preferred model as we go along.[1]

1 SPEED

The first consideration is speed. There are five arguments for this.

Speed hastens arrival

It is better to achieve your objective sooner than later, unless there is a problem of 'more haste, less speed', so that, by hurrying, you end up with an inferior version. There are certainly some forms of rapid privatization that could be most unfair. But, as we show, there is no need for rapid privatization to be unfair. And we now give some reason to suppose that a rapid privatization would lead to a better end-outcome.

---

* In H. Siebert (ed.), *The Transformation of the Socialist Economies: Symposium 1991*. University of Kiel (1991), pp. 27–43.

Speed prevents reversal

There is at present in Eastern Europe, and increasingly in the Soviet Union, an enthusiasm for capitalism. But this could die away, as the birth pains of capitalism become increasingly apparent. Rapid private ownership has three major advantages:

–   It creates at once a whole class of individuals with a share in the new system rather than the old. This was the trick used by Henry VIII of England to prevent the return of the Catholic Church: he gave the church lands to everybody who mattered.
–   Widespread private ownership can also prevent the regrouping of old interest groups, or the creation of new ones, hostile to the standard capitalist model. For ownership does in the last resort give power, at least of a sort (see below).
–   And, if the transfer of ownership includes an element of gift, it may soften the pain of recession, by making the new owners feel that even in the short run there are some pluses. A counter-revolution becomes less likely.

Speed removes uncertainty

Thus speed makes it more likely that we reach our destination at all. It also makes the destination a better one. So long as ownership issues are unsettled, no one has an incentive to invest. This deepens recession, discourages foreign investment, and decreases the fraction of European economic activity and European population that will remain in Eastern Europe at the end of the day. If Eastern Europe is to escape from a low level trap, the first thing to do is to establish private title.

Some writers also argue that privatization will improve wage behaviour and decrease the degree to which workers try to grab the quasi-rents of enterprises. Let us hope so. But the experience of privatization East and West is not unambiguous on this point, and the experience of Western Europe certainly suggests that capitalism as such, without considerable unemployment, is not sufficient to ensure non-inflationary wage behaviour. But in Eastern Europe capitalism has become a necessary condition for a recovery of investment.

Speed protects the budget

Critics (like Kornai) of speedy proposals often argue that there is no point in establishing any form of private ownership that is not the fully mature private ownership found in the West. They condemn intermediate forms of private ownership, set up as staging posts, as tricks that will have no effect. For example, they argue that privately owned holding companies, set up as intermediate forms of ownership, are no different from bureaucracy. We do not accept this. British experience showed that companies like British Telecom, British Airways and British Steel acquired a new commercial ethos before privatization – because they were near to the goal of mature private ownership. Eastern Europe desperately needs this commercial ethos. So long as joint stock companies are state-owned, with no immediate prospect of private ownership, they will not become fully commercial. They will press for, and often receive, bail-outs when they are in trouble. This will be bad for the enterprises, bad for the budget, and bad for the economy.

Speed may help fairness

Finally, there is the danger of privatization from below, in which there is no clear general framework, and in the meantime privileged groups of nomenklatura pick the plums. That runs against our second principle.

2 FAIRNESS

This second criterion is fairness. Many East European economists (especially for Hungary) argue in favour of privatization by sale. The main objection to this is one of fairness. Private domestic financial wealth is far below the true value of the national capital stock. Foreign purchasers are highly restricted in most of Eastern Europe, except for Hungary. It follows that a quick sale at a feasible price would give huge capital gains to the existing owners of financial capital. But the capital stock was acquired through the general saving of the people. A transfer of these savings to a limited fraction of the population would be unacceptable.

It has been suggested that this problem could be overcome by the state lending citizens money with which to buy the capital – thus driving the price of the capital up to a reasonable level. The problem here is that the buyer would have to be sure of being able to service the debt.

This raises the question of the valuation of individual enterprises. There is almost no way this can be done, particularly with larger enterprises that will often need massive restructuring before their ultimate mode of operation becomes clear. Many enterprises will turn out to have no value – think of what happened in East Germany. Thus the administrative problem of debt service collection would be quite horrendous – not to mention the horrendous effects on the debtors and on their views about capitalism.

Thus, if large industrial enterprises are to become rapidly private, *they must be given away, not sold*. Though some shares may be sold, the majority of the productive capital stock should be given to the citizens as soon as possible. Preferably, equal amounts should be given to all citizens, including children.

It is important to stress that there is no standard economic arguments that suggests the superior efficiency of sale over gift.[2] We have here a non-repeatable situation where we can choose the initial distribution of assets. As welfare economics make clear, no one initial distribution is *per se* more efficient than any other. But some are fairer than others.

The wealth distributed should be tradable, and it could therefore be traded for beer. The resulting ownership of wealth would not therefore be equal. But it would be much more equal than if the capital stock were sold. Children's wealth should not be tradable below the age of majority, and this would ensure a steady flow of new capitalists into adulthood for the next two decades. Old people should also receive equal shares, since they lived through the worst of the past and their savings created the capital.

The most powerful argument against privatization by gift relates to the monetary overhang and macroeconomic stabilization. In the Soviet Union private financial assets in 1989 equalled 95 per cent of personal income, compared with a, perhaps normal, level of 80 per cent in 1983–85. This excess helped to create inflationary pressure. The size of monetary overhang varies sharply from time to time as prices change. But at the same time there is a budget deficit, financed by printing money. If we use privatization as an occasion for mopping up the money, this has a favourable once-for-all effect on the equilibrium price level. However, it does nothing to deal with the underlying condition of excess demand, which still calls for a fiscal correction, including sufficient taxes to replace any dividend paid by state enterprises. The proper instrument for stabilization is not a one-off financial ploy but a proper budget balance and a high enough level of interest rates.

3 EFFICIENT CONTROL

But *how* should the capital be given away? The main aim is to ensure that it is efficiently distributed and then efficiently managed. There are a number of considerations.

Administrative simplicity

We cannot give every citizen a share in every firm – the paper needed would consume a forest. Even to give citizens tradable vouchers could be very complicated. And the more complicated the scheme, the greater resources are likely to be devoted to the business of distributing wealth rather than using it. Eastern Europe cannot afford to have its best brains involved in producing financial schemes rather than goods and services. Rewards should go to those who increase the size of the pie, not to those who distribute it. If voucher schemes have the opposite effect, they should be rejected. Distribution by gift is not necessarily the same as distribution by voucher.

One simple scheme would be to give every citizen an equal number of shares in a few well-diversified holding companies. However, administrative simplicity alone is not decisive. What else matters?

Efficient managerial control during restructuring

One thing is certain. The behaviour of management has to change, while at the same time most enterprises need restructuring. Who is to supervise this?

With medium- and small-scale enterprise, the market will do it for you. There are sufficient private funds to permit sale to smallish groups of owners who will ensure efficient management. But with large enterprises, the problem of corporate governance is acute, even in Western countries. And in the East there is the additional task of restructuring, which will take at least a decade.

There are thus three tasks: (1) the appointment of efficient managers, (2) the insistence that they perform, and (3) the restructuring of their enterprises. At the initial stage none of these can be done from within the existing enterprises. But 30 million shareholders of each enterprise could not organize it either. Nor should it be done by government, since private ownership should be established at once. The obvious solution is to have a set of say 5 intermediate holding companies. The numbers could be larger but we shall take the number 5 to explain our proposal.

Each holding company would be the majority owner of a random selection of one-fifth of the larger enterprises – and would simply be given the appropriate number of tradable shares. And citizens would be given tradable shares in each holding company. It is very important that these holding companies should not reproduce industrial ministries – hence the random (conglomerate) nature of their holdings. The holding companies should be majority owners of their enterprises, to give them the power to restructure without excessive costs of negotiation.

Clearly, these holding companies need to include much of the top managerial talent of the country and could usefully draw on foreign talent also, in order to properly supervise the behaviour and restructuring of all newly privatized enterprises. That is why the number of holding companies cannot be as large as would otherwise be desirable. As regards the enterprise managers, many of these will clearly have to stay, since managers are scarce. But the trick will be to change their objectives and performance.

Who will supervise the managers of the holding companies? This is a key question. Clearly the shareholders will have limited influence. It is unlikely that they could sack the managers, nor would the takeover threat be effective. The holding company shares would be tradable and might in due course reflect managerial performance. Public pressure on bad performers could thus develop. But in practice in the initial years the government would have to appoint the holding company managers and fire them.

Thus an economy run in part by 5 holding companies is not a mature capitalist economy. In due course it is essential that this direct ownership of firms becomes more widely spread. *The holding companies should therefore be charged in their articles to sell all (or at least one-half) of the shares of each of their enterprises within a 10-year period.* The shares could be sold to anybody. Obvious candidates would be citizens, workers, foreigners, and domestic institutions. Sale proceeds should be distributed to shareholders as dividends.

Since citizens will have financial wealth as holding-company shareholders, they will have the wealth to buy the enterprises at the full economic price. The money they pay for these shares is immediately recycled as dividends. Equally, if shares are sold to foreigners, the proceeds go directly to citizens – making such sales much more popular than if the proceeds went to the treasury (most human beings finding their vision obscured by veils).

It is thus worth passing quickly to an intermediate stage of capitalism even if it is not the full thing – for two reasons. First, any step towards privatization should help: at least it could do no harm. Second, the method we propose creates the private wealth that will generate realistic asset prices as soon as shares begin to be traded.

But two major issues arise at the point where the firms are sold to direct owners: the issue of corporate governance (yet again) and the issue of competition.

Corporate governance after restructuring

We know that corporate governance is a problem in any economy: how to make managers seek the shareholders' interests. Both logic and empirical evidence suggest that small shareholders exert little control over management. While they could in principle monitor managers and replace them with better ones, the evidence is that they lack the expertise and the incentive to achieve the coordination needed to do this. Proxy fights, in which a majority of shareholders vote to acquire a majority of the seats on the board, are rare and rarely successful. Although takeovers, actual or merely threatened, could in principle force management to be efficient, they are again relatively rare when shareholding is diffuse.[3]

Hence many societies rely on systems where there is a stable core of major equity owners. Japan (and to some extent France) have systems of interlocking ownership between productive enterprises; in Germany universal banks are major owners.[4]

What would be appropriate in Eastern Europe? It is difficult to tell in advance how banks will have developed (though it is sure that in the early days they should not be burdened by the ownership of capital of doubtful value). Pension funds may be appropriate owners, though if they are given special rights of control their freedom to trade must also be limited – to avoid problems of insider trading. Foreign ownership would be very helpful, though it remains uncertain how far foreign firms will want to buy major stakes in existing large state enterprises, rather than setting up on their own.

And what about the holding companies themselves? There are two points of view here. One is that their role will become obscured unless they are charged initially with total divestiture within 10 years. The other is that if a holding company is successful, it would be a waste to disband its expertise. On this view holding companies should be required to sell off at least half their holdings in each firm within 10 years, but could then if they wished remain as effective minority shareholders from then on.[5]

Competition

We have so far dodged the key issue of competition. Many people believe that in the Western mixed economy, the main factor affecting performance is competition, not ownership (Kay and Thompson, 1987). In a formerly planned economy, ownership becomes much more important, but the issue of competition remains formidable.

Many East European enterprises are sole suppliers in their countries. That does not make them monopolists[6] – except probably in the Soviet Union. But it gives them great market power. Where it exists, this must be broken up. The time to do so is *before* the enterprise is sold off into direct ownership. There needs to be a totally independent office of competition, which has to approve every sale into direct ownership in terms of the adequacy of competition.

4 WORKERS, FOREIGNERS, PENSION FUNDS, THE STOCK MARKET AND THE FORMER OWNERS

That completes the core of our proposal. It is however worth pursuing in more detail the possible role of different key groups of potential owners (workers, foreigners, pension funds) and the role of the stock market – ending with the role of former owners.

Workers

In the plan we have sketched, workers would of course be allowed to buy their enterprises, with or without help from others such as banks, but not at an advantage compared to other potential buyers. They could instead be given shares of their own firm from the start, or they could be given preferential treatment in the purchase of their firm from holding companies later on.

On grounds of equity, giving workers a special claim in their own firms is unfair, for two reasons. First, there is no reason why those who happen to work in factories should receive more than those in agriculture or public services. The second reason goes in the opposite direction. What the workers get under worker-ownership are claims that are highly correlated with their other source of income. Workers in dinosaur firms are likely both to lose their jobs and to end up with useless pieces of paper.

There are, however, good historical and political reasons to give workers some special claim. *De facto*, and sometimes *de jure*, workers already have substantial control in their firms. Poland and Czechoslovakia have powerful workers' councils. Those in Poland enjoy wider support from workers than those in Czechoslovakia. In both cases, the practical issue may not be how much control to give workers, but how much to take away.

Leaving aside equity and political considerations, are there good reasons to oppose giving some control and ownership to the workers? The answer is no. First, workers have substantial expertise about their firms that outsiders lack. And the often-heard argument that workers' ownership cannot succeed is based on a simple confusion. Workers as shareholders can mean two very different things.

In the Yugoslav solution, ownership rights are given to existing workers and are not transferable.[7] Logic and experience have shown that this structure of ownership works poorly. The incentives faced by worker-shareholders and thus by managers are wrong: the current workers do not get the proceeds from investment and have strong incentives to give themselves dividends and to opt for very liquid forms of investment, such as foreign exchange. Similar issues arise in the hiring of new workers, since hiring implies the dilution of property rights. The transfer of capital across firms is restricted to debt-like agreements, and there is an excessive tendency for profits to stay within the firm. These biases need to be undone by central government intervention, something hardly practical in a market economy.

In the alternative scheme, ownership rights held by workers in a firm can be sold freely on the stock market (or sold back to the firm when leaving, as in Mondragón, Spain; see Bradley and Gelb, 1983). In that case, the incentives faced by worker-shareholders are, for the most part, the correct ones, and the distortions just analysed should not be present. One problem however, may remain: if workers are majority shareholders, with full voting rights, they have the opportunity to exploit minority shareholders, for example, by relabelling part of profits as wages. This problem can in principle be resolved by restrictions on voting rights and other guidelines, and will be irrelevant as long as the proportion of shares held by workers does not give them a controlling interest in the firms.[8]

Thus, if this is required on political grounds, allocating some percentage of shares to workers, say 20–30 per cent, and the rest to the holding companies may be a simple way of recognizing the initial situation and obtaining consensus on a privatization programme. Workers may then want to use those shares to buy their whole firm through leveraged buyouts, or they may opt either to sell them to other potential buyers or to keep them, in order to have a say in the newly sold company.

Foreigners

Foreign know-how and foreign funds are crucial. Worker ownership will discourage acquisition of existing enterprises. *Tant pis*. But nothing should be done to put limits on the scale of foreign ownership or the repatriation of profit. It is a reasonable guess that much foreign investment will involve the creation of new enterprises rather than the acquisition of existing ones, with all their problems.

Pension funds

There are two separate issues about pension funds. First, there is the issue of using privatization as a way of partially funding the retirement system (see, for example, Schaffer, 1990). At this stage, retirement systems in Eastern Europe, as in most other countries, are run mostly as unfunded systems, with contributions by those who work being used to finance benefits for those who have retired. These systems could be partially funded by giving workers, working or retired, shares in proportion to their past contributions and decreasing the present value of benefits paid by the state. From then on, workers would make contributions to both (funded) pension funds and to the (unfunded) state retirement system and receive benefits from both. In thinking about this option, one must keep in mind that the scope for funding the social security system is limited. The degree of funding of the overall retirement system will depend on the ratio of the value of the privatized firms to the present value of benefits. Under even the most optimistic assumptions about the value of privatized firms, and the assumption that all shares are transferred to pension funds, the degree of funding will still be far below one. Compared to the case in which the state kept the same unfunded retirement system and distributed shares more or less equally to all, the macroeconomic effect of partial funding would be to increase the saving rate, and this is therefore the basis on which to judge such proposals. There are indeed grounds for worry about the saving rate. Thus, allocating some percentage of the shares of holding companies to pension funds set up in the way sketched above may indeed be justified on macroeconomic grounds.

Table 22.1   UK share ownership, 1987 (per cent)

Individuals	18
Industrial/commercial companies	5
Institutions	67
Pension funds	32
Insurance companies	25
Trusts	10
Public sector	3
Overseas	5
Charities	2

Source: Schaffer (1990).

Another, conceptually different issue is that of the role of large institutions such as pension or mutual funds in the development of the financial system. In developed market economies, those large institutions are the major owners of shares. Table 22.1 gives the composition of share ownership for the United Kingdom: institutional investors account for more than two-thirds of share holdings. It is clear that such institutions will have to appear in Eastern European countries as well. As holding companies divest and distribute the proceeds of sales through dividends, there will indeed be a growing demand for such financial instruments as shares in mutual funds. Mechanisms to allow investors to save in such a way are clearly desirable.

The stock market

We have argued that expecting a new stock market with decentralized ownership to do a decent job of valuing individual firms and providing effective control in the current environment is naive. We believe, however, that developing a stock market is essential. The path of development we think appropriate is implicit in what we have already said. In the beginning most of the trading should be concentrated in the shares of a small number of holding companies.[9] Over time, as new firms are created and ex-state firms are sold by the holding companies, the number of stocks traded should increase. And, as more and more firms are sold by the holding companies, mutual funds and other large institutions should play an increasingly larger role.

Former owners

A major hindrance to privatization in Eastern Europe – and to foreign investment on greenfield sites – is the issue of reinstatement of former owners.

To sort out these claims will take years. In the meantime the assets must be used by someone who expects to continue owning them. The only procedure is to establish a permanent owner at once along the lines described above. The claim of the former owner should be limited to compensation, not reinstatement.

5 THE POLISH PLAN[10]

Against this background let us take as a case study the current Polish proposals.[11] Note that plans have changed many times and may still change somewhat. But the broad outline of the government's proposals of June 1991 is quite likely to become reality.

The government will establish a number of investment trusts (perhaps 10–20) with largely Polish boards, but managed by management firms that will be largely foreign. The management firms will be paid on a performance-related basis.

From spring 1993, the investment trusts will be owned by the citizens, each citizen over 18 being given one share in each trust. The trusts, in turn, will own an important slice of Polish industry. In the first instance the aim is to privatize by this method about 400 medium and large firms producing about a quarter of industrial output.

The shares in each firm would be distributed as follows:

- 33 per cent would go to one particular trust, which would thus become the 'lead' shareholder in that firm.
- 27 per cent would go to most or all of the other trusts – small parcels to each.
- Up to 10 per cent would go free to the workers.
- 30 per cent would remain with the Treasury, some of which might be transferred to the national pension fund (ZUS).

Soon after the initial allocation, trade in shares could begin. Individuals could sell their shares in the investment trusts. And trusts could sell their shares in their companies, subject to suitable control by the Anti-Monopoly Office. The firms they manage can also of course borrow, raise new capital and do all other activities necessary for restructuring.

This plan is a remarkable achievement. If enacted, it will reflect a rational form of privatization achieved within four years of the collapse of Communist rule. Happily, the scheme requires no initial choice by the citizen about how to exercise his claims – no vouchers.[12]

How the scheme will work out is difficult to forecast. Since trusts can borrow and raise capital on their own account, the danger of anticompetitive intertrust mergers and takeovers will need watching. This apart, the scheme satisfies our criteria – provided the other firms become privatized soon after.

6 SMALL BUSINESS AND LEASING

Finally, we can turn to the rest of the economy, beginning with the smaller enterprises. Here the sums of money involved are so much less, and the value is so much clearer, that sale (by auction) is feasible. Even so, it is striking that in Poland most sales have been of leasing facilities rather than outright title. Typically, the lease is to incumbent workers or managers. Most of retail trade is already private.

In the Soviet Union leasing by incumbent workers or managers has also become an important feature, even in some large enterprises. According to the 1989 Law on the Principles of Leasing Legislation, the employees and management of a state-owned enterprise have a right not only to lease its assets but also to buy them (at a price determined by the authorities). By early 1991, 2400 industrial enterprises with 1.5 million employees were operating under lease, producing 5.2 per cent of industrial output. They had thus an average size of around 600 workers. In services there was of course much leasing – of 33 000 shops for example.

They are now beginning to be buyouts. By early 1991 in Russia, 14 industrial enterprises, employing 6500 workers, had been bought – as well as 107 service enterprises.[13] But there is substantial political opposition to such privatization that largely benefits the nomenklatura. Indeed, this very fact may account in part for the general opposition to privatization (see Table 22.2). Where large

Table 22.2 Employees' opinions about the future of their enterprise
(USSR, October 1990)

'Our enterprise should':	per cent
Remain in state ownership	40.2
Be reorganized as:	
'Collective enterprise'	14.0
Leased enterprise	8.7
Join venture with foreign capital participation	4.5
Joint-stock company	4.2
Private enterprise with auction sale	4.1
Cooperative	3.5

Source: Goskomstat SSSR, Press Issue, 42 (8 February 1991).

enterprises are leased or bought by incumbent groups, there will always be the danger of a massive rip-off. There is also of course the danger that valuable assets are bought and operated by people who ought to be replaced by more competent alternatives.

7 HOUSING

Finally, there is the key issue of housing. Housing is crucial because without a proper housing market, there will be virtually no labour mobility and mass unemployment will be much more difficult to avoid. It is a complete fallacy to suppose that the stock of housing is fixed in the short run. Given the right incentives, the use of a given space can respond rapidly to economic incentives, making possible major transfers of population from dying areas to centres of growth.

To try to balance housing demand with supply (and to close budget deficits), governments are raising rents. But this will not work. Few countries, if any, operate a system of public housing in which the market clears. In Britain, Mrs Thatcher raised real rents steadily for eleven years. But there are still huge waiting lists for public housing in all high-employment areas, and people coming from outside the region have no chance of obtaining public housing except by subterfuge.

The reason why the policy cannot work is that raising rents is political dynamite. Rent riots are as common as food riots. So the obvious way to create a housing market is to give all houses to those who occupy them. This is little more than the recognition of reality. For at present the existing occupiers have the right of permanent abode, which they can hand on to their relatives. What they cannot do is sell and thus create a market.

One could of course say they should pay something for their houses – or they should pay for extra space above a basic minimum, or some other formula. In our view all formulae would lead to endless delay, as would any scheme for purchase on credit.

There are of course political difficulties with give-away (though less than with any other approach): it gives nothing to those who already own. There is an element of unfairness in this, but there is little that can really be done for existing owners. Fortunately, they are few, compared with the millions of existing tenants who will complain if rents are raised to 'realistic' levels. Of course the grandest houses cannot be given to their nomenklatura occupants and some other solution will be needed there.

One might think that giving people their houses would be immensely popular with those who received them. In Britain, council house sales at knockdown prices are often cited as a major reason for Mrs Thatcher's re-elections. However, give-away may not be greeted with quite such ecstasy in the

East. For, as we have said, it simply ratifies the status quo. And owners would now have to shoulder maintenance charges at least as high as existing rents.

But one thing is certain: give-away would be immensely popular compared with the most likely alternative of raising rents. It should have high priority.

8 CONCLUSIONS

We believe that three main criteria should govern a privatization plan: speed, fairness, and efficient control. From this we derive our optimum scheme, though we recognize that in most countries it needs modifying to existing circumstances:

- Privatization should be by gift, not sale. But distribution by gift does not require distribution through vouchers.
- To ensure efficient control of restructuring, there should be holding companies, each being the chief owner of enterprises drawn from a range of industries. Citizens should be given shares in each holding company. The holding company should be charged to restructure its enterprises and then sell all (or at least 50 per cent) of its shares within a 10-year period. The final pattern of owners would include citizens, workers, foreigners, and pension funds, but provision would be made for some 'stable core' of owners – either interlocking ownership among firms, or major holdings by foreigners, banks or holding companies.
- For smaller companies a different approach would suffice, involving direct sale or leasing.
- If mass unemployment is to be avoided, it is crucial to create a mass market in housing. The only way to do this quickly is to give all houses to their existing tenants.

There is a real danger that Eastern Europe and the Soviet Union will enter a low-level trap where no one has any incentive to invest. Rapid privatization is crucial in preventing this.

Notes

1. We became convinced of the proposed approach after valuable discussions with Stanislaw Gomulka in Poland in April 1990 (see Blanchard and Layard, 1990a, 1990b). Our ideas were improved through discussions with Rudi Dornbusch, Paul Krugman, and Larry Summers, our colleagues in the WIDER Macro-

economic Policy Group, with whom we co-authored Blanchard *et al.* (1991). For Gomulka's own proposals, see Gomulka (1989), which advocates holding companies, and Gomulka (1990), which advocates giving away. For other discussions of the issues, see Lipton and Sachs (1990), Fischer (1991), Tirole (1991), and Gordon (1991).

2. There are of course issues of subsequent managerial efficiency, discussed in section 3.

3. See Grossman and Hart (1980) and Shleifer and Vishny (1986) for further discussion.

4. For a discussion, see Franks and Mayer (1990). For suggestions for Eastern Europe, see Lipton and Sachs (1990).

5. In the initial phase holding companies should not be allowed to borrow money or issue equity on their own account – though their enterprises could do so. Holding companies would thus be prevented from taking each other over.

6. See Blanchard and Layard (1992) for some evidence that Polish enterprises did not increase markups under price liberalization, as might have been expected if there were large monopoly power.

7. For an analysis of the Yugoslav experience, see, for example, Estrin (1990).

8. This issue, as well as the issues associated with workers having both their labour income and part of their wealth invested in the firm, has arisen in the United States in connection with employee share-ownership plans (ESOPs). Those plans transfer shares to workers and are conceptually close to the second approach sketched in the text. Those shares are, after some time, vested. In some cases, firms remain public, with workers being either majority or minority holders. In some cases firms become private, with workers as sole owners; shares of departing workers are then bought at pre-agreed price. In 1989, close to 10 million employees and 10 000 firms were covered by ESOPs. Most firms were small, with a median size of 100 workers. In one-third of the plans, workers were or will become majority holders. Plans often have limitations on workers' voting rights, but the issue of protection of minority shareholders has not been perceived as major. The issue of insufficient diversification of workers' wealth is, however, perceived as important (see Blasi, 1988; Scholes and Wolfson, 1990).

9. Tirole (1991) includes an interesting discussion of the appropriate structure of institutions and remuneration, expressed as a function of the amount of noise in financial signals.

10. See Ministry of Ownership Changes (1991). As this document makes clear, many of the ideas in the scheme were developed by Lewandowski and Szomburg during 1988. Lewandowski is now the minister of ownership changes.

11. For a survey of schemes in other countries, see Estrin (1991) and Grosfeld and Hare (1991).

12. For a scheme involving vouchers, see Frydman and Rapaczynski (1990, 1991).

13. See Filatotchev (1991). See also his DELTA paper (1990). All this activity is arranged by the public holding company, which owns the particular enterprise. Under present arrangements all enterprises are, or are becoming, grouped under these independent public 'concerns'.

References

Blanchard, O. and R. Layard (1990a) 'Economic change in Poland', in J. Beksiak *et al.* (eds), *The Polish Transformation: Programme and Progress* (London: Centre for Research into Communist Economies) (July), 63–83.

Blanchard, O. and R. Layard (1990b) 'Making it safe for capitalism', *Financial Times* (11 July).

Blanchard, O. and R. Layard (1992) 'Post-stabilization inflation in Poland', in F. Coricelli and A. Revenga, *Wage Policy during the Transition to a Market Economy*, World Bank.

Blanchard, O. *et al.* (1991) 'Reform in Eastern Europe', Report of the WIDER Macroeconomic Policy Group (Cambridge, MA).

Blasi, J. (1988) *Employee Ownership: Revolution or Rip-off* (Cambridge, MA: Ballinger Pub. Co.).

Bradley, K. and A. Gelb (1983) *Cooperation at Work. The Mondragón Experience* (London: School of Economics, Industrial Relations Discussion Papers.).

Estrin, S. (1990) 'Labour markets in Yugoslavia: policy issues raised by the current reforms', LSE (August), mimeo.

Estrin, S. (1991) 'Privatization in Central and Eastern Europe: what Lessons can be learnt from Western experience?' Centre for Economic Performance, LSE, mimeo.

Filatotchev, I. (1990) 'Prospects for privatization in the USSR', Département et Laboratoire d'Economie Théoretique at Appliquée (DELTA) (Paris).

Filatotchev, I. (1990) 'Management and employee buy-outs as a form of privatisation in the USSR', Centre for Economic Performance, LSE, mimeo.

Fischer, S. (1991) 'Privatization in East European Transformation', MIT Department of Economics, *Working Paper*, 578 (Cambridge, MA: MIT).

Franks, J. and C. Mayer (1990) 'Capital markets and corporate control: a study of France, Germany and the UK', *Economic Policy Review*, 10, 189–231.

Frydman, R. and A. Rapaczynski (1990) 'Markets and institutions in large scale privatisations: an approach to economic and social transformations in Eastern Europe', New York University, mimeo.

Frydman, R. and A. Rapaczynski (1991) 'Privatization and corporate governance in Eastern Europe: can a market economy be designed?', New York University, mimeo.

Gomulka, S. (1990a) 'How to create a capital market in a socialist country and how to use it for the purpose of changing the system of ownership', mimeo; published in Polish in *Studia Ekonomiczne* (1990).

Gomulka, S. (1990b) 'Stabilisation, recession and growth in Poland', paper presented to a conference in Wilga (April).

Gordon. R. (1991) 'Privatization: notes on the macroeconomic consequences', University of Michigan, Ann Arbor, mimeo.

Grosfeld, I. and P. Hare (1991) 'Privatization in Hungary, Poland and Czechoslovakia" *European Economy, The Path of Reform in Central and Eastern Europe*, Special Edition, 2, 129–56.

Grossman, S. and O. Hart (1980) 'Takeover bids, the free rider problem, and the theory of the corporation', *The Bell Journal of Economics*, 11, 42–64.

Kay, J. and D. Thompson (1987) 'Policy for industry', in R. Dornbusch and R. Layard (eds) (1987), *The Performance of the British Economy* (Oxford: Clarendon Press), 181–210.

Lipton D. and J. Sachs (1990) 'Privatization in Eastern Europe: the case of Poland', *Brookings Papers on Economic Activity*, 2, 293–333.

Ministry of Ownership Changes (1991) 'Mass privatization. Proposed programme', Warsaw (June).

Schaffer, M. (1990) 'On the use of pension funds in the privatization of Polish-owned enterprises', Centre for Economic Performance, LSE (October), mimeo.

Scholes, M. and M. Wolfson (1990) 'Employee stock ownership plans and corporate restructuring: myths and realities', *Financial Management*, 19(1), 12–28.

Schleifer, A. and R. Vishny (1986) 'Large shareholders and corporate control', *Journal of Political Economy*, 94, 461–88.

Tirole, J. (1991) 'Privatization in Eastern Europe: incentives and the economics of transition' (Cambridge, MA: *NBER Macroeconomics Annual*).

23 Post-Stabilization Inflation in Poland (1992)*

with O. Blanchard

In January 1990, as part of its stabilization program, the Polish government fixed the zloty exchange rate and introduced an incomes policy based on partial indexation of wages to the price level. As of April 1991, the parity has held and the incomes policy is still at least nominally in place. But the price level now stands at 4.4 times its level at the inception of the program, and inflation is still running at close to 5 per cent a month. (The behavior of CPI inflation is given in Figure 23.1). How come?

The question is of interest for two reasons. First, the persistence of high inflation after stabilization is a frequent outcome, and the Polish experience provides another case study. Second, the Polish experience is potentially different from those, say of Latin America, in that Poland has embarked on stabilization cum restructuring, putting in place a market environment which was unfamiliar to both firms and workers. Thus, the lessons from Poland are of particular relevance for other Eastern European countries.

Our paper is an exercise in arithmetic. As a matter of arithmetic, one can account for increases in the price level since January 1990 as the results of two sources of shocks, increases in prices over wages, and increases in wages given prices, with wage indexation amplifying the effects of both types of shocks. Our conclusions are that both factors played a role, roughly in equal proportion. Prices have indeed increased faster than wages. Interestingly, the removal of rationing and the exercise of monopoly power appear to have played little role in price increases. Rises in nominal interest payments, in import costs and declines in productivity have been much more important. And wages have increased more than would have been implied just by indexation. This has come from legal loopholes, and in the more recent past, from some relaxation of the rules in response to wage pressure.

---

* Chapter 3 in F. Coricelli and A. Revenga (eds), *Wage Policy during the Transition to a Market Economy. Poland 1990–91*, World Bank Paper, 158 (Washington, DC: World Bank, 1992), pp. 51–72.
We thank Andrew Berg, Fabrizio Coricelli, Stanislaw Gomulka and Jeff Sachs for discussions. We thank Jan Rajski for data and help.

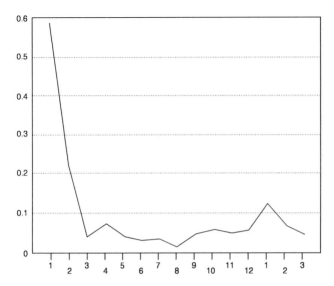

Figure 23.1 CPI inflation in Poland, monthly rate, 1990: 1–to 1991: 3

What are the lessons from the exercise? With the benefit of hindsight, one can think of ways in which price level increases could have been made smaller, and inflation brought under control sooner. Some lessons are obvious: lower indexation would have been desirable, but was and still is politically difficult to implement. Some lessons are less obvious. As we shall see, the mechanics of the incomes policy allowed the firms to pay wages substantially above the norm for some time, forcing them however to abruptly decrease them at the beginning of 1991. The result was a strong reaction against the incomes policy, endangering the policy, forcing concessions from the government, and adding to inflation in 1991; this mistake could have been avoided. Or, to take another example, financial indexation, which is justified on other grounds as well, would probably have led, given the pricing behavior of firms, to much lower price inflation at least at the beginning of the program.

There may also be lessons for the near future. If incomes policies hold in their current incarnation, inflation should indeed be brought under control soon. This in turn raises the larger issues of whether incomes policies can hold, and of whether they should be modified, relaxed or strengthened. We take it up briefly in the conclusion.

Our paper is organized as follows. In section 1, we develop the basic accounting framework, relating inflation to shocks. In section 2, we look at wage behavior. In section 3, we look at price behavior.

1   SHOCKS, INCOMES POLICIES, AND INFLATION

Consider the following simple framework:
  Let p_c and w be logarithms of the nominal consumption price and wage levels. Let p_{c0} and w_0 be the values of p and w at time zero, the month preceding stabilization. Let price behavior be characterized by

$$p_c - p_{c0} = w - w_0 + \epsilon_p \tag{1.1}$$

This equation simply defines ϵ_p as the change in the markup of prices over wages, for whatever reason, from time 0 to time t. Changes in ϵ_p have many sources, which we shall look at later. Let the behavior of the wage be characterized by:

$$w - w_0 = \alpha(p_c - p_{c0}) + \epsilon_w \tag{1.2}$$

If, as a result of incomes policy in Poland, nominal wages had simply been adjusted for the increase in prices with constant indexation coefficient α, the equation would hold with $\epsilon_w = 0$. Again, we shall take the equation as definitional, with ϵ_w capturing all changes in nominal wages not explained by indexation, and leave an explanation of ϵ_w to later.[1]
  Combining the two equations gives a reduced form equation for the price level:

$$p_c - p_{c0} = \frac{\epsilon_w + \epsilon_p}{(1 - \alpha)} \tag{1.3}$$

Thus, the cumulative change in prices from the time of stabilization to any time t is equal to the sum of the two epsilons, times a multiplier which depends positively on the degree of indexation.[2] The decrease in the real wage is independent of the degree of indexation and is just given by ϵ_p.
  What we shall do in the next two sections is to measure and decompose ϵ_w and ϵ_p, thus providing an accounting breakdown of inflation over the last 15 months.

2   THE BEHAVIOR OF WAGES

The wages policy followed since January 1991 has been based on two components, the determination of a wage norm based on partial indexation to the consumption price index, and the use of an excess wage tax.[3] The incomes policy only applies to state firms, not to the private sector. The wage figures we refer to are however overwhelmingly for state firms; information about the private sector wages is still sketchy.

2.1 The mechanics of incomes policy

The evolution of the wage norm has been given by:

$$w_t^* - w_{t-1}^* = \alpha_t(p_{ct} - P_{ct-1}) - \beta_t(n_t - n_{t-1}) + \eta_{1t} \tag{2.1}$$

where w_t^* is the logarithm of the wage norm, p_{ct} is the logarithm of the consumer price index and n_t is the logarithm of employment. The first term gives the effect of indexation. The degree of indexation, α_t has varied through time, from 0.2–0.3 at the beginning of the stabilization plan to 0.6 since August 1990, with a brief increase in July 1990 at 1.0. Monthly values of the degree of indexation are given in the first column of Table 1 below. The second term reflects the fact that, during 1990, firms were free to choose either the wage bill or the average wage as the base for the norm. Thus, as most firms were decreasing employment, they chose the wage bill as the base, allowing the norm wage itself to increase further in proportion to employment. This option was eliminated in 1991. Thus β_t was equal to one in 1990, and to zero in 1991. η captures all other changes in the norm, making (2.1) definitional. Those other changes were unimportant until the end of 1990; they have been at the core of the story since then, and we shall return to them later.

During 1990, the computation of the excess wage tax was as follows. During each month of 1990, each firm would compute the accumulation of differences between the wage and the wage norm since the beginning of the year. As long as its accumulated credit was positive, a firm did not have to pay the excess wage tax. If and when however the accumulated credit was negative, the firm had to pay an excess wage tax on wages in excess of the norm, at the rate of 100 per cent for excesses below 2 per cent, 200 per cent for excesses between 2 and 5 per cent, and 500 per cent for excesses above 5 per cent, and to keep doing so as long as wages remained above the norm. At the end of the year, all credits/debits were to be cancelled, and a new process of accumulation started. As we shall see, this last set of provisions was modified in January 1991.

2.2 The evolution of wages: an informal account

The evolution of the average wage and the average wage norm is given in Figure 23.2. Table 23.1 gives the degree of indexation, the evolution of the average wage, the evolution of the wage norm, bonus payments from profits, the cumulated credit, and the percentage of the wage bill subject to the excess wage tax. The measurement and decomposition of ϵ_w, the excess of the nominal wage above what was implied by indexation, will be given in the next subsection.

For the first six months of the stabilization, wages were substantially below the norm wage. In January, wage inflation was far below that allowed by the

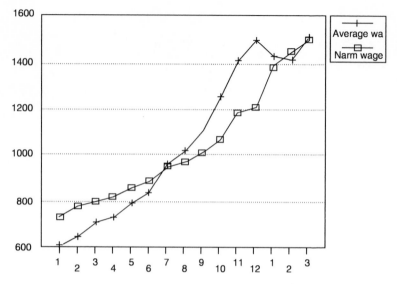

Figure 23.2 Wage and norm wage in Poland, monthly, 1990: 1–to 1991: 3, zl1000

norm. From January to July, wage inflation was in excess of norm inflation, but the wage was still below the norm. The explanation is almost surely to be found in the uncertainty as to what post-stabilization would bring, and the initial attitude of firms and workers was one of restraint. Bonus payments from profits, which always follow a strongly seasonal pattern were high in March and April and lower later.[4]

By July, the average wage had caught up to the norm. But – and the implications of this had not been fully understood before it actually happened – firms had accumulated substantial credit from paying wages below the norm in the first half of the year, which they could use to pay higher wages than the norm, at least until the credit had been exhausted. This was indeed what firms did in the second half of 1990. Actual wage inflation was 45 per cent from July to December, compared to 24 per cent for norm wage inflation. As is shown in column 5 of Table 23.1, aggregate cumulated credit which had peaked in June, became negative in December. Because some firms were above the norm even when the average was below it, some excess wage tax payments were made all through the year. But the percentage of the wage bill subject to the excess wage tax which was very low until October, stood at 3.6 per cent in November, and 7.2 per cent in December (generating considerable revenues for the state in the process).

Table 23.1 Evolution of the wage and the wage norm

				January 1990–March 1991		
Date	Index	Wage	Norm	(Bonus)	Cumulated credit	% of wage bill subject to tax
	(1)	(2)	(3)	(4)	(5)	(6)
1990						
Jan	0.3	613	734	4	125	0.0
Feb	0.2	646	778	56	261	0.1
Mar	0.2	714	797	249	347	0.3
Apr	0.2	732	821	184	439	0.3
May	0.6	795	862	84	509	0.5
Jun	0.6	839	890	52	563	0.7
Jul	1.0	960	945	26	553	1.2
Aug	0.6	1017	972	16	513	1.2
Sep	0.6	1106	1012	9	426	1.5
Oct	0.6	1258	1068	9	246	2.5
Nov	0.6	1418	1187	4	24	3.6
Dec	0.6	1507	1212	63	–234	7.2
1991						
Jan	0.6	1438	1394	65	–45	5.5
Feb	0.6	1423	1459	243	–8	0.8
Mar	0.6	1521	1507	210	–23	0.9

Note:
Monthly, in zl1000. The exchange rate is zl9500 per US dollar.
Source: Institute of Finance, Warsaw; data provided by Jan Rajski.

Thus, as a result of the internal dynamics of the computation of the norm and the excess wage tax, in December the average firm found itself faced with a wage 24 per cent above the norm and, having exhausted its credit, having to pay taxes on the excess of wages above the norm. Compliance with the norm implied a large decrease in nominal wages, a decrease which was just not politically viable. Thus, a number of adjustments were made to the wage norm in January. First, firms with low average wages were allowed an increase in their norm.[5] Second, the principle that accumulation of credit started anew in 1991 was abandoned. For firms with negative credit, credit accumulation was indeed started anew in January 1991. In addition, firms with negative credit were allowed an increase in their monthly norm wage of 1/24 of their negative credit. Thus, a firm which had consistently for example paid wages of 10 per cent above the norm in 1990 would have seen its norm wage increased by 5 per cent in 1991.[6] In contrast, those firms which had unused positive credit from 1990 were allowed to keep it for 1991, in the form of an increase in their monthly norm wage of 1/12 of their unused credit. As a result of these adjustments, the wage norm was increased by 7.7 per cent above what it would have been, given the indexation adjustment for inflation.

Apart from their direct inflation effects, the time consistency dangers of such forgiveness measures are evident. But the government probably had little choice, and these adjustments appeared to have been sufficient for the time being to maintain the incomes policy. In January and February, nominal wages decreased, and wages have stayed roughly within the norm since.

2.3 Accounting for ϵ_w

Given our discussion, we can write the evolution of the wage from December 1989 to any time t as:

$$w_t - w_0 = \sum_{s=0}^{t} \alpha_s (p_{cs} - p_{cs-1}) + [\sum_{s=1}^{t} \beta_s (n_{s-1} - n_s) + \sum_{s=1}^{t} \eta_{1s} + \sum_{s=1}^{t} \eta_{2s}] \qquad (2.2)$$

The first three terms give the evolution of the wage norm. The first is the mechanical effect of indexation. The second is the effect of the use of the wage bill rather than the wage in 1990. The third captures the changes in the norm due neither to price inflation or employment changes; we have discussed them above. The last and fourth term gives the accumulated difference between actual wage changes and wage norm changes since the beginning of the stabilization. For the purpose of our decomposition of inflation later, we shall define ϵ_w as the sum of the last three terms, that part of the change in the nominal wage not due to indexation. The value of each of the four components, and the value of ϵ_w is given in Table 23.2. At the end of March 1991, the cumulated change in the wage was 92.7 per cent. Indexation was responsible for 59.5 per cent, and the cumulated increase in wages over what was implied by indexation was 33.2 per cent. Of that, 18 per cent was due to the decrease in employment up to December 1990, 14 per cent was due to relaxations of the norm, half of it during January 1991, and practically none of it was, by then, due to an excess of the wage above the norm.

3 THE BEHAVIOR OF PRICES

The consumer price index, P_c depends on the price of final goods produced by domestic enterprises, P, as well as the price of other components of the

Table 23.2   Decomposition of cumulative wage change since December 1989

Date	$w - w_0$ (1)	Indexation effect (2)	Employment effect (3)	Residual norm (4)	Residual wage (5)	ϵ_w (6)
1990						
Jan	0.018	0.176	0.011	0.012	-0.180	-0.157
Feb	0.071	0.218	0.022	0.016	-0.186	-0.148
Mar	0.171	0.227	0.035	0.019	-0.110	-0.056
Apr	0.196	0.241	0.048	0.021	-0.115	-0.046
May	0.278	0.268	0.067	0.024	-0.081	-0.010
Jun	0.332	0.288	0.079	0.024	-0.059	0.044
Jul	0.467	0.324	0.095	0.033	-0.016	0.144
Aug	0.525	0.334	0.111	0.034	0.045	0.200
Sep	0.610	0.361	0.125	0.033	0.089	0.247
Oct	0.737	0.395	0.138	0.041	0.164	0.343
Nov	0.857	0.423	0.152	0.104	0.178	0.434
Dec	0.918	0.458	0.183	0.060	0.218	0.461
1991						
Jan	0.871	0.529	0.183	0.128	0.031	0.342
Feb	0.861	0.568	0.183	0.135	-0.025	0.293
Mar	0.927	0.595	0.183	0.140	0.001	0.332

Notes:
(1) Cumulative wage change since December 1989: $\ln w - \ln w_0$; (2) Indexation effect: $\Sigma_{s=1}^{t}\alpha_s(p_{cs} - p_{cs-1})$, with α_s from Table 23.1; (3) $\Sigma_{s=1}^{t}\beta_s(n_{s-1} - n_s)$, with β_s equal to 1 for 1990, 0 thereafter; (4) Cumulative norm inflation not due to inflation or employment; (5) Cumulative wage inflation in excess of norm inflation; (6) cumulative wage inflation in excess of indexation.
Source: Institute of Finance (Warsaw).

consumption basket, such as rents, electricity, and imported final goods. We focus first on P, for which we have detailed information on costs.

Until January 1990, the standard practice for Polish firms – for firms in Eastern Europe in general – was to price according to a markup over total unit cost, adjusted for subsidies and the turnover tax.[7] Thus, a reasonable approach to describing price behavior is to ask what happened to the markup so defined and to the various components of total unit cost after December 1989.

Thus, write P as:

$$P = [(WN + iB + P_mM + \text{Dep} - S)/Y](1 + t)(1 + \mu) \tag{3.1}$$

The term in brackets gives total unit cost. WN stands for the wage bill (including a 43 per cent social security tax, a 20 per cent wage tax and a 2 per cent employment fund tax, all rates which have remained unchanged during the stabilization). iB denotes nominal interest costs, which for most of the period have represented interest costs on working capital, as much of the longer-term debt was wiped out by high inflation in 1989. In Poland, as in most other countries, there is no evidence to suggest that firms made a distinction between nominal and real interest rates in computing costs. Dep stands for accounting depreciation and S stands for subsidies. Y stands for final sales of domestically produced goods. t is the rate of turnover tax. Turnover tax rates have remained unchanged during the stabilization. μ is the markup of price over total unit cost, adjusted for subsidies and the turnover tax. As for our wage equation, our price equation is definitional in that we shall compute the markup as the ratio of the price to the adjusted total unit cost. Our purpose will be to identify the contribution of each of the components to the increase in the price.

3.1 Accounting for ϵ_p

Rewrite (3.1) as:

$$P/W = (N/Y)[1 + (iB + p_mM + \text{Dep} - S)/WN](1 + t)(1 + \mu) \tag{3.2}$$

Define the terms in brackets as X, equal to one plus the ratio of non-wage costs to wage costs. Taking logarithms and rearranging:

$$p - p_0 = (w - w_0) + \epsilon_p, \tag{3.3}$$

where

$$\epsilon_p = (\ln(N/Y) - \ln(N_0/Y_0)) + (\ln X - \ln X_0) + (\ln(1 + \mu) - \ln(1 + \mu_0))$$

The increase in prices of domestic final goods above wages is the sum of three terms, the decrease in labor productivity, the increase in the ratio of non-wage to wage costs and the increase in the markup.

Columns (1)–(3) of Table 23.3 give the evolution of those three components. Column (4) gives their sum, the cumulative increase in the ratio of the price of goods produced by domestic firms to the wage. Column (5) gives the cumulative difference between the consumer price level and the price of domestically produced goods: this difference reflects changes in the relative price of such goods as electricity, rents, or imported goods.[8] And column (6), which is the sum of columns (4) and (5), thus gives the value of ϵ_p.

Table 23.3   Decomposition of cumulative price change since December 1989

Date	Productivity (1)	Non-wage cost (2)	Markup (3)	Sum (4)	Rel. price effect (5)	ϵ_p (6)
1990						
Jan/Feb	0.27	0.32	−0.05	0.55	0.09	0.64
Mar	0.24	0.38	−0.10	0.52	0.14	0.66
Apr	0.32	0.25	−0.11	0.46	0.24	0.70
May	0.26	0.28	−0.06	0.49	0.18	0.67
Jun	0.26	0.28	−0.10	0.43	0.22	0.65
Jul	0.30	0.11	−0.14	0.27	0.29	0.56
Aug	0.21	0.18	−0.12	0.28	0.24	0.52
Sep	0.20	0.16	−0.05	0.31	0.17	0.48
Oct	0.08	0.12	−0.18	0.03	0.38	0.41
Nov	0.11	0.06	−0.15	0.01	0.33	0.34
Dec	0.13	0.36	−0.25	0.24	0.11	0.35
1991						
Jan						0.51
Feb						0.58
Mar						0.57

Notes:
(1) Cumulative rate of labor productivity change: $\ln(N/Y) - \ln(N_0/Y_0)$;
(2) Cumulative rate of change in the ratio of costs to wage costs: $\ln X - \ln X_0$;
(3) Cumulative rate of change in the markup: $\ln(1 + \mu) - \ln(1 + \mu_0)$;
(4) Cumulative rate of change of the price of goods produced by domestic firms: sum of (1) to (3); (5) Cumulative rate of change of the consumer price index relative to the price of domestically produced goods; (6) Cumulative rate of change of the CPI relative to the wage: sum of (4) and (5).

Table 23.4 gives the value of each of the components of X, the ratio of each of the non-wage costs to wage costs. Because of data availability constraints, January and February 1990 are lumped together, and we have no data yet for the cost components for 1991. The reporting practices of firms as well as the assumptions required in the construction of those tables are such that month-to-month movements should be assessed with some suspicion. There appears in particular a curious December effect for the various components of costs. For the time being, the tables use the average for 1989 as the starting point,

Table 23.4   Evolution of non-wage costs in relation to wage costs

Date	Interest (1)	Depreciation (2)	Imports (3)	Subsidies (4)	Sum (5)
1989	0.23	0.60	0.27	0.29	0.85
1990					
Jan/Feb	0.43	1.06	0.39	0.32	1.56
Mar	0.26	1.16	0.40	0.12	1.70
Apr	0.26	1.10	0.31	0.31	1.38
May	0.23	1.06	0.37	0.21	1.46
Jun	0.18	1.01	0.34	0.17	1.44
Jul	0.13	0.87	0.32	0.14	1.07
Aug	0.13	0.86	0.32	0.16	1.23
Sep	0.13	0.88	0.35	0.14	1.17
Oct	0.13	0.88	0.40	0.17	1.10
Nov	0.14	0.89	0.33	0.17	0.96
Dec	0.19	1.25	0.62	0.16	1.64

Notes:
(1) Interest payments as a ratio to wage costs, (iB/WN); (2) Depreciation as a ratio to wage costs, (Dep/WN); (3) Imports of raw and intermediate products as a ratio to wage costs, (P_mM/WN); (4) Subsidies and quasi-subsidies as a ratio to wage costs, (S/WN); (5) Sum of (1) to (3) minus (4), plus other minor costs not included in those columns.

rather than the more appropriate December values of the various components. We hope to get the December values and appropriately modify the computation.

Together, those tables tell the following story for 1990:

(1) The increase in ϵ_p (equivalently the decrease in the measured consumption wage) was largest at the beginning of the stabilization program, and steadily decreased thereafter. In December, it stood at 35 per cent, nearly half its value in January 1990.

(2) The increase in ϵ_p came two-thirds from the increase in P/W, and one-third from the increase in the relative price P_c/P.

(3) The increases in P/W came mostly from the increase in non-wage costs relative to wage costs. This effect was strongest at the beginning, and Table 23.4 tells here a surprising story: Much of the increase in P in January 1990 was due to two factors one might not have thought of before the fact, the increase in nominal interest costs, and the increase in imputed depreciation.

Monthly nominal interest rates were as high as 35 per cent at the beginning of stabilization. While most of the longer term debt had been wiped out by the high inflation of 1989, firms' debt corresponding mostly to working capital was still equal to about 1.5 times their monthly wage bill. Thus, the effect of higher nominal rates was to increase unit cost by close to 10 per cent over the first two months of stabilization.[9] To take into account the effects of hyperinflation in 1989, the book value of capital was multiplied in January 1990 by a factor of 11 (another reevaluation was made in January 1991). This was responsible for a further increase in total unit cost of close to 20 per cent.[10] The importance of these two factors was steadily reduced throughout the year, as nominal interest rates decreased, and inflation reduced the real value of depreciation deductions. The other two non-wage components of costs, the relative costs of imports of raw and intermediate products, and the subsidies to firms, played an increasing role through the year, as subsidies were steadily decreased and, later in the year, the prices of CMEA imports of raw materials were sharply increased.

(4) Another factor in the increase of prices over wages was the decrease in labor productivity due to the sharp decline in sales at the beginning of the stabilization, which was only partially matched by the decrease in employment. The effect on unit costs of this factor by itself was 27 per cent in January. As employment was progressively reduced throughout the year, the effect decreased, but was still accounting for an increase in unit costs of 13 per cent by the end of the year.

(5) Finally, and contrary to widespread expectations before stabilization (including those of the authors), one of the factors which appears to have played no role in the increase in prices was the markup. That the markup would increase as rationing in markets with excess demand disappeared, and as firms were able to exert monopoly power was a plausible forecast. But the markup which had average 45 per cent in December, declined to 38 per cent in January, and kept declining through the year, reaching 24 per cent in November and 13 per cent in December. This decrease should however be kept in perspective, as the markup was unusually high in 1989. Figure 23.3 gives the conventionally defined markup, the ratio of the value of gross sales by enterprises to gross costs minus one, for the years 1989 and 1990. The decline in 1990 is evident, but against a background of an increase in the markup in 1989.[11] Why the markup has steadily decreased is an important question for the future. Increased foreign competition throughout last year is a plausible answer. Only a study across firms according to their degree of exposure to foreign competition will allow us to test this theory.

To summarize, the price shock, ϵ_p was equal to 64 per cent in January, decreasing to 35 per cent at the end of 1990. The two main factors responsible for the increase remaining by the end of the year were the increase in relative non-labor costs, and the decrease in productivity.

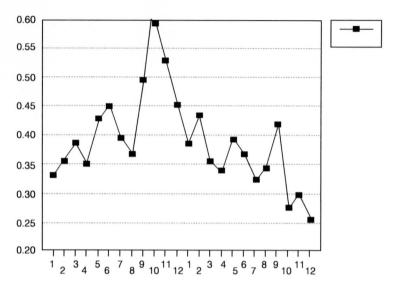

Figure 23.3   Markup over costs net of subsidies, Poland, 1989: 1–to 1990: 12

3.2   Putting things together

Table 23.5 puts our two sets of results together, providing the decomposition implied by (1.3), which we repeat for convenience:

$$p_{ct} - p_{c0} = \frac{\epsilon_{wt} + \epsilon_{pt}}{(1 - \bar{\alpha}_t)} \qquad (3.4)$$

The only complication comes from the fact that indexation has actually not been constant. Thus, for the relation to hold $\bar{\alpha}_t$ has to be defined as average indexation from time 0 to t, that is as

$$\sum_{s=1}^{t} \alpha_s (p_{cs} - p_{cs-1}) / \sum_{s=1}^{t} (p_{cs} - p_{cs-1})$$

Column (1) gives the value of $\bar{\alpha}$. Columns (2) and (3) give ϵ_w and ϵ_p, and column (4) gives their sum. Column (5) gives the sum multiplied by $1/(1 - \bar{\alpha}_t)$, that is cumulated CPI inflation since the beginning of stabilization. The basic conclusions from the table have already been stated. The beginning of 1990

Table 23.5 The proximate sources of inflation

Date	Indexation $\overline{\alpha}$ (1)	Wage shocks ϵ_w (2)	Price shocks ϵ_p (3)	Combined $\epsilon_w + \epsilon_p$ (4)	Cum change in p $p_c - p_0$ (5)
1990					
Jan/Feb	0.29	–0.15	0.64	0.49	0.67
Mar	0.27	–0.06	0.66	0.60	0.82
Apr	0.26	–0.05	0.70	0.65	0.87
May	0.28	0.01	0.67	0.66	0.91
Jun	0.29	0.04	0.65	0.69	0.97
Jul	0.31	0.14	0.56	0.70	1.01
Aug	0.32	0.20	0.52	0.72	1.05
Sep	0.33	0.25	0.48	0.73	1.08
Oct	0.34	0.34	0.41	0.75	1.13
Nov	0.35	0.43	0.34	0.77	1.18
Dec	0.36	0.46	0.35	0.81	1.26
1991					
Jan	0.39	0.34	0.51	0.85	1.39
Feb	0.40	0.29	0.58	0.87	1.45
Mar	0.40	0.33	0.57	0.90	1.50

was dominated by ϵ_p, the contribution of price shocks. The end of 1990 was dominated instead by ϵ_w, the contribution of wage shocks. Since the beginning of 1991, a new set of price shocks has again led to higher inflation.

In retrospect, a number of modifications to incomes policy would probably have allowed for lower cumulative inflation and thus less real appreciation of the zloty. Indexation of debt, for which there are strong arguments in a period of uncertain inflation such as that which follows a stabilization program, could also have reduced the initial shock to ϵ_p by leading firms to include real rather than nominal interest payments.[12] The idea of having a wage rule which determined the level of allowable wages independent of the past path of actual wages – except clearly through their effect on prices –, and allowing credit accumulation for good behavior, appeared to be a good idea. In retrospect, it led firms to put themselves in a position of suddenly having to decrease nominal wages, a situation which put great stress on incomes policy. The same wage rule, but without credit accumulation, would have avoided such stress. Clearly lower indexation, and a longer time between adjustments for inflation would also have led to less inflation: in the absence of indexation altogether, Table 23.5 implies that – *ceteris paribus* – the price level would stand at 2.5 rather than the actual 4.4 times its December 1989 value. But it is not clear that support for the policy would have been maintained with much lower rates of indexation. Are there lessons for the future? Our analysis suggests that, in the near future, the prognosis for inflation control is good if incomes policy is maintained. After the tension of early 1991, incomes policy seems to have survived without drastic relaxation. And after the large additional price shocks of the beginning of the year, no major price shocks are predicted. Thus, given that wages are now constrained by the evolution of the norm, the assumption that inflation will decrease is a reasonable one.

This however assumes that incomes policies remain in place, and raises the much larger issue of the role of incomes policies both in the past and in the near future in Eastern Europe. We discuss this issue, and what we think are the relevant models of wage and price setting for an economy such as Poland in a companion paper (Blanchard and Layard, 1991; see also Layard, 1991 and Commander *et al.*, 1991). In short, we believe that (1) absent incomes policy, there would be an increase in inflation at the current unemployment rate – which stands at roughly 8 per cent; (2) whether the incomes policy can be maintained in the near future depends on the unemployment and profit rates, and that it would not survive much more expansionary monetary and fiscal policies; (3) the incomes policy can be maintained in the near future given current unemployment and profit rates. For the medium run, we believe that (1) the incomes policy can only be phased out when ownership of firms has been clearly defined and collective bargaining is bargaining between two strong sides but (2) the incomes policy, at least in its current form, needs to be phased out to allow for adjustment of the relative wage structure within state firms.

Notes

1. Among the complexities of reality is the fact that the indexation coefficient itself has changed. We ignore this complication for the time being.
2. Note that the cumulative change in price is defined as a log difference. Thus, the fact that the price level at the end of March 1991 stood at 4.4 times its pre-stabilization level corresponded to a cumulative change of 150 per cent. The fact that the wage level stood at 2.5 times its initial level corresponded to a cumulative change of 93 per cent. These are the numbers that we explain and decompose in the tables below.
3. The excess wage tax, which has acronym PPWW is known as Popiwek in Poland. By an extraordinary coincidence, the word means tip, while in English such a tax is known as TIP (for tax-based incomes policy).
4. Our understanding is the limits on bonus payments effectively prevent firms from increasing compensation through bonus payments, avoiding the excess wage tax along the way.

5. The fixing of the initial wage norm for January 1990 at the September 1989 level with some adjustment for inflation from September to December had led, as is usual, to inequities. At the beginning of stabilization, the average wage was roughly equal to the norm. But some industries, which had had a major wage adjustment in October, November or December 1989, were left with a lower relative wage under the wages policy. The intent of the adjustment was in part to adjust those relative wages.
6. This is our understanding of this change.
7. See Schaffer (1990), who gives evidence for the largest 500 firms, from 1983 to 1987.
8. Much of 'food' appears in the final sales of enterprises. And the relative price of food has not been an important component of the overall price story. At the end of March 1991, the food price component of the CPI stood at 3.8 times its December 1989 level, compared to 4.4 for the overall CPI.
9. The implications of the general practice of firms to treat nominal rather than real interest rates as costs were pointed out by Domingo Cavallo (1977).
10. This again assumes that firms treated accounting depreciation as part of cost, and ignored the distinction between marginal and average cost. There is no evidence to the contrary.
11. The behavior of the markup has also been noted by Schaffer (1991). Our number for the markup for December 1989 is lower than in a number of other papers; we have corrected for what we think is a mistake in the 'gross cost of own sales' data for that month.
12. The alternative, which is to have firms use inflation accounting, seems much harder. And there are many other reasons to favor financial indexation of basic borrowing and lending instruments.

References

Blanchard, O. and R. Layard (1991) 'Wage and price determination in Poland, and the role of incomes policy' (Cambridge, MA: MIT), mimeo.
Cavallo, D. (1977) 'Stagflation effects of monetarist stabilization policies', unpublished PhD thesis, Harvard University.
Commander, S., F. Coricelli and K. Staehr (1991) 'Wages and employment in the transition to a market economy', *PRE Working Paper*, 736 (Washington, DC: World Bank).
Coricelli, F. and A. Revenga (1992) 'Wages and unemployment in Poland: recent developments and policy issues', *Wage Policy during the transition to a Market Economy: Poland 1990–91.*
Layard, R. (1991) 'Wage bargaining, incomes policy, and inflation', in S. Commander (ed.), *Managing Inflation in Socialist Economies in Transition* (Washington, DC: Economic Development Institute of the World Bank) (June).
Schaffer, M. (1990) 'How Polish enterprises are subsidized', University of Sussex (mimeo).
Schaffer, M. (1991) 'A note on the Polish state-owned enterprise sector in 1990', Centre for Economic Performance, LSE, *Discussion Paper*, 36.

24 Who Gains and Who Loses from Russian Credit Expansion? (1994)*

with A. Richter

When credit is created, it appears to help those who get it. But this conclusion does not follow, for an increase in credit also causes inflation. This reduces the value of the existing stock of money (or working capital). Thus the process of credit creation also imposes costs. At the same time that it replenishes the working capital of enterprises, it generates further inflation – which erodes that working capital. From the point of view of the economy as a whole, the process is thus largely self-defeating.

To understand the process in full, there are six main steps in the argument, which we develop extensively in this article.

(1) Growth in total credit causes an equal growth in total money (M2), other things being equal.

(2) This growth in money causes inflation. When money growth is constant, inflation equals money growth four months earlier. But when money growth rises, prices rise faster than money, because firms and households react to higher inflation by spending money faster ('velocity increases'). Thus in Russia the inflation rate closely mirrored the growth rate of money four months earlier, but there was also an upward drift in the inflation rate due to higher 'velocity'.

(3) Inflation erodes the real value of money, creating a shortage of real working capital for enterprises and robbing households of their real savings. (A fall in real wealth means that monetary wealth has a lower purchasing power in terms of goods.) Enterprises react to this by seeking still more credit in order to restore their liquidity, while households (who receive little or no credit) can only restore their liquidity by saving more.

(4) Thus inflation imposes an inflation tax on enterprises and households equal to their monetary wealth times the inflation rate (adjusted for any

---

* *Communist Economies & Economic Transformation*, 6(4) (1994), pp. 459–72. This article originally appeared as a Special Report in *Russian Economic Trends*, 2(4) (1993).

interest received on deposits). Thus,

Inflation tax
= Currency × Inflation rate + Deposits × (Inflation rate − Interest rate)

This inflation tax causes a direct reduction in real liquidity.

(5) But, for enterprises, this negative effect has to be weighed against the benefit of new credits. For the direct effect on liquidity from the process of credit creation is

Change in liquidity = New credit − Inflation tax

For enterprises the new credit may well exceed the inflation tax. But for households the opportunity to borrow is negligible. In this way the process of credit creation helps enterprises at the expense of households. It is vital that this reality be understood by all who make decisions about credit emission.

From April 1992 to September 1993 households paid on average an inflation tax equal to 13.3 per cent of GDP each month. This is equal to nearly 30 per cent of all household income.

By contrast, enterprises have paid an inflation tax equal to 12.6 per cent of GDP each month − roughly the same amount as households pay. But to set against this they have received new credits worth 26 per cent of GDP. The process of credit creation has thus gone far beyond what was needed to restore liquidity. No wonder enterprises clamour for more credits, heedless of their direct effect on the well-being of households.

(6) Enterprises may argue that more liquidity is necessary in order to sustain production. But the main forces which can lead to higher output are higher investment and higher productivity. The international evidence shows clearly that these are reduced by high inflation.

We can now examine these arguments step by step.

1 CREDIT GROWTH CAUSES MONEY GROWTH

Money grows mainly due to an increase in credit. This can be seen by looking at the consolidated balance sheet of the banking sector (the Central Bank, the Sberbank and the commercial banks). When their accounts are consolidated, commercial banks' reserves and CBR credit to commercial banks get netted out (see Appendix 1, p. 443). Hence the assets of the banking sector *are* the outstanding credits (see Table 24.1). The liabilities of the banking sector are money (currency and bank deposits) − with net worth making up the difference.

Thus, if credits expand, money expands by the same amount, other things equal. Table 24.2 shows the history of credit growth and money growth in Russia. The bulk of the increase in credit has been credit to enterprises.

Table 24.1   Consolidated balance sheet of banking system

Assets	Liabilities
CBR credit to budget (net)	Currency
CBR credit to CIS states	Deposits
Credit to enterprises (total)	Net worth
Net foreign assets	
Total	Total

The increase in credit has in turn led to a roughly equal increase in money. The discrepancy in 1993 occurs because the profits of the banks, including the Central Bank, have exceeded the growth of Net Foreign Assets.

2   MONEY GROWTH CAUSES INFLATION

This growth of money in turn has raised prices. The effect of money growth on inflation is one of the best documented relationships in all of economics. Figure 24.1 shows the clear working of the relationship in Russia. Monetary growth causes inflation with a lag of about four months. If one estimates the

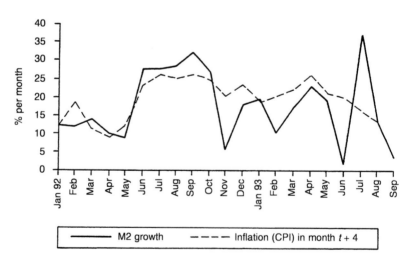

Figure 24.1   Money growth and inflation

Table 24.2 Change in credit and money (Rbillion)

		CBR credit to budget	CBR credit to CIS states	Credit to enterprises	Total credit	Currency	Household deposits	Enterprise deposits	Total money
1992	Q2	240	270	480	990	200	30	350	720
	Q3	330	840	1490	2660	540	50	1400	2420
	Q4	−10	390	2220	2600	720	120	1280	2600
1993	Q1	770	800	3630	5200	890	330	1720	3820
	Q2	−110	920	7040	7850	2530	480	1710	5290
	Q3	3310	840	7770	11920	3450	620	4290	9880

statistical relationship depicted in Figure 24.1, one can accept the standard hypothesis that prices rise in proportion to money (see Appendix 2, p. 444).

There is however one further point that emerges from Figure 24.1. In most of 1993 prices were rising somewhat faster than monetary growth in the corresponding period – by on average about four percentage points a month. Since output was falling by at most two percentage points a month, this means that the velocity of circulation of money was rising. The reason for the rise in velocity is clear. High inflation erodes the value of rubles, so that people decide to keep their rubles for a shorter period.

This dangerous increase in velocity is due directly to the process of credit creation. Velocity in Russia is still far below the level of velocity in most other countries that have Russia's level of inflation. Until now velocity in Russia has been restrained by the slowness of the non-cash payments system, and the fact that cash wages continue to be paid out only twice a month. These delaying factors could easily change – leading to a rapid increase in inflation unless credit growth is further restrained.

An alternative explanation of inflation is often proposed in Russia: that inflation is due to the monopoly power of enterprises. But this explanation does not stand up to scrutiny. It is true that monopoly increases the *relative price* of the monopolist's product. But it does not affect the *general price level*.

For example, suppose that the money stock is constant but we increase the monopoly power of one industry. That industry will raise its money price. So consumers will have less to spend on other goods, and their prices will fall. But once the monopoly has been in existence for a while, it will have no reason to raise its prices further since it will *already* have chosen its optimal relative price. After that it will only raise its prices if all other prices are rising due to an increase in the amount of money.

3   INFLATION IMPOSES AN INFLATION TAX

The rise in prices in turn affects the welfare of different groups in the economy, in particular households and enterprises. We are not here concerned with the impact on real wages, which would be nil if wages rose in line with prices. We are concerned with the impact which inflation has on people and firms as holders of money, who find the purchasing power of their money eroded by the rise in prices.

If somebody owns R100 000 in cash and prices rise by 15 per cent, he loses R15 000 of purchasing power. For him it is exactly as if he had paid a tax of R15 000. We therefore refer to this loss as an inflation tax. There is also an inflation tax on deposits, but in this case the interest rate may have been adjusted upwards in partial compensation for inflation.

Table 24.3   Inflation tax (% of GDP)

		Households	Enterprises	Total
1992	Q2	16.5	11.4	27.9
	Q3	9.4	6.1	15.5
	Q4	19.1	27.2	46.3
	Q2–4	15.0	14.9	29.9
1993	Q1	12.6	17.5	30.1
	Q2	9.3	11.2	20.5
	Q3	10.6	13.9	24.5
	Q1–3	10.8	14.2	25.0

We therefore measure the total inflation tax on all types of money (see Appendices 3 and 4) as

Inflation tax =
Currency × Inflation rate + Deposits × (Inflation rate − Interest rate)

Table 24.3 shows the inflation tax paid by households and enterprises. The size of the tax is truly remarkable.

We begin with the effect on households. In 1992 (Q2–4) households paid in tax 15 per cent of GDP, or 38 per cent of household income. In 1993 (Q1–3) they paid 11 per cent of GDP, or 27 per cent of household income. Most of this tax was a tax on currency, since real household deposits shrunk substantially.

Enterprises paid a nearly equal inflation tax on their money holdings in 1992, and 30 per cent more in 1993. In 1992 (Q2–4) they paid 15 per cent of GDP and in 1993 (Q1–3) 14 per cent of GDP.

4   WHO GAINS AND WHO LOSES?

So who gains and who loses from the process of credit creation? Clearly the households lose, and lose heavily. But the position is different for enterprises, since they also receive the credit which is causing the inflation. This credit increases their liquidity at the same time as the inflation tax erodes it. The balance between these two influences is shown in Table 24.4.

In both years the flow of new credit to enterprises greatly exceeded the inflation tax which they 'paid'. Thus the new credit was much more than was needed to replace their working capital. The corollary of this excess is the inflation tax paid by households.

Table 24.4 Enterprises: credit growth and inflation tax (% of GDP)

		New credit[a] (1)	Inflation tax (2)	Balance ((1) − (2))
1992	Q2	18.5	11.4	7.1
	Q3	39.0	6.1	32.9
	Q4	35.5	27.2	8.3
	Q2 to 4	31.0	14.9	16.1
1993	Q1	22.4	17.5	4.9
	Q2	26.5	11.2	15.3
	Q3	16.6	13.9	2.7
	Q1 to 3	21.8	14.2	7.6

Note:
[a] New credit equals net increase in outstanding credit.

5   IS THE INFLATION TAX SUSTAINABLE?

A inflation tax on the scale we have shown is much higher than ever before recorded. Normally when inflation is high, velocity rises sharply and thus the ratio of money to national income falls. This reduces the inflation tax, since (ignoring interest)

$$\frac{\text{Inflation tax}}{\text{National income}} = \frac{\text{Money}}{\text{National income}} \times \text{Inflation rate}$$

Normally, as the inflation rate rises, the money to income ratio falls, and eventually falls by a greater proportion than the increase in inflation. So there is a maximum ratio of the inflation tax to national income. Generally 10 per cent is the highest value found.

In Russia, however, we find a ratio of 20 per cent in September 1993, and as high as 50 per cent in earlier months. This is because the money to income ratio has so far fallen little (and velocity has risen little) in response to high inflation. Figure 24.2 shows the actual change in velocity, but more relevant is 'underlying velocity' given by our statistical analysis. This has risen by only about one quarter (since early 1993).[1]

Velocity has remained low for the reasons we gave earlier. But it is inevitable that in due course people will understand the burden of inflation tax, and will therefore cut the period for which they hold money. This in turn will reduce the ratio of money to national income.

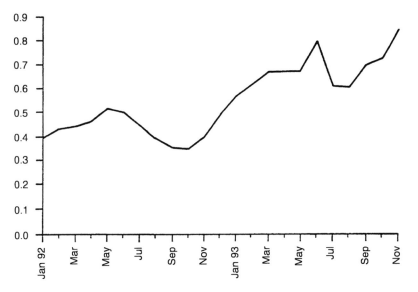

Figure 24.2 Velocity

The only way to sustain the inflation tax (through which enterprises are assisted) will then be to increase further the rate of growth of money and thus inflation. If this response is adopted, it will inevitably lead to hyper-inflation – as it has in all other countries where this approach has been attempted.

Alternatively, Russia can decide that it will no longer fund enterprises at the expense of households. Enterprises will then have to rely mainly on their own earnings, but in return their working capital will no longer be eroded month by month.

6 EFFECT OF INFLATION ON SAVING

The inflation tax on households is no abstraction. It directly affects their living standards. To try and maintain the real purchasing power of their money holdings, people have to save a higher proportion of their income – and spend less on real consumption.

As Table 24.5 shows, households have not in fact been able to save enough to offset the effect of the inflation tax fully. In consequence their real money holdings have fallen sharply – unlike the real money holdings of enterprises (see Table 24.6).

Table 24.5 Saving rate of households

		Inflation tax as % of household income	Saving as % of household income
1992	Q2	45.1	26.4
	Q3	23.1	39.7
	Q4	46.2	21.5
	Q2–4	38.1	29.2
1993	Q1	33.7	30.5
	Q2	24.6	23.3
	Q3	21.7	13.1
	Q1–3	26.7	22.3

Table 24.6 Real money holdings (end of period), R billion (December 1991 prices)

		Households			Enterprises			Total money
		Currency	Deposits	Total	Currency	Deposits	Total	
1991	Dec	162.1	372.0	533.9	11.6	323.6	335.2	869.1
1992	Mar	38.8	64.9	103.7	2.5	87.9	90.4	194.1
	Jun	43.7	43.1	86.8	2.1	89.4	91.4	178.3
	Sep	72.8	35.3	108.1	0.9	169.4	170.3	278.4
	Dec	55.8	22.6	78.4	9.6	136.3	145.9	224.3
1993	Mar	58.0	18.6	76.6	23.7	107.1	130.8	207.4
	Jun	59.9	16.8	76.7	29.5	84.1	113.6	190.3
	Sep	46.2	12.8	59.0	24.4	71.7	96.1	155.1

Appendix 1: The Balance Sheet of the Banking Sector

In a two-tier banking system like Russia's, the impulse for the growth of total credit comes mainly from the growth in Central Bank credit. But, from the point of view of enterprises, it is the total credit which matters, rather than Central Bank credit alone. And it is changes in total credit which, *ceteris paribus*, cause exactly equal changes in the money supply (M2). To show this, we begin with the separate balance sheets of the Central Bank of Russia (CBR) and the commercial banks (including Sberbank, the national savings bank). Both are highly simplified and shown in Table 24A.1. When these balance sheets are consolidated, the starred items drop out.

Table 24A.1 Balance sheets of the Central Bank and of commercial banks

	Assets	Liabilities
Central Bank		
	CBR credit to budget (net)	Currency
	CBR credit to enterprises	
	CBR credit to commercial banks[a]	Commercial banks' reserves[a]
	CBR credit to CIS states	Net worth of CBR
	CBR net foreign assets	
	Total	Total
Commercial banks		
	Commercial banks' reserves[a]	CBR credit to commercial banks[a]
	Credit to enterprises	Deposits
	Banks' net foreign assets	Net worth of banks
	Total	Total

Note:
[a]Credit to the budget should be measured net of government deposits at the Central Bank.

Appendix 2:   The Effect of Money on Inflation

We estimated the following regression for data from May 1992 to September 1993:

$$\pi_t = 0.33 m_{t-3} + 0.27 m_{t-4} + 0.20 m_{t-5} + 3.9D + 3.5$$
$$(3.4) \qquad (3.1) \qquad (2.3) \qquad (2.3)$$

where π monthly inflation (per cent)
 m monthly growth of M_2 (per cent)
 D Dummy $= 1$ after March 1993, 0 otherwise

Note: The positive coefficient on D represents an upward drift in velocity from March 1993 onwards. Specifications more in line with basic theory (e.g. the Sargan–Hendry specification) yielded less usable results.

Appendix 3: Calculation of the Inflation Tax

Tables 24A.2–24A.4 show how the inflation tax is calculated. We assume that all enterprise deposits are in commercial banks and that all deposits in commercial banks are demand deposits. Our approach to measuring the inflation tax is not the same as the standard approach, for reasons explained in Appendix 4. Table 24A.2 deals with the tax on currency holdings: (Tax = Currency × Inflation rate). Table 24A.3 shows the tax on deposits in Sberbank: (Tax = Deposits × (Inflation rate − Interest rate)), and Table 24A.4 shows the equivalent calculation for deposits in commercial banks.

Table 24A.2   The inflation tax on currency

	Currency (R billion)		Monthly inflation (%)	Inflation tax (R billion)		Inflation tax as % of GDP	
	Households	Enterprises		Households	Enterprises	Households	Enterprises
1992							
Jan	179	13	245	417	30	114.8	8.2
Feb	201	15	38	73	5	15.1	1.1
Mar	240	15	30	66	5	11.8	0.8
Apr	298	24	22	58	4	9.0	0.7
May	350	19	12	39	3	5.2	0.3
Jun	437	21	19	73	4	7.7	0.4
Jul	622	24	11	58	2	5.2	0.2
Aug	817	13	9	65	2	5.2	0.1
Sep	986	12	12	108	2	7.7	0.1
Oct	1106	91	23	241	12	13.6	0.7
Nov	1256	193	26	307	37	14.1	1.7
Dec	1464	252	25	340	56	13.2	2.2
Average 1992 (without Q1)						9.0	0.7
1993							
Jan	1983	619	26	464	8	10.3	2.6
Feb	2442	900	25	522	6	10.3	3.5
Mar	2869	1172	20	490	5	8.7	3.4
Apr	3553	1579	23	680	9	8.8	3.8
May	4250	2022	19	671	12	7.7	3.5
Jun	4989	2460	17	780	18	6.6	3.2
Jul	5699	2883	19	1073	28	7.6	3.8
Aug	5548	4444	26	1711	73	10.8	7.0
Sep	7274	3843	21	1589	94	7.9	5.1
Average 1993						8.7	4.0

Table 24A.3 The inflation tax on Sberbank (household) deposits

	Deposits (R billion)		Monthly inflation (%)	Monthly interest rates (%)		Inflation tax (R billion)		Inflation tax as % of GDP	
	Demand	Time		Demand	Time	Demand	Time	Demand	Time
1992									
Jan	206	172	245	0.2	0.8	498	418	137.2	115.1
Feb	217	177	38	0.2	0.8	81	65	16.8	13.6
Mar	231	167	30	0.2	0.8	66	50	11.9	8.9
Apr	241	160	22	0.2	0.8	51	34	7.9	5.3
May	250	157	12	0.2	0.8	29	18	3.9	2.4
Jun	288	130	19	0.2	0.8	50	25	5.2	2.7
Jul	304	126	11	0.2	0.8	32	13	2.9	1.2
Aug	288	154	9	1.3	2.5	23	9	1.9	0.7
Sep	302	154	12	1.3	2.5	32	15	2.3	1.0
Oct	316	155	23	1.3	2.5	67	32	3.8	1.8
Nov	340	157	26	1.3	2.5	81	37	3.7	1.7
Dec	385	168	25	1.3	2.5	86	37	3.3	1.4
Average 1992 (without Q1)								3.9	2.0
1992									
Jan	452	195	26	1.7	6.7	101	35	2.3	0.8
Feb	505	213	25	1.7	6.7	110	37	2.1	0.7
Mar	494	348	20	1.7	6.7	92	38	1.5	0.6
Apr	510	431	23	3.3	8.3	100	58	1.2	0.7
May	550	558	19	3.3	8.3	80	50	0.9	0.5
Jun	498	785	17	3.3	8.3	74	61	0.6	0.5
Jul	732	686	19	3.3	8.3	98	81	0.7	0.6
Aug	807	800	26	3.3	8.3	174	131	1.3	1.0
Sep	859	892	21	3.3	8.3	147	107	0.9	0.6
Average 1993								1.3	0.7

Table 24A.4 The inflation tax on commercial bank deposits

	Deposits (R billion)		Monthly inflation (%)	Monthly inflation rate (%)	Inflation tax (R billion)		Inflation tax as% of GDP	
	Households	Enterprises			Households	Enterprises	Households	Enterprises
1992								
Jan	0	390	245	1.1	0.0	871	0.0	239.6
Feb	2	458	38	1.6	0.4	155	0.1	32.3
Mar	4	544	30	2.1	0.8	139	0.1	24.8
Apr	6	551	22	3.3	1.0	101	0.1	15.6
May	9	596	12	3.6	0.6	48	0.1	6.5
Jun	13	894	19	4.8	1.5	103	0.2	10.8
Jul	17	1 121	11	4.9	0.9	61	0.1	5.5
Aug	19	1 593	9	5.6	0.6	46	0.0	3.7
Sep	23	2 295	12	5.6	1.3	124	0.1	8.8
Oct	28	3 095	23	6.0	4.3	458	0.2	25.9
Nov	33	3 034	26	6.2	6.0	606	0.3	27.8
Dec	41	3 578	25	6.5	6.9	611	0.3	23.7
Average 1992 (without Q1)							0.2	14.3
1992								
Jan	59	4 379	26	6.4	9.7	771	0.2	17.8
Feb	81	4 553	25	6.8	12.5	798	0.2	15.0
Mar	78	5 296	20	7.5	10.0	622	0.2	10.1
Apr	106	6 566	23	8.3	13.7	886	0.2	10.5

Table 24A.4 continued

	Deposits (R billion)		Monthly inflation (%)	Monthly inflation rate (%)	Inflation tax (R billion)		Inflation tax as % of GDP	
	Households	Enterprises			Households	Enterprises	Households	Enterprises
May	95	8 122	19	8.6	9.9	724	0.1	7.7
Jun	117	7 001	17	9.5	8.4	597	0.1	4.9
Jul	189	11 149	19	10.3	13.7	817	0.1	6.0
Aug	228	12 272	26	11.1	31.0	1 745	0.2	12.9
Sep	264	11 288	21	11.2	24.1	1 154	0.1	6.8
Average 1993							0.2	10.2

Notes: Money is defined as cash plus deposits of households and enterprises. Data on money relate to the end of the month.

Inflation tax = (Inflation rate − Interest rate) × Money stock (mid month).

The year's average inflation tax 'payment' as a percentage of GDP is calculated by taking the average of monthly inflation tax payments as percentages of monthly GDP.

Appendix 4: Standard Analysis of the Effects of Inflation on Private Wealth

In the standard analysis there are two main agents in the economy: the government and the private sector. All money except base money is inside money (i.e. where some private agent's assets are equal to another private agent's liability).

When the government runs a deficit, the Central Bank prints base money equal to ΔM_0. In the steady state the velocity of M_0 is constant, as is output. Hence

$$\text{Inflation rate} = \frac{\Delta M_0}{M_0}$$

The inflation tax is a tax on base money only, so that

$$\text{Inflation tax} = \text{Inflation rate} \times M_0 = \Delta M_0$$

Hence the inflation tax is exactly equal to the normal tax which would have been needed to balance the budget. Through the inflation tax the government can obtain the same real resources as it could through the equivalent normal tax.

To see why the inflation tax is only 'levied' on base money consider the following:

$$\text{Base money} = \text{Currency} + \text{Commercial banks' reserves}$$

and (from the banks' balance sheet)

$$\text{Commercial banks' reserves} = \text{Deposits} - \text{Credits}$$

Credits here mean credit from commercial banks. It follows that

$$\text{Base money} = \text{Total money } (M_2) - \text{Credits}$$

Thus the inflation tax can also be thought of as a tax on the difference between M_2 and Credits. This is perhaps the more fundamental concept.

The idea here is that although private agents lose from tax on their money, they gain from the fall in the real value of their debts. As long as the banks make no profit, the interest they pay to money holders will equal the interest they receive from credit recipients. In this case, even if inflation affects the interest rate, it will be true that the conventional calculation of the inflation tax, which is

$$\text{Inflation tax} = \text{Inflation rate} \times (M_2 - \text{Credit})$$

will equal the change in non-bank private sector wealth caused by inflation.

450

For our purposes this analysis has to be substantially adapted.

(i) We want to know the incidence of the inflation tax on households and enterprises *separately*. Even if banks made zero profits (which is not true in Russia) we should need to take interest payments into account, since the interest paid and received by each sector would not normally be equal.

(ii) We need to allow for the fact that owing to negative real interest rates *new credit* issued as part of the inflationary process does not have zero value, as would normally be the case in a Western economy. The present value is very difficult to evaluate because the appropriate discount rate is not obvious. Clearly the present value of one ruble borrowed is less than one ruble, since some real repayment has to be made. The size of repayment is very difficult to know given the scale of subsidised credits. But, if interest rates are low relative to inflation and discount rates are high, the present value of one ruble borrowed may indeed be close to one. For purpose of exegesis we shall call the ratio α.

Therefore if C is credit, the effect of inflation on enterprise wealth per period is:

Effect of inflation on enterprise wealth =
Value of extra credit + Value of erosion of debt − Inflation tax =
$$\alpha \Delta C \quad + \quad C(\pi - i_b) \quad - \text{Inflation tax}$$

Table 24A.5 gives these figures on the assumption that the interest rate paid by borrowers was (thanks to subsidies) one half the unsubsidised borrowing rate. This also enables us to make a rough estimate of α, assuming that the pure time discount rate is 2 per cent per month.

Table 24A.6 column (1) gives the total effect as a percentage of GDP. This calculation has involved many assumptions. And it does not altogether address the question in the mind of the enterprise director. His most immediate concern is with the liquidity of his enterprise, which is given quite simply by

Effect of inflation on enterprise liquidity = ΔC − Inflation tax

This is the expression which we give in the main body of the article, and which is reproduced in Table 24A.6, column (2).

As can be seen, the change in the real wealth of enterprises brought about by the inflationary process was

in 1992 (Q2–4)   27 per cent of GDP
in 1993 (Q1–3)   20 per cent of GDP

This greatly exceeds the increase in enterprise liquidity shown in column (2) of Table 24A.6. It is however a much more tentative figure and for reasons given above we concentrate on the liquidity measure.

Table 244.5 Effect of inflation on net worth of firms

	Total credit	Change in credit (ΔC)	Monthly borrowing rate (i_b)	Monthly inflation rate (π)	$\alpha\Delta C$	$+C(\pi - i_b)$	− Inflation tax	= Total effect
Jan 92	517		0.012	2.450		1 260	900	360
Feb	697	180	0.015	0.383	155	256	161	250
Mar	918	221	0.019	0.298	175	256	143	288
Apr	1 025	107	0.021	0.216	74	201	105	169
May	1 042	17	0.030	0.120	8	94	50	51
Jun	1 393	351	0.037	0.186	212	208	107	313
Jul	1 860	467	0.041	0.110	186	129	64	252
Aug	2 153	293	0.044	0.090	92	99	48	143
Sep	2 878	725	0.045	0.120	302	216	126	392
Oct	3 731	853	0.048	0.230	564	680	470	774
Nov	4 487	756	0.049	0.260	533	945	642	835
Dec	5 102	15	0.051	0.250	423	1 018	667	774
Jan 93	6 177	1 075	0.053	0.258	748	1 267	884	1 131
Feb	7 140	963	0.055	0.247	650	1 371	985	1 036
Mar	8 734	1 594	0.060	0.201	925	1 228	830	1 322
Apr	9 685	951	0.062	0.232	606	1 648	1 205	1 049
May	11 357	1 672	0.064	0.185	894	1 370	1 057	1 208
Jun	15 773	4 416	0.067	0.199	2 477	2 087	987	3 577
Jul	17 380	1 607	0.076	0.220	939	2 511	1 332	2 118
Aug	19 962	2 585	0.077	0.260	1 692	3 663	2 697	2 658
Sep	23 544	3 582	0.080	0.210	1 982	3 073	2 025	3 030

Note: $\alpha = 1 - \dfrac{[(1 + i_b)(1 - \gamma)]^t}{(1 + \pi)^t}$, where i_b is the borrowing rate, γ is the discount rate (here assumed to be 2% per month) and π is the monthly inflation rate.

Table 24A.6 Effects on enterprises (% of GDP)

		Change in real wealth	Change in real liquidity
1992	Q2	21.9	7.1
	Q3	20.6	32.9
	Q4	37.3	8.3
	Q2–4	26.6	16.1
1993	Q1	22.4	4.9
	Q2	18.2	15.3
	Q3	17.7	2.7
	Q1–3	19.4	7.6

Note

1. This is less than the increase in measured velocity. Measured velocity rises when monetary growth falls due to the lagged effect of this upon price inflation. But this must be a transitional phenomenon.

25 Can Russia Control Inflation? (1994)*

SUMMARY

Russia has come near to hyper-inflation and pulled back from the brink. But the position is still delicate. In this paper we review the past history, and then what needs to be done and the difficulties of doing it.

Russian monetary policy since the reform has gone through three phases – first quite tight (in early 1992), bringing inflation down to 10 per cent per month in the summer; then very loose (till late 1992), pushing inflation up to over 25 per cent per month; and then a gradual tightening.

Inflation in spring and summer 1993 was a steady 20 per cent per month. But the Central Bank credit targets adopted for the year would reduce inflation progressively. The recent rise in the real value of the rouble is an encouraging sign. However there are five major question marks.

- Can Central Bank credit really be controlled?
  The pressures are immense. But, on the good side, public opinion is now, since the near hyper-inflation towards the end of last year, quite hostile to inflation. It is also fairly resigned to the economic chaos involved in restructuring.

  However there remain massive pressures, which are exacerbated by the role of enterprises as providers of much housing and health care (where the transfer of responsibility to local authorities takes time).

  For these reasons Russia is not currently planning a 'shock therapy' stabilisation, which could only be mounted with massive foreign aid. There are well known difficulties in a gradual approach. But, if Russia succeeds in reducing inflation in the next year, it is quite likely to be by the gradualist route.

- What about credit to the rouble area?
  As part of the process, inflationary credit to other former republics of the Soviet Union will have to be further curtailed. This would be easier if each country had its own currency, fully convertible with the Russian rouble. But

---

* J.A.H. de Beaufort Wijnholds, S.C.W. Eijffinger and L.H. Hoogduin (eds), *A Framework for Monetary Stability* (Boston: Kluwer Academic Publishers, 1994), pp. 269–81.

credits will still be necessary to sustain good will and some necessary trade links. They should be directly financed by the Russian government as a political decision and only indirectly by the Central Bank.

• Will control of Central Bank credit lead to control of commercial bank lending?

Even if the growth of base money can be controlled, this will not reduce inflation at all rapidly if the money multiplier explodes, as frequently happens in a credit squeeze. It would therefore be wise to require a new higher ratio between extra deposits and extra reserves. Alternatively some reserves could be converted to bonds.

• May not velocity explode?

The velocity of circulation of M_2 (about 7 times per year) is remarkably low given the high inflation rate. It has been held down by the primitive payments system. The payments system will improve. Thus, if dollarisation took hold, velocity could easily explode. This emphasises the importance of a rapid disinflation.

• What about inter-enterprise credit?

One way in which velocity might increase is through an increase in inter-enterprise credit (as a replacement for bank credit). This danger is exaggerated. Inter-enterprise credit is now quite low by international standards, since enterprises are increasingly unwilling to deliver supplies unless payment is assured.

Conclusion

Thus the dangers in the present situation are substantial and are well understood by the reform ministers in the government. So long as the present reform government remains in place Russia is unlikely to experience hyper-inflation. But disinflation could well be a prolonged and difficult business.

1 THE RECORD

In the most essential ways, the generation and control of inflation in Russia happens in the same way as in any other country:

(i) Money affects real interest rates and thus real aggregate demand (with a lag)
(ii) Real aggregate demand affects inflation (with a lag).

In addition, since Russia is a rather open economy (with exports equal to nearly a half of GNP),[2] there is an important transmission mechanism through the exchange rate:

(iii) The real interest rate affects the real value of the rouble, with low real interest rates lowering the value of the rouble and thus directly fuelling inflation.

Let us review the history, beginning with monetary growth and its effect on inflation. This is shown in Figure 25.1.

Monetary policy has gone through three main phases. The first phase from January to June 1992 was one of relative tightness. On 2 January most prices were liberalised and jumped on average by a multiple of 3.5. But the Central Bank did little to accommodate this increase, since the aim of the liberalisation was to eliminate the pre-existing monetary overhang. Instead the Bank pursued a quite cautious policy, which led to a money growth (M2) of around 10 per cent per month up to May 1992.

But by that time strong pressure had developed in favour of greater credit expansion. At the meeting of the Congress of Peoples' Deputies in April, one enterprise director after another spoke of the shortage of working capital, and from June onwards the authorities responded. In the orgy of credit creation in 'phase 2' the Central Bank, which comes under the Supreme Soviet, happily took the lead.[2] But the reform members of the government were also forced unwillingly to agree to large 'directed' credits through the Ministry of Finance. As a result monetary growth leaped up to over 25 per cent per month for the next five months.

This had a disastrous (lagged) effect upon inflation (see Figure 25.1). In response to the relatively responsible policy at the beginning of the year,

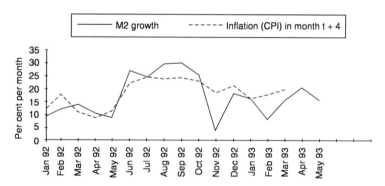

Figure 25.1 Monetary growth and subsequent inflation

inflation had fallen steadily to around 10 per cent per month in August. But it then leapt to a plateau of around 25 per cent per month for the rest of the year. By the end of the year there was a general fear of hyper-inflation.

This led to a third phase of monetary policy (more restrained), which began with Yegor Gaidar's establishment of the Credit Commission in October 1992 and was intensified with the appointment in January of Boris Federov as Deputy Prime Minister for macroeconomics. He at once announced targets for the growth of Central Bank credit up to the end of the year. These were to follow a declining growth path, reaching roughly 20 per cent per quarter in the third quarter and 15 per cent in the fourth. In April the Central Bank agreed to the target for Central Bank credit in the second quarter, and in consequence credit growth fell from 57 per cent in the first quarter of the year to 38 per cent in the second quarter. (The target was 32 per cent). In May the government and Bank agreed with the IMF on the targets for Central Bank credit mentioned earlier, which do not include the credits provided to the government by the IMF. But unfortunately performance in the 3rd quarter was nearer to 40 per cent rather than the target of 20 per cent.

The more responsible 'phase 3' monetary policy has already led to some improvement in inflation, which has fluctuated around 20 per cent a month since March. However sustained improvement will depend heavily on what happens in the rest of the year.

The fundamental problem in controlling inflation is that in the short-run this involves a fall in output. The Phillips curve is alive and well in Russia.[3] Inflation only falls when output falls. Tight money does not immediately reduce inflation. It reduces real balances which in turn reduces output, and thus ultimately inflation.

Figure 25.2 shows the history of real balances and of output (net of trend). As can be seen, the tight money policy of the first half of 1992 led to a steady

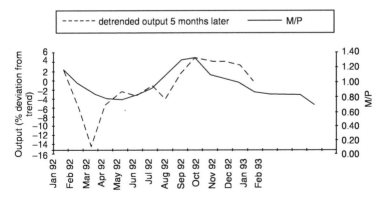

Figure 25.2   Effect of real balances on output (5 months later)

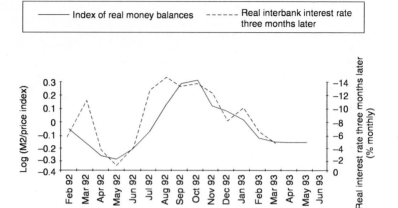

Figure 25.3   Real money balances and the real interest rate

fall in real balances, which in turn accelerated the fall in output. But from June to October real balances rose, leading to a stable level of output from September until early 1993. Since then output has again been falling, due to the tighter stance of monetary policy.

Real balances affect real output through their effect on real interest rates. Market real interest rates have risen from around minus 14 per cent in November 1992 to around minus 4 per cent in mid-1993 (see Figure 25.3). And the Central Bank refinance rate has now moved up to close to the market rate.

The real interest rate affects not only output but also the real value of the rouble, as is predicted by the standard interest parity condition and the notion that in the long-run the real exchange rate is determined by real rather than monetary forces (see Figure 25.4). Real interest rates have risen sharply from around minus 14 per cent last November to around minus 5 per cent in mid-year. This is the main explanation for the sharp real appreciation of the rouble since mid-June. From mid-June to late September (when the Parliament was dissolved) the nominal value of the rouble was roughly constant at around R1000 to the dollar. This is perhaps the most tangible success of the new monetary policy. A rise in the dollar wage (from 25 in November 1992 to 60 in August 1993) can only be good for inflation. Following the suspension of Parliament the exchange rate fell to nearer R1300, due to increased uncertainty. Since then new policy measures have been announced and their effects on the exchange rate remain to be seen.

Can the policy last and can Russia really control inflation? There are a number of major problems which we have to consider:

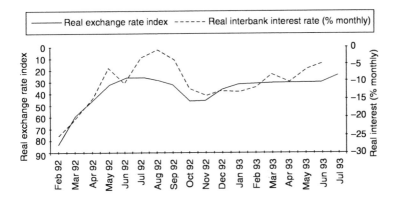

Figure 25.4   The real interest rate and the real exchange rate

(i)   Can Central Bank credit to the budget and to enterprises be controlled?
(ii)   What about credits to the rouble area?
(iii) Will control of Central Bank credit lead to control of commercial bank lending?
(iv)   May not velocity explode?
(v)   What about inter-enterprise credit?

In the rest of the paper we address these issues in turn.

2 CENTRAL BANK CREDIT, UNEMPLOYMENT AND GRADUALISM

The biggest single problem is controlling Central Bank credit. In 1992 the growth in Central Bank credit equalled 40 per cent of GNP.[4] This level of seigniorage is almost without parallel and was only possible because Russia's primitive payments system prevented an increase in the velocity of circulation of money (see below).

If inflation is to be controlled, new Central Bank credit will have to be severely curtailed. According to the agreement reached in May with the IMF, Central Bank credit (excluding that financed by sale of IMF dollars) would grow by the following percentages of GDP:[5]

(1992)	(40)
1993 Q2	14
1993 Q3	7
1993 Q4	5

This would be difficult to achieve because of pressures coming from all three recipients of Central Bank credit – budget, enterprises and other CIS states. In many ways the distinction between finance for the budget and for enterprises is somewhat artificial, since the budget props up enterprises through explicit subsidies, while credits at negative real rates do the same through an implicit subsidy from the banking system.

The budget

Even so, it is worth recording that the budget (and extra-budgetary funds) have not been the main sources of credit creation. In 1992 total taxes (including revenue of extra-budgetary funds, like the Pension Fund) amounted to around 60 per cent of GNP – almost exactly the same as total expenditure.[6] The record of tax collection has been one of the unsung triumphs of the economic reform.

In 1993 the balance of the rouble budget was positive up to the middle of the year – due as before to the principle of sequestering applied by the Ministry of Finance. In July however the Supreme Soviet made a bigger challenge on the budgetary front than ever before and this (together with its attack on privatisation) was a major factor leading to the dismissal of the Parliament.

Given the huge pressure for credit to enterprises, the optimal target for credit to the government (excluding credit to enterprises) is negative. To achieve such a balance will require further efforts to increase government revenue especially from the energy sector. After the July price rise the price of gas was still only about 10 per cent of the West European level (at the prevailing exchange rate), and taxes on gas are minimal (at 15 per cent excise). Russia should be using its huge energy sector as a milch-cow for the budget.

An important step towards non-inflationary budgetary finance would also be the sale of government bonds. The government is currently taking a small step in this direction, but the scope for this is limited due to the current popular distrust of government.

Credit for enterprises

In any event the main problem has been and remains the problem of finance for enterprises (whether 'directed credits' issued through the Ministry of Finance or commercial credits through the commercial banks). This is the area where the main macroeconomic battle has been fought and will continue to be fought. Enterprises want credits above all to pay wages,[7] and to avoid the pain of restructuring. In 1992 inflationary finance provided them with a major transfer of resources from households, as the following figures show:

% of GDP in 1992

Credit to enterprises	31
– Inflation tax on enterprises	– 21
Net transfer to enterprises	10
Inflation tax on households	14

The real money balances of households are now so low that the scope for any future transfer to enterprises is limited. Enterprises now pay nearly all the inflation tax – a fact which should make them less enthusiastic about inflationary finance. But there will still be enormous pressure for finance to avoid layoffs, i.e. inflationary finance which transfers resources from sound enterprises with good bank balances to weak ones that may never repay their debts.

Will such pressures prevail? Two main arguments are used in favour of credits – that they will prevent unemployment and that they will enable enterprises to continue to finance housing and health care.

Unemployment

At present Russia has an official unemployment rate of 1.4 per cent.[8] This is clearly well below any conceivable long-run equilibrium rate of unemployment, which is roughly 9 per cent in Western Europe and perhaps the same in Poland and Hungary. Unless Russia moves at a reasonable pace towards its equilibrium unemployment rate, inflation is bound to increase. Will Russia choose unemployment or hyper-inflation?

There are some grounds for optimism:

(i)   Public opinion polls reveal strong aversion to inflation. Inflation affects everybody. Unemployment will affect a minority, though the fear of unemployment is of course widespread.

(ii) Resignation in the face of misfortune has been a long-standing feature of Russian life. This is reflected in the absence of organised social protest against the economic reform, and in the weakness hitherto of the trade union movement (though this could change in the absence of easy wage increases).

(iii) Even in the West unemployment has on most occasions, but not all, led to apathy rather than unrest.

However there are two special features in Russia which give ground for concern:

(i)   Enterprises are major providers of social services, especially housing, health, kindergartens and holiday facilities. Unless housing and health can be off-loaded onto local government, enterprises will be able to mount a convincing argument that they should be supported. And if these responsibilities are transferred to local authorities, this will put more strain on the budget.

(ii) For the next 9 months Russia will be in an election campaign (for the Duma in December and for the President in June). This will make tough policies difficult, so that it remains quite likely that stabilisation in Russia will happen by stealth.

Gradualism

Such a gradualist stabilisation would be very unusual by world historical standards. Is it conceivable?

There are standard arguments to the contrary, which go roughly as follows. A policy can only work if it shows results. So long as inflation is high, everybody waits till they know what relative prices will prevail. Sales of goods whose prices are held down (like energy) remain low, waiting for future price rises – and this adds to the shortages. Investment is suspended and barter is everywhere. Enterprises with bad debts gain at the expense of those with solid bank balances. On this view the situation deteriorates steadily till a clean break is made.

That view may well be correct for standard capitalist economies. It is not so clear for a transforming economy, where the scope for improvement is so great that it may occur even in an environment of macroeconomic disorder. Indeed some Russians concerned with privatisation believe privatisation will work better in an environment of abundant inflationary finance rather than one of monetary tightness.

I doubt the last of these arguments. My own preference would be for a clean and quick stabilisation. But as a forecaster I would not rule out the possibility of a gradual stabilisation by stealth.

The government's current plan falls in between the extremes of stealth and shock therapy. It involves a clear timetable for disinflation, but no specific moment of stabilisation

The timetable is a timetable for Central Bank credit. This involves not only tight credit for the Russian economy but also tight credit for the other former republics of the Soviet Union.

3 THE ROUBLE AREA

In 1992 about a quarter of new Central Bank credit went to the rouble area outside Russia. This financed the trade deficits of the other states with Russia.

But the roubles thus created were of course paid to Russian enterprises and thus increased the base money supply in Russia.

Up to July 1992 the provision of credit to other states was almost automatic. Each state's Central Bank created its own non-cash roubles, and these could then be used to pay Russian suppliers. But from July 1992 onwards Russia refused in principle to accept net payments from other republics beyond agreed limits. All payments from (say) Kazakh enterprises to Russian enterprises had to be made through the Kazakh Central Bank and the Russian Central Bank and there were agreed limits to the extent of deficit permitted to the correspondent account of the Kazakh Central Bank with the Russian Central Bank. Thus in effect the (non-cash) Kazakh rouble became a different currency from the Russian rouble.

But there was no organised foreign exchange market in Russia for exchanging these currencies. Bit by bit such a market is developing. Kazakh commercial banks can now hold correspondent accounts with Russian commercial banks in Moscow, so that some trade can be financed through direct bank to bank payments rather than through the Kazakh and Russian central banks. This will help the development of this foreign exchange market.

But so far the existence of separate, non-convertible currencies has had a serious impact on inter-state trade. Inflation in each state has also wreaked havoc with trade, both between states and within. Barter is still a major method of inter-state trade.

There are now essentially two possible types of monetary arrangement to restore trade. One, favoured until recently by the IMF and the EC, is to maintain the single currency area with credit rationing by Russia, or at least to operate a fixed exchange rate system with current account convertibility and some kind of Payments Union or Inter-State Bank providing limited credit to deficit countries. The problem of any such system is that the pressure for excess credit creation would be intense.

The alternative is separate currencies, floating against each other. This too would be subject to strong inflationary pressures. For Russia runs a massive current account surplus with most other states. If this is cut speedily, it will cause major hardship and President Yeltsin does not want to sour relations with his neighbours. Thus it is not going to be possible to operate without some on-going rouble credits or subsidies to the successor states.

But these need to be explicit acts of political will, and not a haphazard outcome of monetary operations. Any subsidies or credits to other republics should be included in government budgetary outlays and covered, if necessary, by credit issued to the government.

The second approach seems less likely to lead to excessive credit creation. If eventually the other CIS states want to peg their currency to the Russian rouble, that would be fine. But first they must learn to manage their currencies on their own.

The actual trend of affairs here remains somewhat unclear. In September, 6 countries signed up to a rouble zone controlled in principle by Russia, but involving dangers of massive credit creation.

Foreign aid

The final element affecting the generation of Central Bank credit is foreign aid. If this aid goes to the government (or Central Bank) the dollars can then be sold for roubles, thus reducing base money.

The Russian GNP is so small (under $100 billion) that foreign aid can make an enormous difference. The IMF Systemic Transformation Facility is $3 billion – of which the second half ought to be released and disbursed this year. The proposed Stand-By is $4 billion and if the government now produces a good programme that should begin flowing early in 1994. In addition trade credits should be provided as far as possible to the government – to be sold in exchange for roubles. Subsidised sales of such credits should cease, which will limit demand. But such finance can at least double the flow of dollar sales beyond that provided through the IMF and World Bank,[9] all of which will help to restrain the growth of Central Bank credit.

4 THE PYRAMID OF CREDIT

If Central Bank credit can be controlled, two further links must hold if inflation is to be controlled:

(i)   The money multiplier (M_2/M_0) must not explode, and
(ii)   Velocity (PY/M_2) must not explode.

Let us consider first the money multiplier.

Russia has a two-tier banking system with some 2000 commercial banks, about 10 of which account for the vast majority of banking business. Some of these ten are elements of the old structures (the saving bank, the agricultural bank, the industry and construction bank, the Moscow Business Bank and so on) and some are new.

Commercial banks are subject to a required reserve/deposit ratio of 20 per cent (since April 1992).[10] However they also hold excess reserves which have increased from almost nothing in April 1992 to over 15 per cent of deposits (on average) in the early months of this year. The reasons for this increase are unclear. It is unlikely that the payments system deteriorated since April 1992, so we cannot assume that these excess reserves correspond to a necessary float. It is more likely that they are the accumulated effect of continued emission of Central Bank credit plus increasing uncertainty about the solvency of potential borrowers. The obvious danger is that, if credit emission becomes more restrained, this will lead banks to lend a higher fraction of their assets, thus offsetting in part at least the intended effect of the credit squeeze.

As Rostowski shows,[11] this is a standard pattern in situations where credit growth first expands and then contracts: at first the money multiplier decreases and then (during the stabilisation) it expands. This has been found not only in Latin America but also in Poland and Yugoslavia.

To guard against this danger, a number of policies are available. Raising the reserve ratio is a crude way, which could unfairly penalise banks with low existing ratios. A fairer method along these lines would be a new and higher marginal reserve ratio, so that extra deposits would require a higher addition to reserves. Alternatively reserves above some limit could be converted into bonds. But some kind of action does seem advisable.

The second element in the money multiplier is the currency/deposit ratio. This too has risen from 20 per cent when the reform began to over 30 per cent. Nothing can be done abut this but there is again the obvious risk that, if inflation comes down and payments systems improve, the currency/deposit ratio could fall, increasing the money multiplier. Thus the authorities need to keep a tight watch on M_2 as well as simply Central Bank credit.

5 VELOCITY AND THE PAYMENTS SYSTEM

But suppose bank credit and M_2 remain under control. Is this enough to control inflation? It depends of course on what happens to velocity.

In most countries velocity rises when credit is easy, and it falls when credit is tight. This has not been the Russian experience. Figure 25.5 gives the history of velocity. It is not well correlated with inflation.[12] The remarkable thing is how low velocity has remained, despite a year of 20–25 per cent inflation per month.

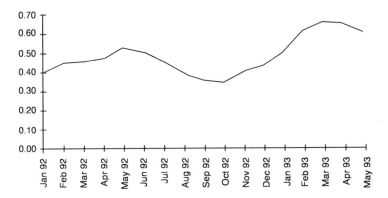

Figure 25.5 Monthly velocity of M_2

The explanation seems to lie in the crudity of the payments system. Firms can only draw currency to pay wages, which is done every two weeks as it has been for very many years. And payment of non-cash money by money order is subject to unpredictable delays and obstruction, making it necessary for enterprises to hold abnormally large bank balances. Dollars are used as a means of payment in quite limited sectors of the economy. But the situation is extremely fragile. The payments system is bound to improve now that correspondent accounts between banks are legal and all clearing does not have to go through the Central Bank. Similarly, dollarisation of transactions can easily spread, if inflation continues. The Tanzi–Oliveira effect is a less likely source of hyper-inflation, as most tax payments are made in advance on the basis of forecast liabilities. But a rise in velocity could quite easily come from nowhere. Enterprises already have dollar deposits of around $11 billion in Russian banks – roughly the same value as their rouble deposits. If the dollar became a regular means of payment, velocity could easily take off. It is this which makes progress in disinflation so vital.

6   INTER-ENTERPRISE CREDIT

There is a widespread belief that monetary policy cannot control inflation in Russia due to the absence of effective bankruptcy laws. According to this argument, if bank credit is squeezed, purchases and sales of goods will continue to occur at ever-rising prices, and firms will become more and more indebted to each other.

This belief was reinforced by the 'arrears crisis' of mid-1992. Under the old Communist system, firms took limited responsibility for paying their bills (which corresponded essentially to the costs of physically allocated supplies). Instead bills were sent to the debtor's bank, which paid them according to pre-assigned priorities as and when money came into the debtor's bank account. During 1992 overdue payments rose sharply from virtually zero to about 3 months' GDP by the middle of the year. Unfortunately, a netting-out process was instituted for all debts up to 1 July – so that all net debtors ended up clear, and net creditors were credited by the Central Bank.[13] Since then many statements have been made ruling out any repeat performance, and urging sellers to check on the liquidity of their customers. More and more sellers now insist on prepayment.

Since last autumn the 'arrears problem' appears to have remained well under control, despite some vociferous complaints. At the middle of 1993 overdue payments to industrial enterprises equalled only half a month's GDP – a quite respectable figure by Western standards.[14]

As the credit squeeze tightens, the figure is bound to rise. But, so long as creditors do not expect to be paid if they sell to bankrupt enterprises, the arrears problem will remain under control. Even in 1992 it was completely wrong to assert that Western style monetary policy could not control inflation in the absence of effective bankruptcy laws. The whole of East European experience demonstrates this fallacy and it is equally fallacious in Russia.

Notes

1. This is at mid-1993 exchange rates which clearly undervalue domestic sales. Using this exchange rate imports were about 20 per cent of GNP in mid-1993.
2. Mr Geraschenko became Chairman in mid-July.
3. There are not enough time series observations to estimate the curve. But on a cross-section of 38 manufacturing industries there is a clear relationship between the change in wages and the change in employment (comparing December 1992 with January–February 1991), see *Russian Economic Trends*, 2, (2), p. 65.
4. Due to high Central Bank profits from interest charges and some accumulation of government deposits in the Central Bank, M_0 grew by only about 25 per cent of GNP.
5. The government's fourth quarter target is now unclear on the assumption that the second tranche of the IMF's Special Transformation Facility is not now provided in the fourth quarter, as originally planned.
6. *Russian Economic Trends*, 2, (2), pp. 8–13. Other estimates are in the range of 52–54 per cent.
7. An incomes policy could be very dangerous in the difficult political situation in Russia.
8. A World Bank/Goskomstat household survey reports a figure of 3 per cent.
9. The Bank is now negotiating a second Rehabilitation Loan of around $0.6 billion.
10. The ratio was 5 per cent in January 1992 and rose in monthly steps up to April.
11. J. Rostowski (1994) 'Dilemmas of Monetary and Financial Policy in Post-Stabilisation Russia' in A. Aslund (ed.), *Economic Transformation in Russia*, Printer Publications, London.
12. The best explanation of velocity comes from the simple equation illustrated in Figure 25.1. According to that

$$\dot{p} = \dot{m}_{-4}$$

where $\dot{p}$ is inflation and $\dot{m}$ is monetary growth. This implies that the change in velocity is $\dot{y} + \dot{p} - \dot{m} = \dot{y} - (\dot{m} - \dot{m}_{-4})$ which is dominated by the term $(\dot{m} - \dot{m}_{-4})$. Thus velocity *rises* in a disinflation, due to the lagged response of price inflation to reduced monetary growth. As we point out later, this relationship could easily change.

13. It appears that total net debt equalled only about 14 per cent of total gross debt (R450 billion, compared with R3200 billion). Most of the R450 billion was used to pay taxes. However one cannot be sure that, without the netting out process, most of the taxes would not have been paid in some other way.
14. Total outstanding payments (overdue and other) to industrial enterprises amounted to just over one month's GNP.

26 How Much Unemployment is Needed for Restructuring? The Russian Experience (1995)*

with A. Richter

1 INTRODUCTION

Transferring labour from old to new jobs is a major problem in any country; in a post-communist country it is even more difficult. There are clearly two ways through which it can be done – the 'pull' route involving direct moves from old to new jobs, and the 'push' route, where displaced workers first enter the pool of unemployment before being hired into new activities. The two routes are illustrated in Figure 26.1.

When Communism fell and Western economists began to think about the process of redeployment, nearly all of them thought of unemployment as a key transfer mechanism.[1] Subsequent experience has cast doubt on this approach – especially experience in Russia.

The original consensus centred around four propositions.

1 To have enough labour available to fill new jobs, there would have to be a substantial *pool of unemployed*.
2 Old state enterprises should, therefore, be encouraged to *lay off* workers during the transition, at rates higher than is usually observed in the West.
3 Unemployment would thus *build up rapidly* to high levels, and then fall as the need for further restructuring diminished.
4 Since high unemployment would be temporary, a suitable form of temporary Western aid would be support for the *social safety net*.

---

* *Economics of Transition*, 3(1) (March, 1995), pp. 39–58.

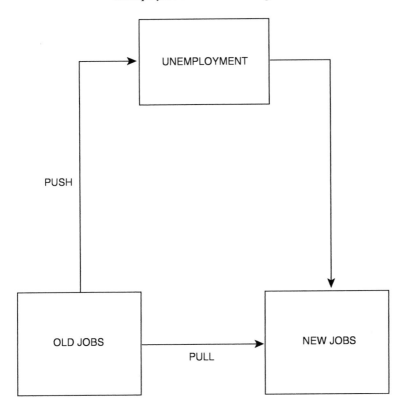

Figure 26.1 Two routes for reallocating labour

In practice, events have not followed this pattern.

1 Most jobs in the new private sector have been filled by people who were still in work rather than unemployed.[2] They reach their new jobs by being 'pulled' out of old ones, rather than by first being 'pushed' into unemployment. Also, most of the unemployed are eventually rehired in old state enterprises rather than in the new private sector.
2 There have been substantial falls in employment in old state enterprises, but these have mainly occurred not through lay-offs but through non-replacement of workers who leave (that is, through natural wastage). As

Table 26.1 Registered unemployment: flows and stocks, 1993

	Inflow rate %	Outflow rate %	Unemployment %	"Standardized" unemployment %
	(1)	(2)	(3)	(4)
Russia	0.3	15.2	1.4	5.5
Poland	0.7	4.9	15.4	13.8
Czech Republic	0.7	20.5	2.8	3.9
Slovak Republic	1.2	8.2	13.5	12.6
Hungary	1.5	6.2	14.3	11.2
Bulgaria	0.9	7.5	16.4	18.5
Romania	0.3	2.4	9.5	n.a.
UK	1.4	12.0	10.4	10.3
USA (1988)	2.0	46.0	5.5	5.5

Sources: Rows 1–6: Columns (1) and (2) from Commander and McHale (1994, Table 1) and Columns (3) and (4) from Boeri (1994, Table 1).
Row 7: Columns (1) and (2) from Commander and McHale (1994, Table 1) and Column (3) from EBRD, *Transition Report* (October 1994).
Row 8: Employment Department, *Employment Gazette* (June 1994).
Row 9: OECD, *Employment Overlook* (1990, Table 1, and Economic Report of President.
Inflow rate = Monthly Inflow/Employment. Outflow rate = Monthly Ouflow/Unemployment

Table 26.1 shows, *inflow rates* to unemployment have typically been lower than in the West. However, unemployment *levels* have been very high in many countries (though not the Czech Republic or Russia). This is because of very low outflow rates from unemployment, so that by now roughly a half of the unemployed in Eastern Europe have been out of work for over a year. This is exactly the same problem as has bedevilled Western Europe and results not from problems of restructuring but from the way in which the unemployed are treated and wages are determined.

3   In most East European countries inflation has not been falling sharply in the last one or two years, suggesting that these countries may be near their equilibrium unemployment rates. It is not surprising, therefore, that an equation to explain equilibrium unemployment rates in OECD countries does quite well at explaining the unemployment rates of different East European countries (Burda, 1994).

In general, one is forced to the conclusion that unemployment policy in most of Eastern Europe has not been a great success. Unemployment rates have been far higher than needed as a transfer mechanism from old to new jobs. However, both the Czech Republic and Russia have so far avoided this high unemployment. The Czech Republic has done so through a remarkably high outflow rate, partly achieved through wage subsidies to employers hiring unemployed people (Burda and Lubyova, 1994). Russia has had a particularly low inflow rate to unemployment. This is because Russia has a much more flexible wage structure than any OECD country.

In this respect Russia conforms better to the OECD's recommendations than any OECD country.[3] If a firm experiences a negative shock its real wages fall sharply, so that few workers are laid off. The others do, however, start looking for other jobs and in due course labour is redeployed to other sectors through the mechanism of voluntary quitting rather than through unemployment.

The purpose of this paper is to document and explain this process, and finally to evaluate whether more unemployment would have been desirable. Section 2 sets out the basic facts about lay-offs and about unemployment – both open unemployment and the hidden unemployment within firms. Section 3 attempts to explain the low unemployment. Section 4 provides a policy evaluation, and section 5 concludes.

1 BASIC FACTS[4]

Flows and redeployment

Let us begin with the flows in the labour market. These are depicted in Figure 26.2. The arrows show what percentage of the workforce flowed in each direction in 1993, and the figures in brackets show the stocks in early 1994.

The main point is the low level of lay-offs. The flow of redundant workers in 1993 was only 1.5 per cent of the workforce. As Table 26.2 shows, this is the total flow recorded by enterprises – the numbers entering unemployment must have been somewhat lower.

How was this low level possible? One possible explanation which quickly comes to mind is that nothing changed – simply stagnation. But this is wrong. There were considerable changes in the pattern of employment.[5] As Table 26.2 shows, employment fell by 8 per cent in industry, but rose in services. And there were further changes at firm level. Even when the majority of industrial firms were contracting their employment, a sizeable minority were expanding (see Figure 26.3).

So how did the redeployment occur without lay-offs? The main reason is that workers quit the declining firms in droves. Altogether 23 per cent of workers

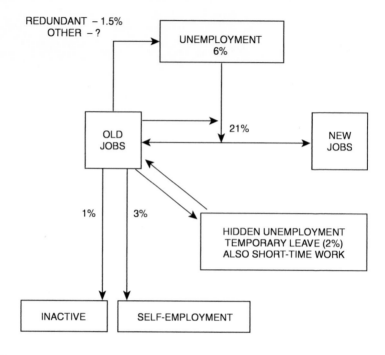

Figure 26.2 Labour force flows, as percentage of labour force in 1993 (stocks, as per cent of labour force in 1994: Q1)

quit their previous employer in 1993 (see Table 26.2). Most of them were hired elsewhere – either into new jobs or into gaps created by workers moving into new jobs. If there had not been a sufficient rate of new job creation, then clearly this chain of hiring would not have occurred, nor probably would the voluntary quits. But in fact, the labour market was remarkably buoyant, with even industrial enterprises reporting a 3.8 per cent vacancy rate in Summer 1993 (Standing, 1994).

Hidden unemployment

A second reason for few redundancies was hidden unemployment within firms. One form of this is involuntary leave. The figures commonly used in public debate here have been wildly exaggerated.[6] In early 1994 some 2 per cent of the workforce were on involuntary leave at any one time – see Table 26.3. (Nearly all of these were in the industrial sector, where they represented some

Figure 26.3 Percentage of industrial firms expanding over the previous month, 1992 and 1993
Source: Russian Economic Barometer 1994(1), p. 52. The data refer to a sample of around 180 medium-sized firms (employing 250–2000 employees). See also Aukutsionek and Kapelyushnikov (1994).

6 per cent of the industrial workforce.) In addition, some 4 1/2 per cent of workers were working reduced hours (short-time). The total hours lost through shorter hours averaged $1\frac{1}{2}$ per cent of the potential hours in the economy.[7] These numbers were a sharp step up from 1993 but there is no evidence of any subsequent increase during 1994. Moreover, hiring continued at the same rate in 1994 as in 1993.

Another coping strategy for firms is simply to delay paying their bills – including the wages they owe (which are normally the second claim upon an enterprise's money after tax payments). By August 1994 total wage arrears in industry, construction and agriculture had reached 44 per cent of one month's wage bill in those sectors – up from around 9 per cent a year earlier. Again there was a sharp rise in early 1994, after which arrears were fairly stable. Of workers interviewed in a household survey in January 1994, 18 per cent had not yet been paid last month's income– up from 10 per cent in the previous quarter.[8]

Table 26.2　Employment during 1993 (organizations with over 200 workers)
(% of employees in the sector)

	Net change in employment	Hirings	Separations	Of which workers made redundant	Vacancies (end of year)
Total	−4.0	21.1	25.1	1.5	1.1
Industry	−8.7	20.1	28.8	1.8	0.6
Agriculture	−3.2	11.3	14.5	0.7	0.3
Transport	−3.1	26.5	29.6	1.1	1.5
Communications	−1.1	32.1	33.2	1.7	1.4
Construction	−5.4	38.7	44.1	1.9	0.8
Retail sales and catering	−5.0	22.7	27.7	2.9	0.5
Wholesale trade	−2.4	21.7	24.1	2.9	0.8
Accommodation services etc.	5.7	36.2	30.5	1.3	2.5
Health, sports, social safety net	0.8	18.0	17.2	0.5	2.5
Education	2.7	15.2	12.5	0.5	1.4
Culture and arts	1.8	15.7	13.9	0.8	2.7
Science and scientific services	−13.0	12.1	25.1	2.0	1.2
Finance and insurance	7.3	22.5	15.2	1.8	2.7

Source: Goskomstat (1994).

Table 26.3　Workers on involuntary leave (paid or unpaid) and short-time
work (percentage of total labour force)

	1993: Q1	Q2	Q3	Q4	1994: Q1
Involuntary leave	0.6	0.5	0.7	1.2	2.1
Short-time working	1.3	1.3	1.5	2.2	4.4

Source: Goskomstat (1994).

Table 26.4 Employment (million)

	1992	1993	1994: Q1	Q2	Q3	Q4
Employees	67.6	64.6				
Self-employed	4.4	6.4				
Total	72.0	71.0	70.5	70.3	70.2	69.6

Source: Goskomstat (1994).

Self-employment and non-participation

A third mechanism for averting mass redundancies has been the growth of self-employment: the net flow into self-employment in 1993 was 3 per cent of the labour force. The final form of adjustment is exit from the labour force altogether; but in 1993 labour force participation in fact fell by only 1 per cent of the workforce.

Employment and unemployment

We can now look at the total change in the numbers employed and unemployed. The available figures provide a fairly consistent picture – with employment falling some 2 per cent between 1992 and mid-1994, and unemployment rising by about $1\frac{1}{2}$ percentage points.[9]
Table 26.4 shows employment. The number of employees fell quite sharply, but some two-thirds of this fall was offset by strong growth in self-employment (including partnerships). Table 26.5 shows unemployment. The measure of increased unemployment is fairly consistent, whether we use the Labour Force Survey or registrations at employment offices.

The Labour Force Survey questionnaire is based on the European Labour Force Survey, and the answers make it possible to calculate the number of people unemployed on the ILO–OECD definition. On this basis people are unemployed if they (i) did no work for pay or profit in the reference week, (ii) sought any work within the last month, and (iii) are available for work. The definition is narrow in one way since it excludes people who did any work (however little), but wide in another since it includes people seeking work of any kind (however little).[10]

Using the ILO–OECD definition, the proportion of Russian workers unemployed rose from 4.8 per cent in 1992 to an estimated 6.7 per cent in

Table 26.5 Stock of unemployed people (percentage of labour force)

	1992	1993	1994 March	1994 Sept
Labour force survey	4.8	5.5	6.2	6.7
Registered as out of work at the FES, of which:	1.0	1.4	1.8	2.3
redundant	0.5	0.5	0.4	0.5
receiving benefits	0.2	0.6	1.2	1.6

Source: Goskomstat (1994 and monthly reports); Federal Employment Service.

September 1994 (see Table 26.5). Of the unemployed, about a fifth were students or pensioners and only a third were looking for permanent work.

The numbers registered as 'out of work' with the Employment Service were little more than a third of the survey figure. But the striking fact is that the Employment Service number had risen by almost exactly the same amount as the survey number – from 1.0 per cent of the workforce in 1992 to 2.4 per cent in October 1994.

We have no detailed data on the duration of unemployment except for those registered at the Employment Service. The percentage of such individuals unemployed for more than one year has been rising but is still low (see Table 26.6). However, *Goskomstat* report that at the end of 1994 roughly

Table 26.6 Unemployment duration of the FES registered unemployed (percentage of those registered as unemployed at end of month)

	March 1993	March 1994
Less than 1 month	15	15
1–4 months	43	40
4–8 months	29	24
8–12 months	11	12
More than 1 ycar	2	9
All	100	100

Source: FES.

17 per cent of survey unemployed had been out of work for over a year, and more than 50 per cent had been out of work for more than 4 months. As regards characteristics, unemployment rates decrease with education, but not very sharply (see Table 26.7). Unemployment is especially high for young people, but it is striking that young people have not so far had more trouble in the labour market. Survey unemployment rates are similar for men and women. Registered unemployment is higher for blue-collar workers – not

Table 26.7   Unemployment rates (survey-based), 1993

	Unemployment rate (%)	% of the unemployed	% of the FES unemployed Jan 94
By education			
Higher education	3.1	10	21
Special secondary school	5.2	32	41
General secondary school	5.8	37	25
Uncompleted secondary	6.0	21	13
Total	5.5	100	100
By age			
15–19		15	5 (up to 18)
20–24		15	13 (18–22)
25–29		11	8 (22–24)
30–49		45	57 (25–)
50–54		6	
55–59		5	
60–72		3	7 (pensioners)
By sex			
Male		51	32
Female		49	68
By occupation			
White collar			29
Blue collar			71

Note: The last column relates to the officially 'registered unemployed'.
Source: Goskomstat (1994).

Table 26.8   Source of unemployment for people registered at the
Federal Employment Service (percentage of total)

	December 1992	December 1993	September 1994
Redundant	41	21	27
Quit	38	47	
Other	**21**	22	
	100	**100**	**100**

Note:
The table refers to those 'out of work', not the narrower number of officially
'registered unemployed'.
Source: FES.

surprising when about a quarter of former white-collar workers getting jobs
through the Employment Service in 1992 got blue-collar jobs.

Unemployment benefit

To understand unemployment one must understand *inter alia* the system of
unemployment benefit. The benefit system, set up in 1991 and administered by
the Federal Employment Service works through a network of 2400 employment offices. Details of benefits are set out in Appendix 2. Broadly, workers
made redundant get paid by the firm for three months. But they need to
register at once with the Employment Service if they are to be entitled to
collect benefit from the fourth month onwards. This benefit is a declining
proportion of their former nominal wage, subject to a minimum benefit equal
to the minimum wage (about 10 per cent of the average wage in the economy in
June 1994). In a period of high inflation the minimum wage soon becomes the
binding constraint. All other unemployed workers are entitled to the minimum
wage (except those who are sacked for disciplinary reasons or refuse job offers,
who can be refused benefit for up to three months).

So how many of the unemployed **have** been made redundant? In September
1994 only one-quarter of the stock of those registered as out of work had been
made redundant (see Table 26.8). Of the inflow to unemployment, redundant
workers formed an even smaller proportion. In 1994, 4.5 per cent of workers
registered a new spell at the Employment Service, but this included only 1.0 per
cent of the workforce who had been made redundant (see Table 26.9).[11]
Interestingly the number of redundant workers who registered a new spell at

Table 26.9 Flows of unemployed people registering with the Federal
Employment Service (percentage of labour force, annual rates)

	All workers		Redundant workers	
	Inflow	Outflow	Inflow	Outflow
1993	2.9	2.8	0.4	0.6
1994: Q1	4.5	2.9	0.9	0.7
June	4.1	3.5	1.1	0.7
September	4.6	4.0	1.0	0.5

Note: See Table 26.5.
Source: See Table 26.5.

the FES in 1993 was under a half of the total redundancies of around 800 000 reported by firms in Table 26.2.

This raises the more general question of why the numbers of unemployed registered at the Employment Service are so much less than the number of unemployed reported in surveys. There are a number of possible reasons.

1 Benefits are low in nominal terms, and their value is quickly eroded by inflation. Even so, it is surprising that young people at least would not claim them.
2 The Employment Service covers a fairly small percentage of placings in the economy. It is said to have on its books a third of all vacancies, but these are skewed towards manual vacancies (about 85 per cent of the total). About one-third of those who leave the Employment Service's register (of those 'out of work') go to a job obtained with the help of the Service. This flow amounts to about 1 per cent of the workforce per year – compared with a total flow of hiring of around 20 per cent (see Table 26.2).
3 The Employment Service has so far provided very little retraining for unemployed workers. In September 1994 the numbers in training were 46 000 – only 3 per cent of the number of unemployed on the books of the Federal Employment Service.
4 Some people do not like to claim money except for work done.
5 Parts of the population are out of reach of the Employment Service.
6 Some of the survey unemployed are lying; in fact they have undeclared earnings.

Those who believe that unemployment in Russia is already high will tend to stress reasons 1–5. Others will tend to stress 6. The truth is that some people who are in desperate trouble (but doing some petty work) may be excluded from both Survey and FES figures, while even the FES figures may include some people who are not in serious trouble.

2   WHY SO FEW LAY-OFFS?

Wage flexibility

Why have there been so few lay-offs? The main possible cause is high wage flexibility. We begin with the average real wage before looking at the more important issue of relative wages. When real aggregate demand fell from 1991 to 1992 the real consumption wage dropped by a third. Recorded real wages in reporting enterprises have remained around that level ever since.

More striking is the fact that, as between industries, the fall in real wages was greater whenever the contraction of demand was bigger (as reflected in the fall in employment). In fact for each extra percentage fall in employment between January/February 1991 and December 1992, industry wages fell by 2.4 per cent.[12]

How does this compare with flexibility in other countries? We have only limited evidence. A similar analysis was done for Poland relating changes in employment and in wages in 20 industries during 1990. In the Polish case a 1 per cent change in employment induced a 1.7 per cent change in relative wages (Jackman, Layard and Scott, 1992). This analysis is for a shorter time interval than the one for Russia referred to above. One would expect the impact to be stronger in the short term than in the long term, since, in industries subject to a once-and-for-all relative decline in demand, relative wages would begin to recover once enough people had left. Thus, if we look at changes in Russia during 1991 a 1 per cent fall in employment was associated with a 5.8 per cent fall in relative wages.[13]

These numbers from post-communist countries can also be compared with some Western numbers. In Britain for changes in wages and employment in the two-year period 1982–4 the coefficient was 0.2 – compared with 2.4 for Russia (and for the period 1983–5 in Britain it was only 0.04).[14]

So why have relative wages been so flexible? One possible explanation would be high inflation. As John Maynard Keynes pointed out in the 1920s, it is difficult to get falls in nominal wages. Thus, one might explain higher relative wage flexibility in Russia by its higher-than-average inflation. However, inflation has been high enough in other post-communist countries to accommodate most of Russia's changes in relative wages.

Table 26.10   Social services provided by enterprises, 1993 (percentage of
surveyed individuals who received these services)

	April	August	December
Free or subsidized meals	14	9	9
Subsidized food and other goods	21	13	20
Retraining and education	6	4	4
Income support for hardship cases	14	12	11

Source: VCIOM Survey of the Working Population (1993).

Worker attitudes

The flexibility of wages is mainly explained by the importance which workers
place on retaining formal ties with their enterprise, as well as opportunities to
earn extra-enterprise income which exist for some workers. Russian workers
appear to be much more willing to let wages fall, if this saves jobs. Why?

There are five main reasons. First, there is the social support provided by
enterprises – above all health care and housing. When a worker leaves his
enterprise, his family may lose access to the enterprise's hospital/clinic or to
financial support for other health care. Housing is different. No one can force a
worker out of his home. But if the enterprise is in financial collapse, it cannot
heat or maintain the housing. Other forms of social support are subsidized
child care, meals, food and vacations – as well as social assistance in case of
hardship (see Table 26.10). However, many of these are already on the decline.

Second, the enterprise is a source of personal identity. As in Japan,
membership of an enterprise structures a person's life much more than in the
West. There is, therefore, greater aversion to open unemployment in Russia
and Japan than in the West.

Third, the alternatives to staying in the enterprise are poor. Unemployment
benefit is low and its earnings-related component unindexed. By contrast, if the
worker stays in his enterprise his nominal wage is likely to rise even if his
relative wage falls. Moving home to find other work is difficult due to a rigid
housing market and local *propiska* systems, so that laid-off workers cannot
easily seek a better life in another city.[15]

Fourth, retaining ties to the enterprise allows workers to continue using the
enterprise's tools and equipment to earn some additional income from petty
jobs. And a significant number of workers are earning income from second
occupations in the private sector. The share of wages in total household

income has been declining steadily. It is due to these extra-enterprise activities, undertaken either by enterprise employees themselves on a part-time basis or by their family members, that wage-earners can survive on lower real wages.

Finally, workers are in general poorly organized to oppose such cuts. Except in mining, worker organization is weak, and trade unions historically have played a minimal role in wage determination. In 1992 only 27 strike days were lost per 1000 workers. This compares with the OECD average of 110 in that year (or 340 on average for 1983–92). For Poland the 1992 figure was 230 (or 100 on average for 1990–92). In Russia the incidence of strikes has been falling: in 1993 only 4 days were lost per 1000 workers, and in 1994 (up to November) less than 1 day per 1000 workers was lost.

Managerial attitudes

Wage flexibility is certainly important but it is not the only reason why lay-offs are low, since managers are certainly keeping on some workers whose marginal productivity is zero. There are probably six main reasons. The first is that workers actually do have some power in the enterprise, especially where they are shareholders.[16] Even if they do not strike, there is an implicit *quid pro quo* of managers promising few redundancies to employees (made possible by low real wages), in exchange for employee-shareholders not voting the manager out of his job. A second reason is that beyond this pressure, many managers see employment as a social good and do not eliminate jobs for paternalistic reasons. They may also be under pressure from the authorities. Third, access to cheap government credit may be directly linked to the number of people earning a living through the enterprise. Fourth, many managers have been overoptimistic about the future. This is nicely demonstrated in Table 26.11.

There are also two important financial reasons why firms may gain little (or sometimes nothing) from laying off workers. One is the excess wage tax, which is incorporated in the profit tax and works as follows.[17] In computing taxable profit, an enterprise can only include as wage-cost the wage bill that would have been paid if the average wage was six times the minimum wage. Hence, average wages above six times the minimum wage are subject to a profits tax rate of around 35 per cent.[18] Thus, enterprises have an incentive to reduce their average wage.

This in turn affects the relative advantage of dismissing a worker, compared with keeping him on but cutting his wage. If the worker is retained but his wage is cut, this reduces the average wage, so that the savings in excess wage tax may well exceed the wage cost of retaining the worker rather than firing him.[19]

The other financial consideration is the substantial cost of severance. If the firm has to pay the worker for another three months anyway (albeit without any wage increase), its immediate gain from a lay-off is small.

Table 26.11 Percentage of industrial enterprises experiencing changes and forecasting changes, 1994: Q1

	Increase	No change	Decrease	Total
Output				
Forecast	18	49	31	100
Actual	8	28	61	100
Employment				
Forecast	6	56	35	100
Actual	2	45	50	100

Note:
These data are from the quarterly Business Survey conducted by the Centre for Economic Analysis and Forecasting. It involves 1400 firms in the majority of manufacturing sectors.
Source: Centre for Economic Analysis and Forecasting (1994), 1994.1.

The soft budget constraint

A quite different explanation for low lay-offs is based on the soft budget constraint. In this case when firms get into financial trouble, it is not the workers who come to the rescue (by accepting real wage cuts) but the government (by providing cheap credit, subsidies and tax relief). Clearly, this has also been an important mechanism in Russia, but one of diminishing importance. Unfortunately there are no comprehensive data on industrial support in Russia. At the federal level there were, by 1994, few subsidies or cheap credits except to agriculture, coal and defence industries. But regional governments also spent 5 per cent of GDP on the 'national economy', which includes substantial targeted subsidies – and they also gave targeted tax relief. Thus, although monetary conditions have frequently been very tight (with average real interest rates strongly positive in 1994), targeted assistance has surely been one method of slowing down the decline of many enterprises.

Outlook

So what is the future prospect? There is a huge amount of adjustment still to be made. Will the pace of lay-offs quicken? Pressure will surely develop as outside owners achieve more control over enterprises and as the scale of subsidies is

cut back. Lower inflation, however, will operate in two opposing directions –
higher real benefits for workers will make wage cutting more difficult, but
higher real severance costs for firms will make lay-offs more expensive and,
therefore, less likely. Also, the general aversion of Russians to unemployment,
after 70 years of full employment, will take some time to change.

3 EVALUATION

How should we evaluate the policies and attitudes which have kept Russian
unemployment so low? First we consider these questions assuming that output
is the only good (employment having no value *per se*). If people are kept in a
firm when they are producing little, this has advantages and disadvantages.

The advantage is that they do not deteriorate through unemployment, while
having every incentive to look for better work (assuming their pay has
plummeted). The experience of Western Europe shows the extraordinary
inefficiency of long-term unemployment, which, in addition to weighing heavily
on the nation's budget, does almost nothing to control inflation and erodes the
nation's human capital.[20] Search on the job is often easier than off, and
preserving the employability of workers increases future output. Similarly,
while it retains surplus workers, the firm has an incentive to think creatively
about new activity for the workers – which may be quite important when there
are so many obstacles to the development of new firms.

On the other hand, it is vital that old enterprises reorganize their shop floors
to raise output per man hour. This can be severely impeded unless the
unproductive labour is kept out of the way – for example, on involuntary leave.
This is the reason why the Federal Employment Service has the power to pay
the minimum wage to workers sent home on involuntary leave.

We can now consider the issue in the wider context where employment and
social harmony matter as well as output. As Clarke and Oswald (1994) have
shown, unemployment is one of the main sources of human misery: the
difference in reported happiness between an unemployed person and the
average person in work (*ceteris paribus*) far exceeds the difference in happiness
between rich and poor. In Russia the psychological effect of open
unemployment could be even more devastating, especially when one considers
the social stigma which has historically been attached to being unemployed.[21]
It should, therefore, be a major policy goal to restructure the economy without
mass unemployment. This is equally important for the sake of social peace,
which has so far survived to a remarkable degree.

There are, however, some basic policy issues which need addressing if
unemployment is to be controlled effectively and at the same time prosperity
enhanced.

Commercial training

A massive retraining effort is needed to match the supply of skills to the new pattern of demand. The training should be almost entirely in commercial skills. In a market economy about a third of workers are employed in jobs for which formal commercial training makes an enormous difference (management, marketing, financial services, retail and wholesale trade, basic accounting and self-employment). For the employed, commercial training will raise productivity and reduce the probability of entering unemployment. For the unemployed it will help them back into work. It is particularly needed by the young so that they have the necessary qualifications to be able to start their adult lives with a job.

In many Western countries, empirical evidence on the rate of return to training unemployed people shows unsatisfactory results. But in the Russian context, where commercial skills are presently so scarce, the returns could not fail to be high.

There are enormous economies of scale in such a training effort if good teaching packages are developed and waves of teacher-trainers are taught to use these packages. Very little of this has been done so far. It should be a top priority.

Public works

It is vital to stop people entering long-term unemployment. This problem has not yet arisen in Russia, with only 10 per cent of the unemployed out of work for more than one year. But it is important that no one unemployed or over a year be paid 'material assistance' for doing nothing. Support for individuals out of work for a long time should be through wages paid for working on a public works project. Plans need to be laid now for projects which are worth developing.

Housing

In some areas it will be extremely difficult to generate enough jobs, even for those older employees who want work. Young people will have to move. Everything must be done to make this possible. This means the abolition of the *propiska* (the residence permit required for some major Russian cities) and of all unreasonable restrictions on the use of housing space. If possible, empty public buildings should be made available as hostels for migrant workers.

Excess wage tax

Like all tax-based incomes policy, this has the objective of increasing the level of employment consistent with stable inflation.[22] It does this in two ways: by encouraging general wage restraint and, implicitly, subsidizing the employment of low-wage labour. Russia's present tax is doing the job well and should be continued. It provides quite sufficient flexibility for changes in relative wages.

Unemployment benefit

Unemployment benefit for people made redundant must be adequate for them to support themselves. If inflation was under control, the present provision would be adequate. For other unemployed people, such as young people entering the labour market and those returning to the labour force, countries like Italy have, until recently, had minimal provision. This may be a sensible model for Russia. At present in Russia the work ethic is in this respect quite well-developed, due perhaps to the Socialist principle 'From each according to his ability, to each according to his work'. It would be a pity to erode these feelings and encourage welfare dependency.

Western aid for the social safety net

Since Russia's unemployment level is not transitional, there is no reason why temporary Western aid should be targeted at paying unemployment benefit. However, there are social activities which require special public expenditure at this time – particularly retraining and the support of housing costs before these can be fully borne by the occupiers. These are indeed suitable objects for Western lending.

4 CONCLUSIONS

Russia has had lower unemployment than most communist countries (6 1/2 per cent in late 1994). This is mainly because lay-offs have been low (around 1 1/2 per cent a year), most employment adjustment being accommodated through voluntary quits. These quits have been high because the hiring rate has remained remarkably high (around 20 per cent) even in former state enterprises. This is due to new job growth and the chain of movement it induces. Thus, most workers have been redeployed through voluntary quitting – moving directly from one job to another.

Unemployment has also stayed low because the duration of unemployment is much shorter than in most post-communist countries. This is partly due to the high hiring rate but also to low unemployment benefits, making workers unwilling to remain unemployed for long.

The reason for low lay-offs is mainly ultra-flexible wages, reflecting the strong unemployment-aversion of the Russian workforce and the possibility of outside earnings. In addition, the Russian managerial tradition has been to provide income through a job and not through a transfer.

This is a basic instinct worth preserving. The objective of employment policy must be to prevent the development of a dependency culture. Instead people need active help to become and remain employable. The natural situation of a person must be to earn his own living. This has so far remained the case in Russia more than in many countries, and with care Russia can avoid the mistakes made in Western Europe.

Appendix 1: Supplementary Tables

Table 26A.1 Numbers employed, including self-employed (million)

	1980	1985	1990	1991	1992	1993
Total	73.3	74.9	75.3	73.8	72.0	71.0
Industry	23.8	24.2	22.8	22.4	21.5	20.8
Agriculture	11.0	10.7	10.0	10.0	9.5	9.6
Transport and Communication	7.0	7.3	5.8	5.8	5.7	5.2
Construction	7.0	7.1	9.0	8.5	8.3	8.0
Trade and Catering	6.1	6.2	5.9	5.6	5.7	
Services				3.2	3.1	3.2
Health, Sport, Social Security				4.3	4.3	4.4
Education, Culture, Art				7.3	7.5	7.7
Science and scientific services				3.1	2.6	2.4
Finance and Insurance				0.4	0.7	
Public Administration				2.0	2.2	2.4

Source: Goskomstat, 1992 Yearbook and *Goskomstat, Monthly Reports* (various issues).

Table 26A.2 Unpaid leave and delayed wage payment, VCIOM survey results for January 1994 (percentage of sample)

	All	Moscow and St Petersburg	Other large cities	Medium and small cities	Rural areas
Did you have to take any unpaid leave in the last 3 months? If so, for how long?					
No	80	87	77	78	85
Yes, less than one week	6	3	8	6	5
Yes, between one week and one month	8	5	9	10	6
Yes, more than one month	5	3	6	6	3
No answer	1	2	0	0	1
Was last month's income paid on time and completely?					
Yes	41	64	45	37	32
Fully but delayed	29	19	27	30	34
On time but not fully	4	4	4	2	8
Delayed and not fully	8	4	9	9	9
Have not been paid yet	18	7	15	22	17
No answer	0	2	0	0	0

Appendix 2: Unemployment Benefit System

SCALE OF BENEFIT

1   A worker made redundant and remaining out of work gets:

First 3 months:	His last monthly wage, unindexed. (This is paid by the employer.)
Next 3 months:	75 per cent of last wage (average of last 2 months, unindexed).
Next 4 months:	60 per cent of his last wage (as above).
Next 5 months:	45 per cent of his wage (as above).
Thereafter,	'Material assistance': up to the minimum wage plus occasional lump sum payments.

2   Other unemployed workers receive the minimum wage for 12 months and 'material assistance' thereafter.

3   Dependents: Benefit is increased by 10 per cent for each dependent but dependents may also receive 'material assistance'.

CONDITIONS

1   Active job search reported when individual signs on (at least twice a month).

2   Those who refuse 2 appropriate job offers or were dismissed from their last job for personal reasons may lose benefit for up to 3 months.

3   To get benefit a redundant worker must register within 2 weeks of losing his job (i.e. at the beginning of the 'first 3 months').

4   No age limit.

Appendix 3: Excess Wage Tax and Employment Incentives

Suppose that in an enterprise worker i would earn W_i and the other $(n-1)$ workers an average of W. Let t_π be the profit tax rate, N the permitted (tax-free) average wage, and t_L the employers' rate of social security taxation.

If worker i is not employed the firm's total labour cost is

$$(1 + t_L)(n - 1)W + t_\pi(n - 1)(W - N)$$

If worker i is employed, the first term changes by $(1 + t_L)W_i$ and the second by $t_\pi(W_i - N)$. It is therefore worth keeping the worker on if the value of the tax offset $(t_\pi N)$ which the firm gains by employing an extra worker exceeds the extra cost of employing the worker $(1 + t_L + t_\pi)W_i$. *This requires*

$$\frac{W_i}{N} < \frac{t_\pi}{1 + t_L + t_\pi}$$

Currently in Russia the profit tax rate is 35 per cent and the social security tax 39 per cent. The permitted (tax-free) wage (N) is 6 times the minimum wage and the average wage in April 1994 was roughly 12 times the minimum wage. Using these figures as an example, it is worth keeping a worker at any wage less than 1/10 the average wage.

Notes

1. See for example Aghion and Blanchard (1993).
2. See for example Blanchard *et al*. (1993, p. 25) and Jackman *et al*. (1993). Much useful evidence is summarized in Boeri (1994).
3. See OECD, *Jobs Study* (1994).
4. We gratefully acknowledge the provision of data and comments by T.L. Gorbacheva of *Goskomstat*.
5. More detailed data are in Appendix 1, which include the self-employed as well as the employed.
6. This is because the raw figures show how many workers have *ever* been placed on involuntary leave during a period. For example they show that 6.5 per cent of workers experienced unpaid leave in 1993. This much-quoted figure is not the number on leave at any one point in time. To find this figure we need to use data on how long the leave lasts – in the first quarter of 1994 the average was around 16 days for workers placed on involuntary leave.
7. This includes only hours lost in industry.
8. VCIOM Survey of the General Population (see Appendix 1, Table 26A.2 for details.
9. This casts doubt on the idea that employers increasingly over-record employment.
10. In the West it is possible to construct a different unemployment rate in which part-time workers wanting full-time *are* counted as half unemployed but unemployed people seeking part-time work are only counted as half unemployed. In the USA this multiplies unemployment by about four-thirds and in Europe and Japan by rather less (*Monthly Labour Review*, March 1993).
11. Annualized rates for up to September.
12. Ellam and Layard (1993); *Russian Economic Trends*, 2(2), p. 65.
13. See Ellam and Layard (1993). Perhaps the best way to analyze these phenomena is the basic model of Chapter 2 of Layard, Nickell and Jackman (1991). In this model wages are set to maximize a function that includes both profits and the welfare of the average worker. Workers' welfare depends in turn on wages and the incomes from the existing employer plus the chances of lay-off and the level of outside opportunities. In such a model an anticipated fall in relative demand in the industry will induce a fall in expected employment and in relative wages. But eventually, if relative demand stopped changing, relative wages would gradually revert to their former level, once enough workers had left the industry. In the model just described managers set employment to maximize profit, after wages have been set and the level of demand has been revealed. In an alternative model, wages and employment would be jointly determined, but in such a model it would be difficult to explain the scale of positive hiring.
14. For three-year changes we have, as we expect, small effects: for 1982–5, a coefficient of 0.13 and for 1983–6, a coefficient of 0.02. The analysis above was kindly conducted by Steve Nickell and covers 59 manufacturing firms, using CBI wage settlement data. Needless to say, the response of firm- or industry-level wages to employment is quite different to the response at the level of the whole economy or region, where labour mobility is much less.
15. A *propiska* (or residence permit) is needed to be able to live in most major Russian cities.

16.	During the voucher programme of industrial privatization in Russia (December 1992–June 1994) the most frequently chosen mechanism of privatization involved 51 per cent of the enterprise's shares going to the enterprise's employees.
17.	For a detailed exposition of the workings of the excess wage tax see Roxburgh and Shapiro (1994).
18.	In 1993 the tax operated on average wages above four times the minimum wage. The tax rate was 32 per cent on excess wages between four and eight times the minimum wage and 50 per cent on the part of excess wages above eight times the minimum wage.
19.	Annex 2 shows the necessary condition.
20.	Layard *et al.* (1991, 1994).
21.	In the Soviet Union until at least the late 1980s, being unemployed for more than a certain period of time was a punishable offence.
22.	See, for example, Layard (1982).

References

Aghion, P. and O.J. Blanchard (1993) 'On the speed of transition in Central Europe', EBRD, *Working Paper*, 6 (July).

Åslund, A. (ed.) (1995) *Russian Economic Reform at Risk* (London: Pinter Publishers).

Aukutsionek, S. and R. Kapelyushnikov (1994) 'The labour market in 1993', *Russian Economic Barometer*, 1.

Blanchard, O.J. *et al.* (1993) 'Unemployment and restructuring in Eastern Europe', paper presented to the World Bank Conference on Unemployment, Restructuring and the Labour Market in East Europe and Russia (Washington, DC) (7–8 October).

Boeri, T. (1994) 'Transitional unemployment', *Economics of Transition*, 2(1).

Burda, M. (1994) 'Unemployment, labour markets and structural changes in Eastern Europe', *Economic Policy*, 16.

Burda, M. and M. Lubyova (1994) 'The impact of active labour market policies: a closer look at the Czech and Slovak Republics', paper presented at the WZB Workshop on The Flow Approach to Labour Market Analysis (Berlin) (1–3 December).

Clarke, A. and A. Oswald (1994) 'Unhappiness and unemployment', *Economic Journal*, 104 (May).

Commander, S. and J. McHale (1994) 'Labour markets in the transition in East Europe and Russia: a review of experience', paper prepared for the World Bank's *World Development Report* (October).

Ellam, M. and R. Layard (1993) 'Prices, incomes and hardship', in Åslund and R. Layard (eds), *Changing the Economic System in Russia* (London: Pinter Publishers).

Jackman, R. (1994) 'Economic policies, employment and labour markets in transition in Central and Eastern Europe', ILO/UNDP (June).

Jackman, R., R. Layard and A. Scott (1992) 'Unemployment in Eastern Europe', LSE, mimeo.

Jackman, R. *et al.* (1993) 'The labour market in Bulgaria', paper presented to the World Bank Conference on Unemployment, Restructuring and the Labour Market in East Europe and Russia (Washington, DC) (7–8 October).

Layard, R. (1982) 'Is incomes policy the answer to unemployment?', *Economica* (August).

Layard, R. and A. Richter (1995) 'Labour market adjustment in Russia', in A. Åslund (ed.), *Russian Economic Reform at Risk* (London: Pinter Publishers).

Layard, R., S. Nickell and R. Jackman (1991) *Unemployment: Macroeconomic Performance and the Labour Market* (Oxford: Oxford University Press).

Layard, R., S. Nickell and R. Jackman (1994) *The Unemployment Crisis* (Oxford: Oxford University Press).

OECD (1994) *Jobs Study* (Paris: OECD).

Roxburgh, I.W. and J.C. Shapiro (1994) 'Excess wages tax', *Socio-Economic Survey*, 17, MFU (Moscow) (January).

The Russian Centre for Public Opinion Research (VCIOM) (1993, 1994, various months) 'Survey of the General Population' and 'Survey of the Working Population' in *Bulletin of Information: Economic and Social Change* (Moscow: Aspect Press).

Russian Economic Barometer (1994) (Moscow: Institute of World Economy and International Relations).

Standing, G. (1994) 'Labour market dynamics in Russian industry in 1993: results from the third round of the RLFS' (Budapest: ILO–CEET) (February).

27 Why So Much Pain?
(1998)*

The collapse of European Communism is the most important world event since the end of the Second World War. At the same time the world's largest country, China, has taken giant steps in the direction of capitalism. But both in Europe, China and Central Asia the transformation is only partly accomplished and it has not begun in Cuba. Sensible strategies for the future depend crucially on learning the right lessons from what has been done so far.

The most striking fact is that in Eastern Europe and Russia the reforms have been accompanied by huge falls in output, followed in Eastern Europe by some recovery especially in Poland (see Table 27.1). By contrast Chinese output has grown steadily, at a rate never seen in Europe. The main challenge facing us is to explain these facts. If free markets and private ownership are meant to increase economic opportunity and welfare, why has their introduction been accompanied by such pain in Eastern Europe and Russia? And why no output fall in China? Were fundamental mistakes made in the European model of change that could be avoided in future?

EASTERN EUROPE AND RUSSIA

Six facts stand out about the European reform process, compared with the Chinese.

State power was weak

The European reforms followed the collapse of Communist rule. The new governments were (a) weak and (b) determined above all to prevent the return of Communism. These facts largely explain what followed.

Price liberalisation was rapid

Most of the reform governments inherited budget deficits and thus an excess of monetary demand over the value of output at current controlled prices. Queues

---

* Chapter 1 in P. Boone, S. Gomulka and R. Layard (eds), *Emerging from Communism: Lessons from Russia, China and Eastern Europe*, The MIT Press, 1998.

Table 27.1 Growth, inflation and unemployment

	Change in GDP (%)		Change in prices (%)		Unemployment
	1989–96	1993–6	1989–96	1995–6	1996
Poland	4	23	16 270	55	13
Czech Republic	–9	12	212	19	3
Hungary	–13	5	479	59	11
Russia	–49	–25	508 010	321	9
China	108	54	118	22	3

Sources: GDP: EBRD, *Transition Report* (1996); IMF, *World Economic Outlook* (October 1996). Inflation rates: EBRD, *Transition Report* (1996); IMF, *World Economic Outlook* (October 1996); OECD, *Economic Outlook* (December 1996). Unemployment: OECD, *Economic Outlook* (December 1996); ILO, *Yearbook of Labour Statistics*, (1995). Unemployment rate for China is for 1994.

were lengthening. Since governments lacked the authority to undertake a monetary reform and no longer had the power to control prices, they had little option but to free most prices within one or two years. This rapidly made the system of state orders inoperable, and both prices and quantities were basically determined by market forces within a similar period. In addition the reformers opened up foreign trade to market forces. And the system of state trading between the former Communist countries was largely abolished in 1991.

As a result, the opportunities facing enterprises changed at an incredible speed. Enterprises dependent on raw materials faced huge increases in the real cost of their inputs and at the same time many found that the demand for their products had disappeared or shifted elsewhere to cheaper producers.

If capital and labour could have been rapidly redeployed there would have been no reason why aggregate output should fall. But this redeployment takes time. The formation of new relationships in conditions of uncertainty always takes time, in business as in private life. But when the participants are quite unused to writing contracts which determine the profits and survival of a business, the process takes even longer. As a result there is massive unused capacity during the adjustment process.

It is striking that the slowest adjustment has been in the Former Soviet Union which suffered 75 years of central planning and absence of markets, and faster in Poland and China, where agriculture at least was mainly private except for a shortish period.[1] Thus in Poland the new private sector has grown rapidly and now accounts for 20 per cent of national output, whereas in Russia new enterprises struggle to get started because of over-regulation at the local level and lack of public support for competitive challenges from new suppliers.

Military demand fell drastically

On top of the rapid shifts in demand and supply resulting from free prices (and reduced subsidies) came a major collapse in the government's demand for defence goods. This too resulted from the weakness of the state – the taxes could no longer be collected to pay for defence. We shall never know precisely, but the defence and space effort probably accounted for around one quarter of GDP in the Soviet Union. The figure was below 10 per cent in the rest of the Warsaw Pact. In all these countries the figure is now below 5 per cent. Such a huge adjustment could not fail to cause a huge fall in total output, especially in Russia.

There was a macroeconomic shift, raising unemployment

Another reason for the fall in output came from a necessary change in the macroeconomic balance of the economy. In Russia and much of Eastern Europe, Communist policy had been to let the level of monetary demand exceed the maximum value of production at the controlled level of prices. This ensured that almost anything that was produced could be sold. And prices were controlled by fiat.

Once prices were freed, they naturally shot up. To control the resulting inflation required monetary restraint, but this restraint only worked through generating sufficient slack in labour and product markets to offset inflation inertia. As these countries moved to free markets, so unemployment, originally negligible, rose to the natural rate. This inevitably involved falls in output. This process was unnecessary in China, which has for years had many free markets and substantial urban unemployment. There inflation has been continuously restrained by responsible monetary policy and generally been in single digits.

Inflation was high

By contrast in Eastern Europe and especially Russia there have been periods of very high inflation. These stem from the weakness of the state. The government no longer had its former power to collect taxes, and this was truer in federal states like Russia than in smaller ones like the Czech Republic. At the same time the pressure for continued subsidies remained high, and, when the Ministry of Finance refused, the pressure shifted to the Central Bank which often obliged with cheap credits. The combination of budget deficits and cheap credits fuelled inflation.

Some countries resisted these pressures better than others, especially those which received strong early support from the IMF, as the Visegrád countries did. In Russia Gaidar consciously agreed to inflationary credits as the price of remaining in power and pushing on with privatisation.

The resulting inflation has been a major factor delaying the recovery. In high inflation it is impossible to plan for the future. Private investment rates are low, and capital flies abroad. Everyone waits for the uncertainty to clear. In Russia, unlike China, high inflation and political uncertainty have been major factors retarding output growth. And, as the Vietnamese experience shows, the control of inflation does not itself have any serious short-run output effects.

Privatisation was rapid

By historical standards, privatisation has also been extraordinarily rapid throughout post-Communist Europe. Two motives have been at work. One, political, has been to create a large enough class of capitalists to prevent the re-election of a Communist government. Henry VIII of England prevented the return of Catholicism by selling off the monasteries, and today's reformers prevented the return of Communism by selling off state enterprises. The second, economic, motive is of course the belief that private ownership is an essential condition for efficiency in the long run.

However, in the short run, privatisation yields slow returns. Managers devote excessive energy to organising the claims on future output, and too little to making sure that output is produced and markets are won. Sometimes key parts of an enterprise are hived off, leaving the total output from the existing capital lower than before. In the end such reorganisation should pay-off, but in the meantime output falls.

Conclusion

Thus it is no longer difficult to understand why output performance has been so disappointing in Eastern Europe and Russia. Much of the reform policy has been driven by the weakness of the government and by the desire to preserve freedom by preventing a return of the Communists. But ideas have also played a role. Many Western economists, including myself, advocated rapid change – partly because we understood the weakness of the government but partly because we believed that it would be better to suffer considerable pain and disorder for a short time than to have perhaps less pain but over a longer period. The argument was that the sum of present and future welfare would be higher if change was rapid, and the new, less distorted economy, established as soon as possible.

Were we right? The evidence is not yet fully in. Certainly there has been substantial pain. Yet, on the best available evidence, rapid reform had no effect, positive or negative, on the extent of the fall in output between 1989 and 1995, but it speeded up the whole process, thus bringing forward the recovery.[2]

If this analysis is right, then rapid reform increases the (discounted) value of the whole path of output. But we are still very close to the beginning of the reform. There have so far been few cases of strong and sustained recovery (except for Poland) and some challenging cases (like Uzbekistan) where reform has been slow and the output fall so far has been relatively small.[3] Certainly output has fallen everywhere, however fast or slow the reform. While the bulk of the evidence is favourable to the case for rapid reform, we cannot yet prove that, if politics had permitted, a more gradual evolution would have been a mistake.

CHINA

In China the initial conditions after Mao died were quite different. Let me highlight three key facts about China.

The Chinese state remained strong

There was no upsurge against the ruling elite and thus no breakdown of state power. Budgets were roughly consistent with low inflation.

China was predominantly rural and desperately poor

The poverty of China provided remarkable possibilities for catch-up, and thus high economic growth, provided the economic framework was right. In some ways China in 1987 was like Europe in 1947 – far behind the technological frontier and with a large reserve of excess labour in agriculture, ready for redeployment in the more productive industrial sector (especially the townships and village enterprises). In this respect China was not unlike Korea and Taiwan in 1960. It could grow by huge transfers of people out of unproductive agriculture into the growing industrial sector, and industrial growth did not therefore depend as in Eastern Europe and Russia on redeployment of people within the urban economy.

Thus China post-Mao grew just like the non-Communist Far East. But this was by no means automatic: North Korea stagnated. Chinese growth was due to some key features of Chinese economic organisation.

The Chinese economy was highly decentralised

China's sensational economic growth has come from five main areas.

(a) *Agriculture.* This had been re-collectivised only in 1966 and was reprivatised in 1978. This shock therapy, which also involved free prices for a substantial share of output, was more drastic than anything applied to agriculture in Russia and Central Europe, and had immediate and spectacular effects.

(b) *Township and village enterprises (TVEs)*. These small-scale enterprises, mostly in agro-industry, were set up by local municipal governments on their own initiative. The bonuses paid were often so large that some enterprises are better considered as coops. But the ability of local municipalities to father these enterprises reflects the strong decentralisation brought about by the Cultural Revolution.

In some ways the Cultural Revolution (1966–72) was equivalent to the recent Economic Reform in Eastern Europe. It dismantled many of the bureaucratic controls and in the process caused a considerable initial loss of output. (National income fell by 14 per cent between 1966 and 1968.) But the decision-making framework that emerged was conducive to high subsequent growth – as it will eventually turn out to have been in Eastern Europe.

(c) *State-owned enterprises*. Even the state-owned enterprises in China have grown. This is actually the only challenging difference between Chinese and East European experience. One reason may be that many of the state-owned enterprises are under the control of regional rather than provincial or central government. But the same was actually true in Eastern Europe, once the size of country is allowed for. Probably more important, subsidies are still used to avert lay-offs; the scope for catch-up is greater; and the rest of the economy is growing.

(d) *The new private sector*. By now the new private sector in towns is producing around 30 per cent of the country's national output. This reflects an environment for new business that is in many ways easier (in terms of regulations) then in Russia or even Eastern Europe. It also reflects the growing opportunities to make money, originating from growth in agriculture and agro-industry.

(e) *Foreign trade*. A final area is foreign trade. China exports 23 per cent of its national output, an exceptionally high figure for such a large country with few natural resources. Due to an open trading policy (including special economic zones with tax breaks for foreigners), the trade sector has grown extremely fast and has led to substantial input of foreign capital and know-how, often financed by overseas Chinese.

So it is no mystery that China has grown so rapidly. It has pursued many of the policies recommended by economic liberals, and has grown like the rest of the Far East. The main difference is over state-owned industrial enterprises. These have not been hit by sudden cuts in defence orders nor in subsidies, and have therefore shared in the general growth.

MAIN LESSONS

Against this background, the members of the Emerging Markets Programme at the Centre for Economic Performance decided to set down what they believed they knew about the causes and consequences of the economic reforms followed in Eastern Europe, Russia and China. The first five chapters are about Eastern Europe and Russia, and the last two about China.

1. Output

Gomulka reviews the various reasons that have been offered for the output drop in Eastern Europe and Russia – some sensible (and already mentioned) and others less sensible. He goes on to discuss the conditions for recovery, stressing the importance of the de novo private sector and of sufficient domestic savings to finance adequate investment.

2. Inflation

One source of low output, and certainly of hardship, has been high inflation. What caused this? Boone and Horder begin by asking why there were very different jumps in prices at the time of liberalisation, ranging from around 30 per cent in Czechoslovakia to 250 per cent in Russia. This was due to the degree to which the public had lost confidence in money and was expecting further subsequent inflation. In most cases these expectations of further inflation proved well-founded.

In general the rate of subsequent money creation was driven by the power of different interest groups – and not to any major degree by programmes of social support. For example in Russia the enterprise lobby was very powerful and in 1992/3 extracted nearly 30 per cent of GDP in credits from the government. In consequence they paid an inflation tax on their existing money holding but since they only held half the money stock their net gain was nearly 15 per cent of GDP. The household sector, and in particular the pensioners, lost an equivalent amount.

So why did the great inflation come to an end? One reason was that inflation so increased velocity and reduced the holdings of real money that the level of inflation needed to generate a given transfer to industry rose and rose. Industry decided it was not worth the candle. Another reason was improved understanding of the inflation process.

So how can further inflation be prevented? Many institutional arrangements can help, such as conditional IMF aid, constitutional budget processes and where appropriate 'poison pills', as when a currency board is put in place.

3. Privatisation and restructuring

While inflation has to be controlled in any economy, the more fundamental elements in economic transition are the establishment of free markets and the establishment of private ownership. Estrin examines the extent to which private ownership has so far contributed to improved performance.

There are of course two ways in which private ownership can develop – through the privatisation of state enterprises as going concerns, and through the establishment of new privately-owned firms (using newly created and older assets). And among privatised companies there are many patterns of ownership which can develop, depending on the form of privatisation that is adopted. Thus owners can be predominantly workers, managers or outsiders. Most theories of corporate governance predict superior performance from companies where ownership is concentrated in few hands, thus short-circuiting the free-rider problem. Thus it might be expected that privatised companies do best if ownership is concentrated in the hands of managers or of outside block-holders, owning a substantial block of shares.

Estrin attempts to test the impact of ownership patterns on enterprise performance. He shows that newly-founded private firms do better than any others. But in the time available no one type of privatisation can be shown to have done better or restructured faster than any other. Only time will tell.

4. Banking reform and privatisation

As economic reform proceeds, it becomes clear that some enterprises are in trouble. If the enterprises have substantial debts to banks, the banks too are in trouble due to the unperforming loans. A major banking crisis looms. This was a major threat in most of Eastern Europe, though not in Russia where high inflation wiped out much of the debt.

Van Wijnbergen addresses the question of how the bad loans should be handled – or, more widely, the role of the banks in the process of restructuring. The sharpest contrast is between the approaches adopted in the Czech Republic and Poland. In the Czech lands, the government took over the bad loans, replacing them in the banks' balance sheets by well-performing government debt. A public agency was then set up to try and collect the bad debts. The problem with this approach is that the agency's officials have inadequate incentive to recover the loans and to force the firms to restructure.

By contrast in Poland, the banks were left with their bad debts – which gave them a strong incentive to force restructuring in order to recover their money. Meantime the banking crisis was averted by a once-for-all re-capitalising of the banks. This worked well and provides important lessons for other countries.

5. Unemployment and restructuring

A major consequence of economic reform has been unemployment – a condition largely unknown under Communism in Europe. A key question is how far high unemployment is necessary to the process of restructuring. According to Jackman and Pauna, it is not.

As they show, the key change which all these economies have to make is a shift from manufacturing into trade, finance and other services. The speed at which this is occurring and new jobs being created in the new sectors is independent of the level of unemployment. This is perhaps not surprising since the new jobs are usually filled by people who are still in work rather than by the unemployed.

Thus unemployment is explained by much the same factors as explain unemployment in non-transition countries. A country like Poland which has open-ended unemployment benefits has high unemployment, while a country like the Czech Republic, which has short-duration benefits and active policies to help the unemployed, has low unemployment.

6. Why China always grew

When we turn to China everything is different. There is a long sequence of reforms from 1978 to the present. And there is steady growth. Does this show that gradualism is best? Wing Thye Woo argues that it does not.

In his comprehensive account growth occurs for all the reasons given earlier in this chapter. One key factor is that the government never lost control. So inflation remained low. This in turn encouraged higher savings and a strong confidence in the future.

Thus, when the production function approach is used to account for the sources of growth, over half the growth is due to capital accumulation. Another key factor is the reallocation of labour out of low productivity agriculture. Total factor productivity growth, though positive, is not particularly large.

A key issue is the role of the state-owned enterprises which employ 18 per cent of the workforce – the same as in 1978. Unlike state enterprises in Eastern Europe, their output grew. Why is this?

The state-owned enterprises have been given increased autonomy, but their rates of profit have declined. In consequence they have received increasing subsidies which are a growing drain on the budget.

Xu and Zhuang argue that there are also other reasons for the relative success of state-owned enterprises in China. Their average size is smaller than in Europe and they are controlled by more localised political structures than was typical in European Communism. Thus in China total factor productivity growth was negative in centrally-owned state enterprises and was positive in those under local control.

But the great growth of industrial production came from the township and village enterprises. Though their pattern of ownership is ill-defined, this did not limit their ability to motivate both managers and workers – given the relatively disciplined framework of society. Thus a clear key to Chinese success has been decentralisation of public and collective enterprises, linked to an economy which is in many ways as capitalist as the nearly capitalist countries of Eastern and Central Europe.

Notes

1. In Poland 6 years (1950–6) and in China 17 (1956–61 and 66–78).
2. See Åslund, Boone and Johnson (1996).
3. For country details see EBRD, *Transition Report* (1986).

Reference

Åslund, A., P. Boone and S. Johnson (1996) 'How to Stabilize: Lessons from Post Communist Countries' in *Brookings Papers on Economic Activity*, 1, 1996.

Appendix: Richard Layard's Publications

1 EDUCATION AND INEQUALITY

Books

(1963) *Appendix Volumes One–Three of Higher Education. Report of the Robbins Committee* (London: HMSO), Cmnd 2154, I, II, II–I, III, see Chapter 18 in this volume.

(1968) *Manpower and Educational Development in India, 1961–86* (London: Oliver and Boyd) (with T. Burgess and P. Pant).

(1969) *The Impact of Robbins: Expansion in Higher Education* (Harmondsworth: Penguin) (with J. King and C. Moser).

(1971) *Qualified Manpower and Economic Performance: An Inter-Plant Study in the Electrical Engineering Industry* London: Allen Lane, The Penguin Press (with J. Sargan, M. Ager and D. Jones).

(1978) *The Causes of Poverty, Background Paper*, 5, Royal Commission on the Distribution of Income and Wealth (London: HMSO) (with D. Piachaud and M. Stewart).

(1979) *Human Capital and Income Distribution*, Special Issue of *Journal of Political Economy* (October) (edited).

(1985) *Trends in Women's Work, Education, and Family Building*, Special issue of *Journal of Labor Economics* (January) (edited with J. Mincer).

(1994) *Britain's Training Deficit* (Aldershot: Avebury) (edited with K. Mayhew and G. Owen).

Articles

(1964) 'Planning the scale of higher education in Great Britain', *Journal of the Royal Statistical Society* (with C. Moser). Vol. 127, Part 4.

(1966a) 'Manpower needs and the planning of higher education', in B.C. Roberts and J.H. Smith (eds), *Manpower Policy and Employment Trends* (London: G. Bell).

(1966b) 'Educational and occupational characteristics of manpower: an international comparison', *British Journal of Industrial Relations*, vol. 4, no. 2, pp. 222–66 (with J. Saigal).

(1970a) 'How profitable is engineering education?' *Higher Education Review* (Spring) (with L. Maglen).

(1970b) 'The LSE as a graduate school', *Universities Quarterly* (Autumn) (with J. King).

(1971) 'The scale of expansion to come' and 'Meeting the cost restraint', in G. Brosan, C. Carter, R. Layard, P. Venables and G. Williams (eds), *Patterns and Policies in Higher Education* (Harmondsworth: Penguin) (with G. Williams).

(1972) 'Economic theories of educational planning', in M. Peston and B. Corry (eds), *Essays in Honour of Lord Robbins* (London: Weidenfeld & Nicolson), Chapter 15 in this volume.

(1973a) 'Denison and the contribution of education to national income growth: a comment', *Journal of Political Economy* (July–August).

(1973b) 'University efficiency and university finance', in M. Parkin (ed.), *Essays in Modern Economics* (London: Longman (with R. Jackman)), Chapter 16 in this volume.

(1974a) 'The screening hypothesis and the returns to education', *Journal of Political Economy*, 82(5) (with G. Psacharopoulos), Chapter 9 in this volume.

(1974b) 'The cost-effectiveness of the new media in higher education', in K. Lumsden (ed.), *Efficiency in Universities. The La Paz Papers* (New York: Elsevier); reprinted in *Minerva* and the *British Journal of Educational Technology* (with Michael Oatey), Chapter 17 in this volume.

(1974c) 'Traditional versus Open University teaching methods: a cost comparison', *Higher Education* (August) (with B. Laidlaw).

(1975a) 'Cost functions for university teaching and research', *Economic Journal* (March) (with D. Verry)

(1975b) 'Capital-skill complementarity, income distribution and output accounting', *Journal of Political Economy*, 83(2) (with P. Fallon), Chapter 10 in this volume.

(1977) 'On measuring the redistribution of lifetime income', in M.S. Feldstein and R.P. Inman (eds), *The Economics of Public Services* (London: Macmillan), Chapter 3 in this volume.

(1978) 'The effect of collective bargaining on relative and absolute wages', in Shorrocks and W. Krelle (eds), *The Economics of Income Distribution* (Amsterdam: North-Holland) and *British Journal of Industrial Relations* (March) (with D. Metcalf and S. Nickell), Chapter 7 in this volume.

(1979a) 'Family income distribution: explanation and policy evaluation', *Journal of Political Economy*, 87(5), Pt 2 (with A. Zabalza), Chapter 4 in this volume.

(1979b) 'The causes of poverty', *National Westminster Bank Review* (February) (with D. Piachaud and M. Stewart), Chapter 6 in this volume.

(1979c) 'Human capital and earnings: British evidence and a critique', *Review of Economic Studies* (July) (with G. Psacharopoulos), Chapter 8 in this volume.

(1979d) 'Education versus cash redistribution: the lifetime context', *Journal of Public Economics*, 12(3) Chapter 5 in this volume.

(1980a) 'Wages policy and the redistribution of income', The Colston Research Society Annual Lecture, in D. Collard, R. Lecomber and M. Slater (eds), *The Limits to Redistribution* (Bristol: Colston Society).

(1980b) 'Married women's participation and hours', *Economica* (February) (with M. Barton and A. Zabalza), Chapter 11 in this volume.

(1980c) 'On the use of distributional weights in social cost-benefit analysis: comment', *Journal of Political Economy*, 88(8), Chapter 13 in this volume.

(1980d) 'Human satisfactions and public policy', *Economic Journal*, 90 (December), Chapter 14 in this volume.

(1982) 'Trends in civil service pay relative to the private sector', in *Report of the Inquiry into Civil Service Pay* (Chairman Sir John Megaw), vol. 2, Cmnd. 8590–1 (London: HMSO) (July) (with A. Marin and A. Zabalza).

(1983) 'Incomes policy and wage differentials', *Economica* (May) (with O. Ashenfelter).

(1985a) 'Why are more women working in Britain?', *Journal of Labor Economics*, 3(1) (with H. Joshi and S. Owen), Chapter 12 in this volume.

(1985b) 'Overseas students' fees and the demand for education', *Applied Economics*, 17 (with E. Petoussis).

(1985c) 'Public sector pay: the British perspective', in D. Conklin *et al.* (eds), *Public Sector Compensation*. Ontario Economic Council, Special Research Report.

(1993) 'The Training Reform Act of 1994', *International Journal of Manpower*, 14 (5) (with K. Mayhew and G. Owen).

(1994) 'The welfare economics of training;, in R.Layard, K. Mayhew and G. Owen (eds), *Britain's Training Deficit* (Aldershot: Avebury).

(1995) 'Lifelong Learning', Centre for Economic Performance Occasional Paper No. 9, London School of Economics (with P. Robinson and H. Steedman).

2 UNEMPLOYMENT

Books

(1969) *The Causes of Graduate Unemployment in India* (London: Allen Lane, The Penguin Press) (with M. Blaug and M. Woodhall), Chapter 11 in R. Layard, *Tackling Unemployment* (London: Macmillan, 1999).

(1982) *More Jobs, Less Inflation* (London: Grant McIntyre).

(1984) *The Causes of Unemployment* (Oxford: Oxford University Press) (edited with C. Greenhalgh and A. Oswald).

(1986a) *Restoring Europe's Prosperity* (Cambridge, MA: MIT Press) (with O. Blanchard and R. Dornbusch).

(1986b) *How to Beat Unemployment* (Oxford: Oxford University press). Translated into Swedish.

(1987a) *The Rise in Unemployment* (Oxford: Basil Blackwell) (edited with C. Bean and S. Nickell), reprint of *Economica*, Unemployment Supplement (1986).

(1987b) *The Fight against Unemployment* (Cambridge, MA: MIT Press) (edited with Lars Calmfors).

(1991a) *Unemployment: Macroeconomic Performance and the Labour Market* (Oxford: Oxford University Press) (with S. Nickell and R. Jackman). Translated into Spanish.

(1991b) *Stopping Unemployment*. The Employment Institute (September) (with J. Philpott).

(1992) *Helping the Unemployed: Active Labour Market Policies in Britain and Germany*, The Anglo-German Foundation (March) (with Richard Disney, Lutz Bellmann, Alan Carruth, Wolfgang Franz, Richard Jackman, Hartmut Lehmann, John Philpott).

(1993) *UK Unemployment*, Studies in the UK Economy (London: Heinemann Educational), 2nd edition 1993, 3rd edition 1997 (with A. Clark).

(1994) *The Unemployment Crisis* (Oxford: Oxford University Press) (with S. Nickell and R. Jackman). Translated into Spanish, 1996.

Articles

(1979) 'The costs and benefits of selective employment policies. The British case', *British Journal of Industrial Relations*, 17 (July), also in the National Commission for Manpower Policy, *European Labor Market Policies* (September 1978)

(1980a) 'The case for subsiding extra jobs', *Economic Journal*, 90 (March) (with S. Nickell) Chapter 17 in R. Layard, *Tackling Unemployment* (London: Macmillan, 1999).

(1980b) 'The efficiency case for long-run labour market policies', *Economica*, 47 (August) (with R. Jackman) Chapter 16 in R. Layard, *Tackling Unemployment* (London: Macmillan, 1999).

(1980c) 'Evidence to the House of Lords Select Committee on Unemployment', *Minutes of Evidence* (London: HMSO).

(1981a) 'Measuring the duration of unemployment: a note', *Scottish Journal of Political Economy* (November).

(1981b) 'Unemployment in Britain: causes and cures', *Work and Social Change*, 6, European Centre for Work and Society (Maastricht), Chapter 13 in R. Layard, *Tackling Unemployment* (London: Macmillan, 1999).

(1982a) 'Efficient public employment with labour market distortions', in R. Haveman (ed.), *Public Finance and Public Employment* (Detroit: Wayne State University Press) (with G. Johnson).

(1982b) 'Youth unemployment in Britain and the US compared', in R. Freeman and D.Wise (eds), *The Youth Labor Market Problem* (Chicago: The University of Chicago Press).

(1982c) 'An inflation tax', *Fiscal Studies* (March) (with R. Jackman).

(1982d) 'Is income policy the answer to unemployment?', *Economica* (August), with Appendix 'Trade Unions, the NAIRU and a Wage-Inflation Tax' (with R.A. Jackman), Chapter 18 in R. Layard, *Tackling Unemployment* (London: Macmillan, 1999).

(1982e) 'Causes of the current stagflation', *Review of Economic Studies* (October) (with D. Grubb and R. Jackman).

(1982f) 'Incomes policy, employment measures and economic performance', in 'Could Do Better', *IEA Occasional Paper Special*.

(1983a) 'Agenda for Liberal Conservatism. A comment', *Journal of Economic Affairs* (January).

(1983b) 'Wage rigidity and unemployment in OECD countries', *European Economic Review*, 21 (with D. Grubb and R. Jackman), Chapter 3 in R. Layard, *Tackling Unemployment* (London: Macmillan, 1999).

(1983c) 'Macroeconomic prospects and policies for the European Community', *Centre for European Policy Studies Paper*, 1 (April) (with R. Dornbusch, G. Basevi, O. Blanchard and W. Buiter).

(1984a) 'Europe: the case for unsustainable growth', *Centre for European Policy Studies Paper* 8/9 (May) (with G. Basevi, O. Blanchard, W. Buiter and R. Dornbusch), Chapter 22 in R. Layard, *Tackling Unemployment* (London: Macmillan, 1999).

(1984b) 'Wages, unemployment and incomes policy', in M. Emerson (ed.), *Causes of Europe's Stagflation* (Oxford: Oxford University Press) (with D. Grubb and J. Symons).

(1984c) 'Neo-classical demand for labour functions for six major economies', *Economic Journal* (December) (with J. Symons).

(1985a) 'The causes of British unemployment', *National Institute Economic Review* (February) (with S. Nickell).

(1985b) 'Cutting unemployment using both blades of the scissors', *Catalyst* (Spring).

(1985c) 'Employment and growth in Europe: a two-handed approach', *Centre for European Policy Studies*, Paper 21 (May) (with O. Blanchard, R. Dornbusch, J. Drèze, H. Giersch and M. Monti).

(1985d) 'European unemployment is Keynesian and classical but not structural', Centre for European Policy Studies, *Working Document*, 13 (June) (with R. Jackman and S. Nickell).

(1985e) 'On tackling unemployment', *Economic Affairs* (July–September).

(1985f) 'Unemployment, real wages and aggregate demand in Europe, Japan and the US', in K. Brunner and A. Meltzer (eds), *Carnegie–Rochester Conference Series on Public Policy*, 23 (Autumn) (with S. Nickell).

(1986a) 'Policies for reducing the natural rate of unemployment', in J.L. Butkiewicz, K.J. Koford and J.B. Miller (eds), *Keynes' Economic Legacy* (New York: Praeger) (with R. Jackman and C. Pissarides).

(1986b) 'The economic effects of tax-based incomes policy', in D. Colander (ed.), *Incentive-Based Incomes Policies* (New York: Ballinger) (with R. Jackman).

(1986c) 'A wage-tax, worker-subsidy policy for reducing the 'natural' rate of unemployment', in W. Beckerman (ed.), *Wage Rigidity and Unemployment* (London: Duckworth) (July) (with R. Jackman).

(1986d) 'A new deal for the long-term unemployed', in P.E. Hart (ed.), *Unemployment and Labour Market Policies* (London: Gower) (with D. Metcalf and R. O'Brien).

(1986e) 'Unemployment in Britain', *Economica Special Supplement on Unemployment*, 53 (with S. Nickell).

(1986f) 'The rise in unemployment: a multi-country study', *Economica Special Supplement on Unemployment*, 53 (with C. Bean and S. Nickell).

(1986g) 'Employment – the way forward', Stockton Lecture, *London Business School Journal*, 11 (Winter).

(1986h) 'Reducing unemployment in Europe: the role of capital formation', Centre for European Policy Studies, 28 (with F. Modigliani, M. Monti, J. Drèze and H. Giersch).

(1986i) 'An incomes policy to help the unemployed', Employment Institute; required in J. Shields (ed.), *Making the Economy Work* (London: Macmillan 1989) and in abbreviated form in *Economic Review*, 5 (November 1987) (with S. Nickell).

(1986j) 'The natural rate of unemployment: explanation and policy', in O. Ashenfelter and R. Layard (eds), *Handbook of Labor Economics* (Amsterdam: North-Holland (with G.Johnson).

(1987) 'The labour market', in R. Dornbusch and R. Layard (eds), *The Performance of the British Economy* (Oxford: Clarendon Press) (with S. Nickell), Chapter 4 in R. Layard, *Tackling Unemployment* (London: Macmillan, 1999).

(1988) 'Innovative supply-side policies to reduce unemployment', in P. Minford (ed.), *Monetarism and Macroeconomics*, IEA Readings, 26 (with R. Jackman).

(1989a) 'On vacancies', *Oxford Bulletin of Economics and Statistics*, 51 (4) (November) (with R.Jackman and C. Pissarides), Chapter 5 in R. Layard, *Tackling Unemployment* (London: Macmillan, 1999).

(1989b) 'Why does unemployment persist?', *Scandinavian Journal of Economics*, 91 (2) and in S. Honkapohja (ed.) *The State of Macroeconomics* (Oxford: Blackwell Oxford 1990) (with C. Bean), Chapter 9 in R. Layard, *Tackling Unemployment* (London: Macmillan, 1999).

(1989c) 'Lessons for another country', in E. Wadensjo, A. Dahlberg and B. Holmlund (eds), *Vingarnas Tryggnet*, Essays in Honour of Gösta Rehn.

(1990a) 'Lay-offs by seniority and equilibrium employment', *Economics Letters*, 32 (Harvard University).

(1990b) 'The real effects of tax-based incomes policies', *Scandinavian Journal of Economics*, 92(2) (with R. Jackman), Chapter 19 in R. Layard, *Tackling Unemployment* (London Macmillan, 1999).

(1990c) 'Is unemployment lower if unions bargain over employment?', *Quarterly Journal of Economics* (August), and in Y. Weiss and G. Fishelson (eds), *Advances in the Theory and Measurement of Unemployment* (London: Macmillan (Spring) (with S. Nickell), Chapter 21 in R. Layard, *Tackling Unemployment* (London: Macmillan, 1999).

(1990d) 'European unemployment: cause and cure, *Revista de Economia*, 4; also in J. Velarde *et al.* (eds), *La Industria Espanola* (*Economistas Libros, Madrid*).

(1990e) 'Wage bargaining and EMU', in R. Dornbusch, C. Goodhart, and R. Layard (eds), *Britain & EMU* (London: Centre for Economic Performance and Financial Markets Group).

(1990f) 'How to end pay leapfrogging', Employment Institute Economic Report, 5 (5) (July), Chapter 20 in R. Layard, *Tackling Unemployment* (London: Macmillan, 1999).

(1991a) 'Does long-term unemployment reduce a person's chance of a job? A time series test', *Economica* 58 (229) (with R. Jackman), Chapter 6 in R. Layard, *Tackling Unemployment* (London: Macmillan, 1999).

(1991b) 'Unemployment and inequality in Europe: what to do', in A. Atkinson and R. Brunetta (eds), *Economics for the New Europe*, IEA Conference Volume 104.

(1991c) 'Mismatch: a framework for thought', in F. Padoa Schioppa (ed.), *Mismatch and Labour Mobility* (Cambridge: Cambridge University Press) (with R. Jackman and S. Savouri), Chapter 7 in R. Layard, *Tackling Unemployment* (London: Macmillan, 1999).

(1993) 'The squeeze on jobs: getting people back to work', *Worldlink (May–June)*.

(1994a) 'Unemployment in the OECD countries', in T. Tachibanaki (ed.), *Labour Market and Economic Performance: Europe, Japan and the USA* (London: Macmillan) (with S. Nickell).

(1994b) 'Preventing long-term unemployment in Europe', in P.-O. Bergeron and M.-A. Gaiffe (eds), *Croissance, Compétitivité, Emploi: a la Recherche d'un Modèle pour l'Europe* (Collége d'Europe); reprinted in various forms in House of Commons Employment Committee, *The right to work/workfare: minutes of evidence* (Tuesday 22 November) (London: HMSO, and in *Work in future. The future of work.*, Alfred Herrhausen Society for International Dialogue (Stuttgart: Schäffer-Poeschel Verlag and as *Preventing long-term unemployment*, Employment Policy Institute (October) and as 'Preventing long-term unemployment', in H. Sasson and D. Diamond (eds), *LSE on Social Science* (London, LSE Books, 1996) and as 'How to cut unemployment', in *Policy Options*, Institute for Research on Public Policy, Montreal,

17 (6) (July–August 1996) and as 'Preventing long-term unemployment', in
J. Philpott (ed.), *Working for Full Employment* (London: Routledge, 1997).

(1994c) 'Subsidising employment rather than unemployment', *Rivista di Politica Economica*, Fascicolo XI, Anno LXXXIV (November).

(1995) 'Reforming national labour markets', in W.D. Eberle, E.G. Corrigan and W. Moller (eds), *The Future of the World Economy* (Washington DC, The Aspen Institute).

(1996a) 'Preventing long-term unemployment: an economic analysis', in J. Gual (ed.), *The Social Challenge of Job Creation* (Aldershot: Edward Elgar) and in D. Snower and G. de la Dehesa (eds), *Unemployment Policy: Government Options for the Labour Market* (Cambridge: Cambridge University Press, 1997), Chapter 14 in R. Layard, *Tackling Unemployment* (London: Macmillan, 1999).

(1996b) 'Vägen Tillbaka Till Full Sysselsättning'(The 1995 Rudolf Meidner Lecture), *Arbetsmarknad & Arbetsliv*, 2(1); reprinted as 'Sweden's Road Back to Full Employment', *Economic and Industrial Democracy* (London: Sage, 1997), 99–118.

(1996c) 'Combatting unemployment: is flexibility enough?', in OECD, *Macroeconomic Policies and Structural Reform 1996* (with R. Jackman and S. Nickell), Chapter 10 in R. Layard, *Tackling Unemployment* (Paris: OECD) (London: Macmillan, 1999).

(1997) 'Preventing long-term unemployment: strategy and costings', Employment Policy Institute Economic Report, 11(4) (March), Chapter 15 in R. Layard, *Tackling Unemployment* (London: Macmillan, 1999).

(forthcoming) 'Labour Market Institutions and Economic Performance' in O. Ashenfelter and D. Lard (eds) *Handbook of Labour Economics* (Amsterdam: North-Holland).

3   TRANSITION

Books

(1991) *Reform in Eastern Europe* (Cambridge, MA: MIT Press) (with O. Blanchard, R. Dornbusch, P. Krugman and L. Summers).

(1992a) *East–West Migration: The Alternatives* (Cambridge,MA: MIT Press) (with O. Blanchard, R. Dornbusch and P. Krugman). Translated into Italian.

(1992b) *Russian Economic Trends*, 4 quarterly issues and 12 'monthly updates' (London: Whurr) (editor and co-author 1992–7).

(1993a) *Changing the Economic System in Russia* (London: Pinter Publishers) (edited with Anders Åslund).

(1993b) *Postwar Economic Reconstruction and Lessons for the East Today* (Cambridge, MA: MIT Press) (edited with R. Dornbusch and W. Nölling).

(1993c) *Post-Communist Reform: Pain and Progress* (Cambridge, MA: MIT Press) (with O. Blanchard *et al.*).

(1994) *Macroeconomics. A Text for Russia* (Moscow: Wiley) (in Russian).

(1996) *The Coming Russian Boom* (New York: The Free Press) (with J. Parker).

(1998) *Emerging From Communism: Lessons from Russia, China and Eastern Europe*, The MIT Press (ed. with P. Boone and S. Gomulka).

Articles

(1990) 'Economic change in Poland', in J. Beksiak *et al. The Polish Transformation: Programme and Progress*, Centre for Research into Communist Economies (London) (July) (with O. Blanchard).

(1991a) 'Wage bargaining, incomes policy, and inflation', in S. Commander (ed), *Managing Inflation in Socialist Economies in Transition* (Washington, DC: Economic Development Institute of the World Bank) (June).

(1991b) 'How to privatise', in H. Siebert (ed.), *The Transformation of Socialist Economies: Symposium 1991* (University of Kiel) (with O Blanchard), Chapter 22 in this volume.

(1992) 'Post-stabilization inflation in Poland', in F. Coricelli and A. Revenga (eds), *Wage Policy during the Transition to a Market Economy, Poland 1990–1991*, World Bank Paper, 158 (Washington, DC: World Bank) (with Olivier Blanchard), Chapter 23 in this volume.

(1993a) 'Prices, incomes and hardship', in A. Åslund and R. Layard (eds), *Changing the Economic System in Russia* (London: Pinter Publishers) (with M. Ellam).

(1993b) 'Eldorados in Russia', in A. Raphael (ed.), *Debrett's Euro-Industry 1993* (London: Debrett's Peerage Limited).

(1993c) 'Why so much pain, and how to reduce it', *Voprosy Ekonomiki* (Questions of Economics), 2.

(1993d) 'The future of the Russian reform', *The Economics of Transition*, 1(3).

(1993e) 'Stabilization versus reform? Russia's first year', in O. Blanchard *et al.* (eds), *Post-Communist Reform* (Cambridge, MA: MIT Press).

(1994a) 'Who gains and who loses from Russian credit expansion?', *Communist Economies & Economic Transformation*, 6(4) (with A. Richter), Chapter 24 in this volume.

(1994b) 'The conditions of life', in A. Åslund (ed.), *Economic Transformation in Russia* (London: Pinter Publishers) (with A. Illarionov and P. Orszag).

(1994c) 'Can Russia control inflation?', in J. Onno de Beaufort Wijnholds, S.C.W. Eijffinger and L.H. Hoogduin (eds), *A Framework for Monetary Stability* (Boston: Kluwer Academic Publishers), Chapter 25 in this volume.

(1994d) 'The current state and future of economic reform', in *European Expertise Service 1992–1994: 1st Review Exercise*, TACIS European Commission (Brussels) (21–22 September).

(1995a) 'Labour market adjustment in Russia', in A. Åslund (ed.), *Russian Economic Reform at Risk* (London: Pinter Publishers) (with A. Richter).

(1995b) 'How much unemployment is needed for restructuring? The Russian Experience, *Economics of Transition*, 3(1) (March) (with A. Richter), Chapter 26 in this volume.

(1996) 'The coming Russian boom', *The American Enterprise*, 7(4) (July–August) (with J. Parker).

(1998) 'Why So Much Pain?', Chapter 1 in P. Boone, S. Gomulka and R. Layard (eds), *Emerging from Communism: Lessons from Russia, China and Eastern Europe, The MIT Press*, Chapter 27 in this volume.

4 GENERAL

Books

(1971) *Cost-benefit Analysis* (Harmondsworth: Penguin) with long introduction; 2nd edition (Cambridge: Cambridge University Press, 1994) (edited with S. Glaister).

(1978) *Microeconomic Theory* (New York: McGraw-Hill) (with A.A. Walters); reissued as International Student Edition (1987). Translated into Japanese.

(1987a) *Handbook of Labour Economics* (Amsterdam: North-Holland) (edited with O. Ashenfelter). Translated into Spanish.

(1987b) *The Performance of the British Economy* (Oxford: Oxford University Press) (edited with R. Dornbusch).

(1989) *World imbalances*, Report of the WIDER (World Institute for Development Economics Research) World Economy Group (with O. Blanchard, R. Dornbusch, M. King, P. Krugman, Y. Chul Park, and L. Summers).

(1990) *Britain & EMU*, Centre for Economic Performance and Financial Markets Group (edited with R. Dornbusch and C. Goodhart).

(1997a) (Signatory) *Promoting prosperity*, Report of the Commission on Public Policy and British Business (London: Vintage).

(1997b) *What Labour Can Do* (London: Warner Books).

Articles

(1972) 'The determinants of UK imports', *Government Economic Service Paper* (with R.D. Rees).

(1976) 'The date of discounting in cost–benefit analysis', *Journal of Transport Economics and Policy* (July) (with A.A. Walters).

(1977) 'The income distributional effects of congestion taxes', *Economica* (August).

(1989) 'The Thatcher miracle?', *American Economic Review, Papers and Proceedings* 79(2) (May); also *Economic Affairs* (December 1989–90), also *Wirtschaft und Gesellschaft*, 4(1989) (with S. Nickell), Chapter 19 in this volume.

(1993) 'Varför Överge den Svenska Modellen?', in V. Bergström (ed.), *Varför Överge den Svenska Modellen? (Helsingborg Nationalekonomiska Föreningen och Tidens Förlag)*.

Index

Note: page numbers in **bold** type refer to illustrative figures or tables.